L.W. Smith

Exceptional Children and Youth

FOURTH EDITION

An Introduction to Special Education

Norris G. Haring

University of Washington

Linda McCormick

University of Hawaii

CHARLES E. MERRILL PUBLISHING COMPANY
A Bell & Howell Company
Columbus   Toronto   London   Sydney

We dedicate this book to the late **Nicholas Hobbs** (George Peabody College, Vanderbilt University), whose belief that society's most important mission is to improve the lives of its children has shaped and sustained the values and practices of several generations of teachers and other professionals in the human services.

Published by Charles E. Merrill Publishing Co.
A Bell & Howell Company
Columbus, Ohio 43216

This book was set in Novarese.
Cover Design: Cathy Watterson
Text Design: Michael Rogondino
Production Coordination: Jan Hall
Cover Photos © Bruce Johnson

Library of Congress Catalog Card Number: 85–62501
International Standard Book Number: 0–675–20467–4
Printed in the United States of America
3 4 5 6 7 8 9—91 90 89 88 87

Photo credits:

pp. xii, 2, 21, 84, 89 ,132, 145, 170, 177, 247, 285, 301, 312, 316, 332, 341, 368, 400, and 491: Strix Pix

pp. 40, 46, 53, 74, 77, 102, 114, 130, 135, 150, 160, 183, 200, 205, 213, 233, 350, 393, 414, 430, 439, 442, 448, 451, 458, 461, 465, 474, and 482: Phillips Photo Illustrators

p. 49: West/Corn's Photo Service

pp. 55 and 58 (left and right): Prentke Romich

pp. 60 (all), 61 (top), 62 (top and bottom), 63, 64, 396, 407, 412, 417, 419, and 422: Hagler/CEM

p. 61 (bottom): VersaBraille, Telesensory Systems

pp. 70, 110, and 221: Johnson/CEM

p. 81: Action's Foster Grandparents' Program/CEM

p. 86: Marie D. Thompson

pp. 94 and 302: Luanna Voeltz

p. 99: Johnson/Corn's Photo Service

p. 107: George Aleman

p. 118: Susan Hartley

pp. 191, 280, and 486: Marjorie McEachron, Cuyahoga County Board of Mental Retardation, Cleveland, OH

p. 259: Miller

p. 270: Andrew Rakoczy

p. 276: E. B. Heston

pp. 281, 290, and 424: Hutchinson/CEM

p. 289: Tom Tondee

p. 296 (left and right): Bonnie Ruth, Diane Talarico, and the Community-Based Instructional Program, Albemarle County Public Schools, Charlottesville, VA

p. 304 (left and right): Trice Lewis, Anne Graham, and the Community-Based Instructional Program, Albermarle County Public Schools, Charlottesville, VA

p. 323: Roman Spalek

p. 328: Marvin L. Silverman

p. 345: J. Mark Rainez

p. 352 (left and right): June Bigge and Barbara Sirvis

p. 356: Charles J. Quinlan

pp. 366 and 381: Jan Smyth

p. 377: Sheila Lowenbraun and Marie D. Thompson

pp. 378 and 383: Northwest School for Hearing Impaired Children, Seattle, WA

p. 389: Early Childhood Home Instruction Program, University of Washington

p. 390: Telex Communications Inc./CEM

p. 408: T. J. Hamilton/Corn's Photo Service

p. 413: Richard M. DeMott

p. 416: Russell Illig

p. 485: Mike Davis

Preface

Significant changes strengthen this volume over all previous editions. Chapter for chapter it is almost a complete rewrite, responding to comments from a systematic review by specialists, professors of special education, teachers of exceptional children, and university students. It encompasses the rapid expansion of continuing research and examines new technology.

This fourth edition offers a fresh perspective from co-editor Linda McCormick, who lends her special competencies in early childhood, language, and communication. Crucial additions to this revision are Don Bailey and Pamela Winton's chapter on families, and a chapter on how computer technology applies to the lifestyle and the teaching of exceptional individuals.

As in the last edition, communication disorders are examined, this time by Linda McCormick; and visual impairments are covered by Rita Livingston. Phil Chin joins Linda in a discussion of cultural diversity, looking at minority students' homes, communities, interests, talents, and learning styles.

Current issues in learning disabilities by Cecil Mercer include a life-span view of learning disabilities; screening, identification, and assessment; program development for secondary and post-secondary transition levels; and approaches where students evaluate themselves, decide about their own learning, and achieve self-control and mastery of attention, memory, and generalization.

In the chapter on behavior disorders, Cullinan and Epstein ask crucial questions: How do we determine whether required behavior changes are of real social value? How can we assure that new skills will be maintained and generalized? What are practical strategies that increase students' self-control?

Patton and Payne, in chapter eight, offer excellent new ideas on innovation and development in mental retardation. Next, in a very comprehensive chapter on students with moderate, severe, and profound handicaps, Marti Snell and Adelle Renzaglia present their thoughts on how integrated activities can motivate positive interactions between severely handicapped students and their nonhandicapped peers; what alternatives there are to competitive placements for some severely handicapped students; and ways to maintain learned functional skills.

June Bigge and Barbara Sirvis, in chapter ten, talk about how transdisciplinary cooperation works—its value in developing comprehensive programs for students with physical and health impairments, and how the cooperative spirit becomes motivated and maintained.

The chapter on gifted and talented, completely updated by Joan Wolf and Tom Stephens, is one of the most comprehensive discussions on this topic available today. They discriminate sharply the most pressing issues, including how to recognize culturally different gifted students; advanced placement for college and university credit; strengthening the curriculum to emphasize the conceptual, creative, and critical as well as the goals of social adaptation, responsibility, and leadership.

Throughout this fourth edition we wanted to sharpen our focus on the diversity of topics now confronting those who work with exceptional children: administrative policies, full integration of the handicapped, prevention through early intervention, peer tutoring and social interaction, self-monitoring, and attention to academic learning time.

As we finished our manuscript, we felt excited and optimistic. We hope this electricity comes through to you. We encourage your interaction with us about what you are about to read.

Norris Haring
Linda McCormick

Acknowledgments

This edition is possible largely with the assistance and patience of others. We are particularly grateful to Jane A. Kortemeier, typing and editing; Ruth Pelz and Jim Pruess, editing; Susan E. Lewis, word processing; Mary Jo Noonan and Norma Jean Hemphill, for many excellent suggestions and manuscript refinement; and to Rosalie Boone, special thanks for assistance with the test bank.

We would also like to thank the reviewers of the complete manuscript:

Dr. August J. Mauser
University of South Florida

Dr. Millie Lusardi
San Francisco State University

Dr. John F. Vokurka, Jr.
Western Kentucky University

Dr. Qaisar Sultana
Eastern Kentucky University

Dr. Margaret M. Noel
University of Maryland

The individual chapter reviewers:

Dr. Deborah Bott
University of Kentucky

Dr. James Delisle
Kent State University

Dr. John Eulenberg
Michigan State University

Dr. George Shepherd
University of Oregon

Dr. Peter Gray
Syracuse University

Dr. Judith Page
University of Kentucky

Dr. John Umbreit
University of Arizona

Dr. Mary Margaret Kerr
Western Psychiatric Institute
University of Pittsburgh

Dr. James Krouse
Bowling Green State University

Dr. Eric Jones
Bowling Green State University

Dr. LaDelle Olion
Fayetteville State University

Dr. John Venn
University of North Florida

Dr. Rosanne Silberman
Hunter College

Dr. Richard Luftig
Miami University

Dr. Maurice Miller
Indiana State University

Dr. Reuben Altman
University of Missouri

Dr. Shirin Antia
University of Arizona

Dr. Laura Kretchmer
University of Cincinnati

Dr. Richard Voorneveld
The College of Charleston

Dr. Mary Jo Noonan
University of Hawaii

Dr. Wesley Brown
East Tennessee State University

And the people who reviewed the third edition and provided suggestions for the fourth:

Dr. John Vokurka, Jr.
Western Kentucky University

Dr. William Reid
University of Florida

Dr. Frank Rocco
Winona State University

Dr. Alfred Lazar
California State University
at Long Beach

Dr. LeRoy Aserlind
University of Wisconsin
at Madison

Contents

8

Mild Mental Retardation   233
James R. Patton, James S. Payne

9

Moderate, Severe, and Profound Handicaps   271
Martha E. Snell, Adelle M. Renzaglia

10

Physical and Health Impairments   313
June Bigge, Barbara Sirvis

11

Hearing Impairments   357
Sheila Lowenbraun, Marie D. Thompson

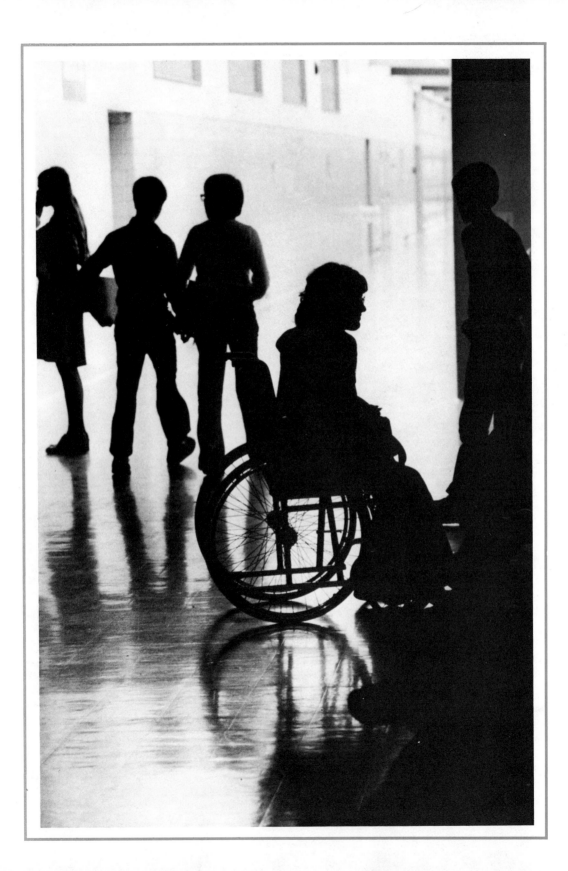

1

Introduction

Norris G. Haring
University of Washington

An understanding of exceptional children and youth begins with an understanding of the range of similarities and differences within the population as a whole. All people are different in some ways, yet all people are more alike than they are different. They all have the same basic needs and are guaranteed the same rights under our Constitution. Moreover, in most areas or activities the similarities among people are much more significant than the differences.

This book concerns itself with individuals who are exceptional from an educational standpoint, that is, who need different educational services from those provided their peers. The type and range of services required depend on the nature and degree of the exceptional person's deviation from "normal" learners. It is important to realize that this deviation may be either higher or lower than the norm. The term *exceptional* is a label for those with disabilities and impairments as

well as for the gifted and talented. It is also important to understand that both *normal* and *exceptional* are relative terms. Like all labels they tell us little about the individuals involved.

The labels used to identify groups of exceptional persons can be very confusing. The terms *disorder, disability, impairment,* and *handicap* are sometimes used interchangeably but actually have different meanings. *Disorder* is the broadest of the four terms. It is a disturbance of normal academic, psychological, or social functioning. The term *disability* is used to refer to a physical disorder such as the loss of a limb or some other crippling condition. It is also used with learning and behavior problems that may or may not be due to a physiological cause. The term *impairment* is usually reserved for sensory deficits: we speak of the hearing impaired and the visually impaired. All three of these terms refer to problems within the individual. The

Handicaps are minimized in classrooms that adapt to special needs.

fourth, *handicap*, is an environmentally related limitation. All of us have had the experience of being handicapped at one time or another. Unless you have had dancing instruction or experience, you are probably handicapped on a dance floor. Unless you are a skilled tennis player, you are handicapped on the court with a tennis professional. Students with physical, sensory, psychological, and/or learning problems are handicapped in a classroom environment that does not accommodate their learning needs.

The exceptional population includes people of all ages. Special education is not limited to what is traditionally thought of as the school-age population. For normal people learning is a lifelong activity that begins at birth and continues through adulthood. The same is true for the exceptional population. Many exceptional individuals need special educational services from infancy through adulthood to enable them to learn from and adapt to their environments.

History of Special Education

Society today has very different attitudes about individual differences and the rights of exceptional persons from those in the past, and special education is a very different field from what it was even 15 or 20 years ago. It is a field that has evolved over time and continues to change according to the influence of several interrelated factors: prevailing social attitudes toward exceptional individuals; relevant laws and government policies; theories about the nature, causes, and treatments of handicapping conditions; and the status of education in general. For each factor historical milestones can be identified, and key trends and issues can be traced.

Most historians trace the beginnings of concern for the exceptional to the Age of Enlightenment at the end of the 18th century, the time of the American and French revolutions. Prior to this time, physical deformities were viewed as the result of witchcraft or a curse imposed by the gods. Emotional disturbances were attributed to possession by the devil. Mentally retarded persons were kept as fools for the entertainment of the rich and royal. In some European cities people paid to stare at asylum residents much as we pay to watch the animals in a zoo. The Greeks, Romans, and other early cultures routinely killed deformed children.

In the Moslem and Christian religions there were those who believed that the mentally ill and retarded were "innocents of God" and deserved to be treated with kindness and care, but these were exceptions. If care was given at all, it was often in crowded, unheated asylums, where the residents were poorly clothed, underfed, cruelly treated, and often chained.

The Age of Enlightenment

The Enlightenment produced new interest in human liberty and equality, expressed by such outstanding political philosophers as Thomas Jefferson and Jean Jacques Rousseau. It also produced reformers in the treatment of the handicapped. These included the French physician Philippe Pinel and his student Jean-Marc-Gaspard Itard. As director of a Paris institution for the mentally ill, Pinel became famous for releasing his patients from their chains. He also pioneered occupational therapy. Despite a basic belief that children suffering from "idiocy and insanity" were incurable, Pinel fought for more humane treatment (Kauffman, 1982). Though it would not be viewed as such today, Pinel's approach was called "moral treatment." It was, at least, a beginning.

Itard was influenced both by his teacher Pinel and by the Enlightenment philosopher John Locke. Locke described the human mind as a blank slate, awaiting sensory input. Itard put these theories to the test when he was given charge of a young boy found living wild in the forests of central France. The nonverbal and "savage" youth was known as the wild boy of Aveyron. Itard named him Victor. After five years of intensive work with Victor in a program based on sensory stimulation, Itard described his efforts as a failure. Although Victor had acquired some language and social skills, he was not "normal." This "failure" is now identified as the first special education program.

Pinel's principles of moral treatment and humane reform were applied in late 18th-century America by Benjamin Rush—a physician, professor, and signer of the Declaration of Independence. Several decades later, in 1837, the French physician Edouard Seguin established a school for the mentally retarded that extended Itard's ideas. Seguin became the first to advocate that *all* mentally retarded individuals could learn.

Although Seguin's school was the first for mentally retarded children, there had been schools for the sensorily impaired since the mid-1700s. A French abbot, Charles Michel Del'Epee, opened a school for deaf students in 1755 using manual methods to teach communication. Thomas Braidwood of Scotland and Samuel Heinecke of Germany became known for their work with the oral method of teaching the deaf. Both methods were studied in Europe by the Reverend Thomas Hopkins Gallaudet of Connecticut, who established the first school for the deaf in this country in 1817.

The history of education of the blind goes back even further. A tactile communication aid for the blind was invented as early as 1651. In 1784 Valentin Haüy, a French educator, established a school in Paris and became the first to use embossed letters as a means of teaching the blind to read. The school's most famous student, Louis Braille, developed the tactile reading system most widely used today. Haüy went on to found schools in Russia and Germany, and by 1820 there were schools for the blind in most European countries. The first such school in the United States was the Perkins Institute, founded in 1832.

Reformers and the Issue of Institutionalization

The reforms and idealism of the Enlightenment were carried into the 19th century by a number of outstanding educators and activists. Samuel Gridley Howe, founder of the Perkins Institute, not only developed new teaching methods for the blind but also convinced the Massachusetts legislature to fund a program for the mentally retarded. Dorothea Dix, an energetic crusader for institutional reform, called for the creation of new institutions—more humane ones—to accommodate the handicapped.

In later years, however, reformers often called for an end to the use of institutions as a treatment strategy. Over the years the institutions had become larger, less personal and familial, overcrowded, and sometimes brutally inhumane. Furthermore, there was growing opposition to the principle of institutionalization itself as people came to feel that it was wrong to segregate the handicapped in separate, isolated environments. Institutions, they argued, should be reserved for those with only the most serious handicaps and the least capacity for leading independent lives.

The movement toward deinstitutionalization did not fully mature until recently, after many decades of simmering debate. On the one hand was the argument that exceptional populations—the deaf, the mentally retarded, the physically impaired, and others—would be better served and more humanely treated in segregated settings, among people who understood them. This position predominated in the 19th and early 20th centuries, as evidenced by residential institutions and segregated special education classes in the public schools. It was opposed by those who advocated greater integration of the handicapped into all areas of life. This group argued against the notion that special education could be carried out only in special places by special persons.

The Nature/Nurture Debate

Another critical and persistent issue in the history of exceptional education has been the question of etiology or cause: Are children's handicaps the unalterable result of heredity (nature) or the product of environmental factors such as stimulation, education, diet, and family interactions (nurture)? Today, virtually everyone in the field acknowledges that both genetic and environmental factors must be taken into account; evidence has shown them to be inseparably interrelated. But for more than a century, the nature/nurture debate was among the most heated in the special education field, and it can be a lively one even now.

Reformers of the early 1800s concentrated on improvements in environmental conditions, as do educators today. But the latter half of the 19th century marked an upsurge of interest in heredity. A major source of this interest was Charles Darwin's writing on evolution. Many people seized on Darwin's theories on the survival of the fittest as an argument for restricting undesirable elements of the population: the handicapped, the poor, and immigrants. These people, it was said, were responsible for all of society's problems and ought to be prevented from reproducing. Policies of forced institutionalization and sterilization of the handicapped became common. Social attitudes toward exceptional populations reached a new low, which lasted until about the time of World War I. The nature/nurture issue receives attention even today with a substantial accumulation of evidence demonstrating the inseparable interaction of the biogenetic contribution and the ecology of the individual.

Changes in the Early 20th Century

It was in the early 1900s that public education came into its own in America. For centuries, both in this country and in Europe, education had been largely a privilege of the rich. In 1876 fewer than 5% of American children between the ages of 5 and 17 were in school. It was common for children to attend classes for only a few years and for just a few months of the year. In a rural, agricultural economy there were interruptions for planting and harvest, transportation problems, and other obstacles. With industrialization came even greater problems. Factory workers were paid so little that all family members had to contribute wages in order to survive. Children as young as six were expected to toil 10 to 14 hours a day.

Compulsory education finally became a reality in all states in 1918. During that Progressive Era educational reformers joined with organized labor to win the first of many child labor laws and to advance the cause of public education nationwide.

The early decades of this century can be seen as a period of change in social attitudes toward all children; young people were no longer to be treated as miniature adults but as individuals with their own desires and needs. During this period there were developments in psychology, educational theory and practice, government policy, medicine, and technology that would help lay the groundwork for the tremendous expansion of special education that was to come.

Studies in the field of medicine, for example, led to important discoveries about the nature and causes of many handicapping conditions. Much of the superstition, fear, and rejection associated with the disabled had been rooted in a lack of understanding. As medical explanations were discovered for epilepsy, cerebral palsy, and other diseases and syndromes, social attitudes changed. With understanding also came advances in treatment, prevention, and in some cases cures. Better care for mothers and infants before, during, and just after birth reduced or eliminated many congenital defects.

Technological developments were also important. The mass production of automobiles, for instance, and advances in public transportation made it possible to serve handicapped children from a large area in centralized day schools. The invention and refinement of such aids as braces, motorized wheelchairs, tape recorders, and hearing aids contributed to special education as well as to other areas.

Equally significant were advances in the field of education itself. The development of reliable testing methods provided a way of accurately measuring students' abilities and disabilities. The French professor Alfred Binet and his student Theodore Simon completed the first draft of a standardized intelligence test in 1905. It was introduced into the United States in 1908, refined and adapted and followed by increasingly accurate testing procedures in a variety of areas, from audiology to emotional disturbance. Along with medical research, accurate assessment contributed significantly to educators' ability to understand exceptionalities and to distinguish one from another. Until these advances in understanding, mental retardation and emotional disturbance, especially, had often been confused.

Tremendous progress was made in educational theory and practice in the early and middle 1900s. Outstanding individuals such as Freud, Piaget, and Skinner and the many researchers who applied their theories in the classroom made a profound impact on the field. Psychiatry, speech pathology, and a host of related fields of study were introduced during this time, and special education teacher training became common in American universities.

The Role of Government

Wars and the problems of dealing with injured veterans have often led to improvements in the care and training of the handicapped. For example, Louis IX is credited with establishing, in the year 1260, treatment for soldiers blinded in the Crusades (Scheerenberger, 1983). Goldstein's (1927) studies of soldiers who received brain injuries in World War I ushered in a new era of research and understanding of the brain and its relationship to learning behavior. In the years following World War II, the federal government provided funds to veterans' hospitals and universities for research in such areas as clinical psychology, speech pathology, and physical medicine. Great advancements were made in the technology of artificial limbs and braces and in mobility training for the blind. The success of retraining programs for wounded veterans also generated new support for the idea of educating handicapped children in regular classrooms.

The United States government has played an active role in many other ways in the development of education in this century. Beginning with the first White House Conference on Children and Youth in 1909 and the founding of the Children's Bureau in 1912, federal agencies have taken a leadership role in studying the needs of our nation's youth. Legislation regarding vocational education and the rehabilitation of disabled adults is another example of federal action in the early decades of the century that would help pave the way for changes in opportunities and services for exceptional children as well as in attitudes toward them. Through a combination of research and development of model programs, incentive funding, and legal requirements, the federal government has played an increasingly important role in bringing about these changes.

The Movement Gains Momentum

One other development that should be mentioned is the founding of advocacy organizations. The earliest of these, now known as the American Association on Mental Deficiency, was initiated by Edouard Seguin in 1866. The 20th century has seen the creation and expansion of organizations at the local and national level for nearly every population and handicapping condition. Many—such as the Council for Exceptional Children, founded in 1922, and the Association for Retarded Citizens, first locally founded in 1933—are primarily for nonhandicapped advocates. Other organizations are made up of the handicapped themselves: the American Federation for the Blind; United Cerebral Palsy Association; the Association for Children and Adults with Learning Disabilities; Association for the Gifted and Talented; the National Epilepsy League; American Speech, Language, and Hearing Association; and the Council on Children with Behavior Disorders.

All of these developments—medical, technological, theoretical, governmental, and organizational—formed the roots of a powerful movement for the advancement of special education in the United States in modern times. This movement rapidly gained momentum in the 1960s, achieved major goals in the 1970s, and continues to mature in the 1980s.

Several factors, in addition to the forces already mentioned, helped initiate this period of intense activity. President John F. Kennedy, who had a mentally retarded sister, did much to bring the concerns of the handicapped before the public. In 1961 he commissioned a Presidential Panel on Mental Retardation which made far-reaching recommendations about prevention, deinstitutionalization, rights, dignity, and care. Ten years later the United Nations adopted a Declaration of General and Specific Rights of the Mentally Retarded, a symbol of the international recognition and support that had been gained. Similar milestones in public recognition were achieved by other handicapped groups.

Outstanding, too, were the achievements in educational research in the 1960s. The behavioral principles described in this book that have proven so effective with special populations were being identified and refined during this period. Other important models, methods, and curricula were being developed; new professional roles were emerging; and professional training programs were expanded and improved. In 1948 only 77 colleges and universities provided training programs in educating the exceptional. By 1954 the number had grown to 122, in 1973 it was over 400, and in 1976 it exceeded 600. Accompanying this increase in trained professionals was a sixfold increase in the number of exceptional students served from 1948 to 1972 (Reynolds & Birch, 1977).

Even more important as a catalyst for change in special education was the civil rights movement. The efforts to integrate racial minorities had both direct and indirect bearing on the movement for integrated education of the handicapped. In *Brown v. Board of Education* in 1954 the Supreme Court ruled against so-called "separate but equal" schooling for blacks and whites. The case affirmed education as a right of all Americans that could not be denied except by due process of law.

The relevance of *Brown v. Board of Education* to the handicapped was quickly apparent. Traditionally, the school system had operated on the assumption that its primary role was to provide an education for the majority, which meant the normal students. All too often exceptional students had been considered disruptive elements that impaired the school's ability to function for the good of the majority. The Constitution's guarantee of equal protection and compulsory school attendance laws notwithstanding, the system handled problem students by segregating them into special classes or by refusing to serve them at all. Although by the middle 1970s about 70% of the states had enacted laws allowing districts to develop programs for the handicapped, many children were specifically excluded (Weintraub & Ballard, 1982). The estimate of exceptional children and youth in the nation receiving no education whatsoever was as high as 1 million (Reynolds & Birch, 1977). The 1980s have seen significant progress toward the provision of services to all exceptional children. Early identification and intervention programs have effectively reduced the unserved population of the handicapped.

Special Education Legislation

Organizing efforts on the part of minority groups brought some concrete grains for handicapped students. For example, one of the first laws to provide federal funds for education of the handicapped (Public Law [P.L.] 89–10, described in Figure 1-1) was primarily directed at meeting minority students' educational needs. Passage of this and other civil rights laws helped mobilize the parents of handicapped children to organize themselves. Throughout the postwar decades parent groups became increasingly active and played a critical role in winning for all handicapped citizens the educational rights they have today. These parent groups argued that the school must provide a free education to *all* children, no matter what their handicap. Moreover, this must be an education that is appropriate to the child's abilities and needs. Parents took their arguments to the local school boards, to the courts, and eventually to Congress. Special education as it exists today was created essentially by law. Beginning in the early sixties, state and federal legislation began to provide the structure and resources for the growth and development of special education.

1965	Elementary and Secondary Education Act (ESEA) authorized federal financial assistance to local educational agencies to help meet the special needs of educationally deprived students (P.L. 89–10).
1965	ESEA Amendments granted federal funds to state agencies for educating handicapped children and youth (P.L. 89–313, Title I).
1966	ESEA Amendments provided assistance to state and local agencies for education of handicapped children and youth (P.L. 89–750, Title VI).
1967	ESEA Amendments created regional resource centers for evaluation of handicapped children and youth and services for deaf-blind children and youth (P.L. 90–247).
1968	Handicapped Children's Early Education Assistance Act established experimental preschool programs for handicapped children (P.L. 90–538).
1969	National Center on Educational Media and Materials for Handicapped Act created national network of educational materials/media for education of handicapped children and youth (P.L. 91–62).
1970	ESEA Amendments enacted Gifted and Talented Education Assistance Act, authorized federal support for gifted-talented and learning disabled children and youth (P.L. 91–230).
1972	Social Security Act was amended to include supplemental security income (SSI) to provide direct financial support for the disabled.
1973	Amendments to Vocational Rehabilitation Act (P.L. 93–112) emphasized provision of services for the most severely disabled, included Section 504—the Bill of Rights for the handicapped.
1974	Educational amendments increased federal funds for Title VI programs (see P.L. 89–750), set forth procedural safeguards, assured education in the least restrictive environment (P.L. 93–380), and identified the gifted and talented as a part of the Special Projects Act.
1975	Education of the Handicapped Act (EHA) (P.L. 94–142) increased federal commitment to providing a free and appropriate education for all handicapped persons.
1977	Amendments to EHA (P.L. 95–49) included the approved federal definition of learning disabilities.
1978	Gifted and Talented Children's Education Act provided money to states for planning as well as grants for personnel training, model programs, and research.
1983	Amendments to EHA (P.L. 98–199) extended a variety of discretionary grants and established new programs for transition of secondary students and evaluation of services as well as financial incentives to expand services for children from birth to 3 years of age.

Figure 1-1 Major federal education laws for exceptional children

One driving force behind such legislation has been the Council for Exceptional Children (CEC). In 1958 CEC joined with the National Association for Retarded Citizens (NARC) to support legislation to provide grants for training special education personnel. As a result of this effort, a special ad hoc committee under the guidance of Leo Connor drafted a policy statement that specified two basic needs for improving federal educational programs for exceptional children. First, it explained the need for reorganization of the Office of Education to meet new demands. Second, there was a need for improvement in the scope and quality of services for exceptional and special children. A number of the objectives in the policy statement were realized by federal action during 1963. Perhaps the most significant was the creation of the Division of Handicapped Children and Youth (the Bureau for Education of the Handicapped) within the Office of Education. Along with this came legislation, P.L. 88–164, that provided federal monies for scholarships, fellowships, and research funds in specific areas of special education.

The Elementary and Secondary Education Act (ESEA) of 1965 provided federal monies to state and local districts for developing educational programs for economically disadvantaged children and, for the first time, provided support for the handicapped. Edwin W. Martin, associate commissioner of the Bureau for Education of the Handicapped, described P.L. 89–10 in this way:

> Of the many programs developed and approved by the 89th Congress and the Administration—programs aimed at the cities, and the aged ("medicare"), etc.—none outranked in brilliance the Elementary and Secondary Education Act of 1965, P.L. 89–10. Its final passage, with its programs of assistance to children in disadvantaged areas (including handicapped children), new instructional materials, centers for innovation and research, and support for strengthening state educational agencies, was precedent-shattering not only in its educational implication, but also in the brilliance of its legislative drafting and strategy which succeeded in overcoming the traditional barriers to federal aid to education. (1972)

Two points are important. First, for the first time federal legislation provided money for research and program development. Second, the precedent was set for providing quality education for exceptional children of all types. The ESEA was a stepping stone to categorical aid to the handicapped. Subsequent federal legislation advanced the basic 1965 law.

But it was 1966 that was the banner year for special education. Administrative supervision was created at the federal level through the National Advisory Committee on Handicapped Children and the Bureau for Education of the Handicapped, and funds were especially earmarked for handicapped children. Other advances included matching funds to state departments of education for direct aid in developing programs for educating the handicapped, expanded services to state institutions and day schools, and extended services to the blind and deaf.

The 1966 legislation was the first step toward national programs to provide all children with the education they need and deserve. This legislation, however, only began to meet the needs of the handicapped. The National Advisory Committee on Handicapped Children advised Congress in 1966 that only one-third of the handicapped children in the country were receiving necessary services. In 1969 P.L.

91–230, the Learning Disabilities Act, was passed. It provided federal funds for service programs on a state level for learning disabled and gifted-talented children.

In 1970 the Elementary and Secondary Education Act Amendments, were signed into law. With this package Congress began to see programs for the handicapped as a single, interlocking whole. Handicapped and exceptional children were recognized as a target population with specific needs. In addition, the efforts of special educators were also recognized, emphasizing the need for humane treatment and educational opportunities and resisting mechanical categorizations resulting from particular descriptions of disabling conditions.

The first major victories were won in the courts. There were three important cases in 1972: *Pennsylvania Association for Retarded Children v. Pennsylvania, Mills v. Board of Education,* and *Maryland Association for Retarded Citizens v. Maryland.* In each case the courts affirmed that handicapped children have a right to a publicly supported education, regardless of the nature of their handicap. Further suits were subsequently brought against states on other related issues, such as discrimination in assessment and identification procedures and the right to be educated in the company of nonhandicapped children. These major judicial decisions are summarized in Figure 1-2.

These court rulings, together with continued pressure from parent lobbying groups, resulted in the passage of two very important federal laws. The first, the Vocational Rehabilitation Act of 1973 (P.L. 93–112), constituted a civil rights law for the handicapped. Section 504 of the act said essentially that handicapped people could not be excluded from any program or activity receiving federal funds simply on the basis of their handicapping condition. *Handicapped* was defined in terms of vocational opportunity, the intended focus of the act. The act was amended in December of 1974 (Section 111a of P.L. 93–516) to have a broader base. It now applies across the board to any recipient of federal funds, forbidding discrimination against the handicapped in employment or provision of services. In addition, the regulations mandate that employers make reasonable accommodations for the special needs of handicapped employees.

Section 504 of this law contains regulations requiring handicapped accessibility not only to jobs, education, and housing, but to virtually all public facilities (the "wheelchair requirement"). The definition of terms used in Section 504 of the Vocational Rehabilitation Act is included here.

"Physical or mental impairment" means (1) any physiological disorder or condition, cosmetic disfigurement, or anatomical loss affecting one or more of the following body systems: neurological; musculo-skeletal; special sense organs; respiratory (including speech organs); cardio-vascular; reproductive; digestive; genito-urinary; hemic and lymphatic; skin; and endocrine; or (2) any mental or physiological disorder, such as mental retardation, organic brain syndrome, emotional or mental illness (including addiction to alcohol or drugs), and specific learning disabilities.

"Major life activities" means functions such as caring for one's self, performing manual tasks, walking, seeing, hearing, speaking, breathing, learning, and working.

"Has a record of such impairment" means the person has a history of or has been misclassified as having a mental or physical impairment that substantially limits one or more major life activities.

1954   *Brown v. Board of Education.* State and local school systems violate black students' rights to equal protection under the Fourteenth Amendment by requiring school segregation; separate education is inherently unequal.

1972   *Pennsylvania Association for Retarded Children v. Pennsylvania.* State and local school districts are required to provide free and appropriate education for all handicapped children, regardless of the nature or extent of their disability; to educate handicapped children with nonhandicapped children to the extent it is appropriate for the handicapped child; to conduct an annual census to locate and serve handicapped children; to stop applying school exclusionary laws; to notify parents before evaluating a child to determine whether he is handicapped or placing him in a special education program; to set up a method for impartial hearings if the parents challenge the school's decisions; to periodically reevaluate handicapped children; and to pay private school tuition if they refer the child for private education. In later years, through such cases as *Fialkowski v. Shapp* (1975), the courts further interpreted the original PARC ruling to mean that schools must use proven, state-of-the-art teaching methods to meet the criteria for appropriate education.

1972   *Mills v. Board of Education.* The District of Columbia is required to provide free and suitable public education to all handicapped children, regardless of the nature or extent of their liability; to not suspend a handicapped child for more than 3 days without first granting him the right to a hearing; to continue his education in home-based or other nonschool programs during his suspension; to conduct an annual census of handicapped children; to properly evaluate each handicapped child's educational needs; to provide compensatory education to illegally excluded children; to notify parents before evaluating a child to determine whether he is handicapped and placing him in a special education program; to set up a method for impartial hearings if the parents challenge the school's decisions; to periodically reevaluate handicapped children; and to give parents the right to see and add to or clarify their children's school records.

1972   *Maryland Association for Retarded Citizens v. Maryland.* All retarded children have a right to free appropriate education and transportation to and from school; the right to tuition subsidies if they are placed in private schools by public schools; the right to be educated in accredited programs; and the right to be educated with nonhandicapped children, if appropriate.

1973   *LeBanks v. Spears* (also 1976). Louisiana schools are required to educate handicapped children suitably; to provide them with elaborate rights to a hearing before they are classified as handicapped or placed in special education programs; and to assure their right to be educated with nonhandicapped children, if appropriate.

1972   *Larry P. v. Riles* (also 1980). Certain IQ tests discriminate against black children because the tests were not validated as ways to determine those children's intelligence; schools may not use those tests for de-

Figure 1-2 Significant judicial decisions

ciding whether to place black children in classes for mildly retarded children; and other ways of assessing minority children must be used instead of IQ tests. A similar decision was handed down earlier in *Hobson v. Hansen* (1967).

1970   *Diana v. State Board of Education* (also 1973). The ruling in this case was the same as that in *Larry P. v. Riles* but applied to Spanish-speaking children. A similar result was reached in *Guadalupe Organization v. Tempe* (1972).

1972   *Frederick L. v. Thomas* (also 1976). Learning disabled children are not educated appropriately, as is their right, when they are not taught by qualified, specially trained teachers.

1975   *Lora v. Board of Education of City of New York*. Emotionally disturbed children must be educated with nonhandicapped children and may not be segregated by race or sex from other children. The court adopted the "mainstreaming" principle.

1979   *Mattie T. v. Holladay*. The state of Mississippi violated Section 504 by failing to include all school-age handicapped children in schools, in the least restrictive settings, and in conformity with nonbiased testing procedures.

1979   *New Mexico Association for Retarded Citizens v. New Mexico*. The state violated Section 504 by failing to include all school-age handicapped children in an appropriate public school program.

1979   *New York State Association for Retarded Children v. Carey*. Retarded children with hepatitis-B, an infectious disease that can be contained by public health practices, may not be placed in separate, self-contained programs in New York City schools. Such placement violated P.L. 94–142 and Section 504 provisions for least restrictive educational placements.

1980   *Battle, Bernard, and Armstrong v. Kline*. Some severely retarded children, enrolled in schools, have a right to 12-month schooling if it can be proved that they will regress during the regular summer vacation; a state 9-month school-year law violates P.L. 94–142 and Section 504.

1982   *Rowley v. Board of Education of Hendrick Hudson Central School District*. School district does not have to provide an interpreter for a deaf child because the child is making adequate progress in school without such special assistance. In this first Supreme Court decision on P.L. 94–142, appropriate education does not require the maximizing of education or assistance potential.

1984   *Irving Independent School District v. Tatro*. The Supreme Court ruled that school systems must provide handicapped students with catheterization to help them benefit from education.

1984   *Smith v. Robinson*. The Supreme Court ruled that parents are not entitled to recover attorney's fees. Also, plaintiffs cannot sue under P.L. 94–142 and Section 504 simultaneously.

"Is regarded as having an impairment" means the person (1) has a physical or mental impairment that does not substantially limit major life activities but is treated by a recipient of federal funds as constituting such a limitation, (2) has a physical or mental impairment that substantially limits major life activities only as a result of the attitudes of others toward such impairment, or (3) has none of the impairments listed above but is treated by a recipient of federal funds as having such an impairment. (34 C.F.R. §84.1)

The provisions of Section 504 are that

1. a zero-reject mandate is included
2. a child-find duty is placed on the schools
3. the schools must educate students without cost to parents
4. the schools must provide related services
5. all services must be provided in barrier-free settings

The next important landmark was the Education Amendments of 1974, P.L. 93–380. This legislation extended the life of several already-existing laws, including the ESEA, and contained several new provisions that indicated the federal government's growing awareness of the needs of exceptional children. This law authorized money to be spent by state and local agencies for planning programs for the gifted and talented. It also provided for money to be spent by the state for teacher and leadership personnel training and for research. In addition, it was a precursor of the Education for All Handicapped Children Act, noting that many handicapped children were not then receiving an education and setting a goal of correcting that defect. P.L 93–380 also required the states to protect the rights of handicapped students and their parents at the time of any change in educational placement and to assure as much mainstreaming as possible. These provisions became nationwide mandates with the passage of P.L. 94–142.

The Education for All Handicapped Children Act

Public Law 94–142—enacted on November 29, 1975—is clearly the most sweeping statement this nation has ever made about the rights of handicapped children to full educational opportunities. Two aspects of the law are especially noteworthy. First, by assuring "a free appropriate public education" to all handicapped children between the ages of 3 and 21, the law rejects the practice of excluding exceptional children because of their differences from normal learners. Second, because of its highly specific provisions for the kind and quality of education that handicapped children are to receive, the law establishes a new principle: the obligation to offer an individually planned education to meet the unique needs of each handicapped child. Because its specific provisions make the act a forceful mandate rather than a mere expression of hope for the exceptional child, those provisions should be examined carefully.

All handicapped children, regardless of the severity of their handicaps, must receive "a free appropriate public education which emphasizes special education and related services designed to meet their unique needs" (P.L. 94–142). Those services must be provided at public expense, without charge to the child or parents; must meet the standards of the state education agency; must include an appropriate preschool, elementary, or secondary education; and must conform to the requirements of the student's individualized education program. Unless it has specific laws or court decisions that rule otherwise, each state must make such an education available to all handicapped children between the ages of 3 and 18 by September 1, 1978, and to all handicapped children aged 3 to 21 by September 1, 1980.

The act provides substantial increases in funding to compensate local school districts for the "excess costs" of educating handicapped children. Using a formula that gradually increases the amount of funding from an additional 5% to 40% of the average amount spent to educate each pupil, the act provides for an eventual federal contribution of over 3 billion dollars for education of handicapped children. In other words, the government's commitment is both legal and financial. However, the government's response to its financial commitment has been very disappointing. As of the administration's 1985 budget, the proposed fund for P.L. 94–142 is less than one-third of what was anticipated.

The focus on serving children who most need help is closely tied to the funding provisions. Thus, while the act defines handicapped children in terms of categorical labels, it demands that funds be spent on the basis of need rather than category. More specifically, it establishes two priorities of handicapped children: (1) the unserved child, who currently receives no education, and (2) the underserved child, who is not receiving all of the special education or services needed to succeed. Among the unserved are the severely and profoundly handicapped, most of whom have received no educational services at all in the past. Among the underserved priority is given within each disability to the most severely handicapped receiving an inadequate program. The effect of these provisions is to concentrate on individual needs rather than on categorical labels as the basis for service.

Consistent with the emphasis on needs rather than categories is the act's requirement that each handicapped child be educated in the "least restrictive environment." The principle of the least restrictive environment is clearly a better guide for the placement of children than is placement according to categories. With the new mandate to serve previously unserved children, the need to "return" mildly handicapped children to regular classes (mainstreaming) is even more critical. Placing these children in less restrictive settings like the regular classroom is necessary to free special education personnel to deal with the needs of "first priority" children. Of course, it is not yet clear whether the regular classroom actually becomes the least restrictive educational setting for the majority of mildly handicapped children. Much of the success of that effort will depend on the flexibility of regular classroom teachers in planning for and meeting the individual needs of their pupils. A large role in the development of that flexibility may fall to special educators, who can share their systematic instructional procedures and experiences with regular teachers. It is important to note that the act does call for a comprehensive system of teacher training and retraining with special emphasis on inservice training of practicing teachers and special attention to promising new educational practices and materials.

Two other critical provisions of the act relate to the rights of the child and the parents. One is the extension and refinement of the requirements of P.L. 93–380 to observe legal due process in labeling and placing a child in special education. Among the specific guarantees is one that allows the parents to secure an independent evaluation of their child; another requires that written notice of pending identification, evaluation, and placement of a child be given the parents in writing and in their native language. Still another sets up guidelines for prompt, unbiased appeal hearings in the event that a parent disagrees with an evaluation or placement decision. A second major provision affecting parents is the requirement to involve them, to whatever extent possible, in formulating the individualized education program (IEP) that must be written for their handicapped child. Specific detail on the IEP is included later in this chapter.

In summary, the following are among the law's key requirements and guarantees:

1. *All children must be provided with a free public education, no matter what their handicap.* This provision is based on the principles that all children can benefit from an education and that all citizens have an equal right to the benefits of their government—education being one of these. As defined in P.L. 94–142, the financial responsibility of government extends not only to the educational program itself but to any services that a child needs in order to benefit from that education (e.g., physical or speech therapy, transportation to the school facility).

2. *All children receiving "special education and related services" must be fairly and accurately evaluated.* In the past many problems and abuses in special education could be traced to poor evaluation practices. All too often children were inappropriately labeled and/or placed in programs with no consideration for their real abilities and needs. Most controversial was the tendency to overidentify minority students as mildly mentally retarded, a problem that was found to be largely the result of culturally biased tests. P.L. 94–142 safeguards the evaluation process by requiring that more than one type of evaluation be used, that all tests be free of ethnic/cultural bias, and that they be used by trained professionals in a proven and appropriate manner. Furthermore, the child's parent(s) must consent to the evaluation process before it is initiated.

3. *A handicapped student's education must be appropriate to his or her individual capacities and needs.* P.L. 94–142 requires the development of an individualized educational plan for each student. The IEP must be based on evaluation of the student and prepared at least once a year by a committee that includes the child's special education teacher, a school district representative, an expert in the child's area of disability, and the child's parents. One member of the IEP committee (or some other qualified person) must be qualified to interpret the

assessment results. The IEP must include statements of the child's present level of functioning, long-term educational goals and short-term measurable objectives, support services needed, and other information. Although not a binding contract because educators cannot be sued if the student fails to meet projected goals, the IEP does represent a serious commitment on the part of the school and should be the most important guide in planning a student's educational program and placement.

4. *Handicapped children and youth must be educated in the "least restrictive," or most normal, environment feasible.* School districts must offer a continuum of placement options from the most restrictive (residential institutional care) to the least (full-time placement in a regular classroom) and must not assign a student to a more restrictive setting unless it can be demonstrated that the most restrictive setting will result in greater gains. Placements must be close to the child's home whenever possible and in the company of the student's nonhandicapped peers as much as possible. When academic integration is not feasible, handicapped and nonhandicapped students should be brought together for such activities as physical education classes, lunch, and assemblies.

5. *Students' and parents' rights must be protected at all stages of the special education process.* In addition to the requirement that parents approve the initial evaluation of their child and play an integral role in developing the IEP, there are other legal (due process) protections written into the law. Parents must be notified in advance whenever the school proposes to change a child's placement or evaluate the child. They have the right to review their child's school records and to request—with cause—that information in the files be changed. They have the right to present complaints with regard to their child's educational program and the right to call for an impartial hearing if disputes cannot be otherwise resolved.

The Individualized Education Program

Of all this law's provisions, one of the most specific and most significant is the requirement for an IEP for each child identified as handicapped. The IEP must be a joint effort of the child study team, which is comprised of a representative (other than the child's teacher) of the local education agency, the child's teacher(s) both regular and special, the parents, and other support staff (like speech therapists, school psychologists, physical therapists), and the child as well whenever appropriate. According to the rules proposed to implement the act, the IEP must include

1. a statement of the child's present levels of educational performance, including academic achievement, social adaptation, pre-vocational and vocational skills, psychomotor skills, and self-help skills;

2. a statement of annual goals which describes the educational performance to be achieved by the end of the school year under the child's individualized education program;

3. a statement of short-term instructional objectives, which must be measurable intermediate steps between the present level of educational performance and the annual goals;

4. a statement of specific educational services needed by the child (determined without regard to the availability of services), including a description of
   a. all special education and related services which are needed to meet the unique needs of the child, including the type of physical education program in which the child will participate, and
   b. any special instructional media and materials which are needed;

5. the date when those services will begin and length of time the services will be given;

6. a description of the extent to which the child will participate in regular education programs;

7. a justification of the type of educational placement that the child will have;

8. a list of the individuals who are responsible for implementation of the individualized education program; and

9. objective criteria, evaluation procedures, and schedules of determining, on at least an annual basis, whether the short-term instructional objectives are being achieved. (*Federal Register*, 41[252], p. 5692)

An example of a completed IEP is shown in Figure 1-3.

We are part of a new era in education in this country. No longer is exclusion either justifiable or legal. No longer is our principal concern whether or not we should provide full educational opportunity to exceptional children; our concern is now how best to do it. The law tells us that we must now plan, in advance of placement, how, where, what, and how fast a child will learn. It tells us that the child has the right to be made aware of his performance and to be protected so that others will not judge him unfairly. It tells us that each exceptional child is to receive an individually planned program of instruction. And probably most important of all, it tells us that the individualized program must be reviewed and evaluated regularly, at least annually.

Of course, the success of any law lies in the effectiveness with which it is put into practice and enforced. The Education for All Handicapped Children Act is no different. But we do have the resources and the knowledge to make full educational opportunity for exceptional children more than just a hopeful phrase.

Categories of Exceptionality

Ten categories of children and youth with handicapping conditions are being served under P.L. 94–142:

learning disabled	multihandicapped
speech impaired	hard-of-hearing and deaf

INDIVIDUAL EDUCATION PROGRAM

Date 11-25-85

(2) Committee

Name: Joe S.
School: Adams
Grade: 5
Current Placement: Regular Class/Resource Room   Age: 11-1
Date of Birth: 10-1-74

	Initials
Mr. Havlichek Principal	Ø.H.
Mrs. Snow Regular Teacher	S.S.
Mr. Bigelow Counselor	C.B.
Mr. Sheets Resource Teacher	A.S.
Mrs. S. Parent	M.R.S.

IEP From 12-1-85 To 12-1-86

(3) Present Level of Educational Functioning	(4) Annual Goal Statements	(5) Instructional Objectives	(6) Objective Criteria and Evaluation
MATH *Strengths* 1. Can successfully compute addition and subtraction problems to two places with regrouping and zeros 2. Knows 100 basic multiplication facts *Weaknesses* 1. Frequently makes computational errors on problems with which he has had experience 2. Does not complete seatwork Key Math total score of 2.1 grade equivalent	Joe will apply knowledge of regrouping in addition and renaming in subtraction to 4-digit numbers.	1. When presented with addition problems of 3-digit numbers requiring two renamings, the student will compute the answer at a rate of one problem per minute with 90% accuracy. 2. When presented with subtraction problems of 3-digit numbers requiring two renamings, the student will compute the answer at a rate of one problem per minute with 90% accuracy. 3. When presented with addition problems of 4-digit numbers requiring three renamings, the student will compute the answer at a rate of one problem per minute with 90% accuracy. 4. When presented with subtraction problems of 4-digit numbers requiring three renamings, the student will compute the answer at a rate of one problem per minute with 90% accuracy.	Key Math (after 4 mos.) Teacher-made tests (weekly) Key Math (after 4 mos.) Teacher-made tests (weekly)
	Joe will multiply 2- and 3-digit numbers requiring regrouping.	1. The student will multiply 2, 3, and 4 digits by 1 digit without regrouping with 90% accuracy. 2. The student will multiply 2 and 3 digits by 1 digit with regrouping with 90% accuracy. 3. The student will multiply 2 and 3 digits by 2 digits with no regrouping with 90% accuracy. 4. The student will multiply 2 and 3 digits by 2 digits with regrouping with 90% accuracy.	Key Math (after 4 mos.) Teacher-made tests (weekly) Key Math (after 7 mos.) Teacher-made tests (weekly)
	Joe will use linear, volume, weight, temperature, and money measurements.	1. The student will write dictated money values up to $200.00 with 90% accuracy. 2. The student will identify various weights in pounds and ounces using a scale with 70% accuracy. 3. The student will read a thermometer with 90% accuracy 4. The student will measure items to the nearest foot, yard, inch, meter, and centimeter.	Teacher observation (daily) Key Math (after 8 mos.)

Figure 1-3 Sample IEP (math portion)

mentally retarded	orthopedically impaired
emotionally disturbed	visually handicapped
other health impaired	deaf-blind

Although there are a large number of subcategories within each of these (e.g., autism, orthopedically impaired, Down syndrome), the above categories provide a functional grouping of handicapping conditions for the purposes of funding and providing services.

We are providing here an even more comprehensive categorization:

1. sensory handicaps, including hearing and vision impairments

2. intellectual deviations, including giftedness as well as mental retardation

3. communication disorders, such as speech and language dysfunction

4. learning disabilities/minimal brain dysfunction, resulting in learning problems without motor involvement

5. behavior disorders, including severe emotional disturbances

6. physical handicaps and health impairments, including neurological defects, orthopedic conditions, diseases such as muscular dystrophy and sickle cell anemia, birth defects, developmental disabilities, and autism

Within each of these categories the degree and frequency of difficulties within the exceptional experience vary widely. For example, a person with only slight problems in visual discrimination may require very little special help to function near the norm socially and intellectually. Someone who is blind, on the other hand, may need the help of many specialists over a long period of time to achieve mobility and social adjustment. Similarly, a mild motor impairment might adversely affect an individual's performance in certain games or sports but not the development of other skills.

It should be noted that, among the exceptional, the gifted and talented are a sadly neglected group. Even though the difficulties they experience and the needs they have are often as great as those of other exceptional individuals, little has been done for them. Few laws make special programs available to them, and schools have been slow to meet their educational and social needs. Indeed, all too often the gifted and talented find hostility rather than concern and interest in their teachers and their peers. Although the term *exceptional* may be used more or less synonymously with the terms *handicapped* and *disabled*, we must not lose sight of its broader sense. The needs of the gifted and talented are discussed in detail in chapter 13.

Social and Educational Differences

The degree and frequency of difficulties that an exceptional individual encounters will determine that person's educational management and, as a result, her social, personal, and intellectual growth. Someone with a very slight deficit can often compensate enough to avoid any significant social or intellectual ill effect. Only an audiologist may know that a given individual has a hearing loss in the high frequencies. Only a podiatrist may know of a person's need for a modified right shoe. For these very slightly disabled persons, no changes in educational programming are needed. Frequently they are not even classified as handicapped. Mildly handicapped persons have problems slightly more severe. They often need an individualized program of instruction but usually do not require placement in special programs. Although they may be two years behind in acquiring academic or motor skills, many can be fully integrated into the regular educational environment.

In contrast to the slightly disabled and mildly handicapped, both the moderately and severely handicapped do need individualized education, special instruction, and quite often placement in special programs. Still, the moderately handicapped can sometimes be grouped successfully with the nonhandicapped—in recreation programs or social activities, for example. And although it may challenge handicapped and nonhandicapped alike, the severely handicapped should be integrated into as many ordinary social situations as possible.

Both handicapped and non-handicapped students benefit from social integration.

American culture has not shown a high degree of tolerance for the handicapped. Throughout most of our history the moderately and severely handicapped were placed in institutions outside the mainstream of society. Only recently have Western societies begun to reexamine their treatment of these individuals. Segregating them merely perpetuates and increases the effects of their handicaps. Integration gives them the opportunity to learn from nonhandicapped partners at work and in social and recreational activities. Fortunately, the focus has shifted to integration, allowing the handicapped full opportunity to develop their abilities and to enjoy normal social activity. The benefits of such integration are reciprocal. As handicapped people enter society and are accepted, they can begin to contribute to society. Unfortunately, however, the very labels that special educators use in order to offer the handicapped a more appropriate education sometimes emphasize not their abilities, but rather their disabilities.

Labeling

Some system for identifying and classifying the exceptional would seem to be the logical first step toward providing services to meet their needs, yet there are implicit dangers in the labels that result from such classification. Exceptional individuals display a wide range of differences. No one category can adequately describe the social, educational, psychological, or physical advantages or disadvantages of an exceptional person. Many of the labels we use today result from the attempts of medical and psychological researchers to distinguish handicaps. Although they serve to simplify information for administrators, placement counselors, educators, and legislators, they frequently do more harm than good to the individuals they identify. Too often a child's individual differences and strengths are obscured by a label, which too often describes only the individual's deficiencies. The negative picture that results can adversely affect the individual as well as the quality of services received.

In 1972 Elliot Richardson—then secretary of health, education, and welfare—urged federal agencies to review the system for classifying and labeling exceptional children. Richardson's concern provided the impetus for the Project of the Classification of Exceptional Children, which culminated in a two-volume study edited by Hobbs (1975). In presenting reasons for and against classifying and labeling exceptional children, Hobbs emphasized the danger of any system of classification.

> Classification or inappropriate classification . . . can blight the life of a child, reducing opportunity, diminishing his competence and self-esteem, alienating him from others, nurturing a meanness of spirit, and making him less a person than he could become. Nothing less than the futures of children is at stake. (p. 1)

A system of classification may be useful, Hobbs acknowledged, if it is directly relevant to education. Thus, to be of value, a system should

> deemphasize the familiar but gross categories of exceptionality. It should specify . . . the services required to assist the child or his family and school in the interest of the child's fullest development. (p. 234)

Clearly there are advantages as well as disadvantages in classifying and labeling exceptional persons.

Advantages of Labeling   Assigning a label can result in increased visibility for a group of people with special needs. For example, parents who were eager to find another term for children labeled "neurologically handicapped," "minimal brain dysfunction," and "slow learners" adopted the label "learning disabled" and formed the Association for Children with Learning Disabilities (ACLD). This association now has chapters in all 50 states and has proved to be an effective special-interest group in lobbying for legislation, federal funding, and special programs for the learning disabled.

Labels also help administrators within the school system provide appropriate services to exceptional students. Undoubtedly, some system of classification is necessary if special education services are to be organized efficiently. Similarly, labels can facilitate specific treatment and promote effective communication among agencies, service providers, and professionals.

Disadvantages of Labeling   Labels are sometimes used indiscriminately to exclude individuals from the regular classroom. Furthermore, in spite of their proliferation among health and education professionals, labels seldom adequately reflect individuals' educational or therapeutic needs. More important, labeling and resultant enrollment in categorical programs of instruction may deflate a person's self-concept, aggravating whatever condition she may have and increasing her vulnerability to ridicule or isolation from peers. In addition, labels suggest a permanent disorder requiring long-term professional treatment.

The use of labels can actually shape a person's limitations and failures. Called the Pygmalion effect, this phenomenon was observed in a study of teachers and their students (Rosenthal & Jacobson, 1968). The teachers were told that certain students in their classes were slow learners, unable to keep up, and that others were late bloomers, likely to catch up with the average students in their classes. The result was that the students' performance exactly reflected their classification, although there had originally been no actual differences in the learning capabilities of the two groups. This experiment has been challenged (Elashoff & Snow, 1971), but other studies support the notion that students will perform much as their teachers expect them to perform (Beez, 1968; Fine, 1970).

Finally, tests used to identify and label the exceptional are suspect. A disproportionate number of minority individuals are classified as mentally retarded, learning disabled, or behaviorally disordered on the basis of questionable testing procedures. It has been estimated that blacks are 7 times and Mexican Americans, 10 times as likely as Anglo Americans to be placed in special classes for the handicapped (Jones & Wilderson, 1976). Conversely, minorities are grossly underrepresented in special programs for the gifted. This discrepancy is due in large part to the cultural bias of IQ tests used to qualify students. One critic of the cultural tyranny in labeling made the following charges:

> Special education is part of the arrangement for cooling out students. It has helped to erect a parallel system which permits relief of institutional guilt and humiliation

stemming from the failure to achieve competence and effectiveness in the task given to it by society. Special education is helping the regular school maintain its spoiled identity when it creates special programs (whether psychodynamic or behavioral modification) for the "disruptive child" and the "slow learner," many of whom, for some strange reason, happen to be Black and poor and live in the inner city. (Johnson, 1969, p. 245)

In the face of such criticism, one may reasonably ask what is being done to correct or justify the use of systems of classification in special education.

Trends in the Perceptions and Labeling of the Exceptional   Educators are now more enlightened about the ways in which cultural and historical factors influence our perceptions of exceptional persons. The recent focus on the problems inherent in our present system of classification, coupled with more strident demands to protect the civil rights of the handicapped, has resulted in an active effort to revamp the classification system. Professionals no longer cling to the excuse that labels are necessary for lobbying and obtaining funding. Instead, there is increased interest in changing legislation and funding procedures that require the use of labels. Educators have grown more sensitive to the dangers inherent in labeling—cultural bias, social stigma, distortion, and oversimplification. They now focus on the levels of skill that exceptional individuals exhibit and the educational tasks needed to improve inadequate skills. Insofar as possible, emphasis on the individual's deviation from the norm is being reduced.

Ultimately, this shift in emphasis will mean a relaxation of popular notions of normality. We will view a far wider range of individual differences as normal, and more handicapped students will be allowed in regular classrooms. This expanded concept of normality will lead to innovations in classroom instruction to allow for more individualized instruction and the realization that many people are exceptional at some time in their lives, that many need individualized instruction— whether in the form of remedial education, psychotherapy, physical therapy, or advanced training in an area in which they excel. Indeed, we all share a need for special services.

Prevalence of Exceptional Children and Youth

The problems with labeling are nowhere more evident than in the effort to determine prevalence—the number of exceptional children and youth at a given time. Prevalence figures are difficult to obtain, variable, and dependent on trends in classification and the provision of services. Estimates of the percentage of children and youth with exceptionalities in the United States have ranged from as low as 5% to as high as 40%.

Incidence Versus Prevalence

The fact that an exceptionality may occur in an individual for only a short period of time further complicates statistical evaluation. Indeed, one study suggests that as many as 80% of all children and youth are in need of special services at some point between their birth and the conclusion of their secondary school years (Rubin & Balow, 1971). Figures such as these assess incidence—the extent to which a condition occurs over time in a population—rather than prevalence. Incidence percentages are usually higher estimates and less reliable than prevalence percentages.

In this text we will confine our discussion to prevalence, using the figures for various categories of handicap reported to the U.S. Department of Education for the school year 1983–1984 by state agencies under Public Laws 94–142 and 89–313. Corresponding figures for the gifted are not available.

Problems in Estimating Prevalence

Even though prevalence figures are generally more reliable than incidence figures, any attempt to accurately assess the prevalence of specific kinds of handicapping conditions inevitably encounters several stumbling blocks. First, the definition of any one condition may be open to subjective interpretation and thus may vary widely, even within small geographic areas. Second, a related problem is the question of which criteria and evaluation procedures should be employed to determine the existence of a handicapping condition. Estimates of prevalence are only as valid as the criteria and evaluating techniques used. Third, funding and professional resources available for services to the handicapped have a significant impact on prevalence figures. Generally, the more funding and resources available, the higher the prevalence figures. If money and professional help are limited, handicapped individuals may not be identified or served. Thus, they are not included in statistical analyses. Finally, in reporting prevalence, state and local governments may include only those handicapping conditions that fall under federal guidelines for funding rather than using more valid criteria.

Current Estimates of Prevalence

Clearly then, any attempt to establish prevalence must take into account all of the above factors and acknowledge a significant margin of error. At present most special educators believe that, on the average across the nation, 12% of all school-age children and youth exhibit some form of handicap. The U.S. Office of Special Education and Rehabilitative Services appears to concur in its national estimate that 12% of all school-age children and youth are eligible for special education funding ("GAO Cites," 1980). In addition, the Office of Gifted and Talented (a part of the Office of Special Education and Rehabilitative Services) estimates that between 3% and 5% of the school-age population in the nation is gifted or talented. These gifted students are not included in the 12% estimate.

Table 1-1 presents the Office of Special Education's figures on the nationwide number of handicapped children and youth, by category of handicap, who received special education and related services in 1983–84 under P.L. 94–142 and P.L. 89–313. The total, over 4 million, is an increase of more than 500,000 since 1978; yet only approximately 8% of the population aged 5 through 17 was served. This compares poorly with the government's estimate of 12% who are eligible. Still, even though the number served falls short of the number assumed eligible, some be-

Table 1-1   Children receiving special education

Disability Group	Ages 3–5	Ages 6–17	Ages 18–21	Total
Mentally retarded	19,052	557,909	76,121	653,082
Hard-of-hearing	3,634	29,622	3,464	36,720
Deaf	1,740	8,682	1,517	11,939
Speech impaired	168,176	941,847	4,666	1,114,689
Visually handicapped	1,736	17,021	2,489	21,246
Emotionally disturbed	5,860	299,536	15,203	320,599
Orthopedically impaired	7,031	34,941	3,227	45,199
Other health impaired	4,015	41,767	3,833	49,615
Learning disabled	19,204	1,699,070	70,592	1,788,866
Deaf-blind	139	1,150	158	1,447
Multihandicapped	12,500	33,083	5,123	50,706
Totals	243,087	3,664,628	186,393	4,094,108

Note: Total school-age population (ages 5–17) was 44,750,000.
SOURCE: From U.S. Department of Education, 1983–84.

lieve that too many are already being served. They feel the eligibility criteria should be more exclusive and more stringently enforced. The Government Accounting Office (GAO), for example, claims that the Office of Special Education's policy of including speech impaired among those eligible for funding is unwarranted. The GAO further claims that the federal estimate of eligible children and youth is too high. Thus, the controversy over labeling persists and extends into the upper levels of our government.

Strategies for Teaching Exceptional Children

Even though many educators of exceptional children had been using individualized educational objectives, P.L. 94–142 standardized that process. Two of the law's requirements were profound and controversial statements about how we should teach exceptional students. The first of these was the mandate that handicapped students should be placed in the least restrictive educational environment in which they can learn successfully. The second was the requirement that every handicapped student be offered an appropriate instructional program to meet specific individual needs. Thus, it is useful to view education for the handicapped in terms of both the settings in which students are served and the instructional practices by which they are taught.

The Settings

Throughout the 1970s educators viewed the various options for placing handicapped learners in special programs as a "cascade" of services (Deno, 1970). One such cascade model is portrayed in Figure 1–4. Within this framework the regular classroom in the public school was viewed as the most natural and therefore the least restrictive of all options, but until the passage of P.L. 94–142 few handicapped students were educated in regular classrooms.

The most widely used public school setting for educating the mildly handicapped in the 1950s and 1960s was the self-contained class for the so-called educable mentally retarded. Teachers of these classes were normally trained to teach one type of exceptionality, but often the classes were filled with students with various handicapping conditions. In the 1960s and early 1970s separate classes for

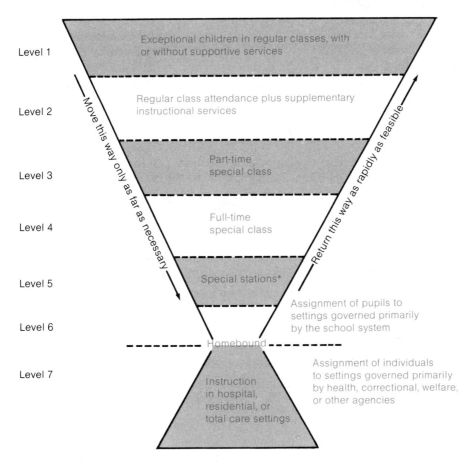

Level 1 — Exceptional children in regular classes, with or without supportive services

Level 2 — Regular class attendance plus supplementary instructional services

Level 3 — Part-time special class

Level 4 — Full-time special class

Level 5 — Special stations*

Level 6 — Homebound

Level 7 — Instruction in hospital, residential, or total care settings

Move this way only as far as necessary

Return this way as rapidly as feasible

Assignment of pupils to settings governed primarily by the school system

Assignment of individuals to settings governed primarily by health, correctional, welfare, or other agencies

Figure 1-4   The cascade system of educational placement

*Special schools in public school system

those with learning disabilities became commonplace, and there also began to be some separate classes for students labeled emotionally disturbed.

Trends in Placement of the Mildly and Moderately Handicapped

Even before the passage of P.L. 94–142 schools had begun mainstreaming the handicapped in limited ways—integrating them into the regular classroom when it was in their best interest educationally. Two ways of doing this evolved. One was to employ specialists such as visual, auditory, learning disabilities, and reading or language teachers as well as speech therapists to act as consultants (or resource specialists, as some states called them). Some consultants traveled from school to school and worked with students individually or in small groups. Others were available to the classroom teacher to help prepare remedial strategies and special materials and to suggest the best procedures to use. They received special training in diagnosis, continuous evaluation, and individualized and systematic instruction.

The other popular model for teaching the mildly handicapped in regular schools made use of special "resource rooms" or staffed "instructional materials centers." Under this plan a child was enrolled in a regular class for part of the day, with special instruction in a separate resource room during another part. Ideally, a resource room had one or more instructional aides to assist the master teacher or resource teacher and special equipment, such as console teaching machines. Both models continue to be used as a means of providing special education in mainstreamed settings.

Significant progress is being made in increasing the numbers of handicapped students in regular classrooms. According to the Sixth Annual Report to Congress on the Implementation of Public Law 94–142, 68% of handicapped students are being educated in regular classes, and 25% are receiving services in separate classes within regular education facilities. The visually handicapped, emotionally disturbed, orthopedically impaired, hard-of-hearing, and deaf are among those students showing an increase in services received in regular classes.

SRI International, a private research agency, concluded in a recent study (1982) that

- there is an increased number of students served in resource rooms

- a number of states have adopted a noncategorical placement option, which has allowed students to remain in their neighborhood schools in many instances

- an increased number of severely handicapped students are being educated in local agencies.

Trends in Placement of the More Severely Handicapped

One of the clearest implications of P.L. 94–142 was the move toward more appropriate and less restrictive settings for the more severely handicapped. Until recently those with severe and multiple handicaps were generally served in public residential settings. About 10% of those receiving special education in this country were in residential schools—variously referred to as training schools, hospital schools, detention homes, or boarding schools. Private boarding schools are still maintained throughout the country, offering services to the blind, deaf, emotionally disturbed, and learning disabled. However, increasing awareness of the rights of the severely and multiply handicapped has led to greater scrutiny of public residential facilities in the past few years. The problems of institutionalizing the handicapped have consequently been more widely recognized.

> Some of the negative characteristics associated with these institutions are regimentation, lack of privacy, impersonal treatment, limited freedom and independence for the residents, and limited interaction between the residents and the "outside" world. The larger the institution and the larger the geographic area that it must serve, the more difficult it is to normalize that environment for its residents. Activities aimed at improving conditions for residents in institutions can legitimately be called deinstitutionalization. (Neufeld, 1977, pp. 15–23)

Instead of noncare, closed-door policies and the isolation of the severely handicapped in the back wards of institutions, new programs are presently being developed. They emphasize the importance of allowing the handicapped to remain in their own community and lead as normal a life as possible through the use of hostels, foster homes, group homes, community training centers, day-care facilities, and community-based social services. There are at least two promising alternatives for the education of the severely handicapped who remain in their home community.

> The "cluster" or self-contained school for special education students offers the advantage of high community visibility, concentrating parents, administrators, and resources—which are apt to be scarce in a community—in one central location. Staff and consultant communication and problem sharing are maximized under this mode. Ancillary professional personnel spend less time in transportation and thus more time in service. Supervised practice teaching and inservice programs are easier to administer, and specialized support services, e.g., medical personnel, can be concentrated in one place.
>
> On the other hand, the "dispersal" model—or the spreading of classes for the severely handicapped throughout several, or many, schools in a district—offers the possibility of integration into community life and normalization (Sontag, Burke, & York, 1973). The students are apt to come into contact with the problems of the severely/multiple handicapped child, and the possibilities for new approaches for remediation are increased. (Sailor & Haring, 1977, pp. 70–71)

The dispersal model is the preferred option. As mildly and moderately handicapped students spend more time in regular school classrooms, more special educators are learning to work with the severely handicapped within the context of the public school system.

Integrating severely handicapped students in regular education facilities actually goes beyond providing the least restrictive environment; and when this is achieved, both the handicapped and nonhandicapped establish productive, instructional relationships. An increased number of successful examples of integration are appearing in the contemporary literature (Gaylord-Ross & Pitts-Conway, 1984; Voeltz, 1984). Among the most interesting and mutually beneficial are those programs that involve the handicapped with the nonhandicapped in meaningful social interaction. The complexity of problems involved in planned integration are numerous, but the advantages of continuous effort toward this goal far outweigh the problems.

Moderately and severely handicapped students have made great gains in shared activities with their nonhandicapped peers. Educational settings should provide for readily planned interactions on a daily and long-term basis. Side-by-side classrooms—that is, special self-contained classes alongside regular ones—is a functional way to achieve this in elementary and secondary schools.

Changing Views Toward Placement

Although the cascade model of providing services to the handicapped has been predominant for a decade or more, it has recently been criticized for overemphasizing place, or educational setting. It is important to realize that providing a special setting for instruction and providing specialized instruction are not the same. By and large, the regular classroom is considered the most appropriate placement for the mildly handicapped, but this placement must be carefully planned with the necessary support services and teacher assistance that provide the individualization necessary for these students. In fact, some special settings have proven to be only diluted versions of regular classrooms. Conversely, the currently popular model of integration into the regular classroom does not necessarily mean better educational opportunities. True, it may remove the stigma of segregated education; but if it fails to meet the individual needs of the exceptional person, it can also, like the segregated classroom, be detrimental to the student. To summarize, educators are becoming increasingly aware that effective services to handicapped students are those that emphasize the quality and individualization of programs within the most integrated settings possible.

A recent article by Stainback and Stainback (1984) presents a very convincing rationale for merging special and regular education. The authors argue that maintaining dual systems of education, separate professional organizations, separate personnel preparation programs, and separate funding patterns may inhibit the integration of the handicapped and reduce the effectiveness of education. They point out that a single educational system could improve the quality of instruction for the handicapped and nonhandicapped alike. While such a merger is not imminent, the idea is an important one.

Services Outside the Schools

While educators and parents have pressed the schools to assume more responsibility for educating severely handicapped children and youth, services for the handicapped have also grown and improved outside the schools. Among these are new programs for handicapped preschoolers and adults. Preschool programming has been promoted through federal funds attached to P.L. 94–142 and the Handicapped Children's Early Education Act, which has supported model programs for the preschool handicapped around the country.

There have also been notable improvements in services for handicapped adults. There is a new emphasis on placement in competitive employment; today's community-based, on-the-job training programs have a higher success rate than previous vocational rehabilitation programs in activity centers and sheltered workshops. This success is due largely to the fact that clients are trained at the job site itself and the employer and co-workers as well as the clients are prepared for eventual integrated employment. In addition, more attention is being given to helping the handicapped make a successful transition from school to adult life. This involves coordinating support services to assist the handicapped adult in achieving a more independent work and life style. The active support of community leaders and parents is now more clearly recognized as a critical factor in the adult's integration into the community. Equally important is training that gives the handicapped person the social skills necessary to relate successfully to co-workers and other members of the community. Although many nonhandicapped and mildly handicapped students make the transition to adult life with minimal support from public services, severely handicapped students will need explicit transition planning and ongoing public support (Wilcox & Bellamy, 1982). Their success will depend on three factors: preparation in the schools, the transition period, and the quality of adult services.

Approaches to Teaching the Exceptional

On one level the history of special education has been characterized by a common effort among educators to expand and improve services to meet the needs of all handicapped individuals, regardless of their age or the severity of their handicaps. On the classroom level, however, the field has seen perhaps more disagreement than agreement. A large part of this controversy, no doubt, has stemmed from the fact that special education is a hybrid of several older disciplines, particularly medicine, psychology, and education. Thus, special educators over the last several decades have relied on varying explanations of what causes a given type of handicap and have proposed varying strategies for maximizing performance in the face of that handicap.

Much of present practice in special education, for example, has its roots in the medical model that physicians use to treat their patients: they diagnose an illness or injury in terms of what has caused it and then prescribe medication, surgery, or some other remedy to cure it. In fact, the term "diagnostic prescriptive teaching" is still used in current articles (Gettinger, 1984). Others in the field of special education use models from psychology to explain how children acquire, retain, and apply information. Depending on which theories seem most sound, these specialists may hypothesize that children are ready to learn certain kinds of information only at certain ages, that certain children learn better from visual rather than auditory stimuli (or vice versa), or that some children need help in learning processes (such as memory) before they can acquire basic skills (such as reading). Still others involved in special education see themselves primarily as scientists. The scientific model seeks to systematically arrange all aspects of the learner's environment and collect information on the learner's progress in order to identify changes in the environment that might result in increased learning.

Apart from these differences in points of view, special educators do share a common conviction about teaching handicapped students. This common ground is their view that handicapped students require more detailed assessment of strengths and needs, greater individualization of instruction and curriculum, and more careful and systematic monitoring of performance to prevent them from falling behind on tasks that normal students might be expected to master almost independently. In other words, it is likely that even special educators who disagree on the precise causes of a given student's handicap, or even on the need to identify the precise causes, might nevertheless work with that student in strikingly similar ways. Both would select special materials and activities to develop needed skills and would carefully monitor the student's progress. And both would adjust the materials and activities if progress was not satisfactory.

Systematic Instruction

One highly successful and scientifically based approach to teaching handicapped learners relies on systematic instruction and the application of behavioral principles in the classroom. Systematic instruction is based on the principle that focusing on the behavior of each individual provides us with the best information about that individual's abilities and needs.

> The specific curricula, materials, and instructional tactics which are required in teaching will vary with the needs of the pupil and the limitations of the situation in which instruction must take place. In order for teaching to be consistently effective, therefore, it must consist in part of procedures designed to determine and monitor the needs of the individual learner. Consistently good teaching is a process of learning— learning how to help others learn. . . . Unless the teacher is prepared to observe the behavior and learning patterns of each student carefully, noting particular needs and reactions to the instructional plan, some of the children will fail. A teacher must have the tools and skills necessary to learn from each child what best facilitates that child's growth. (White & Haring, 1980, p. 5)

As its name implies, systematic instruction is an organized body of plans and procedures—a technology for teaching. It is based on

gathering objective data regarding the student's performance level at the start of the program,

establishing priorities among the skills the student needs to learn,

identifying the prerequisite behaviors that are necessary to develop those skills, carefully assessing progress in acquiring new skills, and

using data from progress assessments to revise instructional procedures before the student fails.

Task Analysis   To guide the student from simpler to more complex responses, systematic instruction relies on breaking down a task into a series of small steps. Whenever a student cannot master a specific task, the teacher reduces it to smaller, more manageable units arranged in a careful sequence. The goal of teaching a severely handicapped student to feed himself may be reasonable, for example, but it is hardly precise enough to allow for carefully planned instruction. By dividing the skill into small instructional objectives, the teacher can sequence them so that one subskill builds on another. Thus, if the student has difficulty in chewing food, the teacher knows not to begin mealtime with instruction on how to use a spoon. The first step must be the most fundamental one.

Observation and Measurement   Systematic instruction might quickly become a rigid set of inflexible procedures without the continual updating of information on student progress. After specifying a skill that the student must have in order to succeed in the world (for instance, adding simple math facts), the teacher must then measure the student's progress in terms of her ability to do that task. The information that comes from this direct observation is used to set up an instructional program. The direct measurement of several such target skills tells a teacher what the student can do and what she must learn. This information is organized into long-term and short-term objectives that help the teacher place the student in the curriculum and sequence instructional activities.

The teacher continues to collect and use information to make any necessary changes in the instructional plan. By collecting the information frequently—even daily in many cases—the teacher can change a plan before the student actually fails (White & Haring, 1980). And when the student demonstrates mastery of a skill, the information tells the teacher to advance the student to the next objective in the sequence. This process is called a data-based approach to instructional decisions.

Planned and Individualized Instruction   To carry out such a finely tuned instructional program, the teacher must specify an educational program for each student, the steps within the program, the sequence of tasks, preparations and procedures, a record of correct and incorrect behavior, and criteria by which change can be measured. Specifying all of this information makes it possible for any person on the teaching staff, as well as parents, to work with the student on a one-to-one basis.

Thus, by following the simple steps of assessing the student's performance, choosing the exact skills he needs to learn, and measuring and evaluating the student's mastery of each of those skills, teachers can monitor each student's progress. Plans can be made and modified to provide meaningful success for each individual.

It should be noted that systematic instruction does not end with the simple acquisition of skills and knowledge. Instruction must continue until students achieve consistent and fluent performance in a variety of settings. The ability to apply a skill learned in one setting to other situations with other individuals is called generalization; it is a key focus of instructional programming especially for severely handicapped students.

Systematic instructional procedures are just as applicable to teaching mildly handicapped and nonhandicapped individuals as they are to teaching the severely handicapped. This point is perhaps the most important of all. The need to be more precise, more careful, and more effective in helping the severely handicapped learn has led to the refinement of teaching skills in general education. With the legal mandate to improve instruction for all handicapped students and the accompanying return of many mildly handicapped individuals to regular classrooms, perhaps these students can bring with them—through consultation with special educators and comprehensive in-service training efforts—the systematic instructional approaches that have been developed to help them. And perhaps instruction for all students can be made more systematic and more effective.

Almost all special educators who have experienced success in teaching exceptional children have applied a certain degree of systematic instruction to their approach. Yet the idea of precise and systematic approaches is still controversial among many practitioners Those who favor systematic instruction maintain that evidence of change in academic and social performance cannot be demonstrated without a record of performance during instruction or before and after an instructional segment. In addition, in order to be able to identify the conditions under which the changes occurred, a detailed description of the instructional plan—including the instructional arrangements, conditions, and materials—is necessary. These are considered the technical aspects of teaching (Tawney & Gast, 1984).

On the other hand, Guess and Siegel-Causey (1985) believe the special education teacher must go beyond being systematic.

> It is our position that technicians can be taught to follow carefully prescribed instruction programs. With instruction, technicians can be prepared to systematically and accurately move a severely handicapped learner toward successful completion of an identified educational objective. It is a teacher, however, who can provide a broader approach to the educational process by modifying the instructional environment to enhance untargeted emerging skills that demonstrate movement toward more complex and adaptive levels of functioning. (p. 242)

The Teaching and Management Professionals

For most of our history the teaching of all students was the responsibility of the regular classroom teacher; those who were too seriously handicapped to succeed in a regular classroom simply did not go to school. By the middle of this century, however, the regular teacher began to serve handicapped children and youth—mainly by identifying those students in the class who seemed unable to keep up with their peers or whose behavior created serious discipline problems. Once identified, these students were referred to a school psychologist or other evaluator. This individual determined whether or not they should be placed in a separate, special education class, where they would receive more individualized attention. Once placed, they became the responsibility of the special education teacher rather than the regular classroom teacher. Now, however, the move toward mainstreaming has changed the regular teacher's role. Educating children and youth in the least restrictive environment means that the regular classroom teacher must once again assume more responsibility for teaching handicapped pupils.

Regular and Special Education Teachers   Over the years what has distinguished the regular classroom teacher from the special education teacher has not been simply the students' level of skill, but the teachers' methods and curricula as well. For the most part, the regular classroom offers the standard curriculum of the school system to groups of students. There is relatively little one-to-one instruction (Hall, 1979), although over the years more and more elementary teachers have broken their classes into groups of faster- or slower-paced pupils for reading and perhaps for math or spelling instruction. There remains a heavy premium placed on order and control (Silberman, 1970), not only to maintain classroom discipline but also to socialize children and youth as members of an orderly society.

In short, the differences between special education and regular classroom teachers are primarily differences in the degree to which each uses systematic instructional procedures. Special educators employ a greater degree of individualized assessment, planning, and instruction than do their counterparts in regular classrooms. Of course, not all special education teachers follow these steps with all students, and the degree of precision with which teachers follow them varies considerably also. Even so, this system represents increasingly common practice in the field.

In addition to regular and special education teachers, an impressive number of other professionals may join in serving an exceptional learner.

Paraprofessionals.   Trained paraprofessionals are employed in every kind of special education setting, and they work with persons with all levels of handicaps. They may perform any of a wide variety of clerical, instructional, and other tasks— observing students, writing reports, assisting in preparing instructional materials, reinforcing learning with small groups, and (with the severely handicapped) performing housekeeping duties (Tucker & Horner, 1977).

Reading Specialists   These specialists, trained in diagnosis and remediation of reading problems, most frequently work with reading problems in children not specifically labeled as handicapped.

The reading specialist may be a classroom teacher who has had a well-structured program of advanced preparation, a special resource teacher who assists others in a variety of educational matters, or a remedial reading teacher. . . . The well-prepared reading specialist usually proceeds through a series of diagnostic steps that are sequenced to obtain the largest possible amount of information about a child's problems with the smallest amount of time and testing that can be expended to achieve the desired results. . . . The excellent reading teacher provides a program of developmental instruction as the foundation for remedial work and adds heavy amounts of additional work to fill the gaps in the child's skills that have been identified. (Sartain, 1976, pp. 492–493)

Communication Disorder Specialists Although the communication disorder specialist (also called speech pathologist, speech-language clinician, speech therapist) may work in private practice, hospitals, clinics, rehabilitation centers, or government agencies, 70% of these professionals work in the schools (Stick, 1976). Formerly, they had relatively large caseloads (around 50 students), with whom they worked once or twice a week—often requiring them to travel to several different school buildings each day. The majority (probably 80%) of the cases involved articulation problems (Stick, 1976). In recent years, however, more emphasis has been placed on the larger problems of language delays and language disabilities evidenced by many handicapped children (see chapter 7). Since so many severely handicapped individuals are nonvocal or have serious communication delays and problems, continued growth in programs and services for this population will require substantial increases in the numbers of these specialists.

School Psychologists/Educational Diagnosticians Traditionally, the school psychologist conducted the psychoeducational diagnosis of each student referred for possible placement. This "workup" usually consisted of administering a battery of standardized tests, including an intelligence test, academic achievement tests, and one or more tests of social or emotional development. The school psychologist's recommendation was frequently the principal basis on which a student was labeled handicapped or not. In recent years the school psychologist's evaluations have included more direct observations of the student's behavior in school. Many school psychologists now act as consultants to regular and special teachers, particularly in such areas as collecting data on student performance, applying systematic instructional principles, and establishing behavior management programs.

Vocational Education Teachers These teachers, with their skills in providing work experiences and job training for students, are essential in special or mainstream programs to prepare handicapped students for adult careers. Unfortunately, few vocational education teachers have had sufficient training in working with handicapped students, and several studies report that these teachers have largely negative views toward integrating handicapped students into regular vocational education programs (Comptroller General, 1976; Minner, Knutson, & Aloia, 1979). Perhaps one explanation of this reaction lies in the fact that in 1974 only about 500 of the 266,000 vocational education teachers in the country had received special training in working with the handicapped (Comptroller General, 1976). Although some progress has been made in changing attitudes and providing training for these educators (Minner & Knutson, 1980; Regan & Deshler, 1980), far more must be done to involve them fully in planning and programming for handicapped students.

Guidance Counselors Guidance counselors can assist handicapped students in career planning (Nelson, 1980) and can play an important role in helping handicapped students adjust to school life—by counseling, offering management suggestions to teachers, and serving as liaisons between home and school (Wallace & McLoughlin, 1979).

Physicians Physicians play a crucial role in identifying children with potential handicaps, primarily because they are often the first professionals to assess the development of infants and young children. And since serious medical problems threaten so many severely and physically handicapped children, the physician's evaluation and direction is very important. Physicians are frequent sources of support and guidance for parents of mildly handicapped students as well. They often prescribe medication to change the behavior of learning disabled youngsters, particularly those considered hyperactive. And although many educators criticize the overuse of such medication, teachers and physicians can work together productively. In one instance, for example, when teachers directly measured pupils' academic performance, they were able to give physicians pertinent, reliable data on how differences in medication affected their students' schoolwork (Scranton, Hajicek, & Wolcott, 1978).

Nurses Nurses specially trained to work with handicapped children can assist in early screening and assessment of handicapped preschoolers, even observing their parents' perceptions and needs (Erickson, 1976). They can also advise and assist teachers of the severely handicapped in the development of nutrition and social skills programs and in the use of medication as it relates to classroom management. They can set up guidelines and procedures for illness and emergency care and can even help develop programs to teach self-help skills, such as menstrual care for retarded girls (Blackard, Hazel, Livingston, Ryan, Soltman, & Stade, 1977). Nurses can also take responsibility for providing genetic counseling for families with handicapped children.

Physical and Occupational Therapists These professionals survey the muscular abilities of the handicapped and prescribe and implement appropriate programs for them. At the earliest stage of infant intervention, they coach the parents on how to manage their handicapped child, and they later work to ensure that the disabled individual is handled and placed in normal positions for proper physical development. Therapists also recommend adaptive equipment—wheelchairs, prone boards, pillows, scooters, standing tables, walkers—to help handicapped individuals function more independently in their environment. Physical and occupational therapists provide assessment, treatment, and consultation on the development of both gross and fine motor skills, as well as self-help skills (like feeding) when motor problems may interfere with progress. They often administer individual therapy, and many also train classroom teachers and paraprofessionals to implement appropriate motor development programming.

Adaptive Physical Education/Recreation Therapy Specialists These professionals can help handicapped students participate in physical education programs in schools, an important step in integrating them into the mainstream of school life. Many are also working now in state and local agencies that provide recreation and leisure programs, most often called therapeutic recreation. Their goal is to help handicapped individuals experience the same physical, emotional, and social benefit of recreation and leisure activities that nonhandicapped people enjoy (Heward & Orlansky, 1980).

Social Workers Caseworkers from social welfare agencies are frequently involved in working with families of handicapped children from poor socioeconomic circumstances, families of delinquent youths, and handicapped children placed in orphanages and foster homes. They can sometimes give educators information on the home environment that is relevant in planning for appropriate placement or programs; they can also represent the school's decisions to parents or guardians. They can even help monitor the effects of home-based intervention efforts with children in preschool and Head Start programs. Some schools employ social workers as regular members of their staffs.

School Administrators The building principal or administrator in charge of special education services can provide IEP team members with support and access to resources, such as transportation to a special center or a sign langage interpreter for a deaf student. The administrator is primarily responsible for seeing that all the requirements of due process and confidentiality have been met, scheduling IEP meetings, making certain that all necessary information is available for the team's decision making, and even making the final recommendation when the team cannot reach a consensus (Pasanella, 1980).

Conclusion

The field of special education has changed drastically since Itard spent five years working with the wild boy of Aveyron, instituting what is considered the first special education program. Several decades later, Seguin argued that all mentally retarded individuals could learn, paving the way for further development of the field. The early 20th century saw more gains in the education of special individuals: Binet drafted the first intelligence test in 1905 and compulsory education was mandated in 1918, advancing the cause of all public education. Later in the century, in 1954, *Brown v. the Board of Education* affirmed education as the right of all Americans, a right that could not be denied except by due process of law.

The mid-20th century has witnessed growth in the interest and services for the handicapped. Along with this growth, classification and definitions of exceptionality have developed. Exceptional people differ significantly from the norm in ways that affect their success in personal, social, or educational endeavors. The gifted and talented are included in the term *exceptional*, but not *handicapped*. Exceptional people are classified by the type of deviations they have: sensory, mental, communication, learning, behavior, or physical. Labeling is the means of classifying people according to their major deviation in order to facilitate special services; however, labels cannot adequately describe nor can they indicate the appropriate services needed.

Study Questions

1. What were some developments in psychology, education, medicine, technology, and public policy during the 20th century that paved the way for the growth and expansion of special education?

2. Why is P.L. 94–142 an important landmark in federal legislation?

3. What are the minimum requirements of an individualized education program (IEP)?

4. Discuss the advantages and disadvantages of labeling as a process for identifying and classifying exceptional students. Is there an alternative to labeling?

5. Discuss the problems in establishing the prevalence of special kinds of handicapping conditions in the general public.

6. What are some characteristics of systematic instruction?

7. In addition to regular and special education teachers, what other professionals are called upon to provide services to exceptional learners?

2

Technological Applications for Children with Special Needs

Linda McCormick
University of Hawaii

Norris G. Haring
University of Washington

Machines that process information and communicate the results of that processing have been with us for a long time. However, there have been substantial gaps in progress toward realization of the practical potential of these "thinking" machines.

The first mechanical computers were developed by Charles Babbage in 1835. He called one the "difference engine" and the other the "analytical engine." Augusta Ada Byron, the poet Lord Byron's daughter, developed the first program in 1857. Unfortunately, Babbage was not able to complete his machines because the technology of the time was not capable of producing the necessary parts, so Byron never actually ran her program.

A century later, in the 1930s and 1940s, Howard Aiken and other British scientists applied Babbage's principles to produce a machine that had all the elements of a modern computer. However, the real excitement about computers began in the sixties, when silicon chips made miniaturization, enhanced memory, and processing possible. Since that time technology has moved ahead at an amazing speed. We have become accustomed to such marvels as solar-powered calculators, computer-controlled car engines and microwave ovens, and talking computers that would have startled our grandparents.

The computer revolution of the eighties is like the Sputnik revolution of the fifties: it has stimulated an unprecedented curriculum reform movement. The number of computers in schools has almost doubled every year since 1980. A 1983 survey reported that 42% of elementary schools and 77% of secondary schools owned at least one microcomputer (Becker, 1983). These figures were up from 23% and 53% respectively in 1982 and from 10% for both in 1981. If this growth rate continues, the vision of computers in every classroom, which has been described and debated by regular and special educators for more than 20 years, may be realized by 1990. By the year 2000 we will probably have trouble remembering how we taught without computers.

The dramatic cost reduction of computers in the eighties is the major reason for the explosion in school computer use: The computers of the eighties are affordable. They are also decidedly more powerful, easier to operate, and considerably smaller than their ancestors. What was once a room-sized machine is now small enough to sit on a desk or table and lightweight enough to be moved from one location to another. The newest microcomputers, which can fit easily into a standard briefcase, weigh little more than a hardback dictionary.

The development of software and hardware for handicapped students began to attract some attention in 1980, when researchers at Johns Hopkins University undertook the National Search for Personal Computing to Aid the Handicapped (Schiffman, Tobin, & Buchanan, 1982). This year-long search, which offered nearly 150 cash awards and prizes, was the first nationwide attempt to find creative software and hardware applications for special needs students. Interestingly, 22 of the 97 best entries dealt with nonvocal communication.

Use of Microcomputers in Special Education

The broad purpose of education for both regular and exceptional learners is to prepare them to function in and contribute to society. Microcomputers can provide efficient and effective solutions to many of the problems educators face in attempting to meet this goal. As a tool for teachers and students, computers are both a medium and an object of instruction. Teachers can create individualized instructional environments and can manage and generate instructional, research, and administrative data. For some students the computer is a learning tool; for others (the physically and sensorily impaired) it is also a communication device and a means of environmental control. It can also provide both recreational and vocational opportunities. The only limitations, which are fast dissipating, are the lack of appropriate software and the shortage of teachers skilled in creating and/or adapting courseware to their curriculum needs.

Computer technology is particularly attractive as an educational tool for special needs students because, as Behrmann and Lahm (1984) have noted, there are

many similarities among computers, instructional methods used in special education, and the learning characteristics of handicapped children. These similarities include the ability to individualize and to provide needed repetition and the computer's infinite patience in drill and practice. The computer can also be programmed using the principles of applied behavioral analysis to provide consistent and systematic feedback and reinforcement for children. Another similarity is in the logical sequencing using in programming computer software and the special education instructional medium for defining and objectively measuring progress toward mastery criteria in instructional tasks, allowing teachers to collect and analyze more data on student performance than previously possible within the parameters of their classrooms. (p. v)

Attempts in special education to differentiate instruction solely on the basis of students' characteristics (called aptitude-treatment interaction) have not been particularly successful (Lloyd, 1984). However, there are some methods that have proven effective with most handicapped students:

1. reducing distracting and irrelevant stimuli
2. simplifying and repeating task directions
3. providing for substantial practice after a concept or skill is initially acquired
4. modeling and demonstrations
5. providing prompts and cues
6. breaking instruction into small, manageable steps
7. delivering immediate and frequent reinforcement and feedback

With well-designed software the computer can provide these instructional supports. It can be used for everything from drill-and-practice to simulations of real life events; it is a vehicle for teaching logical thinking, deductive reasoning, and creative writing skills. However, its greatest potential, even more significant than enhancing academic learning, may be in the areas of communication, motivation, and self-esteem.

A single chapter cannot begin to answer all the questions teachers have about integrating microcomputers into their programming for special needs students. We can provide only a general overview of the types of software available for instruction, management, and job preparation. Ultimately, after you have learned about microcomputers and used them in your classrooms, it will be up to you to evaluate their role in helping you prepare your students to function in and contribute to society. Figure 2-1 provides definitions for some basic terms that are apt to be encountered in a discussion of computers.

Assessment and Instructional Software

Assessment   With the appropriate software, computers can perform a number of assessment tasks, including (1) test construction, (2) test administration, (3) scoring and analysis, and (4) filing/storage of test results. Teachers can construct tests from their own or commercially available pools of testing items. They can then print the test and administer it in a pencil-and-paper format or use on-line test administration, where students interact directly with the computer. Advantages of on-line administration include highly individualized testing, reliable error analysis, and efficiency. The most often used individualization technique is branching, which adapts the test during administration according to student responses.

The use of computerized test-scoring programs frees professionals from such repetitive and tedious tasks as adding raw scores and reading tables of normative scores. Such programs also decrease the likelihood of computational error. Edu-

Cursor: A visible sign that moves around the screen to indicate where the next symbol will appear.

Disk (or disc): A round plate coated with magnetic material on which are stored the programs for operating the microcomputer. There are two primary kinds of disks—the hard disk, which is made of metal and permanently mounted inside the computer; and the changeable, plastic (floppy) disk, which is inserted into a disk drive.

Disk drive: The record-player part of the computer. It reads or writes data on the disk and moves data between the disk and the computer's memory.

Input device: Any peripheral that permits the communication of information to the computer. The most common input device is a keyboard. Other input devices include the mouse, which is a sort of pointer used with the Apple Macintosh; the Koala Pad, which is a graphics tablet; and a joystick, used for arcade games.

Memory: The computer's information storage capacity. The computer has two types of memory. Random-access-memory (RAM) is something like instant recall. When the power is turned off, information stored in RAM is lost unless it has been transferred to another memory device. Read-only-memory (ROM) is the permanent memory necessary for the computer's operation. This information cannot be altered or lost, and it can be recalled by the user.

Modem: A device (usually peripheral) that links the computer to a telephone line for communication with other computers. The transfer of information between two or more computers via the telephone network is called telecomputing.

Peripheral: Any equipment or accessory that can be attached to the computer. Peripherals include disk drives, monitors, printers, separate keyboards, cassette players, joysticks, and modems.

Software: The sets of instructions (programs) that tell the computer (the hardware) how to do specific tasks. These instructions are written in a computer language and stored on disks.

Figure 2-1   Basic computer terms

cational diagnosticians save further time by using word processing software for automatic report-style formatting and rapid printing of reports. Assessment data and reports can be filed and stored in an easily accessible form for subsequent development of instructional goals and objectives or for monitoring and research purposes.

Instruction   There are at least five interrelated applications of computer-assisted instruction (CAI): (1) drill-and-practice programs, (2) tutorials, (3) simulations, (4) problem-solving programs, and (5) word processing. Each application uses a somewhat different delivery method that matches the type of learning required. CAI can be used to supplement instruction provided by the teacher, or it can be used in place of teacher presentation.

Drill-and-practice programs present material in a repetitive fashion until the student reaches some prespecified criterion. Though the terms *drill* and *practice* are often used interchangeably, there is some value in their differentiation because they involve somewhat different teaching and learning processes (Dennis & Kansky, 1984). Drill involves associative learning; it is basically the process for teaching established facts, such as spelling and the multiplication tables. Practice, on the other hand, teaches step-by-step procedures, such as word-attack skills and sentence parsing. In both cases learning requires repetition and feedback, but the presentation formats and the outcomes are quite different.

The computer is ideal for drill and practice. In addition to being more palatable to students than workbooks or flash cards, computer drill-and-practice programs save teachers (and parents) time and patience. The computer can generate a large number of individualized problems or examples of a given type, present those problems at a pace commensurate with the student's ability, provide corrective or reinforcing feedback, keep records, and determine when a satisfactory performance level has been attained.

Tutorials are designed to help students acquire new information and/or skills. Ideally, the level of sophistication and the direction of the dialogue are determined by the student's responses. Branching and reinforcement strategies provide an individualized program for each student. A typical format is the presentation of paragraphs of material interspersed with a succession of carefully planned questions. Programs that teach a programming language, typing, algebra, shape discrimination and letter recognition, and basic math concepts are examples of tutorials. Tutorials can be as much fun as games, or they can be as boring as worksheets.

Simulations are teaching games. Good simulations provide a realistic context for problem solving. Some model real social and physical phenomena and associated decision making, and others use fictional situations. These programs can provide students with exposure to such adventures as piloting an airplane, running a nuclear reactor, or crossing America's wilderness with the pioneers. Students are required to make decisions as to what data to collect, how to alter the environment, and when to seek the advice of authorities. In most simulations there is more than one path to successful resolution of the problem, each with specific consequences. The effect of reading deficiencies can be minimized by presenting information graphically or with a speech synthesizer.

Problem-solving programs take a somewhat more direct approach to teaching problem-solving skills than do simulations. They teach students to apply step-by-step decision-making procedures to the translation of data into information and conclusions. Students learn how to structure problems in a logical form, express ideas as algorithms (procedural rules for problem solving), use computer models to simulate real systems, and analyze data.

Word processing programs can be used to improve students' writing, grammar, spelling, and even reading skills. The word processor allows changes in text with relatively simple keyboard commands: paragraphs can be rearranged, spelling corrected, and new words or phrases inserted. Word processing programs can improve the possibility of creative expression and give students a product to be proud of when they finish an assignment. The motivational potential of a word processing

Teaching games motivate as well as instruct.

program depends on two factors: the student's proficiency in using the program and the teacher's creativity in assigning interesting activities.

Authoring Systems

Teachers do not have to be skilled programmers in order to create individualized programs for their students; authoring materials are available. There are basically two categories of authoring systems—relatively simple programs that allow creation of drill-and-practice or question-and-answer lessons and more complex programs with which teachers can develop interactive courseware that identifies student error and tells the nature of the error. Even with very little programming know-how, teachers can formulate drills and exercises based on a student's particular capabilities. Most authoring systems include a print option so that word lists and games can be printed out for pencil-and-paper use. The more complex systems allow teachers to use graphics and sound to develop problem-solving programs, games, and simulations. Some of these systems permit development of interactive programs, enabling teachers to present concepts in narrative form and then ask questions about the material.

Special Education Management Software

Management of the educational plans and records of special education students is no small task. State and federal regulations designed to ensure equal educational opportunity for handicapped students place enormous demands on special education teachers and administrators. Computer-managed instructional (CMI) systems free professionals from some of these tasks so that they can spend more time in direct instruction. At the same time these systems provide a more concise and comprehensive documentation of student needs and progress to assist decision making.

With the appropriate software computers can assume major responsibility for planning and assigning learning activities, monitoring and evaluating student progress, and managing data. They can also assist IEP development and decision making. An example of the latter is a program developed by Hasselbring and Hamlett (1984) using decision rules developed by Haring, Liberty, and White (1980) to help teachers know when an instructional program should be changed and what type of change should be made. This program, titled AIMSTAR, also helps teachers manage student performance data and carry out graphing and flow-chart analysis.

Job Preparation and Career Information

We can only speculate as to what employment requirements will be in the year 2000, but there is little question that many future job opportunities will depend on the knowledge and skills necessary to apply, maintain, and/or service computers. Knowing how to use computers may, in fact, be a standard requirement for all jobs. Computer technology and the job market have led to the development of new curricula and revised approaches to job counseling for disabled students.

There are a number of systems specifically designed to provide students with information about career opportunities in technological fields. Foremost among these is VOCOMP, developed by Guidance Information Services and marketed by the Houghton Mifflin and Timeshare Corporation. VOCOMP provides 875 occupational descriptions in its data base. This service assists rehabilitation counseling and also makes recommendations for client placement based on interest and aptitude ratings. Because VOCOMP considers local job market trends, it has the ability to suggest jobs available in the client's geographic area.

Recreation and Motivation

Many nonhandicapped children and adults spend leisure time playing computer games, and this use of computers should be equally available to handicapped persons. As an interactive medium, computer games have decided advantages over passive media such as radio, television, and movies (Cain, 1984). However, most severely handicapped students require training, and possibly some adaptations to the peripherals, in order to benefit from recreational use of computers.

There is also potential for the use of the computer as a reinforcer. Earning time for computer games and other applications by completion of traditional assignments is a powerful reinforcement for some students (Budoff & Hutten, 1982).

Applications with Special Needs Students

Judy was diagnosed at 8 months of age as having athetoid cerebral palsy. She has only very restricted use of her limbs with the most marked problems on the left side, and she cannot coordinate her breathing and orofacial muscles to produce intelligible speech. Judy is not able to walk or hold a pencil, but at 19 she is a college freshman majoring in computer science. First introduced to a computer at age 15, she uses a modified joystick and a headpointer to input information and create her own programs and graphics with Logo. (Logo is a programming language that is easy to learn but powerful enough to permit sophisticated programming.) In her specially equipped dormitory room at college, she also operates the telephone and a music synthesizer with her joystick and the C2E2 (Control, Communications, Education, and Entertainment system developed at the University of Alabama in Birmingham).

Four students in a special education resource room are sitting around a computer, discussing the type of weather (air pressure, humidity, wind, and temperature) required to make plants grow. There seems to be some disagreement as to whether the plant needed to sustain the life of Lowboz, an alien accidentally left on the planet Earth, can survive with clouds or overcast skies. After some discussion there is a decision to check out the possibility. One of the girls hits a key on the Apple keyboard to see what effect their weather decision has on the plant. There is an air of suspense as they all lean forward, peering expectantly at the screen. They are using a program called Weather Makers from the Center for Human Growth in Honolulu.

These are two of many possible examples of how computer technology is helping special needs students overcome barriers to learning and performance. For some students like Judy computers are more than just teaching machines; they are a means to reduce and compensate for the debilitating effects of sensory impairments, malfunctioning muscles, and damaged nerve pathways. For other students microcomputers are aids to learning important academic content, problem solving, inductive reasoning, and interpersonal communication skills.

Software is the key to effective use of the microcomputer. In some ways the selection of computer applications is similar to the selection of other types of curriculum aids; however, there are many more ways in which it is quite different.

Mildly Handicapped

Whether classified as learning disabled, behaviorally disordered, or mentally retarded, the overwhelming majority of mildly handicapped students demonstrate significantly below-average academic achievement. Among the factors contributing to their lack of success in academic areas are attention problems, retention deficits, and lack of motivation. Many have expressive and/or receptive language problems that affect communication and success in reading and spelling, and most demonstrate behaviors suggesting low self-esteem.

Substantially more data are needed to state with certainty that computers have a positive impact on the education of mildly handicapped students. However, some of the capabilities of CAI do seem to make it well suited to their needs.

1. *Reduction of distraction and irrelevant stimuli.* The stimulus value of important information can be heightened with verbal cues, animation, sound effects, and/or external prompts such as arrows that highlight relevant stimuli. Also, text pre-

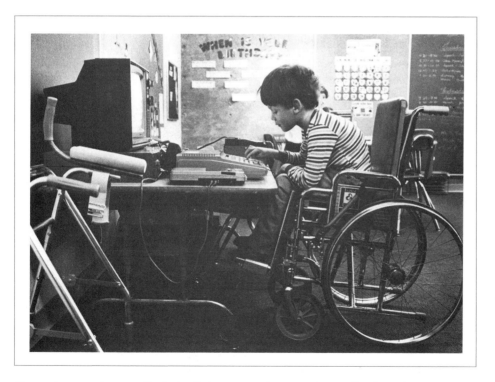

Computers can be coordinated with tape recorders or voice synthesizers for simultaneous audio and visual presentation.

sentation can be delayed so that the student sees only one letter, word, or phrase at a time.

2. *Simplification and repetition of task directions*. Task directions can be presented in a printed format and/or with a speech synthesizer at a level appropriate to the student's reading ability or receptive vocabulary. Repetitions can be provided as often as necessary at whatever pace the learner can handle.

3. *Practice for "overlearning."* Drill-and-practice programs are ideal for any skills and concepts such as math facts, spelling, and sight words that require repetitive presentation. An added advantage is student control of the pace of presentation.

4. *Modeling and demonstration*. There are two ways to have simultaneous audio and visual presentation. One method is to add a special switch, making it possible to synchronize a tape recorder with the text on the screen. Another method uses a speech synthesizer. A synthesizer such as the Echo II "speaks" the text as it appears on the screen. It is also possible, of course, to present a visual model or demonstration on the same frame with the instructions or immediately before it.

5. *Prompts and cues*. CAI offers the possibility of errorless learning. There are any number of ways to prompt and/or cue responses. Among the most popular are sound, color, and animation.

6. *Instruction in small, manageable steps*. CAI lends itself well to delivering instruction in small steps with frequent responses.

7. *Immediate and frequent reinforcement and feedback*. In addition to providing immediate corrective feedback in a nonthreatening manner, the computer has numerous reinforcement possibilities. Students can be reinforced for a correct response with a personalized praise statement, graphic displays, or brief game segments. As Hagan (1984) points out, students are less likely to punish themselves for wrong answers with CAI. They come to think of incorrect responses as "goofs"—a nonjudgmental attitude that encourages continued practice rather than giving up.

In addition to the application of methods that have proved effective with mildly handicapped populations, the microcomputer has other educational possibilities. Word processing and programming are uses of the computer that are unique to the medium; students can learn to think and be creative with these programs. In a sense the computer becomes both a learning tool and a teaching tool. Learning is at the same time student controlled and computer controlled. Students can experiment and discover within limits, but they must also follow some procedures because the computer has its own system of logic.

A word processing program is an intriguing tool for teaching and learning. Bank Street Writer and some other word processing programs have tutorial disks that help students learn the commands. Some programs also have command charts that can be posted above the computer as memory aids. With a program such as Bank Street Writer, even young children can produce a written product that is a source of pride rather than an embarrassment, and they can do it without the enormous concentration and effort that pencil-and-paper writing requires. Word processing programs can help students with language-learning problems overcome their "writer's block." Students become more creative and, equally important, begin to submit legible assignments. These programs also help students appreciate the importance of spelling as a functional tool rather than just another academic exercise.

Programming is, in a sense, a form of discovery learning. Logo, a programming language developed by mathematician Seymour Papert and colleagues, encourages exploration of the fundamentals of programming, mathematics, logic, and a variety of other subjects through the use of "turtle graphics." The student conceptualizes a specific design and then uses a small triangular cursor called a turtle to develop a program to create that design. According to Papert (1980), Logo is more than a language. It is a philosophy of learning based on two of Piaget's (1976) premises: children learn many important things without formal instruction, and they have an innate predisposition to make and revise theories about the interaction of objects and events in their environment.

In addition to being a tool for discovery learning, Logo can be used as an interactive programming language. It has been proven to be particularly successful with mildly handicapped students because Logo activities emphasize methods of doing things rather than answers (e.g., Weir, Russell, & Valente, 1982). It is the discovery and learning processes that count, not the product. Programming shifts control of the learning environment to the students, who become teachers challenged to instruct the computer to perform specific tasks. In the course of developing and testing their own instructional hypothesis, they learn about symmetry, design, angles, geometric forms, and mathematical logic.

Two problems that compound the learning difficulties of many mildly handicapped students are a poor self-concept and lack of social interaction skills. Considering the significant role that school experiences play in shaping how students feel about themselves, one can understand why many students with learning problems have a poor self-concept. The feeling of being a loser then affects future academic performance (a loser does not risk trying a difficult task) and social-emotional development. Failure and poor self-concept become part of a vicious cycle. The quantity and quality of both academic performance and peer relationships are affected. The potential of computers to interrupt this cycle may well be their most important contribution to the education of mildly handicapped students. With appropriately designed software, teachers can assure successful academic experiences, and mastery of an "electronic wizard" in itself goes a long way toward improving a student's self-concept.

In addition, it is possible to design experiences to facilitate peer interactions and group problem solving, even though this aspect of the technology has not received much attention. Computer experiences need not be one-to-one activities. All that is needed is to design the learning environment so that students must pool their mental resources to accomplish mutually desired objectives. This may or may not require special software. Programming is a particularly good vehicle for group problem solving. Assigning a small group of students the task of developing a sample program is one way to encourage cooperation and sharing of ideas. The process involves considerable communication and the testing of various alternative solutions. Student responses are often similar to those of a winning athletic team: there is much cheering and congratulatory hand slapping.

Another way to facilitate peer interactions and group problem solving is to develop or adapt software that requires collaborative decision making. The four students in the scenario described earlier were working with a program of this type called Weather Makers. Interpersonal communication is increased and enhanced by the requirement to collaborate to solve a problem, in their case to provide the right growing conditions for a plant. Each child had to assume the role of one of four weather elements—sun, wind, clouds, or rain. The content of this simulation program was designed to augment the science curriculum for grades 4 to 6.

Despite a plethora of literature discussing the characteristics of CAI that make it particularly well suited to the educational needs of mildly handicapped students, there has been relatively little research into effectiveness. The research of Alice Chiang (1978) and her associates in California represents one of the few large-scale studies in this area. Chiang and her associates concluded that the content of available CAI software was too difficult, the pacing was too fast, and the steps were too large. They then went on to develop an authoring system called Assist, which has lesson formats into which teachers can program the material from their existing curricula that they want to teach.

Teachers in four elementary and four junior high schools used the Assist program to create lessons for 200 mildly handicapped students. In all cases the computer instruction was a supplement to traditional methods. The average student had 5.3 lessons and 33 minutes of CAI per week during the school year. Cognitive impact was measured by gains (from pretest to posttest) on the Peabody Individualized Achievement Test (PIAT) and Keymath Tests. Significant differences on the reading recognition subtest of the PIAT were reported for two of the junior high classes in the treatment group. Overall, students who received CAI made positive (but not significant) group gains in three-fourths of the measures, and 83% of the teachers reported being highly pleased with the program. (Participating teachers created a total of 687 language arts and 124 mathematics lessons over a year's time.) Of particular interest are Chiang's data concerning student use of the lessons. Greater student usage was related to (a) fixed scheduling of computer time, (b) higher student reading ability, (c) individualized (as opposed to group) instructional formats, and (d) teacher enthusiasm.

In another study Watkins and Webb (1981) compared the pre/post math gains of two groups of learning disabled students and maintained equal amounts of instructional time for students in the experimental and control groups. The experimental group received 10 minutes of math drill and practice each day while the experimental group received 10 minutes of traditional instruction. Students were pretested on the math computation section of the California Achievement Test (CAT) and posttested on the Math HELP, a criterion-referenced test. CAI students achieved significantly greater gains than the traditional-instruction group.

Peer interaction can be improved through computer programs that foster group problem solving.

Kleiman, Humphrey, and Lindsay (1981) also considered the effects of CAI in math, but their findings (at least in terms of skill gains) with 18 children described as hyperactive are not quite so optimistic. Performance on problems administered by a computer was compared with performance in the traditional pencil-and-paper format. The children worked on the computer and with pencil and paper on alternate days. Accuracy, number of problems attempted, and speed in problem solving were compared. Results indicated that the only differences between the two methods were in the number of problems the children attempted and the time commitment. They attempted almost twice as many problems on the computer and spent almost twice as much time working on the computer, but there were no differences in accuracy or speed of problem solving. The computer seemed to be highly motivating; it increased the attention span, but did not seem to affect learning.

The learning disabled students in a study by Trifiletti (1982) began with at least a two-year delay in math, as measured by the Keymath Diagnostic Arithmetic Test. Students in both the CAI experimental group and the control group received 40 minutes of instruction each day. An added incentive for students in the CAI group was the opportunity to earn 5 extra minutes a day to play computer games if they completed homework sheets. The CAI students gained about twice as many skills as the control group during the initial 5 months of the study. Over the full academic year they achieved a mean of 8 months' academic gain compared to a mean gain of 3 months for the control group.

Another study by Lally (1981) considered the effectiveness of the computer as an adjunct for teaching sight words to mildly handicapped students. Eight students were assessed and provided with supplemental CAI instruction in sight-word recognition. The control group received only traditional instruction. Lally noted that the purpose of this study was to demonstrate the usefulness of CAI as a supplement to traditional instruction, so there was no attempt to equalize the amount of instructional time for the two groups. Results indicated that for the CAI group the number of sight words recognized increased from 38 to 70, whereas the number for the control group increased from 38 to 47. A probe conducted after a 7-week vacation indicated that the CAI group had retained all 70 of the recognized words.

The results of these studies suggest some advantage for CAI over traditional instructional methods with mildly handicapped students, but a caveat is necessary. Some studies have found no differences in effectiveness of CAI instruction as compared with conventional methods (e.g., McDermott & Watkins, 1983). Substantially more research is needed before we can discount the possibility that some of the advantages of CAI are a function of the novelty of the technology (Clark, 1983).

Communication Disordered

Speech, language, and/or communication difficulties are associated with most handicapping conditions. Language and communication disorders are prevalent in mildly handicapped students—particularly students classified as learning disabled or mentally retarded. In addition, many severely handicapped persons have difficulty with speech and language because requirements of language and communication are demanding in both cognitive and motor senses. A third large group (chapter 7) has primarily a speech, language, and/or communication disorder.

To date, some of the most exciting and successful uses of electronic technology to facilitate interpersonal communication have been with nonverbal students and those with severe language disorders. There has been a diverse array of developments in this area since 1957, when LaVoy published the first report on an electronic communication device. Some 20 years later Vanderheiden (1977) located more than 100 different communications devices in use in North America and western Europe. With the current availability of relatively inexpensive, lightweight, battery-operated computers, such devices are becoming as practical and manage-

The Touch Talker is a communication aid that allows the language disordered individual to communicate needs. Because the device is lightweight, portable, and increasingly inexpensive, it is becoming as practical and manageable as eyeglasses or a hearing aid.

able as hearing aids and eyeglasses. Most important, communication aids are now also versatile. Some manufacturers, such as Prentke Romich in Ohio, have up-graded communication devices so that they can interface with microcomputers.

The same type of pointing devices that allow physically disabled students to control a computer keyboard are used with communication boards. A headpointer is probably the most common input device. Output devices include speech syn-thesizers, which can convert print to speech, and the printers themselves.

Most research has been concerned with technological development and selec-tion of appropriate communication devices and systems. Some of the questions that researchers must address now are these: Does the student initiate interactions with handicapped peers? Does the complexity of interactions increase over time? Does the student use the system wherever communication is appropriate? Is the student able to express his full range of knowledge? How does the introduction of an augmentative communication system affect cognitive and social development?

Use of microcomputers to assist speech and language training has not pro-gressed quite so rapidly as applications for augmentative communication—for sev-eral reasons. Until fairly recently the inferior quality of speech synthesizers pre-cluded their use as a speech therapy aid, and it was difficult to present pictures or animations as rapidly as desired. Another reason for the slower progress concerns the nature of language learning. Under optimal conditions a young child's interests, capacities, and needs stimulate adult responses and dictate the content of communicative exchanges. Research and design of interactive systems that can simulate caregiver-child exchanges are only now beginning to take place.

One example of this new focus is the pilot research project of Behrmann (1984) at George Mason University in suburban Washington, DC. Behrmann is using microcomputers to help handicapped infants (11 to 30 months) develop some control over their environments. Training begins by establishing simple cause-effect relationships: the babies learn to press a switch to make a happy face appear. (Some have a hand-operated switch, whereas others use switches that are activated by the head, foot, or eyebrow.) At the second training level they learn to choose between two possibilities—turning on a radio or activating a mechanical toy. At the third level they play a game and match a stimulus picture to one of two choices on the microcomputer. A correct match permits operation of the toy or radio. The next level of training offers more choices, and the baby receives a verbal prompt and encouragement (from the computer's voice synthesizer or the teacher). At this level the concept is more abstract because the child must associate a verbal symbol with the picture on the computer screen. There are about 12 options offered at this level, expanding the number of ways that the baby can interact with the environment. The next two levels of training provide four more options and introduce the concept of categorization. Eventually, the babies will be able to manipulate their surroundings with a small, maneuverable robot that brings toys and objects and signals for help.

Meyers (1984) describes another example of how the microcomputer can be integrated into language interventions with severely handicapped toddlers. She reports an application with a 26-month-old child who was blind, nonvocal, and diagnosed as having cerebral palsy. When the parents were asked what routines and games the child enjoyed, they reported that he showed the most pleasure when being sung to. The task then was to program the computer so that when the child touched any location on a plastic keyboard overlay (12″ × 12″), the speech synthesizer would produce the word *sing*.

In the first session the mother began singing a song and then stopped and asked, "Do you want me to sing?" If the child smiled or moved his head, the mother sang another verse. Then the requirements for control of this reinforcing event were increased. The mother said, "If you want me to sing, say *sing*. Touch the keyboard to say *sing*." She demonstrated by placing the child's hand on the keyboard. Initially, the child's lack of motor control precluded switch activation. However, by the end of the 20-minute session, he was holding his hand on the keyboard long enough to produce an output. The mother would sing a verse of a song, then stop and say, "What do you want me to do?" He would respond immediately by touching the keyboard to say the word *sing* and then smile and shift position in anticipation of continued singing. Once during this first session, to everyone's amazement, the child even said the word *sing* after touching the keyboard. In later sessions the same techniques were used to teach the request of a desired food and a favorite sound-making toy. Subsequent goals included modification of the keyboard to allow more varied and sophisticated requests.

Physically Impaired

A physical impairment can affect a student's range of motion, physical strength, coordination, communication, and interaction with instructional materials. The primary and most devastating effect of these problems is restricted opportunity to learn about and control the environment. The standard computer can help overcome and compensate for these restrictions. The first task is to adapt the turn-on switch and devise a means whereby the student can load software into the disk drives without assistance. Moving the turn-on switch to the front of the machine and attaching a pressure-sensitive switch solves the first problem. Hagen (1984) suggests constructing a small ramp for the disk drives to solve the second problem. If the student does not have sufficient coordination to slide the disk up the ramp with his hand or a mouthstick, the alternative is a completely automated system. Such a system operates something like the selection and storage system of the old jukebox; disks can be changed simply by pressing a button or activating a switch.

The next concern is how the student will input information—an access mode. Very often the standard input mode, a keyboard, can be made accessible to physically impaired students by repositioning it in some way, modifying the keys, or adding a keyguard. The addition of a keyguard or a change in the size and spacing of the keys prevents the student from striking more than one key at a time. One type of keyguard, available for Apple computers, has keyholes with a 5/8-inch diameter and a 3/4-inch space between keys.

Other students need more specialized access peripherals. At one time the majority of such devices were designed and custom-built in bioengineering laboratories and specialized clinics. Now there are a variety of reasonably priced, commercially available peripherals, such as the joystick, which can be used as is or adapted if necessary. The wires intended to control game paddles can be connected to whatever type of switch the student can manage. Single or multiple switch interfaces can be plugged directly into the microcomputer's game-control socket.

One of the newest input devices is the brow-wrinkle switch. This device has an adjustable headband, a body switch, and a small wheel that responds to movements of the body surface on which it rests. The students can control a scanning system simply by raising an eyebrow. Other input devices include head pointers, manual pointers, light pointers, and laser devices. There are also a variety of pressure-sensitive switches, such as breath switches, foot trolley switches, and tip switches. In addition to their use as computer input devices, these switches are useful for controlling electronic communication devices, tape recorders, record players, radios, slide projectors, appliances, and mechanical toys.

Another readily available input device that is functional for some physically handicapped students is a graphics tablet. Known as digitizing tablets, these devices look something like a small slate. They have a flat surface that is activated by the touch of a special stylus. The tablet can be covered with a grid template containing words, phrases, pictures, or letters. The size and number of symbols and, of course, the symbols themselves, depend on the needs and abilities of the user. The program in the computer decodes the x-y coordinates of the point of

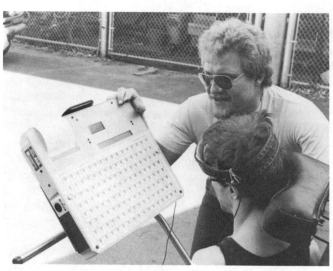

An adjustable headband gives a physically impaired student input capability that depends merely on eyebrow movement.

contact with the tablet and processes the input. In addition, some students with more control are able to use touch screens and light pens as input methods.

Students with some ability to vocalize may use voice entry to input information. The only requirement for voice entry (also called speech pattern recognition) is consistent signals. The computer is programmed to "hear" and match the student's sounds to others stored in memory. It can respond to sounds that are indiscernible by the human ear. Speech recognition technology permits voice control of any computer functions that a keyboard can access.

There is now a fairly wide selection of software adapted for use with alternative access devices. An example is the "handicapped typewriter," which is actually an Apple II with custom programs. This scanning system operates with single-switch input (Smith & Graystone, 1981). An array of letter and number symbols are displayed on the screen and sequentially highlighted by the scanner. When the desired symbol is highlighted, the student activates the switch to input that symbol into the computer. The handicapped-typewriter program has 26 files of commonly used phrases and sentences that can be personalized according to the communication requirements of different environments. This program can also control such peripherals as a calculator, a telephone, and an environmental-control system.

Until fairly recently the need to use a switch scanning system meant that physically handicapped students were limited to adapted software programs unless they could purchase the costly hardware necessary to run standard software programs. In order to use standard software, one needs what is called "transparent control"—a means of fooling the computer into thinking that input is coming from a keyboard, when it is really coming from a scanning system. One way to get transparent control is to use a keyboard emulator driven by a separate computer, but this is expensive. A much less expensive interface device, called the adaptive firmware card, is now available for the Apple II. This card permits access with 10 different input modes, including a number of scanning techniques, Morse code (or another code), or direct selection. It consists of a specially designed, printed circuit card that is inserted into a slot on the computer and a small plastic box that snaps onto the side of the computer. Installation requires only a few minutes. The significance of this device is that it enables physically disabled students to use virtually any software that will run on the Apple computer.

Other technological devices have been designed to increase mobility and personal independence. One example of a computer-based innovation is the electronically controlled wheelchair. Controlling these chairs is similar to and as easy as changing a television station with a remote control. For quadriplegics the control switch can be placed near the head; if manual control is not feasible, the chair can be controlled by a voice-activated device.

Another means of extending the functioning range of the physically handicapped is with robotics. Schneider, Schmeisser, and Seamone (1981) describe a worktable system with a computer-aided robotic arm, which can be activated by a quadriplegic through manipulation of a mouthpiece. The robotic arm can locate, manipulate, and position a typewriter, typing paper, reading materials, a telephone, and self-feeding equipment. Other electronic arms using microcircuitry allow physically impaired persons to control prosthetic arms by nerve impulses on the skin. In time these devices will replace the complicated array of straps and levers now used to control prosthetic limbs.

Visually Impaired

An earlier example described the application of a computer to language instruction of a blind child. The Kurzweil Reading Machine is another system designed for blind or visually impaired persons; it converts print into speech to help visually handicapped students "read." The printed material is placed face down on a scanning device, in much the same way as a printed page is placed on the screen of a photocopying machine. This device can read as many as 200 different type faces at a speed of up to 250 words per minute and can convert the input to speech. Other devices for the visually impaired include a speech synthesizer, which, when attached to the keyboard, says what is being typed; a talking directory, which provides both auditory and visual output of the appropriate telephone number when a name is supplied; and the Optacon, which translates print into tactile letters.

Other advancements in communication for the blind, described by Ruconick, Ashcroft, and Young (1984), are the electronic braille devices. These microprocessor-based systems use magnetic tapes or disks to store and retrieve information written in the braille code. For example, VersaBraille, manufactured by Telesensory System, allows the user to send information directly to the computer in braille; information sent from the computer is displayed in a line of movable pins representing 20 or more characters of braille data. Students can read electronic braille more rapidly than they read tactile letters, such as those of the Optacon.

Julie's using the Kurzweil Reading Machine to listen to Greek plays.

The scanner (to her right) reads a page placed on the glasstop.

The machine is programmed to read English, French, Spanish, or Arabic, depending on the tape used.

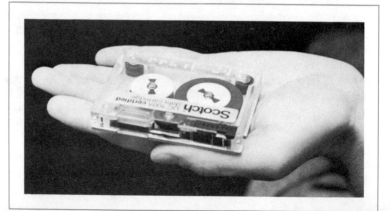

VersaBraille offers the listener about 200 pages of braille per 30 minutes of cassette (1,000 words per page).

Electronic braille devices permit computer input and output in braille.

Chuck uses an optical-to-tactile converter, the Optacon, with his counselor.

Greg adjusts the voice synthesizer on his talking IBM PC, which he is just learning to use. As an employee of the Ohio State University Disability Services Center, Greg helps track down articles for handicapped faculty and staff. He hopes to use his computer to access the library catalog. "And to think two weeks ago I thought *Pascal* was a 17th century philosopher," he says.

Synthesized speech devices provide the blind with another means of access to microcomputers. Information Through Speech (ITS), a Hewlett-Packard product modified by the Maryland Computer Services, is one device that utilizes synthetic speech to say or spell words, say whole lines of words, or say all the information on the screen. The student can control the rate of speech, pitch, tone, and volume. Another adaptation particularly valuable for the partially sighted allows the computer to generate enlarged print, through closed circuit television or magnifying devices.

Electronic technology can also provide greater independent mobility for the blind. One of the most recent mobility devices is the electronic travel aid (ETA). This device sends out electronic signals to sense the environment within a certain range, processes the data, and furnishes the user with relevant information. The most widely used of the ETAs are the Pathsounder, Mowat Sensor, Sonicguide TM, and Laser Cane (Hill & Bradfield, 1984).

Hearing Impaired

Developments in microcomputer technology are also aiding the deaf and hearing impaired. Hannaford (1983) reports the development of a bioear, a small disk con-

Peggy, a secretary, uses a closed-circuit TV hooked up to her typewriter so she can proofread individual letters. It can also split the screen so that she can copy from a printed page and check her typing at the same time.

taining a microprocessor that is implanted behind the ear. This tiny device receives auditory stimuli and converts them into a series of impulses, which are then passed to the brain via the auditory nerve.

The same speech recognition systems that permit the blind to read with synthesized speech also allow the deaf to see in print what others are saying to them. The computer hears the words or sounds spoken into a microphone, matches each to a pattern stored in its memory, and displays the message on the screen.

Another recent innovation is Deafnet, a computer-based telecommunications network. Although this system does not solve the isolation problem experienced by deaf persons, it does expand their potential for social interaction with both deaf and hearing populations because it can be accessed by either telecommunications devices for the deaf or standard computer terminals. Deafnet is like an electronic post office with private mailboxes, into which messages are sorted and saved until collected by intended recipients with a coded key (password). The network includes an electronic bulletin board, where users can post items of interest.

Gifted

Throughout this chapter we have emphasized the role of microcomputers in augmenting the quality of education and the learning environment. In no area is this more crucial than it is for gifted students. Feldman (1979) reminds us that Einstein's remarkable achievements were as much a function of the state of physics during Einstein's lifetime as they were a function of his talents. The co-occurrence of the individual and the environment produces gifted performance. The challenge is to design a learning environment in which gifted students can explore what computers can and cannot do, how widely and deeply they are affecting our society, and what ethical questions surround their use (Edwards, 1984).

Learning to program promotes logical, deductive thinking and strengthens creative thinking skills and problem-solving abilities. Other applications popular with gifted and talented students are word processing and data processing. Word processing programs allow gifted students to record and edit their creative ideas without having to be concerned with handwriting. They can use data processing programs (also called database management) to organize and manipulate data from their research, a function particularly appealing to gifted students.

The fundamental considerations in selecting software for this population are whether it stimulates higher-level thinking skills and provides opportunities for collaboration to strengthen vital peer relationships. Ideally, it should encourage or require divergent thinking, risk taking, and problem finding and problem solving; and it should be easily individualized.

One of several demonstrations of CAI with gifted students is found in a discussion by Walkington and Babcock (1984), who have used CAI successfully with gifted underachievers in developing subject skills. (Several producers have software and courseware available to cover the full range of subject areas.) According to the authors, the gifted enjoy programming computers to help teachers manage classroom chores such as grade computation, to provide tutoring assistance to other children, and to simulate favorite games.

As Turkle (1984) points out, children with different personalities and learning styles approach computers differently; the opportunities offered are as varied as the students themselves. Some students are attracted to computer programming as an opportunity to develop their mastery of abstract concepts and skills of analysis, organization, and logic. For students who are gifted in the arts and humanities, the computer's potential for direct manipulation and graphic display may bridge the gap to the otherwise unappealing worlds of mathematics and abstract thought. Open-ended, exploratory programs such as Logo offer unique possibilities for the development and expansion of gifted students' potential in a variety of learning areas.

Evaluation of Instructional Software for Special Needs Students

The greatest obstacle to wider use of microcomputers for instructional purposes is the lack of software. This holds true for teachers of both handicapped and nonhandicapped students. Compounding the problem is the fact that much of the software that is available is not good. Moreover, there are very few programs designed specifically for special needs students.

The major reason for the lack of special needs software is economics; publishers put their resources where the potential return is largest—that is, the regular education market. Another reason relates to the finding that well-designed software is often as effective with handicapped as with nonhandicapped students (Taymans & Malouf, 1984). Adaptations for students with physical and sensory impairments can be accomplished through hardware modifications, as previously described.

Hannaford (1983) suggests three criteria to consider when selecting software for use with special needs students: (1) educational appropriateness, (2) design, and (3) technical adequacy. These are what Taber (1983) calls "internal evaluation criteria"—questions that teachers and other school system personnel should ask before making software purchases. This type of evaluation requires preview of the software. Software evaluation may also be external, or based on information from outside sources (other agencies, organizations, or magazines).

The first question related to educational appropriateness is, Is it necessary? If learning can be accomplished as effectively and efficiently with worksheets and other printed materials, then microcomputer instruction may not be the best medium. The educational advantage may not be significant enough to justify the additional cost.

Another concern within the area of appropriateness is congruence of the software and specific student needs. Because the computer is basically a visual medium, the majority of programs require reading skills. It is important to determine precisely what reading level a program requires: sometimes the reading level is much higher than the content level. Also important is the spacing of the text: single-space lines and many lines of text in each frame can cause problems for special learners. The size of the letters, their clarity and spacing, and the use of upper- or lowercase should be considered. Use of a speech synthesizer can eliminate the reading problem, but these output devices also have some limitations. Very often the output is only marginally intelligible, so a speech synthesizer is generally not appropriate for language instruction or for use with hearing impaired students.

Careful attention should also be given to the program's pacing, prompts, and cues. Some special needs students must have delays between portions of text presentation and cues, such as, "Stop and think before you answer." Others need animation, directive arrows, and highlighting to focus their attention. A final consideration related to both student characteristics and design adequacy is reinforcement and feedback. Good programs provide immediate reinforcement for correct answers and specific and nonthreatening error feedback.

Another important question of appropriateness is whether the software is compatible with the curriculum philosophy and your instructional style (Hannaford, 1983). Some teachers do not like software that requires considerable monitoring. Others eliminate software that does not include adequate supplementary materials. It is possible, of course, to modify and update the program's content and presentation format, but many teachers do not have the skills or time required.

The second criterion is design adequacy. Hannaford lists important design features.

1. Specific objectives should be formulated with particular audiences in mind. There should be evidence of extensive content analysis of the topic, and this analysis should correspond to student needs. Additionally, the developers should indicate student entry level: what knowledge and skills the student must have in order to benefit from the program.

2. Content, organization, terminology, and spelling must be correct. Topics should be properly sequenced, and there should be provisions for recall and review to enhance retention.

3. Material must be presented in an attractive and instructionally sound manner, pace should be learner-controlled, and directions should be clarified with examples.

4. Response requirements must be at the same level of sophistication as the reading level and content, and they must be appropriate to the student's response capabilities. How the program evaluates the responses and how it provides feedback and reinforcement are also important considerations.

The third criterion is technical adequacy. It is often necessary to reject software packages because they have technical defects, or "bugs." Another consideration is whether the program makes use of all of the features of your particular computer. If your computer has color, graphics, and sound capabilities, these features should be incorporated in whatever software you purchase. If you have peripherals, such as a light pin, the software should also make use of these devices.

Hannaford and Taber (1982) also emphasize the importance of determining the extent to which the program can be modified and controlled (by teacher and/or student). Some programs cannot be modified because of safeguards to prevent unauthorized duplication. Also, students should be able to begin the program, select a desired module, obtain operating instructions from the program if needed, and exit when desired. Many programs are not flexible enough to allow this degree of learner control.

Another consideration of technical adequacy has to do with how fragile the program is. If software is vulnerable to random input, it may be damaged within a very short time, whether it is being used by handicapped or nonhandicapped children. All of these evaluation issues are critical to decision making. Judicious evaluation prior to the purchase of software can prevent costly mistakes.

Innovation and Development

It is extraordinary that a tiny silver-gray fleck of silicon no larger than an infant's fingernail has reached into every area of modern life and has influenced the naming of an age. Even more awesome are the predictions that there will be tinier chips with more power in the future and that artificial intelligence will become a reality by 1990 (Boraiko, 1982).

Many new developments are under way. One of them, the optical video disk, makes visual material available on a surface that is many times more durable than tape. The rapid and random access capabilities of the video disk allow users to select their own route through the 54,000 frames on the disk and hop back and forth as desired. When integrated with a computer and other peripherals, this technology makes possible the presentation of lifelike pictures controlled by student responses (Hofmeister, 1983). As yet this medium has not had a broad effect on education because most educators do not view it as cost-effective. An exception is Thorkildsen, Bickel, and Williams' (1979) work with retarded students.

The next generation of computers will be able to recognize both natural speech and written language and automatically translate and type any kind of document. All that will be necessary is to speak a command. If the computer does not understand a spoken or written command, it will ask questions. It will be able to draw inferences and make judgments, based on knowledge of meanings as well as numbers.

The computers of the future will have other advantages over our present machines. Besides being very small (about the size of a pocket calculator), they will be easily affordable, extremely reliable, and specifically designed to expedite the educational process. As Evans (1982) has commented, "Teachers working in schools where anything smaller than an elephant has to be chained to the floor" (p. 14) may question the advantage of further miniaturization. However, the reduced size will be accompanied by drastically reduced manufacturing costs, making computers as inexpensive and readily available as calculators.

In Evans's (1982) opinion economics is the key to understanding the future role of computers in education and their impact on society in the next decade. He contends that edcuational applications of computers are one of the biggest untapped commercial markets in the world and predicts a rush by commercial organizations to "pump colossal sums of money into investigating the nature of the teaching process and developing powerful and effective teaching programs" (p. 16).

Evans's (1982) prediction is thought-provoking and auspicious. Perhaps the promise of lucrative markets is what it will take to stimulate the much-needed economic support of educational improvements. In any event we know that it is possible to move from a noncomputerized society to a computerized one in a single generation. The development of artificial intelligence will have an impact on what and how we teach our children, to say nothing of the way we live. As technology makes increased learning and independence possible, the concept of handicaps may have to be redefined.

Study Questions

1. List some reasons why computer technology is particularly useful as an educational tool for special needs students.

2. List and briefly describe the various applications of computer technology to assessment and instruction.

3. Distinguish between CAI and CMI.

4. What are some uses of word processing programs with special needs students?

5. Give some examples of computer applications with severely handicapped infants.

6. Describe input devices for persons with severe physical impairments.

7. Describe the benefits of each of the following computer-aided devices for the sensorially impaired: Kurzweil Reading Machine, Optacon, VersaBraille, ITS, Pathsounder, Bioear.

8. List and discuss the three criteria to consider when selecting software for use with special needs students.

9. What are some predictions about the next generation of computers?

3

Families and Exceptionality

Donald B. Bailey, Jr., and Pamela J. Winton

University of North Carolina at Chapel Hill

Throughout history society has established numerous institutions—political, economic, educational, and religious—to help regulate and guide its members. These social institutions come and go: their philosophies, direction, and very existence are affected by time and the current zeitgeist. However, one institution—the family— has remained relatively impervious to change; the roles of various family members and the organization of families may change over time, but the fundamental importance of the family has remained constant.

Preparation of this manuscript was supported in part by Special Education Programs, Special Education and Rehabilitative Services, U.S. Department of Education, Contract Number 300–82–0366. The opinions expressed do not necessarily reflect the position or policy of the U.S. Department of Education, and no official endorsement by the U.S. Department of Education should be inferred.

The relationship between the family and other social institutions, particularly education, has not been equally constant, however. The general trend has been for the family unit to relinquish greater responsibility to the established educational system. In many ways such a trend is appropriate. As societies become increasingly diverse and sophisticated, it becomes impossible for the individual family to provide the range and depth of experiences required for successful integration into the adult world. However, such a trend also has its costs. For example, families may rely too heavily on the schools to teach children social, ethical, and moral concepts. Also, there exists the risk that families and educational institutions may operate in isolation.

In the case of exceptional children, this trend has operated in reverse. Parents have been given new and expanded roles in their child's education and are expected to function effectively as teachers and as educational decision makers. This increased involvement has been mandated in part by law. In addition, it has grown out of the efforts of parents and professionals who believe that a close working relationship between schools and families is essential for the optimal development of exceptional children and their families.

The trend toward increased involvement of parents in the education of their handicapped child has meant that special educators have needed to expand their knowledge and skills in working with families. Bailey and Simeonsson (1984) cite three fundamental reasons that skills in working with parents are essential. First, families have a legal right to a certain minimal level of involvement. Second, parents can serve as teachers of their children and thus may be able to assist in introducing new skills or in helping children apply skills learned in school.

Finally, families themselves may need to be the targets of intervention.

Each of these reasons provides guidance for special educators and represents an increasing level of sophistication. On the simplest level special educators should know the laws and regulations governing the rights of exceptional children and their families and should be able to implement each aspect of the law accurately, consistently, and fairly. On another level special educators need to know how to help other persons (e.g., parents, siblings, grandparents) effectively teach the exceptional child. On the most complicated level special educators need to be able to assess the needs of parents and other family members and design individualized programs of support for them. This level requires a knowledge of theories and concepts of family functioning and development and a basic understanding of the family as a complicated and unique system.

The Law and the Family of the Exceptional Child

As stated in chapter 1, P.L. 94–142 established the right of all handicapped children to a free, appropriate public education. One area of the law in which a number of specific requirements exist is the area of family involvement. In all areas special educators need to recognize that many families are not fully aware of their rights or their responsibilities. An important role for professionals, in addition to complying with the law, is informing families of their rights. Only through full awareness of their status can parents participate fully and effectively in planning and implementing programs for their children.

The Right to Be Informed and Give Consent

First, families have a right to be informed before the schools initiate any preplacement evaluation procedures. A complete and fair evaluation must be conducted prior to designing an individual program for a child and placing the child in any specialized classroom or program. Parents must be informed as to what the evaluation will consist of and must give their written consent before any testing can begin.

The implications of this provision for special educators are several. Special educators must be aware of the mandatory requirements of an appropriate evaluation, as described in chapter 1. In addition, they must be familiar with the issues and guidelines surrounding the notion of informed consent. Special educators may not simply obtain permission for testing. Rather, they must first inform the parents of the rationale for testing. The obligation for providing full information rests on the party seeking the consent. Thus, if parents claim that they did not understand something they signed, the school system may be ultimately liable if it did not adequately inform parents about the procedure. In a recent study by Roit and Pfohl (1984) investigating the readability of written materials on P.L. 94–142 provided to parents in 25 states, those authors found that the reading level is often such that the information may not be comprehensible to a large number of parents. We should not assume that simply providing written information to parents fulfills the requirement of informed consent.

Parents also have the right to withdraw their consent for evaluation (or any other activity) at any time. They should be informed, in writing, of this right. Furthermore, parents have the right to obtain an outside evaluation by a private consultant if they are not satisfied with the evaluation provided by the school.

Participation in Program Planning

As discussed in chapter 1, the law mandates that an IEP be written and implemented for each exceptional child. Special educators need to be aware of the rationale for developing IEPs, and they should know the legal requirements for involving parents in the developmental process and should actively encourage parent participation. The law clearly specifies the important role of parents in the development of an IEP: at least one parent should attend the IEP meeting. The purpose of this regulation is to ensure that parents have the opportunity to provide input regarding their own educational priorities for their child and to react to goals and services proposed by other team members. Furthermore, parents must approve and sign the IEP before it can be implemented.

Although the role of families in the IEP meeting is an important one, research to date suggests that, in actuality, parent involvement is neither encouraged nor practiced. For example, the National Committee for Citizens in Education (1979) surveyed approximately 2,300 parents of handicapped children; over half of them reported that the IEP had been completed by the professional team prior to the team meeting. Such a practice tends to reduce the IEP meeting, and thus parent involvement, to an approval process rather than a developmental process. In a survey of educators participating on interdisciplinary teams, Yoshida, Fenton, Maxwell, and Kaufman (1978) found that team members supported relatively passive roles for parents (e.g., gathering and presenting basic information) and were not in favor of more active roles (e.g., monitoring programs and becoming involved in the schools). Likewise, Gilliam and Coleman (1981) found that team members generally felt that parent contributions to and influences on the team decision were minimal. Ysseldyke, Algozzine, and Mitchell (1982) observed 34 team meetings and found that in 73% of the meetings parent input was requested only occasionally or rarely.

Parents play a central role in developing their handicapped child's IEP.

Only 27% of the meetings were judged to consist of language that was at a level parents could understand.

Approval of the IEP and Right to Due Process

Before an IEP can be implemented, the child's parents or guardian must agree that it is an appropriate plan of goals and services and must sign the IEP to indicate their agreement with it. P.L. 94–142 clearly states that parents have the right to disagree with the program offered by the school system and to appeal to another authority to serve as mediator. This right, referred to as the *right to due process,* actually encompasses a variety of situations:

1. Parents may disagree with the class placement of their child.

2. Parents may disagree with the label assigned to their child.

3. Parents may disagree with the program offered their child.

4. Parents may be denied access to information the school has about their child.

5. Parents may not be allowed to obtain an independent evaluation of their child.

If any of these circumstances exist, parents have a right to a formal hearing. The nature and format of such a hearing vary considerably from state to state (Strickland, 1983). Federal law specifies that the hearing officer must neither be employed by an agency involved in the education or care of the child nor have a personal or professional interest that would interfere with her objectivity. The law also guarantees that both the school system and the parents may have an attorney or an educational agent present, may prepare evidence and cross-examine witnesses, and may obtain a verbatim record of the hearing and a written finding of facts and decisions. The hearing officer weighs all of the evidence and makes a decision. Either party, if dissatisfied, may request a review by the state education agency. If this review is not acceptable, either party may file a civil action in either a state or federal district court.

Due process hearings are both time-consuming and expensive. However, they are an important and necessary component of comprehensive services for families. All families should be made aware of their right to appeal. They should be clearly informed of this option and assured that their child's program will not be negatively affected in any way if they choose to pursue a formal hearing.

Implications for Special Educators

What can be done to improve parent involvement? On the most basic level special educators should inform parents of the importance of their role and their active participation in the team meeting. This approach alone may not be adequate for all families, however. Goldstein and Turnbull (1982) compared two strategies to increase parent participation in IEP conferences. The first strategy involved sending questions to the parents to consider prior to the meeting. The questions concerned their goals for their child, the child's educational potential, and the development of an IEP. The second strategy had the school guidance counselor present at each conference in the role of parent advocate. Counselors introduced parents at the conference, asked questions of them, gave positive feedback on their contributions, and helped to summarize discussions at the end of the conference. Results indicated that (1) a significantly larger number of fathers attended the meetings after receiving the questionnaire and (2) the parent advocate strategy significantly increased parent participation in the meetings.

Other variables can also affect parent participation and satisfaction. For example, Witt, Miller, McIntyre, and Smith (1984) found three characteristics of team meetings that were positively associated with parent satisfaction: longer meetings in which fuller discussions were possible, the attribution of blame for the child's problems to sources other than the parents, and active participation by more than one or two professionals. Turnbull and Strickland (1981) have proposed an extensive training model to prepare parents for participation. Training is conducted in group sessions with videotape examples and role-play organized around six topics: preconference preparation, initial conference proceedings, interpretation of evaluation results, development of the curriculum portion of the IEP, placement decisions and related services, and conclusion of the meeting.

Probably the most important strategy is actively encouraging parent involvement during the IEP meeting itself and providing positive feedback whenever parents do participate. This feedback should be given naturally, acknowledging and following up on parent contributions, rather than artificially responding to parent suggestions in a way that is different from the reactions to contributions of other team members.

On the most fundamental level every special educator should be aware of all rights and legal provisions pertaining to families with exceptional children. Each special educator should also inform families of the rights they have. Finally, each should serve as an advocate for families though this may place him in the precarious position of opposing the efforts of school administrators. For example, a special educator and a parent may feel strongly that a child needs speech therapy, whereas the administrative staff may not feel the situation warrants the expense. The challenge is for special educators to go about advocacy efforts in a positive fashion, which achieves the intended results yet does not place them or the parents in an adversarial relationship with the schools.

Family Members as Teachers of Their Children

A number of reasons have been offered to support the importance of helping family members become good teachers of their exceptional child (Bailey & Simeonsson, 1984). First, family members may have a better rapport with the child than nonfamily members have and may thus be more likely to elicit cooperative participation. Second, family members remain relatively constant during the child's life, whereas teachers come and go. Therefore, the family can serve as long-term teachers. Third, successful participation in teaching activities may enhance feelings of competence and control for family members.

Numerous studies have shown that family members can indeed be taught teaching skills and can use those skills in helping a child acquire new behaviors or apply the behaviors learned in a school setting. Although the majority of studies have been directed toward parents, a number of studies have demonstrated that siblings also can become effective teachers (see Simeonsson & McHale, 1981; Simeonsson & Bailey, in press, for reviews).

When conducted in the proper way and under the right circumstances, parent training can be a useful activity. However, several cautions are worth noting. First, parents often report that they do not wish to serve as teachers of their child (Winton & Turnbull, 1981). Similarly, siblings may resent being asked to spend extensive amounts of time in relatively structured teaching activities. Teaching is an imposition on personal time and has the potential to alter the relationship between parents and child or between siblings. Special educators should be sensitive to this issue and should not assume that all parents or siblings are interested in this type of involvement.

A second caution has to do with the presumption that the teacher automatically knows more than the parent. Although most parents have had no formal training in working with their child, many have developed an effective and efficient set of strategies. Furthermore, many teachers do not realize what it is like to be a parent, particularly a parent of an exceptional child, and families may resent or discredit their suggestions. At least two solutions exist for this problem. First, a teacher can demonstrate competence with the child in the classroom. Second, a teacher can establish a cooperative relationship with the family, in which each party's opinions are respected and needs for additional training are identified in a collaborative effort.

Implications for Special Educators

Effective training is an important skill. Special educators need to be able to identify family needs for training and to design acceptable strategies to help family members acquire needed skills. Teachers should first be aware of reading materials available for parents. Three of the more popular books are *Living with Children* (Pat-

Special educators help parents understand and cope with their child's needs.

terson & Gullion, 1976), *Parents Are Teachers* (Becker, 1971), and *Families: Application of Social Learning to Family Life* (Patterson, 1977). Bernal and North (1978) reviewed 26 manuals for parents, as well as the research documenting the manuals' effectiveness. They concluded that manuals alone can be useful when parents are dealing with a specific, limited problem. However, as problems become more "diffuse, complex, multiple, and generalized across settings" (p. 541), the teacher's role in working with and guiding parents becomes increasingly important. Another strategy for teaching parents is a didactic group training session. The fundamental assumption underlying such a session is that parents need a certain set of basic skills for approaching problem situations. Some advantages of group training are the efficiency in reaching a large number of parents and the opportunity for parents to discuss common problems and solutions. However, if parents need only very specific assistance, then individualized help is preferable. Examples of comprehensive programs for training parents are provided by Harris (1983) and Kozloff (1973).

Training sessions for family members are more likely to be successful if several criteria are met. First, topics should be concrete and tied to specific problems encountered by parents. Second, training should include modeling, either through videotapes or through live observation. Third, training should allow the opportunity to practice new skills and to receive feedback regarding the effectiveness of the teaching behavior. Fourth, training should be positive in orientation, focusing on parent strengths and providing techniques that are consistent with family values and the established family system. Finally, the skills taught should be easy to implement and should be relevant to the child's needs.

The Family as a System

An important factor affecting the provision of services to exceptional children and their families is the professional view of the family. Although professionals have increasingly recognized the importance of including parents in intervention efforts, this inclusion has generally been restricted to parent performance of certain roles (primarily those of teacher and educational decision maker) and participation in a predetermined set of activities. In spite of the special educator's expertise in individualizing services for exceptional children, individualizing programs for families has not been common practice.

Special educators have begun to recognize the need to expand their focus. Concepts drawn from theories and models of family functioning as generated by psychiatrists (Minuchin, 1974) and sociologists (McCubbin & Patterson, 1983; Olson, Russell, & Sprenkle, 1983; Tseng & McDermott, 1979) have been used increasingly to achieve a broad understanding of families. A central theme is the recognition of the family as a unique system of interrelationships that demonstrate both stability and change.

Families Have Unique Needs and Values

No two families are identical. They differ in terms of the number of family members, extended family relationships, cultural style, attitudes toward child rearing, outlook on life, and role expectations for various family members (Turnbull, Summers, & Brotherson, 1983). Although it is easy to identify the needs of families of handicapped children as a group, professionals need to recognize the individuality and diversity of these families and plan for family involvement that is appropriate to their unique needs and characteristics. Unfortunately, special educators tend to offer families a prescribed set of activities, often educational. If parents do not participate, they may feel guilty and the professionals may feel discouraged.

Families Perform Many Functions   As many as nine family functions have been identified in the literature (Benson & Turnbull, in press): economic, physical, rest and recuperation, socialization, self-definition, affection, guidance, education, and vocational. These nine functions and the specific tasks associated with each are listed in Table 3-1.

Table 3-1   Family functions

Economic	Physical	Rest and Recuperation
Generating income Paying bills and banking Handling investments Overseeing insurance and benefit programs Earning allowance Dispensing allowance	Food purchase and preparation Clothes purchase and alteration Health care and maintenance Safety and protection Transportation Home maintenance	Individual and family-oriented recreation Release from demands Development and enjoyment of hobbies
Socialization	**Self-definition**	**Affection**
Interpersonal relationships Social skills	Establishing self-identity and self-image Recognizing strengths and weaknesses Providing a sense of belonging	Nurturing and love Companionship Intimacy Emotional expression
Guidance	**Education**	**Vocational**
Problem solving Advising and giving feedback Shaping basic beliefs and values Transmitting religious values	Continuing education for parents School work Homework Cultural appreciation	Career choice Development of work ethic Support of career interests

SOURCE: From *Working with Families with Disabled Members: A Family Systems Approach* (p. 36) by A. Turnbull, J. Summers, and M. Brotherson, 1984, Lawrence: Kansas University Affiliated Facility. Copyright 1984 by Kansas University Affiliated Facility. Reprinted by permission.

If parents are expected to spend much time on any one family function, they will have less time for the others. An example of overload in one area of functioning is the situation in which a child has several therapists, each of whom asks the parents to engage in a different home therapy program. Although the individual tasks required by each program may be manageable, the sum of these tasks may be overwhelming.

Families Respond Differently to Stress   It is well documented that the exceptional child represents a persistent source of stress for family members. Evidence suggests that the kinds of stress most likely experienced include the following: additional financial costs, stigma, interruptions of family sleep, large amounts of time required for the personal care of the exceptional family member, social isolation, difficulty in finding the time and energy for shopping and other normal household routines, difficulty in handling behavior problems, limitations in recreational activities, and pessimism about the future (Moroney, 1981).

Special educators have looked to family crisis models generated by sociologists (Hill, 1949; McCubbin & Patterson, 1983) to better understand how families adapt to or cope with the stress associated with an exceptional family member. McCubbin and Patterson (1983) emphasize that a family's response to stress is both an intrafamily (member to member) and a transactional (family and community) process. Intrafamily strategies include *passive appraisal* (avoiding or denying the problem in the hope that it will resolve itself) and *reframing* (redefining the problem so that it seems less stressful). Transactional strategies include the use of social, spiritual, and formal support. Thus, a family's reaction to stress depends on both their definition of the stressful event and their use of resources to deal with it.

Implications for Special Educators   The most important step in providing families with support is a careful assessment of individual needs. Although we generally have good models and instruments for assessing exceptional children's needs, it is much more difficult to assess the needs of families. Using the coping strategies identified by McCubbin and Patterson as a guide to determine a family's perception of their own needs and resources is one approach to a family-needs assessment. Any intervention should make full use of a family's existing resources and supplement where resources are lacking. For example, the formal support offered by professionals can be directed in any of three different areas: social-emotional, instrumental, and informational.

Social-emotional support can be defined as the presence of one or more individuals who empathize with the family member and are available to hear and discuss problems. Such support may be provided by a spouse, a friend or neighbor, an extended family member, a professional, or another parent. Social-emotional support is important for several reasons. Families with handicapped children have many concerns about both the present and the future. They may worry about their own competence as parents. They may fear that something they did caused the handicapping condition. They may be grieving or may be quite angry that adequate services are not being provided for their child. They may feel rejected or stigmatized by other parents or community members. They may sense that their lives are

Extended family members can provide significant support.

out of control, with no clear direction or hope. Although some of these problems have the potential for immediate solution, many do not. What family members need is a network of social support that they can rely on throughout their child's development.

If families do not have supportive friends, neighbors, or relatives, it may be important for professionals to facilitate the development of this network. Putting families in touch with other families of exceptional children, with existing parent support groups, or with parent advocacy groups is an important way of helping families develop their network. Group meetings can be organized around specific topics generated by either the teacher or the parents. Perhaps the most important benefit of group meetings is that they give parents the opportunity to meet other parents of exceptional children, thus paving the way for a more personal support network outside the group context. Parents can support each other in ways that no professional ever could. Similar groups can also be formed for siblings of exceptional children.

Instrumental support can be defined as support that helps a family or family member accomplish specific tasks. For example, a mother of a handicapped child may find it impossible to care for her exceptional child and still have time for other important family functions. Mothers in one study (Winton & Turnbull, 1981) reported a pressing need to be able to relax and take a break from the daily responsibilities of caring for their exceptional child. Other research indicates that finding willing and competent babysitters is a problem.

Professionals can play an important role by developing or helping families locate respite care services, day-care programs, after-school activities, or recreational outlets appropriate for exceptional children. In some communities agencies have enlisted volunteers as citizen advocates or companions for exceptional individuals. Not only do these services provide families with a break from the care of the exceptional family member, but they also help families mainstream or integrate the exceptional person into the community.

Informational support provides the family with needed information or access to such information. Since families have many important decisions to make about their child, they need and generally want as much information as possible. Some information is desired simply for understanding. For example, families may want to read about their child's disability or about other families who have had experience with a handicapped child. Helpful books of this type include *We Have Been There: A Guidebook for Parents of People with Mental Retardation* (Dougans, Isbell, & Vyas, 1983), *A Difference in the Family: Living with a Disabled Child* (Featherstone, 1981), and *Parents Speak Out* (Turnbull & Turnbull, 1985). In addition, parents may want information on the laws, advocacy, potential programs for their child, effective educational decision making, or dealing with the educational system. Recommended books on these topics include *Negotiating the Special Educational Maze* (Anderson, Chitwood, & Hayden, 1982), *How to Organize an Effective Parent/Advocacy Group and Move Bureaucracies* (DesJardins, 1980), and *Selecting a Preschool: A Guide for Parents of Handicapped Children* (Winton, Turnbull, & Blacher, 1984). Finally, information is needed to help parents with parenting tasks. For example, parents may need information on how best to toilet train their child or to reinforce at home what the teacher has taught at school. Selected books on parenting skills have been mentioned earlier in the chapter.

There are several ways in which special educators provide families with informational support. They can set up a resource center or clearinghouse of information about services and programs available at the local level. Such centers can help families deal with fragmented and uncoordinated services, and mothers of preschool handicapped children have identified the absence of such centers as a concern (Winton, 1981). Special education teachers can also share information informally with families. Mothers of preschoolers identified this type of information sharing with their child's teacher as their most preferred type of parent activity (Winton & Turnbull, 1981). Special educators can also help families interpret and evaluate information received from other professionals. Frequently families of exceptional children must deal with a variety of specialists with a variety of recommendations. Special educators can help families evaluate and prioritize these recommendations to suit their unique situation.

Finally, it is important to remember that no one person could or should provide all of the support needed by a family. Teachers should guard against investing all of their emotional and physical energy in certain families with many needs. First of all, families need to develop their own support systems, which will extend beyond their typically short involvement with a particular teacher. In addition, teachers need to avoid professional burnout resulting from intense emotional involvement with family problems. Teachers must realize that they are only one facet of an overall family support system.

Family Members Are Bound Together

A family is bound by affection, heredity, and law. These ties create a bond that endures through time and space. However, for some handicapped children the affectional bonds between parent and child are at risk; a strong parent-child attachment requires a mutually satisfying relationship. Parents and children typically engage in many behaviors and routines during infancy that facilitate the development of that relationship: gazing, holding, talking, smiling, and playing games. Cute babies who smile and cuddle generally have a powerful effect on adults: they cause them to do things (e.g., talk abnormally, and exaggerate their facial expressions) that they would never do in the presence of peers alone. An unresponsive child or an extremely fussy one is not so enjoyable and may prompt less frequent parent interaction. An unpredictable child or one whose needs are not easily identified is also frustrating for parents.

Professional interest in the area of attachment and parent-child interactions within exceptional populations has been high because of the documented stress associated with parenting a handicapped child and because of the high incidence of child abuse associated with this population (see Meier & Sloan, 1984, for review of this literature). Typically this research has focused on the mother-child dyad. Increasingly, however, professionals are noting that examination of selected interactions of selected family members does not give an accurate picture of the dynamics of family interaction (Stoneman & Brody, 1984).

Implications for Special Educators   An important aspect of the interrelatedness of family members is the recognition of reciprocal influences. Any change affecting one family member will affect all others. This basic concept is frequently overlooked by professionals designing intervention programs. The two most common approaches to parent involvement—parent counseling and parent training—are not family oriented; they focus on the individual or the mother-child dyad rather than the total family system (Foster & Berger, 1979). There are numerous problems with this type of approach. Engaging one family member's time and energy in a disproportionate way with another family member makes it more difficult to carry out other roles and functions within the family. It may also cause a spouse or siblings to feel isolated and unsure of their roles. And it usually means that the needs of the spouse, siblings, and extended family members are overlooked. This approach can do more harm than good if it undermines a family's support system and coping abilities.

Certain precautions should be taken when involving family members in intervention. The fact that siblings can function as effective teachers of exceptional children does not automatically mean that every sibling should be engaged in a teaching program. Reviews of the literature on sibling relationships in families of handicapped children indicate that siblings vary in their adjustment and reactions (Simeonsson & McHale, 1981; Simeonsson & Bailey, in press). Clearly, intervention tasks should not be assigned without first considering individual needs. Similarly, a nationwide sample of normal families indicated a great deal of discrepancy in the way husbands, wives, and their adolescent children described their own families (Olson et al., 1983). Their findings illustrate the danger of using information from one family member to determine intervention for the entire family.

The single-parent family is another case in which faulty assumptions may result in less effective intervention. In a review of the literature on single mothers with exceptional children, Bristol (in press) reports that the child's father and the father's relatives are among those who help regularly with child care tasks. Yet single-parent families are often treated as if the other parent is not involved. All relevant family members should be included in a thorough needs assessment before individualized, family-oriented intervention is begun.

Siblings of handicapped children have their own needs and unique reactions to their family circumstances.

Professionals also need to know that an exceptional child may be at risk for impaired affectional ties and developmentally inappropriate parent-child interactions or even child abuse. They can help parents to understand and identify their child's needs so that they can interact with the child in an appropriate fashion. Special educators can also spot evidence of child abuse and should know how to intervene. Intervention programs for families of young exceptional children include the Family, Infant, and Toddler Project at George Peabody College of Vanderbilt University (Gabel & Kotsch, 1981) and the Family Intervention Project at Georgia State University (Berger & Fowlkes, 1980; Foster & Berger, 1979).

The Family Is Always Developing

Few educators would ignore the importance of viewing each child from a developmental perspective. However, it is easy to ignore the fact that families are also constantly developing. Tseng and McDermott (1979) have described five stages in the life of a family: the primary family (early stages of marriage), the childbearing family, the child-rearing family, the maturing family (children in adolescence and young adulthood), and the contracting family (adult children, aging spouses, declining health, loss of a family member). One way to look at the stages in family life is as a series of relatively calm plateaus punctuated by transition events that are frequently a source of family stress. These events require the family to make certain modifications in their established routines and to renegotiate roles in order to adapt to the new stage.

Transitions are even more difficult when there is an exceptional family member. Wikler, Wasow, and Hatfield (1981) have suggested 10 critical periods in the development of families with mentally retarded children. Five of these represent landmarks in normal development (walking, talking, beginning of school, onset of puberty, and 21st birthday). These periods are crises because they often draw attention to the discrepancies in the handicapped child's development as compared to that of other children. The other five critical periods may occur at any age and include the following: when the child is identified as handicapped, whenever placement decisions occur, when younger siblings surpass the skills of the handicapped child, when unusual behavior or health crises occur, and when guardianship and long-term care are decided. This section will discuss the unique needs of families of handicapped children at three different stages.

The Family with a Handicapped Infant or Preschooler   Childbearing years are exciting times for almost every family. Parents of young children build up tremendous expectations of what their children will be like, even before their birth. The early childhood years represent the time when children accomplish major developmental landmarks. In the space of five or six years they go from a seemingly helpless newborn to a being who walks, controls a complex symbol system known as language, and manages almost every self-help task.

For many parents of exceptional children, however, the early childhood years are difficult; during this period many children with moderate to severe handicapping conditions are identified. Some children are identified at birth, particularly those with obvious physical impairments or chromosomal disorders. Other children are not identified until they show delays in attaining developmental landmarks.

One of the identified needs of families with handicapped infants or preschoolers is support in coping with the fact that their child is handicapped. The professional literature over the past 20 years has produced numerous models describing the process families go through when they become aware that their child is handicapped (see Blacher, 1984, for a description and review of these models). Although each model is different, commonalities do exist. One typical model has been proposed by Drotar, Baskiewicz, Irwin, Kennell, and Klaus (1975), who describe a series of five stages of parental reaction and adjustment to the awareness of their child's handicap. The first stage is that of shock, followed by a period of denial. During these two stages parents may be confused and disorganized. They may not accept the fact that their child is handicapped and may take the child to numerous specialists, seeking either an alternative diagnosis or a cure. In the third stage the inevitability of the handicap becomes apparent, and families often experience intense feelings of sadness, anger, and anxiety about the future. This period is most difficult for families, since the potential impact has begun to sink in. Parents worry about the happiness of their child and the possibility of permanent caretaking responsibilities. The fourth stage is a gradual adaptation to having a handicapped child, and the fifth stage represents reorganization and long-term acceptance of the situation. Although these models are useful, too often professionals have interpreted them to mean that parents should reach a final stage of acceptance. The

Parental acceptance of a child's handicap can lead to an effective helping relationship.

10 critical periods of Wikler et al. (1981) illustrate clearly that transitional events and crises punctuate the entire life cycle of a family with an exceptional child. There may be periods of acceptance, but the need for readjustments and adaptation will be ongoing.

Another special need of families with young handicapped children is for an agency or person to help them in identifying and providing appropriate services for their child. Parents of school-age children deal primarily with one agency—the public schools. Services for younger children, however, are much more diverse and fragmented. In addition, the laws mandating preschool and infant services vary from state to state. In some states parents may find a broad range of publicly supported programs, whereas in other states few services for preschool-age handicapped children exist. Furthermore, families may need to interact with many different service providers: mental health agencies, social service agencies, public schools, physicians, therapists, private programs, church-sponsored programs, and organizations such as the Association for Retarded Citizens or cerebral palsy hospitals. When parents of young handicapped children find no one agency to meet all of their needs, they themselves must serve as advocates and decision makers for their children. However, many families may not be able to evaluate options effectively. Should we keep our infant at home, or should he be in a program of some sort? Is mainstreaming an appropriate option for our child? Our therapist says she needs to see our child twice a week, but is it worth the expense? These questions are always difficult to answer. However, they are particularly difficult when a myriad of agencies exist, often with little communication among themselves, and when no one agency or person takes a leadership role as an advocate and "broker" for families with special needs.

One final area of special need of families with young handicapped children is parent-child interaction. Families normally go through a bonding process with their children, often referred to as attachment (Ainsworth, 1973; Bowlby, 1969). As mentioned earlier, this process is at risk in families with young handicapped children (Blacher & Meyers, 1983) for several reasons. First, some families may be so caught up in the grieving process that they may emotionally divorce themselves from their child. Second, some handicapped children do not encourage normal parent-child interactions. The child who is always fussy, cannot be consoled, does not smile, is limp, or does not like to be touched or held is not likely to elicit the same quality or quantity of parenting behavior as the child who is cute, cuddly, and highly responsive to social interactions. Finally, some families of handicapped children react in the opposite way. They may be overattentive or overprotective of their children or may tend to baby them longer than they should.

The Family with a School-Age Child   Families of school-age handicapped children continue to need social-emotional, instrumental, and informational support, although the nature, form, and direction of that support generally change. There are also some unique needs that are often observed during the school years. As opposed to the early childhood years, when parents had to deal with a multitude of agencies and programs, services at this age are generally provided by the public schools. P.L. 94–142 established the right of every handicapped child of school age to receive a free, appropriate public education. "Appropriate education" was further defined to encompass any need the chld has related to learning and/or development, including the need to learn basic self-help skills, to have appropriate adaptive equipment, to develop appropriate social interaction skills, to acquire basic prevocational skills, and to receive therapy—physical, speech, or occupational. Thus, schools are now mandated to provide almost all necessary services, with the exception of health care, for handicapped children. This situation is both a blessing and a curse. When school systems serve as advocates for families and provide a comprehensive program of services for children, it is a blessing. When school systems resist providing comprehensive or appropriate services, it is a curse because families generally have nowhere else to go. They must accept the services offered, fight for what they and their child need, or pay for private services.

The school years are particularly difficult for some parents because many children are formally identified or labeled as handicapped during this period. Although most moderately or severely handicapped children have been identified before they enter public school, a large number of mildly handicapped children are not identified until they enter school and are unable to meet customary age-level expectations. Included in this group may be many children who are labeled as educable mentally handicapped, learning disabled, or emotionally disabled. Also, many children with mild hearing or visual problems may not be identified until their teachers realize they cannot see the chalkboard or follow directions adequately.

In some cases parents may have suspected a problem prior to school entry. For them, although the diagnostic and labeling process may be a difficult one, it may be a relief to have finally documented what they suspected all along. Other families may have had no idea that their child was in any way incapable of performing up to expectations. For these parents the identification and labeling process may be a very difficult time, and many parents may go through the various stages of response described for parents of younger children. Unfortunately, although parents often need considerable support at this time, school systems generally are not prepared to offer it. In many ways the agencies and systems designed to serve younger handicapped children are more sensitive to these needs for family support and counseling, and they often have staff members responsible for facilitating that support. Although exceptions exist, public schools are typically more child focused than family focused. The process of informing and supporting parents often is left either to special education teachers, who may or may not be well trained in working with families, or to a school psychologist, who may or may not have expertise in the area of exceptional children. Thus, families of school-age children are more likely to have to seek out and establish their own support systems.

The school-age years often force parents of handicapped children to reframe their expectations for their child. For example, it is during this period that many families of handicapped children become aware that their children may not be able to succeed in college or may have difficulties that will not be cured by the schools. It may become apparent that the child will have to cope with a disability throughout adult life.

Although it can happen at any age, it is during the school-age years that the self-concept of many handicapped children is eroded. It may be during this period that a younger sibling matches or exceeds the handicapped child's academic performance. Furthermore, it is during the school-age years, when children's peer relations are so critical, that handicapped children are more likely to experience re-

The school-age years challenge an entire family to support the positive self-concept of a handicapped member.

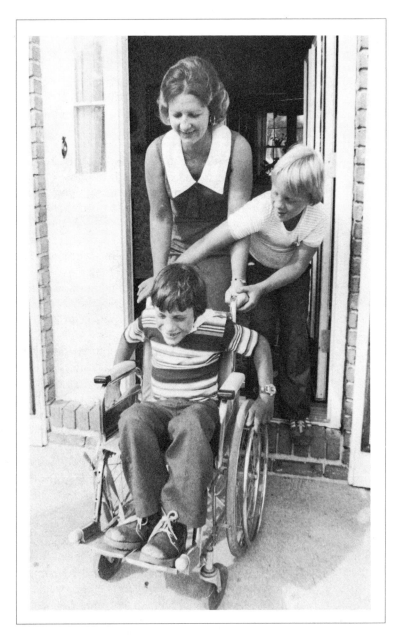

jection or overt teasing or hostility from their nonhandicapped peers, particularly during the late elementary and early junior high school years. Thus, parents of school-age handicapped children bear the extra responsibility of helping their child develop and maintain a positive self-concept.

Finally, it is during the school-age years that most children reach puberty. This developmental milestone can be a challenging one for all parents. However, for many parents of handicapped children it can be a traumatic period. Puberty is a clear sign that the child is becoming an adult in a physical sense. This new maturity can accentuate any delays in academic or social development. In addition, many parents have not viewed their handicapped children as sexual beings. Puberty forces parents to address a host of important issues regarding their child's sexual development as well as related concerns about the future, such as vocational and independent living possibilities for their child.

The Family with a Handicapped Adult   The transition from childhood to adulthood is one of mixed emotions for almost all families. A person's 21st birthday is generally celebrated in symbolic recognition of this passage to independence. Even though most parents are happy to see their children reach adulthood, many also have feelings of sadness and loss. For families with handicapped children this transition can be especially difficult.

First of all, parents find themselves once again in the situation that existed when their child was very young: they must deal with a variety of service providers, no one of which will take a leadership or advocacy role for their child. Since public schools are no longer responsible after age 21, parents and handicapped adults must deal on their own with groups such as social service agencies or vocational rehabilitation centers.

The specific problems encountered during this phase are greatly dependent upon the level of handicapping condition. However, most concerns relate to the areas of employment, independent living, social/recreational outlets, and planning for the future. Since adults in our society are generally expected to work and contribute to the economy, one responsibility of parents is to help their children seek and secure appropriate opportunities for employment. Many parents have mixed feelings about the option that is best for their handicapped child. Typical of the many questions asked during this stage is this: Should a moderately retarded young adult work in a sheltered workshop with other handicapped persons, or should she seek competitive employment? In a sheltered workshop the handicapped person will probably be accepted by peers and staff and will receive training and work assignments commensurate with her skill level. However, there will be fewer opportunities to make a decent salary and interact with nonhandicapped peers. In competitive employment the person will have the opportunity to participate in normal work experiences and to earn competitive wages. However, she must compete with other workers. Employers may or may not provide adequate training. Furthermore, co-workers may or may not accept the handicapped employee, and social interactions may be far less frequent.

Another major concern is living arrangements. Many handicapped individuals can live alone and care for themselves. Placement in a public facility, such as a local group home, may be the most appropriate alternative for others. A third, smaller group of individuals with significant health and physical management problems may require lifelong care in a restrictive environment.

Parents are also concerned about their child's long-term social development. Dating, marriage, and childbearing are normal transitions that often pose difficulty for the family of an adolescent or young adult with a handicapping condition. The individual's judgment or ability to accept responsibility may be an issue. Appropriate use of free time is another problem because many handicapped persons have not learned to participate in enjoyable and age-appropriate recreational activities. Recreational opportunities available in the community may need to be sought out and developed.

A final problem is long-term care and guardianship. Many handicapped and disabled adults are capable of making their own decisions and seeking out their own resources, but others will never be able to accept this level of responsibility. As parents begin to realize that their handicapped child will probably outlive them, they are faced with the issue of who will be responsible. This anxiety can be particularly traumatic, especially for parents who have had to take an active and involved role in the care of their child. Their fundamental concern is whether anyone else would devote the time and energy necessary to ensure a life of as high a quality as possible. Many parents can imagine their child living out his days in some back ward of an institution or in some cold and lonely apartment with no one to love and care for him. Although service agencies exist, they do not have feelings and are not emotionally invested. Only individuals can make that kind of enduring commitment. However, unless another family member volunteers to assume this role, parents are often hesitant to ask anyone to accept such a lifelong responsibility. Thus, this decision can be a very difficult one for parents and calls for much support and assistance.

Implications for Special Educators   An understanding of the stages and transitions of the family life cycle will help special educators recognize that not only do different families have different needs, but the same family has different needs at different times. Research with normal families (Olson et al., 1983) suggests that families use different coping strategies at different life stages. Although research of this type with exceptional populations has not been carried out, one can assume that they, too, utilize different ways of coping with different transition events. The task for special educators is to support or strengthen each family's unique way of coping, offering services or programs in areas of identified need.

An intervention program of this sort exists at the University of Kansas. Research conducted by Turnbull and her associates (1983) indicated that there was a lack of communication in many families about future plans for exceptional family members. Consequently, they designed an intervention program in which all relevant family members and friends were helped to develop together appropriate future plans for the exceptional adult.

Families with Gifted Children

This chapter has focused on the families of handicapped invididuals. Families with gifted children experience a different set of problems. However, most of these families also have need for social-emotional support, instrumental support, and informational support. Many myths exist about gifted children. One is that gifted children were born gifted: that the child's genes are the major contribution of the child's parents. Although a genetic component of giftedness probably exists, parents play a crucial role in providing an environment that allows the child to find and use her abilities. In a study of world-class pianists, mathematicians, and Olympic swimmers, Bloom (1982) concludes, "It is safe to say that not one of these individuals has reached this level of talent development on his or her own" (p. 511). Likewise Dewing (1978), in a review of family influence on creativity, emphasizes the importance of parent contribution to creativity and suggests three important parent variables: "(1) an unpossessive relationship which encourages the child to be self-reliant and independent, (2) permissive child-rearing methods, and (3) diverse and intellectual interests of parents" (p. 400). Parents do play an important role in encouraging the development of their gifted and creative children.

Just as with handicapped children, a frequent difficulty of families with gifted children is obtaining an educational experience appropriate for their child. Although many fine private schools exist and parents in most communities can obtain private lessons in certain skills, parents may also feel that public schools should be meeting their child's needs. Even though P.L. 94-142 does not address gifted children, approximately half of the states include them in their mandates for exceptional children. Nonetheless, obtaining truly individualized and comprehensive services is often difficult. One reason parents of the gifted have to fight continuously for service is the prevailing assumption that gifted children are already blessed with unique abilities far exceeding those of most other children. Why then should these children be provided extra service when many other youngsters need help just to survive? Gallagher (1979) describes America's "love-hate relationship" with the gifted. Although we admire, respect, and need individuals who are truly gifted, we are reluctant to provide any type of program that could be considered elitist. Thus, parents of gifted children often need social-emotional and instrumental support in their search for service.

A related difficulty is identifying the types of programming for which parents should advocate. A common dilemma is whether to advocate for a highly structured program designed to advance skill acquisition in certain content areas or for a less rigid program designed to encourage free thinking and creativity. Thus, another need of parents is for informational support.

Parents of gifted children may also need help and support in developing a quality interpersonal relationship with their child. These parents may take one of two extremes. One is to make the child's development the focus of all family activities. For example, the family of a talented tennis player may devote all of their weekends to trips to tennis tournaments, ignoring the needs and interests of other members of the family. The other extreme is to ignore or even resent the gifted child's unique needs. Most parents want what is best for their child, but parents of gifted children may feel a great deal of pressure to provide stimulating experiences. Thus, these parents, like those of handicapped children, need support and guidance in determining a realistic course of activities and services that are acceptable to all family members.

Study Questions

1. What factors argue for individualization of services to families?

2. Assume that you have been given the responsibility of designing a brochure and training activities to ensure that parents of handicapped children are aware of their legal rights. What information would be included? What else could be done to help parents actively strive to achieve those rights?

3. Assume that you have been given the responsibility of helping prepare parents for participating in IEP meetings. What information would you include?

4. Provide a rationale for providing services to families. Be sure that your rationale extends beyond legal rights.

5. What are the critical skills that a teacher of handicapped children should develop in the area of working with families?

4

Cultural Diversity and Exceptionality

Philip C. Chinn
East Texas State University

Linda McCormick
University of Hawaii

Paquita is a 7-year-old second grader in a small town in the Southwest. The only child of Mexican immigrants, she was born shortly after her parents arrived in this country. Her father works as a farmhand and her mother is a part-time seamstress. Paquita is bilingual, although her English is poor compared to the other Mexican-American students in her class.

Although well-behaved and polite in class, Paquita never participated in class discussions or volunteered for any classroom activities. When asked whether she understood lessons or instructions, she always responded affirmatively. Her poor work, however, suggested a complete lack of comprehension—in performance she was at the bottom of her class of 26 students. After 3 months of intensive effort and individual tutoring to no avail, she was referred for evaluation of suspected learning disabilities or possible mental retardation.

Paquita was evaluated bilingually by a school psychologist. Because she understood English, the English version of the Wechsler Intelligence Scale for Children, Revised (WISC-R) was administered with the assistance of a Spanish-speaking interpreter. All instructions were given in both English and Spanish, and Paquita was told she could respond in either language. Most of her verbal responses were in Spanish, although occasionally she answered in English.

On the Wechsler she achieved a full-scale IQ of 71, but the results of other testing indicated a low self-concept. Her responses in the testing situation were limited to yes and no. The psychologist suspected a severe language disability compounded by a low self-concept and recommended further educational testing.

An educational diagnostician recently trained in the use of the System of Multicultural Pluralistic Assessment

(SOMPA) administered it to Paquita. The Medical Model Profile indicated no medical or organic problems, and Paquita's adaptive behavior score was in the 81st percentile, indicating that she was functioning well for a child in her cultural group. Her estimated learning potential (ELP) was in the mid-90s, suggesting that her behavior was in the normal range at home and in her own community and that her ability to learn was masked by her low socioeconomic status and lack of acculturation.

The assessment team concluded that although Paquita's WISC-R score (with norms based on white, middle-class children) was low, her potential to learn, as evidenced by her high level of adaptation to her environment, was actually in the average range when compared to that of Mexican-American children in the same cultural and economic group. She was recommended for placement in a bilingual class for 2 years, after which time her English was expected to be fluent. Her progress will be monitored, and if her achievement in the bilingual class is as expected, Paquita will be ready for regular class placement.

Numerous and complex problems are associated with the provision of equal educational opportunities for all children. Whether the result of physical, emotional, or learning problems or superior abilities, the special education needs of culturally diverse (minority) children challenge the system at every level, from teachers to policymakers. The first prerequisite for a creative and productive interface between multicultural education and special education—one that assures maximally effective and appropriate educational experiences for every child—is informed educational personnel.

History

Despite America's historical reputation as a country where people of all nationalities are welcomed and treated equally, until 1954 there was little concern (at least at an official policy level) for the education of minority students. That year, in the landmark ruling *Brown v. Topeka Board of Education*, the Supreme Court outlawed racially segregated schools. The court held that segregation of black and white children in separate schools denied black students their right to an equal educational opportunity, as guaranteed by the Fourteenth Amendment. A decade later, with passage of the Civil Rights Act, there began a clarification and precise definition of what constitutes "equal education opportunity."

In 1968 Congress passed the Bilingual Education Act (also known as Title VII of the Elementary and Secondary Education Act), which made available $7.5 million to fund bilingual programs in 76 school districts. This was the first federal acknowledgment that a lack of English proficiency impedes equal access to educational opportunities. To be eligible for one of these programs, children had to be identified as having limited English-speaking ability and as coming from low-income families where the dominant language was other than English. This law provided for native language improvement, study of the history and culture associated with the student's native language, and efforts to enhance the child's self-esteem. Subsequent amendments in 1974 and 1978 expanded the population of eligible students and substantially increased the amount of the appropriation.

Assessment of minority students began to attract considerable attention in the early seventies. In California parents of six black children who had been classified as mentally retarded (on the basis of their performance on standardized intelligence tests) initiated a class action suit against the San Francisco Unified School District (*Larry P. v. Riles*). Citing the disproportionate number of black students in special classes for the educable mentally retarded and the fact that their own children were found to have normal intelligence when retested, the plaintiffs succeeded in restraining school personnel in California from continuing their minority assessment practices. A preliminary injunction was handed down in 1974 and became permanent in 1979, setting a precedent for the rest of the country. Many school systems began restricting or abolishing IQ tests.

In 1974, at the height of the concern for discriminatory assessment practices, a class action suit further legitimized the search for bilingual education alternatives. *Lau v. Nichols*, filed on behalf of 1,800 Chinese children, alleged that non-English-speaking students were being discriminated against because instruction was provided in a language they could not understand. The Supreme Court decision held that "there is no equality of treatment merely by providing students with the same facilities, textbooks, teachers, and curriculum; for students who do not understand English are effectively foreclosed from any meaningful education" (414 U.S. 563). This suit and another notable suit filed in California on behalf of Mexican-American students, *Diana v. State Board of Education* (1970), were among the numerous court actions that led to the amendments of the Bilingual Education Act and enactment of the Education for All Handicapped Children Act (P.L. 94–142).

There have been two other important class action suits since the enactment of P.L. 94–142. In both cases the impetus for the suits was inappropriate identification, assessment, and placement of minority students in special education programs. *Lora v. New York City Board of Education* was filed on behalf of black and Hispanic children assigned to special day schools for the emotionally disturbed. In 1979 the U.S. District Court ruled that these students were not being properly placed, and the school board was ordered to develop and engage in more extensive assessment and evaluation procedures. A second suit, *Dyricia S. v. New York City Board of Education*, was filed on behalf of Puerto Rican and other Hispanic students with handicaps and limited English proficiency; it included others who require bilingual special education programs for which they have not been promptly evaluated and placed. These cases led to a consolidated judgment in 1980, calling for the provision of appropriate bilingual programs for all handicapped students.

The laws and court actions summarized here played a significant role in stimulating progress toward meeting the special needs of exceptional minority students. However, building support for change is only half the battle; the other half is implementing the desired change. Minority students are still being misdiagnosed and misplaced, and some of those who need special services are not being served (Ysseldyke & Mirkin, 1981). There are still some fundamental issues related to minority assessment and placement decisions that remain unresolved. Certainly there has been progress, but we are still far from educational equality. Educators have just begun to address the complexities involved in bilingual or multicultural special education. Notable beginning efforts include the topical conferences of the Council for Exceptional Children (CEC) that have addressed the concerns surrounding the exceptional black child and the exceptional bilingual child.

Definition

The Council for Exceptional Children defines a *minority* group as "any group which because of racial or ethnic origin constitutes a distinctive and recognizable minority in our society. Present examples . . . include Blacks or Afro-Americans, American Indians, Mexican Americans or Chicanos, Puerto Ricans, and Oriental Americans" (Fuchigami, 1980, p. 241). Minority students are not necessarily disadvantaged, unless their environmental conditions include economic poverty; their cultural background is as significant and rich as that of students belonging to the majority culture.

It is important to remember that minority cultural groups are no more homogeneous than the dominant cultural group. With the exception of beliefs that can be traced directly to family values and influences, ethnic group members share few educationally relevant characteristics. Thus, stereotypic characterizations of different minority groups as having different patterns of ability, learning styles, or problem-solving approaches are of no value to educators. More important and worthy of attention are discontinuities between the home/neighborhood environment of minority students and the classroom environment. Identification and exploration of the different expectations and demands of those environments can provide educationally relevant information.

A term that appears often in the multicultural education literature is *cultural pluralism*—the belief that society is strengthened and enriched by the contributions of different cultural groups. A policy statement formulated by the multicultural education commission of the American Association of Colleges for Teacher Education (AACTE) captures the essence of this concept:

> To endorse cultural pluralism is to endorse the principle that there is no one model American. To endorse cultural pluralism is to understand and appreciate the differences that exist among the nation's citizens. It is to see these differences as a positive force in the continuing development of a society which professes a wholesome respect for the intrinsic worth of every individual. Cultural pluralism is more than a temporary accommodation to placate racial and ethnic minorities. It is a concept that aims toward a heightened sense of being and of wholeness of the entire society based on the unique strengths of each of its parts. (AACTE, 1973, p. 246)

Teachers who recognize and appreciate the contributions of all cultural groups to the development of our society are generally more adept at recognizing and providing for individual needs and differences among culturally diverse students

Cultural pluralism emphasizes the rich contribution of individual differences.

than are those who believe that minority students should blend into the main-stream of society. The mainstream or melting pot theory, called *cultural assimilation*, is basically the opposite of cultural pluralism. Inherent in cultural assimilation is the belief that diverse cultures should be merged into a single homogeneous society with common life styles, values, language, and cultural practices. This concept is offensive to many minority groups because it denies the significant contributions of their particular culture to the society as a whole.

The AACTE (1973) defines *multicultural education* as education that values cultural pluralism. It includes four major elements:

1. teaching values that support cultural diversity and individual uniqueness

2. encouraging and accepting the qualitative expansion of existing ethnic cultures

3. supporting exploration in alternative and emerging life styles

4. encouraging multiculturalism, multilingualism, and multidialectism

Multicultural education is for all students, not just those who happen to belong to a minority culture. Rodriguez (1982) argues for incorporation of multicultural concepts in every facet of education: "The concept of multicultural education is not based on the premise that there are ethnic minority students in the classroom, but that there are differences in students within any classroom and that all of those students live in a pluralistic society" (p. 227). It is a way of teaching that recognizes some basic truths about our society. It should be reflected in every lesson or unit of study at all levels of the curriculum. According to Rodriguez, an effective multi-cultural approach is also a way of learning. All students, regardless of cultural background, benefit from exposure to different people, beliefs, and ideas; they learn to relate to and evaluate new perspectives.

Although some children from minority cultures are quite competent in English, others enter school with few English language skills. Rodriguez (1982) de-scribes *bicultural* or *bilingual education* as education that reinforces the student's language and culture while at the same time teaching the ability to function in another language and behave on occasion according to patterns of the second culture. Parker (1978) defines bilingual education as instruction through the medium of two languages. This usually means teaching skills and subject content in English as well as another language.

A program sometimes confused with bilingual education is English as a Second Language (ESL) (Baca & Cervantes, 1984). An ESL program may be one component of a bilingual education program, but it does not alone constitute that program. Bilingual and ESL education share a common goal—promoting English proficiency—but bilingual education is more comprehensive in nature. It enhances and encourages the students' development of their native language and culture as part of the instructional process, whereas ESL instruction focuses exclusively on English as both the goal and the medium of instruction.

Prevalence

During the 1980-1981 school year 350,000 children received assistance in Title VII programs. However, the National Foundation for the Improvement of Education estimates that some 3.5 million children in the United States could benefit from bilingual programs (NFIE, 1982).

Characteristics

Most learning and behavioral differences of nonhandicapped minority students can be traced directly to the family. Cultural beliefs affect family values, which affect child-rearing practices. Child-rearing practices, in turn, influence cognitive, language, and social development. The home experiences of minority children may not prepare them for the demands and expectations of schools and teachers. Behaviors that are acceptable at home may be considered inappropriate at school, and vice versa. The same is true, of course, of exceptional minority children except that, in addition to learning and behavioral differences attributable to family values, they also demonstrate sensory and/or physical impairment or some characteristics associated with one of the categories of exceptionality.

The way in which a student typically approaches learning is called cognitive style. How students respond to a teacher or whether they respond at all often depends on the interaction of the teacher's instructional style and the student's cognitive style (Fuhrmann, 1980; Johnson, 1976). There is evidence (from experimental and ethnographic research) of cultural differences in two dimensions of cognitive style—field sensitivity/field independence and sensory modality strength (Cazden & Leggett, 1981).

The first dimension refers to individual differences in how information is received, conceptualized, and retained. Field-sensitive students are heavily influenced by the background or context in which an item is embedded; they like to work with others to achieve a common goal and tend to seek guidance and demonstrations from the teacher. Field-independent students are not influenced by background or context stimuli. They tend to work independently and to be very task oriented; they are better able to use elements out of context to solve a problem (Witkin et al., 1977). Relative to interpersonal behavior, the field-sensitive person makes greater use of social cues and shows a need for friendship and a readiness to reveal feelings and emotions. Field-independent persons tend to rely more on internal or physical cues from the environment, prefer solitary activities, and demonstrate more concern for ideas and principles than for feelings. They can see themselves apart from others rather than relying on interpersonal relationships (Kagan & Buriel, 1977).

The second dimension in which there is evidence of cultural differences—visual and auditory modality strengths—refers to the sense through which a person best receives information. Visual learners perform better when material is presented on the chalkboard or projection screen, whereas auditory learners perform better when material is received auditorily.

Whether child-rearing practices affect sensory strengths and preferences is unclear. However, the effect of socialization and child-rearing practices on the development of field sensitivity/field independence has received some attention (Cazden & Leggett, 1981). When cultural values lead parents to emphasize conformity and obedience, children tend to be field sensitive. Because their cultural group stresses cooperation, they are likely to be attuned to social cues. Kagan (1977) suggests that Mexican-American children may fit this profile; they are often more concerned with cooperative ventures than with competitive activities. Cooperation is also an important value of American Indians (Pepper, 1976) and native Hawaiians (Jordan, 1981). Those children whose culture emphasizes independence and competition are typically more attentive to the characteristics of objects and activities than to social variables. In a comparison of black, Mexican-American, and Anglo students, Madsen and Shapira (1970) found that black and Anglo students were more competitive than their Mexican-American peers.

There is no evidence that field-sensitive and field-independent students differ significantly in their ability to learn or retain information. Where they do differ is in the kinds of materials they are able to respond to and assimilate most easily and in the strategies they apply to achieve their goals. Teachers who are able to match their teaching style to their students' learning style improve the students' chances of learning.

Minority students are handicapped by an inflexible educational system, not by their cultural background.

It is most important to remember, when considering the learning characteristics of bicultural children, that even though low socioeconomic status is a strong predictor of school failure (Cole & Bruner, 1971), minority group membership is not. The academic failures of minority children and their disproportionate placement in classes for handicapped students must not be viewed as an incrimination of their home and community environments. Rather, these problems reflect the system's inability to develop unbiased assessment procedures and its lack of flexibility and skill in dealing with individual differences. It is the educational system that handicaps these children, not their cultural diversity.

Minority student dropout percentages verify the failure of the system to accomplish its mission—the education of all students, regardless of race, religion, sex, national origin, or creed. In comparison to their enrollment, fewer than 75% of blacks and Hispanics complete high school. Nationally, about 10% of all students drop out of school each year, compared to 15% of black students, 20% of Hispanic students, and 22% of American Indian students (Dearman & Plisko, 1981). Data suggest further that knowledge of the dominant culture language is a determinant of whether students complete their high school education: foreign-born Hispanic adolescents with non-English language backgrounds had significantly higher drop-out rates than Hispanics with predominantly English language backgrounds.

Language Differences

Some minority children are quite competent in English; others have had minimal exposure to it prior to entering school. They may speak Spanish, the second most common language in the United States; one of the many Asian languages; one of the many native American dialects (e.g., black English, Hawaiian pidgin); or any one of a dozen or so less common languages, such as Arabic or Tongian. In California alone there are students representing some 70 to 80 linguistic backgrounds (Wong-Fillmore, 1981). Bilinguals and children who use a dialect are a diverse group, but they share a common problem. They are faced with learning a second language while receiving academic instruction in that language.

Estimates indicate that 7% to 10% of the school-age population exhibits some type of language-learning problem (American Speech-Language-Hearing Association, 1980). The prevalence of these disorders among school-age bilinguals may be even greater. Based on a Chicago study of predominantly Mexican-American and Puerto Rican areas, Toronto (1972) reported that 20% of the Spanish-speaking children under the age of 6 years had inadequate language skills in their native language and in English. More recent studies of bilingual children have confirmed this finding (Hoover, 1981). As Matluck and Matluck (1982) point out, accurate identification of these children depends on the ability of an assessment system to distinguish between bilinguals who have not yet learned English and bilinguals who have a genuine language disorder. Such an assessment system does not presently exist because there is little agreement as to what constitutes linguistic proficiency for bilingual children (Langdon, 1982; Matluck & Matluck, 1982). Because most assessment procedures focus on the structural aspects of language, the scores they yield do not reflect the totality of the bilingual child's language knowledge and skills.

Multicultural Giftedness

Nationally, ethnic minority students constitute approximately 26.7% of the general student population and 18% of the gifted population (Office of Civil Rights, 1982). As with handicapped students, the disproportionate numbers of minority students in classes for the gifted and talented must not be viewed as a reflection of ability distribution in minority cultures. At the Guidance Institute for Talented Students at the University of Wisconsin, observation of talented children and adolescents from minority cultures is beginning to yield some interesting findings (Perrone & Aleman, 1983). Gifted children from minority cultures possess a variety of talents that are valued and nurtured within their own cultures but are often ignored in school. New and innovative identification techniques are being developed in an attempt to provide these students with the educational opportunities they need to fulfill their potential.

Assessment

The fact that some minority groups are overrepresented in classes for the mentally retarded and emotionally disturbed and underrepresented in classes for the gifted highlights the need for nondiscriminatory assessment practices. P.L. 94–142 was an attempt to establish guidelines by requiring all state and local education agencies to ensure that

> assessment procedures are selected and administered in a manner that is not racially or culturally discriminatory,

> tests have been validated for the specific purpose for which they are used and are administered by trained personnel in the child's native language or other mode of communication,

> assessment procedures are administered by a multidisciplinary team, and

> no single test or procedure is used as the sole criterion for determining placement.

The law also includes procedural due-process safeguards guaranteeing the rights of parents to a meaningful role in the assessment-intervention process. As detailed in chapter 1, parents have the right to examine all relevant records; obtain an independent evaluation; receive written notices in their native language concerning any school actions taken on behalf of their child; present complaints with respect to any matter relating to identifying, evaluating, or placing their child; participate in a hearing conducted by an impartial hearing officer; and file an appeal.

Despite the important assessment and due-process safeguards of P.L. 94–142, there are still numerous problems related to assessment bias and placement inequities. Reports abound regarding disparities in the percentages of the total school-age population and the school-age minority population enrolled in special education programs (OCR, 1982). The greatest overrepresentation of minority students is in self-contained special classes. Blacks constituted 38.7% of students served in classes for the educable mentally retarded (EMR) (more than twice the percentage found in the general population), 27.6% of the students served in classes for the trainable mentally retarded (TMR), and 25.2% of the students in classes for the seriously emotionally disturbed (SED). In those states with a large Hispanic population, Hispanics are also overrepresented in special education classes. For example, in New Mexico, where 46.5% of the school population is Hispanic, EMR classes have 60.4% Hispanic enrollment, TMR classes have 57.8%, and severe learning disabilities (SLD) classes have 48%. In addition, both blacks and Hispanics are underrepresented in gifted/talented classes. The renaming of intelligence tests has not changed the fact that language proficiency is the primary factor being measured. In such a situation, when children's cultural and language experiences determine their test scores, those test scores cannot be considered an accurate measure of learning ability.

Other possible biasing factors in the assessment process are children's reactions to the testing situation as well as the examiner's personality and methods of interacting with the students. There is some evidence that minority children react differently to the testing situation than do their dominant culture peers (Mercer, 1973).

The search for a solution to the problem of biased assessment procedures has stimulated considerable activity in the field of psychometrics. One procedure that shows promise is the System of Multicultural Pluralistic Assessment (SOMPA) (Mercer, 1979). According to the author, the SOMPA has three basic purposes:

- to reduce the overlabeling of non-Anglo children as mentally retarded and the underlabeling of non-Anglo children as gifted, a result of unidimensional assessment that does not take the sociocultural distance between the family and the culture of the school into account in interpreting the child's performance

- to provide sufficient information concerning each child's sociocultural background, health history, current performance in non-academic social systems and estimated learning potential to enable the schools to develop educational programs that treat each child as an individual

- to identify the educational needs of children who are not being served by present monocultural, monolingual, Anglo-centric programs of the public school (p. 28)

The SOMPA has three models: medical, social-system, and pluralistic. The health component includes measures of visual acuity, auditory acuity, weight by height, health history, physical dexterity, and the Bender Visual-Motor Gestalt Test. The second system includes a social measure—the Adaptive Behavior Inventory for Children—and the Wechsler Intelligence Scale for Children, Revised (WISC-R)—an index of academic role performance. The third system includes pluralistic measures designed to assess children's performance in relation to age and the expectations of their sociocultural group. In this third component the WISC-R scores are transformed into estimated learning potentials (ELPS) to indicate the position of the child's score relative to the scores of others from similar sociocultural backgrounds. Thus, the SOMPA permits measurement of three aspects of performance: adaptive behavior, school performance, and learning potential. An assumption of SOMPA and other supposedly culture-fair tests is that there are some tasks common to all culture groups. Figure 4-1 shows a sample SOMPA profile.

The Kaufman Assessment Battery for Children (K-ABC) (Kaufman & Kaufman, 1983) is another instrument that may have promise in the assessment of ethnic minority children. The battery is designed to be individually administered to children 2½ to 12½ years old. It has four global areas of functioning: sequential processing, simultaneous processing, mental processing composite, and achievement. The K-ABC has received considerable attention from those concerned with the assessment process. Standardization, based on 1980 census data, included proportionate numbers of white, black, Asian, native American, and exceptional children; ethnic minority reviewers were utilized in statistical analysis of item bias. The authors and the publisher suggest that this battery is especially sensitive to the diverse needs of preschool, minority, and exceptional children. Undoubtedly, the K-ABC will receive close scrutiny from psychologists and diagnosticians. Research with the instrument will eventually determine its usefulness with minority group children.

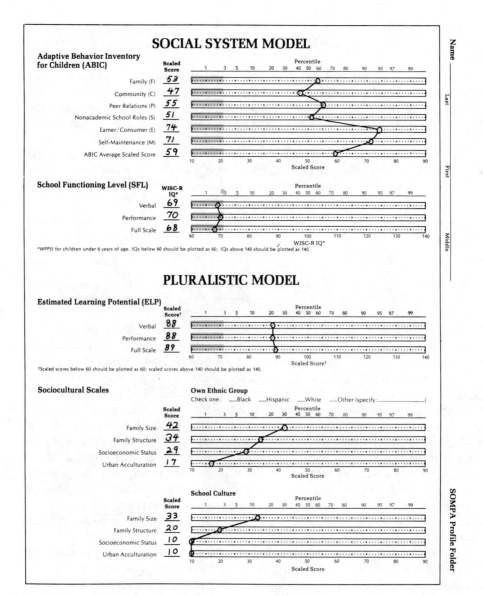

Figure 4-1   Sample SOMPA profile

SOURCE: Reproduced by permission from the System of Multicultural Pluralistic Assessment.
Copyright © 1977, 1979 by the Psychological Corporation, New York, NY. All rights reserved.

Tests that attempt to include only those items that do not discriminate among cultural groups are a promising alternative to traditional instruments. However, there is a strong possibility that the tests used with minority children are not the only culprit in placement inequities. In fact, researchers have failed to find clear evidence of bias in cognitive tests when used with American-born minority groups

What are teacher's preconceptions about their minority students?

(e.g., Cole, 1981; Reynolds, 1981). These findings suggest a need to look beyond the measurement devices to other possible sources of unfairness in assessment—at least for this subgroup of the larger minority population.

Ysseldyke's (1979) suggestion that educational personnel may be at fault, particularly those responsible for educational decisions, is worth considering. Supporting the possibility of bias in decision making is evidence that regular education teachers (1) expect minority children to have higher incidences of handicaps than other groups (Ysseldyke et al., 1980); (2) judge minority children as less competent than their peers (Kelley, Bullock, & Dykes, 1977; Spring, Blunden, Greenberg, &

Yellin, 1977); and (3) disproportionately and erroneously refer minority children for special education evaluation (Greenleaf, 1980; Tobias, Cole, Zibrin, & Bodlakova, 1981). Supporting this position are reports that children found eligible for EMR placement but not placed are disproportionately white and that black children placed in EMR classes tend to be more capable than their white peers (Mercer, 1973).

Teachers tend to refer students who bother them (Rubin & Balow, 1978), and different teachers are bothered by different kinds of students. Too often referral reflects a negative interaction between the teacher's beliefs and the student's characteristics, not a learning or behavior problem. Referral for special education assessment and placement is a teacher's way of saying that he is having trouble coping with a particular child (Ysseldyke & Algozzine, 1984). Newly arrived immigrant children are often referred for special education assessment even before there has been sufficient time for them to become familiar with the demands and expectations of the system.

Current practices result in a high probability that referred students will be found eligible for special education services. A 1981 study by Ysseldyke, Algozzine, and Allen analyzed videotapes of placement team meetings to determine the degree and type of participation of various team members. Regular education teachers were not active participants. Their total contribution most often consisted of data on classroom performance. Less than 10% of their participation involved recommendations or suggestions for service options. Consistently, special education teachers, school psychologists, and principals were the most active participants in team meetings, even though regular classroom teachers had been most closely involved with the students.

Also of interest are the findings of another study by Ysseldyke and colleagues (Ysseldyke, Algozzine, Richey, & Graden, 1982). Using the test scores presented at team meetings, they objectively identified students as learning disabled or not. These identifications were then compared with the decisions made by the placement team. Students classified as learning disabled by the test scores were not classified as such by the placement teams. The fact that the relationships between score-based and team decisions were very low suggests that the teams were using information other than test data. At least in the case of mildly handicapped students, they seemed to be operating under the assumption that teacher referral is a more reliable and valid indicator of the need for special services than are test scores. In essence, the team was relieving the teacher of a difficult-to-teach child. The purpose of the assessment process seemed to be to confirm the teacher's judgment that special placement was indicated. The implications of this type of decision making for minority group children are distressingly clear.

One conclusion seems indisputable—the concept of bias is complex and not well understood. The disproportionate representation of minority students in special education classes is not the effect of a single factor. The system can break down at any one of a number of points in the assessment-placement process, and any one of a number of factors can effect the breakdown. The fallibility of the system highlights the need for educational personnel to be constantly alert to tacit ethnocentrism—judging competence and performance only in the context of specific roles and value standards.

Intervention

Despite the inappropriate placement of minority group children in special education classes, it is important not to forget that there are many bicultural students
who do in fact, require special education services because of significant limitations
unrelated to their minority group membership. They need bilingual special education, which is defined in ideal terms by Baca and Cervantes (1984) as "use of the
home language and the home culture along with English in an individually designed program of special instruction" (p. 18). Goals and procedures for these students will be similar to those for their dominant culture handicapped peers. However, there will be important differences in teacher competencies needed to achieve
these goals and some differences in teaching strategies.

The primary goal of both regular and bicultural special education is to bring
about a greater degree of academic and social competence and educational independence. In line with the provisions of P.L. 94–142, educational personnel must
identify student strengths and disabilities, the level and type of instruction needed,
the means by which it will be provided, and the setting(s) for instruction. The
educational setting must not restrict the student's learning and social options; the
student's IEP should call for specially tailored instructional activities and enhancement of English proficiency. Annual goals and objectives should reflect the needs
of the student and support the specific culture of the family.

The language of instruction should be the language through which the child
learns most effectively and efficiently. If that language is other than English, placement must be with a teacher who is fluent in that language, knowledgeable about
the student's cultural beliefs and values, and well versed in the theory and process
of first and second language acquisition. If no bilingual personnel are available,
then special education intervention requires that the child be provided a structured
program in English as a Second Language with intervention initially focused on
development of the language skills necessary to function in a totally English language curriculum (Baca & Cervantes, 1984).

Analysis of the home and community and creation of an educational environment more closely matching that of the home may eliminate some of the factors
contributing to the child's academic failures. The Kamehameha Early Education
Program (KEEP) for Hawaiian and part-Hawaiian children demonstrates application
of this concept (Jordan, 1981). This program has attained significant language and
reading gains by using teaching strategies compatible with Hawaiian culture.

There are implications for teaching style in the idea that much of the school
failure experienced by minority group students may be the effect of a disparity
between their cultural values and learning styles and those of their teachers; that
is, performance problems may be a function of nonproductive teacher-student interaction patterns rather than problems residing in the student or the home environment. A field-sensitive teaching style (most appropriate for children with a field-
sensitive cognitive style) would be characterized by overt expressions of approval
and warmth (social reinforcement), a great deal of encouragement, clear presentation of tasks with directions for each step, lots of demonstrations, and group work
assignments. Care would be taken to point out and discuss how concepts relate to
the students' own personal experiences. A field-independent teaching style would

Effective intervention with a special needs child of any age requires personnel fluent in the child's language and knowledgeable about his culture.

be more formal and authoritative, with an emphasis on individual effort, competition, and inductive learning. Students would be encouraged to adopt a discovery approach and learn through trial and error.

Materials most appropriate to the field-sensitive teaching approach are those that lend themselves to fantasy, humorous play, and expression of feelings. A most important characteristic of these materials is their potential for cooperative play or learning projects. Materials for the field-independent teaching approach have high intrinsic appeal. They draw attention to factual details, stimulate the search for unique solutions, and lend themselves to competitive activities.

Instructional materials should enhance rather than detract from the student's self-concept. In a discussion of the self-concept of American Indian students, Pepper (1976) suggests

teaching the history of different minority groups and the value of these cultures to all students,

providing clear behavioral evidence that students are valued and accepted as they are,

using words that build self-esteem and feelings of adequacy, demonstrating faith in students so that they believe in themselves, and planning learning experiences in which success is guaranteed.

Teacher Competencies

The new standards of the National Council for Accreditation of Teacher Education (NCATE) which became effective in 1979, explicitly address multicultural education. In order to receive full accreditation by NCATE, teacher training institutions must provide prospective teachers with some knowledge and skills related to multicultural concepts. Teacher training programs must also recruit culturally diverse students. In 1976 the Equal Employment Commission reported that of the 2,046,088 teachers in the United States, only 35,767 (approximately 2%) were Hispanic. This is an alarming statistic, considering the estimate that there are some 13.2 million persons of Spanish origin in the United States (Bureau of Census, 1981). The Office of Civil Rights (Killalea Associates, 1980) reports that 24% of all special education students come from minority backgrounds, but only 11% of all teachers are from a minority group (Baptiste, Baptiste, & Gollnick, 1980).

Minority special education students with adequate English proficiency to benefit from instruction in English obviously do not need teachers with second language competencies. However, they do need teachers with special cultural awareness in their attitudes and skills. Most important, they need teachers who can establish an atmosphere that accommodates the differences in each student's cultural reality. In addition to subject matter and teaching competencies, teachers who work with minority students should

1. understand how their own cultural perspective affects the teaching/learning relationship and be willing to continuously explore the effects of their cultural limits on the educational process;

2. provide for and encourage an atmosphere in which cultural differences can be explored on attitudinal and affective, as well as cognitive, levels;

3. draw upon the cultural experiences of students and parents to generate authentic cultural perspectives in the curriculum;

4. adjust to and accommodate different learning styles;

5. scrutinize assessment practices to assure that they are as fair as possible;

6. understand and convey that there are no culturally deprived or culture-free individuals—that every culture has an integrity, validity, and coherence; and

7. expand the students' knowledge of themselves culturally and their capacity to appreciate and deal with differences in others (Benavides, 1980).

Family Interactions

Many professionals seem oblivious to the pressures on a family to raise their handicapped child to conform to linguistic and social patterns. They fail to recognize that parents are getting many mixed messages—conflicting opinions and advice from professionals, other family members, and other members of their cultural community (Linder, 1983).

Minority culture parents often feel alienated by the school and misunderstood by teachers. Some have had negative experiences during their own school years, when insensitivity and discrimination on the part of school personnel precluded the possibility of positive experiences. They may now tolerate the seeming impertinence and insensitivity of school personnel because they hope for better experiences for their children. However, they may find it impossible to convey positive feelings toward the educational system, thus sending their children to school without the motivation necessary for school success.

To further compound the problem of negative attitude, some minority group students are justifiably suspicious and distrustful of all adult authority figures in law enforcement and educational systems. The inequitable treatment of these systems has been clearly recognized and resented by minority group students. Differential treatment can take many forms, including reverse discrimination. Teachers who are overly solicitous or patronizing to minority students are as resented as those who are overtly negative.

It is the responsibility of school personnel to develop a positive school environment and positive interactions with parents. Equally important is their responsibility to assure that parents understand their rights as parents of bilingual exceptional children and the nature of available bilingual resources (Baca & Cervantes, 1984). Diagnosis, service plans, and evaluation strategies should be explained in detail as often as is necessary. Transmittal of this information in such a way that it will be understood requires more than simply translating the words of the law: it requires a basic commitment to what these words represent.

Curriculum Implications

There are extremely few curricular materials specifically designed for bilingual special education. Most teachers adapt curricula intended for monolingual special education students or curricula for bilingual nonhandicapped students. Baca and Cervantes (1984) list the eight essential steps in developing and implementing a comprehensive curriculum for bilingual exceptional children:

1. *Planning.* Converting and adapting the curriculum to each student's special cultural and linguistic background takes extensive planning. The content, scope, sequence, pace, and learnability of the materials must be considered.

2. *Becoming familiar with each student's background of culture and language.* Before and during planning bilingual special education teachers must familiarize themselves with each student's cultural heritage and find out how the particular culture deals with different exceptionalities. Excellent sources of information, beyond parents and bilingual education personnel, are national and state organizations serving culturally diverse populations.

3. *Becoming familiar with each student's special learning style and educational needs.* As discussed earlier, children's cultural experiences seem to influence their learning

styles. Maximizing each student's chances for academic success requires matching teaching style and materials to student learning styles. Also, of course, the design of instructional experiences must consider special learning needs that may be an effect of the student's handicapping condition.

4. *Preparing individual instructional plans.* Teachers typically perform some classroom assessments to verify the pre-IEP assessment results and to specify more precisely where instruction should begin. In addition, the teacher must determine the sequence of instruction, realistic time limits for units, corrective feedback/reinforcement options for each student, and evaluation procedures.

5. *Developing individualized lessons and materials appropriate to the student's exceptionality.* The primary information source for this step will be available special education curricula.

6. *Modifying individualized lessons and materials using a "cultural screen" and sensitivity.* The following questions should be considered in modifying and screening materials:
    a. Are the pictures/objects familiar in the children's environment and relevant to their learning needs?
    b. Do the students have the necessary preskills to benefit from the materials?
    c. Are the directions in the students' native language or an approved translation?
    d. Do the materials present any material that contradicts the students' cultural beliefs?
    e. Are the methods culturally appropriate?

7. *Referring to resource staff for assistance and arranging coordination of services.* Like other special education teachers, bilingual special education teachers must draw from the contributions of other professionals and paraprofessionals, making joint decisions and coordinating service delivery.

8. *Evaluating students' progress and revising instruction.* Evaluation procedures should flow logically from students' goals and objectives. Teachers should plan both process and product evaluations prior to implementation of any curriculum procedures.

In summary, the steps in developing and adapting curriculum for a bilingual special education student are not significantly different from those in developing and adapting curriculum for any other student with special learning needs. The keys to success are planning, individualization, and careful monitoring.

Mainstreaming

Johnson and Johnson (1980) define mainstreaming as "providing an appropriate educational opportunity for all handicapped students in the least restrictive alternative, based on individualized educational programming and aimed at providing

Constructive interaction is the key to effective mainstreaming.

handicapped students with access to and constructive interaction with nonhandi-capped peers" (p. 152). The important phrase in this definition is "access to and constructive interaction with nonhandicapped peers."

If handicapped students are accepted by their peers and teachers and if they have constructive interactions with their peers and teachers, only then can their presence in a regular classroom and in other school settings with their nonhandi-capped peers be termed mainstreaming. Whether a handicapped student belongs to a minority culture or the dominant culture, the issue is the same—acceptance and constructive, positive interactions. Some studies have demonstrated that placement of handicapped students in a regular classroom may result in greater prejudice, stereotyping, and rejection (e.g., Gottlieb, Cohen, & Goldstein, 1974). However, there is also evidence that the placement of handicapped students in a regular classroom can positively influence the attitudes of their nonhandicapped peers (e.g., Wechsler, Suarez, & McFadden, 1975). The teacher seems to be the single most important determinant of whether placement of handicapped students in a regular classroom qualifies as mainstreaming. General strategies to maximize the possibilities of success are (1) structuring a cooperative learning atmosphere, (2) providing detailed and specific information about the potential of all persons, and (3) providing students with the opportunity to discuss, question, and clarify their beliefs and attitudes about individual differences (Gearheart & Weishahn, 1984).

Innovation and Development

This chapter has emphasized the problems surrounding the provision of equal and appropriate educational opportunities for exceptional, culturally diverse students because understanding is a requisite to change. Since human and economic resources are finite, some choices must be made. We can do more than just hope for more equitable treatment of culturally diverse students; we can advocate for and actively support the distribution of resources to multicultural and bilingual education. What we have achieved in this area represents years of effort by parents, advocacy groups, and public-interest organizations; whatever we achieve in the future will be the result of more years of hard work.

Looking specifically at the future of special education services for culturally diverse students, Baca and Cervantes (1984) make certain predictions:

1. The number of non-English-speaking handicapped children will likely increase at a greater rate than the rest of the student population because of an increased number of immigrants.

2. Assessment procedures will continue to improve as research and training efforts in this area improve and as more bilingual professionals become available.

3. The trend toward educationally relevant (as opposed to etiologically based) classification will continue because of the increasing concern for the negative stigma attached to labels.

4. Individualized education programs (IEPs) will improve as a result of teacher training programs and litigation that continue to focus on the language, social, and academic needs of minority group students.

5. There will be an increased emphasis on early intervention with minority group children as cost-benefit data become available.

6. Self-contained classes for bilingual special education will decrease in number as we gain more experience in facilitating successful integration.

7. The use of computers with culturally diverse exceptional students will increase as the new technology becomes more advanced and readily available.

Increased understanding of the interrelationship of learning and teaching, cognitive styles, and cultural values will enable educators to keep minority students in school, nurture their self-concepts, and assure them a productive and independent future. However, these objectives will require planning, research, and commitment if we are to continue learning and translating what we learn into practice.

Summary

This chapter introduced some basic concepts and issues related to provision of appropriate educational services for exceptional minority group students. Several significant court cases in the 1970s focused attention on discriminatory assessment and placement practices, but they continue to be a problem. There remains an underrepresentation of minority students in classes for the gifted and an over-representation in classes for the handicapped. These data, together with current dropout statistics, suggest an educational system that is not adequately responding to individual differences.

Exceptional minority students require bilingual special education provided by teachers with special competencies. Development and implementation of an appropriate curriculum should follow certain definite steps; constructive interaction with nonhandicapped peers should be a distinct objective.

Much has been accomplished in the education of culturally diverse exceptional students; much remains to be done. As citizens, these students are entitled to the same rights and privileges that their majority group peers enjoy.

STUDY QUESTIONS

1. Describe the effects of legislation and litigation in securing equal educational opportunities for minority group students.

2. Differentiate between cultural pluralism and cultural assimilation.

3. State the rationale for multicultural education, and discuss how multicultural education differs from bilingual education.

4. How do family values and child-rearing practices affect the learning and behavioral characteristics of minority students?

5. Discuss assessment and decision-making biases as they relate to special education placement inequities.

6. Contrast the special education services and teacher competencies required for minority group handicapped students and those required for other handicapped students.

7. Contrast the field-sensitive teaching style and materials and the field-independent teaching style and materials.

8. What are some strategies to maximize the success of mainstreaming efforts?

1. As you identify the different ethnic groups in your classroom, become informed about their characteristics and learning styles.

2. Encourage and assist students in sharing their culture in the classroom; you can start the process by sharing your own cultural values and traditions.

3. Avoid textbooks and materials that present cultural stereotypes.

4. Know as much as possible about minority students' home and community, interests, talents, skills, and potentials and develop an instructional program accordingly.

5. Find out how the minority students in your class wish you to refer to their ethnic group; for example, some Mexican-Americans prefer to be called Chicanos while others may take offense at the term.

6. Include ethnic studies in the curriculum to help minority students gain a more positive self-image.

7. Make parents your partners in helping minority students.

8. Treat all students equally; do not fall into the trap of reverse discrimination.

9. Be sure assessment techniques used are appropriate and take into account cultural differences.

10. Avoid imitating speech patterns of minority students; rather than an aid in education, this may be viewed as mockery.

TIPS FOR HELPING

5

Learning Disabilities

Cecil D. Mercer
University of Florida

Jason has brown hair and brown eyes, wears glasses, and is a little small when compared to his fourth-grade classmates. However, his size does not restrict him from being the most noticeable character in a group. Jason talks loudly and continuously and is forever in motion. "Out of seat," "short attention span," and "forever asking questions" are phrases his teachers use to describe him. On the playground Jason lacks coordination. He has trouble catching, kicking, hitting, and throwing a ball. Although his IQ is in the superior range, Jason has severe problems with word attack, handwriting, and spelling. In a recent evaluation his grade-level achievement in word attack was 1.2; spelling, 1.0; and reading comprehension, 1.8. His math achievement, 3.7, appears adequate. The learning disabilities resource room teacher works with Jason daily for one 50-minute period. She

concentrates on reading skills and assists the regular teachers with behavior management suggestions. Jason does not have many friends, and his parents were recently considering putting him on medication to control hyperactivity and enrolling him in a private school. Then the learning disabilities teacher suggested that Jason increase his time in the resource room to three periods a day. She felt that a highly structured approach, combined with behavior modification, instructional games, peer teaching, and a language-experience reading program would help Jason's social-emotional adjustment and academic achievement. In the two months since Jason began his new schedule, he has improved his relationships with his peers, and recent achievement tests have shown gains from 3 to 6 months in all academic areas. Jason is labeled learning disabled.

Although there is some confusion regarding the nature of learning disabled individuals, some basic descriptions do exist. All learning disabled students have an academic problem in one or more areas; and this problem is not primarily due to emotional disturbance, mental retardation, visual or auditory impairment, motor disability, and/or environmental disadvantage. In their problem area(s) they are not achieving in accordance with their potential ability. Social-emotional problems may or may not be present.

History

By 1960 most public schools provided special education services to some handicapped students. Programs and services were extended to some mentally retarded, emotionally disturbed, blind, deaf, speech impaired, and physically handicapped students. Still, there remained a group of youngsters who had serious learning problems but did not fit any of the existing categories of exceptionality. Many had average or above-average intelligence and appeared to be physically intact. Because there were no apparent reasons for their learning problems, their parents and teachers sought help from professionals in a variety of fields.

Numerous theories emerged from medicine and psychology to explain the problems of these students. Explanations included laziness, brain damage, perceptual handicaps, dyslexia, and neurological impairment. A multitude of terms were introduced to describe the characteristics the students exhibited. Confusion, frustration, and eventually growth resulted. Initially, the medical profession concentrated on identifying students with learning problems. Psychologists joined in the effort, studying characteristics. Yet in both these fields treatment recommendations were few and limited. In the early 1960s it became apparent that educators would have to involve themselves in treating students with complex learning problems.

Local associations of parents formed to organize classes and provide services not offered in public schools. The number of local groups and state organizations increased rapidly, and in 1963 a national conference was held in Chicago to organize a national association. At this conference Kirk introduced the term *learning disabilities* (LD). Parents, who had been dissatisfied with existing terms, received this new term enthusiastically and formed the Association for Children with Learning Disabilities (ACLD). Kirk's introduction of the term and the formation of ACLD are viewed as the official beginning of the LD movement, although the stage had been set for this development by other distinct movements, whose interaction has been traced by several authorities (Hallahan & Cruickshank, 1973; Wiederholt, 1974). Six primary movements influencing the LD field are identified in Table 5-1—spoken language, written language, perceptual motor skills, reinforcement theory, interest groups, and government policy. Significant developments presented later in this chapter are charted here according to their area of origin.

In 1968–69 several key events occurred. First, the National Advisory Committee on Handicapped Children (NACHC) was established to develop a definition. Under Kirk's leadership the committee drafted a definition that is still used today. Second, the Council for Exceptional Children (CEC) established the Division for Children with Learning Disabilities (DCLD). Through the efforts of ACLD and DCLD, legislators were made aware of learning disabled children and the paucity of educational services available to them. As a result of intense lobbying the Children with Learning Disabilities Act of 1969 was passed into law (P.L. 91–230). This legislation provided for a 5-year program of teacher training, research, and the establishment of model education centers for LD children. In 1975 learning disabilities was included as one of the handicapping conditions in P.L. 94–142, and a more precise definition was requested. The 1975–77 period was highlighted by much debate and controversy over the LD definition and identification practices. On December 29, 1977, the *Federal Register* was released with regulations for defining and identifying LD. These regulations remain in effect for P.L. 94–142 practices.

Definition

In no other area of special education has so much effort been expended in developing a definition (Kass, 1969). The major definitions formulated over the years have reflected terminology that can be classified in three primary categories: brain injury, minimal brain dysfunction, and learning disabilities (Mercer, 1983). The first description of students with learning problems was based on the assumption of brain injury (Strauss & Lehtinen, 1947). However, parents disliked the term and the permanence it implied; professionals claimed that it was of little use in classifying, describing, or teaching children. During the 1960s the term *minimal brain dysfunction* (MBD) emerged. MBD theorists proposed that minimal or minor brain injury was linked with learning problems. However, the MBD definition was never widely accepted either. Educators found the MBD label no more useful in planning educational intervention than the brain injury label.

In time the medical emphasis was replaced with concern for psychological and educational variables. Special educators preferred to refer to students with learning problems as educationally handicapped, language disordered, or perceptually handicapped. Finally, both parents and educators endorsed the term *learning disability*. With the responsibility for funding special education programs for LD children came the need for a clear and functional definition. The definition developed by the National Advisory Committee on Handicapped Children (NACHC) and incorporated into P.L. 91–230, the Learning Disabilities Act of 1969, is included here:

> Children with special learning disabilities exhibit a disorder in one or more of the basic psychological processes involved in understanding or in using spoken or written languages. These may be manifested in disorders of listening, thinking, talking, reading, writing, spelling or arithmetic. They include conditions which have been referred to as perceptual handicaps, brain injury, minimal brain dysfunction, dyslexia, developmental aphasia, etc. They do *not* include learning problems which are due primarily to visual, hearing or motor handicaps, to mental retardation, emotional disturbance or to environmental disadvantage. (U.S. Office of Education, 1968, p. 34)

Acceptance of this definition was widespread. By 1975, 31 states were using the NACHC definition or some variation of it (Mercer, Forgnone, & Wolking, 1976; Murphy, 1976).

Table 5-1 Highlights in the field of learning disabilities

	Spoken Language	Written Language	Perceptual Motor Skills	Reinforcement Theory	Interest Groups	Government Policy
	Circa 1940s: Osgood, Myklebust, Wepman, Kirk	Circa 1930s: Orton (brain-dominance theory), Monroe, Gillingham, Stillman, Spalding	Circa 1940s: Strauss, Werner, Lehtinen, Cruickshank, Kephart, Doman & Delacato, Frostig	Circa 1950s: Skinner, Haring, Lindsley	Circa 1950s: Fund for Perceptually Handicapped Children, New York Association for Brain-Injured Children	No direct legislation
	Psycholinguistic teaching	Multisensory remedial reading techniques; phonics	Delineation of characteristics of brain-injured children; reduced stimuli techniques	Operant conditioning; precision teaching		
1963	←—Kirk's speech to parents suggesting term *learning disabilities* —→				ACLD formed	Task forces I, II, and III planned
	ITPA and psycholinguistic teaching widespread	Remedial reading emphasis; 3 Rs stressed	Extensive use of P-M tests and training activities	Lovitt's application of precision teaching to LD	ACLD expansion to international organization	Clements' use of MBD term
1968	Growing criticism of psycholinguistic approach—led by Hammill and colleagues	Rapid development of commercial programs (e.g., DISTAR); shift from ability to skill model	Growing criticism of P-M approach—led by Hammill and colleagues	Growing use of precision teaching; direct instruction stressed by Stephens; criticism of ability model	DCLD formed Continuing ACLD multidisciplinary emphasis; DCLD teacher-oriented emphasis	NACHC definiton P.L. 91–230, the LD Act
1975						P.L. 94–142 identification of learning disabilities as handicap and request for precise LD definition

——— Controversy over definition extensive in 1975–77 period ———→

Table 5-1 Highlights in the field of learning disabilities (continued)

	Spoken Language	Written Language	Perceptual Motor Skills	Reinforcement Theory	Interest Groups	Government Policy
1977	Process tests and treatments minimized in 1977 Federal Register; value questioned by researchers	Proliferation of commercial materials spurred on by IEP requirement in P.L. 94–142	Severe criticism of P-M approach; P-M minimized in 1977 Federal Register; value questioned by researchers	Appearance of commercial precision teaching programs	Increased attention on process vs. ability; controversy within and between ACLD and DCLD	1977 Federal Register Federal funding of LD research institutes
1980	Oral language training provided mainly by language specialists. Commercial language tests expanding rapidly. A subgroup of LD—the language learning disabled (LLD)—becoming more prominent	Widespread criterion-oriented commercial programs. More emphasis in the literature on the LD adolescent and more adolescent-oriented commercial programs. Computer-assisted instruction for LD students available on a large scale	P-M widely criticized; some resurgence in occupational therapy; Ayres influential. P-M test introduced by Barbe and Swassing	Directive teaching and precision teaching gaining in use. Journal of Precision Teaching published	National Joint Committee for LD (NJCLD) formed from 6 organizations. LD definition proposed by NJCLD. DCLD withdrawal from CEC (Hammill-led movement) and formation of the Council for Learning Disabilities (CLD). A new CEC division called Division for Learning Disabilities (DLD) begun by a cadre of former DCLD members	Beginning of federal de-emphasis of education. Much support for LD in public hearings; LD category intact at the federal level
1984			Detroit Tests of Learning Aptitude revised; Ayres revising sensory-integration test; supportive data for P-M still lacking	Precision teaching content included in the majority of college teacher-training programs		

During the 1979–84 period various professionals recommending cognitive approaches; others, an ecological approach combining both ability and skill orientations

Nonetheless, when P.L. 94–142 was passed in November 1975, it required that LD be defined more precisely, and the Office of Education was charged with this task. After two years the regulations for defining and identifying LD students appeared in the *Federal Register*. These regulations endorse a definition of *specific learning disability* that is almost identical to the earlier NACHC definition:

> "Specific learning disability" means a disorder in one or more of the basic psychological processes involved in understanding or in using language, spoken or written, which may manifest itself in an imperfect ability to listen, think, speak, read, write, spell, or to do mathematical calculations. The term includes such conditions as perceptual handicaps, brain injury, minimal brain dysfunction, dyslexia, and developmental aphasia. The term does not include children who have learning problems which are primarily the result of visual, hearing, or motor handicaps, or mental retardation, or emotional disturbance, or of environmental, cultural, or economic disadvantage. (U.S. Office of Education, 1977, p. 65083)

Although the definition remained virtually the same, the regulations included criteria for identifying LD students that helped to clarify the LD definition:

Academic Component, Qualified by Discrepancy Factor

1. A team may determine that a child has a specific learning disability if:
   a. The child does not achieve commensurate with his or her age and ability levels in one or more of the following areas when provided with learning experiences appropriate for the child's age and ability levels: oral expression, listening comprehension, written expression, basic reading skill, reading comprehension, mathematics calculation, or mathematics reasoning.
   b. The team finds that a child has a severe discrepancy between achievement and intellectual ability in one or more of the same areas listed in the preceding statement.

Exclusion Component

2. The team may not identify a child as having a specific learning disability if the severe discrepancy between ability and achievement is primarily the result of:
   a. a visual, hearing, or motor handicap
   b. mental retardation
   c. emotional disturbance
   d. environmental, cultural, or economic disadvantage (*Federal Register*, 42 (250), pp. 65082–65085)

The identification criteria focused on academic skills of concern and interpreted academic problems within the context of a discrepancy factor. A discrepancy exists when a student's academic performance falls far below her estimated ability in one or more subjects. A student may have average intelligence yet function in reading or math several grade levels behind her chronological age. Many authorities consider the discrepancy factor to be the common denominator of learning disabilities. However, both the definition and the criteria state that a child cannot be labeled LD if the discrepancy between academic achievement and estimated ability is due to physical or sensory handicaps; mental retardation; emotional disturbance; or environmental, cultural, or economic disadvantages. This is known as the *exclusion component*.

Reactions to the 1977 *Federal Register* definition and criteria remain controversial. Dissatisfaction with the definition resulted in the formation of the National Joint Committee for Learning Disabilities (NJCLD), which reached agreement on a new definition in 1981:

> *Learning disabilities* is a generic term that refers to a heterogeneous group of disorders manifested by significant difficulties in the acquisition and use of listening, speaking, reading, writing, reasoning, or mathematical abilities. These disorders are intrinsic to the individual and presumed to be due to central nervous system dysfunction. Even though a learning disability may occur concomitantly with other handicapping conditions (e.g., sensory impairment, mental retardation, social and emotional disturbance) or environmental influences (e.g., cultural differences, insufficient/inappropriate instruction, psychogenic factors), it is not the direct result of those conditions or influences. (Hammill, Leigh, McNutt, & Larsen, 1981, p. 336)

This definition omits reference to basic psychological processes, recognizes the existence of learning disabilities in all ages, and stresses the medical orientation.

A recent survey (Mercer, Hughes, & Mercer, 1985) of all state departments of education reveals that of the six components commonly used in defining and/or identifying LD, three (academic problem, exclusion, and discrepancy) have increased in usage, and three (process, neurological involvement, and intelligence level delineation) have decreased since a similar survey was conducted in 1976 (Mercer, Forgnone, & Wolking). These trends are consistent with the survey's parallel finding that 72% of the states use the 1977 *Federal Register* definition or some variation of it, as compared to 62% in the 1976 study.

Prevalence

The lack of accurate estimates of the prevalence of learning disabilities in the population reflects the problems of definition and identification. Figures vary depending on the stringency of the criteria used. For example, if mildly disabled learners are included, a prevalence figure of around 4% will probably be found. The federal government's count of learning disabled children and youth served under P.L. 94–142 indicates that 4.63% of the population aged 3 through 21 received service in 1983–84 (U.S. Office of Education, 1984). However, if only severe specific learning disabilities are considered, the figure may well be much lower, around 1.5%. It should be noted that a learning disability is very difficult to identify at the preschool level. LD is primarily an academic learning problem and is frequently not detected until the child faces formal academic instruction. To assess prevalence among older students, Schmid, Algozzine, Wells, and Stoller (1980) conducted a national survey of secondary LD teachers and found that the average incidence of LD among adolescents was 2.01%. Certainly the learning disabled comprise one of the largest groups within the handicapped population.

Causes

In the majority of cases the cause of a student's learning disability is unknown. Nonetheless, numerous factors have been proposed as possible causes, and they can be grouped into three basic categories—organic and biological, genetic, and environmental.

Organic and Biological Factors

Some authorities with a medical orientation believe that brain injury is the primary cause of learning disabilities. Because they do not consider the brain damage severe, they use the term *minimal brain dysfunction* (MBD). Several problems exist regarding this theory. First, procedures for detecting minor brain injury are unreliable. The diagnosis of MBD depends heavily on inferences made from anecdotal reports (developmental history), observations of behavior, and the electroencephalogram (EEG). The validity of the EEG is questionable. EEG readings of 200 normal and 200 LD children showed abnormal brain wave patterns in 29% of the normal children and 42% of the LD children (Boshes & Myklebust, 1964). Furthermore, there is a lack of evidence that MBD causes learning disabilities. Clinical evidence of MBD is not present in all LD children, and not all children diagnosed as brain injured are learning disabled.

Some researchers maintain that biochemical disturbances are the cause of learning disabilities. For example, Kittler (1970) reported studies in which the behavior of some MBD children improved when allergens such as chocolate and milk were excluded from the diet. The notion of linking allergies to learning disabilities was popularized when Feingold (1975, 1976) linked allergies to hyperactivity. He claimed that learning disabilities could be caused by allergic reactions to salicylates and artificial colors and flavors in food. For treatment he recommended the Kaiser-Permanente (K-P) diet, which eliminates foods such as apples, tomatoes, oranges, peaches, and a variety of berries that contain natural salicylates; foods containing artificial colors and flavors; and miscellaneous items such as toothpastes, perfumes, and compounds containing aspirin. Although there are some avid supporters of the K-P diet, well-conducted studies of the diet's effect indicate that it helps only a small percentage of hyperactive children (Spring & Sandoval, 1976).

It has also been suggested that learning disabilities can be caused by the blood's inability to synthesize a normal supply of vitamins (Cott, 1972). Consequently, some recommend megavitamin therapy, in which large daily doses of vitamins are administered to overcome vitamin deficiencies. There is, however, no conclusive evidence to support the claims made for megavitamin therapy (Silver, 1975). In fact, large doses of vitamins did not improve the performance of LD children in one study conducted to test the therapy (Kershner, Hawks, & Grekin, 1977).

Several investigators have suggested that the immaturity of some LD students is related to a lag in the development of central nervous system components (Bender, 1968; Rourke, 1978). A variety of factors have been proposed as possible causes of such lags, including complications during pregnancy, early trauma, infection, or poor nutrition. However, a lag does not necessarily indicate a structural deficiency or limitation of potential (Bateman, 1966). Thus, a child whose learning disability is the result of a lag may partly overcome some behavior and learning difficulties with increasing age (Bryant, 1972).

Poor nutrition is also cited as a cause of learning disabilities. It seems to affect the growth of the central nervous system (Cravioto, 1973). The results of one study suggest that protein-calorie malnutrition may lead to delays in intersensory integration (Cravioto, DeLicardie, & Birch, 1966). Yet because malnutrition is usually associated with economic and cultural variables that adversely influence cognitive and social development, its relationship to learning disabilities remains uncertain.

Genetic Factors

Heredity does appear to play a role in some learning disabilities (Critchley, 1970). A study of 276 dyslexic cases (individuals with reading problems) revealed a high enough prevalence of reading and language problems among relatives to justify a conclusion that genetic factors were involved (Hallgren, 1950). Furthermore, studies indicate that both identical twins, individuals who develop from the same egg, are more likely to have reading disabilities than are both fraternal twins, who develop from different eggs (Hermann, 1959).

Environmental Factors

A growing number of educators feel that inadequate or poor learning environments significantly contribute to the learning and behavior problems of many LD children (Engelmann, 1977; Lovitt, 1978). There is evidence that the problems of many LD students are corrected through direct, systematic instruction (Bijou, 1973; Lloyd, Cullinan, Heins, & Epstein, 1979). Poor instructional programming, lack of motivating activities, and inappropriate methods, materials, and curricula have, in fact, been found to cause childhood learning disorders (Wallace & McLoughlin, 1979).

Characteristics

The identification criteria presented in the 1977 *Federal Register* provide an initial framework for examining LD characteristics, with the focus on academic difficulties and language difficulties. Kirk and Gallagher (1983), along with numerous others (Bryan & Bryan, 1978; Lerner, 1985), broaden the range of difficulties to include perception, motor, social-emotional, metacognitive, memory, and attention problems. The importance of various characteristics is likely to be debated for some time.

As we review the proposed characteristics, we need to keep four points in mind. First, each student is unique and may exhibit a learning problem in one area but not in others. Second, characteristics used in identifying a student as learning disabled must persist over time. Many students who are not learning disabled exhibit LD characteristics for brief periods—hyperactivity surrounding a field trip, for instance. Third, in identifying learning disabilities, it is preferable to describe characteristic behaviors rather than to label the student. Finally, as noted earlier, learning disabilities are identified in terms of a discrepancy between achievement and estimated ability.

Academic Learning Difficulties

Academic learning problems are the most widely accepted characteristic of LD individuals. Mathematics, reading, and written expression are the areas in which these problems occur, with reading the most common area of difficulty. Reading problems are manifested in a variety of ways; Table 5-2 presents selected difficulties related to the reading habits, word recognition, comprehension, and phrasing of learning disabled students.

Arithmetic problems exist at all ages. During the primary years children with arithmetic disabilities cannot sort objects by size, match objects, understand the language of arithmetic, or grasp the concept of rational counting. During the later elementary years they have trouble with computational skills (Otto & Smith, 1980). Bryant and Kass (1972) add that it is also important to examine such areas as measurement, decimals, fractions, and percentages in dealing with arithmetic disabilities. The math deficits of many secondary students are similar to those of younger children (e.g., place value problems and difficulty with basic math facts). Although the specific error patterns of each student must be considered individually, it is helpful to examine some of the research regarding types of errors that students exhibit across grades. In a study of the computational errors of third graders, Roberts (1968) identified four primary error categories:

Wrong operation. For example, the student subtracts when he should add.

Obvious computational error. The pupil applies the correct operation but makes an error in recalling a basic number fact.

Defective algorithm. An algorithm includes the specific steps used to compute a math problem; it is the problem-solving pattern used to arrive at an answer. An algorithm is defective if it does not deliver the correct answer when basic facts are recalled correctly.

Random response. In a random response no discernible relationship is apparent between the problem-solving process and the problem.

Language Difficulties

Perhaps 50% of LD individuals have language and speech problems (Marge, 1972). This may account for the increasing interest in and attention to language disorders (Wiig & Semel, 1984). Language and speech difficulties reflect deficient skills in oral expression and listening comprehension.

Table 5-2 Selected reading problems of learning disabled children

Characteristics	Manifestations
Reading habits	
Tension movements	Frowning, fidgeting, using a high-pitched voice, lip biting
Insecurity	Refusing to read, crying, attempting to distract the teacher
Loss of place	Losing place frequently (often associated with repetition)
Lateral head movements	Jerking head
Holding material close	Deviating extremely (from 15 to 18 inches)
Word recognition	
Omissions	Omitting a word (e.g., *Tom saw cat.*)
Insertions	Inserting a word (e.g., *The dog ran* [fast] *after the cat.*)
Substitutions	Substituting one word for another (e.g., *horse* for *house*)
Reversals	Reversing letters in a word (e.g., *no* for *on, was* for *saw*)
Mispronunciations	Mispronouncing a word (e.g., *mister* for *miser*)
Transpositions	Reading words in the wrong order (e.g., *She away ran.*)
Unknown words	Hesitating for 5 seconds at a word
Slow, choppy reading	Not recognizing words quickly enough
Comprehension	
Poor recall of basic facts	Being unable to answer specific questions about a passage
Poor recall of sequence	Being unable to tell the sequence of the story read
Poor recall of main theme	Being unable to recall the main idea of the story
Miscellaneous symptoms	
Word-by-word reading	Reading in a choppy, halting, and laborious manner with no attempt to group words into thought units
Strained, high-pitched voice	Reading in a pitch higher than conversational tone
Inadequate phrasing	Inappropriately grouping words and splitting up natural phrases with unnatural pauses

Source: From *Students with Learning Disabilities* (2nd ed.) (p. 309) by C. D. Mercer, 1983, Columbus, OH: Charles E. Merrill. Copyright 1983 by Bell & Howell Company. Reprinted by permission.

Perceptual Disorders

Perception involves using the senses to recognize, discriminate, and interpret stimuli. Individuals unable to perform these tasks are said to have perceptual disorders. Specialists in learning disabilities have given much attention to perceptual problems that affect learning, focusing primarily on visual and auditory perception. The following list indicates specific perceptual areas in which the LD student may be deficient.

Facility with math may reveal itself in early ability to distinguish object size.

1. *Visual perception* refers to the ability to make visual sensory stimuli meaningful. The student may have difficulty discussing a slide show or a picture.

2. *Visual discrimination* refers to the ability to perceive dominant features in different objects and, thus, to discriminate one object from another (e.g., a *b* from a *d*).

3. *Visual memory* refers to the ability to recall the dominant features of a stimulus item or to recollect the sequence of a number of items presented visually (e.g., remembering the sequence of letters in a word).

4. *Auditory perception* refers to the ability to recognize and interpret stimuli that are heard. A student may have difficulty participating in a discussion or following oral directions.

5. *Auditory discrimination* refers to the ability to recognize differences between sounds and to identify similarities and differences between words. A student may have difficulty distinguishing such sounds as *d*, *b*, and *p*.

6. *Auditory memory* refers to the ability to recognize and/or recall previously presented auditory stimuli. The student may forget oral instructions or have difficulty remembering the sounds of letters.

Although several leading authorities in the field continue to stress that perception and neurological involvement are key factors in defining learning disabilities (Cruickshank, 1976), emphasis on perceptual problems has diminished in recent years. In 1975 a committee under the auspices of the Project on the Classification of Exceptional Children defined a learning disability as "a substantial deficiency in a particular aspect of academic achievement because of perceptual or perceptual-motor handicaps, regardless of etiology or other contributing factors" (Wepman, Cruickshank, Deutsch, Morency, & Strother, 1975, p. 306). However, the 1977 *Federal Register* does not refer to perceptual disorders at all in its evaluation criteria.

Motor Disorders

There are at least three dominant areas of motor disabilities: hyperactivity, hypoactivity, and incoordination (Myers & Hammill, 1982). *Hyperactivity* is a condition manifested in excessive, nonpurposeful movement. The hyperactive student is unable to sit or stand still, constantly needs to be moving about the classroom, and translates the need to be active into finger and foot tapping when confined to a seat or station in the room. *Hypoactivity* is the term used to describe a state of unnatural inactivity. The hypoactive child may sit quietly for long periods at school and accomplish very little work. *Incoordination* refers to a lack of muscular control. A student with gross motor control problems may walk with an awkward gait or have difficulty throwing and catching a ball, skipping, or hopping. Difficulties in fine motor control may be evident in cutting with scissors, buttoning, or zipping. Like perceptual disabilities, motor problems have traditionally received much attention; however, both are now being de-emphasized. The 1977 *Federal Register* does not include motor problems in its identification criteria.

Social-Emotional Problems

LD students experience several types of social-emotional difficulties: poor self-concept, low frustration tolerance, anxiety, social withdrawal and social rejection, task avoidance, poor self-management skills, and slowness in work. Frustrated by their learning difficulties, many learning disabled students are disruptive in social settings and develop negative feelings about their worth. Their emotional devel-

A hyperactive student has difficulty sitting still.

opment seems to differ from that of normal children (Rappaport, 1975). They tend to learn in terms of what they "can't do" rather than what they "can do." This, of course, often results in poor self-concept and self-esteem.

Research has also shown that classmates often view an LD student as someone they do not want as a friend (Bryan & Bryan, 1978). Investigators have suggested that the social-emotional problems of some LD youngsters are due to their social imperceptions. In other words, many LD students lack skills in perceiving the feelings and subtle responses of others (Bryan, 1977).

Metacognitive Deficits

Literature is accruing that suggests that selected learning disabled students exhibit metacognitive deficits (Baker, 1982; Wong, 1982). Basically, metacognition consists of two factors: (1) an awareness of the skills, strategies, and resources that are needed to perform a task effectively and (2) the ability to use self-regulatory processes (such as planning moves, evaluating effectiveness of ongoing activities, checking the outcome of effort, and remediating difficulties) to ensure the successful completion of a task (Baker, 1982).

Hresko and Reid (1981) report that the study of metacognitive variables in learning disabled students may lead to a better understanding of how these variables function, resulting in more productive educational interventions. To date, metacognition holds promise for helping practitioners understand the learning disabled; however, like other new theories, investigations are needed to determine its usefulness.

Memory Problems

Much interest surrounds the memory problems LD students exhibit. Learning disabled students generally have memory problems with both auditory and visual stimuli (Kaufman, 1976). Teachers frequently report that LD students forget spelling words, math facts, and directions. Few conclusions, however, can be drawn from the research completed thus far in this area.

Attention Problems

To succeed in school, a student must initiate and sustain thought processes relevant to classroom tasks. Students with attention problems are unable to concentrate on specific tasks long enough to complete them—they have a short attention span. Typically, they cannot screen out extraneous stimuli. Neither can they resist the appeal of irrelevant stimuli—they are highly distractible. In addition, individuals with attention problems often are hypersensitive and hyperactive. Attention problems in LD students have been well documented in research (Hallahan & Kauffman, 1982).

A good example of this hyperactive/short-attention-span phenomenon outside the classroom occurred recently in a little league football setting. William, one of the team's 10-year-old players, was classified as LD in his elementary school. At football practice William constantly picked fights, generally goofed off, talked back to coaches, and used questionable language. After a long practice in which William had been especially difficult to manage, the head coach asked the players to gather in front of him. William obeyed. In no uncertain terms the coach told them to listen to what he was about to say because he did not want to repeat his instructions. After he was assured that everyone was listening, he proceeded to tell them that the next practice was on Monday at 5:30 and they should have their helmets and pads. Then he asked whether there were any questions. William raised his hand. The coach responded, "Yes, William?" William replied, "When's the next practice?" The coach, obviously upset with the question, responded, "William! What was the first thing I said?" William thought for a moment and replied, "Listen."

The Learning Disabled Adolescent

Most of the literature about LD characteristics focuses on children, not adolescents. However, since many differences exist between children and adolescents, it is not appropriate to simply apply the characteristics of young children to young adults. The teen-ager should be viewed as an adolescent first and then as an exceptional student. Many of the characteristics of the adolescent period (e.g., puberty, independence, peer group pressures) interact with the learning difficulty and the demands of the high school curriculum to create a myriad of academic and social-emotional problems.

In an effort to understand the characteristics and needs of the learning disabled adolescent, much activity has occurred recently in this neglected area. For example, Deshler and his colleagues at the Learning Disability Institute at the University of Kansas are focusing on the adolescent. Some of their most pertinent findings (Schumaker, Deshler, Alley, & Warner, 1983) are summarized here:

1. Most LD adolescents exhibit severe academic achievement deficits and typically score below the 10th percentile on achievement measures in reading, written language, and mathematics. Moreover, the majority of LD adolescents perform poorly in all achievement areas.

2. The academic skill development of many LD adolescents levels off during the secondary grades, reaching a plateau by the 10th grade. For example, LD students' average reading and written language achievement in seventh grade is at the high third-grade level and plateaus at the fifth-grade level in the senior high grades.

3. Most LD adolescents demonstrate deficiencies in study skills. A majority of the students perform poorly in such areas as test taking, note taking, listening comprehension, proofreading, and scanning.

4. Many LD adolescents exhibit social skill deficiencies. Problem areas include accepting negative feedback, giving feedback, negotiating, and resisting peer pressure.

The relationship between learning disabilities and juvenile delinquency is currently being investigated. Some feel that learning problems contribute to an adolescent's sense of failure and frustration, which, in turn, leads to aggressive behavior (Unger, 1978). Preliminary results of a 4-year study of the LD/JD link show that the proportion of individuals with learning disabilities is greater among delinquents than among nondelinquents (Keilitz, Zaremba, & Broder, 1979). However, although there appears to be a relationship between learning disabilities and juvenile delinquency, no empirical evidence exists to support the theory that learning disabilities cause juvenile delinquency. Lane (1980) states, "Although research has not established that a significant causal relationship exists between learning disabilities and juvenile delinquency, it has uncovered a range of possible relationships between the two variables" (p. 433). However, many agree with Bachara and Zaba (1978): "It is time to take the question of juvenile delinquency beyond the correlation phase" (p. 245) and provide academic remediation to the delinquent. Crawford (1984) found that after a course of academic remediation (55 to 65 hours during a school year), the delinquent behavior of one group of juvenile delinquents decreased significantly.

Heterogeneity of Learning Disabilities

Most special educators agree that learning disabled students are a heterogeneous group. A youngster may qualify as learning disabled by exhibiting a discrepancy between ability and achievement in one or more of the seven areas listed in the

Academic frustration can turn into aggression problems.

1977 *Federal Register* and by satisfying the conditions of the exclusion clause. Thus, at one end of the continuum is a student who exhibits one academic-discrepancy problem. On the other end is a student with a discrepancy in all of the seven academic problem areas. Moreover, as mentioned previously, many agree that a much broader range of LD characteristics exists than that included in the *Federal Register*. In addition to the academic-discrepancy areas, cognitive and social-emotional characteristics are commonly attributed to learning disabled individuals. Thus, theoretically, an LD student could have any one or all of the identified cognitive or social-emotional problems in addition to any one or all of the academic-discrepancy problems. When the severity of each problem area is considered, the possible combinations are myriad.

The heterogeneous nature of learning disabilities and the complexity of learning disabled students should prompt professionals to follow certain guidelines:

1. Beyond the common denominator of an area of academic discrepancy, each LD individual has a unique set of cognitive and social-emotional behaviors.

2. Professionals must avoid stereotypic descriptions of LD individuals that assign characteristics that may or may not exist.

3. Professionals must delineate the subgroups of learning disabilities. As McKinney (1984) points out, "The emerging literature on LD subtypes supports a multiple syndrome approach to theory in the field and offers a new paradigm for research which seems to accommodate the heterogeneity produced by the complex collection of disorders encompassed" (p. 49).

4. Educators must design educational and behavioral interventions to meet individual needs.

Nonetheless, the heterogeneity of LD does not require a different treatment for each unique individual. Direct and systematic educational and behavioral interventions can be effective with many students with many different characteristics. Intensity of intervention is often the factor that individualizes treatment.

Learning Disabilities Across the Life-Span

Characteristics must be viewed within the context of an individual's age. In the past, LD has focused primarily on the elementary-age child; however, recent directions encompass a life-span view of learning disabilities. Within the context of problem areas, Table 5-3 presents the most prominent problem areas for each age group.

Assessment

Diagnostic Approaches

Methods of assessing learning disabilities for the purpose of prescribing appropriate educational programs vary. There are two diagnostic approaches: the ability model and the skill model (Stephens, 1977). The ability model is based on the premise that the cause of the learning problem is within the student. According to this theory, the processes essential to learning are impaired in LD students. Visual and auditory perception, attention, and perceptual-motor processes are some of the areas stressed in this approach. Three assumptions about these process problems are basic to this model: (1) they underlie academic problems, (2) they can be

Table 5-3 Life-span view of learning disabilities

	Preschool	Grades K-1	Grades 2-6	Grades 7-12	Adult
Problem Areas	Developmental milestones (e.g., walking) Receptive language Expressive language Visual perception Auditory perception Attention Hyperactivity	Academic readiness skills (e.g., alphabet knowledge, quantitative concepts, directional concepts) Receptive language Expressive language Visual perception Auditory perception Gross and fine motor skills Attention Hyperactivity Social skills	Reading skills Arithmetic skills Written expression Verbal expression Receptive language Attention Hyperactivity Social-emotional skills	Reading skills Arithmetic skills Written expression Verbal expression Listening Study skills (metacognition) Social-emotional skills Delinquency	Reading skills Arithmetic skills Written expression Verbal expression Listening Study skills Social-emotional skills
Assessment	Prediction of high risk for later learning problems	Prediction of high risk for later learning problems	Identification of learning disabilities	Identification of learning disabilities	Identification of learning disabilities
Treatment Types	Preventive	Preventive	Remedial Corrective	Remedial Corrective Compensatory	Remedial Corrective Compensatory
Treatments with Most Research and/or Expert Support	Direct instruction in language skills Behavioral management Parent training	Direct instruction in academic and language areas Behavioral management Parent training	Direct instruction in academic areas Behavioral management Self-control training Parent training	Direct instruction in academic areas Tutoring in subject areas Direct instruction in learning strategies (study skills) Self-control training Curriculum alternatives	Direct instruction in academic areas Tutoring in subject or job area Compensatory instruction (i.e., using aids such as tape recorder, calculator, computer, dictionary) Direct instruction in learning strategies

measured, and (3) they can be reduced or eliminated. Tests commonly used in the ability model include the following:

- Illinois Test of Psycholinguistic Abilities (ITPA)
- Detroit Tests of Learning Aptitude
- Woodcock-Johnson Psycho-Educational Battery (cognitive subtests)
- Southern California Sensory Integration Tests

Rather than trying to assess deficiencies in learning processes, the skill model focuses on the student's ability to perform academic tasks (reading, writing, and math). In contrast to the ability model, the skill model assumes that the learning problem is primarily external—the result of inadequate experiences—and that direct instruction in skills that are lacking will remedy it. The purpose of assessment in this model is to determine the academic skills in which the student is deficient. Although the skill approach uses standardized academic achievement tests, the major assessment procedures are informal. Frequently, a scope and sequence skills list is used in assessment. The hierarchy of skills necessary in a subject area is defined, and the student's skill level is assessed in terms of this hierarchy. Instruction begins at the level of the lowest skill not mastered.

Both approaches are used extensively, but much controversy exists regarding the relative merits of each. For assessment purposes the application of each model is clear. In the skill model assessment provides information that leads directly to a plan for daily instruction. This information, however, has limited use for identification and classification. Instruction is an important outcome of assessment in the ability model. Because the ability model stresses the existence of a learning problem within the child, it is best for identification and classification of exceptional students. A thorough approach to assessment will combine both.

Identifying a Learning Disability

As we have noted, the 1977 federal criteria for identifying learning disabilities include an exclusion component, an academic component, and a discrepancy factor. In addition, numerous definitions include a process component. Each of these functions in the identification of an LD individual.

Exclusion Component This component serves to distinguish the learning disability from other categories of handicapping conditions. Beginning the diagnostic process by checking for all the excluded handicaps can save time. These excluded categories and the minimal characteristics an individual must exhibit in order *not* to be classified in them are listed in Table 5-4.

Academic Achievement Component A student's level of academic achievement can be reasonably accurately measured by standardized achievement tests in the following areas: reading, writing, arithmetic, and preacademic skills. Of course,

Table 5-4 Excluded categories and LD characteristics

Excluded Category	Characteristics the LD Student Must Exhibit
1. Mental retardation	A score better than or equal to two standard deviations below the norm on an individual intelligence test interpreted by a certified psychologist
2. Visual impairment	Visual acuity in the better eye with best possible correction of 20/70 or better
3. Hearing impairment	No more than a 30 dB loss in the better ear unaided, and speech and language learned through normal channels
4. Motor handicaps	No evidence of a motor handicap directly related to the child's learning deficit
5. Emotional disturbance	No emotional disturbance so severe as to require a systematic therapeutic program
6. Environmental, cultural, or economic disadvantage	An environment with ample opportunity to learn

NOTE: To check Items 2, 3, and 4, either a review of recent medical records or a physical exam is required. Teacher observation may be adequate to determine the presence of Items 1 and 5. In borderline cases, however, testing must be done by a psychologist.

in diagnosing a learning disability, low academic achievement is significant only in contrast to learning potential.

According to the 1977 *Federal Register*, however, a learning disability does not automatically exist even when achievement falls markedly below potential. A learning problem may be only the result of limited educational experiences; an alternative educational strategy will remedy this type of problem. To be classified as learning disabled, a student must have a learning problem that exists even when he is provided with a wide variety of appropriate educational experiences. This criterion requires that the use of alternative educational strategies (e.g., a different basal reader, a math program involving manipulatives, a behavior modification program) must be documented in identifying an LD student.

Discrepancy Component Mercer, Hughes, and Mercer (1985) report that three types of criteria are the most prominent in determining a discrepancy between ability and achievement: deviation from grade level, percentage lag, and standard scores. Of the 38 states using criteria to determine severe discrepancy, 80% report using deviation from grade level; 15%, percentage lag; and 19%, standard score (Mercer, Hughes, & Mercer, 1985). Percentage lag requires a student to be below a certain percentage in her functioning when compared to peers. Standard score comparison determines the discrepancy between the scores on standardized tests of ability and achievement.

Operationalizing the discrepancy component, or translating it into behavioral terms, has become a major concern of researchers and state departments. Forness, Sinclair, and Guthrie (1983) compared the performance of eight formulas used to operationalize discrepancy and concluded that each yielded different results. Cone and Wilson (1981) discuss several procedures (grade level deviation, expectancy formula, standard score comparisons, and regression analysis) for quantifying a discrepancy. They conclude that standard score comparisons and regression equations offer potentially viable methods for operationalizing discrepancy.

Process Component   In diagnosing learning disabilities numerous authorities still consider it important to assess—insofar as possible—the basic psychological processes that underlie academic achievement and language development. These authorities employ standardized tests to measure the following types of processing.

1. visual—perception, memory, association, and reception
2. auditory—perception, memory, association, and reception
3. haptic—tactile, kinesthetic
4. integrated sensory—visual-motor, auditory-motor, auditory-vocal, and visual-auditory.

The problems in measuring psychological processes are one reason the process component has been looked upon with disfavor by some.

Early Identification Perspectives and Guidelines

The identification of learning disabilities in the young child is extremely difficult because LD is primarily an academic learning handicap. Thus, a preschool diagnosis becomes more a matter of prediction than of identification. Infants and preschool children who are likely to experience learning problems in the primary grades are referred to as at-risk or high-risk children. During the last decade the early identification of these children has received substantial support from parents and professionals in medicine, psychology, and education. They feel that many learning, social-emotional, and educational problems can be prevented or remediated if identification and intervention are provided before the child enters school.

Based on her review of prediction studies and her own early identification research, Badian (1976) concludes:

> It may be difficult to identify children with potential learning problems because, as some authors have pointed out, among kindergarten children there are very few consistent and identifiable patterns of characteristics associated with future learning problems. Certainly, from the point of view of administrative expedience, as well as from that of predictive accuracy, kindergarten teacher judgments, perhaps based on a behavioral checklist, together with a simple test of ability to name letters and shapes, would seem to contribute as much or even more toward the identification of children likely to underachieve, as the test batteries specially designed for such identification. (p. 29)

Although Badian's (1976) comments are consistent with the more recent findings of Hammill and McNutt (1981) and Busch (1980), the latter studies indicate that the use of a group-administered intelligence test is warranted. The following tests and procedures would be an excellent beginning in formulating an early identification program for 4- to 6-year-olds.

1. A test of alphabet knowledge (e.g., Alphabet Knowledge Subtest of the Metropolitan Readiness Test or Letters and Sounds Subtest of the Stanford Early School Achievement Test)

2. A test of intelligence (e.g., Lorge Thorndike or Cognitive Abilities Test: Primary I, Form 1)

3. Teacher perception (e.g., checklist, rating scale, or teacher-developed informal measure)

4. A test of spoken and written language, for older preschoolers (e.g., Test of Language Development or Boehm Test of Basic Concepts)

5. Parent involvement (Tjossem, 1976) focusing on the tenuous nature of diagnosis, the need for supportive services at home, and the potential harmful effects of lowered expectations.

Prediction data are being gathered in several major early identification projects. Mardell and Goldenberg (1975) are collecting data from Project DIAL (Developmental Indicators for the Assessment of Learning). It features a battery that concentrates on gross and fine motor skills, concepts, and communication skills. Its usefulness must await meaningful follow-up data. Projects such as DIAL often provide the practitioner with information, techniques, or forms that can be adapted.

In summary, determining whether a learning disability exists is a difficult task. Scores on the various instruments can serve only as guidelines. Nothing can replace the clinical judgment of a diagnostician or a team of professionals who examine the test data in light of other types of diagnostic information. The 1977 *Federal Register* requires that such a multidisciplinary team determine the eligibility of students for LD programs and that each member of the team sign a statement indicating agreement or disagreement with the eligibility decision.

Intervention

P.L. 94–142 identifies a learning disability as a handicapping condition that requires special education. Moreover, the identification criteria call for a severe discrepancy in specific learning areas. Some educators mistakenly view all learning disabilities as mild learning problems and conclude that learning disabilities should be served entirely within the regular classroom or, at most, in a resource room. Learning disabilities include handicapping conditions that range from mild to severe (Weller, 1980), and a full spectrum of service arrangements for LD children and youth is needed. The service or placement options for LD students are

Table 5-5   Advantages and disadvantages of LD service models

Model	Advantages	Disadvantages
Regular classroom model (LD student remains with regular class all day.)	Is least restrictive setting Provides for interaction of handicapped and nonhandicapped peers Prevents needless labeling	May compound learning disabilities May include large number in class population Lacks special teacher training
Consultant teacher model (Consultant teacher works with regular teacher concerning LD programming.)	Able to reach many teachers Can supply specific instructional methods, programs, and materials Can serve more children Influences environmental learning variables Coordinates comprehensive services for the child	May not consider consultant a member of the teaching staff Lacks firsthand knowledge of child that comes from regular teaching May separate assessment and instruction
Itinerant teacher model (Itinerant teacher travels to various schools to consult with regular teachers about LD students.)	Aids in screening and diagnosis Provides consulting help Provides part-time services Covers needs of children in different schools or areas Serves mild problems economically	Does not provide consistent support Lacks staff identification Presents difficulty in transporting materials Lacks continuity of program Lacks regular follow-up
Resource room model (LD child spends a portion of school day, 45–60 minutes, with resource room teacher; most widely used model in LD.)	Reduces stigmatization Supplements regular classroom instruction Separates handicapped learner from nonhandicapped peers for limited periods of the school day Provides individualized instruction in problem areas May provide a consultant for the child's regular teachers Works toward mainstreaming the child Retains responsibility for student's instructional program with regular classroom teacher	Cannot provide services for the severely learning disabled Creates scheduling problems Struggles with overenrollment Can misunderstand teacher role Generates role conflicts Provides little time to assess and plan

Table 5-5 Advantages and disadvantages of LD service models (*continued*)

Model	Advantages	Disadvantages
Special class model (LD child spends majority of school day in special class for LD students.)	Is least restrictive setting for severe cases Provides environmental conditions to serve LD children with severe problems Provides individual or small group instruction Maintains self-esteem Directs full-time attention toward one teacher Provides full-time highly specialized learning conditions	Is segregated Permits extremely limited interaction with nonhandicapped peers Stigmatizes Can be a mistake May become inappropriately permanent Restricts mild and moderate cases unnecessarily Models inappropriate behaviors Fosters low teacher expectations Does not usually involve regular classroom teachers in educational programming
Special day school model (LD child spends entire school day at a special school.)	Can serve a large number of moderate and severe cases of LD Centralizes diagnostic, teaching, and consulting services Provides the means to develop a model program for later replication Provides a special environment while permitting a child the advantages of remaining in the home and community	Is self-contained Permits no interaction with nonhandicapped peers during the school day Is not the least restrictive environment in all cases Can be expensive Removes pressures for the development of local services
Residential school model (LD child lives at a special school.)	Provides occupational training Gives attention to diet and necessary medical treatment Provides opportunities for involvement in all facets of normal school life within the school program Demonstrates appropriate diagnostic and teaching procedures	Segregates residents from mainstream of society Entails financial expense Shows low incidence of exits May not be the least restrictive environment May diminish quality control

SOURCE: From *Learning Disabilities: Concepts and Characteristics* (2nd ed.) (pp. 373–374) by G. Wallace and J. A. McLoughlin, 1979, Columbus, OH: Charles E. Merrill. Copyright 1979 by Bell & Howell Company. Adapted by permission.

listed in Table 5-5 along with their respective advantages and disadvantages. The resource room is now the most prevalent service arrangement for learning disabled pupils.

The span of services detailed in P.L. 94–142 is required for handicapped students at the secondary as well as the elementary level. LD adolescents have been neglected, although junior and senior high schools are now beginning to make provisions for older LD students. In their survey McNutt and Heller (1978) found a variety of services offered at the secondary level: resource room only; resource room and integrated classroom; resource room, integrated classroom, and self-contained classroom; resource room and self-contained classroom; integrated classroom only; self-contained classroom only; and work-study and/or vocational education only. Almost 90% of the respondents in the survey used a service arrangement that involved a resource room. In a national survey of 741 secondary LD teachers, Schmid et al. (1980) found that 78% worked in a resource room and 85% were employed full-time in one school.

Curriculum Implications

Curriculum planning for LD students is naturally influenced to a large degree by the theories of the curriculum planners regarding learning disabilities. These theories affect both program content and teaching strategies. Obviously, skill development is an important aspect of all programs devised for LD students. However, what skills are emphasized, how they are taught, and how their mastery contributes to the overall education of an LD student are issues determined by the curriculum developer's perspective.

Perceptual-Motor Approach

Some maintain that the learning problems of LD children originate in inadequate perceptual-motor (P-M) skills—visual, auditory, and motor. These theorists believe that improving poor P-M skills may improve academic skills (Barsch, 1967; Cratty, 1971; Kephart, 1971). The training program P-M theorists prescribe may include activities involving gross and fine motor skills, body image, eye-hand coordination, visual perception, and auditory discrimination. Tapes, pictures, balls, puzzles, beads, pegboards, boxes, stencils, and designs are commonly used materials in this approach. Educators might do any of the following:

- Prepare an obstacle course consisting of tires, hoops, chairs, and balance beams. Instruct the child to move through the course at various rates, pretending that he is moving around breakable objects.

- Construct a road system on paper and instruct the child to guide a toy car on it while verbalizing turns and directions.

- Construct a gadget-manipulation board by attaching a zipper, a buttonhole strip from a shirt, nuts and bolts, a belt buckle, a shoelace, and various other devices to a thin piece of plywood. The child can practice these functional fine motor skills by manipulating the items on the board.

P-M skills are assessed in many programs, and instruction is designed to correct inadequate P-M areas. Reviews of the literature on P-M research, however, indicate that the impact of P-M training on academic growth is not impressive (Hallahan & Cruickshank, 1973; Hammill, Goodman, & Wiederholt, 1974). Kavale and Mattson (1983) reviewed 180 perceptual-motor training studies and concluded that it is not an effective intervention for improving academic or cognitive skills.

Language Approaches

Proponents of psycholinguistic teaching assume that inadequate psycholinguistic skills result in academic learning problems. In the area of learning disabilities, they tend to focus on the input-association-output model developed by Osgood (1957). *Input* refers to the individual's receiving information (reception); *association* is the process by which the individual relates this information to known information; and *output* is the act through which the individual responds to the information (expression). Typically, the psycholinguistic approach uses the Illinois Test of Psycholinguistic Abilities (ITPA) for assessment purposes and emphasizes the development of reception, association, and memory skills in the visual and auditory channels.

Language experiences enrich the curriculum of the learning disabled.

For example, to strengthen visual reception, a student may circle similar drawings on a page containing varied drawings. There are numerous psycholinguistic instructional programs and books on the market, including the Peabody Language Development Kits (Dunn, Smith, Dunn, Horton, & Smith, 1981), the MWM Program for Developing Language Ability (Minskoff, Wiseman, & Minskoff, 1972), and Aids to Psycholinguistic Teaching (Bush & Giles, 1982). However, there is little solid evidence to support the position that instruction aimed at improving psycholinguistic deficits positively influences academic growth. On the whole, there is not much empirical support for using the ITPA as either a diagnostic tool or as the basis for remediation programs. The controversy continues and data are needed from good empirical studies.

Other language-linguistic approaches exist that are based on different assumptions. Most LD teachers work cooperatively with language clinicians when these programs are provided for LD students. Some programs, such as the Developmental Syntax Program (Coughran & Liles, 1974) and the Interactive Language Development Training Program (Lee, Koenigsknecht, & Mulhern, 1975), are based on the work of developmental linguists and language theorists. The programs focus on the particular language skills the child should have and the best way to train her. These programs do not deal with etiology; they are meant to strengthen only syntax skills and do not include training procedures for the other language components.

The Developmental Syntax Program can easily be implemented in a public school. Based on reinforcement theory, this approach includes programs and training procedures for articles, pronouns, possessive pronouns, adjectives, verbs, and plurality. The second program, the Interactive Language Development Training Program, provides remedial guidelines for training individuals or small groups of young children. The program uses a conversational setting to teach both receptive and expressive language skills. The interactive feature provides a means of assessing and training the child's syntactic language skills. Research findings indicate that this program is well suited to its stated purpose (Wiig & Semel, 1976).

Multisensory Approach

A multisensory approach is based on the premise that learning is facilitated for some students if information is received through several senses rather than just one or two (vision and hearing). Frequently, kinesthetic and tactile stimulation are used along with visual and auditory stimulation. The multisensory programs that feature seeing, hearing, tracing, and writing are often referred to as VAKT (visual-auditory-kinesthetic-tactile) programs. To increase tactile and kinesthetic stimulation, sandpaper letters, finger paint, sand trays, and raised and sunken letters are used.

Both the Fernald (1943) method and the Gillingham and Stillman (1966) method are reading approaches based on VAKT instruction. The Fernald method stresses whole-word learning. The Gillingham-Stillman method derives from the work of Orton (1937) and features sound blending, the process of taking isolated sounds and blending them into a word. Slingerland (1971) adapted this approach to develop a multisensory language arts program for LD students.

Another multisensory approach used with individuals who have severe reading problems is the neurological impress method. In this approach the student and teacher read together aloud and rapidly. The student follows by moving his or her finger along the words. It is reasoned that hearing the words provides stimulation and feedback. The research on this method, however, is inconclusive.

Multisensory approaches feature distinct instructional procedures and may be viewed as independent of specific content. These procedures are often used with individuals who have severe learning problems.

Precision Teaching

Precision teaching was developed in 1964 by Lindsley; its main feature is charting. The teacher pinpoints a target behavior the student must learn and charts the student's progress in learning that single skill. The behavior might be, for instance, to see words and say them. The student's mastery of the targeted behavior is tested regularly—often daily—through the number of correct and incorrect responses given in a specified time period (frequently 1 minute). Rate of performance is emphasized. The results of each test provide the data for the chart. Mastery is usually defined in terms of a certain rate of correct responses—for example, reading 100 to 140 words per minute with two or fewer errors. Precision teachers record the daily performance of each student and chart the results. The Standard Behavior Chart is commonly used to graph the student's performance on a specific behavior (the vertical axis) over time (the horizontal axis). The student is able to note his progress by examining either the slope of the graph or the recorded raw data.

Although charting is frequently used to develop skills within a specified skill hierarchy, it is a procedure that is independent of the identified skill. Precision teaching is a refinement of the task analysis approach. Its value lies in the fact that it incorporates a direct, continuous, and precise measurement system, which provides a sound basis for instructional decisions. Teaching in the precision model is usually direct and simple. It can involve any number of materials and methods, including commercial materials, drill sheets, flash cards, games, media, modeling, and positive reinforcement. Precision teaching has impressive research support (Lovitt, 1977; White & Haring, 1980).

Direct Instruction

Teachers who do not wish to use rate data in charting student progress can use direct instruction. It is a criterion-referenced approach for providing data-based instruction and involves systematic instruction. The pupil is assessed in terms of a scope and sequence skills list in a subject area, and instruction begins at the lowest skill not mastered. Many commercial programs follow this format by providing placement tests for assessing the student's entry level and mastery tests for monitoring student progress. In essence, this approach involves four steps:

1. The student takes a pretest on a criterion skill—for instance, multiplication facts for one-digit numbers.

2. The student is directed to a specific instructional activity based on the pre-test—for example, a game in which the student multiplies the number of dots on two dice.

3. The teacher periodically administers the criterion test until mastery is demonstrated—the student responds correctly to, say, 95% of the multiplication problems.

4. When mastery is achieved, a new skill is introduced, and the cycle is repeated.

Stephens (1977) provides a detailed description of direct instruction. There is also extensive research support for this method (Nelson & Polsgrove, 1984; Treiber & Lahey, 1983).

Direct instruction is similar to precision teaching in that both approaches use direct and frequent measurement, base instructional decisions on student performance, establish instructional aims, stress task analysis, require records of student performance, and emphasize principles of behavior modification. The approaches differ primarily in the frequency of data collection and in the type of data collected. In precision teaching, rate data are usually collected daily, and proportional charts are used to record student progress. In direct instruction student performance is recorded on a checklist, and assessment is based on number or percent correct and not on rate. Also, the frequency of data collection may vary from daily to weekly in the two programs.

Ability Versus Skill

Just as with assessment, the ability-versus-skill issue influences curriculum. Stephens (1977) states the major assumptions of the ability approach:

1. Reliable and valid aptitude measures exist.

2. Aptitude deficits can be corrected.

3. Aptitude weaknesses are causally related to performance deficits.

In addition, he lists the major assumptions of the skill approach:

1. Direct skill instruction corrects inadequate responses.

2. Behavior change is a function of its consequences.

3. Pupils can learn to generalize specific responses across conditions.

Stephens (1977) reports that the ability approach is based upon more unproven assumptions than the skill approach. He agrees with Quay (1973) and Ysseldyke and Salvia (1974) in recommending the skill-oriented approach.

Research supports the position that the most effective approach for improving the academic skills of school-age LD students is to teach directly to those skills. For example, for improving reading skills, direct reading instruction has consistently yielded better reading performance than instruction that focuses on developing perceptual-motor, visual, auditory, or sensory-integration abilities. Thus, the issue of what to teach LD students clearly favors direct academic skill training. Likewise, the advantages of direct, specific, and frequent measurement of student progress are apparent in providing individualized programming.

Programming for the Learning Disabled Adolescent

The provision of secondary programs for LD students is relatively new. Successful demonstration programs have been developed in many states, and the federal government has funded several projects (Riegel & Mathey, 1980). Although few programs have been empirically validated, the recent surge of programs and literature has certainly increased our knowledge about secondary LD programming.

Deshler and his associates at the University of Kansas Institute for Research in Learning Disabilities have contributed some very helpful information. They examined the demands placed on students in secondary, mainstreamed classrooms. Schumaker and Deshler (1984) summarize the literature and discuss their findings in three general areas: work habit demands, knowledge acquisition demands, and knowledge expression demands. Work habit demands require that students be able to work independently with minimum feedback or help from the teacher. Students must be able to complete assignments and follow classroom rules. Knowledge acquisition demands are numerous. Students must be able to listen to presentations and take accurate notes. They must gain information from materials written at a secondary level, and they must be able to study. Knowledge expression demands are vital to success at the secondary level. Students must be able to demonstrate their knowledge on classroom tests and on minimum competency tests. They must also be able to express themselves in writing, both descriptive and narrative prose. In addition, they must participate in classroom discussions.

When the LD adolescent with her complex needs enters the secondary setting with its extensive demands, the need for a diversity of services becomes apparent. At least five types of program services are required: regular course work with supportive instruction, academic remediation, instruction in learning strategies, training in functional living skills, and career-related instruction (Mercer & Mercer, 1985). No one service approach is appropriate for all adolescents with learning disabilities. Deshler, Schumaker, Lenz, and Ellis (1984) report that the real challenge is not in determining which approach is right or wrong but in ascertaining under what conditions and with whom a given service is most effective.

In planning programs for LD adolescents, many questions arise: Should basic skill instruction continue throughout the high school years? Should the LD student take regular subject area courses? Should the curriculum emphasize functional living skills? Should vocational training be stressed? Answers to these questions depend, of course, on the individual needs of each student. Some students with learning disabilities are able to complete regular courses. Many continue their education in colleges or trade schools. Others, more severely disabled, need to acquire vocational and functional living skills to prepare them for productive life after high school. The secondary program should include basic placement options rele-

Like all adolescents, the learning disabled enjoy "nonacademic" subjects that teach a wide variety of skills.

vant to the LD student's long-range development and should support those options with a strong counseling program.

Mainstreaming

Mainstreaming does have its rationale. First, the research has failed to demonstrate that handicapped youngsters progress more quickly when segregated (Birch, 1974; Kaufman, Gottlieb, Agard, & Kukic, 1975). Second, it is believed that the stigma associated with special-class placement does not affect the handicapped child who remains in the regular class (Kaufman et al., 1975). Prillaman (1981) used a sociometric device to examine classmate acceptance of learning disabled elementary students in a mainstream environment and found that the learning disabled students did not rate lower in popularity than their peers. Third, interaction with peers

Model Program

The University of Florida's Multidisciplinary Diagnostic and Training Program (MDTP) is a team of professionals from neurology, psychology, language, and special education who serve K–6 children with complex medical, behavioral, and/or learning problems. Although the majority of the children are learning disabled or emotionally handicapped, students from all exceptionalities have been served by MDTP. After a child is referred—from approximately 12 school districts in north and central Florida—an MDTP liaison teacher visits the student's classroom for observation and consultation with the teachers. Next, the child goes to the University of Florida campus for a medical and language evaluation at Shands Teaching Hospital and an educational and psychological evaluation at the College of Education. After the evaluations are completed, a case conference is held with school district personnel and MDTP staff. At this conference a diagnosis is determined and intervention plans are detailed.

It may be decided to return the child to her home school and to assign the MDTP liaison teacher to work with local school personnel to implement the intervention plan. Or the decision may be made to enroll the student in the MDTP diagnostic and training classroom. This class is located in the College of Education, and students may attend it for a period of from one to six weeks. Children attending the class receive intensive treatment aimed at documenting effective teaching and management strategies for the child. Data-based instruction is used to determine the effectiveness of instructional programs (e.g., reading, language, math, spelling) and management techniques (e.g., point system, contingency contracts, parent involvement).

When effective interventions are documented, the child's local school teacher visits the class to observe and learn the interventions. Then the child is returned to her local school, and the MDTP liaison teacher continues to work with the teacher to implement the intervention plan. To date, over 100 children have attended the diagnostic class, and all have made excellent progress in their problem areas. Much emphasis is placed on designing interventions that are feasible to implement in the school districts. Peer teaching, self-correcting materials, computer-assisted instruction, instructional games, contingency contracts, parent management training, and charting progress are some of the techniques that are extensively used.

In addition to serving hundreds of children with complex problems, MDTP is a valuable resource for preservice training in special education, curriculum and instruction, counselor education, speech and language, educational psychology, and medicine as well as in-service training. Moreover, the parent training component offers services to parents and provides university students with the opportunity to be involved with parent training. The program operates at no cost to the families of the children.

Although the advantages of MDTP are numerous, some disadvantages do exist. The expense of the program would prohibit some school districts and universities from initiating it. Also, because the diagnostic classroom is well equipped and has a low pupil-teacher ratio, some teachers think it is impossible to teach these children in their own classroom settings.

John J. Ross, M.D., and Cecil D. Mercer, Ed.D., are codirectors of the program.

is often educational and emotionally healthy (Kaufman et al., 1975). Fourth, many parents do not want segregation. Fifth, regular classroom teachers trained in mainstreaming techniques are likely to respond better to the special education needs of students with periodic or situational problems (see Morsink, 1984). Finally, court decisions now specify that regular class placement is preferable (Kaufman et al., 1975).

Although the mainstreaming movement is spreading rapidly, some educators regard it skeptically. For example, Cruickshank (1983) claims that no definitive research shows one type of placement to be less restrictive than another. He feels that most teachers lack the preparation to serve exceptional students and that many administrators, who do not understand the nature of the problem, do not provide adequate support to teachers. Similarly, Lovitt (1978) points out that mainstreaming has been primarily promoted by legislators, who have not consulted with the school personnel charged with implementing it.

Clearly, if regular classroom teachers are to teach handicapped children, they must learn how to do it well. They must learn to understand how handicaps affect learning, recognize handicaps and develop prescriptive learning experiences, individualize instruction, understand the emotions of handicapped students, use the services of supportive personnel, and communicate effectively with parents of handicapped youngsters. Smith, Neisworth, and Hunt (1983) note that the key to success for the exceptional child placed in the regular classroom is the regular classroom teacher. This teacher has an enormous responsibility and must receive the proper preparation and support.

The resource room model, which serves the majority of school-age LD students, also represents a mainstreamed approach because the students spend the majority of the day in regular classes. The resource room teacher is located in the school building and works closely with numerous teachers to coordinate the instructional programs of the LD pupils, approximately 20 per day. Obviously the role demands a highly competent, personable individual. The resource room model can accommodate the different needs of both students and teachers through a variety of intervention arrangements:

1. special materials introduced into the regular classroom

2. special consultation with the regular classroom teacher

3. student pulled out of the regular classroom for group or individual work weekly

4. student pulled out of the regular classroom for group or individual work daily

5. referral for outside help or special class placement

Speece and Mandell (1980) questioned 228 regular educators about resource room services. The teachers considered the following support services to be critical: attending parent conferences, meeting informally to discuss student progress, providing remedial instruction in the resource room, providing information on behavior, providing academic assessment data, scheduling meetings to evaluate student progress, providing materials for the classroom, suggesting materials for the classroom, and providing written reports of students' activities and progress. Since many of these services involve consultation, Speece and Mandell recommend more training programs that focus on consultation skills.

Roddy (1984) believes that the widespread practice of taking LD students out of the regular classroom for resource room instruction needs to be reexamined. He believes that more emphasis needs to be placed on improving instruction in the most natural environment, the regular classroom. Although the resource room is gaining in popularity, its effectiveness has not been extensively measured.

Innovation and Development

The area of learning disabilities has accomplished much in its brief existence. Public interest has been generated, litigation initiated, legislation written and passed, educational programs developed, and professional organizations established. Despite continuing controversy several noteworthy trends can be identified:

1. A transition from the medical model to the educational model has occurred. Now the behavioral orientation is receiving much attention.

2. The practice of identifying and directly teaching specific academic skills has increased, whereas the practice of identifying and teaching specific ability processes that influence learning has decreased. Tests designed to assess information-processing abilities and process-related instruction continue to be criticized severely (Cook & Welch, 1980).

3. ACLD has become the forum for presenting viewpoints from many disciplines; the Council for Learning Disabilities (CLD) stresses an educational orientation.

4. The use of precision teaching appears to be increasing. Commercial precision teaching materials are beginning to emerge.

5. Speech and language clinicians are now the key professionals responsible for the oral language of LD students. Recognition of the language learning disabled (LLD) subgroup appears to be gaining acceptance. A variety of language tests are now available.

6. The written language movement shifted to a criterion-oriented academic intervention approach, serving as a catalyst for the proliferation of commercial academic programs. Today, publishers are a major force in LD instruction.

7. Extensive criticism of perceptual-motor tests and training has diminished the popularity of the P-M movement. Currently, the primary advocates of this movement are found among occupational therapists who stress the work of Ayres.

8. Primarily through the work of Deshler and his colleagues and Zigmond and her colleagues, a promising emphasis on the LD adolescent has emerged. Deshler's learning strategies approach is having a widespread impact, and commercial programs in this area are growing.

Since 1978 the five LD research institutes (at the Universities of Chicago, Kansas, Minnesota, and Virginia and at Columbia University) have exerted strong influence. Certain issues and developments within several areas of the LD field deserve particular attention.

Definition

The field continues to struggle to find a precise and universally accepted definition. Currently, the 1977 *Federal Register* definition is widely used, but dissatisfaction remains. The discrepancy factor, a key component in identifying LD students, is apt to be included in any forthcoming definition. A taxonomy of learning disabilities may also be developed in the near future. In view of the heterogeneous nature of LD students, many experts agree that such a structure would be very helpful in dividing learning disabilities into subgroups of handicapping conditions.

Assessment

Ysseldyke and his colleagues at the University of Minnesota's LD institute are very critical of the assessment practices in learning disabilities (Ysseldyke et al., 1983). In essence, they recommend that less time and fewer resources be allocated to assessment and more time, to instruction. Too much time is spent on assessment that gathers data of too little use. For example, numerous tests are based on ill-defined psychological constructs presumed to underlie learning problems. Although an abundance of commercial standardized tests does exist, the need persists for reliable, valid, and instructionally relevant ones. Perhaps some of the recent and forthcoming tests will be beneficial. To help the practitioner, Brown and Bryant (1984) have provided an excellent consumer's guide for evaluating tests.

Teacher Preparation

The concern for quality teacher training has become a national issue. Throughout the country, states are initiating competency tests for teachers, introducing merit pay plans, and challenging colleges of education to develop viable teacher education programs. Specific competencies that should be required of LD teachers have been offered by CLD but have not as yet been widely endorsed. Thus, the problem of teacher preparation has been recognized, and this area should see active developments.

Cognitive Approaches

The influence of the research institutes at Virginia and Columbia is apparent in the promotion of a cognitive approach to understanding and treating learning disabilities. In addition to the metacognition discussed previously, information-processing theory and cognitive behavior modification are being applied to LD.

Information-processing theory resulted from the joining of information theory and computer technology (Loftus & Loftus, 1976); it focuses on what and how information is acquired. These theorists examine how people select, extract, maintain, and use information in the environment. Information-processing theory generally holds that (1) all individuals are active in their own learning and rely on all available resources; (2) there is an integrative and reciprocal relationship among attention, memory, and perceptual functions; and (3) higher order mental processes control attention, memory, and perception. Maker (1981) acknowledges that recent findings indicate that some children are unable or unwilling to apply the appropriate strategies for solving a problem. The learning disabled, as well as the immature child, do not appear to use active strategies for learning or problem solving (Lloyd, 1980; Loper, 1980). Furthermore, literature supports the position that these strategies can be taught to learning disabled students. Maker (1981) provides an excellent resource of teaching suggestions to help learning disabled children learn problem-solving strategies. Information-processing theory appears to hold much promise for helping educators. Its validation must await more empirical studies.

Cognitive behavior modification combines behavior modification techniques with self-treatment methods (e.g., monitoring, instruction, evaluation, and verbalization). The basic tenet of this approach is that cognitions (of which inner speech is one) influence behavior and that, by modifying cognitions, behavior can be changed. Essentially, inner speech is viewed as behavior that is subject to the same learning principles that overt behavior is subject to. Keogh and Glover (1980) discuss the respective roles of cognitive and behavior therapy in cognitive behavior modification:

> It is *behavioral* in that it is structured, utilizes reinforcement techniques, is usually focused on particular problems or complaints, and is not concerned with antecedents or etiology of the problem. It is *cognitive* in that its goal is to produce change in the individual by modifying his thinking. (p. 5)

Meichenbaum (1975), the pioneer of cognitive behavior modification, describes the steps of a self-instructional program:

1. An adult model performed a task while talking to himself out loud (cognitive modeling);

2. The child performed the same task under the directions of the model's instruction (overt self-guidance);

3. The child whispered the instructions to himself as he went through the task (faded, overt self-guidance); and finally

4. The child performed the task while guiding his performance via private speech (covert self-instruction). (pp. 16–17)

Hallahan (1980) and his colleagues at the University of Virginia have conducted most of the research on this strategy in connection with LD. Hallahan and Kauffman (1982) found it useful because it stresses self-initiative and helps the student overcome passivity in learning; it offers specific methods for solving problems; and it seems applicable to poor attention and impulsiveness.

Minimum Competency Testing

In an effort to establish or maintain credibility in the educational system and improve educational services, many states are instituting minimum competency tests. Primarily, these tests are used to ensure that students who are being promoted or graduated possess certain basic skills. The relationship of minimum competency tests and the learning disabled student is currently being examined. Some alternatives are being explored:

- exempting learning disabled students from minimum competency testing

- providing test modifications for learning disabled students (Grisé, 1980)

- including minimum competency skills in the LD student's IEP

- using minimum competency test results to design remediation programs for learning disabled students

Minimum conpetency testing appears to be an educational trend that will require the development of certain policies and procedures for learning disabled students.

Life-Span View of Learning Disabilities

Until recently the LD field has focused primarily on the school-age child. Professionals are now beginning to gain information about the older LD individual. Horn, O'Donnell, and Vitulano (1983) reviewed the literature reported since 1960 on long-term effects of learning disabilities and uncovered a variety of conflicting results. However, an analysis of the findings reveals some of the factors that affect those results:

1. For most LD persons basic academic skill deficits persist into adulthood. This finding seems to be highly correlated with lower socioeconomic status and severity of initial academic deficits.

2. Follow-up of educational/vocational attainments reveals that LD persons do attain educational levels and vocational status commensurate with normal learners in the general population" (Horn, O'Donnell, & Vitulano, 1983, p. 553). This finding suggests that many LD adults are able to compensate for their academic skill deficits. Also, evidence indicates that LD adults tend to become involved in educational experiences and vocations that do not rely heavily on verbal skills. Moreover, the literature reveals that these comparable educational/vocational attainments take longer for the LD person to achieve.

3. The follow-up studies of the social-emotional adjustments of LD persons yielded mixed results. To date, studies exist that indicate both good and poor adjustment. Additional research is needed.

The development of college programs for LD individuals is currently receiving much attention. Vogel (1982) reports that the 1980s represent a time when higher education will respond to the needs of LD adults, and she outlines extensive guidelines for developing LD college programs. Cordoni (1982) provides a directory of college programs, support groups, and resources for youth and adult LD persons. Knowles and Knowles (1983) found that the *American College Test*, the *Standard Test of Academic Skills*, and grade-point average identified LD college freshmen with 84% accuracy. As previously mentioned, Deshler and his colleagues at the Learning Disabilities Institute at the University of Kansas have contributed much to the understanding and treatment of the secondary LD student (Schumaker, Deshler, Alley, & Warner, 1983); their learning strategies interventions continue to hold much promise.

Single-Subject Research

When group designs are used and individual scores are averaged, it is possible that the mean score is not representative of any individual's performance since the learning disabled are a heterogeneous population. Single-subject research is tailored to evaluate the effects of treatments on individual performance, and its use has been recommended by numerous authorities (Haring & Schiefelbusch, 1976; Lovitt, 1975). Moreover, the recent guidelines (CLD Research Committee, 1984) for selecting and describing LD subjects for research, if followed, should help alleviate a major problem of LD research—the variability of LD subjects among studies.

Microcomputers

The influence of microcomputers on the teaching of LD students is extensive. For example, both the *Journal of Learning Disabilities* and *Learning Disability Quarterly* feature sections on computers in every issue. Microcomputers are used for initial learning, drill, and practice. They offer teachers the opportunity to provide individualized instruction efficiently. Likewise, LD students with microcomputers in their homes have an extended learning opportunity. Finally, microcomputers represent a viable resource to help LD adolescents and adults compensate for their learning deficits.

Summary

All learning disabled students have an academic problem in one or more areas and are not achieving in accordance with their potential ability. In this chapter the recent history of the field of LD is traced, and the major definitions and criteria for identifying LD students are presented. Prevalence estimates indicate that the learning disabled comprise one of the largest groups within the handicapped population.

The causes of learning disabilities are discussed in terms of three categories: organic and biological, genetic, and environmental factors. Each LD student is unique, and LD characteristics may include one or more of a range of problem areas, such as academic learning, language, perception, motor use, social-emotional adjustment, metacognition, memory, and attention.

Methods of assessing learning disabilities are discussed in terms of two diagnostic approaches (ability model and skill model); and four components in the identification of LD (exclusion, academic achievement, discrepancy, and process) are examined. In addition, early identification perspectives and guidelines are presented.

Service or placement options for LD students are listed with their respective advantages and disadvantages. Five approaches to teaching the learning disabled are discussed—perceptual-motor, language, multisensory, precision teaching, and direct instruction—as well as programming considerations for the LD adolescent. The rationale and criticism of mainstreaming are presented briefly, and the resource room model is described as a mainstreaming approach.

Recent innovations and developments in the field of LD involve areas such as teacher preparation, cognitive approaches, minimum competency testing, life-span view of LD, and microcomputers. The field of LD is an active and exciting area that is making great strides in facilitating the identification and instruction of persons who are learning disabled.

Study Questions

1. Discuss the evolution of the term *learning disabilities*.

2. Write the 1977 *Federal Register* definition of learning disabilities. Compare the components of the definition and the identification criteria.

3. Discuss five characteristics of learning disabilities.

4. Why are individuals with learning disabilities considered to be a heterogeneous group?

5. What are the basic issues in the ability-versus-skill approaches? Which model has the most research support?

6. Outline the beginning of an early identification screening/testing program.

7. Discuss five intervention approaches for the learning disabled.

8. According to Deshler and his associates, what are the demand areas for secondary LD students?

9. What are some of the recent findings regarding the learning disabled adult?

10. Discuss five innovations and/or developments in the field of learning disabilities.

TIPS FOR HELPING

1. Provide support; be cheerful, complimentary, and enthusiastic.

2. Provide structure; clearly specify rules, assignments, and duties.

3. Establish situations and tasks that lead to success.

4. Use simple vocabulary in giving directions and in interacting with students.

5. Use self-correcting materials to minimize students' public experiences of failure and to provide immediate feedback.

6. Practice skills frequently; use instructional games and otherwise vary drill formats as much as possible to maintain interest.

7. Allow older LD students who have difficulty writing to record answers on tape and provide extra time to complete tests to students who work slowly.

8. For older LD students who have difficulty organizing and understanding material, provide outlines to be filled in as they read or listen to lectures.

9. For older LD students, tape lecture material and provide them with class time to listen to tapes in order to check notes, review, and study.

10. Pair LD adolescents with peer helpers, and provide class time for these pairs to work on specific assignments, play instructional games, and study materials such as vocabulary and concept cards.

11. Use microcomputers for drill and practice of basic academic skills.

12. Teach self-instruction techniques and learning strategies to help LD students learn in varied situations.

Why
People
Take
Drugs

6

Behavior Disorders

Douglas Cullinan and Michael H. Epstein
Northern Illinois University

Pupils passing the guidance counselor's office, surprised by the screaming from within, have formed a small crowd. Some listen quietly, others are making jokes and giggling; a teacher appears and orders them to move along. Sandy is standing in the corner of the counselor's office, tearfully wailing and begging to call her father to take her home. Sandy's homeroom teacher escorted this eighth grader to the counselor's office after she vomited during homeroom period—the fourth such incident in the first 2 months of this school term. The principal is trying to reach her father now.

Sandy is often the last student to enter a classroom and always tries to sit apart from the other students (a fact for which her nearest peers were most grateful this morning). She also avoids social interactions by staring straight ahead when she walks in the halls and mumbling short answers (often "I don't know") when called on by a teacher. If

required to be with others in classroom activity groups or mandatory assemblies, sometimes she suddenly begins to sob and runs away. When questioned about this by a teacher or administrator (often an angry one), she attributes her behavior to attacks of nausea, dizziness, headaches, menstrual pain, or other illnesses. Teachers have also noticed that Sandy avoids dark rooms and areas of the school at all costs. For example, the stairway and hall leading to the basement cafeteria are not well lighted, and Sandy habitually walks halfway around the school to enter the cafeteria by an outside door. Schoolmates tease her a good deal about this and other fears she has.

Last year, Sandy's first at this school, she was absent 36 times; this year she has already missed 16 days. A conversation with her mother revealed that most of these absences occur when Sandy awakes with pains or nausea; when the parents insist that she attend, Sandy typically becomes highly upset, may vomit, and has even fainted. Examination by a physician revealed no medical basis for these complaints.

To a couple of teachers whom she trusts, Sandy has confided great concern over schoolmates making fun of her, not being fair to her, and hating her. Another worry is her academic problems: she usually does adequately on homework assignments and in-school exercises, but she chokes on tests, frequently completing only a small number of the items. She has never failed a grade but realizes that this is a distinct possibility.

Parents, school staff, and Sandy have expressed a need for and willingness to attempt corrective action, but no one is certain what should be done. For now, she visits the guidance counselor three times a week during her study period. A conference involving teachers, counselor, principal, and parents will take place in 2 weeks. Unless dramatic improvement occurs, various possibilities will be brought up by the principal, including having Sandy see a therapist and placing her in another school where special education services are available.

Students who do and say things that substantially interfere with the appropriate functioning of others and themselves are often described as showing *behavior disorders.* Sandy is an example of such a student. Behavior disorders, sometimes referred to as emotional disturbance or maladjustment, can take a wide variety of forms. There may be little or no classroom participation, play, communication, or other interaction; excessive physical aggression, threats, disobedience, destructiveness, or inappropriate movement; a lack of basic academic and school-readiness skills, as well as any organized learning strategies for acquiring them; verbal and other expressions of extreme fear, sadness, guilt, or self-doubt. Children and adolescents with the most severe behavior disorders often show strange movements and postures, profound language handicaps, a lack of basic self-care skills, and fundamental cognitive disturbances. No behaviorally disordered young person will show all of these problems, but few will show only one.

History

Special education for students with behavior disorders is a modern development shaped by earlier ideas and practices. Our ancestors believed that supernatural powers controlled all sorts of phenomena that were difficult to understand—stars, seasonal changes, reproduction, and deviant behavior. Behavior disorders were often interpreted as evidence of possession by evil spirits that needed to be exorcised. In addition, very early versions of today's biological, psychodynamic, and behavioral ideas existed.

Special Education

Child labor and compulsory schooling laws in the 19th century helped make public education a major social institution that had to deal for the first time with children and adolescents having a variety of physical, sensory, learning, and behavior disorders. By about 1900, provisions for delinquent and hard-to-manage pupils were not uncommon in large cities. In the early years of the 20th century, education was sometimes provided for the behaviorally disordered in institutions and special schools, but it was seen as an extra, often an extension of therapy. Public school students showing behavior disorders were commonly suspended or excluded.

As special education college courses and state certification requirements became widespread, some behaviorally disordered students began to be placed in special classes for the retarded, or brain injured. Only in the 1950s and 1960s, as psychoeducational and behavioral models became influential, did contemporary features of special education for the behaviorally disordered emerge. The Council for Children with Behavioral Disorders (CCBD)—a special-interest division of the Council for Exceptional Children—was founded in 1964. During the 1970s education for students with behavior disorders was broadly affected by both the letter and spirit of public policy developments—litigation and laws, especially P.L.94–142—involving educational and other rights of exceptional children.

One major treatment for behavior disorders is, of course, drug therapy. Natural sources of drugs that change behavior have long been known, but drug treatment became common only in the past four decades with the availability of synthetic compounds with more predictable effects. In 1938 it was reported that the stimulant drug amphetamine improved the educational and behavioral functioning of a group of behaviorally disordered children (Conners & Werry, 1979). Since then treatment of children's behavior and learning disorders with stimulants and other drugs has been studied extensively, but many questions still remain about their effectiveness (Conners & Werry, 1979) and the larger social implications of drug treatment (Grinspoon & Singer, 1973).

Psychodynamic Psychology

Psychoanalysis, developed by Sigmund Freud and revised by other theorists and therapists, forms the basis of psychodynamic psychology, which is concerned with the development and interaction of mental processes and sees behavior disorders as symptoms of abnormal processes. Psychodynamic psychology has influenced treatment of children and adolescents in two main ways. First, psychoanalysis and other psychodynamic therapies have been used to treat youngsters in clinics, institutions, and schools. In 1950 Bettelheim relied heavily on psychoanalysis to create his Orthogenic School with its permissive "therapeutic milieu," where behaviorally disordered young people could be freed from their intrapsychic anxiety. Play therapy (Axline, 1969) and transactional analysis (Berne, 1964) are two examples of the many psychodynamic therapies for behaviorally disordered students.

Second, modified psychodynamic principles have produced the psychoeducational model, which has deeply influenced special education for behaviorally disordered students. Its beginnings can be traced to the work of Fritz Redl at Pioneer House (Redl & Wineman, 1951); his program stressed acceptance but expected behavior improvement and enforced program limits. Redl's adaptations of psychodynamic treatment included the life-space interview technique for crisis exploration and strategies for managing surface behavior problems. William Morse (1965, 1971, 1976) later conceptualized the crisis-helping teacher, and Nicholas Long (1974) established a program for training teachers to use psychoeducational interventions and developed a curriculum to promote student self-control.

Behavioral Psychology

Beginning in the 1930s B. F. Skinner's laboratory research identified important relationships between behaviors and environmental stimuli and established a science of behavior known as *operant conditioning*, which holds that behavior can be predicted fairly accurately and modified substantially with knowledge of and control over the appropriate stimuli. Operant conditioning has been applied even to complex human behavior patterns such as language and education (Skinner, 1957, 1968).

Behavioral psychology began to be used systematically to help students with behavior and learning problems about 1960. Early reports focused on intervention with individual children, but before long there were organized school and institutional programs based on operant conditioning. In one of the pioneering applications, Haring and Phillips (1962) operated a highly structured class for behaviorally disordered pupils, focusing on the predictability and consistency of the child's everyday home and school environment. Frank Hewett (1968) developed and evaluated the engineered classroom plan, which used a system of tokens and praise to reinforce task accomplishments within a carefully structured educational environment. Herbert Quay and his colleagues (Quay, Glavin, Annesley, & Werry, 1972) showed how behavioral principles could be used in a resource room program for the behaviorally disordered. Under the direction of Hill Walker, the Center at Oregon for Research in Behavioral Education of the Handicapped (CORBEH) developed, evaluated, packaged, and disseminated interventions to correct classroom acting out behavior, poor academic readiness skills, social withdrawal, and aggression outside the classroom (Walker, Hops, & Greenwood, 1984).

To summarize, contemporary special education for behaviorally disordered students has been shaped by diverse influences. Prominent have been developments in education, medicine, and psychodynamic and behavioral psychology (for details see Achenbach, 1974; Cullinan, Epstein, & Lloyd, 1983; Kauffman, 1981; Kazdin, 1978; Sarason & Doris, 1979; Zilboorg & Henry, 1941). This diverse background is a strength in many ways, but it is also one cause of continuing disagreement on fundamental issues.

Definition

Children and youth with behavior disorders are certainly not rare, and most of us have observed or dealt with such young people. Ironically, though, there is no generally accepted definition of behavior disorders. One of the major stumbling blocks is the diverse and sometimes conflicting viewpoints about the nature of behavior disorders. Another issue is the subjectivity of standards for determining exactly what is a behavior disorder: standards of normality can vary by age, sex, subculture, community, politics, and economic conditions. Another obstacle involves problems of assessment. Presently there are too few instruments that can accurately measure the social, emotional, and behavioral problems of school children, thus requiring an uncomfortable degree of subjectivity in identifying behaviorally disordered pupils and specifying their problems. One further problem is the potential harm in labeling pupils—the lowered self-concept, loss of popularity and acceptability among peers, and decreased teacher expectations.

Table 6–1 presents a few definitions selected from among dozens available. The federal definition is used by the Office of Special Education as it administers financial support and other federal activities related to research, teacher training, and state programs. Other government agencies have separate administrative definitions (Epstein, Cullinan, & Sabatino, 1977). The next four definitions in the table reflect various perspectives on behavior disorders. The last definition reflects aspects of behavior disorders that are of particular interest to educators. Its key phrases should be examined closely.

Behavior characteristics. Educators are concerned about their students' behavior—their movements, language, and obvious physiological responses, such as tears or a flushed face—and the effects this behavior has on objects and people in the environment. Even mental or emotional problems are deduced from an observation and interpretation of behavior.

Deviation from educators' standards of normality. There is, of course, no clear-cut boundary that divides normality from abnormality. We all have expectations about what is typical in school situations—expectations that take into account age, sex, and other characteristics. Behavior disorders usually involve familiar behaviors that occur with a frequency and/or intensity that is too great or too small relative to the educator's expectations. Teachers are likely to tolerate moderate behavior problems for a while but become concerned if they persist. Most often, then, the educator's standard of normality involves a range of behavior perceived as typical of some group of students. Behavior that goes beyond this range may be identified as disordered.

Impaired functioning of the student and/or others. Some behavior disorders involve substantial personal distress, as indicated by self-deprecating remarks, unrealistic anxieties, sadness and depression, or an inability to make friends. Other disorders interfere with the young person's personal, emotional, or educational development: a lack of essential academic skills, short attention span, and excessive dependence on the teacher are examples. Still other behavior disorders—including aggression, bizarre statements or actions, and disruptive rule violations—impede the productive performance of other individuals. Of course, few behavior disorders impair the functioning of only the student or only others. Behavior that is personally distressing or that interferes with self-development usually disturbs other people sooner or later; conversely, the student whose behavior disturbs others is likely to experience social and personal repercussions as well.

Table 6-1 Definitions of behavior disorders

Federal

Seriously emotionally disturbed children . . . . exhibit one or more of the following characteristics over a long period of time and to a marked degree:
(1) An inability to learn which cannot be explained by intellectual, sensory, or health factors;
(2) An inability to build or maintain satisfactory interpersonal relationships with peers and teachers;
(3) Inappropriate types of behavior or feelings under normal circumstances;
(4) General pervasive mood of unhappiness or depression; or
(5) A tendency to develop physical symptoms, pains, or fears associated with personal or school problems (20 U.S.C. 1401 [13])

By perspective

(1) Biological
A *biogenic mental disorder* is a severe behavior disorder that results solely from the effects of biological factors, including both gene action and the effects of the physical-chemical environment. (Rimland, 1969, p. 706)
(2) Psychodynamic
A child suffers *emotional conflict* whenever anything interferes with the satisfaction of his instinctual drives and his frustration produces a state of tension. (Lippman, 1962, p. 3)
(3) Behavioral
Psychological disorder is said to be present when a child emits behavior that deviates from an arbitrary and relative social norm in that it occurs with a frequency or intensity that authoritative adults in the child's environment judge, under the circumstances, to be either too high or too low. (Ross, 1980, p. 9)
(4) Ecological
Emotional disturbance [is] a reciprocal condition which exists when intense coping responses are released within a human community by a community member's atypical behavior and responses. The triggering stimulus, the rejoinder of the microcommunity, and the ensuing transaction are all involved in emotional disturbance. (Rhodes, 1970, p. 311)
(5) Educational
Behavior disorders of a student are behavior characteristics that (a) deviate from educators' standards of normality and (b) impair the functioning of that student and/or others. These behavior characteristics are manifested as environmental conflicts and/or personal disturbances, and are typically accompanied by learning disorders. (Cullinan, Epstein, & Lloyd, 1983)

Environmental conflicts, personal disturbances, and learning disorders. It is convenient to discuss behavior disorders of children and adolescents in terms of these three general aspects. Environmental conflict refers to aggressive-disruptive, hyperactive, and social maladjustment problems, whereas personal disturbance includes anxiety and social withdrawal problems. Many pupils with these difficulties also have learning disorders that must be addressed by teachers.

Prevalence

Prevalence information is important to persons responsible for funding, personnel development, and other administrative issues in educating the behaviorally disordered. It can also tell us how behavior disorders differ according to age, sex, socio-economic status, or geographic area; and this information has implications for our ideas about causes and interventions.

Most prevalence estimates are of two types: those based on actual surveys of young people with behavior disorders and "guesstimates" derived from the opinions of others as to how widespread behavior disorders are. There have been many prevalence studies of behavior disorders in children and adolescents in schools and communities (see Glidewell & Swallow, 1968; Graham, 1979), but for various reasons—especially differences among research methods—the resulting estimates have varied from less than 1% to more than 30% of the school-age persons. Administrative guesstimates do not vary so widely: Schultz, Hirshoren, Manton, and Henderson (1971) found that most state education agency prevalence estimates fell within the range of 2 to 5%. The official federal guess is that 2% of students are "seriously emotionally disturbed."

Recent data on services provided nationally under federal special education legislation suggest that considerably fewer than 1% of students are being served as seriously emotionally disturbed (behaviorally disordered) Kauffman and Kneedler (1981) suggest that, because P.L. 94–142 requires that special education be provided to all students found to be handicapped, many districts may be finding only as many behaviorally disordered students as can be served within existing personnel and budget limitations.

Highly accurate prevalence estimates will probably remain elusive as long as there are major discrepancies among definitions and continuing assessment problems. Our own guesstimate, based on individual studies and prevalence reviews, is that behavior disorders among students may follow a rule of one-third: in any school year about one-third of all students show behavior problems that concern their teachers to some extent. One-third of this group (about 10% of the total student population) show disorders to an extent that moderate to substantial alterations of ordinary educational procedures are needed. And about one-third of this group (roughly 4%) exhibit behavior disorders severe enough to justify special education and/or other intervention services (Cullinan et al., 1983). Included within this 4% would be the very small number of children (less than 1 in 1,000) diagnosed as autistic or otherwise severely behaviorally disordered (Werry, 1979a).

Causes

What do we mean by *cause*? To scientists trying to understand behavior disorders, a most helpful kind of cause is the necessary-and-sufficient condition (Achenbach, 1974). When a necessary-and-sufficient condition operates, the behavior disorder will definitely occur; when it does not, the behavior disorder cannot occur. Therefore, to remedy the problem one simply needs to identify and control the necessary-and-sufficient condition. Unfortunately, such powerful and uncomplicated causes have not yet been identified. Instead, the vast majority of causes are contributory conditions—situations that increase the risk that a behavior disorder will occur. Research indicates that some conditions increase this risk more than others, but in most individual cases the causes of behavior disorders cannot be pinned down. Given the complex nature of human behavior and behavior disorders, necessary-and-sufficient conditions may never be identified for most behavior disorders.

Fortunately, effective intervention is possible even when the initial causes of behavior disorders are not known; in fact, knowing the causes may have little relevance for effective intervention. For instance, many contributory conditions—brain damage or severe child abuse, for instance—involve historical events that cannot be undone, yet effective intervention can reduce or eliminate the impairments.

It would take several pages to list every condition that has been suggested at one time or another as a cause of behavior disorders. However, these factors fall into just a few categories. First, research points to a number of biological and psychological conditions that can be important determinants of an individual's development, both normal and abnormal. Second, there are several models of behavior disorders; the psychoeducational, behavioral, and ecological models are particularly relevant. Each of these models involves certain ideas about how behavior disorders are produced and perpetuated, and each provides intervention principles that have been translated into special education practices.

Biological Conditions

Recent research has begun to reveal how a child's characteristics are influenced by the genetic material inherited from parents. Genes control critical chemical chain reactions in our bodies, so gene defects that produce a broken link in these chains may cause drastically disturbed functioning. Defects of chromosomes (collections of genes) can also cause serious physical and behavioral problems. Certain long-term research strategies have been especially designed to discriminate the effects of nature and nurture on human adjustment, and results increasingly point to heredity as a contributory condition in some behavior disorders (Lahey & Ciminero, 1980).

Many events operating before, during, and after birth can produce brain disorder (structural damage to the brain or dysfunctions such as abnormal electrical activity). The relationship between brain disorder and behavior disorders continues to intrigue and baffle researchers. One major obstacle to a definitive determination is the technical inadequacy of assessment procedures for brain disorder (Werry, 1979a). Nevertheless, reviews of the available evidence (Ross, 1980; Werry, 1979a) suggest several main conclusions: (1) severe-profound behavior disorders, especially infantile autism, are probably strongly associated with brain disorder; (2) hyperactivity can be caused in various ways, one of which is brain disorder; but (3) most behavior disorders are not caused by brain disorder, and most children with brain disorders do not show behavior disorders.

Research indicates that severe, chronic deprivation of either general nutritional needs or certain specific dietary substances can cause not only physical and mental retardation but behavior disorders as well (Lahey & Ciminero, 1980). Orthomolecular psychiatry (Pauling, 1968) is based in part on the concept that if a person's highly individual needs for certain vitamins are not met, behavior disorders such as hyperactivity or psychosis may result. Feingold (1975) has proposed that salicylic acids in certain foods and additives produce in many children an allergic reaction that causes hyperactivity. Orthomolecular psychiatry and Feingold's hypothesis have become popular but are backed by relatively little scientific evidence (Conners, 1980; Lahey & Ciminero, 1980).

Psychological Conditions

The family is universally recognized as a fundamental influence on the development of children and adolescents, and much research and theory have focused on family structure and functioning as possible causes of behavior disorders. Some major family variables related to behavior disorders include (1) divorce and separation; (2) father or mother absence due to other reasons; (3) conflict between parents; (4) a behaviorally disordered parent (especially psychotic or severely antisocial); (5) parental hostility, neglect, or abuse; and (6) inconsistent or extremely lax discipline (Hetherington & Martin, 1979; Willis, Swanson, & Walker, 1983). However, it appears that none of these family variables are necessary-and-sufficient conditions for behavior disorder. The influence of each seems to vary according to the child or adolescent's sex, age, and socioeconomic status. However, evidence does indicate that these family variables (and others) often operate as contributory conditions; each one increases the risk of behavior disorders.

Normal and abnormal socialization can also be shaped by peers, the school, media, socioeconomic disadvantage, and other influences beyond the family. Peer interaction is a central aspect of child development, providing opportunities for companionship, social status, self-understanding, personal maturity, and adjustment to society. Behavior disorders seem to cause poor peer relations, and vice versa; in either case children and youth with poor relationships with their peers are not likely to be happy or effective pupils (Oliver, 1974). Furthermore, even satisfying peer relationships can contribute to some disorders since peer groups often encourage behaviors that deviate from the standards of teachers, parents, and others.

Kauffman (1981) has described how schools can contribute to behavior disorders through insensitivity to student individuality, inappropriate expectations for students that become self-fulfilling prophecies of failure, teacher ineptitude in providing management and instruction, and preoccupation with irrelevant tasks and routines. On the other hand, of course, schools can be immensely important in preventing and correcting behavior disorders.

Socioeconomic disadvantage refers to a collection of unfortunate circumstances—including poverty, family breakdown, inadequate educational and other services, frequent exposure to deviant persons, and minority racial status—that overlap so much that it has not been feasible to isolate the effects of any one alone. It is known that socioeconomically disadvantaged persons are at increased risk for behavior disorders and have less chance of obtaining appropriate treatment (Nathan & Harris, 1980). Chan and Rueda (1979) point out that socioeconomically

The impact of television violence on minors is a subject of continuing concern and investigation.

disadvantaged children often enter school without all the skills and behaviors that primary grade teachers commonly expect of pupils. Consequently, they are educationally handicapped from the very beginning.

Television and other mass communication media play an ever greater role in the socialization of children and adolescents. Concerned individuals and organizations have protested the extent to which sexual and aggressive programming appears on television. Some scientific support for their concern comes from research on televised violence (Liebert & Wicks-Nelson, 1981), indicating that a large percentage of the programs watched by children involve violence and that televised violence can promote aggression in its viewers.

Stress generally refers to a situation in which the adaptive resources of a person are strained or exceeded by demands in the environment or within that person (Monat & Lazarus, 1977). Physical, social, or psychological events that initiate stress—injury, loss of a loved one, frustrated attempts to reach a goal—are called stressors. Stressors may produce physiological changes (e.g., in breathing, circulation, or blood chemistry); they can disrupt attention, problem solving, language, and performance; and they can prompt fear, anger, or other strong emotions. Many observers in the classroom and clinic are convinced that stress can lead to disorders of thought, feeling, and behavior. Stress is a key feature of a major psychoeducational concept of behavior disorders, the conflict cycle (Long, 1974), which is described later.

Interaction of Biological and Psychological Conditions

Biological and psychological conditions have been discussed separately, but few theorists believe they operate in isolation. One conception of how biological and psychological conditions interact to produce children's behavior disorders is the work of Thomas and Chess (1977) on temperaments, styles of behaving that are observable from early childhood. Their research on individuals from birth into adolescence led them to formulate nine categories of temperament that, in various combinations, significantly determine children's development. Thomas and Chess found that a child's particular pattern of temperament usually influences which child-rearing practices his parents adopt; in turn, these parental practices influence the child's behavioral development. Children whose temperaments include (1) irregularity of feeding, sleeping, and other biological functions; (2) avoidance of and poor adaptation to new situations; and (3) frequent intensely negative moods and behaviors are especially difficult for parents to manage and are more likely to experience school problems.

Research on temperament indicates that children exhibit certain identifiable patterns of behavior early in life—patterns quite possibly determined by biological conditions prior to birth. These early temperaments help shape parenting practices and other environmental influences (perhaps including teachers' reactions). In turn, such environmental influences have an important impact on the child's behavior and development.

Models

The psychoeducational, behavioral, and ecological models provide different explanations of the causes of behavior disorders and recommendations about appropriate intervention. This section will consider the views of causation.

Psychoeducational Model   The psychoeducational model adapts ideas and practices of psychodynamic psychology for use in schools, institutions, camps, and other educational-therapeutic settings for children and adolescents with behavior disorders. Long (1974) has provided a psychoeducational perspective on behavior disorders called the conflict cycle. In this view, if parental or societal expectations interfere with the child's or youth's attempts to satisfy her own basic needs, an improper self-image will develop. She will also view the world as hostile, restrictive, or incompetent and will behave according to this negative view. Typical academic and social demands encountered in school will likewise be viewed negatively and will create stress in the individual. Such a young person will feel anxious and behave defensively and immaturely. These behavior patterns ordinarily provoke negative reactions from teachers and peers that perpetuate the individual's maladaptive feelings and behaviors, thus creating a self-perpetuating cycle of conflict and failure. Long believes that teachers who conceptualize a student's behavior disorders in terms of the conflict cycle will better understand how those behaviors are tied to disturbed emotions and how the student can be supported and helped to modify her view of the world, leading to more adaptive behavior.

Behavioral Model Originating mainly in Skinner's principles of operant conditioning, the behavioral model has profoundly influenced the helping professions, including special education. A fundamental concept in the behavioral model is that most human behavior is learned. Drives, emotions, thoughts, and feelings are not believed to be major determinants of behavior. Instead, principles of operant conditioning are used to explain the origin, perpetuation, and modification of normal and abnormal behavior. For example, if reinforcement is provided for dependent, aggressive, withdrawn, incompetent, or other undesirable behavior, it will occur more frequently or more intensively. On the other hand, if prosocial, skillful, or other desirable behavior is not reinforced, it may decrease (Cullinan, Epstein, & Kauffman, 1982).

When students engage in disruption, aggression, disobedience, hyperactivity, and other inappropriate behavior patterns, teachers often react in a variety of ways. They may give a reminder about a broken rule, reprimand or publicly ridicule the students, engage them in a discussion about the necessity of being good citizens, and so on. Though diverse in many ways, these reactions have one important element in common: they provide attention from an adult as a consequence of inappropriate behavior. Such attention can reinforce disordered behavior (Becker, Madson, Arnold, & Thomas, 1967), and classroom research has demonstrated that teachers do tend to pay much attention to problem behavior while ignoring on-task and prosocial behavior (Walker & Buckley, 1973). Behaviorists point to this process as one major way in which behavior disorders arise and are perpetuated.

Additionally children can learn inappropriate behavior through models (Bandura, 1973). Modeling can be a particularly powerful source of problem behavior if the student's home, school, or community contains many peers or adults who demonstrate aggression, delinquency, anxiety, nonparticipation, or otherwise maladjusted behavior and who fail to demonstrate cooperative, achievement-oriented, and other prosocial behavior. As noted earlier, television and other popular media also provide models of deviant behavior (Bandura, 1973).

Ecological Model Educators of the behaviorally disordered have recently begun to examine ecological concepts used in anthropology, ethology, psychology, sociology, and other disciplines (Cullinan et al., 1983). The ecological model emphasizes the need to examine overall patterns of interaction among the individual's capabilities and behaviors, along with the social and physical environments in which these behaviors take place. Expectations, restrictions, and demands are present in any behavior ecology system (ecosystem); when the person's behavior is in harmony with these, there is a goodness-of-fit. In the ecological model a behavior disorder is really lack of goodness-of-fit; it is a disturbance in the patterns of interaction between an individual and the ecosystem, not a property of either the student or the ecosystem alone. Unfortunately, people involved in the disturbed ecosystem do not always see it this way. For instance, when ecological goodness-of-fit is disturbed, the student is prone to blame peers or the teacher; at the same time teachers, administrators, and authoritative persons often initiate a labeling process that locates the source of disturbance in the student.

Characteristics

In the most general sense, the characteristics of students with behavior disorders can include any behavior patterns that prompt others (especially educators) to identify the student as behaviorally disordered. Most teachers of the behaviorally disordered will sooner or later have to deal with a wide variety of maladaptive functioning. However, research and teacher observations indicate that certain behavior-problem characteristics are much more likely to be identified than others, and educators should be especially aware of and skilled in these areas.

Evidence from various sources—especially research on prevalence and classification of the problems of behaviorally disordered youngsters (Achenbach & Edelbrock, 1982; Cullinan & Epstein, 1984; Quay, 1979)—shows rather clearly that the major behavior-problem characteristics that are exhibited by pupils with behavior disorders fall under two general headings: environmental conflict and personal disturbance. This evidence further suggests that environmental conflict includes at least three behavior patterns—which may be termed aggression-disruption, hyperactivity, and social maladjustment—and that personal disturbance includes at least two—anxiety-inferiority and withdrawal. Further, pupils with behavior disorders often show some degree of learning disorders that may appear as cognitive disabilities or academic skill deficits.

The characteristics and representative behaviors are summarized in Table 6-2 for the more common mild-moderate behavior disorders and the infrequent severe disorders. The severe disorders involve some behavior problems that appear to be extreme expressions of the characteristics in mild-moderate behavior disorders. However, the behavior similarities do not necessarily imply similar causes, outcomes, or appropriate treatments.

Mild-Moderate Behavior Disorders

Aggression-Disruption   Aggression, broadly defined, is commonplace, and under some circumstances is even admired and encouraged. However, behaviors that produce destruction, pain, or disadvantage to others most often disturb adults and children and may produce counteraggression. Disorders of aggression-disruption may involve cruelty, bullying, threats, fighting, screaming, tantrums, disobedience and disrespect to the teacher, and hostile resistance.

Table 6-2 Summary of major characteristics of children and youth with behavior disorders

Characters	Representative Behaviors	
	Mild-Moderate Disorders	Severe-Profound Disorders
Environmental conflict		
Aggression-disruption	fighting, cruelty, bullying, tantrums, violating rules, disrespect, negativism, threatening, destruction	self-injury, primitive assaults, destruction, negativism
Hyperactivity	overactivity, attention deficits, impulsivity; accompanied by aggression-disruption	repetitive, bizarre motor and verbal acts that appear to provide self-stimulation; other overactivity
Social maladjustment	peer-group-oriented stealing, fighting, vandalism, other illegal acts; substance abuse, sexual irresponsibility, truancy	
Personal disturbance		
Anxiety-inferiority	low self-confidence situation-specific avoidance, crying, physiological overarousal, statements of worry, skill disorganization	extreme upset over minor changes in a familiar situation
Social withdrawal	failure to initiate verbal or motor behavior toward peers and others, failure to reciprocate the initiations of others; incompetent or aggressive social initiations resulting in peer rejection	same, but in more severe degrees; apparent indifference to interpersonal activity, even toward parents and siblings; play skills usually lacking
Learning disorders	low-normal intellectual performance; substantial deficits in basic academic skills and general educational achievement	often, moderate to profound mental retardation; substantial deficits in language, attention, memory, and other abilities; deficient self-help skills

Aggression-disruption represents a very common characteristic of children in special education and mental health treatment (Gilbert, 1957; Morse, Cutler, & Fink, 1964). Boys are three to six times as likely to show this characteristic as girls are, and it concerns teachers of the behaviorally disordered substantially more than other problems (Bullock & Brown, 1972). This concern with aggression-disruption is probably well placed, because follow-up research on children and adolescents has consistently indicated that youngsters often do not grow out of this disorder (Gersten, Langner, Eisenberg, Simcha-Fagen, & McCarthy, 1976). No matter what their age when first identified, highly aggressive children are much more likely than nonaggressive youngsters to remain in conflict with persons in their environment. In fact, such behavior puts the child at high risk for juvenile and adult delinquency and other forms of maladjustment (Robins, 1979).

Hyperactivity   This term is used to describe pupils who show inappropriate overactivity (restlessness, moving about without permission), attention deficits (inability to sustain attention on a task, tendency to be distracted by task-irrelevant happenings), and impulsivity (interrupting and interfering with others, hasty and mistaken decision-making processes). Children may, but do not necessarily, show hyperactivity in more than one situation (e.g., school, home). Very rarely would a child be considered hyperactive in every situation, primarily because restraint and sustained attentiveness are not necessary for acceptable performance in many low-structure situations (e.g., games, play activities). Many hyperactive pupils— some estimates go higher than 50% (Safer & Allen, 1976)—exhibit learning disabilities. Some children with hyperactivity also show aggression, learning disorders, and/or "soft" neurological signs (questionable evidence of brain dysfunction, such as minor disabilities in coordination, reflexes, and visual-motor perception). However, there is a growing consensus that these are not central features of hyperactivity (Routh, 1980): aggression, learning disorders, brain dysfunction, and other problems can but often do not coexist with hyperactivity. Hyperactive students who are also aggressive would probably be particularly likely to be identified as behaviorally disordered.

The reported prevalence of hyperactivity has varied widely, with more careful recent studies ranging from about 1% to 5% of elementary-age pupils (Bosco & Robin, 1980) and identifying four to seven boys for each girl. Approximately half of the referrals to child guidance clinics are related to hyperactivity (Paternite & Loney, 1980). The disorder is usually first noted by about 7 years of age, and only rarely are adolescents identified as hyperactive. However, hyperactive children, especially those who also show aggression, are at increased risk for experiencing various kinds of maladjustment in adolescence (Barkley, 1983; Paternite & Loney, 1980).

Social Maladjustment   This term refers to behavior that violates actual laws or conventional standards of the school or community but conforms to the standards of some social subgroup. Social maladjustment may include gang- or group-related vandalism, stealing, fighting, truancy, sexual precocity, substance abuse, and other acts. Extremes of these behavior patterns often seem intended to achieve the approval and admiration of subgroup peers and tend to be associated with socioeconomic disadvantage. Males are five or six times as likely to show this disorder as females.

Social maladjustment provides an especially clear illustration of the difficulties of conceptualizing and defining behavior disorders, because some socially maladjusted behaviors are commonly performed by many adolescents (Nye, Short, & Olson, 1958) and because the norms and expectations for some of the behavior patterns involved (sexual activity, alcohol and drug usage) can change rapidly and vary from community to community. Further, socially maladjusted behaviors do not necessarily result in personal distress for the performer; in fact, interpersonal functioning, at least with subgroup peers, is often enhanced rather than impaired.

On the other hand, social maladjustment clearly impairs the functioning of other persons, as is obvious from official statistics, media reports, and unfortunate personal experiences of teachers, students, and other victims. Even the grim statistics cannot fully portray the actual consequences in terms of unreported crimes, lost instructional time, a school climate of fear and discouragement, and so on (Epstein & Cullinan, 1979). Research indicates that socially maladjusted adolescents are at high risk for many kinds of adult disorders (Glueck & Glueck, 1968; Robins, 1966), especially those youth identified as juvenile delinquents and placed in correctional institutions (Robins, 1979).

Anxiety-Inferiority Students with this behavior pattern may refuse to speak up in class, be visibly nervous when presented with an assignment, become ill when it is time to go to school, and claim a total lack of self-confidence in performing common school and social behaviors. The anxious child or adolescent is likely to experience a strong anticipation of danger, feel physiological arousal and discomfort, become disorganized in thinking, and avoid the feared situations (Mischel, 1971; Morris & Kratochwill, 1983).

About 4% of boys and girls aged 5 to 17 using outpatient psychiatric clinic services were diagnosed as having "anxiety reaction" (Rosen, Bahn, & Kramer, 1964). Younger children are more likely than older to be diagnosed as having anxiety disorders. The sex ratio is approximately equal through early adolescence, but anxious older adolescents are more likely to be female. Anxiety disorders show some tendency to diminish with age (Gersten et al., 1976; Rutter, Tizard, Yule, Graham, & Whitmore, 1976): children and young adolescents exhibiting anxiety disorders are not particularly likely to show serious maladjustment in adolescence or adulthood. However, anxiety disorders in later adolescence do appear to predict adult maladjustment (Gersten et al., 1976).

Social Withdrawal This characteristic is evidenced by students who rarely take part in play and other informal peer interactions and resist joining in formal educational activities. They often appear uncommunicative, extremely shy, self-conscious, and moody. Greenwood, Walker, and Hops (1977) have described two variations of social withdrawal that can be termed noninteraction and rejection. Noninteractive students have poorly developed social skills and may fear interactions with others; they often appear to prefer solitary activities. Rejected children and youth do initiate social interactions but in such aggressive, immature, or otherwise inappropriate ways that they turn off their peers; thus, their interactions are usually avoided or ignored by other children. About 15% of child clinic referrals are for social withdrawal (Gilbert, 1957).

Social withdrawal indicates a mild or moderate behavior disorder.

It seems self-evident that social withdrawal reduces the developing individual's opportunities for friendships and other important aspects of childhood and
can interfere with chances of profiting from classroom and informal learning activities. Surprisingly, however, mild-moderate social withdrawal, in and of itself, does
not seem to be a strong predictor of later maladjustment (Gersten et al., 1976;
Kohlberg, LaCrosse, & Ricks, 1972).

Learning Disorders In our society a young person's adjustment is closely linked
to how well he acquires and applies information presented at school. Failure to
learn basic academic skills, poor performance in the various subject areas, and a
lack of vocational preparedness are severe obstacles to proper adjustment. Among
students in general, behavior problems are clearly associated with lower achievement and ability (Oliver, 1974; Roberts & Baird, 1972). Students identified as behaviorally disordered are usually substantially behind in reading, arithmetic, and
spelling achievement (Kauffman, 1981; Rose et al., 1981); these deficits seem to
grow larger as the student passes through school (Cullinan et al., 1983); and most

teachers of the behaviorally disordered see academic retardation as an important accompaniment of behavior disorders (Morse et al., 1964). Evidence is not so clear on the cognitive abilities of those with mild-moderate behavior disorders. Although the measured intelligence of these students can range from 70, or even below, up to high levels of intellectual giftedness, their IQs appear most likely to fall in the 80 to 100 range (Kauffman, 1981). These students may also display some of the specific ability problems commonly associated with learning disability, such as impulsivity and attention deficits (Denton & MacIntyre, 1978; Firestone & Martin, 1979).

Neither mild achievement deficits nor slightly below-normal intelligence is a strong predictor of maladjustment in adulthood (Kohlberg et al., 1972). However, children who show poor achievement together with a significant degree of environmental conflict are at substantial risk for a wide variety of adult maladjustment (Robins, 1979).

Severe Behavior Disorders

Children with severe and profound behavior disorders (*psychoses*) have been assigned a confusing variety of labels, reflecting the fact that these disorders are largely a mystery. Some authorities believe that qualitatively different varieties of child psychosis do exist; some say these are only different manifestations of essentially the same disorder(s); others do not take a stand, on the grounds that this issue is irrelevant to effective treatment. The bulk of the evidence seems to support the existence of at least two distinguishable disorders (Russo & Newsom, 1982; Werry, 1979b)—infantile autism and childhood schizophrenia. Psychotic disorders are found in less than 1/10 of 1% of children, and about 75% of these children are boys. Psychotic children rarely become well-functioning adults, and most continue to require extensive supervision and care (Mesibov, 1983). The best predictor of eventual functioning seems to be childhood intellectual level (Werry, 1979b).

There has been considerably more research on infantile autism than on childhood schizophrenia. The best evidence to date links infantile autism to severe brain disorders that interfere with the individual's social and cognitive development (Rutter & Schopler, 1978; Werry, 1979b). Children with infantile autism commonly bite, scratch, and pick at themselves, bang their heads, and otherwise inflict grievous self-injury; they may assault others in primitive ways and destroy furnishings, toys, and other objects. They show activity disorders that seem to be linked with attention and perception disturbances: inappropriately excessive locomotion, extended periods of virtually motionless staring, and various repetitive, stereotyped vocalizations and body movements that seem intended to provide self-stimulation. Autistic children often show reactions resembling extreme anxiety when they detect minor changes in their surroundings and routines. They are socially withdrawn, rarely initiating interactions toward peers and having few appropriate play or social skills; they often seem totally indifferent to friendship or love, even from family members. Typically, serious learning disorders are shown by autistic children: normal or higher IQ levels are possible, but most are mentally retarded (many, severely); language, if present at all, is fundamentally abnormal; attention, perception, and memory disorders are common, as are deficits in feeding, dressing, toileting, and other self-help skills. Detailed reports on infantile autism are provided by Rutter and Schopler (1978) and Werry (1979b).

Scientific evidence on childhood schizophrenia is very sketchy. In some cases it may be an early form of adult schizophrenia, perhaps caused by genetic defects in brain chemistry that make the individual highly vulnerable to various stressors. The name of this disorder may be misleading because few cases become apparent before early adolescence. The major characteristics of the problem include tantrums, repetitive or otherwise bizarre movements and postures, withdrawal and social rejection, and unpredictable emotional changes, such as an extreme display of fear (Cantor, 1982). Intellectual functioning is generally higher than in autism, but there can be cognitive disturbances like those found in adult schizophrenia—delusions (unfounded beliefs), hallucinations, and disjointed, confused language and reasoning (Ross, 1980; Werry, 1979b).

Assessment

Assessment involves the gathering and use of information pertaining to a behavior disorder. Often it is most useful to gather this information in the form of numbers—such as test scores—that represent the student's status or functioning on some behavior characteristic or other area of interest to the educator. With an appropriate assessment device or procedure, educational strengths and problems as well as medical disorders, family and community situations, and other important areas can be represented conveniently in numerical terms. These numbers can then be used in such activities as classifying and researching. Assessment is perhaps most important to educators in screening for behavior disorders, placing the student in an appropriate program, designing an intervention plan, and monitoring the student's progress under that plan.

Assessment Methods

Most of the methods of assessing a pupil's school problems are of three types: They may focus on (1) actual functioning in a natural situation, (2) actual functioning in a contrived situation, or (3) reported functioning.

It is often important to assess the student as she engages in classroom activities. In the direct observation method (Kazdin, 1980; Tawney & Gast, 1984) carefully defined behaviors are observed by the teacher or aide, and the number of times each behavior occurs can be recorded. For example, a pupil's aggression might be assessed each day for several weeks by counting how many times she hits, pushes, and argues with classmates. The resulting daily totals provide a concrete representation of important aspects of aggression. The totals can be checked for a trend or compared to other students' totals to help decide just how different this student's aggression is. A variation of this assessment method is scoring products of the student's behavior, such as daily performance on academic assignments or other tasks that demonstrate a skill.

It is sometimes more convenient to set up a standardized testing situation in which the behaviors assessed are intended to be representative of what the child does in natural situations. For example, a standardized test of intelligence is made up of numerous tasks intended to call for the intellectual ability needed in real-world situations. There are also standardized tests of specific psychological abilities (e.g., auditory perception and fine motor coordination), knowledge and achievement (e.g., reading and language development), adaptive behaviors (e.g., social interaction skills), and other important characteristics.

Many characteristics are assessed by using reports of the student's functioning, which may come from the student, peers, teachers, parents, or some other informed source. Important information can be obtained through an interview with the student or other informant. Interviews that involve a structured format (standard questions about specific problems, situations, and behaviors) are more useful for educational purposes than unstructured interviews. Another measure of reported functioning is the behavior rating scale. Such a scale generally contains a standard group of items, each one describing a behavior or a behavior problem. For each item there is a scale of two or more points indicating the extent to which a student shows that behavior or problem. For example, an item about social withdrawal might have to be marked by the teacher as either "no problem," "mild problem," or "severe problem," reflecting his judgment of how much the student shows social withdrawal. Sociometric techniques require a group of persons to identify desirable and undesirable members of their social group. For example, each student can privately identify at least one peer with whom she likes to interact and at least one who is disliked or avoided. By tabulating the responses of all members of the group, it is possible to identify a few students who are generally admired, some who are actively rejected, and others who are simply ignored.

Uses of Assessment

Screening is designed to sort pupils who do not need special education at the present time from those who may and to do so with relatively little time and effort. Bower's (1969) screening procedure for behavior disorders uses data on a student's social and personal functioning as reported by the teacher, classmates, and the student himself. These data are combined to indicate who should be further assessed.

For each student thus identified detailed assessments may be made of school behavior, academic achievement, cognitive abilities, home and community situation, neurological and other medical status, feelings, and so on. Such diverse information is presented at a conference that often includes the child's regular teachers, principal, parents, special educators, psychological diagnosticians, and other professionals. The purpose of this conference is to decide whether special education is needed and, if so, to develop an IEP.

Once the student is placed, teachers have to perform further assessment to translate educational objectives into effective intervention. Teachers usually need to know about the student's problems in detail—how many arguments and fights, how many positive interactions with classmates, what percentage of assignments completed acceptably per day—in order to select appropriate teaching techniques and set realistic goals for improvement. Direct observation is particularly useful for these purposes and for monitoring the student's progress toward goals.

Unfortunately, many traditional assessment practices have little relevance to the educational needs of behaviorally disordered students, particularly at the point of designing and monitoring intervention. When pupils are referred for maladaptive school behavior, it is reasonable to question the logic of extensive efforts to assess medical, mental, home, and other conditions that usually play an unknown causal role, often cannot be remedied anyway, and seldom indicate either educational goals or teaching procedures (Cullinan et al., 1982; Kauffman, 1981).

Age-Level Distinctions

Each assessment method has been used at various student levels, but different ages often call for differences in the complexity and content of assessment. For example, a sociometric procedure for preschool and early elementary students is included in the *Test of Early Socioemotional Development* (Hresko & Brown, 1984). The names of three friends are solicited privately from each student in a class, and a group tabulation can identify unpopular youngsters who may need assistance. In contrast, Bower's (1969) *Student Survey* sociometric for secondary school students presents a list of positive and negative behavior descriptions; for example, "A student who gets into fights or quarrels with other students" (p. 207). Each student writes the name of a classmate who best fits the description, and a tabulation may reveal a consensus of peer perceptions. It can be important to identify a student perceived negatively by many peers, as well as a student not suggested for either positive or negative descriptions. In similar ways, the objectives and content of other assessment methods for behavior disorders vary by the age of the student.

Intervention

The psychoeducational, behavioral, and ecological models involve intervention principles and techniques that are compatible with the different views of behavior disorders they represent. How each of these models looks at the nature of behavior disorders and the role of education in helping these youngsters is reviewed briefly in Table 6-3.

Psychoeducational Interventions

Surface behavior management (Long & Newman, 1976) includes practices designed to prevent or minimize the unfortunate results of disordered behavior on the student herself, fellow students, or the ongoing program. Management techniques include (1) designing the structure, schedule, and other program aspects so as to avoid behavior problems; (2) letting students know which behaviors are permitted or at least temporarily tolerated; and (3) interfering with behaviors that cannot be tolerated by giving verbal or physical expressions of support, changing tasks, or sep-

Table 6-3   Comparison of psychoeducational, behavioral, and ecological models

Model	Nature of Behavior Disorder	Appropriate Educational Intervention
Psychoeducational	Biological energies and parental actions together influence the child's personality development for better or for worse. Maladaptive behavior and emotions are signs of improper personality development. Though not always apparent, these personality weaknesses can be activated by stress created by home, school, or other problems; the result often is behavior disorders.	The teacher must help students understand their problems and effectively cope with them. This is best accomplished when the teacher develops a trusting and respectful relationship with students, teaches them to recognize and manage stressful situations, and helps them to develop appropriate personal strengths for dealing with future challenges in life. School activities often need to be individualized for each student. Games, simulations, arts, and other nontraditional activities are favored.
Behavioral	Psychologists have discovered key principles of learning that describe how behavior is learned and maintained. These principles apply even to behavior disorders. For instance, children can learn maladaptive behaviors and emotions by observing them in a peer or parent. Also, when teachers pay attention to disruptive, strange, or self-defeating behavior, they may be reinforcing these maladaptive behaviors unintentionally but quite effectively.	The teacher must identify deficient behaviors to increase and excessive behaviors to decrease. Identified behaviors are measured often, so that the teacher remains aware of behavior changes. The teacher teaches and reinforces adaptive social, academic, or other behaviors in order to increase them. On the other hand, maladaptive behaviors must not be reinforced. Students can be taught to take control of their own education by learning to identify, measure, and reinforce behaviors needing improvement.
Ecological	Each child operates as a part of various social systems, including systems involving the school. The child's behavior may fit harmoniously with the other parts of the system; if it does not, the system may become disturbed and not function smoothly. Other persons in the system (e.g., teacher, classmates, principal) react by identifying this child as disordered. But in fact, the system—not any one part of it—is what is disordered.	The teacher must understand all parts of the disturbed system so that a variety of changes can be tried to eliminate disturbance. The student may be taught new competencies or helped to give up maladaptive behavior patterns. But just as important are other changes: modifying the expectations and attitudes of teachers, classmates, parents, and others, obtaining resources needed to provide a more supportive educational situation; and helping to mobilize psychological, health, or other services that impact systems outside the school.

A life-space interview explores what's involved in a crisis, leading to an attempt to foster self-control.

arating the student from a provocative situation. The *life-space interview* (Redl, 1959) is an on-the-spot verbal exploration of a crisis situation in which the teacher's goal is (1) to help the young person overcome strong emotions and return to ongoing activities (emotional first aid) and/or (2) to promote the student's insight into environmental, emotional, and other factors that lie behind her maladaptive behaviors (clinical exploitation of events). *Reality therapy* (Glasser, 1969) and *transactional analysis* (Harris, 1976) are examples of here-and-now psychodynamic therapies that have been adapted for use in special education situations; their emphasis is on personal responsibility for one's own life and a commitment to reasonable and fairly specific behavior changes.

Psychoeducational curricula are collections of activities intended to provide students with understanding and greater control of feelings and thoughts. For example, the Self-Control Curriculum (Fagen, Long, & Stevens, 1975) shows how to assess and teach eight personal skills believed necessary for a student to control her own emotional impulses: attention, memory, sequencing, anticipating, understanding feelings, coping with frustration, delaying actions, and relaxing.

Behavioral Interventions

Behavior modification interventions rely on a relatively few basic teaching strategies. *Positive reinforcement* is a procedure in which a particular behavior is followed by a reward, with the result that this behavior is more likely to be performed in the future. For example, if a student shares academic or play materials with a peer and is then positively reinforced by the teacher's compliments and praise, he is more likely to share in the future. *Negative reinforcement* is also a procedure for making a behavior more likely to occur; it involves the removal of unpleasant stimuli after a specific behavior is performed. For instance, a teacher might tell students that the arithmetic assignment is in two parts and that anyone completing the first part with perfect accuracy will not be required to do the second part. The behavior of a student who completes the first part perfectly will be negatively reinforced by removal of the requirement to complete the second part, and that student will be more likely to complete such assignments accurately in the future. *Punishment* is a process in which a behavior is made less likely to occur again in the future because it is presently followed by some aversive consequence. If a student who throws books and supplies on the floor is required, as a consequence, not only to clean up his own mess but to straighten and clean the room, his trashing behavior is punished and made less likely to recur. Alternatively, behavior can be punished by consequences that either (1) withdraw a specific amount of reward (*response cost* procedure) or (2) prevent access to rewards for a certain period of time (*time out* procedure). For example, the teacher can discourage unauthorized moving about the classroom by either removing a specified privilege or withdrawing a few minutes of recess. *Extinction* is a procedure to decrease the likelihood of behavior that has formerly been reinforced. For example, some teachers attend to and thereby unintentionally reinforce excessively dependent behaviors, such as repetitious requests for clarification or approval. A teacher who recognizes that she has been encouraging dependency in this way may decide to ignore unnecessary requests. This procedure is extinction if it succeeds in reducing the dependent behavior. For details of these and related operant conditioning principles, see Ferster and Culbertson (1982) and Schwartz (1984).

These basic procedures can be combined in various ways to yield other useful teaching techniques. A *token economy* is a simulated economic system based on some sort of token reinforcer, such as check marks, stickers, points, or play money (see Kazdin, 1977). This highly versatile procedure can control a broad range of behavior problems in various settings. Individual students or groups may earn tokens for some specified behaviors and lose them for others. Tokens can be redeemed for desirable items and privileges. Teachers can even simulate economic features of society such as saving, lay-away, interest, inflation, and price reductions. Educational programs based on token reinforcement have been used to improve academic skills, conduct, and other behaviors relevant to the normalization of behaviorally disordered pupils.

A *behavioral contract* is a written description of the relationships between a person's behaviors and the consequences for performing them. A contract should specify (1) responsibilities—the target behaviors to be performed; (2) monitoring—the ways in which the pupil's performance is to be observed and recorded; and (3) privileges—reinforcers earned by the pupil upon completion of the responsibilities. The various aspects of the contract should be agreeable to both teacher and pupil; some negotiation may be required.

Recently behavior modification procedures have been developed for groups of pupils, even entire classrooms. Two advantages of *group contingencies* are that the power of the peer group is utilized to encourage appropriate behavior and teacher time and effort is saved to be more appropriately used (Litow & Pumroy, 1975). The two main types are interdependent and dependent group-oriented contingencies. In an interdependent contingency the performance of the group as a whole determines the consequences for each member of that group. In a dependent contingency the performance of one member of the group can determine the consequences for each member of the group.

Overcorrection (Azrin & Besalel, 1980) consists of two basic components—restitution and positive practice. The restitution procedure requires the person to correct the disruption resulting from his inappropriate behavior; he must restore the environment to its condition before the behavior took place or to an even better state. The positive-practice procedure requires the person to practice behaviors repeatedly that are related to but more adaptive or useful than the inappropriate target behavior. Overcorrection procedures are intended to be tailored to a particular inappropriate behavior, so a wide variety of specific applications exist.

Although many behavior modification procedures feature the teacher as planner, recorder, and implementer of behavior change, it is also possible for a student to serve in these roles. Although many aspects of behavioral *self-management* are still poorly understood and controversial (see Bandura, 1978; Catania, 1975), there clearly are useful self-management techniques relevant to the needs of the behaviorally disordered (Meichenbaum, 1977; Polsgrove, 1979). These varied techniques generally involve students in observing, recording, instructing, rewarding, and/or punishing their own behaviors.

Behavior Modification with Severe Behavior Disorders Autistic and other severely disordered children have received extensive attention from behavioral researchers (see Schreibman & Mills, 1983). The work of Ivar Lovaas and his colleagues (Lovaas & Newsom, 1976) was pivotal in establishing behavioral techniques for teaching important skills to individual autistic youngsters. Recently these techniques have been extended to groups of autistic students. Koegel, Russo, and Rincover (1977) have identified five teaching skills as particularly crucial: (1) giving clear, concise instructions; (2) providing sufficient physical guidance, demonstrations, and other prompts for the desired behaviors and knowing how to remove these prompts gradually as the pupil begins to respond properly without them; (3) providing immediate, effective consequences—primarily edibles and praise for correct behaviors, extinction or time out for inappropriate behaviors; (4) presenting each instruction as a separate response opportunity so the student will not become distracted or confused; and (5) knowing how to shape a desired final behavior by reinforcing responses that are each one step nearer the goal.

In addition to how autistic students should be taught, it is important to consider what they should be taught. Most behavior goals must be approached on a step-by-step basis, so teachers need task analysis and instructional programming skills to specify the steps. Fortunately, carefully specified step-by-step instructional programs for some of these important skills are now available (Lovaas, 1977). Guidelines for teaching autistic students individually, in groups, or even in a regular classroom are provided by Koegel (1981) and Koegel and Schreibman (1981).

Ecological Interventions

Proponents of the ecological viewpoint have provided some general recommendations relevant to education for the behaviorally disordered (Apter, 1982). First, they suggest that the educational system (indeed, society as a whole) should become more accepting of deviant behavior so that fewer students are labeled as behaviorally disordered. Further, when treatment is needed, changes in the educational environment should be targeted as carefully as modifications in the student's behavior (Rhodes, 1970). In addition, it is emphasized that a localized ecosystem, such as the classroom, is subtly but significantly interrelated with other ecosystems, such as the home and community; therefore, the only effective intervention is one that goes beyond the local problem to bring about changes on a larger scale. Thus, ecological special educators argue for a redefinition and expansion of teaching practices to include work with other teachers, involvement with parents and the community, and active child advocacy to help others recognize the needs and rights of children.

Juvenile Corrections

The exact relationship between juvenile delinquency and behavior disorders is unclear; but certainly some juvenile delinquents experience severe disorders, many evidence mild to moderate disorders, and special education needs to play a larger treatment role in the field of juvenile corrections. Educators of these youths should be aware of the programs available to juvenile delinquents. The following two program descriptions represent innovative approaches.

Teaching-Family Model The teaching-family model (T-F) (Phillips, Phillips, Fixsen, & Wolf, 1972) is a community-based group-home program developed by behavioral psychologists. About 6 to 10 youths (delinquents or predelinquents) live in the typical T-F home with a specially trained wife-husband team (teaching parents). The teaching parents establish a realistic home environment; teach the youths the daily routine of living in a family; instruct various academic, vocational, interpersonal, self-management, and other adaptive skills the youths need; and teach them to recognize the consequences of their actions.

The T-F model uses numerous well-developed and evaluated features to establish effective handling of two important areas: the environment in which the youths reside and the treatment strategies. To provide an environment that will aid treatment and simplify running the T-F home, attention is given to assigning specific responsibilities to specific staff, training staff carefully, using professional consultants, and developing a realistic home atmosphere. Several T-F procedures facilitate effective treatment. First, a curriculum is used that outlines the skills necessary for successful adjustment in the community. Upon entry into the program each youth is assessed to identify those skills that need attention. Second, identified skills are taught through positive reinforcement of appropriate behavior. Third, a multilevel token program is used to motivate and acknowledge youth participation and improvement. A self-government system allows youth the opportunity to discuss and actually exert control over accomplishments, goals, house rules, and problems of day-to-day life. The teaching parents also maintain close contact with the local schools and work with teachers to manage school behavior. Finally, substantial training and follow-up consultation are given to the youth's family so that behavior improvements taught in the T-F home are maintained upon return to the natural home. The T-F model has undergone extensive scientific evaluation and has fared well, particularly in comparison to the poor record of most programs for delinquents.

TA for Delinquents

The use of transactional analysis (TA) for incarcerated juvenile delinquents was studied in the Youth Center Research Project (Jessness, 1975). Youths assigned to Close School, a major California detention facility for youths, took part in the TA intervention. Each youth and his caseworker explored important life problems (the life script) in order to negotiate TA treatment contracts that focused on educational, personal, and social behavior. During the negotiations the youths were encouraged to select specific goals to address problems that they wished to correct. Small-group meetings and individual conferences allowed each youth further opportunities to set, evaluate, and move toward the established goals; progress was evaluated by a treatment team as well. Another aspect of treatment was the "community meeting" held three times weekly in each residence hall, giving youths and staff the chance to discuss a wide array of matters, particularly situations that interfered with orderly living in the residence halls. TA principles were also applied in classrooms and in everyday management of the youths. Careful scientific evaluations of the project indicated that this approach holds considerable promise.

Age-Level Distinctions

Each intervention technique can be used with any behaviorally disordered student, but age may need to be considered in determining the objectives and application of an intervention. For example, behavioral self-management techniques have been employed with students of all ages. In the *Think Aloud* program (Camp & Bash, 1981; Camp & Ray, 1984) aggressive primary-grade students have been taught to give themselves appropriate instructions, use new skills to avoid problems in social situations, and evaluate their decisions, resulting in beneficial effects on the behavior and thinking of these young boys. Socially maladjusted junior high students can be taught similar but more complex anger-control techniques (Feindler, Marriott, & Iwata, 1984), including how to reinterpret provocative situations in order to reduce arousal and conflict and how to envision adaptive, nonaggressive responses to such situations. Self-management has also been useful with older adolescent girls in a correctional institution (Seymour & Stokes, 1976). These young people were taught to record their own productive educational and vocational-training behaviors, and the self-recorded behaviors clearly improved. Like behavioral self-management, other intervention techniques often have to be applied in ways that take into account the age level of the student.

Curriculum Implications

Curriculum development for use with behaviorally disordered pupils has lagged behind the progress made in some other areas of special education. Although the characteristics and classroom behaviors of such children and adolescents are known, there are very few empirically based, commercially available curricula. The main exception to this void is in the area of social-skills training. Social skills have been defined by Cartledge and Milburn (1980) as "those behaviors which involve interaction between the child and his peers or adults when the primary intent is the achievement of the child's or adult's goals through positive interactions" (p. 7). Since behaviorally disordered pupils often possess significant social-skills deficits, curricula designed to enhance competence in this area are of special interest to their teachers.

Age-Level Distinctions

School Age The ACCEPTS (A Curriculum for Children's Effective Peer and Teacher Skills) Social Skills Curriculum (Walker et al., 1983) was designed to teach critically important social behavior skills necessary for successful adjustment to the behavioral demands of mainstream settings. The primary goal of the ACCEPTS program is to prepare handicapped children in kindergarten through sixth grade to enter and succeed within less restrictive settings. A related goal is to teach skills that enhance classroom adjustment and contribute to peer acceptance. ACCEPTS includes 28 skills that are grouped into five major content areas: (1) classroom skills, (2) basic interaction skills, (3) getting along, (4) making friends, and (5) coping skills. The classroom skills area focuses on those competencies essential for successful classroom adjustment as defined by teachers (e.g., listening to instruction, following directions). The other four areas focus on skills needed for competent interaction with others.

The ACCEPTS curriculum is based on a direct instruction model that emphasizes clearly defining and sequencing the skills to be taught, providing examples and nonexamples to clearly communicate the skills, utilizing a variety of practice activities during instruction, and using systematic correction procedures when errors are made. The instructional format allows for one-to-one, small group, or large group presentation. Depending on the rate of pupil progress, the program can be completed within 5 to 10 weeks. In controlled evaluations the ACCEPTS program not only taught social behavior skills but led to observable changes in the behavior of handicapped children in classroom and playground settings.

Secondary   A secondary school social skills curriculum is Structured Learning (Goldstein, Sprafkin, Gershaw, & Klein, 1980). The Structured Learning curriculum includes four major components—modeling, role-playing, feedback, and transfer training. Modeling refers to presenting a group of pupils with a demonstration of the skill behaviors the pupils are to learn. Following the demonstration, the pupils are given an opportunity to role-play and practice the skills that were demonstrated. In the feedback component the teacher and other pupils provide the role-

---

Model Program

A model education program for adolescents with behavior disorders is the Stemmers Run program (Heaton, Safer, & Allen, 1982; Heaton, Safer, Allen, Spinnato, & Prumo, 1976; Safer, Heaton, & Parker, 1982). Designed for educating multiply suspended students showing aggression-disruption and social maladjustment, this program is staffed by regular education teachers, an aide, and an assistant principal, with outside consultant support.

The Stemmers Run program is oriented toward academic remediation and behavior modification that relies heavily on a token economy. The school day is divided into morning and afternoon phases. The morning phase consists of one period each of English, math, social studies, and science, taught in the special class by regular teachers. Individualized remedial instruction is managed through behavioral contracts that clearly tie specified work to specified grades. During the morning phase students work on a token economy, earning points for promptness,

learning readiness, being on-task, and other appropriate behaviors, including conduct outside the classroom. For misconduct the student is warned on the first offense and sent to the assistant principal for a brief detention and "cooling off" on the second offense.

The afternoon phase is largely concerned with providing reward opportunities. Based on points earned earlier, students can buy access to a reinforcement room to play card games, table tennis, slot racing, pool, or records and can even buy early dismissal for that day. If insufficient points are earned in the morning, a student has to continue academic assignments to earn enough points for afternoon rewards.

Parent participation is encouraged. Parents can deliver home rewards based on weekly report cards of progress and can receive training and support from the school staff. The Stemmers Run program prepares students for regular class reentry by gradually removing daily points and afternoon rewards, teaching students to self-evaluate their daily performance.

player with encouragement and perhaps suggestions for improvement as the behavior becomes more like the model. Finally, transfer of training involves a number of procedures designed to increase the likelihood that the behavior will be performed in real-life situations.

The Structured Learning curriculum includes 50 skills that fall into the following six content areas: (1) beginning social skills, (2) advanced social skills, (3) skills for dealing with feelings, (4) skill alternatives to aggression, (5) skills for dealing with stress, and (6) planning skills. To be placed at the appropriate position in the curriculum, the student is rated for competence on each of the 50 skills by a teacher or other individual familiar with the student's behavior. Pupils with similar skill deficits should be grouped together. For each of the 50 skills the developers have written a behavioral description and have given tips to facilitate training as well as suggestions for the content of the modeling and other helpful recommendations. The curriculum is presented in a small-group format of five to eight pupils and two adults. Several studies have evaluated the use of Structured Learning with aggressive, antisocial adolescents. The findings consistently showed that the program successfully trained such social skills as empathy, negotiating, assertiveness, following instructions, self-control, and perspective taking (Goldstein et al., 1980).

The ACCEPTS program and Structured Learning are curriculum packages designed to improve the social skills of handicapped children. Evaluations indicate that social-skills curricula can bring about important changes in the social competence and adjustment of the treated pupils. Further work is needed to see how the important behavior changes can be better maintained over time and extended to other settings. Also, as Walker et al. (1983) point out, social-skills training alone is not likely to remediate all the problems of behaviorally disordered students. They recommend the use of powerful behavior modification procedures to control inappropriate behavior along with social-skills training to provide the student with adaptive, socially acceptable ways of dealing with people.

Mainstreaming

Mainstreaming behaviorally disordered pupils successfully is a complex task. Once such pupils are removed from regular classrooms and placed into educationally segregated settings, regular classroom teachers and administrators are likely to feel relieved and less responsible for the pupils' education. Regular teachers do not always look forward to the pupils' return. Thus, prior to removing a pupil from a regular class, every effort should be made to provide consultation and other help to the regular teacher in order to maintain that pupil in the regular class setting.

We believe that the concept of mainstreaming behaviorally disordered pupils is appropriate. At present, though, many questions exist as to how best to put such a concept into practice. Unfortunately, research on the efficacy of mainstreaming such pupils is not common, so research provides few guidelines. Two well-developed ideas that appear to have much potential for integrating students with behavior problems into regular education are described here.

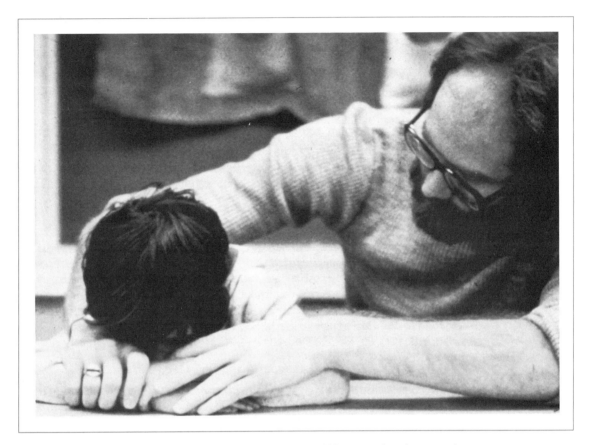

Meeting the needs of a behaviorally disordered student within a regular class requires skill and commitment.

Madison School Plan

The Madison School Plan provides special education support according to pupils' readiness for regular classroom functioning. Four levels of programming are offered, based on students' competence. The lowest level, Preacademic I, emphasizes basic skills of attending, following directions, and being on-task. It is essentially a special class with extensive behavior modification, remedial work, and other highly structured features. Preacademic II stresses taking part in activities and getting along with others. Here there are fewer students and more natural reinforcers (e.g., praise instead of treats), assignments resemble regular class work, and there is some regular education participation. As students develop competencies, they move to levels that emphasize the development of academic skills. At the third level, Academic I, there is a simulation of the regular classroom, with grades given on a daily or hourly basis and natural reinforcers only. Also, there is substantial regular class participation and regular class work. Finally, the Academic II level is full participation in a regular classroom, with close cooperation of regular and special teachers.

The Madison plan uses two average-size classrooms that are subdivided into the three special or transitional settings. Thus, pupils can begin at the lowest level (self-contained) and gradually move into the regular classroom as they develop the necessary skills. Also, students may be placed originally at some level other than the lowest, as appropriate.

The Madison School Plan was not originally designed exclusively for the behaviorally disordered. However, it has high logical appeal for use with these students. Unfortunately, there is at present no research support for the efficacy of the Madison plan in reintegrating behaviorally disordered students.

CLASS Program

Contingencies for Learning Academic and Social Skills (CLASS) is designed to allow regular classroom teachers to control the aggressive and disruptive behavior of a pupil. It integrates several separate behavioral interventions into a teaching package. Prior to intervention, baseline data are collected on disruptive behaviors in the regular class. This information is compared with other referral information to clarify selection decisions and goals of intervention. The student's teacher, principal, parents, and the targeted student herself are then presented with the CLASS package.

The CLASS program itself contains several elements. First, there is a classroom group-oriented contingency. The targeted pupil earns points for displaying appropriate classroom behavior and following the teacher's rules. The teacher also praises the pupil each time a point is earned. Second, if enough points are earned during the day, the entire class shares in a preselected reward (extra recess, playing a game, or the like). Third, arrangements are made with the parents to provide a home reward such as extra TV time or treats when the pupil brings home a satisfactory daily report card, which is available only if the pupil has earned a sufficient number of points.

CLASS is initially carried out and demonstrated by the consultant, but the classroom teacher very soon begins to assume an active role. Within several days he is implementing CLASS with little or no consultant help. As this program moves to completion, the use of points is phased out as teacher praise begins to maintain the pupil's appropriate behavior. The CLASS program is designed to be completed in about 2 months.

Research supports the efficacy and replicability of CLASS for elementary school students with behavior problems. CLASS has usually been implemented to prevent the need for additional special services. However, it appears to be quite suitable for use as an aid to reintegration of a behaviorally disordered student into regular education.

The success of programs such as the Madison School Plan and CLASS is dependent on many factors, including implementation of the total program. Unfortunately, not many teachers are able to implement composite programs. A number of common sense strategies for regular classroom teachers to use in integrating behaviorally disordered pupils are included in the Tips for Helping section at the end of the chapter.

Age-Level Distinctions

Mainstreaming students with behavior disorders is not an exact science by any means, and many factors need to be weighed to ensure its success. Some of these factors are the attitudes and behavior of students, teachers, and others involved; the similarity of the student's functioning and the performance expected in the regular classroom; the range and quality of support for the mainstream effort; and the personal characteristics, such as age, of the mainstreamed student. For instance, some plans for educating behaviorally disordered students in regular classes rely extensively on parents' ability to present or withhold reinforcers at home. But as children grow older, parents seem to control fewer and fewer powerful reinforcers. Thus, some mainstreaming practices are poorly suited for older age levels. Similarly, mainstreaming practices that rely on extensive verbal material may be more appropriate for use with older students having better verbal proficiency.

Innovation and Development

Serving the Underserved

P.L. 94–142 places a priority on special education for underserved groups of handicapped students. Historically, children with behavior disorders have been underserved (Kauffman & Kneedler, 1981), but two subgroups have been most neglected: those with severe behavior disorders and adolescents. By requiring that these individuals receive a free, appropriate education, P.L. 94–142 ushered in significant program development and progress in these areas.

Autism and other severe disorders have always been of great interest to special educators, but until recently they have generally been seen as belonging in the realm of medicine and psychotherapy. Neurological deficits, parental mistakes, or other suspected causes were diagnosed; but unless the family could support expensive private treatment, the child was usually given only meager services in clinics or custodial care in public mental hospitals. Recent legal developments have established the rights of severely disordered children and youth to appropriate educational and related services, and many school districts are beginning to provide for such students.

One special program for these children and adolescents is the Treatment and Education of Autistic and Related Communication Handicapped Children (TEACCH) program. Under the direction of Eric Schopler and associates (Lansing & Schopler, 1978; Schopler & Mesibov, 1983; Schopler, Reichler, & Lansing, 1980) TEACCH has evolved into a multidiscipline, multiagency effort located in and supported by North Carolina. TEACCH is an organization of regional centers for assessment and intervention; each center is associated with special education class-rooms in local public schools. Upon referral to a center, the child is assessed to determine learning needs. Educational goals and strategies are developed, parents are taught how to provide education at home, and the child may be assigned to a TEACCH-style special classroom near the home.

Several concepts or features distinguish TEACCH. First, parents are central to all aspects of service. They are consulted in assessment, trained to teach their children at home, expected to help teach and otherwise participate at school, and assisted in organizing advocacy and communication networks. Further, TEACCH is built on a maturational-developmental concept that influences assessment and teaching activities. Third, assessment and intervention are highly individualized for each student. Such individualization can be difficult for severely handicapped students, who often have rare problems and are geographically spread out, but the TEACCH staff works with many agencies to secure appropriate services in the student's home communities.

Appropriate special education is not widely available for adolescents, and services for adolescents with behavior disorders are especially underdeveloped. There are several reasons for this situation: (1) secondary education is more subject oriented than student oriented; (2) most practices in special education assessment, intervention, administration, and teacher training programs were developed with younger students in mind; and (3) behaviorally disordered adolescents often act in ways that discourage educators from offering help. Only recently have special educators widely acknowledged the need to develop programs uniquely designed for adolescents with behavior disorders (Cullinan et al., 1983).

Professional Issues

Since the passage of P.L. 94–142 there have been political, economic, and other changes. For example, the advisability of extensive government regulations and the cost of government social programs have been passionately debated, and such debates have touched P.L. 94–142 as well. There have even been attempts—unsuccessful so far—to amend critical aspects of this law. Further, there is reason to believe that some education agencies have circumvented the intent of the law. Although the federal guesstimate is that 2% of all students are behaviorally disordered, fewer than 1% have actually been identified. This discrepancy may stem from administrative reluctance to actively identify all students who should receive services for the behaviorally disordered because P.L. 94–142 requires all identified handicapped students to be provided with appropriate education and related services (Kauffman, 1980). Clearly, we need to understand and carefully monitor our profession's relationship with government and our implementation of policy as we plan for improvements in appropriate education for behaviorally disordered students.

Another issue is the degree of attrition among teachers of the behaviorally disordered, estimated at more than 50% over a recent 5-year period (Huntze & Grosenick, 1980). One probable reason is burnout, defined as "emotional exhaustion resulting from the stress of interpersonal contact" (Maslach, 1978, p. 56). The teacher who experiences burnout has difficulty coping with the continued stress of teaching and may lose concern and emotional feeling for the students she is responsible for helping. Stress and the potential for burnout are certainly not unique to teachers of students with behavior disorders, but the significance of special education for these students makes it especially important to develop methods of coping.

Maintaining the capability to teach well is one important countermeasure against burnout. Competent teaching also increases the satisfaction that results from seeing students improve in social, personal, academic, and self-help areas. Research is sorely needed to identify specific details, but general areas of competency can be described (see Pattavina, 1984; Polsgrove & Reith, 1980). For example, teachers of behaviorally disordered students should be able to (1) select, administer, and interpret procedures to assess student functioning; (2) state and evaluate progress toward teaching objectives; (3) manage and improve the learning and behavior of individual students and groups of students; (4) communicate and work with other professionals, paraprofessionals, parents, and others who can help with the remediation effort; and (5) plan, implement, adapt, and evaluate instructional methods and curricula.

Research

Until recently there was very little empirical research based on behaviorally disordered students, and much more needs to be done to determine the best ways to identify, assess, and educationally treat students with behavior disorders. A few of the more pressing research questions are discussed here.

How can special educators more effectively and efficiently intervene with the behavior disorders of children and youth? Many widely used and often-recommended teaching procedures have not yet been objectively evaluated with behaviorally disordered students (Epstein, Cullinan, & Rose, 1980). Also, educational procedures often consist of several component parts; thus, even if it has been shown that a certain procedure works, it is not known whether some of the components can be omitted without loss of effectiveness. In cases where some components are expensive, time consuming, or dependent on extensive teacher training, component analysis research may show how the intervention procedure can be streamlined. In addition, when two or more well-developed intervention procedures or programs exist, they can be directly compared in a study. For example, direct comparisons have shown the feasibility of using behavior modification interventions as an alternative to drug therapy in treatment of hyperactivity (Kazdin & Wilson, 1978). If research shows that one procedure produces superior results, there may be implications for school program changes, teaching competencies, and the like.

How can we determine whether behavior changes are of real value? A wide variety of areas of student functioning may be selected for intervention; changes in functioning may be great or small. Recently, researchers have begun to focus on ways to evaluate whether changes produced by an intervention result in practical, personally and socially worthwhile improvements. Such evaluation, often referred to as *social validation* (Kazdin, 1977), may involve (1) determining whether the changes have brought the student's performance within the range of acceptable levels (social comparison technique) and/or (2) having teachers, parents, and other important individuals in the student's social environment judge their level of satisfaction with the behavior change (subjective evaluation technique). Social validation deals with how closely the student's functioning fits expectations of appropriate performance, a major consideration in the definition of behavior disorders.

Are the improvements in student functioning generalized to other settings and maintained over time? Most behavior changes that are not durable are of only limited importance to special educators. In addition, an intervention capable of improving student functioning in the classroom would be of far greater practical value if it also led to similar improvements in other settings without the need to reapply the intervention in each setting. To date, there is too little research on the generalized effects of educational treatments for behaviorally disordered pupils. Both the generalized and enduring effects of educational procedures demand attention.

Can students with behavior disorders be taught self-control? Teachers of behaviorally disordered pupils have become increasingly interested in the training of self-control skills. The very nature of self-control is debated from a number of viewpoints. Behaviorists view self-control training as the teaching of specific self-management behaviors—self-observation, self-recording, self-instruction, self-reinforcement, or punishment—so that a student can use these behaviors to modify his functioning in other areas. Psychoeducationists see self-control training as developing the student's inner capacity to monitor and regulate personal behavior flexibly and adaptively (Fagen et al., 1975). Both behavioral and psychoeducational teaching procedures and curricula are available for teaching self-control (e.g., Bash & Camp, 1980; Fagen et al., 1975). Ironically, however, there is relatively little scientific research on self-control of the behaviorally disordered, and existing results are equivocal (Epstein et al., 1980). Researchers need to identify the variables associated with effective self-control training for behaviorally disordered students and evaluate the efficacy of these training programs.

Teachers of the behaviorally disordered can hardly be expected to make major research contributions, but they must keep abreast of the issues, be critical consumers of research findings, and demand reasonable evidence of the value of any intervention that is recommended by an expert. Perhaps more than any other single factor, the movement toward better research holds the key to advances in special education for students with behavior disorders.

Summary

Contemporary special education for students with behavior disorders is a recent development that has been diversely influenced. Developments in education, medicine, and psychodynamic and behavioral psychology as well as social and economic trends have all affected education for students with behavior disorders.

Although there have been many attempts to define behavior disorders, no definition is universally accepted by special educators or other professionals. However, there are two broad areas common to most authoritative definitions. Children with behavior disorders (1) deviate from standards or expectations of behavior and (2) impair the functioning of others or themselves. Federal prevalence estimates cite less than 1% of the school-age population as being behaviorally disordered—a questionable figure.

Many factors contribute to normal and atypical development. Heredity, brain disorder, diet, broken families, home conflict, improper discipline, peer influence, schools, poverty, and stress are some of the factors that contribute to behavior disorders. Some behavior disorders arise from the interaction of biological and psychological conditions. Three major models have evolved to explain behavior disorders. The psychoeducational model is based on mental conflicts, especially conflicts that are set in motion by stress. The behavioral model explains disorders in terms of the effect of specific environmental events. The ecological model views a behavior disorder as an imperfect interaction within an ecosystem.

The major characteristics of behavior disorders fall under the general categories of environmental conflict, personal disturbance, and learning disorders. Environmental conflict is characterized by aggression-disruption, hyperactivity, and social maladjustment. Anxiety and social withdrawal are associated with personal disturbance. Typically, students with behavior disorders exhibit learning disorders, including below-average academic achievement and intellectual abilities.

Severe to profound behavior disorders are mainly of two types: infantile autism and childhood schizophrenia. Pupils with severe behavior disorders may show aggression, over- and underactivity, self-stimulation, social withdrawal, and cognitive disorders.

Psychoeducational, behavioral, and ecological models involve intervention principles and techniques compatible with their different views of behavior disorders. Psychoeducational techniques use surface behavior management, the life-space interview, and several here-and-now therapies including reality therapy and transactional analysis. Behavior modification strategies use positive and negative reinforcement, punishment, extinction, token economy, behavior contracts, group contingencies, overcorrection, and self-management to alter behavior. Ecological techniques call for modifications of the total environment and stress child advocacy.

Curriculum development for behaviorally disordered pupils has not kept up with progress in some other areas of special education. The exception is in the area of social skills. Behaviorally disordered pupils often possess significant social-skill deficits that limit their chances to be placed in regular settings. The ACCEPTS Social Skills Curriculum and Structured Learning are curriculum packages designed to improve the social competence of handicapped children. Social-skills training that provides adaptive, socially acceptable ways of interacting with others will improve pupils' chances of being mainstreamed. There are also a number of common sense strategies for teachers to use in mainstreaming pupils.

P.L. 94–142 placed a priority on special education for underserved groups of handicapped students. Pupils with severe behavior disorders and adolescents have been among the most neglected. Although a few exemplary educational programs are available, much remains to be learned through research.

Study Questions .

1. How have developments in education, medicine, and psychodynamic and behavioral psychology shaped contemporary special education for behaviorally disordered pupils?

2. Describe the factors that contribute to the problem of finding a consensus definition of behavior disorders.

3. A definition of behavior disorders with a special education orientation was provided. Discuss the aspects of that definition that make it relevant to special educators.

4. Differentiate causes of behavior disorders that are necessary-and-sufficient conditions and those that are contributory conditions.

5. Research has identified several biological and psychological conditions that can be important determinants of behavior disorder. Discuss the educational implications of these conditions, particularly as they relate to teachers of pupils with behavior disorders.

6. The psychoeducational, behavioral, and ecological models provide different explanations of the behavior disorders of children and adolescents. Describe how each model would explain the disordered behavior of Sandy in the opening profile. Then discuss the interventions likely to be implemented by each model.

7. Environmental conflict and personal disturbance are the major behavior problems exhibited by pupils with behavior disorders. Describe how these problems are likely to be displayed in classroom settings.

8. Describe the intellectual functioning and academic performance of typical students with behavior disorders. How would this affect day-to-day expectations and planning for appropriate education?

9. Many traditional assessment practices have little relevance to the educational needs of behaviorally disordered students. What are some questions that teachers should consider when choosing assessment instruments and reviewing assessment data?

10. Behaviorally disordered pupils often possess significant social-skill deficits. Identify curriculum programs designed to enhance competence in this area and the components of these curricula that make them effective.

11. Several educational programs and curricula were mentioned as models for appropriate education. What features separate these programs from others for behaviorally disordered pupils?

12. If you had recently been hired as a mainstreaming consultant for a local school district, what would your recommendation be to the staff for establishing a mainstreaming program for behaviorally disordered pupils?

13. Much more research needs to be done on the best ways to identify, assess, and educationally treat students with behavior disorders. Given that such research will be done within the next decade, identify the significant educational innovations or changes likely to result from such research.

TIPS FOR HELPING

1. Provide a carefully structured environment with regard to physical features of the room, scheduling and routines, and rules of conduct. If there are to be unstructured activities, you must clearly distinguish them from structured activities in terms of time, place, and expectations.

2. Let your pupils know the expectations you have, the objectives that have been established for them, and the help you will give them in achieving those objectives. When appropriate, seek input from them about their strengths, weaknesses, and goals.

3. Reinforce appropriate behavior; inappropriate behavior should be ignored or mildly punished. Model appropriate behavior and refrain from behavior you do not wish students to imitate.

4. Do not expect behaviorally disordered students to have immediate success; work for improvement on a long-term basis. Reinforce approximations to or attempts at the desired behavior. Continue with the intervention strategy being used when a student is making progress toward an objective; try another way if there is no progress.

5. Be fair, be consistent, but temper your consistency with flexibility.

6. Be sensitive to your students as individuals and as a class; balance individual needs with group requirements.

7. Try to understand the frustrations, hopes, and fears of your students and their parents.

7

Communication Disorders

Linda McCormick
University of Hawaii

John is an active 6-year-old who spends part of the school day in a special class for children with communication disorders. The remainder of the time he is mainstreamed in a regular kindergarten class. As a baby he was colicky and seemed uninterested in play routines such as pat-a-cake and peek-a-boo. His parents cannot remember his ever pointing or waving bye-bye, but his early development seemed normal otherwise. Sometime after his second birthday they began to be concerned about his language progress because he was producing only two words: "mama" and "baba" (for *bottle*).

John is remarkably skilled at fine motor tasks such as puzzles and mosaics. His hearing and vision are within normal limits, and nonverbal assessments indicate near age-level functioning in cognitive areas (abstraction, classification, and problem solving). However, his expressive language is at the level of a 3-year-old, and his receptive

vocabulary is not substantially higher. John's social development is also below age level, but he has shown marked improvement as a result of 2 years in a mainstream preschool program where there was special programming to increase his social interaction skills. Still, he is more likely to play beside peers than with them, and he rarely initiates an interaction without prompting from the teacher. He tends to use gestures rather than words (even when he knows the appropriate words) and rarely produces action requests (e.g., "Push me" when on the slide). John seldom asks a question and answers most questions with gestures or single words.

John belongs to a subgroup of communication disordered children whose language learning problems cannot be attributed to cognitive, sensory, or motor impairment. His teacher's major goal is to expand his existing skills and help him learn the linguistic and social prerequisites to conversational competence.

Language/communication objectives on his IEP are to increase (1) the meanings that John expresses with his present vocabulary, (2) the range of functions that he can accomplish with his present vocabulary, and (3) his question asking and vocalizations to initiate interactions.

What does it mean to be able to talk and why is John having so much trouble learning the talking skills that his peers have acquired so effortlessly? On the surface, learning to talk may seem relatively simple and straightforward. After all, the overwhelming majority of babies begin talking even before they are out of diapers. However, learning to share information through the medium of arbitrary symbols with culturally prescribed rules is *not* an easy task. The fact that very young children learn to talk and to understand language tends to obscure the enormous complexity of the language system and the oral language learning process. Both are enormously complex—so much so, in fact, that until fairly recently researchers were not able to identify the bases of language or provide a satisfactory description of normal acquisition processes. There is still much to be understood in this important area of human learning, but we have taken some giant steps forward in the past decade. We are now a little closer to the goal of ensuring that all children, even those with the most severe handicaps, learn to communicate effectively and appropriately.

Although we will discuss some communication disorders associated with or resulting from other disabilities, we will be most concerned here with students for whom speech, language, and/or communication disorders are a primary disability. The majority of these students do not demonstrate cognitive, sensory, or motor problems. According to the report on the implementation of P.L. 94–142 (U.S. Department of Education, 1984), this classification is one of four subgroups (the others being the mentally retarded, emotionally disturbed, and learning disabled) that account for more than 75% of the handicapped students served in America's schools. This subgroup is by far the largest being mainstreamed in regular classes.

History

Research

In the 1950s there were two major theories concerning the nature of language and language acquisition. Chomsky (1957), the leading psycholinguist of that period, presented an elaborate description of the grammatical knowledge (psychological processes) underlying language. According to psycholinguistic theory, infants have an innate language acquisition mechanism that assists them in learning their native language. In contrast, behaviorists, notably Skinner (1957), were concerned with the functions served by different types of utterances. They stressed the role of parent modeling and selective reinforcement in language acquisition.

The fifties debate was essentially a variation of the nature-nurture controversy: Do children come equipped with an innate knowledge of language structure and rules that is somehow activated through contact with the language of their culture (the psycholinguistic position); or are they born with no knowledge of language, and do they then learn it through experience (the behaviorist position)? Neither the psycholinguists nor the behaviorists of the fifties were particularly concerned with language disordered children. Other investigators in the disciplines of neurology, psychiatry, pediatrics, and deaf education were beginning to generate some data concerning children's language disorders, but their research provided few practical intervention guidelines (Kirchner & Skarakis-Doyle, 1983).

In the late sixties, just about the time that researchers in speech pathology were beginning to ask meaningful questions about the nature of language disorders, there was a single significant study that redirected the attention of all those interested in language acquisition. Lois Bloom (1970) reported data suggesting that the emergence of language is heavily dependent on the infant's cognitive attainments; in other words, meaning or semantics is the basis of language. Almost simultaneously, three other researchers (Brown, 1973; Schlesinger, 1971; Slobin, 1970) came up with practically identical lists of the concepts underlying children's earliest utterances. The maxim of this new perspective, which came to be called the "semantic revolution," was very simple and logical: children talk when they have something to talk about, and they talk about what they understand (Cromer, 1974). The semantic perspective had important implications for intervention with language disordered children. It suggested a need for concern with the cognitive attainments that Piaget (1952, 1954, 1962) described as occurring during the sensorimotor period.

The semantic revolution was short-lived. By the mid-seventies some researchers had begun to question the premise that cognitive development alone is sufficient to account for early language acquisition (Bates, 1976; Bruner, 1975). The spotlight shifted to the *why* of language. Researchers presented evidence suggesting that effective communication, learned in the context of early caregiver-child interactions, is the motivation for language and learning (Bates, 1976; Bruner, 1975). Their basic premise was that the child learns language in order to affect the environment, and their focus was on the functional and interpersonal characteristics of language and language learning.

Clinical Practice

Both the psycholinguistic and the behavioral perspectives had some influence on clinical practices in the sixties. However, the lack of agreement on the nature of language and normal acquisition processes posed problems for clinicians. They needed to know precisely what to teach and what order in which to teach it. The lack of practical information and the many unanswered questions may explain the appeal of the specific abilities approach that came on the scene then. Specific abilities tests such as the Illinois Test of Psycholinguistic Abilities (ITPA) (Kirk, McCarthy, & Kirk, 1968) and the Detroit Test of Learning Aptitude (Baker & Leland, 1967) were touted as capable of identifying the perceptual and processing deficits underlying language disorders. It was comforting to clinicians to feel that some of the guesswork had been taken out of assessment and intervention decision making. Unfortunately, the specific abilities approach did not result in the anticipated improvement in language function. Evidence substantiating the validity of the tests and/or the effectiveness of the intervention procedures never materialized (e.g., Hammill & Larson, 1974; Hammill & Wiederholt, 1973).

In the middle to late seventies clinicians began to take note of the research concerned with the role of semantic and pragmatic knowledge and skills in early language learning. At last there was a theoretically and rationally sound base for both assessment and intervention with language disordered children. At this point the research-practice gap narrowed very rapidly until, by the end of the decade, the findings from investigations of communicative development were becoming fairly well integrated into clinical practices. There were major revisions of assessment and therapy procedures, with a focus on teaching children to use language to accomplish functional goals. Clinicians began to move out of the clinic into the real world of classrooms, playgrounds, and homes.

Definition

Terminology

Understanding communication disorders requires a basic knowledge of the three areas involved in the ability to talk—speech, language, and communication. Talking requires that you know the speech sounds (*phonemes*) of your native language and the ways to combine them to form words. A baby spends much of her first 1½ years experimenting with her vocal mechanism and learning and practicing sounds. Later comes the ability to modulate voice quality and use appropriate intonation and rate.

Being able to talk also requires the ability to encode and decode messages. You must know the words (symbolic code) to represent your knowledge of the world and the rules for sequencing these units to form grammatically correct and meaningful sentences. With practice young children learn to use their culture's finite set of language symbols and syntactic rules to create an infinite number of sentences.

Competent communicators also know how to use nonlinguistic devices to ensure that their messages are conveyed effectively and that the messages of others are understood. They have learned to use gestures, body posture, facial expressions, eye contact, and physical distance to help them suit their messages to the context and listener, and they have learned how to be an appropriate participant in a conversation.

Speech Speech is verbal expression of the language code. It is a complex motor behavior that requires precise control and manipulation of the vocal tract and oral musculature. To produce speech, a child must learn to coordinate respiration

Good communication includes nonverbal signals.

(breathing), phonation (the production of sound with the larynx and vocal folds), resonation (the vibratory response controlling the pitch, intensity, and quality of sound), and articulation (sound formation with the lips, tongue, teeth, and hard and soft palates). By their first birthday normal infants have gained sufficient control over these mechanisms to produce simple words or simplified forms of more complex words. Though speech is a physically and neurologically demanding medium, it is also an extremely effective and flexible vehicle for the transmission of an idea.

Language   Language is the knowledge and use of a set of symbols to represent ideas and intentions (Bloom & Lahey, 1978). A language is a set of symbols and the rules to be followed in combining the symbols. Both the symbols and the rules have been agreed upon by members of the culture as a system through which they will exchange information. Language is essentially a code that allows its user "to represent an object, event or relationship without reproducing it" (Bloom & Lahey, 1978, p. 5).

Traditional descriptions of language included five components—phonology, morphology, syntax, semantics, and pragmatics. (Pragmatics refers to the rules governing the use of language in a social context.) Bloom and Lahey (1978) collapse these five components into three: form, content, and use. *Form* includes phonology, morphology, syntax—the surface or structure aspects of language that connect to and express meaning. *Content* is the meaning or semantic aspect of language—something like a mental dictionary. It includes cognitive information (concepts about the physical and social world) and the links with linguistic knowledge (understanding of how to express concepts). *Use* is the pragmatic or social interaction of language. Hymes (1971) defines it as "tacit knowledge of who can say what, in what way, where and when, by what means and to whom" (p. 12).

The relationship between the rules governing language form and the rules governing language use is similar to the relationship between the rules of a game and actual playing strategies (McCormick, 1984). Take backgammon, for example. The rules of backgammon are straightforward and relatively easy to learn, but they are not the key to being a good player. Winning depends on learning and using certain playing strategies (and, of course, some luck with the dice). Playing strategies are difficult to explain and to learn because their use depends on such variables as the stage of the game and the other player's positions and skill. The same is true of language use strategies. Mastery requires considerable practice, but pragmatic skills are the key to being a really competent communicator. The ability of infants to learn these strategies (e.g., turn-taking, code-switching, establishing and maintaining a topic) at the same time they are acquiring form and content is one of the many wonders of normal language acquisition.

Communication   Communication is the broadest of the three terms. It refers to the act of sharing experiences; more specifically, the exchange of ideas, feelings, and information. The key word is *exchange*. For communication to occur, there must be a message, that message must be expressed, and it must be accurately received. Though not essential, language is a very useful communication tool. You can communicate some concepts and emotions without language—through gestures, facial expressions, body movements, or pictures. For example, an English-speaking person can probably succeed in ordering a meal in a restaurant where the menu is not in English and the waiter does not speak English. However, communicating abstract concepts without language is all but impossible. Imagine trying to discuss politics or religion with someone who does not speak your language.

Communication is not unique to humans (Menzel, 1969). The communication skills of other species are not as well understood as those of humans, but it seems that there is communication, both within and across species. The meaningful exchanges between domesticated animals and humans are an example of cross-species communication. Pets can convey many messages through such devices as tail wagging, growling, jumping, and purring. They also seem to decode many messages accurately.

Category Labels

The importance of differentiating among *speech, language,* and *communication* can be seen in the confusion resulting from the P.L. 94–142 category label and definition. The category label is *speech impaired,* but it is defined as "a communication disorder, such as stuttering, impaired articulation, a language impairment, or voice impairment, which adversely affects . . . educational performance" (U.S. Government Accounting Office, 1981, p. 36). Use of the broader term *communication disorders* would more accurately include the broad range of disorders. However, it seems we must be reconciled to mixed terminology in this area. Theoretically speech, language, and communication disorders are distinct, but few use the terms precisely.

Prevalence

The U.S. Department of Education report for 1983–84 indicated that 2.37% of students were receiving services as speech impaired. However, there is considerable variability in prevalence figures across the states. One reason is the states' adoption of different category definitions. Other reasons include the tests used for eligibility determination, tester variables, and placement decision-making practices.

Another point to keep in mind when considering prevalence figures is the practice of assigning children to the category of their primary disability. The strong relationship between language/communication disorders and learning disabilities makes it extremely difficult to determine which is the primary disability. Longitudinal studies of preschool children identified as language disordered indicate persistent and chronic problems with academic experiences, particularly reading and writing (e.g., Aram & Nation, 1980). And as mentioned in chapter 5, spoken and written language problems are used as defining characteristics of learning disabilities. The question is whether the impaired learning strategies associated with learning disabilities contribute to language problems, or vice versa.

Two studies involving language disordered preschoolers may provide a better estimate of prevalence than the federal data cited here. Silva (1980) and Stevenson and Richman (1976) found that approximately 7% to 8% of the 3-year-olds in their studies demonstrated significant delay in receptive or expressive language functioning.

Causes

Table 7-1 lists factors thought to be necessary for the normal development of speech, language, and communication competencies. Miller (1983) has grouped these variables into three broad categories: neuropsychological factors, structural and physiological factors, and environmental factors. A delay or dysfunction related to any one of these 10 factors can cause a child to have difficulties learning and using speech, language, and/or communication. For example, delayed cognitive development (mental retardation), whether mild or severe, means that the child is not acquiring knowledge of the world at a rate commensurate with her peers. This delay will, of course, affect the acquisition of semantic knowledge; it will also affect the rate at which the child acquires morphological and syntactic rules as well as language use strategies. Whether or not cognitive delay is accompanied by motor control and coordination problems or sensory impairment, there will be a direct relationship between the extent of the cognitive delay and the rate of language

---

Table 7-1 Factors affecting speech, language, and communication acquisition

---

Neuropsychological factors

1. Cognitive development
2. Information-processing strategies (selective attention, discrimination, concept formation, memory)
3. Motor, output capabilities (neuromuscular control/coordination)
4. Social-emotional development and motivation

Structural and physiological factors

5. Sensory acuity (auditory, visual, tactile, gustatory, olfactory)
6. Oromuscular capabilities
7. Speech transmission mechanisms

Environmental factors

8. Social-cultural variables (socioeconomic level, language culture, dialect)
9. Experiences (caregiver-child interactions, linguistic input, caregiver responsiveness)
10. Physical context (availability of toys, pictures, manipulatable objects)

SOURCE: Adapted from "Identifying Children with Language Disorders and Describing Their Language Performance" by J. F. Miller in *Contemporary Issues in Language Intervention* (p. 63) by J. F. Miller, E. D. Yoder, and R. Schiefelbusch (Eds.), 1983, Rockville, MD: American Speech-Language and Hearing Association.

development. In this case the language difficulties would be considered secondary to the primary disability, mental retardation.

The 10 factors presented in Table 7-1 are all interrelated. For example, a visual impairment affects the young child's interactions with caregivers and the physical environment, which, in turn, affect the rate and course of early language development. Semantic development and acquisition of language use strategies are affected by the inability to see and interpret nonverbal language cues; experience with objects is hindered by the lack of mobility. Thus, the visual impairment has caused an experiential deficit; both physiological and environmental factors have interfered with the child's development of early language and communication competencies.

Although identification of the factors contributing to a child's speech, language, and/or communication difficulties may be relatively straightforward in many cases, it is not always possible to predict the nature and severity of the disorder. The effect will be proportional to (1) the degree of the deficit, (2) the type of deficit (e.g., structural and physiological factors may have a more detrimental effect than environmental factors), (3) the time of occurrence, and (4) the time of identification and treatment. Children with the same etiology may differ markedly in their speech, language, and communication characteristics and in their intervention needs.

Etiological factors do have some usefulness as indicators of at-risk status. Severe problems in the neuropsychological, structural, and physiological areas presented in Table 7-1 are identifiable at birth or shortly thereafter. The presence of one or more of these problems indicates that the child is at risk for speech, language, and/or communication problems. Also, if there is reason to suspect a problem in any one or a combination of the environmental factors, some intervention is indicated. Identification of less apparent deficits must await later developmental milestones for comparison with normal expectations.

Speech Disorders

Speech is considered to be disordered if it draws unfavorable attention to itself, interferes with the speaker's ability to communicate, or causes difficulties in social relationships (Van Riper, 1978). There are three major types of speech disorders: articulation disorders, voice disorders, and fluency disorders.

Misarticulation, the abnormal production of phonemes, may be due to a variety of causes. Developmental articulation problems are attributable to a disturbance in the learning process (Shriberg, 1980); one possible cause is hearing impairment. Other causes of articulation problems are associated with structural defects or neuromuscular deficits. Structural defects include gross abnormalities of the oral structures, such as clefts of the lip or palate, which occur during the first trimester of pregnancy and only once in approximately 700 to 770 live births. *Dysarthria* is a group of articulation disorders resulting from neuromuscular deficits—damage to components of the central and/or peripheral nervous systems. The misarticulations of a child with dysarthria are due to lack of precise control over the muscles used in breathing, the larynx, the soft palate and pharynx, the tongue, the jaw, and/or the lips. Another articulation disorder attributable to neuromuscular deficit is *apraxia*. Apraxia involves an impaired ability to organize the necessary motor commands to the speech musculature so that the sounds in words are properly sequenced.

Voice disorders are deviations of voice pitch, loudness, or quality. They may be caused by structural differences in the larynx or neurological damage to the brain or nerves controlling the oral cavity. Physiological causes of disordered voice include growths within the larynx (nodules, polyps, or cancerous tissue), infections of the larynx, damage to the nerves supplying the larynx, or accidental bruises or scratches on the larynx. Another cause of voice problems is vocal abuse, such as excessive yelling at ball games or, for preschoolers, excessive crying. Hearing impairment can also cause voice disorders because the child may not learn to speak with an appropriately resonant voice.

The most common *fluency disorder* is stuttering. Many fluency problems are associated with neurogenic disorders, but researchers have not been able to determine the origin of stuttering. There is some agreement, however, on several points:

It most often begins between the ages of 2 and 7.

Onset is marked by fragmentation of syllables and words.

It fluctuates in severity so that the course of development is not steady.

It changes with time: beginning forms of stuttering differ from advanced forms. (Perkins, 1980, p. 456)

Language and Communication Disorders

Language and communication disorders may stem from problems related to any one or a combination of the factors in Table 7-1. *Aphasia*, a severe disorder of language that affects the child's ability to use symbols, is the result of damage to the central nervous system. The child may demonstrate problems with expressive language, receptive language, or both. The precise nature of the problems depends upon which portion of the brain is involved.

Characteristics

Speech Disorders

Characteristics of the three major types of speech disorders—articulation disorders, voice disorders, and fluency disorders—are relatively easy to distinguish. Children with articulation disorders may demonstrate one or more of the following types of errors: sound omission, substitution, distortion, and addition. Omission, the failure to pronounce all of the expected sounds in a word, constitutes the most serious misarticulation because the resultant speech may be unintelligible. Omissions occur most frequently among young children. In substitution errors the substituted sound is generally somewhat similar to the replaced sound. An example of a substitution error is "thilly" for *silly* or "wed" for *red*. There are many types of distortions; the most common example is the lisp. The way the child produces the phoneme is similar to but not quite like the way it is supposed to be produced. An addition, an extra sound inserted into a word, occurs most often in the speech of young children, especially in the context of consonant blends. Generally speaking, children under 8 years of age probably do not need articulation therapy unless the number of sounds correctly produced places them at least one standard deviation below the norms for their chronological age (Bernthal & Bankson, 1981).

Dysarthria is a separate group of articulation disorders that are manifested in an inability to speak with normal muscular speed, strength, precision, or timing (Aronson, 1981). The lack of muscular control is apparent in the melody, stress, and rhythm patterns. Sometimes dysarthria is so mild that it is imperceptible except to a skilled clinician. At other times it is so severe that the child's speech is totally unintelligible.

Apraxia is characterized by inconsistent articulation errors. Misarticulation errors tend to vary with the degree of complexity of the sound being produced. The basic impairment is an inability to select and sequence the appropriate movements for speech production. The child may also have difficulty with such nonspeech behaviors as coughing, puffing out the cheeks, and blowing and may demonstrate general clumsiness in motor tasks.

In fluency disorders the natural, smooth flow of speech is interrupted with inappropriate hesitations, pauses, and/or repetitions. Some fluency problems are considered normal because they do not call undue attention to the speaker. For example, repetitions of words and phrases and hesitations usually indicate that the speaker is reflecting on what to say. Listeners expect and accept this lack of fluency. What distinguishes a true fluency disorder such as stuttering from a normal fluency problem is muscular tension and the fact that the stutterer's lack of fluency is with speech sounds, not words and phrases (Perkins, 1980).

A fluency problem that is sometimes confused with stuttering is cluttering. Van Riper (1978) compares the clutterer's speech to the pileup of keys when a beginning typist's speed exceeds control. It is rapid, garbled speech with extra sounds or mispronounced sounds and sometimes mixed-up sentence structure.

There are two types of voice disorders—resonance disorders and phonation disorders. Children with resonance disorders demonstrate either hypernasality (an excessive nasal quality) or hyponasality (abnormally reduced nasal quality). Hypernasality sometimes characterizes the speech of children with cerebral palsy or an unrepaired cleft palate. In phonation disorders the child's speech may be harsh, breathy, hoarse, or husky. In some severe cases there is no voice at all. Voice disorders are less common in children than in adults.

Language Disorders

Bloom and Lahey (1978) describe a language disorder as "any disruption in the learning of a native language" (p. 290). They differentiate five subgroups within the language disordered population:

1. children with a form problem—those who have difficulties learning and using a language code

2. children with a content problem—those who have difficulties in formulating ideas or conceptualizing information about objects, events, and relations

3. children with a use problem—those who have difficulties speaking or understanding in certain contexts and/or adjusting their language for different purposes

4. children with an association problem—those who have difficulties with proper association of content, forms, and use

5. children with delayed language development—those who lag behind their same-age peers in all language dimensions

Form Problems   Form is the means for linking sounds, words, and word sequences to meaning. It includes the understanding and use of the sounds (phonemes), the words and morphological inflections (prefixes and suffixes), and the syntax or structure of a language. In order to understand and/or produce language, children must learn the code and their culture's rules for applying the code. Children with form problems have difficulty learning and using the phonological, morphological, and syntactic rules of language. What is most apparent about these children is their problem with the mechanics of language. They cannot say what they mean or understand the meanings intended by others.

Included in this category are some children labeled as learning disabled or aphasic. A recent study comparing the language abilities of children with acquired aphasia and children with language difficulties accompanied by learning disabilities found striking similarities in the patterns of language deficits of these two groups (Miller, Campbell, Chapman, & Weismer, 1984). As you would expect, children with hearing impairments experience form problems. They do not hear and therefore cannot learn the conventional symbols and structures of language without intensive therapy.

Content Problems   Because cognitive development plays a significant role in language and communicative competence, a child's cognitive development is usually somewhat more advanced than his linguistic and social development. However, if a child's performance on cognitive measures is significantly lower than his performance on measures of morphology and syntax, it would be considered a content problem.

There are relatively few children in this subgroup. Among them are blind children and some children with spina bifida. For blind children and some orthopedically handicapped children the disparity between language form and use skills and their content skills is a result of restricted mobility, which limits their experience with the range of objects, events, and relationships available to their nonhandicapped peers.

Use Problems   New knowledge generated by the study of the development of pragmatic abilities in children has led clinicians to look beyond the form and content of utterances to language use strategies. Who can say what, how, where, when, and to whom? Some children produce syntactically well formed and semantically accurate utterances but have problems with communicative interaction strategies, such as turn taking and initiating and maintaining a dialogue. They talk about things that are out of context and string together ideas tangentially without regard for the listener's perspective. These children seem to have difficulty receiving and/or interpreting cues; they fail to adjust their language to the social context. Often there is no attempt to establish and maintain eye contact or employ other nonlinguistic communication devices that serve communicative interactions.

Some learning disabled children demonstrate use problems, as do autistic children (Duchan & Palermo, 1982). The source of these problems is not well understood. They may be an effect of attention, perception, or memory deficits or a primary deficit in social skills.

Content-Form-Use Association Problems   An inability to represent meaning with relevant, meaningful, and/or functional linguistic forms may indicate association difficulties. Sometimes associations among dimensions are weak or distorted, or there may be difficulties related to transfer across dimensions. Children with association or transfer difficulties produce age-appropriate forms and structures, but they do not use these linguistic devices correctly to convey intended meanings in appropriate contexts. One example of an association problem is an autistic child who recites nursery rhymes or television commercials in a conversation.

Content-Form-Use Delay Very often a child's language is almost exactly like that of a younger normal language learner. Development is simply proceeding at a slower rate. Many mildly and moderately retarded children fit this subgroup; they demonstrate a generally depressed performance level in all three language dimensions.

Assessment

Besides screening tests, which are designed to identify children in need of additional assessment, there are two major types of assessment instruments to assist in the determination of intervention objectives and procedures. There are broad

Certain assessment instruments permit in-depth testing of specific skill areas, such as language.

focus tests that permit an overall estimate of the student's development compared with that of same-age peers, and there are other tests that focus narrowly on one or more specific dimensions of speech, language, and/or communication. Tests that fall into this latter group include those that permit in-depth evaluation of voice, fluency, articulation, morphology, syntax, semantics, and pragmatic skills.

In addition to standardized tests, informal checklists, interviews, and observations, many speech-language clinicians use speech samples to evaluate productive language. They record a communication exchange with the student, either on tape or in writing. A transcription of the recorded speech sample (if taped) or the record itself is then analyzed for evidence of performance delays and deficits. For example, if expressive syntax is the concern with a particular student, the speech-language clinician might compare the student's complex sentence development with charts outlining milestones in the use of complex sentences.

The relative importance assigned to assessment information will vary somewhat according to the child's age. However, the questions that assessment seeks to answer will be the same across age groups. When there is reason to suspect a speech disorder, the speech-language clinician will be concerned with these questions:

1.   Does the student have a developmental articulation delay or disorder? If so, what type?

2.   Is the student able to discriminate among words with only initial or final consonant differences?

3.   Is the student's voice deviant in pitch, loudness, or quality?

4.   Does the student's speech flow in a natural and smooth manner?

5.   What phonological rules, if any, is the child using?

If there is reason to suspect a problem with language form, the speech-language clinician will seek answers to these questions:

1.   How does the student's understanding and production of morphological inflections compare to that of same-age peers?

2.   How does the student's understanding and production of grammatical structures compare to that of same-age peers?

Assessment of language content will consider these broad questions:

1.   How does the student's cognitive development compare to that of same-age peers?

2.   Is the student able to talk about the variety of objects, actions, events, and relationships that characterize the language of same-age peers? (In other words, how does the student's vocabulary compare with developmental norms?)

Assessment of language use focuses on these questions:

1. Does the student understand and use the variety of language functions used by same-age peers (e.g., requests, assertions, denials)?

2. Is the student able to engage another student in conversation and direct or regulate the flow of conversation as well as same-age peers?

3. Does the student have age-appropriate strategies for achieving social goals through communicative interaction?

Age-Level Distinctions

Early Childhood   Procedures to identify infants at risk for speech, language, or communication problems begin at birth. Consideration of the three risk categories delineated in Table 7-1—neuropsychological factors, structural and physiological factors, and environmental factors—is useful for determining risk status. The earlier the intervention with at-risk infants and their caregivers, the greater the possibility of preventing or ameliorating language deficits, reducing the likelihood of confounding problems, and enhancing development.

Screening tests that assess general language performance include the Language Subtest of the Denver Developmental Screening Test (Frankenburg & Dobbs, 1970), the Fluharty Preschool Speech and Language Screening Test (Fluharty, 1978), and the Communication Screen (Striffler & Willig, 1981). The Bankson Language Screening Test (Bankson, 1977) and the Northwestern Syntax Screening Test (Lee, 1971) consider specific aspects of language, but they are classified as screening instruments because of the general information they provide.

The preschool period can be divided into five stages according to the average, or mean, length of children's utterances. This *mean length of utterance* (MLU) is a predictor of the complexity of language until the child attains an MLU of 4.0 (Brown, 1973). An MLU is computed by counting the number of words or morphemes in a sample of 50 consecutive utterances and then dividing the total number of words or morphemes by 50. When the MLU has been computed, the clinician can determine whether the child demonstrates a significant developmental delay or deviation by comparing vocabulary, evidence of semantic knowledge, syntax, and communication skills with normal development data, as presented in Table 7-2.

Three standardized instruments that are also useful for evaluating the language and communication development of preschool children are the Receptive-Expressive Emergent Language Scale (REEL), developed by Bzoch and League (1971); the Sequenced Inventory of Communicative Development (SICD), developed by Hedrick, Prather, and Tobin (1984); and the Initial Communication Processes Scale (ICP), developed by Schery and Glover (1982).

With preschool as well as older students observations are particularly important in the assessment of language use and communication skills. Observations answer such questions as (1) how the young child gains the attention of another, (2) how she initiates play with caregivers and peers, (3) whether she anticipates

Table 7-2 Five stages of development during the preschool period

Stage	Attainments
I (MLU: 1.0–2.0) (Approx. age: 12–26 months)	*Speech* Produces some words consistently but varies others greatly; limits initial words in the number and type of syllables and in the different phoneme types; gradually comes to be governed by phonological rules *Language* Uses single-word utterances naming specific objects and classes of objects (animate and inanimate) or expressing a relational meaning (existence, nonexistence, disappearance, recurrence); uses successive single-word utterances; uses two-word combinations to express existence, negation, recurrence, attribution, possession, location, agent-action, action-object, agent-object *Communication* Uses gestures to express intentions; uses gestures plus vocalization to communicate desires and direct the behavior of others; uses multiword utterances to perform a range of functions
II (MLU: 2.0–2.5) (Approx. age: 27–30 months)	*Speech* Begins to follow phonological rules that provide for consistent speech performance *Language* Begins producing morphemes: *in, on,* present progressive (-*ing*), regular plural (-*s*), irregular past tense, possessive ('*s*), uncontractible copula, articles, regular past (-*ed*), irregular third person, uncontractible auxiliary, contractible copula, contractible auxiliary; produces some pronouns (*I, you, them, they, he/she, we, it*) *Communication* Responds to a conversational partner and engages in short dialogue; uses terms such as *here* and *there* to direct attention or to reference
III (MLU: 2.5–3.0) (Approx. age: 31–34 months)	*Speech* Articulates all English vowels and the majority of consonants *Language* Continues to experiment with and modify simple declarative sentences; begins to produce negative, interrogative, and imperative sentence forms *Communication* Learns to become a better conversational partner, taking turns and using contingent queries and questions; uses a greater variety of forms to attain desired objects and services; can take the perspective of conversational partner
IV (MLU: 3.0–3.75) (Approx. age: 35–40 months)	*Speech* May reduce or simplify words and consonant clusters *Language* Produces questions in the adult form; produces embedded sentences and other complex constructions; uses negative contractions including *isn't, aren't, doesn't,* and *didn't;* uses the modal auxiliaries *could, would, must,* and *might* in negatives and questions *Communication* Seems to have a better awareness of the social aspects of conversation; uses some indirect requests
V (MLU: 3.75–4.5) (Approx. age: 41–46 months)	*Speech* Produces a few consonant clusters and blends *Language* Has mastered regular and irregular past tense in most contexts; uses the third person singular and the contractible copula; inverts auxiliary verbs appropriately in questions; uses *and* and, later, *if* to conjoin clauses *Communication* Switches codes (produces simplified utterances) for younger children; uses most deictic terms correctly; can talk about feelings and emotions; produces indirect requests in which the goal is embedded in a question or statement

Table 7-3 Suggestions for classroom observations

Context	What to Observe
Group activities	Amount/extent of participation Appropriateness of interactive behaviors Attention and control strategies Response to directions (individual and group)
Task-oriented situations	Material and object preferences Duration of material/object manipulations Appropriateness of material/object manipulations
Social interactions (with adults and peers)	Type of communication devices used to secure desired objects and events Proportion of initiations versus responses Variations in the frequency of communicative behaviors with different adults and peers Agreement between verbal and nonverbal communicative efforts Amount/extent of turn taking (in verbal and nonverbal exchanges)
Free play	Context of play (isolate, parallel, or interactive) Basis of play (actual or vicarious experiences) Substitution of one object for another in pretend play Appropriateness of pretend activity sequencing

and takes turns, (4) what the nature of routine communication events (both verbal and nonverbal) is, and (5) when and with whom the most appropriate interactions occur. Informal observations also provide important information about the child's learning strategies and interests.

Ideally, observations are conducted in a variety of natural contexts with different physical and social variables. Initial observations of infants and young children usually attempt to answer general questions about the child's communication competencies. Table 7-3 provides some suggestions on what to observe in a preschool setting.

School Age Prior to initiating speech and language assessment of school-age children, limitations on sound production should be considered (Schriberg, 1980). The clinician can evaluate tongue and lip mobility by asking the child to perform speech movements as rapidly as possible (e.g., "Say 'pa-ta-ka' as fast as you can for five seconds"). If there is reason to suspect hearing loss, the clinician arranges for audiological testing that includes at least a pure-tone hearing test and impedance audiometry (see chapter 11). Children with voice disorders are referred to a physician for medical evaluation of the respiratory system and larynx (Boone, 1980).

There is some debate regarding the precise relationship of auditory processing and language development (Rees, 1981, 1983). However, most professionals in the area concede that auditory processing does play a role in language comprehension. Therefore, assessment of auditory discrimination is the next step. Discrimination of sounds and sound sequences is assessed either with a standardized test or through informal observations.

By the time children with normal speech development enter school, they are able to make all the phonological discriminations necessary for word identification and production (Menyuk, 1983). Articulation errors in the primary grades are reason for referral for speech assessment. The assessment process can be accomplished through imitation tasks, ranging from imitation of hand-clapping patterns to syllable sequences to words and phrases. Another method presents pictures to elicit production of consonants in different positions. Articulatory proficiency is judged by comparing the child's omissions, substitutions and distortions, and additions with chronological age expectations. The clinician combines information from these analyses with a rating of overall intelligibility to determine whether there is a need for speech therapy.

Although the rate of morphological development varies among children, the order is fairly consistent. School-age children may still have some difficulty with strong nouns such as *feet* and irregular verbs such as *brought*, but most have entered school with the ability to apply plural and tense markers appropriately (Menyuk, 1983). As reading ability develops in the early school years, children learn to segment words into phonological components, rhyme words, and generate words with the same initial sounds (e.g., *ball, bat*). Later, they learn rules of stress to create different syntactic categories (PER-mit versus per-MIT), ways to create nominal compounds (*birdhouse*), and, eventually, rules of phonological change to create different syntactic categories (*discuss/discussion*). These skills are the primary focus of morphological assessment of school-age children. Syntax and semantics are also assessed to determine whether the child's problems are related to an understanding and production of syntactic structures or a delay in semantic development. Assessment procedures include analysis of a speech transcript and use of standardized instruments.

Formal assessment devices to evaluate phonology, syntax, and semantics include the Test of Language Development (TOLD) (Newcomer & Hammill, 1982), which assesses form in addition to other aspects of language. The TOLD-P is designed for use with children aged 4 to 8. A similar instrument, the TOLD-I, is available for intermediate-age children (ages 8 to 12).

By the time most children enter school, they have developed a large repertoire of language use and communication strategies (Dore, 1979). They know how to accomplish social functions (e.g., requesting, acknowledging, and answering questions) and how to participate appropriately in conversations (Keenan, 1977). Assessment of language use and communication strategies is particularly important with language and learning disabled children because they tend to demonstrate deficits in these skill domains.

Secondary/Transition   There is very little available information concerning the nature of semantic and syntactic delays in adolescents and young adults with language-learning disabilities. The one thing that does seem clear is that children with language and communication disorders do not grow out of their problems when they reach adolescence (e.g., Donahue, Pearl, & Bryan, 1982; Wiig & Semel, 1980). Wiig (1984) notes significant delays and differences in concept formation, semantic development, acquisition of syntax, and memory when language disordered adolescents are compared to their normal peers. Further, they seem to differ from their peers in three aspects of communicative competence: (1) adapting communicative intentions to listener and situational characteristics, (2) conveying and comprehending information, and (3) initiating and maintaining cooperative conversational interactions (Donahue, Pearl, & Bryan, 1983). With intervention language and communicative abilities do improve over time. However, the gap between the skills of language disordered students and those of normal students does not seem to narrow.

Although some tests designed for younger children extend into adolescence, there is only one standardized instrument designed specifically for students 11 to 18 years of age. The Test of Adolescent Language (TOAL) (Hammill, Brown, Larsen, & Wiederholt, 1980) assesses spoken and written semantics and syntax, both receptively and expressively.

It is important to re-emphasize that clinicians consider all aspects of verbal and nonverbal communicative abilities and their interaction. They use a variety of formal and informal procedures to discover and describe what children can do, what they are ready to learn, and what is the best way to teach them. In addition, clinicians have primary responsibility for assuring that assessment results guide intervention.

Intervention

The remaining sections of the chapter will focus exclusively on language and communication, the information most important to teachers. Speech-language clinicians typically assume full responsibility for remediation of speech disorders. The broad purpose of language intervention is to bring about certain outcomes judged necessary for successful academic, social, and vocational functioning. Specific intervention goals vary according to the ages and needs of the students. However, the key intervention issues are the same for all students:

- Intervention goals (What do we want students to be able to do?)

- Procedures and strategies (How do we get them to do it?)

- Instructional contexts (Where, when, and with whom should training occur?)

Intervention Goals

The first and most crucial intervention question is, What do we want students to be able to do? A broad answer is, To understand and use language appropriately and effectively in present and future age-appropriate contexts. Results of the assessment process should provide sufficient information about the student's abilities and disabilities and relevant environmental and interactional variables to formulate a specific answer to this question, thus determining the long-term speech, language, and/or communication goals. Questions such as the following are then asked to assist development and prioritization of instructional objectives.

1. What do same-age peers know about language?

2. How do same-age peers use language?

3. What does the student need to learn now for at least minimal success in social situations? Or how can he be viewed more favorably by peers and adults?

4. What does the student need to learn now for at least minimal success in academic and eventual vocational areas? Or can he understand directions, ask relevant questions, and decode and produce written symbols?

If intervention outcomes are to be meaningful, instructional objectives must go beyond what the students say and how they say it and must include the ability to use language to learn other age-appropriate skills.

Procedures and Strategies

The key word in recent language intervention trends is *natural*. Natural intervention procedures are characterized by naturally occurring training opportunities, natural rather than contrived consequences, and more attention to communication functions and conversational skills. This trend has implications for school-age students and adolescents as well as infants and young children.

Natural intervention procedures are drawn from research into normal language acquisition, which indicates that the majority of a normal language learner's communicative efforts are acknowledged with attention, followed by an immediate confirming response, or rewarded by compliance (Bowerman, 1976; Nelson, 1977). These consequences teach children that language is an extremely effective tool for regulating the behavior of others, obtaining desired objects and events, and maintaining pleasurable social interactions.

Highly structured practice formats have not been altogether eliminated. However, they are now most often limited to sessions that focus exclusively on practice of morphological, syntactic, or semantic structures. A focus on expansion of verbal skills through communicative interactions has replaced total reliance on highly structured task formats. Target responses are now taught in the context of daily routines and ongoing activities to increase the probability of generalization.

Instructional Contexts

The term *context*, broadly defined, means environment or surroundings. In the past the primary context for remediation of language problems was the therapy room. It was assumed that if the what of language was taught, the child would somehow figure out the where, when, and who. Students were expected to generalize what they learned from talking to a clinician to talking to others and to apply what they learned from pictures to real objects and activities. Sometimes the expected generalizations from the therapy room to the real world actually occurred. More often they did not.

The primary caregiver can be shown ways to stimulate the infant's communication through everyday routines.

We know now that intervention can begin in a therapy room, but it must move out of this restricted context as soon as possible. The instructional environment should be arranged to maximize the elicitation, enhancement, and maintenance of appropriate language and communication skills. Among the most important contextual variables are interesting materials, objects, and events; opportunities and consequences for language use; and judicious use of scheduling and routines. In addition, the social elements of the environment are at least as important as physical and temporal variables. Parents, teachers, siblings, and peers arrange for or participate in most of the cognitive, social, and linguistic experiences from which any child learns about language and its use. The challenge for a teacher of a communication disordered student is to maximize the positive instructional role of these experiences—to capitalize on their potential for communication training.

Age-Level Distinctions

Early Childhood Important early communication skills for infants and very young children include requesting, greeting, giving, and showing. The focus of early intervention is on developing these communicative functions. A second goal is to promote manipulation of objects and events that will lead to construction of sensorimotor concepts. Infant intervention programs train the primary caregiver to provide stimulation in the context of play and caregiving routines (e.g., feeding, diapering). Over time the caregiver shapes primitive communicative signals such as smiling, touching, whining, and pointing into more sophisticated communicative behaviors.

Programming for children who understand and use some multiword utterances focuses on shaping more complex forms and establishing a greater variety of communication functions. Semantic-syntactic concepts such as location, possession, and action-object relations are also important goals at this stage. Objectives for language delayed/disordered preschoolers include

1. increased participation (verbal and nonverbal) in group activities;

2. increased communicative initiations and responses;

3. increased and more sophisticated requests for desired objects, events, and services;

4. increased compliance with individual and group directions; and

5. increased and more sophisticated use of conversational strategies such as turn taking.

A most important feature of natural language training procedures is assuring that the children experience the rewards of their communicative efforts. Questions, commands, praise statements ("Good talking"), and corrections are avoided because they tend to constrain and inhibit communicative efforts. Instead, adults follow the child's lead in play and in talking. They may use such facilitative techniques as parallel talking (talking about what the child is playing with), expansion (expanding the topic, syntax, semantic truth of the child's utterances), and labeling (naming objects and events as they attract the child's attention and interest) to facilitate the learning process.

Many of these intervention strategies for infants and preschoolers derive from an intervention model called "incidental teaching" or "milieu therapy" (Hart & Risley, 1975, 1980; Hart & Rogers-Warren, 1978). The primary goals of incidental teaching are to teach children to use language to obtain objects and attention and to use appropriate forms of language in a social context. The basic teaching procedure is to arrange the environment so that the child has to request desired stimuli and assistance. Desired and interesting materials are placed within view but out of the child's reach. Children are initially prompted to use whatever communicative devices they have already acquired to ask for toys, materials, or assistance. When they are consistently producing some type of request form, compliance is made contingent on more intelligible, complex, or semantically correct request forms. Incidental teaching is used in a variety of unstructured and structured classroom settings—free play, snacks and meals, transition periods, art and music periods, and instructional sessions. The only requirement is a variety of attractive and interesting materials, toys, and events and, of course, one or more adults.

School Age   Intervention for children with severe speech disorders begins in preschool or the primary grades. Sometimes identification of less severe disorders does not occur until the middle grades. Intervention approaches for school-age children with articulation problems vary, according to the clinician's training and experience and assessment information. The one characteristic common to all approaches is the involvement of teachers and parents to facilitate transfer to communicative interactions.

A language disorder is not an isolated and easily packaged category of behavior. As the child gets older, it becomes increasingly more difficult to separate language disorders and learning disabilities. Because the two seem to be on the same continuum, many professionals have begun to use the term *language learning disabilities* to describe the problems of these school-age children (e.g., Stark & Wallach, 1980). Table 7-1 presented a broad array of factors that, if delayed or disordered, can cause language and communication disorders. These deficits, in turn, cause an even broader array of academic and social problems, and it is difficult to deal with the language and/or communication difficulties without attention to their effects. In fact, when children start school, the criterion for judging the severity of their language problems and the type of intervention required is the degree to which academic and social functioning is affected.

Panagos and Griffith (1981) provide a useful differentiation of language teaching and learning contexts and their role in intervention with school-age children. They include the linguistic as well as the social and physical contexts. Language targets should be taught in relation to surrounding forms (e.g., nouns in relation to verbs, consonants in relation to vowels) and the entire language system. The key is to assure that the child learns relationships as well as the targeted behaviors. Topical context is also important. Language targets should be taught in the instructional and referential contexts where they are most likely to be used so that the child knows when to incorporate trained skills into discussions and conversations. Further, language should be taught in a variety of physical settings so that relevant physical variables become cues for producing the trained skills. Materials may be viewed as part of the physical context or as a separate context. In either case they give the child something to talk about; they set the occasion for learning and use of meaningful forms and structures. Finally, there is the social context, which must involve significant others if the child is to learn important social communication skills.

Language and communication objectives can be embedded within all kinds of classroom activities and study units. For example, an alternative to drill-and-practice routines is to introduce meanings and functions of new words and concepts into discussions and activities associated with a topic the student is particularly interested in. Children are more likely to apply important learning strategies such as selective attention, concept formation, and memory if they have selected the topics to pursue.

The preferred intervention approach is to teach targeted skills within the context of normal academic instruction and normal social interactions. As Pickering (1981) points out, classroom teachers are central, often emotionally significant figures in a child's world. Thus, they are the most effective and natural change agents. Though the social and academic requirements of the regular curriculum usually have to be modified to accommodate the needs of a child with a language learning disability, the benefits of keeping the child with normal peers far outweigh the costs in time and effort.

Thus, just as language affects the environment, the environment will affect what the child learns about language and communication. Working together, clinicians, teachers, and parents can devise a wide range of interesting and age-appropriate activities and strategies to expand language learning opportunities. However, the primary goal must be sufficient language to succeed in academic and social areas, not well-articulated speech.

Secondary/Transition   Secondary settings place complex demands on students. As Schumaker and Deshler (1984) point out, secondary students are expected to

gain information from materials written at secondary reading levels;

complete homework and other assignments with little or no help from the teacher;

gain information from auditory presentations such as lectures, discussions, and student reports;

participate in discussions;

express themselves well in writing; and

pass minimal competency examinations.

There is not substantial research concerning the language problems of adolescents, but available data indicate that these skills are precisely the areas that constitute a problem for learning disabled adolescents (Schumaker & Deshler, 1984). They read very poorly, often failing to apply whatever learning strategies they have. They have difficulty working independently but rarely ask for help. They have problems producing both oral and written language, and their spelling is poor. To compound their problems at a time when the peer group is particularly important, they have significant deficits in the area of social skills (Deshler, Schumaker, Alley, Warner, & Clark, 1981). The major intervention approaches for adolescents are the structuring of social and academic experiences to increase opportunities to learn language and communication skills and the training of learning strategies.

Curriculum Implications

A curriculum is a composite of objectives and activities designed to result in attainment of long-term goals. Some commercially produced language curricula include either suggestions for or precise descriptions of training procedures; others specify only the instructional content. The primary contribution of any curriculum is delineation of what to teach.

Table 7-4 presents a sampling of important language goals in form, content, and use for infants, preschoolers, and elementary-age students. The suggestions for teachers follow from the discussion on intervention. The focus is on natural teaching strategies in a wide range of physical, social, and temporal contexts to promote communicative competence.

Goals for adolescents are not included in Table 7-4 because there have been very few investigations of curricula for this age group. Among the few curricula are several packages developed at the University of Kansas. One focuses on teaching three types of learning strategies: strategies for gaining information from written and oral materials, strategies for expressing information in permanent products (e.g., assignments, tests, reports), and memory strategies (Schumaker & Deshler, 1984). A second curriculum package focuses on social-communication skills.

The learning strategies curriculum is designed to be used in academic settings to overcome some of the major learning and performance deficits of adolescents who are language learning disabled. It is appropriate for students with a reading level as low as fourth grade. All strategies are taught in a structured, systematic

---

Model Program

The Preschool Language Training Project of the Bureau of Child Research at the University of Kansas exemplifies many of the concepts identified in this chapter. Developed by Ken Ruder, Betty Bunce, and Charlotte Ruder (1984), this program provides an integrated classroom for eight language deficient/delayed children and four nonhandicapped children. All 12 children are between the ages of 3 and 6. As in many preschool programs for handicapped children, activities are planned around specific goals and objectives; but in this program there is a special emphasis on development of language and communication skills. The speech-language clinician, the teacher, and the parents share responsibility for intervention planning and implementation.

Special features of this program are described by Ruder, Bunce, and Ruder (1984):

1. Language training is provided in the classroom in the context of routine preschool academic and preacademic activities.
2. Training is designed to be intensive and to yield generalized outcomes.
3. The teacher is responsible for all language training as well as classroom management.
4. Parents are an integral part of the intervention.

Intake evaluations yield baseline data that are reported on a Test Summary Chart. Structures the child is using (and the times he uses them), transpositions, omissions, and other incorrect usages of language structure are identified and reported on a skill progress report, which is updated at regular intervals as the child acquires targeted skills. These data, together with information provided by the parents, are then used to develop an individualized speech and language program.

Training focuses on teaching concepts, vocabulary, grammar, and language use. In concept training children learn to match, categorize, and sequence objects and events. Vocabulary training teaches words that the child experiences most frequently and seems to want to learn. The goal in training grammar is development of the basic grammatical relations (agent-action-object) and then expansion of these relations. Activities such as free play, snack time, and show-and-tell are used for teaching appropriate and spontaneous language use.

Table 7-4 Selected curriculum goals and teacher behaviors

Age	Form Goals	Content Goals
Infant (birth to age 3)	React to sounds Vocalize single vowel sounds in play and in response Attend/respond to tone of voice Babble repetitive syllable sequences Imitate nonspeech sounds and speech sounds Say "da-da" and "ma-ma" and respond to "no-no" Respond to own name and simple action requests Point to familiar persons, toys, and animals on request Use 2-word sequences Point to body parts (on self and doll) Produce expanded noun phrases Use present progressive inflection (-ing) Use more and different words to encode semantic relations Use intelligible speech (at least 75% of the time)	Look at, manipulate, and search for objects Understand functional relationships Understand the functions and social meanings of a large number of objects Understand that an object can exist, cease to exist, and then reappear Understand the location of two objects in relation to one another Understand possession and attribution Recognize and name colors Match 2 identical items Group objects by a single dimension Apply previous experiences to new problems Remember objects and events
Preschool (ages 3–5)	Produce expanded noun phrases (demonstrative + article + adjective + noun) Use to be as copula, on, possessive 's, some contractions Imitate sentences up to 6 words Begin to use past tense Achieve MLU of 5.5 words Use intelligible speech (at least 95% of the time)	Remember daily routines Know shapes, sizes, positions, and colors Know time (day/night) and seasons Know number symbols (1–10) Understand most prepositions Understand most adjectives Follow 3-action commands Ask and answer wh- questions
Elementary (ages 5–12)	Use verb tense (present possessive, simple past, third person present, irregular past and future) Use 5–6 words per utterance Begin complex structural distinctions Extend and modify word meaning with prefixes Use the five basic sentence patterns competently	Understand all prepositions and adjectives Understand basic linguistic concepts (coordination, class exclusion and inclusion, spatial sequences, temporal sequences, cause-effect, instrumental, and revision) Understand spatial, temporal, and kinship relations Use word definitions (lexicon) resembling those of an adult

Use Goals	Facilitator Behaviors
Smile, coo in response to voice and adult smiling Show anticipation if about to be picked up or fed Discriminate strangers Vocalize to initiate interpersonal interactions Use gestures to direct adult attention Gesture and vocalize to request desired objects and events Vocalize immediately following the utterance of another person Add information to the prior utterance of communicative partner Ask increasing number of questions Use utterances to call attention, regulate others, request, participate in social routines, comment, and play	1. Imitate child's utterances in the course of exploratory activities 2. Provide a variety of interesting materials, objects, and events that invite sensory exploration 3. Encourage exploration and manipulation of the physical environment 4. Talk about the child's activities and object and event preferences 5. Draw attention to physical, temporal, spatial, and social relationships 6. Acknowledge and respond to the intent of the child's communicative efforts 7. Encourage nonverbal and verbal turn taking 8. Encourage all types of interactive play 9. Model and encourage such social rituals as greetings, polite requests, and responses
Change tone of voice and sentence structure to adapt to listener's level of understanding Use alternative forms that take context differences into account Demonstrate some ability to assume another perspective temporarily Show some ability to think about and comment on language Metalinguistic awareness	10. Teach to heterogeneous groups and plan activities that promote group interaction 11. Provide comments that preserve the child's semantic intent 12. Allow the child to select conversational topics
Initiate and maintain conversations Consider the listener's perspective when encoding messages Respond to listener feedback by altering the message if necessary Understand direct and indirect speech acts	1. Begin with what students can do and build on their strengths 2. Avoid language exercises in favor of training in natural context 3. Design instructional activities around student interests and topics being studied by peers 4. Focus on functional communication skills that will contribute to social and academic competencies 5. Use games and self-correcting materials as needed to target specific linguistic structures 6. Modify the language of instruction (e.g., verbal and written directions) and adapt reading materials to maximize student chances of succeeding

fashion using a nine-step teaching methodology (Deshler, Alley, Warner, & Schumaker, 1981):

1. Make the student aware of current learning habits.
2. Describe the new learning strategy.
3. Model the new strategy.
4. Have the student verbally rehearse the strategy.
5. Have the student practice the strategy with controlled materials.
6. Provide feedback.
7. Have the student practice the strategy with grade-level materials.
8. Provide feedback.
9. Test.

After skill mastery has been demonstrated, a three-phase generalization procedure is begun: (1) an orientation phase in which students are made aware of different settings and contexts where a particular learning strategy can be used, (2) an activation phase in which students are given practice with the strategy with a variety of materials and contexts, and (3) a maintenance phase with periodic probes to ensure continued application of the strategy.

The social skills curriculum is composed of materials to train 30 general social skills. Learning disabled adolescents who have learned these skills have demonstrated the ability to apply them in a variety of ongoing activities within the school setting.

Mainstreaming

Education of handicapped children in the most normal environment possible is a federal mandate. For the vast majority of students with a primary classification of speech impairment or communication disorder, the most normal environment possible is the regular classroom. Some students may have individual sessions with the speech-language clinician, but more often the clinician works with and through the classroom staff. Clinicians assist in the adaptation of materials and procedures, monitor progress toward specified goals and objectives, and help the teacher learn to recognize and use routine instructional and social interactions as the medium for remediation of language and communication delays.

Bailey and Wolery (1984) suggest the following general guidelines, based on research by Fredericks et al. (1978), to facilitate language learning in a preschool mainstream setting.

1. Reinforce all verbal and nonverbal communication by the handicapped child.
2. Direct nonhandicapped peers to verbalize to the handicapped child and reinforce the peers for those interactions.

3. Reinforce nonhandicapped children when they initiate and/or respond to handicapped children.

4. Involve the handicapped child in appropriate play situations to increase interactions with nonhandicapped peers.

5. If a peer does not respond to the handicapped child, model a response and provide reinforcement for peer imitation of the modeled response.

6. Encourage the handicapped child's use of increasingly more complex utterances when interacting with peers.

Wiig (1982) suggests some guidelines for teachers in elementary and secondary mainstream settings:

1. Encourage and reward all communicative efforts with undivided attention, a smile, or a confirming response.

2. Attend carefully to nonverbal and contextual cues to facilitate understanding and interpretation of communicative efforts.

3. Be as natural as possible—use a natural facial expression, natural gestures, and a natural voice when interacting with children with language and communication problems.

4. Use familiar words and relatively short and simple phrases and repeat or rephrase directions or questions if the child looks puzzled or does not respond.

5. Avoid ambiguities by giving verbal messages that match the attitudes, feelings, or intentions expressed by your tone of voice, facial expressions, and body language.

6. Seat the communication disordered student in a location where he can watch for nonverbal cues and hear your voice at all times.

7. Provide multisensory materials and opportunities for overlearning through task repetition in a variety of formats.

Innovation and Development

Despite significant strides in the past two decades there are still many unresolved issues in speech, language, and communication intervention. Rees (1983) notes that some are questions of definition: for example, what is the difference between language intervention, language stimulation, and language teaching? Other questions have to do with content boundaries: Who should deal with written language? Should English as a Second Language (ESL) teachers be speech-language clinicians? There are also philosophical issues to be resolved: Should the goal of language intervention always be normal performance? How desirable is it for all students to talk the same? Other questions are of a methodological nature: Can all intervention procedures and outcomes be described in behavioral terms? What kind of research do we need to evaluate the effectiveness of our intervention procedures?

These questions are by no means unique to the field of speech-language pathology, but they remain important. Most will be answered in the coming decade, as will other questions related to increasing a child's chance for success. One of the areas where the need for continuing research is most evident is interactive influences. Traditional assessment and intervention procedures often acknowledged the existence of interactive effects, but they rarely attempted to measure or change any conditions other than those attributed to the child. Professionals are now beginning to give serious attention to interacting variables that may result in a handicapping environment. Future intervention research will also answer important questions about the characteristics of physical and social interactions that promote desired child behaviors. There is a need for professionals to become more skilled in manipulating these variables to effect positive change. There is also a need for data concerning the best possible match between students and facilitating situations.

Another area of both research and training where there is sure to be increased activity is consultation. Consultation has been recognized for some time as a desired competency for speech-language clinicians. However, at this time it is not a standard component of preservice professional training programs. The next decade should see an expanded emphasis on improving consultation and cooperative planning skills and models so that speech-language clinicians can better assist teachers to arrange and develop their classrooms for optimal language learning.

Finally, as discussed in chapter 2, there are sure to be innovations and developments in the use of technology with communication disordered children. The use of microcomputers as prosthetic devices will increase, as will the use of optical video discs in language training.

Summary

This chapter has provided an introduction to the complex problems surrounding assessment and intervention services for students with delayed or disordered speech, language, and/or communication. The chapter presented some practical information for teachers and stressed the importance of collaborative planning and intervention. Among the predominant themes are (1) the importance of focusing on effective interpersonal communication as a primary intervention goal, (2) the need to integrate planning in cognitive, social, and linguistic domains, (3) the importance of teachers, parents, and speech-language clinicians working as a team to develop optimal language learning environments, and (4) the importance of assessing and teaching language and communication in the context of routine activities in the natural environment.

Study Questions

1. Differentiate speech, language, and communication; describe the three components of language.

2. Trace the history of research and clinical practices in language disorders.

3. How do the definitional problems in the area of communication disorders affect prevalence figures?

4. What are the broad factors affecting speech and language acquisition; how is knowledge of these etiological factors useful?

5. Describe the defining characteristics of the various speech and language disorders.

6. Summarize the questions that speech and language assessment procedures should address, and discuss the role of observation in assessment of communicative competence.

7. What are the important issues to address in arriving at appropriate intervention objectives?

8. Contrast natural and artificial/contrived language intervention procedures.

9. Discuss how different contexts affect language learning.

10. Describe intervention strategies and curricular trends for preschool, school-age, and secondary students.

TIPS FOR HELPING

1. Provide materials, objects, and events that invite and encourage high levels of involvement and communication.

2. Create opportunities for language by arranging group activities and projects that make cooperation and communication obligatory.

3. Arrange for communication disordered children to engage in cooperative activities with peers who are good language models.

4. Place desired and interesting toys and materials in a location where they are visible but out of reach so that the young child learns and practices the requesting function.

5. Talk about shared perceptions at the time the objects or events are the focus of the child's attention.

6. Expand the young child's imitations and spontaneous utterances (taking care not to change the meaning).

7. Use incomplete sentences and encourage the child to supply the missing elements.

8. Use pitch, special intonations, rhythm, rhymes, and repetitions to gain the child's attention and increase the salience of new forms.

9. Reinforce children's attempts to communicate by giving your attention, a confirming response, and/or the object or event that the child has requested.

10. Strive to make the who, where, when, and what of language training as natural and normal as possible.

11. Avoid language practice sessions in favor of training through activities.

12. Modify the language of instruction and instructional materials to maximize the students' chances of success.

8

Mild Mental Retardation

James R. Patton
University of Hawaii

James S. Payne
University of Virginia

Remember how it feels to be called on in school when you haven't done your homework?

That's the way Tommy feels now. He's the eight-year-old standing by the blackboard, with the faded T-shirt hanging out over his blue jeans.

His teacher has asked him to add 46 and 24. She may as well have asked him to solve a problem in nuclear physics. It's true that he didn't do his homework, but if you can't read, what's the point in looking at a book?

Yesterday, Tommy was called down for not knowing his address. In the last two years he has moved from his mother's to his grandmother's, and now to his aunt's.

No one has told him the address.
. . . Each month Tommy drops further and further behind in his schoolwork. Now he is no longer just a slow learner; his ability to learn has become limited. How long it will

remain limited depends on the kind of help he receives.

Tommy is mentally retarded.

In the most important growing period of his life, between birth and five years, when he was learning to talk and becoming aware of the world around him, there was no one who could afford to give him more than the bare physical necessities.

No one could provide him with the luxuries of fondling, talking to him, reading to him, or stimulating his mind and emotions.

His early years were his big opportunity for learning. And he missed the opportunity.

. . . Year after year he will probably be given a "social promotion," until he drops out of school at around 15, if he follows the usual pattern. By then he will be in the tenth grade, though he may still be reading on second grade level.

Chances are that his mounting frustration will find expression in behavior problems, and for the rest of his life he will remain emotionally and socially a young adolescent, his potential for a productive maturity lost.

. . . Essentially, he is a normal person whose learning capacity has become limited because of the mental and physical hardships of poverty. (President's Committee on Mental Retardation, 1978, pp. 1-3)

Mental retardation is a condition that historically has been susceptible to confusion and misunderstanding. In great part the confusion has arisen from an uncertainty and naïveté about the characteristics, needs, and capabilities of mentally retarded people. Tommy's situation exemplifies the scenario for many students who have been considered mildly retarded. Many such individuals experience their greatest frustrations, disappointments, and problems during their school years. It is unwarranted to reproach the educational system solely as the grand contributor to this problem, for there are many other factors operating. The salient point is the critical role that early experiences and appropriate educational programs can play in maximizing the potential of these students. This fact gains significance when we realize that 1 out of every 10 Americans has a direct involvement (e.g., a family member) with some form of mental retardation (*Facts on Mental Retardation*, 1973).

History

Throughout history many services have been gained for mentally retarded people. Even though many of these gains have been due to the efforts of specific individuals or groups, powerful sociopolitical influences have also been involved (Payne, Patton, & Beirne-Smith, 1985).

> Many people . . . think that the issues facing special education today are new. But if you read the historical literature of special education, you will see that today's issues and problems are remarkably similar to those of long ago. Issues, problems, and ideas arise, flower, go to seed, and reappear when the conditions are again right for their growth. (Payne, Patton, Kauffman, Brown, & Payne, 1983, p. 164)

With this in mind we can examine briefly how retarded people have been treated in times past.

Antiquity

As far as mentally retarded persons are concerned, the time prior to the 18th century is antiquity. For centuries there was much misunderstanding of retardation and much inconsistency in its treatment. In some societies the more severely retarded were given the role of buffoons or jesters. In others they were viewed as capable of divine revelations or condemned as demons. During this period the concept of mild mental retardation really did not exist. Those people receiving some type of special treatment were more severely impaired. Mildly retarded individuals were not noticeably different from nonretarded people. Because academic skills (the ability to read, write, and calculate) were not stressed, most mildly retarded people blended into society and were not recognized as having difficulties.

The Rise and Fall

During the 1700s a social climate characterized by humanism and openness developed. To a great extent this climate evolved from the Renaissance of the 14th, 15th, and 16th centuries. For the first time sincere and systematic attempts were made to intervene in the lot of retarded people (e.g., Itard's work with Victor). A resounding optimism dominated the early part of the 1800s and lasted for well over half of the century. As the 19th century progressed, optimism turned to pessimism. In this country the Civil War brought disharmony and trauma. The dramatic transition from an agrarian society to an urbanized and industrial one was accompanied by many internal problems. An attitude arose toward mentally retarded people that we can best describe as disillusionment.

Many factors contributed to this change. People had soured on the grandiose and overzealous claims of early optimists who predicted that mentally retarded people could be cured. In addition, a number of other crucial events had tragic repercussions for the mentally retarded. A eugenics movement arose, aiming to eliminate the proliferation of feeblemindedness through very selective breeding; Mendel's laws of inheritance provided theoretical support. Finally, through the efforts of Binet, the mental scale was born, providing the capacity to identify mild forms of retardation and resulting in much more retardation being diagnosed. This population explosion added fuel to the fire; suddenly mental retardation seemed a problem of enormous proportions. Repression and mistreatment of retarded people became commonplace. Segregation of many retarded individuals in secluded, dehumanizing institutions and the enactment of sterilization legislation were evidence that optimism had waned.

Renewed Encouragement

In the 1950s treatment of retarded persons underwent some noticeable changes. Foremost among these was the development of a national policy. A renewed climate of encouragement was created, in which "the demands of parents, the enthusiasm of professionals, and federal, state, and private funding gave new impetus to progress in the area of mental retardation" (Hewett & Forness, 1977). The 1960s gave special education the spotlight. Funding became available, and with it came the expansion of services for many disabled people. Chief among the changes was the recognition of the rights of retarded persons, affirmed by landmark litigation and legislation in the 1970s.

This time period also witnessed the first major challenge to the prolific growth of special education classes and to the procedures by which they were being run. In his often-cited article, Dunn (1968) notes that many culturally diverse students who were not retarded were being placed in these settings. With the passage of the Education for All Handicapped Children Act of 1975, a federal mandate to provide an appropriate education was given to the nation. The implementation of this law brought a major effort to mainstream disabled students whenever possible. The implications of this procedure for mildly retarded students are just now being realized.

Reexamination

The late 1970s witnessed a heavy reliance on the resource room model to provide educational services to many mildly handicapped students. With much professional attention being given to the needs of the previously unserved severely retarded, there was a noticeable shift in interest away from the mildly retarded (Strichart & Gottlieb, 1983). Haywood (1979) acknowledges a related "shift of resources away from mildly and moderately retarded persons" (p. 429).

Another recent development is the changing nature of this population: there has been a decrease in the number of students who are now classified as mildly retarded (i.e., educable mentally retarded), and this group has become "a more patently disabled group" (MacMillan & Borthwick, 1980, p. 155). One is inclined to ask, Where have all the mildly retarded students gone? Some have been reclassified and placed in classes for the learning disabled; others have been decertified and have joined the ranks of the "slow learners," for whom there are few services.

As the decade of the 1980s progresses, a number of pressing questions are being raised: What are the characteristics of this new mildly retarded population? How successful are those formerly classified as mildly retarded who are now in regular education? Can this new mildly retarded population be successfully integrated into the mainstream of regular education (Polloway, 1984)?

Definition

One way to understand the concept of mental retardation is to examine the terms used to describe it. Different labels have been fashionable at different times, reflecting the prevailing views of the period:

Past
feebleminded, moron, imbecile, idiot, mental defective, fool, educationally subnormal, incompetent, dull, dumb, retardate, dunce, immature, stupid

Present
mentally retarded, retarded, developmentally disabled, educable mentally retarded (EMR), trainable mentally retarded (TMR), mentally disabled, mental impairment, mental subnormality (used in Great Britain)

Today's new awareness and sensitivity toward disabled individuals makes certain past expressions offensive. Terms such as *retard, retardate, idiot, imbecile,* and *feeble-*

minded are inappropriate today; terms such as *retarded, mentally impaired,* and *mentally disabled* are much more acceptable (Biklen & Bogdan, 1977).

Generally speaking, mental retardation refers to a condition characterized by restricted intellectual ability and difficulty in coping with the social demands of one's environment. Although there is much variability within this population, all mentally retarded people demonstrate some degree of impaired mental abilities, usually most apparent in academically related areas. Moreover, a retarded person displays an intelligence quotient (IQ) significantly below the average and a mental age (MA) appreciably lower than the chronological age (CA). Thus, retarded people do not possess the range or quality of mental abilities that nonretarded individuals have. In addition, retarded persons demonstrate more inappropriate and less mature social behavior. In the case of mild retardation this discrepancy in social competence can be subtle. The mildly retarded are challenged most dramatically by the school setting, between the ages of 6 and 21; their inability to cope may be seen in problems with peer relationships or noncompliance with teacher-initiated directions.

The AAMD Definition

The most widely accepted definition of mental retardation is the one developed by the American Association on Mental Deficiency (AAMD). Its earlier definition (Grossman, 1973) was incorporated into P.L. 94–142, thus becoming the accepted legal definition at the federal level. Its 1983 revision differs in wording and meaning:

> Mental retardation refers to significantly subaverage general intellectual functioning resulting in or associated with concurrent impairments in adaptive behavior and manifested during the developmental period. (Grossman, 1983, p. 11)

As is evident from this statement, mental retardation is defined in terms of three important factors: intellectual functioning, adaptive behavior, and age of onset.

Intellectual functioning can be conceptualized as a conglomeration of abilities, such as the capacity to learn, solve problems, accumulate knowledge, adapt to new situations, and think abstractly. Performance on an intelligence test, the device used to evaluate intellectual functioning, is considered significantly below average if it is approximately two standard deviations below the mean. The vagueness of the definition and of this interpretation is an attempt to allow for flexibility. The 1983 AAMD definition suggests the use of an upper IQ range of 70 to 75 rather than an exact cutoff point of 70, even though the committee realizes that not all professionals will agree with this flexible criterion:

> [Differing points of view] graphically illustrate the impossibility of developing a classification system that is responsive to different ideologies and that at the same time applies objective standards for identifying persons in need by virtue of intellectual and behavioral impairments. (Grossman, 1983, p. 18)

Figure 8-1 graphically demonstrates the relationship of IQ and retardation.

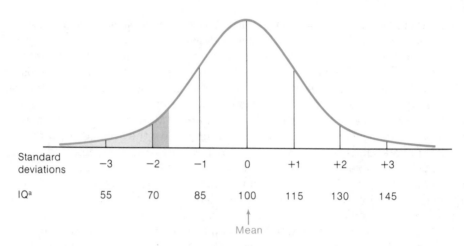

Figure 8-1   Assumed normal distribution of intelligence
[a]Based on Wechsler scales.
NOTE: Shaded areas indicate the mental retardation range.

An individual's level of *adaptive behavior* is determined by the degree and efficiency with which the individual meets "the standards of maturation, learning, personal independence, and/or social responsibility that are expected for his or her age level and cultural group" (Grossman, 1983, p. 11). In other words, the term refers to how well people cope with the demands of their immediate environment. As the definition indicates, there can be a close relationship between intellectual functioning and adaptive behavior. Two major components of adaptive behavior are the level of skill development present and the relationship of acquired skills to developmental and chronological age. The skills of particular importance are those necessary to function independently in a range of situations and those necessary to maintain responsible social relationships (Coulter & Morrow, 1978).

The criteria for assessing adaptive behavior vary according to developmental age and situational context. It is important to be aware that people function in a number of different roles, in a variety of social contexts, and within a multicultural and pluralistic society (Mercer & Lewis, 1977). Accordingly, behavior is strongly influenced by situational and cultural factors. A good example of cultural influence can be found in the area of eating skills. In many Southeast Asian cultures it is quite acceptable to use one's fingers extensively while eating; this same behavior is usually considered inappropriate in most Anglo cultures.

The *developmental period* is defined as that period of time between conception and 18 years of age. Below-average intellectual functioning and deficits in adaptive behavior must appear during this period to be considered indicative of mental retardation. When manifestations of retardation occur after this time period, the condition is classified as dementia (Grossman, 1983).

According to the 1983 AAMD definition, deficits in intellectual functioning and adaptive behavior must exist *concurrently*. This requirement is important because, as

Adaptive Behavior	Intellectual Functioning: Retarded	Intellectual Functioning: Not retarded
Retarded	Mentally retarded	Not mentally retarded
Not retarded	Not mentally retarded	Not mentally retarded

Figure 8-2 Twofold specification in 1983 AAMD definition of mental retardation

SOURCE: From Classification in Mental Retardation (p. 13) by H. J. Grossman (Ed.), 1983, Washington, DC: American Association on Mental Deficiency. Copyright 1983 by American Association on Mental Deficiency. Reprinted by permission.

Figure 8-2 illustrates, only when and if both of these conditions are met, should a person be classified as mentally retarded.

In an effort to allow for exceptions to the general rule, the concept of *clinical judgment* was introduced in the 1977 manual on definition and retained in the most recent definitional perspective. It permits diagnostic teams to classify as mentally retarded certain individuals who display severe problems in adaptive behavior even though their IQ scores are above the 70 to 75 upper range. On the other hand, it is possible that certain students with lower IQs may not be considered retarded because of their demonstrated competence in adaptive behavior. Any classification of an individual as mentally retarded should be based on current functioning and should not indicate an ultimate or permanent status (Payne, Patton, & Beirne-Smith, 1985). Diagnostic teams must exercise sound professional judgment and assume responsibility for misdiagnosis. The present trend—in cases where clinical judgment has been applied—has been to define mental retardation more conservatively, reflecting a reluctance to misplace students in special education. The result has been a sharp reduction in the number of students being classified as mildly mentally retarded in most states.

Alternative Perspectives

Developmental Disabilities Perspective The relationship of mental retardation to developmental disabilities is one of much overlap. The definition of developmental disabilities being used today evolved from the Developmental Disabilities Assistance and Bill of Rights Act of 1978 (P.L. 95–602):

> A severe chronic disability of a person which (a) is attributable to a mental or physical impairment or combination of mental or physical impairment; (b) is manifested before the person attains age twenty-two; (c) is likely to continue indefinitely; (d) results in substantial functional limitations in three or more of the following areas of major life activity (self-care, receptive and expressive language, learning, mobility, self-direction,

capacity for independent living, economic self-sufficiency); and (e) reflects the person's need for a combination and sequence of special, interdisciplinary, or generic care, treatment, or other services which are of lifelong or extended duration and are individually planned and coordinated.

It appears that developmental disabilities imply severe limitations and thus apply to a moderately or severely retarded population (Grossman, 1983). Although the term may be appropriate for certain mildly retarded individuals during some parts of their lives, for the most part it does not refer to this group.

Sociological Perspective   Mercer (1973, 1975) developed a social system framework from which to examine mental retardation. In this conceptualization normality is defined by the prevailing society, and deviance is behavior that does not conform to the existing standards. As a result, mental retardation becomes an "achieved social status" (Mercer, 1973) that varies from one social system to another. Indeed, there are people who legitimately achieve this status in most if not all situations, but many others achieve this status only in certain situations. Mercer advocates a definitional arrangement that encourages consideration of social status, development of multiple norms so that multicultural factors are taken into account, and acknowledgment of an individual's social and cultural background.

Behavioral Perspective   This approach emphasizes the need to focus on observable, measurable, and objectively determined relationships that control behavior (see Bijou, 1966, for a detailed explanation of this orientation). In other words, consideration is directed toward the "relationship between an individual's behavior and the events that either precede or follow that behavior" (Cegelka & Prehm, 1982, p. 10). This perspective discounts any process that strives to uncover underlying constructs such as defective intelligence or biological abnormalities because these are not educationally relevant; more importance is given to a person's observable interactions with the environment. This attention might include investigation of the parent-child interaction or the instructional design of an educational/vocational program. Retardation is seen as external to the individual; level of performance is a function of how well skills have been acquired through systematic programming and contingent reinforcement.

Social Behavioral Perspective   Like the behavioral perspective, the social behavioral perspective emphasizes observable, measurable, and objectively defined behaviors. The theory of social behaviorism, originally developed by Staats (1975), extends beyond the strict behavioral orientation by acknowledging and explaining personality variables. This personality dimension is made up of basic behavioral repertoires (emotional-motivational, language-cognitive, and sensory-motor). Learning is explained as the cumulative hierarchical acquisition of complex systems of behaviors, requiring utilization of the three behavioral repertoires. Retardation is considered in light of these learning conditions and principles, that is, as a problem in the acquisition of these complex systems of behaviors. Such a problem is due mainly to deficits in or inappropriate development of the basic behavioral repertoires—most notable in the language-cognitive area. As in the behavioral approach, there are no assumptions or explanations of etiology. Primary focus is on skill development, the conditions of learning (i.e., the environment and the reinforcing elements operating within it), and the basic behavioral repertoires that are essential for learning to occur. This perspective conveys a positive attitude toward learning and retardation by emphasizing skill acquisition and individual development. (See Staats & Burns, 1981, for a more thorough discussion of the relationship of this orientation to mental retardation.)

Classification of Retardation

Mental retardation can be classified in two ways: by etiology and by severity. Although classification by etiology does not provide practical information to educators, it is essential that professionals in the field have at least some working knowledge of this area. The other method of classifying retardation—by severity—is more frequently used by a wide range of disciplines. The system of classification that is cited most often is the AAMD system, which uses the terms *mild, moderate, severe,* and *profound.* In school settings, however, a different system is often utilized, with terms such as *educable* and *trainable* corresponding to mild and moderate. Thus, it is not uncommon to hear of students classified as EMR (educable mentally retarded) or TMR (trainable mentally retarded).

Classification by severity can use either intellectual functioning or adaptive behavior data. The most recent AAMD breakdown of levels as a function of intellectual functioning (Grossman, 1983) differs from earlier AAMD systems. The nonspecific IQ ranges exemplify the flexibility of this new definitional perspective and make it more consistent with the other major classification systems—the *Diagnostic and Statistical Manual of Mental Disorders,* (DSM-III) of the American Psychiatric Association (1980) and *International Classification of Diseases,* (ICD-9) of the World Health Organization (1978) (see Table 8-1).

A breakdown of severity as a function of adaptive behavior is not as amenable to graphic summarization because the variable of chronological age must also be considered. However, there are illustrations of this type of information in appendix A of the AAMD manual (Grossman, 1983).

Table 8-1   Classifications of mental retardation as a function of intellectual functioning

Level	Classification Source		
	AAMD (1983)	DSM-III (1980)	ICD-9 (1980)
Mild	50–55 to approx. 70	50–70	50–70
Moderate	35–40 to 50–55	35–49	35–49
Severe	20–25 to 35–40	20–34	20–34
Profound	below 20–25	below 20	under 20

Relationship of Mild Retardation to Other Conditions

There is great commonality among individuals who are mildly retarded and those who are labeled learning disabled or slow learners. The relationship of mild mental retardation to learning disabilities remains somewhat confusing because the definition of learning disabilities is ambiguous and difficult to apply. On a conceptual level there is a clear distinction between these two categories, based on the level of measured intellectual functioning. However, these two categories share many learning, social, and emotional characteristics. There are strong indications that many mildly retarded students have been reclassified as learning disabled (Gottlieb, Gottlieb, Schmelkin, & Curci, 1983; Patrick & Reschly, 1982; Smith & Polloway, 1983; Tucker, 1980).

The relationship of mildly retarded students to slow learners is also confusing. By a process of elimination, slow learners are neither mildly retarded nor learning disabled. Yet they can present problems in learning, social skills, and emotional maturity that are much the same as those of the other two groups. On a practical level it is very difficult to distinguish a student who functions near the upper borderline of the retarded range from a slow learner. Again, many students formerly classified as mildly retarded have now been labeled slow learners. The problems arising from this slow learner group will continue to be a major concern for school systems.

Prevalence

Various estimates of the size of the total mentally retarded population are available—frequently ranging from 2% to 3%. In recent years the validity of the 3% figure (the equivalent of more than 6 million Americans) has been challenged, and a more conservative estimate of 1% or less has been suggested (Mercer, 1973; Ramey & Finkelstein, 1981). This lower figure more accurately reflects the number of individuals who meet both criteria of subaverage general intellectual functioning and deficits in adaptive behavior. Tarjan, Wright, Eyman, and Kerran (1973) provide some additional insights regarding this lower figure:

> Many preschool children and adults, however, do not show major impairment in general adaptation even with relatively low IQs. As a consequence, the clinical diagnosis of mental retardation, particularly when it is of mild degree, is age-dependent. It is usually not established before school age and often disappears during late adolescence or young adulthood. (p. 370)

Analysis of federal data reporting the number of children aged 3 to 21 served under P.L. 94–142 and P.L. 89–313 reveals some interesting developments. Smith and Polloway (1983) report that between 1976 and 1981 there has been a decrease of approximately 13% nationwide in the number of students classified as mentally retarded. Since mild retardation constitutes as much as 75% of the total mentally retarded population, these changes are largely attributable to this group. A more recent analysis that considered changes between 1976 and 1984 indicates that a

Table 8-2 Number of children nationwide (ages 3–21) served under
P.L. 89–313 and P.L. 94–142 and classified as mentally retarded

Year	Number of Students
1976–77	969,547
1977–78	944,980
1978–79	917,880
1979–80	882,173
1980–81	844,180
1981–82	802,264
1982–83	780,558
1983–84	653,082
Change in number	−316,465
Amount of change	−32.6%

SOURCE: From U.S. Department of Education, Office of Special Education.

32.6% decrease has occurred nationwide (Patton, 1984). Table 8-2 delineates these changes.

Causes

We can talk definitively about the causative factors of retardation in fewer than 20% of all cases (Payne, Patton, & Beirne-Smith, 1983). In fact, the less severe the retardation, the less likely it is that we can determine a single cause with any certainty. "The majority of the retarded population . . . appear to be neurologically intact [and] have no readily detectable physical signs or clinical laboratory evidence related to retardation" (Grossman, 1983, p. 13). Implicit in this statement is the notion that most retarded people are mildly retarded and the causes of their condition are closely related to environmental factors.

The AAMD has designated nine general categories for classifying the causes of mental retardation (Grossman, 1983). These categories are identified in Table 8-3. There are, however, essentially two major groups of causes: biological and psychosocial. Biological causes, frequently easier to identify, are most often involved in the more severe forms of retardation. Thus, although we can talk specifically about most of the biological cases of retardation, we recognize that these known causes relate to a small percentage of retarded people. Psychosocial causes appear to play a significant role in the vast majority of cases of retardation (i.e., mild retardation), perhaps interacting with multiple genetic factors. Psychosocial causes are also more complex, involving different sets of factors.

Table 8-3   Various causes of retardation according to the 1983 AAMD medical classification (Grossman, 1983)

Type	Example
Infections and intoxicants	rubella, syphilis, toxoplasmosis, herpes simplex, bacterial and viral infections, drugs, poisons, smoking, caffeine, alcohol, lead
Trauma or physical agent	hypoxia, irradiation, trauma
Metabolism or nutrition	lipid storage diseases (Tay-Sachs, Hurler's, Hunter's), carbohydrate disorders (galactosemia, hypoglycemia), amino acid disorders (phenylketonuria), endocrine disorders (hypothyroidism), other (Prader-Willi syndrome)
Gross brain disease (postnatal)	neurofibromatosis, Sturge-Weber, tuberous sclerosis, Huntington's chorea
Unknown prenatal influence	anencephaly, microcephaly, Apert's syndrome, meningomyelocele, hydrocephalus
Chromosomal abnormality	Cri-du-chat, Down syndrome, Klinefelter's syndrome
Conditions originating in the prenatal period	prematurity, postmaturity, low birth weight
Psychiatric disorder	psychosis
Environmental influences	psychosocial disadvantage, sensory deprivation

There has long been controversy over the degree to which environmental and genetic factors operate to cause subnormal intellectual functioning. Most researchers now agree that there is some interaction between both kinds of factors in the majority of cases. In effect, genetic endowment may impose a range of intellectual potential; however, this potential is greatly influenced by a host of environmental variables. Ramey and Finkelstein (1981) compiled a list of the various environmental factors associated with psychosocial causes and identified by researchers:

- maternal factors (IQ below 80, little education, little positive involvement with child)

- poverty (low socioeconomic status)

- family factors (disorganization, large numbers of children)

- poor prenatal care

- spoken language patterns of lower complexity

Often, when the environment seems to be a major factor in retardation, attention to the individual's physical needs is warranted also. It is possible that some of these physical and/or psychosocial factors cause subtle neurological deficits that are not identified by existing techniques (Ramey & Finkelstein, 1981).

For the purposes of distinguishing among the causes of mild mental retardation, we can describe three basic groups of mildly retarded individuals: (1) the neurologically impaired, (2) the multiply handicapped, and (3) the psychosocially disadvantaged. These three groups are adapted from a model of five subgroups originally delineated by Dunn (1973). In the first group, the neurologically impaired, retardation is due to a known, mildly handicapping biological condition. For example, a child might have Down syndrome but nonetheless function at a relatively high level when compared with other individuals thus afflicted. in the multiply handicapped mild retardation combines with other conditions such as emotional problems, sensory impairments, motoric problems such as cerebral palsy, severe language difficulties, or convulsive disorders such as epilepsy. The psychosocially disadvantaged have difficulty in school but often function adequately within community and family settings. These distinctions are useful theoretically; however, on a practical basis the psychosocially disadvantaged group has been the predominant one and has prompted much difficulty and confusion in diagnosis and placement. There is a great deal of effort today to avoid including as mentally retarded those individuals who are merely culturally, ethnically, or linguistically different.

Characteristics

Generally speaking, mildly mentally retarded individuals are capable of functioning adequately on a number of levels in a variety of contexts. However, there are times when they do have difficulty coping with environmental demands. As a group they encounter their greatest difficulties in school.

Three important considerations need to be understood before characteristics are examined. First, retarded persons have the same basic physiological, social, and emotional needs that nonretarded people have. Second, retarded individuals differ greatly among themselves in many ways. Not every mildly retarded person possesses all of the characteristics discussed here. Nonetheless, we can make some generalizations that can provide a framework for our understanding of retarded behavior if we apply them carefully to classroom settings, Third, due to changes occurring in the mildly retarded student population, the traditional characteristics associated with this group may not be so valid as they once were, necessitating continual reconsideration.

Personal/Motivational

Although the importance of cognitive and linguistic characteristics is well recognized, the critical value of personal and motivational factors has often been overlooked (Baumeister & Brooks, 1981). The characteristics discussed here are intimately related to the functional disparity between retarded and nonretarded persons.

Expectancy of Failure   Because many mildly mentally retarded students frequently meet with failure in their early school careers, they are likely to develop an expectancy of failure. To escape the unpleasant experience of failing, they tend to avoid failure-producing situations and consequently may set lower aspirations and goals for themselves (Zigler, 1973). Individuals who are seldom successful in their academic pursuits will soon want to avoid such situations. Motivation is negatively affected.

Dependence   It has also been noticed that mentally retarded people generally rely on other people for solving problem situations. This sometimes is a result of their distrust of their own abilities (Zigler, 1966). Many teachers have heard their students say, "I can't do this," or "This is too hard." Most of the time this type of verbal expression is routine, and the task is attempted. However, some retarded students require or demand the assistance of teachers, aides, or fellow students.

External Locus of Control   Often, mentally retarded individuals perceive the consequences of their own behavior, both positive and negative, to be the result of forces such as fate or chance or other factors beyond their control. This perception is similar to learned helplessness, or the "psychological state that frequently results when events are uncontrollable" (Seligman, 1975, p. 9). It is developmentally appropriate for very young children to feel this way; but as they mature, most normal children shift to an internal locus of control (Lawrence & Winschel, 1975).

Poor Self-Concept   Although the literature is somewhat mixed on this matter, most studies support the view that retarded people possess an inferior self-concept. They simply do not hold strong, positive feelings about their own abilities and potential. Obviously, there is considerable correlation between negative self-concept and chronic failure.

Social/Behavioral

The definition of mental retardation states that adaptive behavior deficits must exist. Areas that can be problematic for mildly retarded persons include self-direction, responsibility, and social skills. In addition, any number of maladaptive behaviors (e.g., destructive or rebellious behavior) may be present. It is not uncommon to observe that mildly retarded individuals have poor interpersonal relationships. Gottlieb and Budoff (1973) found that the more inappropriate the behavior of the retarded individuals, the more likely they were to be rejected. Subsequent research (Gottlieb, Semmel, & Veldman, 1978) indicates that this rejection results from the nonretarded students' perception of behavioral inappropriateness rather than of academic incompetence. These findings have important implications for the integration of mildly retarded students into regular educational settings.

A mirror prompts a mildly retarded student's exploration of interpersonal communication.

Learning

To educators, learning and motivational characteristics of mentally retarded people loom as critically important. Learning has been defined as "the process whereby practice or experience results in a change in behavior which is not due to maturation, growth, or aging" (Payne & Patton, 1981, p. 126). The learning process is complex, and a vast amount of research has been conducted on how retarded individuals learn. Some of the major findings appropriate to mildly retarded students are highlighted here:

1. *Attention variables.* Retarded people seem to have significant difficulty in the three major components of attention (Alabiso, 1977): attention span (length of time on task), focus (inhibition of distracting stimuli), and selective attention (discrimination of important stimulus characteristics). Extensive research in this area has been conducted by Zeaman and House (1963).

2. *Mediational strategies.* Retarded learners are less likely to employ effective techniques for organizing information for later recall (Spitz, 1966). Typical tech-

niques of mature learners include verbal rehearsal and repetition, labeling, classification, association, and imagery. Research indicates that retarded students have difficulty producing these strategies (Bray, 1979; Robinson & Robinson, 1976), perhaps because they tend to be "inactive learners" (Strichart & Gottlieb, 1983)—a previous description of learning disabled students (Torgesen, 1982).

3. *Memory.* In general, research has shown that retarded learners have difficulty in the area of short-term memory (STM) but retain information over the long term. Indeed, their long-term memory (LTM) is usually comparable to that of nonretarded learners (Belmont, 1966). Certain STM problems involving nonserial tasks have been associated with deficits in the spontaneous use of mediational strategies (Cohen, 1982).

4. *Transfer, or generalization.* Mentally retarded students tend to show deficiencies in the ability to apply knowledge or skills to new tasks, problems, or stimulus situations (Stephens, 1972). They fail to use previous experience to formulate rules that will help solve future problems of a similar nature.

5. *Abstraction.* The ability to engage in abstract thinking or to work with abstract materials is limited (Dunn, 1973; Kolstoe, 1976). Symbolic thought, as exemplified by introspection and hypothesizing, is restricted.

6. *Incidental learning.* There is some indication that retarded students are relatively inefficient learners because they tend to pay more attention to incidental information. As nonretarded children get older (i.e., sixth or seventh grade), they become better able to ignore irrelevant information and to attend selectively to essential aspects of the task. This is not the case with retarded children. (See Hardman & Drew, 1975, for a further discussion.)

Speech/Language

Since the development of speech and language is closely associated with intellectual development, it is not surprising that mentally retarded people display more problems in speech and language than nonretarded people do. Specifically, there is a higher prevalence of speech problems in the retarded population (MacMillan, 1982; Spradlin, 1963); difficulties with articulation (e.g., substitution and omission of sounds) occur most often. In addition, language deficiencies are common among the retarded, including delayed oral language development (Dunn, 1973), restricted vocabulary, and incorrect grammatical usage (Spradlin, 1968). Language skills can be one of the greatest hurdles that retarded individuals must overcome if they are to be fully integrated into society (Polloway & Smith, 1982).

Physical/Health

In the mildly retarded population physical and health characteristics do not differ dramatically from those of nonretarded comparison groups. Among the mildly retarded the psychosocially disadvantaged often display no distinctive physical and health characteristics. Typically their performance, particularly in motor skills, is significantly better than that of the neurologically impaired or multiply handicapped (Dunn, 1973). With these latter groups the very nature of their handicapping conditions causes them to differ physically from nonretarded individuals. Overall, we can make certain generalizations about the differences in physical capacity and health between the mildly retarded and the nonretarded population:

1. *Body measurements*. Mildly retarded individuals are below comparative standards for nonretarded persons (equated by age) in height, weight, and skeletal maturity (Bruininks, Warfield, & Stealey, 1978).

2. *Motor development*. A study of mildly retarded young people indicates that they perform significantly below their nonretarded peers in all areas of motor proficiency (Bruininks, 1977).

3. *Physical impairments*. Some mildly mentally retarded individuals—principally the multiply handicapped and neurologically impaired—display concomitant physical problems such as cerebral palsy, convulsive disorders, sensory impairments, and injuries resulting from child abuse (Soeffing, 1975).

4. *Health-related problems*. Inappropriate and unbalanced diets, susceptibility to disease and illness, inadequate health care, and dental problems have all been found to be characteristic of many mildly retarded persons.

Academic

The mildly retarded do not achieve in school subjects at a level commensurate with their intellectual potential (Kirk, 1964). They tend to be underachievers (Hallahan & Kauffman, 1976, 1982), typically in all academic areas. All aspects of reading, but particularly reading comprehension and word attack, cause mildly retarded students great difficulty (Dunn, 1973). In arithmetic fundamentals—addition, subtraction, multiplication, division—they are typically able to achieve at a normal rate, but they are usually deficient in arithmetic reasoning (Dunn, 1973).

Vocational/Occupational

Some information about occupational characteristics has been collected. Crain (1980) studied the postschool economic and vocational status of mildly retarded graduates. She found that most were in the civilian labor force (68%), but the majority of these held unskilled (e.g., dishwashers, maids) and semiskilled (e.g., nurse's aide) positions. Of those employed, only one was earning a yearly income as low as the poverty level. There is little information on those individuals who were not employed.

In general, mildly retarded adults are capable of obtaining and maintaining gainful employment, although a critical factor is their ability to demonstrate personal and social behaviors that are appropriate for the workplace. For many mildly retarded adults, successful adjustment is augmented by families, benefactors, and/or various adult service providers. As Kehle and Barclay (1979) point out, many mildly retarded adults become self-sufficient but feel "a consistent lack of quality in their lives" (p. 51).

Assessment

Assessing mental retardation is a comprehensive collection of information through various techniques: formal and informal testing, interviews, observations, and cumulative records. The process examines intellectual functioning, academic achievement, social and emotional dimensions, adaptive behavior, medical condition, and language development. Various aspects are assigned varying degrees of importance depending on the age of the individual.

Age-Level Distinctions

Early Childhood Since mild retardation is basically a school-related phenomenon, the major focus of assessment at the preschool level is to identify children who are at risk for being classified as mildly retarded later in their lives. Keogh and Daley (1983) have noted some confusion in the definition of risk. In summarizing previous attempts to delineate the types of children at risk (Keogh & Kopp, 1978; Tjossem, 1976), Keogh presents three major types of risk: (1) established risk (e.g., known medical conditions), (2) environmental risk (e.g., life situations associated with possible problems), and (3) biological risk (e.g., early developmental histories suggesting possible problems).

Simner (1983) reviewed the research and found that there are effective and ineffective warning signs. According to Simner, effective measures for predicting school failure include in-class attention span, distractibility or memory span, in-class verbal fluency, in-class interest and participation, letter or number identification skills, and printing errors.

For preschool-age children it is also common to examine different developmental areas. As these children get older, it becomes necessary to determine not only whether they have acquired general prerequisite skills but also whether they demonstrate certain skills that are situation-specific to their subsequent environments (McCormick & Kawate, 1982). Concern should also be given to family needs (Rogers-Warren & Poulson, 1984) and environmental factors that put children at risk for school failure (Ramey & Finkelstein, 1981).

School Age The primary focus at this level is the measurement of intellectual functioning and adaptive behavior. Other areas (e.g., academic achievement) are typically examined, but the identification and classification of students as mentally retarded requires confirmation of problems in these two areas.

There are many theories of what intelligence is. One fairly comprehensive definition describes intelligence as "the ability to adapt, achieve, solve problems, interpret incoming stimuli to modify behavior, accumulate knowledge, or respond to items on an intelligence test" (Payne & Patton, 1981). Intelligence tests sample a cluster of behaviors from which we can infer levels of intellectual functioning. The resulting score—the IQ (intelligence quotient)—is an index of how well an individual performed these behaviors on the test. Most intelligence tests being used to make eligibility decisions in school systems today are individually administered, verbal in nature, scored with reference to age norms (thus comparing mental age with chronological age), and considered reliable and valid.

Traditionally, the most commonly utilized instruments have been the Wechsler Intelligence Scale for Children-Revised (WISC-R) (Wechsler, 1974) and the Stanford-Binet Intelligence Scale (Terman & Merrill, 1973). Recently, the Kaufman Assessment Battery for Children (K-ABC) (Kaufman & Kaufman, 1982) and the Woodcock-Johnson Psychoeducational Battery (Woodcock & Johnson, 1977) have been introduced and are being used regularly in various parts of the country. One innovative approach to assessing individuals is entitled the System of Multicultural Pluralistic assessment (SOMPA). The design of the SOMPA, created by Mercer and Lewis (1977), acknowledges that an individual must function in a number of different cultural and social contexts.

Much controversy exists over the use of intelligence tests in the schools. Some of the issues involved are:

- *The definition of intelligence.* There is considerable disagreement as to what intelligence is.

- *The overemphasis on the intelligence component.* To this day deficits in intellectual functioning are more heavily weighted than deficits in adaptive behavior.

- *The stability of IQ scores.* If intelligence is a basic, enduring attribute, then why do IQ scores fluctuate?

- *Cultural bias.* Critics emphasize that the verbal nature and middle-class standards of the commonly used tests discriminate against ethnic minority and economically disadvantaged students. Figure 8-3 lets you experience briefly what it is like to be asked culturally specific questions.

Assessing adaptive behavior is just as important as assessing intelligence. However, the consideration of adaptive behavior has suffered from an imprecision in definition and psychometric unsophistication. Criticism of the use of such measures has resulted in part from practical problems (e.g., administration of the instruments). Nevertheless, the assessment of adaptive behavior should be supported and encouraged. To date, a number of formal adaptive behavior scales have been developed and are available commercially. Some of the most frequently used instruments, suitable for evaluating mildly retarded students, are the AAMD Adaptive Behavior Scale—School Edition (Lambert & Windmiller, 1981); the Vineland Adaptive Behavior Scales (Sparrow, Balla, & Cicchetti, 1983); and the Adaptive Behavior Inventory for Children (Mercer & Lewis, 1977), which is part of SOMPA. Table

The following questions are biased toward people who have lived in Hawaii for a period of time. Answers appear at the bottom.

1. A woman who is *hapai* is _____.
   a. available
   b. married
   c. pregnant
   d. sexy
   e. a mother

2. A *puka* is a _____.
   a. fish
   b. star
   c. curve
   d. hole
   e. vine

3. If you live on the *mauka* side of the street, then your home is probably _____.
   a. on the east side
   b. on the west side
   c. on the south side
   d. toward the mountains
   e. toward the ocean

4. "*Pau hana* time come by my house" means _____.
   a. When you have a chance, come to my house.
   b. After dinner come over to my house.
   c. Come over to my house this evening.
   d. Come over to my house after work.
   e. Come over to my house in the morning.

Answers: 1, c; 2, d; 3, d; 4, d

Figure 8-3 Examples of culturally specific test questions
SOURCE: from the Hanna-Butta Test by Warren Gouveia. Reprinted by permission.

8-4 lists various skill areas that are integral components of adaptive behavior. These areas reflect somewhat the type of content found in adaptive behavior instrumentation.

Secondary/Transition   Since most mild retardation is identified at the elementary level, the issues of identification and eligibility are not so crucial at this level. In fact, as mildly retarded students leave the school environment, they may no longer be considered retarded. The major assessment needs at this level are concerned with preparation for successful adjustment to the community and adult life. It is important to obtain information about students' occupational interests and aptitudes, general job skills, practical knowledge of everyday realities (e.g., knowing

Table 8-4   Developmental components of adaptive behavior

During infancy and early childhood

1. Sensory-motor skills
2. Communication skills (including speech and language)
3. Self-help skills
4. Socialization (ability to interact with others)

During childhood and early adolescence

5. Application of basic academic skills in daily life activities
6. Application of appropriate reasoning and judgment in mastery of the environment
7. Social skills (participation in group activities and interpersonal relationships)

During late adolescence and adult life

8. Vocational and social responsibilities and performances

SOURCE: From *Classification in Mental Retardation* (p.13) by H. J. Grossman (Ed.), 1983, Washington, DC: American Association on Mental Deficiency. Copyright 1983 by American Association on Mental Deficiency. Reprinted by permission.

how to renew a driver's license), and certain life skills (e.g., parenting skills, assuming family responsibilities).

Intervention

A variety of programming alternatives are presently available for mentally retarded individuals; most of them are for school-age children. Two major issues dominate the topic of intervention: lack of services (for certain age groups) and efficacy of existing services. Older retarded individuals find that when formal schooling ends, so do most of the beneficial educational services. The second concern involves what Turnbull and Barber (1984) call the cost-yield issue. They suggest that the effectiveness of special education be approached from two different perspectives: a cost-benefit basis (economic perspective—does it save money?) and a cost-effectiveness basis (personal perspective—do individuals prosper and progress?).

Age-Level Distinctions

Early Childhood   Public education is required by federal law for preschool-age handicapped youngsters; however, specific policy varies from state to state. As noted earlier, most mildly retarded children are not identified until they enter school. As a result, many of them may not be specifically identified at this age level. Those who are identified may be served in preschool classes for handicapped children; often these children are classified as learning impaired. However, a larger number of potential mildly retarded youngsters may be identified as at risk and served in various early childhood programs, which may or may not be special education related.

Considerable research has pointed to the positive effect of early intervention on the later growth and development of mildly retarded children (Rogers-Warren & Poulson, 1984). Lazar and Darlington (1982), in their review of early education efforts, found a number of positive outcomes—one of which was that fewer numbers of these children were assigned to special education classes. Arguments still remain as to which type of program orientation is most effective. Evaluation of the Follow Through Project, established to sustain the early gains of children enrolled in Head Start programs, has indicated that a teacher-directed orientation has produced significant student gains (Stebbins, St. Pierre, Proper, Anderson, & Cerva, 1977). Even though the importance of early intervention has been validated, the delivery of such services remains confused and inadequately coordinated (Johnson & Chamberlin, 1983).

School Age   Public school systems offer a number of programmatic options to students who are mildly retarded. The four most common educational arrangements are regular education placement; resource services, with students spending only a few hours in special education settings; self-contained classes, with students spending most or all of the school day in special classes; and special school settings. In addition, many mildly retarded students may also receive one or more related services, such as speech/language intervention, occupational therapy, physical therapy, mental health counseling, or special transportation. The current trend is to mainstream mildly retarded students in regular education settings as much as is appropriate and ultimately successful. Some higher functioning students have been reclassified and are now being served in classes for learning disabled students (Mascari & Forgnone; 1982; Smith & Polloway, 1983; Tucker, 1980). However, regardless of the educational arrangement selected, it is important to consider any placement a tentative commitment, subject to change as needed.

Secondary/Transition   Today, many of the same educational arrangements available to retarded children of elementary age are also available to mildly retarded adolescents—regular education classes, resource services, self-contained classes. However, the instructional emphases are, or at least should be, quite different from those of the elementary level. Intermediate and high school programs are usually characterized by predominant instructional orientations (cf. Deshler, Lowrey, & Alley, 1979), which vary considerably.

Each instructional orientation reflects curricular decisions that have been made with implicit educational goals for these students. For instance, if a functional skills approach is adopted for a group of students, then the implication is that these students cannot function in a traditional curriculum. It is important to recognize that other retarded students may be able to succeed in regular classroom settings, performing the traditional academics with minimal assistance from various support systems. Appropriateness of placement and program can be determined only on an individual basis, taking specific factors into account. Mercer and Mercer (1981) affirm that students' educational programs must be predicated "on the basis of individualized planning and supported by a strong counseling program relevant to students' long-range development" (p. 376).

Historically, a vocational orientation has been utilized in programs for retarded adolescents (Brolin, 1982; Brolin & Kokaska, 1985; Smith & Payne, 1980). However, the quality, comprehensiveness, and success of the approach has varied greatly. One popular method for giving students the skills needed for the workplace is the work/study option. This technique attempts to match academic-related skills of practical utility with the demands of specific vocational settings. A description of a work/study program is presented in Table 8-5.

Handicapped students in general have been underrepresented in both secondary vocational programs and postsecondary school environments (*Office of Civil Rights Report*, 1980). Recently, the Office of Special Education of the U.S. Department of Education established transition from school to work as a priority for funding and programmatic efforts, attempting to maximize "student performance and movement through programs, while increasing awareness of interests, aspirations and educational needs, as well as increasing the availability of appropriate programming options" (*Hawaii Transition Project*, 1984, p. 2).

Not all retarded young adults adjust successfully to the demands that life and society make on them after they leave school; some require additional services. They may need continuing education to adjust to everyday living or develop new vocational skills. In a society that is constantly changing and becoming more technologically complex, some mildly retarded workers may be replaced by technology and will need retraining. These individuals may also need regular assistance in finding and utilizing community resources and services. In one study of retarded adults living in community settings, three major areas of everyday life were found to be particularly problematic: (1) making a living; (2) management of sex, sexuality, and marriage; and (3) use of leisure time (Edgerton, 1967). Retarded adults also frequently have difficulty obtaining and maintaining housing, gaining public acceptance, and establishing meaningful relationships with others.

The availability of continuing education for mildly retarded adults is largely restricted to what is available to the general public. Just as regular education was problematic for many members of this group, so these adult offerings pose obstacles as well. Some mildly retarded adults who need assistance can qualify for vocational rehabilitation services. Unfortunately, rehabilitation counselors usually contract out for such services and thus face the dilemma of limited options. Adult services and training opportunities do exist in most communities, but they are too few and have long waiting lists. In some rural areas these services may not exist at all. There have been some isolated attempts to provide vocational training to mildly retarded adults at community colleges. Other innovative programs for securing jobs for retarded adults have been developed and should be replicated.

Table 8-5   A typical work/study program

Grade 10

Academics—Emphasis is on development or remediation of skills in the areas of English, math, or social studies depending on the entry level skills of the student. In most programs, classes or courses associated with these content areas take up about one-half of the school day.

Physical Education/Health—Work/study participants usually take these courses with all other students during one academic period each day.

Preliminary Vocational Training—Specific vocational information concerning the student is gathered at this time (if it has not been secured previously). Basic courses dealing with the fundamentals of work are taken by all students in the program. These basic courses include such topics as using hand tools, developing homemaking skills, making simple repairs. This training encompasses approximately one-fourth to one-half of the school day.

Grade 11

Academics—Emphasis in this area is shifted to use of basic skills in vocational areas. For example, in the area of English the student might work on letter-writing skills. In the area of math the student might work on units concerned with budgeting, buying on credit, or paying taxes. This part of the program continues to require approximately one-half of the school day.

Physical Education/Health—One period each day.

Vocational Training—Depending on a number of factors, such as the student's interests and aptitude and the prevailing as well as projected job market, each pupil is offered specific vocational training. This training may be in such areas as the building trades, clerical work, food service, patient care, or handling materials. At this time students are given the opportunity to display their work skills through in-school job performance. This portion of the work/study program continues to require approximately one-fourth to one-half of the school day.

Grade 12

Academics—Skills directly related to job training continue to be emphasized. These skills include reading newspapers and other written materials to obtain job information and refining job interview skills through effective use of oral and written communications. This portion of the program begins to require less than one-half of the school day.

Work Experiences—During this phase of the program each student participates in a number of specific job experiences in the local community for approximately one-half of the day. Whether at work in the morning or in the afternoon, each student reports to the school every day to participate in academic courses, as well as to receive any necessary counseling.

SOURCE: From *Teaching Exceptional Adolescents* (p. 59) by J. E. Smith and J. S. Payne, 1980, Columbus, Ohio: Charles E. Merrill. Copyright 1980 by Bell & Howell Company. Reprinted by permission.

Mentally Retarded Offenders

Recently, more attention has been directed toward the issues surrounding the incarceration of retarded and other disabled offenders. The relationship of mental retardation and delinquency/criminality is not precisely known; nevertheless, it seems to be more a contributing factor than a cause.

Juvenile Offenders   Morgan (1979) studied national prevalence data indicating the number of handicapped individuals in juvenile correctional facilities. He found that approximately 7.7% of the incarcerated population was educably mentally retarded. Even though this figure was probably inflated, the magnitude of the situation is alarming. Even a figure somewhat lower than 7.7% differs significantly from the 1% of mental retardation existing in the general population.

Plausible explanations for the high rates of retardation among juvenile offenders are much like those describing the relationship of learning disabilities and juvenile delinquency (Keilitz & Miller, 1980): (1) as students these disabled individuals experience a sufficient amount of a school failure to precipitate delinquent behavior; (2) they possess certain behavioral characteristics that make them more susceptible to delinquency; and (3) they are treated differently by the juvenile justice system. There is still much debate as to which of these factors are responsible.

Even though determining cause is critical for preventing or minimizing the occurrence of delinquency, there is also a need to consider ways to intervene in existing situations. Some of the major issues and problems of providing services to this population are presented here:

1. *Responsibility for education.* A major issue questions who is responsible for educating these students; efforts must be directed to straightening out the problem of overlapping authority. Keilitz and Miller (1980) suggest that the best chance for meeting the educational needs of incarcerated students will occur if responsibility remains within the educational system.

2. *Correctional education.* What should be taught to these students? It seems logical that the curriculum should emphasize preparing these individuals to function in whatever subsequent environment seems likely for them. This may require attention to vocational skill development or preparation for postsecondary education. Other requisite areas include social skill development and life skill preparation.

3. *Personnel preparation.* To date, there are few college or university programs that prepare professionals to work in correctional settings. This type of training must differ from that provided to prospective teachers in typical public or private school settings. Some suggestions for correctional training have been offered (Mesinger, 1976).

4. *Staff development.* Because of the paucity of preservice programs for correctional teachers, it becomes especially important to provide comprehensive and continual in-service training to those who do work there (Brown & Robbins, 1979).

5. *Awareness.* There is also a great need to increase professional interest in and public awareness of issues related to an appropriate education for this population.

Adult Offenders Data collected a few years ago estimated the prevalence of mentally retarded offenders to be approximately 10% of the prison population. Like the figures for younger offenders, these are probably inflated; nevertheless, an inordinate percentage of the prison population is retarded. The reasons that mentally retarded individuals enter the criminal justice and correctional systems have been discussed elsewhere (Payne, Patton, & Beirne-Smith, 1985). Most attempts to explain their overrepresentation revolve around two ideas: (1) certain characteristics of mentally retarded individuals make them more likely to enter these systems, and (2) the nature and functions of the legal/correctional system tend to facilitate entry of this group into the system.

The issues surrounding this adult group are similar to those surrounding the juvenile group. The major difference is that there is no legal mandate to provide an appropriate special education to adult offenders. Although some correctional facilities have initiated distinct units within the institution for providing specialized education and training, these programs continue to receive low funding priority. Prisons were not designed to treat (i.e., educate, habilitate, or train) mentally retarded persons (Marsh, Friel, & Eissler, 1975).

Curriculum Implications

Before considering the content and sequence of what mildly retarded students should be taught, we need to establish a few basic guidelines. First, all curricular issues should be examined with a view to maintaining students in settings that are as close to normal as possible. Second, curricula and instructional procedures should challenge students to maximum growth and development. Excessive frustrations should be avoided, but so, too, should skill levels where mastery has already been achieved. Third, as the age of the student increases, emphasis on vocational and everyday living skills should grow stronger. It is crucial for students to develop those skills needed to function successfully in a community context and for teachers to design programs for that transition. Fourth, instructional programs need to be teacher-directed and based upon carefully selected and well-designed instructional techniques (cf. Becker & Carnine, 1980). Fifth, curriculum modification may have to be made to accommodate lower functioning students; content, sequence, and pace of instruction may have to be adjusted.

Adapting a curricular model originally presented by Campbell (1968), Dunn (1973) presented a comprehensive overview of curricular content appropriate for mildly retarded students. We have further adapted the model as a reference for articulating curricular needs and have presented it in Figure 8-4. It divides curricular content into four major areas:

- basic readiness and practical academic development

- communication, language, and cognitive development

As a mildly retarded student grows up, increasing emphasis is placed on everyday skills offering independence.

- socialization, family living, self-care, recreation/leisure, and personality development

- career and vocational development

Educational goals and curricula for mildly retarded students vary widely, as do the students themselves. Consequently, this model should be considered a general framework for reference rather than a definitive schedule.

Age-Level Distinctions

Early Childhood During this period attention is focused on providing children with experiences to develop their cognitive, psychomotor, and social/affective skills—those readiness skills that are requisite for successful performance in kin-

Level (approx.)	Preschool	Elementary School	Intermediate school	High School	Postschool
Age (approx.)	CA[a] under 6 yrs.	CA 6 to 11 yrs.	CA 12 to 14 yrs.	CA over 15 yrs.	—
Grade	—	K–6	7–9	10–12	—

Instructional emphases (percent): 100, 90, 80, 70, 60, 50, 40, 30, 20, 10

Area I. Basic Readiness and Practical Academics Development

Motor development
Sensory training
Perceptual training
Physical education
Reading
Writing
Arithmetic
Art and music
Science
Social studies
Newspaper usage
Practical social studies
Practical science
Law
Problem solving
Insurance
Budgeting
Consumer buying
Driver education

Area II. Communication, Oral Language, and Cognitive Development

Oral language development
Listening skills
Concept development
Memory training
Associative thinking
Learning strategies

Area III. Socialization, Family Living, Self-care, Recreation, and Personality Development

Manners
Self-care
Dramatics
Citizenship
Family living skills
Death and dying
Drug and alcohol abuse
Sex education
Deportment
Art
Grooming
Sports
Dancing
Cooking
Social roles
Child care
Housekeeping

Area IV. Prevocational and Vocational Development, Including Housekeeping

Group play
Safety
Music
Career awareness
Following instructions
Independent work habits
Household chores
Group work habits
Practical arts
Career orientation
Career exploration
Field trips to job sources
Placement services
Job training
Labor laws
Career preparation
Work study

Employment

Figure 8-4 Curriculum content areas for mildly retarded students as a function of developmental level
SOURCE: Original model developed by Campbell in 1968, adapted by L. M. Dunn (Ed.) in Exceptional Children in the Schools: Special Education in Transition (2nd ed.), 1973, New York: Holt, Rinehart & Winston.
[a]CA represents chronological age.

dergarten and the primary grades. Both academic and nonacademic skills must be developed, including the ability to get along with other students in group activities and the ability to pay attention for a given period of time.

By attending to children's deficits, we often fail to notice or identify their strengths. Even at this early age it may be important to recognize areas in which mildly retarded students can succeed and perhaps excel. Dettre (1983) captures the essence of this point:

> In a field where the first concern is usually remediation, identifying and developing strengths is often overlooked. Still, at-risk children, more than any others, need to find something they do better than the average student. (pp. 62–63)

School Age   From the time that students enter elementary school until the time they leave, there is much attention on basic academic skill development in areas such as reading, mathematics, and language arts. Certainly no one would argue against the importance of these basic areas. Unfortunately, other critical content areas such as science and social studies are relegated to secondary status. A strong case for the inclusion of these areas has been made elsewhere (Polloway et al., 1985). The basic argument is that these subjects present the type of information that broadens students' knowledge and experiential base. Too often mildly retarded students receive no instruction, inappropriate instruction, or poor instruction in these areas. If we are to identify student strengths, we should also explore students' ability in the areas of music, art, drama, and dance. Like science and social studies, these areas are regularly given much less attention.

Another important skill area in great need of attention, especially if students are to be integrated into regular education, is social skills. Programs such as the ACCEPTS curriculum developed by Walker and colleagues (1983) and presented in chapter 6 assist in the development of successful classroom adjustment and positive peer relationships.

Another area that deserves attention in the curriculum of mildly retarded learners is that of thinking and problem-solving skills. Winschel and Ensher (1978) have clearly articulated this need:

> There is a need for a new curricular approach in which facts and routine academic skills are consciously subordinate to the processes of intellectual development, and imposed knowledge is secondary to the opportunities for learning and discovery. (p. 132)

The implication here is that students need to become more independent learners because assistance will not always be available to them. Computers offer teachers a perfect opportunity to focus on these skills.

Secondary/Transition   As indicated in Figure 8-4, there is a shift in curricular emphasis at the secondary level. Curricular decisions must be based on the individual educational goals and probable subsequent life styles of mildly retarded students. For some students an academic-oriented program may be appropriate; for others the focus may need to be on vocational and everyday living skills. The

Model Program

Parents and professionals alike are genuinely concerned that retarded adults become productive and reliable members of the work force. One effort designed to achieve this result is the Community Training and Employment Program (COMTEP). COMTEP is a community-based vocational training and placement program that serves adults with mild or moderate retardation. It possesses some unique features. Funded in 1983 and administered through the Association for Retarded Citizens of Hawaii, COMTEP is structured around three primary phases of operation: vocational assessment, job matching, and prevocational training; COMTEP-employer training partnership; and supported employment.

The first phase is concerned with identifying vocational areas in which clients are interested and for which they possess the requisite skills. Assessment activities include formal vocational evaluations as well as situational assessments. One month of prevocational training may also be necessary for some clients; it can address appropriate interaction and communication skills as well as work responsibility and career planning.

The second phase of the program requires the participation of both COMTEP and the employer. After a suitable employment site is found by program staff, both parties agree to certain provisions. The employer provides (1) direction and supervision to the new employee, (2) reasonable accommodation, and (3) wages. COMTEP provides (1) a training facilitator (job coach) for up to 3 months to maximize the success of the placement by providing individualized training to the new employee and by minimizing the disruption to the business; (2) liability coverage for the new employee and the trainer during this on-site training period; (3) access for the employer to the Targeted Jobs Tax Credit Program (TJCP), in which the employer receives substantial tax benefits; and (4) work-related support (e.g., employment counseling, job club) to the retarded employee.

During the third phase COMTEP provides ongoing support for a full year to the employer and the client by troubleshooting, upgrading certain skills, and/or retraining.

The value of the COMTEP model is that it focuses on individual needs and trains individuals on the job, in contrast to the typical classroom setting from which retarded clients must generalize to real situations. The program is attractive to employers for two major reasons. It eases the responsibility and the extra time required to assist retarded employees in adapting to their new setting. In addition, the employment of such individuals entitles employers to certain tax advantages. Thus, COMTEP provides positive outcomes to all parties involved.

overriding objective is preparation for life after high school—in whatever environment is chosen.

There are a number of everyday living skills that must be taught if these students are to adjust successfully to adulthood. Knowles (1978) has identified a host of situations that young adults must be ready to manage. These "life problems" are categorized into six areas: vocation and career, home and family living, personal development, enjoyment of leisure, health, and community living. In addition, topics such as human sexuality, approaches to parenting, human reactions to death and dying, methods of coping with emotional crises, and problems that result from drug and alcohol abuse have long been neglected in curricula for nonre-tarded as well as mildly retarded students. An understanding of these and related topics is important to the individual's adjustment in adolescent and adult life. Particularly in the case of the mildly retarded, who are not likely to take initiative in learning about these subjects, it is crucial to incorporate such topics into the curriculum.

The assumption underlying the model in Figure 8-4 is that individuals leaving school need a wide variety of competencies to adjust successfully to community living. At the same time, though, the model reflects the increasing importance of vocational preparation as retarded students progress through school. Whatever model is used to delineate curricular content for mildly retarded students, empha-sis must be placed on individual needs, desires, and abilities. Furthermore, it is essential that students learn strategies and skills that are not situation-bound.

Mainstreaming

During the last few years continuing attention has been given to integrating handi-capped students into regular education settings. Unfortunately, the implementa-tion of this policy has preceded a firm research base to support it. Gottlieb (1981) captures the nature of the problem:

> More disturbing is the lack of clearly conceptualized and articulated goals for main-stream education. At this point in time, special-educators are more involved with placing children in the least restrictive environment than with educating them in the least restrictive environment. (p. 122)

We should be as concerned with what happens to these students after they are placed in mainstream settings as we are with how to get them there.

Age-Level Distinctions

Early Childhood   For a vast majority of mildly retarded children, the issue of mainstreaming may be a moot point at the preschool level; they probably have not yet been identified. However, for those children who have been identified as re-tarded, learning impaired, or at risk and who may be receiving some type of ser-vices, the issue of mainstreaming becomes real. In these situations we must decide what is the least restrictive environment. Since most public schools do not provide early childhood programs for nonhandicapped students, a usual setting for main-streaming handicapped students is not available. Some school systems have cho-sen to contract with private preschool programs; however, the financial implica-tions can become substantial.

School Age   A substantial amount of research has examined the effects of inte-grating educable mentally retarded students into regular classrooms. However, a cautionary note is warranted. As Gottlieb (1981) has suggested, the results of earlier research on mainstreaming EMR students may not be applicable to the present EMR population. This new, lower functioning EMR group may not be so capable of being mainstreamed (MacMillan & Borthwick, 1980). Overall, the research permits no definite conclusions about the success or failure of mainstreaming efforts. Nevertheless, some observers (Gottlieb, 1981; Gresham, 1982) have identified tendencies:

> In the area of academic achievement EMR students do as well in regular settings as they do in special settings.

> Mainstreamed EMR students are not well accepted by their nonretarded peers. In fact, some evidence suggests that nonintegrated retarded students are better accepted. Correspondingly, there is little interaction between integrated EMR students and their nonretarded classmates.

> Mainstreamed EMR students do not model the behaviors of their nonretarded classmates.

These mixed results suggest that we must continue to evaluate EMR mainstreaming, especially in light of changes in this population.

Any effort to mainstream EMR students if it is to be successful, will need to

1. identify and analyze successful mainstreaming efforts (Mascari & Forgnone, 1982),

2. pay more attention to preparing EMR students for regular class placement by examining the skills and behaviors required in that setting,

3. develop appropriate social skills in EMR students (Gresham, 1982),

4. structure situations in which retarded and nonretarded students have an opportunity to work together cooperatively on tasks that retarded students can perform reasonably well (Gottlieb & Leyser, 1981),

5. investigate the daily interchanges between retarded students and their classmates and teachers (Gottlieb, 1981), and

6. continually reassess the quality of the mainstreamed programs into which EMR students have been placed (MacMillan, Meyers, & Yoshida, 1978).

Secondary/Transition   Efforts to mainstream mildly retarded students can occur at the secondary level; however, there may be limitations on the types of integration that are possible. Clark (1975) has raised four major concerns with mainstreaming mildly retarded adolescents: lack of data to support such efforts, inappropriate curricular focus of regular education, limited attention to career education, and inflexibility in administrative procedures. Students who have had a history of low academic achievement may be difficult to move into regular classes requiring a relatively high level of academic prowess. On the other hand, nonacademic classes (e.g., art, drafting) and extracurricular activities may prove to be viable options in mainstreaming these students.

When formal schooling ends, most mildly retarded individuals are naturally mainstreamed back into the community. As previously discussed, some individuals may require continued assistance of various types. If social acceptance is a function of behavior rather than of academic performance, it may linger on as a problem for retarded young adults. The effectiveness of mainstreaming young adults into society has been described somewhat in the literature on community adjustment.

Innovation and Development

Even though we have gained much knowledge about mental retardation, we have much to learn. As we have mentioned repeatedly, the mildly retarded population is going through a metamorphosis. The significant drop in the number of students being classified as mildly retarded and the inclusion of a lower functioning group in classes for the mildly retarded are forcing us to reexamine whom we are now serving and how we can serve them most propitiously.

Prevention

It is interesting to note, as Begab (1981) has, that few prevention efforts are directed toward eliminating the root causes of retardation. Most programs have been designed to deal with retardation after the fact. In 1976 the President's Committee on Mental Retardation set two goals regarding prevention:

Goal: At least 50% reduction in the incidence of mental retardation from biomedical causes by the year 2000

Goal: Reduction of the incidence and prevalence of mental retardation associated with social disadvantages to the lowest level possible by the end of this century (pp. 135, 137)

It is, of course, the latter goal that is of utmost concern in relation to mild retardation. If social disadvantages are to be significantly lessened, then drastic social changes are in order. Unfortunately, such changes are not likely (Payne, Patton, & Beirne-Smith, 1985). Thus, it is perhaps more realistic for research to reexamine the ambiguous concept of cultural deprivation, as well as its relationship to mild mental retardation, and to investigate methods of implementing services for individuals before they reach school age.

Early education, whether for classified special students or for children at risk, has become an important mechanism for preventing the school failure associated with mild retardation. However, Meyen (1984) warns that, of the many services created for mentally retarded people in the last decade, early childhood education may be the most vulnerable to budgetary reductions. This possibility is alarming and must be challenged.

Education

There are numerous issues relevant to the education of mildly retarded individuals that require further investigation. The cost-yield issue raised by Turnbull and Barber (1984) will become even more critical in times of fiscal restraint and programmatic reevaluation. Improvements in the decision-making process are needed as well, especially in relation to culturally different children.

Instructional changes may be necessary if the EMR population continues to undergo current changes. Attention to curricular modifications and teaching practices must continue. Emphasis on direct teaching and maximizing student time in active learning should also be sustained. Regardless of the student population, attention must be given to preparation for young adulthood and life in the community. Currently, federal funds are being earmarked for the support of projects addressing transition from school to work/community. We hope that the development of innovative and effective approaches will result.

Specific educational uses of computers have been described (see Polloway et al., 1985). The need to acquaint students with this technology is twofold: it can be an effective, interest-driven way of providing certain types of instruction, and it is the unavoidable technology of the future. If we are to prepare students for adulthood, then we must introduce them to the technology that will be utilized in many facets of our lives.

A major problem about which school systems have long known but have done little involves students with significant learning-related problems who may not qualify for special education services. As mildly retarded and learning disabled students continue to be decertified in many school districts, there is an even greater need to provide services to this group of problem learners. As Meyen and Moran (1979) have suggested, special services may need to be available to *all* students who need special assistance, regardless of how briefly the services are needed. One suggestion is to move to a system that is more concerned with labeling services than students, thereby allowing students experiencing problems to obtain the needed services without determining eligibility (Smith & Polloway, 1983).

Life Style

Research topics pertaining to the adjustment of the mildly retarded in community settings cover a wide range. It is important to assess community attitudes toward the retarded, the needs of families in which there is a mildly retarded individual, and service delivery in rural areas. In addition, criteria for judging successful community adjustment need to be established and variables that predict successful adjustment, identified. Most important, researchers must strive to obtain firsthand information from mentally retarded individuals themselves. Often programs are designed and goals set for retarded individuals based on what we think they want rather than what they think and feel. For instance, some programs have been designed in which the ultimate goal is to enable retarded persons to live independently. Frequently, however, the people for whom these efforts were made have indicated that they do not enjoy living independently and were happier when they were living in a group arrangement, where companionship was readily available. In our haste to improve the quality of the lives of the mildly retarded, we must not forget to consider their desires, feelings, and attitudes.

We must also be sensitive to the changing demands of living in an increasingly technical society. Turnbull and Barber (1984) comment on this state of affairs:

> If there are dramatic breakthroughs in bio-engineering for retarded people, there will be dramatic implications for their education, their employment, and their residential placement. Such breakthroughs also will affect the current debate about their educability, employability, and adaptability to "normalized" environments. (p. 5)

The field of mental retardation is an exciting one; it always has been and will continue to be. Like most fields it is not static, and for this reason we must continually reexamine what is happening and how it is affecting those about whom we are concerned.

Summary

Mental retardation is a condition subject to confusion. Like other disabilities, it can be classified along a continuum from mild to profound. Mild retardation affects the majority of those classified as retarded and deserves the attention of professionals in education and human services. The condition is complex and highly variable.

Historically, the treatment of retarded individuals has been a function of sociopolitical influences and the efforts of certain individuals and groups. Within the last 30 years retarded people have gained many rights and services. Nonetheless, there is still much work to do. One current development is the changing nature of the retarded population. There are significantly fewer students being classified as retarded, and the mildly retarded group is lower functioning. These changes pose immediate problems for providing appropriate services to this group.

The definition of retardation has changed over time. The most frequently cited definitional perspective is that of the American Association on Mental Deficiency (AAMD). The latest definitional revision (Grossman, 1983) retains the three major components of the earlier definitions: significant subaverage general intellectual functioning, deficits in adaptive behavior, and manifestation during the developmental period. The concept of clinical judgment was retained also. The AAMD definition reflects a clinical perspective; other definitional perspectives continue to exist. Most professionals suggest that the prevalence of all levels of mental retardation is approximately 1%, although higher figures can be found in the literature.

There is no one cause of mild mental retardation. Instead, there are three general categories under which more specific causes can be grouped: neurological impairments, multiple handicaps, and psychosocial factors. Most mild retardation falls into the third category. Unfortunately, this category is the most complex. In general, the psychosocial domain suggests that retardation is the result of heredity and environment.

Mildly retarded individuals are able to function adequately in various environmental contexts. However, they encounter problems in certain settings, particularly educational ones. Mildly retarded people have normal human needs and differ greatly among themselves in many ways. The major areas of difficulty include personal/motivational, social/behavioral, learning, speech/language, physical/health, academic, and vocational/occupational.

The importance and positive effects of early intervention for high-risk children are clear. It may be important not only to teach preacademic skills but also to address specific nonacademic skills needed for survival in kindergarten. At the elementary level curricula and methodology for mildly retarded students may be similar to those of regular education. However, some specialized materials may be used, and the pace may be different. When mildly retarded students progress to the secondary level, some major curricular decisions must be made. For many of these students an academic-oriented curriculum may be desirable and appropriate. For others a more functional and career/vocational program may be chosen. All students must be prepared for the transition to life after high school. Particularly important is the need for life skills.

An often-overlooked topic needing professional attention is the area of retarded offenders. An inordinate number of retarded persons are represented within the juvenile and adult correctional systems. Although the relationship of mental retardation and delinquency/criminality is not empirically known, the practical implications warrant attention. Key among the pressing issues is the question of how best to provide education and training.

Study Questions

1. Evaluate the treatment of mentally retarded people today as compared to that 20 years ago and 10 years ago.

2. Explain the major components of the latest AAMD definition (Grossman, 1983).

3. How has the mildly retarded population changed over the last 10 years, and what might be some plausible explanations of this phenomenon?

4. According to the major categorical distinctions of neurological impairments, multiple handicaps, and psychosocial factors, what are possible causes of mild retardation?

5. How can personal/motivational and social/behavioral characteristics of mental retardation affect learning?

6. Defend continued funding of early intervention programs for at-risk children.

7. What implications does the lower of the mildly retarded population have on curricula and mainstreaming?

8. Based on the information presented in this chapter, what are the requisite components of successful integration efforts?

9. What postsecondary options are available to mildly retarded students, and what relationships do most school settings have with these postschool environments?

10. What are the major issues concerning juvenile and adult retarded offenders?

TIPS FOR HELPING

1. Set goals that are realistic for the individual and the community in which the individual lives.

2. Assign tasks that (a) are personally relevant, (b) are carefully sequenced from easy to difficult, and (c) allow the learner to be highly and frequently successful.

3. Recognize the individual's strengths and weaknesses, provide incentives for performance, and establish necessary rules for behavior.

4. Explain required tasks in terms of concrete concepts.

5. Pay close attention to the individual's responses to tasks; reward good performance and correct inappropriate responses objectively.

6. Encourage the individual to take part as fully as possible in everyday events, even when participation involves a reasonable degree of risk.

7. Train the individual who cannot achieve total self-reliance (who is not able to generalize problem-solving skills) how to obtain necessary support services.

8. As your position permits, create learning, living, or work opportunities for the mildly retarded that will enhance the quality of their lives.

9. Include retarded individuals in decision-making processes that affect them.

10. Remember that mentally retarded people are much more like than unlike their nonretarded peers.

9

Moderate, Severe, and Profound Handicaps

Martha E. Snell
University of Virginia

Adelle M. Renzaglia
University of Illinois

Lynn is 6 years old, but she does not look that old. She sits limply in a well-padded wheelchair without much expression as her aide wheels her toward her new classroom at the Hillstead Elementary School. The third-grade teacher nods and smiles sympathetically as they pass in the hall; then she shakes her head and wonders what Lynn can possibly learn over the next 9 months.

Lynn has had hypotonic cerebral palsy and severe mental retardation since she was born; her low muscle tone makes her movements floppy, and she does not do what other 6-year-olds do even though she has already attended special classes for two years. Lynn can recognize pictures of her parents, brother, and former teacher and will choose a toy or food by looking at the one she wants. Lynn can help take her clothes off by straightening her arms at the right time, and she does not cry on the school bus anymore.

What will Lynn learn this year? Lynn's new teacher is still getting to know her, even though she first met Lynn during the summer. The teaching objectives on her IEP include many activities in which Lynn will learn to assist a teacher or a peer as they feed her or brush her teeth or take off her coat. With the help of a speech therapist, Lynn will learn to use an electronic communication board to "talk." Lynn will push a pedal to move a light across the board until it comes to pictures representing activities or things Lynn needs. Whenever she sees her new communication board, Lynn smiles and laughs. She seems anxious to get started. Lynn will also learn to greet others in the hall and at recess and to play taped music and operate electronic toys with other children from the first grade.

Lynn has a big year ahead of her and is ready to learn.

The subject of this chapter is a small fraction of the mentally retarded population—the moderately, severely, and profoundly mentally retarded. Often, particularly with those who are profoundly retarded, other handicaps are present, such as movement, sensory, or emotional impairments. Like Lynn in the opening profile, these people are the most severely handicapped of all. They are people who need intensive training to master skills that most of us take for granted—skills such as running a washing machine, riding a bus, making change, or going to the restroom. But these individuals do learn. Such widespread differences exist among the individuals in this group that some might consider it ill-advised to discuss them as a single group. Yet the diversity of problems and traits these individuals reveal is offset by the fact that intervention on all three of these levels of retardation involves rather common programming characteristics and behavioral principles.

History

Our history of educating people with severe or profound handicaps is not long. Many of these individuals died at an early age; in earlier days some were even killed (Scheerenberger, 1982). However, the past 25 years have been more hopeful. In 1961 President John F. Kennedy stated that improvement of the quality of life and services for persons with mental retardation was a national goal. Thereafter, the President's Panel on Mental Retardation provided annual reports that stimulated a multidisciplinary effort to prevent mental retardation and to develop improved services for those who were retarded. Ten years later advocates and parents of 13 mentally retarded children brought suit against the Commonwealth of Pennsylvania (see Figure 1-2 for a summary of the PARC case and other significant judicial decisions). The court ordered the appropriate education of all handicapped children, including those with severe handicaps, and laid the foundation for P.L. 94–142, which still challenges our public schools a decade later.

The combined influence of these events had a favorable impact on all mentally retarded individuals. However, the impact was the least for those with the most severe handicaps. In fact, Pennsylvania came under siege again in 1979 when parents filed a second suit (*Fialkowski v. Shapp*) against the school system of Philadelphia, where programs had remained unchanged for students with extensive handicaps. The result is that severely handicapped students in Philadelphia now attend schools with their nonhandicapped peers; they are taught by teachers who have received extensive training; and their programs reflect state-of-the-art characteristics. Although Philadelphia is not alone in the field, there are many school programs that fall far short of these standards.

One missing piece in this progress, the presence of a professional advocacy organization for persons with severe handicaps, came into being in 1974. Initially known as the American Association for the Education of the Severely and Profoundly Handicapped (AAESPH), the group later changed its name to The Association of Persons with Severe Handicaps (TASH) and grew quickly. Today its more than 5600 members include both parents and professionals.

Definition

Definitions and classification have advantages and disadvantages. They are, for purposes of discussion, research, and provision of services, necessary evils. The currently accepted AAMD defintion of mental retardation was cited in chapter 8. Within the broad category of mental retardation, the moderately, severely, and profoundly retarded are divided into subgroups on the basis of their performance on tests of intelligence and adaptive behavior, both of which were described in chapter 8. Table 9-1 identifies the ranges of test performance that identify an individual as mildly, moderately, severely, or profoundly retarded. A person can score at different levels on intelligence tests and adaptive behavior tests. Once it has been determined that a person has an adaptive behavior deficit, then that person's level of retardation is indicated by her level of measured intellectual functioning, as shown in Table 9-1. The table identifies the levels of retardation with the same terms as those used in previous AAMD manuals. The IQ ranges are generally consistent with those suggested by the American Psychiatric Association in their *Diagnostic and Statistical Manual* (3rd ed.), but a narrow band at each end of each level is used to indicate that clinical judgment of all information is necessary in determining level. Thus, someone whose Wechsler IQ is 53 might be diagnosed as either mildly or moderately retarded, depending on other factors.

Severely Handicapped

Over the past 10 years the term *severely handicapped* has become popular. In general usage the severely handicapped are those who exhibit mental retardation ranging from moderate to profound, as measured by their performance on intelligence and adaptive behavior tests. In addition, they may possess other minor or serious handicaps, either emotional (e.g., autism) or physical (e.g., visual, auditory, or orthopedic impairment).

Table 9-1 Level of retardation indicated by IQ range (obtained from measure of general intellectual functioning)

Level	IQ range
Mild mental retardation	50–55 to 70 (approx.)
Moderate mental retardation	35–40 to 50–55
Severe mental retardation	20–25 to 35–40
Profound mental retardation	below 20–25

SOURCE: From *Classification in Mental Retardation* (p. 13) by H. Grossman (Ed.), (1983), Washington, DC: American Association on Mental Deficiency. Copyright 1983 by American Association on Mental Deficiency. Reprinted by permission.

The following often-quoted, graphic description of the severely handicapped population lists some possible pretreatment characteristics.

> Those who are not toilet trained; aggress toward others; do not attend to even the most pronounced social stimuli; self-mutilate; ruminate; self-stimulate; do not walk, speak, hear, or see; manifest durable and intense temper tantrums; are not under even the most rudimentary forms of verbal control; do not imitate; manifest minimally controlled seizures; and/or have extremely brittle medical existences. (Sontag, Burke, & York, 1973, p. 21).

This description does not mean that all severely handicapped individuals possess all, most, or even some of these traits. It merely illustrates that the behavior and skills exhibited by this group are widely diverse and that when appropriate intervention is absent, maladaptive behavior is likely to predominate.

The severely handicapped population overlaps completely the severely and profoundly retarded, but less so the higher functioning moderately retarded. One exception in this overlap is those persons in the severe or profound retardation range whose low scores are more a function of emotional or physical problems than of mental retardation. These individuals might be referred to as functionally retarded and given other diagnostic labels, such as autistic or cerebral palsied, to explain their poor test performance. Such fine discriminations are based primarily on clinical judgment. For all practical purposes, parents and educators should focus on educational programming relevant to the individual rather than on a more precise description of the causes involved. Retarded individuals learn slowly; and many, because of low-quality or sporadic programming, have enormous ranges of untapped potential. Emphasis on preventive or remedial programming can bring them closer to their potential.

Throughout the remainder of this chapter, the term *severely handicapped* will be employed frequently to refer to the entire group of moderately, severely, and profoundly mentally retarded. It is less cumbersome and perhaps more accurate, given the difficulty of differentiating among levels of retardation and between actual and functional retardation.

Prevalence

In a review of 19 separate prevalence studies, Abramowicz and Richardson (1975) set an upper IQ boundary of 40 in order to determine a more representative prevalence rate for persons with severe or profound retardation. They found that these studies were remarkably consistent in estimating about 4 in 1,000 persons to be severely or profoundly retarded. This rate is much higher than we would expect from the standard distribution curve for intelligence in the total population. Theoretically the rate should be 1.2 per 1,000. However, the much higher rate reflects the number of individuals who incur damage to the central nervous system in accidents. This same population raises the expected percentage in the moderate to severe ranges only slightly (Robinson & Robinson, 1976). These figures mean that accidental brain injuries have a significant effect on the prevalence of retardation, particularly profound retardation.

Causes

Despite the fact that a broad range of conditions are known to lead to mental retardation, it is frequently impossible to identify the precise cause in a given case. Of the known causes of retardation approximately one-third are acquired rather than genetic or inherited. These acquired causes may strike before, during, or after birth and include such factors as infections, a lack of oxygen, and poisons. Genetic causes are responsible for about two-thirds of the cases of mental retardation and include numerical or structural chromosomal abnormalities, specific enzyme deficiencies, hormonal deficiencies, cell membrane disorders, malformation syndromes, and hereditary multisystem diseases (Milunsky, 1983).

Well-established genetic causes of severe handicapping conditions include chromosomal abnormalities, particularly Down syndrome, and metabolic disorders such as untreated phenylalanine hydroxylase, commonly referred to as phenylketonuria, or PKU. Although some of the children affected are only mildly retarded or of borderline intelligence, Down syndrome does account for roughly one-sixth to one-third of the severely handicapped population (Abramowicz & Richardson, 1975). With the availability of amniocentesis prenatal tests can now be made to determine whether a fetus has inborn errors of metabolism (e.g., hydrocephalus, spina bifida) or chromosomal abnormalities (e.g., Down syndrome, trisomy 18). Mandatory screening of all newborns for PKU will continue to reduce the frequency with which this enzyme disorder causes mental retardation.

More accurate and extensive research is needed to isolate factors present before or at birth that result in severe retardation. Length of labor and poor conditions immediately after birth have now been found to be related to retardation, but toxemia and delivery complications (including use of forceps, multiple births, and breech presentation) are cited more often in the medical histories of severely retarded children (Abramowicz & Richardson, 1975). Also, severely retarded persons are likely to be premature or to weigh less than average at birth. Unlike mild mental retardation, moderate to profound retardation does not seem to be associated with socioeconomic status. Occurrence tends to be random rather than associated with any particular environmental variables (Abramowicz & Richardson, 1975; Stark, 1983).

Characteristics

Severely handicapped individuals display a wide variety of physical and psychological traits, as well as skill deficits and maladaptive behaviors. Institutionalization and lower intelligence seem to be correlated with increased amounts of maladaptive behavior and decreased skill levels. The absence of mobility, on the other

Institutionalization is often correlated with reduced skill levels.

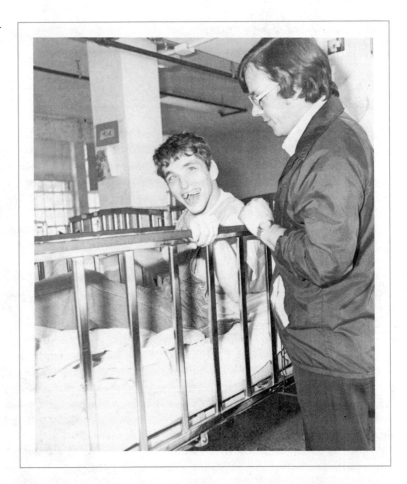

hand, is often related to a decrease in skills but not necessarily to an increase in maladaptive behavior (Landesman-Dwyer & Sackett, 1978). Although maladaptive behavior and institutionalization appear to be interrelated, the research does not point to a clear-cut, cause-and-effect relationship. For example, maladaptive behavior is more frequent in institutionalized retarded persons than in retarded individuals residing in the community (Eyman & Call, 1977). Yet it is also true that (1) persons with maladaptive behavior are institutionalized more often than those without (Eyman, O'Connor, Tarjan, & Justice, 1972); (2) persons functioning at the severe and profound levels of retardation are more likely to be institutionalized (Eyman, Moore, Capes, & Zachofsky, 1970); (3) the frequency of maladaptive behavior does not appear to change when institutionalization occurs (Baumeister, 1978); and (4) maladaptive behavior that is self-injurious, aggressive, or self-stimulating is more prevalent in lower functioning persons (Baumeister, 1978). Thus, even though maladaptive behavior seems to be correlated with institutionalization, we cannot conclude that the latter causes the former.

Multiple Handicaps

Among the moderately to profoundly retarded, the presence of a second handicap is relatively common; 25% to 50% of this group (1 to 2 per 1,000 in the total population) suffer from both severe retardation and one or more serious handicaps (Abramowicz & Richardson, 1975). Serious handicaps include inability to walk, incontinence, psychiatric or behavior disorders, sensory impairment, seizures, absence of speech, and cerebral palsy.

In some cases these handicaps can be reduced, if not eliminated, through intervention. For instance, although incontinence may be caused by damage to the nerves responsible for bladder and bowel sensation, the inability to control elimination is also a likely result of an absence of instruction. Likewise, signing or picture systems can effectively replace speech; and concentrated instruction in functional speech may reduce the effect of a speech handicap.

Adaptive Behavior

Habilitation is the process of developing a capacity to perform the routine tasks required to attain some degree of self-sufficiency. Recently, the subject of debate both in and out of the courtroom has been the probability of successful habilitation of the severely handicapped. If given an appropriate public school program, how much and what types of behavior changes would constitute successful habilitation of a person with severe handicaps? Because of tremendous differences in the severely handicapped population that are not accounted for by IQ differences, no simple answers are possible. Institutionalization, ability to walk, uncontrolled seizures, and amount and history of maladaptive behavior appear to be far better predictors of educability (more accurately, relative ease and speed of skill acquisition) than IQ. As Berkson and Landesman-Dwyer (1977) have observed,

> The main impact of the research during the last 20 years has been to change our view of what severe and profound mental retardation means. Severely-profoundly retarded persons are not simply "vegetative" or "animal-like." They are sentient humans who can learn and are social. Their behavior development is very slow and, because of multiple handicaps, can also be pathological. We do not know why it is sometimes bizarre. (p. 438)

Amid the debate some findings relevant to the habilitation of the severely handicapped have emerged:

1. Behavior modification techniques are used most often with the severely handicapped.

2. Successful habilitation occurs most often at the moderate level of retardation, less frequently at the severe level, and least often at the profound level.

3. Most often little or no change occurs in adaptive behavior of individuals who manifest profound retardation, seizures, and major motor impairment.

4. Educators have had success in developing basic attention, imitation social skills, communication, functional academics, daily living and self-care skills, leisure time and recreation abilities, and vocational tasks across most levels of retardation.

5. The severely handicapped have particular difficulty in generalizing skills.

Maladaptive Behavior

As with skill development the frequency of abnormal behavior is highly variable within the severely handicapped population. Some of the characteristic inappropriate behaviors are aggression toward property and people, tantrums, self-injurious behaviors (head banging and hand biting, for example), and stereotypic behaviors (meaningless, repetitive movements such as rocking and hand waving). More bizarre behaviors that occur less often are vomiting and rumination, disrobing, pica (eating inedible objects), stealing, material hoarding, and other attention-seeking responses. Institutionalized, profoundly retarded persons are most likely to exhibit these behaviors (Eyman & Call, 1977). Behavior that causes self-injury is often associated with institutionalization and a medical diagnosis of brain injury—two traits relatively characteristic of the profoundly retarded. Behavioral intervention procedures have been successful in eliminating each of these behaviors in the severely retarded.

Assessment

To create an appropriate educational program for any student, both initial and ongoing assessments are necessary. In the case of students with severe handicaps, however, traditional diagnostic techniques such as norm-referenced, standardized intelligence and aptitude tests, achievement tests, and language assessments may be of limited utility for instructional programming. A teacher cannot determine educational goals or objectives for students with severe handicaps on the basis of intelligence, achievement, or developmental age scores. Furthermore, since the standard error of measurement of many norm-referenced tests increases for extremely low scores (and extremely high ones), it may be very difficult to obtain reliable scores for learners with severe handicaps.

Assessment information that is more relevant to educational programming for students with severe handicaps can be obtained by collecting general background and performance information, conducting structured observations of specific behavior and skills, and administering general assessment instruments. Figure 9-1 provides a model of an educational planning process in which assessment results in instructional objectives and a daily schedule. Although we will examine the process as it relates specifically to students with severe handicaps, it is also applicable to students with other handicapping conditions. The process does not change for

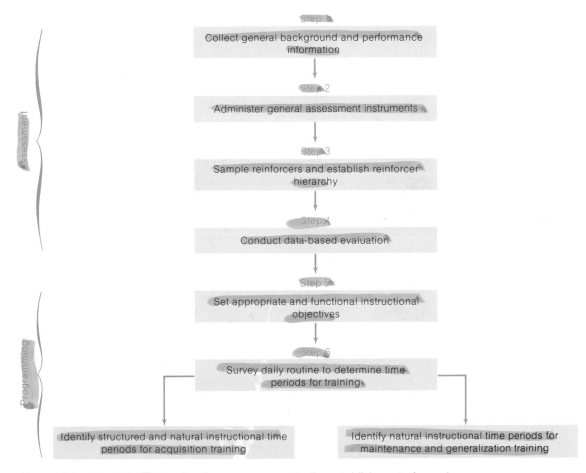

Figure 9-1 Educational planning from assessment to the establishment of an educational program

students of varying ages, although the specific instruments used in Step 2 will be different if the child is very young.

Collecting General Background and Performance Information

Initial procedures for assessing students with severe handicaps are likely to be informal and unstructured. Evaluating past records, interviewing parents, and directly observing the student in a home and/or school environment may all be part of the early strategy. Past records, of course, should be used cautiously. However, the information they provide regarding previously learned skills and skills targeted for instruction may be useful in identifying areas for further evaluation and training. In addition, past records may indicate what instructional techniques have been successful.

Parents and educators should focus on educational programming relevant to the individual.

Similarly, parent interviews serve to identify priorities for instruction as well as particular problems parents are experiencing at home with their child. Especially at the preschool age, parents should be integrally involved since they are likely to be responsible for the majority of their child's educational programming. Parents can provide valuable information for developing successful instructional programs, including the student's preferred foods, toys, and activities—which can be used as reinforcers; the skills the student has mastered in the home setting; and the opportunities the student has to engage in independent self-help, language, daily living, and leisure/recreation skills in the home. All this information assists the teacher in selecting instructional objectives and developing and evaluating instructional programs.

Although past records and parent interviews do aid in initial student assessment, it is unwise to rely solely on secondhand information. Firsthand observations of the student in his natural environment should always be a part of this phase of assessment. Initial observations are usually informal and may be conducted in both the home and school settings. If informal observation follows parent interviews and evaluation of past records, a teacher can use these observations to validate the presence or absence of skills and behavior problems that were identified by others.

Valuable assessment can be
made from watching specific
skills and behavior.

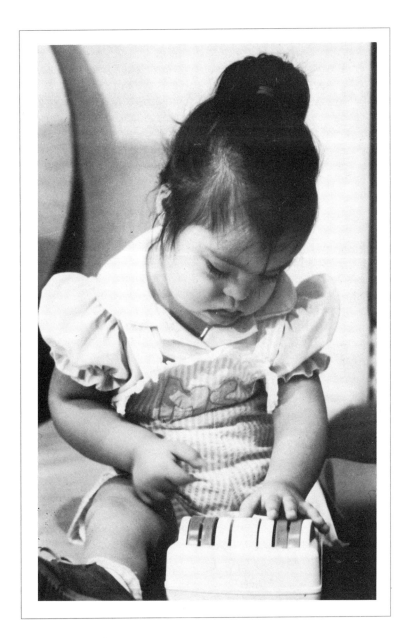

Administering General Assessment Instruments

In the second step of the process validated commercial instruments are used to
obtain information about a student's entry-level skills. Acceptable standard instruments include the AAMD Adaptive Behavior Scale (Lambert, Windmiller, Cole, &
Figueroa, 1975), the Camelot Behavioral Checklist (Foster, 1974), the TARC Assessment Inventory (Sailor & Mix, 1975), the Uniform Performance Assessment System

(Haring, White, Edgar, Affleck, & Hayden, 1981), and the Scales of Independent Behavior (Bruininks, Woodcock, Weatherman, & Hill, 1984).

The formal assessment should provide a general record of the student's skills in curricular and behavioral areas relevant to placement in the least restrictive environment. For example, the AAMD Adaptive Behavior Scale allows a general evaluation of independent functioning skills (such as eating, toileting, cleanliness), physical development, using numbers and telling time, domestic activity, vocational activity, self-initiation, responsibility, socialization, and inappropriate and maladaptive behavior. It was developed for use with a wide range of ages and handicapping conditions.

Instruments used in this step of assessment should also yield information that contributes to educational programming; the assessed skills must be pertinent to the student's educational goals and objectives. Frequently commercial instruments include a number of items that are not relevant. However, when the majority of items are irrelevant, the instrument is inappropriate and should not be used.

Similarly, many general assessment instruments are designed for use with a particular age group and are inappropriate for other age groups. For instance, the Developmental Activities Screening Inventory (DASI) (Dubose & Langley, 1977) and the Bayley Scales of Infant Development (Bayley, 1969) are designed for use with very young children. In a number of items on the Bayley Scales the individual being tested is required to play with, retrieve, or respond to a rattle. Although rattle play may be acceptable and even targeted as an instructional objective for infants, it is obviously not an appropriate objective for older students with severe handicaps, regardless of their skill levels. When such items are administered to an individual of the wrong age, the information gained is educationally irrelevant.

Teacher-made checklists are also useful in assessing skill domains relevant to programming. Although they are not standardized and do not correlate results with an equivalent age or developmental level, they can assess the specific skills necessary to move a student into a less restrictive environment.

In addition to general educational assessment, related assessments by professionals in other fields should also be conducted. For example, visual, audiological, neurological, and motor skills should be tested to determine students' needs for ancillary services.

Sampling Reinforcers and Establishing a Reinforcer Hierarchy

The identification of objects, foods, and activities arranged in order of the student's preference assists the teacher in developing the most effective instructional program. In most cases the use of items and activities to reward appropriate behavior facilitates learning in students with severe handicaps. The preferred items and activities are identified and ordered in a hierarchy of reinforcers by several methods involving observation:

1. Observing a student in a free-time situation and recording the activities she engages in most often.

2. Providing the student with an array of items—for example, a toy, food, and consumables such as perfume—and recording the student's choice after requesting that she select the most desirable item

3. Recording the effects of using a particular item as a reward for specific appropriate behavior

Conducting Data-Based Evaluation

General assessment instruments do not identify where instruction must begin. After completing a general assessment, the teacher must identify skill areas that have not been mastered and need further evaluation. This fourth step, like the preceding one, involves structured observations and data collection. In order to evaluate the student's skills on a specific task, a teacher must observe the student performing the task. However task analysis is necessary prior to observation in order to determine exactly which skills are involved in the task. Assessment of specific skills should be conducted in a consistent fashion, more than once, preferably across days, to provide a valid measure of the student's competence. As soon as this has been done, instructional objectives can be set.

Especially with students with severe handicaps, it is important to teach the component steps of a task and regularly evaluate student progress in achieving them. Evaluation of proficiency in specific skills should be done at least weekly in the same way the initial assessments were made. This schedule will enable the teacher to observe progress toward skill acquisition, which frequently occurs in small increments. An example of task analysis is shown in Figure 9-2.

Problem behavior that has an impact on educational programs—such as self-stimulation and self-abuse, aggression toward others, noncompliance, and tantrums—cannot be measured with task analytic assessment. However, these behaviors frequently are targeted for intervention and therefore must be measured in some way. One method uses planned observations. The teacher records the frequency of the behavior or its duration, depending on the target of intervention. When a frequency count is taken, the observer must be sure that each observation session lasts the same length of time. If observational periods differ in length, the numbers recorded cannot be compared unless the figures are first converted into numbers per time period. As with task analytic assessment, measurement of maladaptive behavior should not terminate when intervention begins. It must be regularly and consistently repeated to determine program effectiveness.

Although regular and consistent measurement of student behavior is needed, teachers frequently have difficulty designing manageable data collection systems. Strain, McConnell, and Cordisco (1983) have suggested the following strategies: (1) use simple recording sheets, (2) keep recording sheets in accessible locations, (3) schedule data collection at feasible times, and (4) use mechanical aids (e.g., counters, stop watches) to assist in data collection. These strategies can help teachers use data-based decision making in their educational programs for students with severe handicaps.

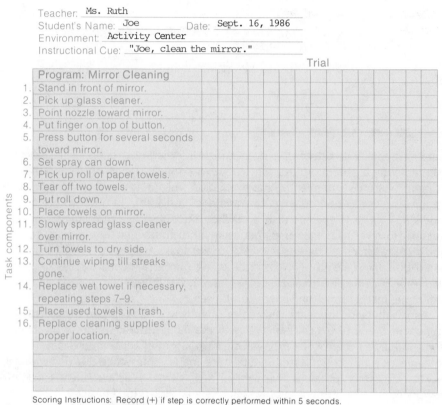

Teacher: __Ms. Ruth__
Student's Name: __Joe__   Date: __Sept. 16, 1986__
Environment: __Activity Center__
Instructional Cue: __"Joe, clean the mirror."__

Trial

Program: Mirror Cleaning													
1. Stand in front of mirror.													
2. Pick up glass cleaner.													
3. Point nozzle toward mirror.													
4. Put finger on top of button.													
5. Press button for several seconds toward mirror.													
6. Set spray can down.													
7. Pick up roll of paper towels.													
8. Tear off two towels.													
9. Put roll down.													
10. Place towels on mirror.													
11. Slowly spread glass cleaner over mirror.													
12. Turn towels to dry side.													
13. Continue wiping till streaks gone.													
14. Replace wet towel if necessary, repeating steps 7–9.													
15. Place used towels in trash.													
16. Replace cleaning supplies to proper location.													

Task components

Scoring Instructions: Record (+) if step is correctly performed within 5 seconds.
Record (−) if step is incorrectly performed or there is not response within 5 seconds.

Figure 9-2   Task analysis and recording form for mirror cleaning
SOURCE: Task analysis developed by B. Ruth. Reprinted by permission.

Intervention

When the initial assessment process is completed, an intervention program must be developed for each instructional objective. Due to the high frequency of multiple handicaps experienced by persons with moderate to profound retardation, transdisciplinary programming is necessary. With the involvement of so many specialists, the plan for providing services must be tightly organized. An integrated services model provides for ongoing consultation to classroom instructors and other care providers (Sternat, Messina, Nietupski, Lyon, & Brown, 1977). The specialists often work directly with the student on a regular basis in addition to teaching classroom teachers and care providers appropriate methods of intervention. Thus, the training process is ongoing rather than sporadic and is conducted consistently in all environments and by all trainers. For example, in an integrated

Multiple handicaps require the ongoing interaction and cooperation of numerous specialists.

services approach the positioning and handling techniques that a physical thera-pist determines to be appropriate for a student are taught to and utilized by all staff and care providers who come into contact with that student. The daily sched-ule in Table 9-2 illustrates the complexity of service delivery to a severely handi-capped student.

Constant collaboration between school personnel and one or both of the stu-dent's parents or a guardian is not only mandated by P.L. 94–142 but is vital for students with severe handicaps. Because of the frequent health problems and ma-jor skill deficits experienced by these students, a united approach throughout all their environments facilitates their progress. Teachers must establish contact with significant persons and survey student needs. This interaction will assist in estab-lishing priorities for individual students and may help care providers take a lifelong approach to planning for this child. In addition, teacher support for a family's ef-forts to train and maintain their child in their home may be a deciding factor in preventing institutionalization.

Table 9-2 Sample instructional program for a severely handicapped student

This schedule was designed for Marsha, an 11-year-old severely retarded quadriplegic confined to a wheelchair that she cannot operate independently. Marsha's class of eight severely handicapped students between the ages of 6 and 12 is housed in a public elementary school for nonhandicapped students. Marsha has multiple handicaps, including limited vision, no oral communication skills, and no toileting skills. She can raise her arms off her tray and, without precision, reach and touch items on her tray. She communicates with yes or no head movements in response to questions.

	Activity	Students	Teacher	Setting
8:30	toileting and handwashing	Marsha	Mr. Jackson[a] and occupational therapist	bathroom
8:50	language: communication board—two tactile symbols	Marsha, Bob, Steve, and Randy	Ms. Smith[b] and speech therapist	classroom
9:20	money recognition: money game	Marsha, Paul, Susan, and Karen	Ms. Smith	classroom
9:35	money: vending	Marsha, Susan, and Karen	Ms. Smith	lounge vending machines
10:00	snack: finger foods	Marsha, Bob, Steve, Randy, Paul, Karen, Susan, Linda, and two fourth graders	Ms. Smith and occupational therapist consultation	snack area
10:20	toileting and handwashing	Marsha	Mr. Jackson with consultation from occupational therapist if needed	bathroom
10:40	toothbrushing: electric toothbrush	Marsha and Paul	Ms. Smith	bathroom
10:55	communication board—two tactile symbols to reach and touch	Marsha, Bob, and Steve	Ms. Smith and speech and occupational therapists consultation	classroom

Table 9-2 Sample instructional program for a severely handicapped student
(continued)

	Activity	Students	Teacher	Setting
11:20	handwashing	Marsha, Karen, and Randy	Mr. Jackson	sink in room
11:30	lunch: chewing, grasping spoon for feeding, and cup drinking; communication board	all students	Ms. Smith, Mr. Jackson, and occupational and physical therapists consultation	cafeteria
12:15	toileting and handwashing	Marsha	Ms. Smith and occupational therapist consultation	cafeteria and bathroom
12:35	toothbrushing: electric toothbrush	Marsha and Paul	Ms. Smith	cafeteria and bathroom
12:50	dressing for adapted physical education	all girls	Ms. Smith and occupational therapist	gym locker room
1:15	physical education: adapted bowling and cooperative ball toss	all students and five nonhandicapped fourth–fifth graders	Ms. Smith, Mr. Jackson, adaptive PE teacher, and physical therapist	gym
1:45	changing to school clothes	all girls	Ms. Smith and occupational therapist	gym locker room
2:05	toileting and handwashing	Marsha	Ms. Smith	gym locker room
2:25	leisure time: operating record player, communicating with staff and peers	all students and four third-grade volunteers	Mr. Jackson and Ms. Smith	library
2:40	get ready for bus	all students	Mr. Jackson and Ms. Smith	classroom
2:45	get on bus to go home	all students	Mr. Jackson and Ms. Smith	bus

[a]Mr. Jackson is the classroom aide.
[b]Ms. Smith is the classroom teacher.

Curriculum Implications

Developing instructional objectives is the fifth step in Figure 9-1. Educational programs for severely handicapped students should have certain characteristics:

1. Chronological-age-appropriate curricula

2. Emphasis on functional activities

3. A detailed daily schedule

4. Organization in accordance with curricular domains

Chronological-Age-Appropriate Programs

To a great extent, chronological age should determine placement and instructional curricula in educational programs for the severely handicapped. In accordance with the normalization principle, severely handicapped elementary students should be placed in classes in regular elementary schools, and severely handicapped secondary students should be placed in regular high school settings whenever feasible. Age-appropriate placement does not mean that severely handicapped students will attend all classes that nonhandicapped students attend. In fact, the least restrictive educational setting for most severely and profoundly retarded students may be a self-contained class in an age-appropriate school. Often they are included in the activities of nonhandicapped students only in nonacademic classes and activities such as music, art, physical education, lunch, and recess periods. Nonetheless, the self-contained classroom should also reflect the chronological age of the students. For example, pictures, posters, bulletin board themes, and other items displayed in the classrooms should be geared to the appropriate age and interests of the students.

IEP objectives, too, should reflect the chronological as well as the developmental age of severely handicapped students. For example, instead of teaching severely handicapped adolescents to play with a preschool wind-up music box or a busy box, the operation of a record player should be taught using current music. Selection of IEP objectives should also be based on the projected usefulness of a skill for future independent living in a community setting (Brown, Nietupski, & Hamre-Nietupski, 1977).

The social interactions of severely handicapped students should also reflect their chronological age. It is important to limit conversation as well as physical contact to the type most typical of nonhandicapped students of the same age. Greetings accompanied by handshakes or waves rather than hugs or kisses, for example, are appropriate for adolescents. Chronological age appropriateness is a significant factor in normalization and challenges the traditional mental age criterion (IQ) frequently used to select learning objectives and materials for the retarded. Educational practices that are compatible with chronological age are likely to facilitate the acceptance of severely handicapped students by nonhandicapped peers and prepare students for eventual placement in heterogeneous community settings.

Opportunities outside of class to become friends improve the awareness of nonhandicapped peers.

Functionality

Closely related to age appropriateness is the selection of functional educational goals and activities. Functionality refers to the usefulness of a particular skill or activity in a student's present and subsequent environments (Brown, Branston, Hamre-Nietupski, Pumpian, et al., 1979). For example, sorting 1-inch blocks by color is unlikely to be a functional skill. However, if a severely handicapped student will be required to do his own laundry in an assigned group home setting, then sorting clothes according to color would be considered a functional objective. Skills that are frequently used in many settings and are maintained by naturally occurring events are functional and therefore of high instructional priority.

A Daily Schedule

When functional objectives have been selected, a teacher must organize the day to maximize learning, the final step in the process in Figure 9-1. Classroom organization should be described in a precise, timed, daily schedule that is posted for all staff and visitors to observe. For each student the schedule should detail (1) each educational objective and activity, (2) the other students involved in each activity, (3) the instructor for each activity, and (4) the instructional setting for each activity. A detailed schedule of this sort facilitates classroom structure, efficiency, and trainer consistency from day to day. Table 9-2 illustrates such a schedule.

Learning how to set the table can eventually lead to more independent self-care.

Curricular Domains

It is primarily the school's responsibility to teach toward self-sufficiency. However, the school usually has fewer than 15 years to achieve habilitation, and severely handicapped students learn slowly and generalize poorly. Thus, the selection of curriculum is a responsibility of utmost importance so that precious time is not wasted.

The most effective method of curriculum planning for the severely handi-capped uses a *top-down approach* in selecting long- and short-term educational goals (Brown, Branston, Hamre-Nietupski, Pumpian, et al., 1979). In this approach the skills the student needs to function in particular home, school, work, and commu-nity environments serve as the base for developing instructional goals and objec-tives. This community referencing differs from an approach based on the results of developmental testing, which Brown and his colleagues describe as a *bottom-up approach.* The top-down approach is more likely to identify those unique skills that are necessary for a given student's successful performance in her community. This strategy for curriculum planning involves six steps:

1. The curriculum is organized into domains. These generally include domestic living, leisure and recreation, community functioning, and vocation.

2. Natural environments that are and will be part of a particular student's life are identified. Examples are the school, group home, workshop, and grocery store.

3. Within the natural environments subenvironments are delineated. These are likely to include the kitchen, bedroom, bathroom, living area, bus stop, gymnasium, and cafeteria.

4. The functional activities that occur in each subenvironment are identified. There will be many of these, and they will vary from student to student; but they are likely to include clothing care, making a snack, toileting, and riding in a car or bus.

5. Each of the skills necessary for participating in the identified activities are determined. For example, clothing care involves folding, hanging, and putting away, as well as using a washer and dryer and sorting dirty laundry.

6. The teacher must establish priorities for the skills and design programs for teaching the most important ones. The following profile of Richard illustrates how a top-down strategy can be used to develop a curriculum for a specific student. Table 9-3 provides a breakdown of the subenvironments, activities, and skills Richard will require in order to participate in a work program.

Richard is a teenager with a variety of serious handicaps besides moderate retardation. He is visually impaired, with only light perception in his left eye and limited vision in his right eye. Richard's hearing is also impaired, with a bilateral profound loss. He has complete use of only one limb, his right arm, and is therefore confined to a wheelchair. The muscles of his left arm are contracted, preventing weight support. Though currently under medication control, Richard is prone to seizures as well. His condition was caused by rubella, which his mother had during the first trimester of pregnancy.

In spite of all these handicaps, Richard is an alert and active young man. Currently residing at the school for the blind, he has acquired a large number of skills. He signs a limited number of nouns and verbs and appears to have the potential for signing many more but is limited by having the use of only one hand. His teachers are investigating the possibility of a picture communication board to expand his expressive capabilities.

Richard lives in Mississippi. Unless services improve in his community, he will live at the Ellisville State School after graduation from the school for the blind. At Ellisville Richard will likely work at a work activity center on campus, alongside others who are similarly handicapped. He will be trained in daily living skills as well as vocational skills. If he is able to master the necessary daily living skills and at least 50% of the work skills of a normal worker, he will go on to Hazelhurst, to the workshop of the Royal Maid Association for the Blind, and will live in a group home for blind, multihandicapped adults. In its emphasis on learning work and daily living skills, Richard's program is an example of the top-down strategy of curriculum development. (Adapted with permission from C. M. Dennis, 1980)

Table 9-3 Vocational domain (subenvironments, activities, and skills required for Richard to participate in the Ellisville State School work activity center environment)

A. Travel/Mobility Subenvironment

Learns workshop layout
1. visually recognizes areas
2. reads signs
3. learns routes
4. names areas
5. goes to areas on request

Manipulates wheelchair
1. ramps
2. halls
3. doors
4. bathroom
5. cafeteria
6. work area

Gets on transportation
1. arrives on schedule
2. rolls on/off lift
3. secures lift
4. cooperates in physical assist
5. operates lift

Gets off transportation
1. disengages lock
2. rolls on/off lift
3. cooperates in physical assist
4. operates lift
5. continues to destination

Rides nondisruptively
1. secures position
2. socializes
3. looks out window
4. sits quietly
5. uses lap activities

B. Bathroom Subenvironment

Toileting
1. transfers toilet/chair
2. uses toilet paper
3. asks assistance when needed
4. unhooks pants
5. waits if necessary for toilet stall

Checking appearance
1. hands
2. face
3. hair
4. clothes
5. short time

Washing hands/face
1. mixes water temperature
2. operates soap dispenser
3. checks hands
4. checks face
5. does not splash

Drying
1. operates towel dispenser
2. dries hands completely
3. throws towel away

Cleaning bathroom
1. throws towel away
2. throws toilet paper in toilet
3. does not splash
4. indicates to authority if paper is gone

C. Work Area Subenvironment

Communicates needs
1. feels sick
2. needs help in bathroom
3. needs help at work station
4. needs material
5. sees danger

Follows schedule
1. comes on time
2. leaves on time
3. goes to next event
4. watches light signal
5. tells time
6. uses time clock

Follows instructions
1. looks at instructor
2. follows 2-word directions

Programs of Skill Development

To put the research in this area in perspective, we need to remember that the majority of the severely handicapped population is institutionalized. Thus, much of this habilitation research has taken place in institutional settings rather than in the community, and very little of it has involved persons with limited motor skills (Berkson & Landesman-Dwyer, 1977).

Self-Help Skills   Basic self-help and grooming skills are usually priorities for instruction regardless of the targeted domain. The development of independent toileting, for example, is essential for functioning in home, community, and work environments. Similarly, eating, dressing, and grooming skills are required to some degree in all skill domains within various environments.

Table 9-3   Vocational domain (subenvironments, activities, and skills required for Richard to participate in the Ellisville State School work activity center environment) *(Continued)*

3. responds immediately after each instruction
4. remembers instruction more than 30 minutes

Works independently
1. works 6-hour day
2. works 2-hour shifts
3. does not leave station inappropriately
4. works without supervision
5. continues to work while observed

Displays work skills
1. packaging
2. assembling object of 4–5 parts
3. counting (10)
4. weighing
5. using drill press
6. using screwdriver

D. Cafeteria Subenvironment

Selects food
1. points to choice
2. puts food on tray
3. manipulates tray
4. communicates server's mistake
5. selects a balanced diet

Carries tray
1. manipulates tray on counter
2. lifts tray
3. balances tray
4. places tray on table
5. cleans spills

Displays eating skills
1. cuts food
2. passes food on request
3. asks for condiments
4. makes small talk
5. wipes spills

Cleans up cafeteria
1. wipes spills
2. carries tray
3. throws paper trash away
4. puts silver in dish pan
5. puts up tray

Socializes
1. smiles appropriately
2. makes small talk
3. responds to others
4. greets others
5. does not stare

E. Snackroom Subenvironment

Manages money
1. identifies coins
2. selects appropriate amount of money
3. counts change
4. keeps own money
5. communicates money loss

Uses beverage machine
1. puts money in slot
2. selects type (push)
3. retrieves beverage
4. opens beverage
5. gets change

Uses candy machine
1. puts money in slot
2. selects type (pull)
3. gets candy
4. gets change

Cleans snack room
1. wipes spills
2. throws trash in can
3. puts bottles in rack

Socializes
1. smiles appropriately
2. makes small talk
3. responds to others
4. greets others
5. does not stare

SOURCE: From *Top-Down Curriculum for Richard* by C. M. Dennis, 1980, Charlottesville: University of Virginia. Unpublished manuscript. Adapted by permission.

Intensive training programs for teaching self-initiated toileting skills to severely handicapped students of all ages have been tried with notable success. Techniques used include (1) training for long periods of time (up to 8 hours), (2) increasing the individual's liquid intake to increase the number of toileting trials, (3) using an automated signaling device that is activated by elimination, (4) providing frequent and positive feedback for staying dry, and (5) administering an accident procedure for inappropriate elimination (the teacher might let the student feel his wet pants, say "No. Wet pants!" and then require the student to change his pants and rinse them out). Extending the use of intensive training techniques through day and night has also been found to be effective in achieving bladder control (Azrin, Sneed, & Foxx, 1973).

More recently, research has examined procedures less intrusive than these. The encouraging findings indicate that toilet training can be accomplished within the normal daily program, rather than occupying 6–8-hour blocks of time daily (Lancioni & Ceccarani, 1981; Richmond, 1983), and further that urine detection equipment is not always necessary. Brief and simple reprimands for accidents are sufficient (Richmond, 1983).

A variety of eating skills have been taught to severely handicapped students. Reduction of tongue thrust during mealtime in a cerebral palsied, profoundly retarded young boy was accomplished by presenting him with food in response to an absence of tongue thrust and administering mild punishment for tongue thrust throughout the meal (Thompson, Iwata, & Poynter, 1979). In addition, appropriate meal behavior—including use of utensils (Nelson, Cone, & Hanson, 1975; O'Brien, Bugle, & Azrin, 1972), family-style eating, table clearing (Barton, Guess, Garcia, & Baer, 1970; O'Brien & Azrin, 1972), and eating at an acceptable speed with minimal sloppiness (Favell, McGinsey, & Jones, 1980; Knapczyk, 1983)—have all been successfully taught to severely handicapped learners through systematic prompting, reinforcement, and error-correction procedures.

Far less research exists in the area of teaching eating skills to persons with extensive motor involvement. In one notable exception Sobsey and Orelove (1984) demonstrated that prefeeding exercises (e.g., general relaxation routines, stroking around the mouth) led to some improvements in lip closure, rotary chewing, and spillage reduction for four nonambulatory students, of whom three had spastic cerebral palsy and two were blind.

Systematic instruction and intensive procedures have also been used effectively to teach dressing and undressing skills to severely handicapped learners (Azrin, Schaeffer, & Wesolowski, 1976). A number of grooming skills have been the focus of systematic intervention as well. Individuals of varying ages have succeeded in learning toothbrushing (Horner & Keilitz, 1975), hand and face washing (Westling & Murden, 1978), the use of sanitary napkins (Hamilton, Allen, Stephens, & Duvall, 1969), showering (Matson, DiLorenzo, & Esveldt-Dawson, 1981), and maintaining well-groomed appearances (Doleys, Stacy, & Knowles, 1981).

Although many instructional programs for the severely handicapped concentrate on developing self-help skills, we still do not have solid information on what training techniques are the most efficient. Most self-help intervention programs combine procedures, making it difficult to determine which of the techniques actually result in success.

Communication Skills   A large number of the severely handicapped are able to listen and comprehend spoken language as well as to speak understandably. Others, particularly those who are more severely handicapped, do not master speech even with intensive training. For those individuals a nonvocal system of communication is necessary. Usually this means manual signing or use of a communication board that displays pictures, objects, pictographs, or printed words. At times it is best to avoid a bulky communication board and substitute a number of pocket-size pictures secured by a ring and selected specifically for a particular activity and location. Other students may be taught to communicate with signs in some situations and with pictures in nonschool settings, where there often is an absence of persons who comprehend signs. Nonvocal alternatives do offer the individual a viable means of expressing wants and needs.

As in other areas of training, the skills taught the severely handicapped for purposes of communication must be functional. Communication research with this population offers several suggestions:

1. Words that label events that are familiar and enjoyable may be learned most quickly (Goetz, Schuler, & Sailor, 1979).

2. Label comprehension seems to be acquired faster when the student is allowed to use the labeled object (Janssen & Guess, 1978).

3. When one reinforcer is employed to reward the use of one particular label, as opposed to using the same reinforcer for all responses, learning appears to progress more quickly (Saunders & Sailor, 1979).

4. Providing natural opportunities for teaching communication seems to promote spontaneity, an essential feature of functional communication (Halle, Marshall, & Spradlin, 1979; Sosne, Handleman, & Harris, 1979).

Daily Living Skills and Related Functional Academics Self-sufficiency depends most of all on an individual's ability to carry out the tasks of daily living. The presence of needed skills determines in large part what kind of residential setting the individual can manage. The more self-sufficient a handicapped individual is, the less restrictive her environment needs to be. Some techniques for teaching daily living skills have been developed, but primarily for the mildly and moderately retarded.

A number of studies relate to the development of household skills. Cronin and Cuvo (1979) taught five moderately retarded youths to sew hems and seams and put on buttons. A related area of personal grooming—color coordination of clothing—was taught to severely retarded women in preparation for deinstitutionalization (Nutter & Reid, 1978). Snell (1982a) instructed four severely retarded young men to make a partially unmade bed, strip a bed, and make up a clean bed. In another study (Schleien, Ash, Kiernan, & Wehman, 1981) a profoundly retarded woman was taught to prepare a variety of foods—baking a TV dinner, broiling cheese toast, and boiling an egg.

Being mobile in a community generally necessitates pedestrian skills and an ability to use public bus systems. These and related skills have been successfully taught to mildly to profoundly retarded individuals. Generally, the more handicapped the learner, the more important it is to teach these skills in the actual setting. For example, Marchetti and his colleagues (1983) found that students taught pedestrian skills on a 4' × 4' street model were far less likely to transfer that knowledge to real outdoor sidewalks than were students who were taught outdoors. Vogelsburg and Rusch (1979), who also taught pedestrian skills, initially included special safety features to reduce danger (two instructors for one client and a quiet intersection). In still another study profoundly retarded institutional-

Learning to make purchases is a complex process. This student's teacher has found a way to teach the essentials of using money to make a purchase at a fast food restaurant. Instruction occurs both in the classroom and in the actual restaurant.

ized adults were taught to walk from their school to their living unit independently, a skill that greatly reduced staff supervision time (Gruber, Reeser, & Reid, 1979). Other research has focused on the use of public transportation to go to and from work (Sowers, Rusch, & Hudson, 1979).

Those skills in reading, writing, and math that are essential for survival in a community setting are called *functional academics*. Examples are money usage skills and the reading skills necessary for shopping and using public transportation. It appears better to limit academic instruction to naturally occuring tasks identified as functional for a given person. Thus, coin values would be taught through vending machine use (Browder, Snell, & Ambiogio, 1984; Sprague & Horner, 1984). Also, adults might be taught to pay meal costs at a fast food restaurant by rounding up to the nearest dollar, rather than counting out the exact amount (van den Pol et al., 1981).

Leisure and Recreational Skills Up to 50% of an adult's waking hours are available for leisure activities. Yet unlike most nonhandicapped persons, those with severe handicaps infrequently engage in leisure and recreational activities without systematic training. The need to develop leisure skills is underscored by a study of 128 mildly to severely handicapped graduates of work-training programs (Katz & Yekutiel, 1974). Even though 50% of these graduates held competitive jobs in the community, all lacked social contact with peers and failed to engage in recreational activities that required active participation. Their most frequently initiated leisure activities were watching TV or listening to the radio.

Acquiring leisure and recreational skills may result in a number of positive gains for the handicapped beyond increased social integration. Physical fitness, mobility skills, and social skills all may be enhanced. Furthermore, many leisure activities provide a medium for learning other skills. Table games, for instance, provide opportunities to increase counting, word recognition, language, and social skills. In addition, some leisure activities involve skills which handicapped students are able to master, thus permitting them to compete and socialize with nonhandicapped students.

Finding age-appropriate leisure and recreational activities for students with severe handicaps is difficult but essential. Ideally, the individual should learn active and passive as well as individual and cooperative activities, appropriate both at home and in community settings. With this type of repertoire, the individual should be able to select an appropriate leisure activity at any time. Some of the active leisure skills that have been taught through systematic instruction to students with severe handicaps are physical exercises (Wehman, Renzaglia, Berry, Schutz, & Karan, 1978), ball skills (Wehman & Marchant, 1977), use of a sliding board and skateboard (Wehman & Marchant, 1977), throwing darts (Schleien, Wehman, & Kiernan, 1981), and playing pinball (Hill, Wehman, & Horst, 1982). Passive skills that have been successfully taught include playing ticktacktoe or other commercial table games (Marchant & Wehman, 1979; Wehman et al., 1978), playing teacher-made table games (Bates & Renzaglia, 1982), and engaging in social conversation with peers (Matson & Andrasik, 1982).

Vocational Skills   Job placement is frequently a prerequisite for acceptance in many community group homes. Consequently, we cannot overestimate how important a vocation is to the independence of retarded adults. In many instances students with severe handicaps work in sheltered rather than competitive settings. Typically, they perform industrial assembly or packaging tasks in sheltered workshops designed specifically for handicapped adults. The work tasks are usually subcontracted from local industries.

Even though sheltered workshops have been in existence for many years, they have only recently begun to provide work for persons with severe handicaps. In fact, a majority of workshops still do not hire individuals with severe and profound retardation. Within the past decade, however, vocational skill instruction for adolescents and adults with severe handicaps has received increased attention, and the potential vocational competence of these persons has been demonstrated (Rusch & Mithaug, 1980; Wehman, 1981). Through systematic instruction severely handicapped adolescents and adults have acquired the skills necessary to assemble a variety of products in sheltered or simulated sheltered settings—complex bicycle brakes (Gold, 1972), drill presses (Crosson, 1969), and cable harnesses (Hunter & Bellamy, 1976).

Production rate is also a significant factor in the employment of handicapped individuals. Persons with severe handicaps can learn to perform work tasks at an acceptable rate. Indeed, through the application of consistent production contingencies (i.e., requirements for reinforcement), the work rate of severely handicapped workers has been raised from one unacceptable for sheltered employment to one approaching that of nonhandicapped workers in industrial settings (Horner, Lehren, Schwartz, O'Neill, & Hunter, 1979).

Although past emphasis has been on training persons with severe handicaps for sheltered employment, recent investigations have evaluated the efficacy of

Model Program

The Community-Based Instructional Program (CBIP) was initiated in response to a growing need in Albemarle County, Virginia, and the surrounding areas for appropriate services for school-age students with severe and profound handicaps. Prior to the establishment of the program, these students were being served inappropriately in preschool classes, classes designed for students with mild or moderate handicaps, or on a home-bound basis with instruction of no more than 6 to 8 hours weekly.

CBIP established three classes in integrated school settings: an elementary, a middle school, and a high school class. Each class serves up to eight students on a daily basis for a regular school day. All three school settings primarily serve nonhandicapped students; therefore, interaction with nonhandicapped age-appropriate peers is possible daily. School activities and facilities that are available to nonhandicapped students are also available to severely handicapped students in these integrated settings. The programming emphasis in each classroom varies according to the age, ability level, former programming, and physical involvement of the students.

The high school class, which serves students 16 to 21 years of age, is located in a high school serving approximately 2,000 nonhandicapped students. Although a classroom in the high school serves as home base for the CBIP students, their school day is spent in a variety of locations within the community in order to train skills where they will actually be performed. All of the high school students are ambulatory; two have mild to moderate hearing losses. One of these two and a second student have visual deficits. All students have limited verbal expressive language, and the speech of three of the students is highly unintelligible.

The emphasis in classroom programming is on community, leisure/recreational, vocational, and domestic skills training. Vocational training is a major focus. Three students, 20 to 21 years of age, receive up to 5 hours of training daily in selected competitive employment sites; the younger, less skilled individuals receive 2 hours of training daily in community training sites or the community sheltered workshop. Domestic skills are trained in two sites, a group home in which two of the high school students live and a home in the community. Domestic skills targeted for instruction include personal care skills (e.g., shaving, showering, face washing, and hair combing) and home care and survival skills, such as preparing simple meals, cleaning the bathroom, using the telephone, dusting, vacuuming, sweeping the floor, washing the table, doing the laundry. Community skills are trained on location (e.g., pedestrian skills and bus riding skills) or in the classroom (e.g., shopping or using vending machines) with generalization assessed and trained in the actual community environment. Opportunities for socialization and integration with peers exist via Night College (held weekly at the university) and the high school Advocacy Club.

The middle school class (ages 12 to 15) is located in a middle school serving approximately 375 nonhandicapped students. The CBIP students exhibit a wide range of handicapping conditions. Four of the students are severely motor impaired (spastic cerebral palsy) and capable of only limited partial participation in most self-care skills (e.g., feeding, dressing, toileting). These students are also nonverbal, and one is severely visually impaired. The remaining four students are ambulatory, have some verbal skills (although frequently inappropriate or unintelligible), and exhibited several major behavior problems (e.g., aggression, self-stimulation, noncompliance, off-task behavior, inappropriate social behavior).

The emphasis in classroom programming for the middle school class is on (1) providing vocational training on real jobs in the school setting, (2) training domestic skills in a school-based apartment setting, (3) teaching showering and grooming skills in the gym locker room, (4) training community mobility skills, (5) teaching appropriate leisure/recreational activities, and (6) training several functional academic skills (e.g., time telling and money skills). Instructional tasks are adapted to meet the needs of the students with physical handicaps. In addition, vigorous behavior management programs have been implemented.

Students 6 to 11 years old are served in a classroom in an elementary school serving approximately 225 nonhandicapped students. The elementary students have fewer skills in all areas than the students in the other two CBIP classes. These children have difficulty with basic self-care skills. For example, only one student is even partially toilet trained. Two children are verbal, but their speech is infrequent and often inappropriate. Five of the children have severe motor impairments and use wheelchairs.

For this class the emphasis is on basic self-care skills, such as toileting, appropriate mealtime behaviors, dressing, receptive and expressive language skills, compliance with instructions, appropriate use of leisure time, motor skills in the context of functional activities, mobility skills, and appropriate social behaviors. Four of the children are involved in simple domestic skills, including table setting and snack preparation. All children participate in a physical education program daily, in which they have an opportunity to interact with nonhandicapped elementary students who participate in the activities and assist the teacher with instruction. An effort is made to make all skills age-appropriate, functional, and specific to current and future home and community settings.

All classroom programs are systematic and data-based. Each student has a classroom notebook that contains all current instructional programs as well as those previously mastered. Program records are kept in the notebook, too, and all instructional data are graphed daily. Each of the classrooms is staffed by a teacher and an instructional aide. In addition, a domestic/home living specialist and a vocational/community specialist work cooperatively with classroom teachers in providing instruction in functional, age-appropriate skills across the domestic, vocational, community, and leisure/recreational skill domains. The two specialists are responsible for surveying community facilities, acting as liaisons between the community and the schools, and increasing parental involvement. Classroom teachers are ultimately responsible for IEP development and instructional programs. However, program staff works cooperatively to meet student needs with specialists from other disciplines, including speech and language therapists, occupational and physical therapists, adaptive physical education teachers, and vision specialists. A transdisciplinary approach is taken to provide students with continuity in programming and to maximize instructional time and student progress.

Parent priorities are assessed for all CBIP students through home visits and interviews and are taken into consideration in IEP development and program selection. Parent involvement is encouraged by all program staff. Home contacts are made regularly by the domestic/home living skills specialist, who also takes programs into student homes for family involvement.

training them for competitive jobs within the community (e.g., Rusch, 1983). Demonstrated successful placements in competitive jobs have been increasing rapidly. Since payment and potential benefits of competitive jobs far surpass those of sheltered employment, the focus of vocational training has been shifting to effective methods of preparing and training severely handicapped students for such jobs as well as placing them after training.

Mainstreaming

The term *mainstreaming* is usually used in reference to educational programs for students with mild handicaps. Typically, it refers to situations in which handicapped students participate in classes with their nonhandicapped peers and study the same material to some extent. Mainstreaming is an alternative to self-contained classrooms for many students with mild handicaps. It is unlikely, however, that students with severe handicaps will be placed in mainstreamed classrooms; therefore, mainstreaming may not be the most descriptive term to use when discussing educational programs for students with severe handicaps. Instead, integration with nonhandicapped peers (of the same chronological age) better describes the activities that are likely to be a part of the educational programs for severely handicapped students.

In order to provide an opportunity for integration with nonhandicapped peers, self-contained classes for students with severe handicaps should be placed in integrated schools consistent with their chronological ages, as mentioned earlier. For very young children integration means living at home and participating with the family in community activities while receiving home instruction from a visiting teacher and the parent(s). For preschoolers integrated education is likely to take place in an elementary school or in a building that houses other preschool classes.

Once in integrated settings, students with severe handicaps and their nonhandicapped peers can interact on many levels. At a minimum these students can interact on the school grounds, in the halls, on the school buses, in the cafeteria, and at school assemblies or other schoolwide events. Beyond these basic interactions, teachers can and should establish integrated educational programs whenever possible. Frequently, students with severe handicaps can successfully participate with their nonhandicapped peers in nonacademic classes, including physical education, art, and music, or in extracurricular activities such as school-sponsored clubs. Additional planned interactions might include peer tutoring programs, in which nonhandicapped students serve as instructors in selected programs for students with severe handicaps, or leisure/recreational activities conducted on a regular basis for both handicapped and nonhandicapped students.

Such integration of students with severe handicaps and their nonhandicapped peers has potential benefits for everyone involved:

1. Nonhandicapped students serve as appropriate peer models for their handicapped classmates (Moon, 1982; Rynders, Johnson, Johnson, & Schmidt, 1980).

Extracurricular activities such as camping integrate the severely handicapped with their peers.

2. Nonhandicapped students serve as models of age-appropriate behavior for teachers of severely handicapped students (Brown, Branston, Hamre-Nietupski, Johnson, et al., 1979).

3. Aware of the skills that nonhandicapped students use for independent functioning, teachers can more easily identify functional objectives for severely handicapped students (Brown, Branston, Hamre-Nietupski, Johnson, et al., 1979).

4. Nonhandicapped students can frequently serve as teachers or helpers for their handicapped peers (Voeltz, 1980, 1982).

5. Nonhandicapped students can learn to accept and appreciate the differences in people within a community (Brown, Branston, Hamre-Nietupski, Johnson, et al., 1979; Voeltz, 1980).

Integration of severely handicapped students in community-based instruction also has a number of benefits. When students learn a skill in the very place in which it will be used, they are more likely to use that skill. In addition, instruction in the community provides handicapped students with an opportunity to interact with community business people and residents. The students are made aware of the heterogeneous nature of the community and learn to cope with it to whatever extent they are able. Furthermore, the more visible severely handicapped students are, the more likely it is that they will be accepted by the nonhandicapped community.

Youngsters even at early ages like taking part in the instruction of their handicapped peers.

Innovation and Development

There still remain more questions than answers on how best to teach persons with severe handicaps. As we have noted, the education of the moderately to profoundly retarded population has been largely neglected until recently. A few important issues require attention and solution in order to teach this group more effectively.

Issue: How Are Self-Help Skills Best Taught?

Earlier we mentioned that most self-help intervention programs combine a variety of training procedures. It is likely that not all of those procedures are essential to skill acquisition. The effects of specific program components need to be analyzed systematically to make these programs less complex.

Partial participation in self-help skills is another subject that deserves investigation (Brown, Branston-McClean, et al., 1979). Many severely handicapped students are orthopedically impaired and incapable of total independence in self-help skills. We need to know much more about how to encourage and teach partial participation in self-help skills to these individuals.

Issue: How Are Communication Skills Best Learned?

Recent reviews of research challenge the traditional notion of teaching prerequisites before delving into speech or nonvocal expression. It may not be important to teach motor imitation before vocal imitation, or word understanding before word use. This position gains support from the findings of a language program piloted by Guess, Sailor, and Baer (1976), which involved over 400 severely handicapped persons. The researchers did not teach tongue control to persons with Down syndrome, yet they found that tongue control improved on its own after the students learned to speak and were reinforced for improvements in articulation (Sailor et al., 1980). With further validation of these programming trends and those described earlier, the success of language intervention is likely to improve for this population. Still more study needs to be focused on nonvocal methods of communicating.

Issue: What Leisure and Social Skills Should Be Learned?

A wide-ranging body of research is needed to determine what kinds of leisure, recreational, and social skills are most appropriate and valuable for individuals with severe handicaps. The investigations conducted have been relatively unrelated and, in most cases, methodologically inadequate. Research should place particular emphasis on two specific needs: developing age-appropriate activities for persons with the most severe handicaps and exploring adaptations of equipment and activities for orthopedically handicapped students.

Recently, educational researchers have begun to investigate the use of electronic devices to enable persons with severe handicaps to participate in appropri-

 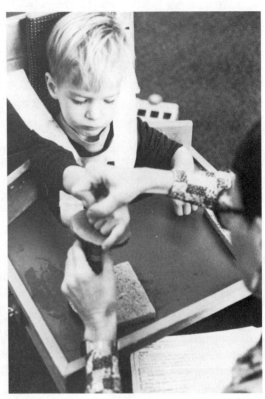

These students are learning to wash and dry their hands.

ate leisure activities. For example, switches have been designed to activate music (Hasket & Hollar, 1978) and toys such as electronic robots (Caro & Renzaglia, 1984). Further research is needed to maximize the opportunities for persons with physical disabilities. Identification of appropriate adaptations for individual students should also be investigated.

Issue: What Type of Integrated Activities Best Promote Positive Relationships Between Severely Handicapped Students and Their Nonhandicapped Peers?

With recent legislation mandating opportunities for integration of students with severe handicaps and their nonhandicapped peers, teachers are faced with making decisions about the type of interactions that would most benefit their students. Activities in which integration might occur vary and include nonacademic classes, extracurricular activities, informal periods throughout the school day, and planned integration activities (Taylor, 1982). Past research has demonstrated an increase in positive attitudes of nonhandicapped students toward severely handicapped students resulting from structured rather than nonstructured interactions (Voeltz, 1980, 1982). However, more information must be gathered regarding the type of interaction that promotes the greatest gain for both types of students. Perhaps the benefits of reciprocal interactions, in which nonhandicapped and handicapped students are equally dependent, are different from tutorial interactions. More research is needed to identify the circumstances that should govern the selection of one type or another.

Issue: Are Competitive Job Placements Appropriate for All Students with Severe Handicaps?

With the recent success in placing students with severe handicaps in competitive jobs, the question arises of whether competitive jobs should be targeted for all students. Perhaps educators should investigate the options in competitive employment for handicapped students who have previously been excluded from gainful employment. Part-time employment, job sharing, and enclaves within community businesses may be more desirable than employment in sheltered workshops. Job sharing, in particular, might enable two workers to match strengths and weaknesses to complete a whole job that neither could complete alone. Enclaves in community businesses could provide severely handicapped persons with the opportunity to work in a competitive location but to receive compensation consistent with work production. Thus, enclave workers could experience all the benefits of working in integrated employment at no added expense to an employer. Although educators are beginning to discuss these options, there are few demonstrations of implementation. This area needs further investigation.

Issue: What Teaching Strategies Will Promote Generalization of Functional Skills?

There has been recent emphasis on the need for persons with severe handicaps to generalize acquired skills to new settings and materials and in the presence of persons who were not part of the original training environment. Instruction that takes place in natural settings encourages generalization of functional skills. Thus, whenever possible, skills need to be taught in the environment in which they are most likely to occur—the community, home, or work setting. In fact, when instruction is conducted in the classroom, the teacher must not consider a skill learned until the students demonstrate its mastery in the appropriate situation. Educators have suggested a variety of techniques that are thought to be effective in facilitating generalization. However, the relative effectiveness of these techniques has not been established. Instructional strategies include training multiple examples of the target skill, training the general case, training loosely, using natural cues, and training in natural settings. Although we have information to suggest that each of these techniques may be effective in facilitating generalization of some skills, no guidelines exist for selecting the most effective techniques for specific skills. In addition, more research is needed to assist educators in designing educational programs that maximize the likelihood of skill generalization. Thus, we need to know much more about both how to encourage skill use across untrained settings and materials and how to promote generalization of specific skills.

Future Directions

Teacher Training   Teachers, parents, and administrators are only beginning to accept the characteristics of intervention described earlier. The average educational program for the severely handicapped may be as many as 10 to 20 years behind the research. To lessen this gap, university teacher training programs, as well as in-service training programs, need strengthening. More recognition needs to be given to the difficulty of teaching the severely handicapped population. Master's level training, pretraining experiences with exceptional individuals, and extensive practical experiences during training were identified by administrators as "superior" characteristics of special education teachers (Westling, Koorland, & Rose, 1981). These findings are consistent with the recommendations of Sontag et al. (1979) that teachers of this difficult-to-teach population be trained at a graduate level and possess a minimum of 2 years' experience with the severely handicapped before being accepted into teacher training programs.

It seems probable that more school systems will adopt a longer year as a result of the *Armstrong v. Kline* decision in Pennsylvania—clearly, the severely handicapped need sustained training (Leonard, 1981). Although teacher burnout has not actually been documented as a cause of turnover in trained staff (Weiskopf, 1980), the work intensity of a longer school year could threaten classroom teachers of the severely handicapped even more. It may be possible to reduce the problem of teacher burnout; school system modifications should include a variety of teacher supports:

1. trained classroom aides

2. responsibility for a reasonable number of students (four to eight, depending on the severity and multiplicity of handicaps)

3. administrative support in the school building and system

4. access to needed interdisciplinary staff (behavior analysts; occupational, physical, and speech therapists; and nurses) and needed equipment (wheelchairs, communication boards, home settings for teaching domestic skills)

A teacher who can rely on these supports has a good chance of developing high-quality instructional programs while maintaining professional sanity.

Changes in Public Attitude   The quality of instruction for the severely handicapped is likely to increase as public attitudes toward and expectations for this small fraction of the population are modified. The average person is misinformed about the potential of even the mildly retarded, and misinformation tends to show itself as fear, as evidenced by the frequent opposition to the establishment of group homes for the retarded in residential neighborhoods. Funding of programs for the severely handicapped has also been victimized by an ignorant voting public. The Kennedy family's influence in the early 1960s reduced public ignorance and prejudice toward the mildly and moderately retarded population. The public today needs visible demonstrations of the human and cost-effective benefits of habilitating the severely handicapped.

Service Delivery Future programs for the severely handicapped should be characterized by some major modifications in case management, deinstitutionalization, and community-based residences. Currently infant and postschool intervention programs in many states are under the control of departments other than education. At the age of 2 to 5, the severely handicapped child is usually included in a school's special education program and continues this placement until the age of 21. At this time, if the locality has a relevant postschool program, the individual tends to start anew in a sheltered workshop or an activity center. When no postschool program exists, institutionalization is frequently the only choice.

A more sensible approach would be to assign a lifelong *case manager* to each severely handicapped individual. The case manager would presumably be associated with the state agency responsible for services to the retarded and would have a close connection to educational programs for the retarded from infancy to adulthood, including community residential programs. To avoid the pitfalls of sporadic intervention and to assist parents in formulating a realistic future for their child, the case manager would work with parents to develop a lifelong plan for the child. That plan should include provisions for (1) coordination of services from infancy to preschool through all the school and postschool years to avoid the inefficiency of programming in isolation and deviating from established life goals; (2) consistency in educational methods and objectives across teachers and settings; (3) centralization of relevant medical information to avoid expensive duplication of diagnosis; and (4) some type of supervised community residence when the individual is 18 to 21 years old.

The trend toward *deinstitutionalization* of retarded persons began at least 25 years ago when President Kennedy stated that the practice of institutionalized segregation from the rest of society was immoral. In 1967, for the first time, the number of institutionalized retarded persons declined. In 1970 President Nixon established a 10-year goal of reducing this population by half, and in the first four years of that decade the reduction rate accelerated to 25% (Braddock, 1977). Unfortunately, Nixon's goal was not achieved by 1980, and deinstitutionalization still falls far short of the goals set by others. Some find the trends toward deinstitutionalization mildly encouraging (Gollay, Freedman, Wyngaarden, & Kurtz, 1978); others find them disappointing (Braddock, 1977). Braddock notes some discouraging facts to support his opinion:

- There are far too few community-based residences to receive individuals ready to leave institutions.

- Many superintendents of institutions believe that over half of their present residents could live successfully in community-based residences.

- One-fourth of the admissions made in 1973 were of mildly to moderately retarded children who should never have been institutionalized.

Public philosophy that supports institutionalization of the severely handicapped appears to be fairly ingrained still today. According to Braddock, "There is still much administrative inertia in our service delivery systems promoting segregation of the deviant and concentration of services" (p. 97).

Partial deinstitutionalization has led to other developments. First, a disproportionate percentage of the retarded currently institutionalized are severely or profoundly retarded (more than 80% according to O'Connor, 1976), thus slowing the community placement process. Second, a wave of court cases has focused on the unfulfilled promises of deinstitutionalization and the value of habilitation. And finally, a number of professional organizations relevant to the field of mental retardation have expressed their opposition to the use of institutions for the retarded in our society. In order to advance the process of deinstitutionalization, public support is required; the abolishment of institutions will depend on public understanding of the habilitation potential of the severely handicapped and the debilitating effects of institutionalization.

Community residential facilities (CRFs) are homes intentionally located in residential neighborhoods. They are small in size (7 to 20 rooms), house an equally small number of persons, and are meant to be either a permanent residence or a transitional training residence for retarded adults. CRFs are varied in nature, ranging from loosely supervised apartments to group homes with live-in house parents (Baker, Seltzer, & Seltzer, 1977). Not only do CRFs appear to be a more cost-efficient type of residence for retarded persons (Intagliata, Wilder, & Cooley, 1979; Zigler & Balla, 1977), but their capacity to promote habilitation in a more humane environment seems indisputable (Blatt, Ozolins, & McNally, 1979; Roos, 1979).

Presently, far too few CRFs exist to meet even current demands, a factor often blamed for the slowed process of deinstitutionalization (O'Connor, 1976). In addition, CRFs tend to serve primarily the less retarded. O'Connor's study of 611 CRFs in 1976 revealed that 80% of the residents had IQs higher than 40. A drastic increase in the number of CRFs is clearly a pressing need, for they stand as the primary alternative to institutionalization.

Summary

Persons with moderate, severe, and profound retardation constitute only a small part of the mentally retarded population. This group is comprised of those whose performance on tests of intelligence is three standard deviations below the mean. The group is often referred to as the *severely handicapped*.

Causes of severe handicaps include chromosomal abnormalities, metabolic disorders, toxemia, and complications during birth. Moderate to profound retardation does not seem to be associated with the socioeconomic status of the family. The severely handicapped have a variety of physical and psychological characteristics. As many as 25% to 50% may have a concomitant handicap other than mental retardation.

Relevant assessment procedures for the severely handicapped include collecting background and performance information (past records and parent interviews), methodologically observing the individual's behavior and skills, and administering general assessment instruments. A goal of intervention should be to provide education in the most natural environment possible so that students will learn the functional skills necessary to live in the community. Curriculum objectives must be functional and appropriate to the student's chronological age. Programs need to be developed in self-help, language, leisure and recreation, daily living skills and related academics, and vocational skills.

Numerous issues relevant to the severely handicapped remain unresolved. The first is the trend toward deinstitutionalization and the community's reluctance to accept responsibility for providing residences, habilitation, and employment for persons with severe handicaps. In addition, there is a need for appropriate educational programs in which specially trained teachers focus on functional objectives, using techniques proven to be effective with severely handicapped students. A final issue relates to the importance of teaching persons with severe handicaps in integrated settings that allow regular interaction with nonhandicapped peers.

Study Questions

1. What part of the retarded population is comprised of the moderately, severely, and profoundly retarded?

2. How does this group perform on tests of intelligence?

3. What are some identifiable causes of moderate to profound retardation?

4. Is the occurrence of moderate to profound retardation associated with socioeconomic status?

5. What percentage of the severely handicapped also have an additional handicap?

6. Describe three assessment procedures used with persons having severe handicaps.

7. Why should persons with severe handicaps be taught in natural settings?

8. How does a top-down, or functional, curriculum differ from a bottom-up, or developmental, curriculum?

9. Give three reasons for the importance of educating persons with severe handicaps in integrated settings.

10. What is partial participation? Why is it an important programming concept?

11. Why should teachers use the chronological age of students with severe handicaps as a criterion for selecting teaching materials, classroom decor, interaction styles, and teaching activities?

12. Describe four recent legal and/or societal issues affecting the education of persons with severe handicaps.

TIPS FOR HELPING

1. Involve the student's parents or care providers at every step of programming, from initial selection of skills to be taught to teaching and evaluation.

2. Seek parental assistance in assigning priorities to teaching objectives.

3. Use teaching methods that minimize errors.

4. When errors occur, provide corrective feedback.

5. Use teaching materials, reinforcers, and tasks suited to the student's chronological age.

6. Teach any given skill on at least a daily basis.

7. Teach and assess in natural settings and at natural times whenever possible.

8. In order to promote skill generalization, teach a given skill across a variety of settings, trainers, and materials.

9. Once a skill is mastered, schedule appropriate opportunities for regular use.

10. Provide as many natural and planned opportunities for interaction with nonhandicapped peers as possible.

10

Physical and Health Impairments

June Bigge
San Francisco State University

Barbara Sirvis
University of Illinois

Tim is a 14-year-old student who has recently transferred from a special education school to a junior high school resource program for students with physical disabilities. He is severely physically handicapped as a result of athetoid cerebral palsy and uses an electric wheelchair for mobility. His cerebral palsy, a result of brain damage during the birth process, caused severe impairment of his motor coordination, which makes his speech unintelligible with the exception of a few words. Lack of control of his shoulder and arm muscles makes it difficult for him to write with a pencil. He reads at the primary level.

The staff of the special education school felt that the junior high school would be the least restrictive environment for Tim because he is keenly aware of his environment, and his IEP emphasizes age-appropriate social skill development. Tim's parents were reluctant for him to attend junior high school because he had had limited opportunity to interact with

nondisabled peers, and they were afraid he would be hurt by teasing. However, since Tim wanted to make the change, his parents concurred with the recommendation.

Since effective communication is assumed to be one of the factors in successful mainstreaming, special education personnel had developed communication boards for Tim. Small pictures of items, symbols representing ideas, printed words, numerals, and the alphabet were placed under clear plastic on stiff cardboard sheets approximately 18″ × 22″. In this way he could point and communicate his ideas to others. Initial training was begun in the special school and is being continued with the resource personnel. Tim has one multipurpose communication board he can use at home, in school, and in the community. He has additional topical boards for specific school subjects. He now knows which board to use in different situations but has difficulty with accurate pointing. Resource personnel helped regular class teachers, administrators, and students by giving them a demonstration with Tim.

Although initially Tim was anxious about new situations and the other students were unsure of how to communicate, Tim has done an excellent job of relieving their discomfort (with lots of support from the resource teacher and his parents). He is functioning successfully in the social environment of a new school and seems more motivated to improve his academic skills. The greatest challenge is to expand his use of the communication boards until he can express all that he wants to say and all that he knows. He needs to learn to spell so that he can type what he wants to report from his lessons.

Tim is able to function in a regular class with some help. Although he can think on levels similar to those of lower functioning junior high school students, he cannot read enough to learn his lessons from texts. He studies by listening to lectures, to others reading to him, and to tapes of textbooks provided by volunteer readers or by the Library of Congress. With the aid of a keyguard he is learning to type some of his lessons on a portable typewriter or microcomputer. He communicates with some limited speech, head signals, and a microprocessor-based communication device that he is just beginning to use functionally. Occasionally, he points to the symbol for "Bug off!" and humorously turns a teasing

situation into a positive interaction with a classmate.

Recent technological developments have provided electronic communication options. Tim will be involved in a training program to learn to use the microprocessor-based communication aid. It is expensive but can be just as important to him as his wheelchair. It has a matrix of many cells about 1-inch square, coded with small pictures, alphabet letters, and other symbols similar to those on his communication boards. Each press of a cell retrieves either a single letter (like a typewriter) or a whole word or sentence, and a small printer prints the message. Tim can even talk through this device. He can store messages, and a speech synthesizer will then say the message for others to hear. The device can be attached to his wheelchair and can be with him wherever he goes.

Options for competitive employment are uncertain at this time because of Tim's severe physical disabilities and difficulties with reading and spelling. Career education programming in school will continue to explore vocational and leisure opportunities. He is now being trained to use a microcomputer word processing program to copy and format short drafts of school bulletins. He has one week to complete each job and presently needs a great deal of help; the goal is for total independence in this and other service jobs. A special effort will be made to explore opportunities for contract jobs in which Tim can use his developing skills with microcomputers.

Individuals with physical disabilities are members of your community and perhaps your class. They may be like Tim and use wheelchairs for mobility or electronic devices for communication, but they have the potential to be active members of the community. Some may be enrolled in college and university programs. Others may receive technical training for employment. Individuals with physical disabilities and health impairments have interests and opinions as far-ranging and as diverse as those of their nondisabled peers.

History

Physical disabilities have been documented through the ages, and programs for disabled individuals have grown from extermination, ridicule, and isolation to acceptance, education, and treatment. Poliomyelitis is thought to have occurred over 6,000 years ago, and there is evidence of cerebral palsy in early times (Denhoff & Robinault, 1960). However, it was not until the late 19th century that programs began to emerge for children with physical handicaps.

Early programs emphasized physical care and surgery for those with cerebral palsy; true educational programming began with children hospitalized for disabilities resulting from such diseases as polio and tuberculosis. Then, gradually, there was recognition that children with more severe disabilities should have educational opportunities as well.

The first public school class in the United States for children with physical handicaps was established in 1899 in Chicago. Early classes were in hospitals, day camps, and convalescent and residential homes. Many facilities were designed as open-air schools for delicate children—those with pretuberculosis, cardiac problems, diabetes, and poliomyelitis. Schools for children with cerebral palsy were the last to begin because many of these children had multiple physical and learning problems and were more difficult to teach. In 1913 the first public school teachers were assigned to teach homebound children with physical disabilities in New York City, and by the 1930s children with physical handicaps were benefiting from legislation to reimburse local school districts for the added costs of educating children with handicaps. A team approach to intervention gradually evolved and gave educational programming equal status with medical services. Although a variety of disciplines contributed to the development of such programming, its roots lie in medicine and related fields (Mackie, 1945, 1969).

Volunteer groups of parents and concerned professionals emerged during the first quarter of the 20th century. Their lobbying efforts greatly influenced the establishment of early education programs for students with physical handicaps. Many of these groups have evolved into agencies that now function as advocates at the local and national levels (e.g., National Easter Seal Society and United Cerebral Palsy Association).

World Wars I and II expedited advancements of complicated orthopedic and rehabilitation procedures for such disabilities as amputations, traumatic spinal cord injuries, and communication and motor coordination impairments due to brain injury. Rehabilitation needs resulted in intensive collaboration of professionals in medicine, therapy, counseling, education, and rehabilitation engineering. Individuals with physical disabilities have benefited from advances in artificial limbs, lifesaving health care, physical therapy, methods for improving physical independence, vocational options, posture and movement improvement, and self-care and communication aids.

Henry Viscardi, Jr., was one of the first Americans to demonstrate that people with handicaps can learn to work and earn their own way (Viscardi, 1972). In early 1950 he collaborated with a small group of disabled individuals to set up a shop in Albertson, Long Island. In this shop, Abilities Incorporated, persons with handi-

Many children with physical handicaps do well in regular classes.

caps found real jobs, not contrived work or charity. This pioneering crew of five persons, served by five good arms and one good leg, became the nucleus of the nationally prominent Human Resources Center and its school for students with severe physical disabilities.

Education and services for students with physical disabilities are now supported by legislation, including P.L. 94–142, P.L. 95–602, and P.L. 98–199. Students have moved from the isolation of hospitals and custodial institutions to public school classes. Education is now characterized by an increasing trend toward placements in less restrictive environments, with options for mainstream placements or individually designed itinerant or resource room programs. Removal of architectural barriers and a decrease in attitudinal barriers have led to acceptance of students with physical disabilities and health impairments in regular classes. Indeed, some are able to compete with their nonhandicapped peers for academic honors; others enjoy social integration in nonacademic situations.

Definition

We refer to individuals with handicapping physical conditions with such terms as *crippled and other health impaired* (COHI), *physically handicapped*, and *physically disabled*. The terms are used more or less interchangeably by professionals, parents, and disabled individuals. Confusion can result from use of the term *physically handicapped*, however, since some people apply this label to individuals with vision and/or hearing impairments.

The guidelines established for P.L. 94–142 attempted to resolve definitional questions by dividing physical handicaps into two broad categories. *Orthopedic impairments* are those disabilities that relate primarily to disorders of the skeleton, joints, and muscles, including these examples:

1. clubfoot, the absence of some member, or other congenital anomalies

2. impairments caused by diseases such as poliomyelitis or bone tuberculosis

3. impairments caused by cerebral palsy

4. amputations

5. contractures (permanent shortening of some member) caused by fractures or burns (*Federal Register*, 1977, p. 42478)

The second category, *health impairments*, is comprised of physical conditions that affect a youngster's educational performance, including "limited strength, vitality or alertness due to chronic or acute health problems such as a heart condition, tuberculosis, rheumatic fever, nephritis, asthma, sickle cell anemia, hemophilia, epilepsy, lead poisoning, leukemia, or diabetes" (*Federal Register*, 1977, p. 42478).

Physical disabilities are frequently accompanied by one or more additional handicaps—communication disorders, speech problems, vision and hearing impairments, behavioral disorders—that interfere with functioning and learning. Wald (1971) has offered a description that reflects the diversity of this population:

[It includes] those children and adults who as a result of permanent, temporary, or intermittent medical disabilities require modifications in curriculum and instructional strategies. Frequent separation from family and a lack of adequate parental guidance contribute to secondary emotional problems . . . The child's physical limitations are often the basis of functional retardation as well as sensory, perceptual, and other conceptual deficits. (p. 95)

Prevalence

Because physical disabilities and health impairments often occur in combination with other handicapping conditions, it is difficult to classify individuals with these disabilities. Some, particularly those with health impairments, may be considered to have a primary disability belonging to another category. Others may be counted as having both a physical disability and, for example, a learning disability or hearing impairment. Determining a relatively valid prevalence rate for physical disabilities is challenging and perhaps impossible.

Nonetheless, we can obtain some indication of prevalence from the data collected by the federal government on children and youth served under P.L. 94–142 and P.L. 89–313. The figures for 1983–84 show a total of 94,814 individuals 21 years old and younger classified as having physical disabilities or health impairments (U. S. Department of Education, 1984). These counts and estimates, however, do not tell all. We do know that within the population identified as primarily physically disabled, the greatest percentage of individuals have cerebral palsy. And we can be certain that a large number of individuals considered multiply handicapped also have a physical disability.

Causes

Causes of physical disabilities and health impairments are as varied as the disabilities themselves. The factors involved may be *prenatal* (before birth), *perinatal* (during the birth process), or *postnatal* (after birth). There are two general groups of causes that play a role before birth: genetic factors and factors outside the fetus. Genetic defects in one or both parents may be transmitted to a child. These defects may not be evident in the parents, and in some cases several children in the family may also carry the defective genetic trait without having the disability themselves (recessive genes). For instance, muscular dystrophy, a hereditary disorder rarely found in females, is generally caused by a sex-linked recessive gene that is transmitted through unaffected mothers to their sons. Hemophilia is also a sex-linked genetic disorder passed from an unaffected mother to her son.

While developing in the womb, the fetus may also be adversely affected by a number of external influences (teratogens). A mother's inadequate prenatal medical care and diet, smoking, excessive consumption of alcoholic beverages, or use of drugs such as marijuana or heroin during pregnancy are potentially harmful to the fetus and may result in physical disability. So, too, is prenatal trauma, injury to the fetus resulting from injury to the mother, as might occur in a serious fall (Crain, 1984).

The perinatal period begins with the first labor pain and ends with the infant's first normal breath. It is a time during which there is great risk of trauma or anoxia (lack of oxygen). If a child is not in the appropriate position for delivery, attempts to change the position can cause physical impairments. In addition, any obstruction of the oxygen supply to the fetus—for instance, strangulation by the umbilical cord—can result in physical handicaps. Cerebral palsy is often the result of a severe reduction in the oxygen supply to the fetus during the birth process (Batshaw & Perrett, 1981).

Postnatal time periods can technically encompass the neonatal period (1st to the 28th day), infancy (28th day to 1 year), early childhood (first 2 years), and childhood (after 2 years), as well as adolescent and adult problems. More commonly, it refers to the period from birth to 2 years. Physical disabilities can result from accidents, the most common being bicycle and car accidents. Accident-related spinal cord and head injuries are frequent postnatal, or acquired, causes of lasting physical impairment. Some accidents, of course, result in only temporary disabilities. Infection is another primary cause of postnatal physical disabilities and health impairments; bacterial and viral infections that attack the central nervous system can result in permanent damage. Infantile encephalitis, a viral inflammation of the brain, can result in muscular weakness. Meningitis (inflammation of the membrane covering the brain and spinal cord) is caused by microorganisms and can result in symptoms similar to those of cerebral palsy. These two infections can occur anytime but often occur within the first 2 years of life.

Characteristics

Different psychological and emotional problems have been associated with disabilities present at birth (congenital) and those that are acquired later. It has been suggested (Wright, 1960) that individuals with congenital disabilities have a sense of difference, of not being like other people, whereas those with acquired disabilities typically experience a sense of loss. In her classic text on psychosocial aspects of disability, Wright (1983) suggests that numerous social, psychological, and environmental factors affect the psychosocial development of individuals with disabilities. She suggests that some individuals develop coping mechanisms and strategies that assist in acceptance and successful adjustment, whereas others have negative experiences and succumb to the negative impacts of disability, "giving scant attention to the challenge for change and meaningful adaptation" (p. 194). Teachers need to understand the potential psychosocial implications of physical disabilities and health impairments as well as the physical and behavioral characteristics.

This section will describe some of the more common physical disabilities found in children and adolescents. There are many other syndromes and birth defects that warrant educational consideration even though they occur infrequently. The chapter reference list at the end of the book includes some sources of information regarding these other disabilities.

Orthopedic and Muscular Impairments

Cerebral Palsy This condition accounts for the largest percentage of students with physical disabilities. It involves motor handicaps that have "in common an impairment of the coordination of muscle action with an inability to maintain normal postures and balance and to perform normal movements and skills" (Bobath & Bobath, 1975, p. 29). It is nonprogressive, that is, the condition of the person does not worsen, except that skill potential is lost without intervention. Although typically resulting from damage to the brain during the birth process, cerebral palsy can also result from trauma during prenatal development or after birth. Prematurity, difficult labor, lack of oxygen at birth, and childhood trauma are problems that increase the risk of cerebral palsy (Bobath, 1980; Holm, 1982).

The amount of physical ability remaining to an individual with cerebral palsy varies greatly. Some youngsters have only slight fine motor coordination problems; some walk with extreme difficulty; others are confined to wheelchairs.

Classification of cerebral palsy is based on the limbs affected or on the nature of the abnormal movement. The following terms reflect the limbs involved:

monoplegia	one limb
paraplegia	both lower limbs
hemiplegia	both limbs on the same side
diplegia	all four limbs with the greater disability in the legs
quadriplegia	all four limbs with approximately equal disability

Movement may follow any of these patterns (Bleck, 1982; Bobath, 1980; Denhoff, 1976; Thompson, Rubin, & Bilenker, 1983):

Spasticity. Muscle tone is increased (hypertonia), and muscles are tight and overactive. Unable to contract normally, they resist movement, which is slow and jerky if it occurs at all. Rigidity is a severe form of hypertonia.

Athetosis. Fluctuating muscle tone causes uncontrolled and irregular movement patterns. Flailing limbs may be difficult to control even for gross movements, and the severity of the abnormal movement increases when individuals are under stress or are emotionally excited.

Ataxia. Lack of coordination is related to poor control of balance and movement. It is difficult to maintain upright posture and to control balance reactions.

Mixed. The movements described here commonly occur in combination.

A number of secondary disabilities are associated with cerebral palsy, including sensory impairments and behavioral and social-emotional problems. Learning handicaps are common as well. However, there is considerable confusion as to the type and extent of secondary problems because physical disabilities make valid assessment difficult.

Muscular Dystrophy   In muscular dystrophy the muscles suffer from loss of protein, and muscle tissue is gradually replaced by fatty and other tissue. The voluntary muscle system gradually becomes useless. Although muscular dystrophy has several adult forms, in childhood it usually appears in the Duchenne, or pseudohypertrophic, form. This form of the disability is typically evident by the time a child is three years old and causes a progressive weakness of the skeletal muscles, often in conjunction with a seeming overdevelopment (pseudohypertrophy) of the calf muscles. Initial symptoms may include difficulty in running or climbing stairs; later the child becomes unable to maintain balance even on a level surface. A characteristic waddling gait, giving the impression of awkwardness or slowness, usually appears before muscle weakness becomes so severe that the child needs to use a wheelchair. Weakness in the upper extremities may appear with the awkward gait or somewhat later (Chutorian & Engel, 1982; Lyle & Obringer, 1983).

Individuals with muscular dystrophy tire easily. Even those who can still walk may need wheelchairs for extended trips. With their weakened muscles these individuals fall easily and may have trouble performing simple tasks, such as opening doors. Treatment is limited to therapy to delay the development of muscle contractures (shortening of muscles). The disease progresses fairly rapidly toward death, usually in the late teens. Of concern to educators is the accompanying mild mental retardation; some research suggests that as many as 50% of students with the Duchenne form may be retarded. However, as with most students whose performance on assessment instruments may be affected by environmental and physical ability, educators should use caution in judging potential for academic performance.

Myelomeningocele (Spina Bifida) Spina bifida takes several forms and may be called *meningocele* or *myelomeningocele,* depending on its extent. In this disease a portion of the spinal cord is not enclosed by the vertebral arches, and a distortion of the spinal cord results. In myelomeningocele, the more complex and involved form of the disability, damage to nerve roots results in a neurological disorder and related deformities. Neurological impairment increases with the degree of distortion of the spinal cord, varying from minor sensory and/or motor loss to paraplegia with incontinence (lack of bladder control). Urinary tract disorders, orthopedic deformities, and problems related to skin sensitivity may also be involved. In many children a blockage causes fluid to accumulate in the head. This condition, referred to as hydrocephalus, can cause mental retardation if not corrected by surgical implantation of a shunt. Children with spina bifida require considerable medical attention, often including physical therapy to assist them to develop gait (walking) patterns, usually with braces and crutches, and/or to become skilled wheelchair users (Anderson & Spain, 1977; Howell, 1978).

Spinal Cord Injury Spinal cord injuries and resultant paraplegia or quadriplegia have ramifications beyond the limitations they place on mobility. Potential problem areas include urinary tract infections, respiratory infections, decubitus ulcers (pressure sores) that occur when lack of movement slows circulation, and muscle contractures. Rehabilitation procedures are long and involved and rarely result in total return of lost function. Emotional problems may develop and require psychological intervention. However, adaptive aids may help the child recover maximum function—for example, wheelchairs for mobility, hand controls for driving, electric typewriters for writing, buttonhooks for dressing, and utensils with large handles for eating. Another procedure is to develop alternate muscle groups to perform activities normally done by the nonfunctioning muscles (Donovan, 1981).

Spinal Muscular Atrophy Spinal muscular atrophy is a hereditary, progressive disorder that causes muscular wasting. It has a variable course, ranging from slow and chronic to rapid, ending in early death. Usually, atrophy first affects the legs and then progresses to the muscles of the shoulder girdle, upper arms, and neck. Often when individuals with the slower form lose their physical independence, they experience a renewal of previously felt feelings of resentment and frustration (Koehler, 1982).

Osteogenesis Imperfecta Defective development in the quantity and quality of bone causes osteogenesis imperfecta, sometimes called "brittle bones." Bones are imperfectly formed and do not grow normally in length and thickness. Consequently, they are so fragile that even simple activities may cause fractures. Dwarfism and dental defects are commonly associated secondary disabilities. Of concern to teachers should be the potential for development of a severe hearing impairment; a child's hearing may actually deteriorate. Academic ability is not affected; however, absence due to hospitalization for treatment of multiple fractures may affect performance (Molnar, 1983).

Legg-Calve-Perthes Disease This childhood disease, often referred to as Legg-Perthes or simply Perthes, is characterized by a change in the density, or porousness, of the round end (femoral head) of the long thigh bone, where it fits into the hip socket. Usually only one hip is affected, but the ability to walk is impaired. The cause of this disease is unknown. Recovery depends on the amount of bone that has been affected and the amount of permanent damage done during the course of the disease. A child can usually recover after 1 to 2 years of treatment, usually involving a brace to hold the hips turned away from midline and keep the femur in proper relation to the hip socket. Some walking is possible with the brace. In 80% of the cases the individuals regain their ability to walk adequately within 18 to 24 months. Although this disease does not affect learning potential, it may—like other disabilities acquired after birth—affect a student's attitude toward learning and the world in general. Again, negative attitude toward the sudden loss of independence may develop (Rab, 1982).

Limb Deficiency Whether congenital or acquired, limb deficiency (the absence of one or more limbs) may present a major obstacle to physical activity and normal functioning. The extent of the limb deficiency (level of functional loss) affects physical ability. The nature or severity of associated psychological problems depends on the age of onset, the severity of the deficiency, and the attitudes of parents and other significant people who work with the child with a limb deficiency. Children may choose to use a prosthetic device (artificial limb) or rely on the remaining portion of their deficient limb. Child and parent perceptions of the functional value of the artificial limb are major considerations in this decision. Parent participation in the rehabilitation process and early intervention by rehabilitation personnel are crucial in developing maximum function, whether a prosthetic device is used or not (Marquardt, 1983). Motivation may be a primary factor in the extent to which a child learns to use a prosthetic device.

Juvenile Rheumatoid Arthritis A chronic, painful, inflammatory disease of the joints and the tissue around them, juvenile rheumatoid arthritis has many forms, all of which usually develop in early childhood. Fever spikes (quick, abnormal, extreme increases in temperature), rash, and morning stiffness are characteristic

Crucial in adjusting to a limb deficiency is the attitude of friends, teachers, and family.

symptoms that often cause absence from school. Sitting for long periods of time may cause the joints to "gel"; thus, children with this disease need freedom to move about at home and in school. Casts, splints, braces, and a variety of assistive devices may be necessary as medical intervention and/or to facilitate independent functioning. Many children show improvement and remission of major symptoms by the age of 18. Residual effects are individualized and vary greatly (Hanson, 1983).

Health Impairments

The physical disabilities described here are usually visible. However, many of the physical problems that we refer to as health impairments are not. This lack of visibility can cause problems for disabled persons when other people do not understand that their unique behavior patterns are a result of or an adaptation to their disability.

Asthma   Asthma is the most common childhood pulmonary disease. Characterized by inflammation and resultant blockage of the airways, attacks are triggered by allergens, infections, irritants, exercise, and emotional responses. Symptoms vary widely; treatment includes identification of provoking factors (e.g., pets, chalk dust, certain foods), environmental controls, and appropriate medications. Participation in physical education may be limited if exercise is a major cause of asthma attacks. Of particular concern to parents and teachers is the identified relationship between emotional stress and asthma attacks. Stress creates attacks, and attacks create stress; thus, specific interventions have been designed to assist children in developing healthy coping strategies. Absence from school may cause problems with peer relations and affect academic performance.

Epilepsy   Epilepsy is manifested in seizures that may or may not be associated with another physical problem, such as cerebral palsy or a brain tumor. There are several types of seizures, all of which are caused by abnormal, excessive electrical brain function due to a group of conditions that overstimulate the brain's nerve cells. However, the alteration in brain function associated with seizures does not imply learning problems or mental retardation. Academic ability varies among individuals with epilepsy as it does among nonhandicapped persons. Not all seizures are even readily visible; only some involve a change in state of consciousness or obvious physical movement. Two categories of seizures have been identified by the International League against Epilepsy: generalized and partial (Low, 1982).

Generalized seizures include grand mal, petit mal, myoclonic, and akinetic seizures—all of which usually occur without warning and involve a loss of consciousness. The most striking, grand mal, involves extraneous, uncontrolled movement of all portions of the body symmetrically (equally on both sides). Salivation increases, and bladder and bowel control may be lost. Most such seizures last only a minute or two, after which the individual may sleep for hours. Petit mal seizures may go unnoticed, and obvious behavior changes very little. Sometimes the only clue may be a slight disorientation in the midst of an activity—for example, a word missed during a dictation assignment. Myoclonic seizures are characterized by a sudden, brief muscular contraction that may or may not be symmetrical and recurring. The myoclonic jerk—a quick upward movement of the arms and bending of the trunk of the body (flexion)—can cause an individual to fall from a chair. In akinetic seizures there is a sudden loss of muscle tone and posture control. Individuals have no ability to break their fall during an akinetic seizure. Unless a protective helmet is worn at all times, the danger of head injury is great.

Partial seizures may affect both motor function and behavior. They occur in many patterns, ranging from brief loss of consciousness to extended periods of purposeless activity. During a psychomotor seizure individuals may appear to be conscious when, in fact, they are not at all aware of their abnormal behavior—even, for example, if they are running around the room (Jacobs, 1983; Low, 1982).

Controversy exists about appropriate medical intervention, which may include multiple medications. Although mental retardation is not necessarily associated with epilepsy, medication can cause problems with academic performance. Teachers should monitor changes in performance and/or behavior (e.g., drowsiness, inattentiveness) and report these to medical personnel for possible reevaluation of medication programs.

Juvenile Diabetes Mellitus   Often hereditary, juvenile diabetes mellitus is a metabolic disorder characterized by the body's inability to use sugars and starches (carbohydrates) to create energy needed for normal functioning. The pancreas does not make enough insulin, causing the glucose level in the blood to rise because glucose cannot get into the cells without insulin. Without glucose in the cells the body has no energy and cannot function (Christiansen & Hintz, 1982).

Youngsters with this disorder must take insulin and consequently may manifest two different types of characteristics. Insulin reaction, which occurs when individuals have too much insulin in their system, is indicated by rapid onset of headache, nausea, vomiting, palpitations, irritability, shallow breathing, and/or cold, moist skin. The recommended treatment is to give orange juice, a candy bar, a sugar cube, or other sugar on which the insulin can act. Symptoms of ketoacidosis, the condition that results from an inadequate supply of insulin, are gradual onset of fatigue, increased water consumption, frequent urination, excessive hunger, deep breathing, and/or warm, dry skin. The treatment, of course, is to give insulin (Christiansen & Hintz, 1982).

Children can be taught at a relatively young age to monitor their insulin levels. Regularity in diet and exercise patterns is crucial to maintenance of insulin balance. Generally, there will be no impact on classroom function unless there is a significant change in routine related to physical exercise or excessive amounts of foods containing sugar.

Hemophilia   Hemophilia typically appears in males and is characterized by poor blood clotting. Although massive blood loss due to external injury is, of course, very dangerous, internal hemorrhaging is a more common and most difficult problem for hemophiliacs. Bumps that would merely cause bruising in a normal child may cause massive internal bleeding in an individual with hemophilia. Blood may pour into joints, destroying surrounding tissue, and causing temporary immobility and pain and possibly permanent disability from joint degeneration. Treatment once involved massive transfusions of whole blood, but modern technology has isolated Factor VIII and Factor IX (clotting factors), which are missing in hemophiliacs. These factors are prepared in a substance called cryoprecipitate, which may be given when needed (Corrigan & Damiano, 1983).

Although learning problems are not directly related to hemophilia, frequent short absences from school because of internal bleeding may retard academic progress. Participation in physical activity and noncontact sports should be encouraged to facilitate healthy physical development.

Cystic Fibrosis   A hereditary disorder found more often in Caucasians, cystic fibrosis is characterized by abnormal mucus secretion by all secreting glands except those that secrete into the bloodstream. The disease begins in the pancreas and soon impacts the normal functioning of the intestine. There is an abnormally high salt level in the sweat of children with cystic fibrosis. Respiratory symptoms—including a dry, nonproductive cough; susceptibility to acute infection; and bronchial obstruction by abnormal mucus secretions—are a major problem. Cystic fibrosis may not be obvious for several months after birth, or it may cause intestinal problems in a newborn child. Recent medical advances have improved what was once a very poor prognosis, and early diagnosis may extend life expectancy into adulthood. Treatment may include taking antibiotics, replacing deficient pancreatic enzymes, modifying diet, and doing breathing exercises.

Children with cystic fibrosis are encouraged to cough to loosen the thick coating on their bronchial passages. In addition, diet and medication needs may require allowances during the school day. Participation in physical activity should be encouraged as much as possible. Learning potential is not directly affected by the disease, although psychological adjustment may periodically interrupt attention to academic performance (Harvey, 1982).

Sickle Cell Anemia   Sickle cell anemia is a hereditary disorder more prevalent among, but not limited to, blacks. It is a blood condition in which abnormal hemoglobin in the red blood cell is distorted into a rigid, sickle (crescent) shape to create a cell that does not pass easily through blood vessels. As a result, blood supply to some tissues may be blocked (vaso-occlusive episode), causing severe pains in the abdomen, legs, and arms; swollen joints; fatigue; and high fever. Blockage of the blood supply can cause a stroke or damage tissues and result in degeneration of joints and related orthopedic problems, including paralysis. Other outcomes can include headache, convulsions, and possible progressive renal (kidney) damage. The symptoms are chronic and recur at irregular intervals. They tend to be more likely in situations of emotional stress, strenuous exercise, chilling, or infection. Although learning potential is not directly affected by sickle cell anemia, frequent absence from school may affect academic performance (Corrigan & Damiano, 1983).

Cardiac (Heart) Conditions   Cardiac conditions may be either congenital or acquired. If acquired, they usually result from some type of infectious disease, such as rheumatic fever. Some heart defects present at birth are not detected until later, making their impact essentially the same as that of an acquired disability. Most students with cardiac problems can attend regular schools and need only minor restrictions on physical activity, dependent on the severity of the condition. Inappropriate severe limitations on physical activity can reduce motivation to perform academically.

Cancer   The causes and cures of the uncontrolled irregular cell growth known as cancer are still largely unknown. In children, leukemia (a disease in the blood-forming organs) and tumors of the eye, brain, bone, and kidneys are the most common forms. The prognosis usually depends on the type of cancer and the time of intervention. Treatment may involve radiation, chemotherapy, and/or surgery. Emotional problems, fatigue, extreme weight loss or gain, nausea, susceptibility to upper respiratory infection, headaches, and baldness are possible side effects of the disease or treatment (Link, 1982). Physical discomfort, irritability, and hospitalization may mean lost time from school or other instructional programs. The teacher's understanding of the progress of the disease and the resultant periods of emotional difficulty will help the child continue to participate in school and interact with peers. Focus should be on qualitative aspects of life, not on negative aspects of death.

Other Syndromes and Birth Defects

We have noted here only the most common physical disabilities found in children and adolescents. Our list is not comprehensive; there are many syndromes and birth defects which occur infrequently but nonetheless warrant major consideration in educational programming. The chapter reference list at the end of the book indicates some sources of information regarding these other disabilities.

Assessment

Self-help, daily living, academic, social, and personal skills all have a role in making independence possible. For most individuals with a physical disability or health impairment, the greatest challenge lies in resolving the problem as much as possible and finding ways to achieve optimum, age-appropriate independence. Assessment can hold the key.

Assessment Team

Medical personnel are frequently the first people involved in physical diagnosis and follow-up medical assessments of individuals with physical disabilities and health impairments. Their role includes not only determining the person's physical condition but also communicating potential physical limitations and needs to parents and educational professionals. Physicians evaluate, then prescribe needed medication, surgery, special therapy, or equipment (such as catheters and wheelchairs). Medical personnel, with the cooperation of teachers, also assess the effects of medication on students. Physical therapists constantly evaluate the individual's quality of movement and use special techniques to alter motor patterns. The role of occupational therapists overlaps and complements that of physical therapists (Bleck, 1982). Occupational therapists have traditionally focused on rehabilitation so that persons can perform activities of daily living (ADL). Both types of therapists evaluate positioning for various school activities and ADL. They assess students' physical characteristics and match them with adaptive equipment and devices. Their roles are varied and are ever changing to meet the needs of special students in regular schools. Rehabilitation engineers recommend and construct special mobility and seating systems; they also design special controls for devices such as tape recorders and wheelchairs. The school health nurse attends to students' specialized health needs.

Special education teachers and resource personnel provide methods and materials for systematic and ongoing assessment. They also demonstrate how learning environments and teaching techniques can be adapted to individual needs, suggesting such things as alternatives to handwriting for students with severe dexterity problems. School principals and classroom teachers have important perspectives to share in regular assessment conferences. Others—including parents, speech pathologists, and social workers, as well as students—also contribute to the assessment process as appropriate.

Special Emphases

An early determination to be made is the types of skills a physically impaired child needs to achieve maximum independence in physical functioning. Continual assessment of self-help skills and ADL—including feeding, dressing, maintaining personal hygiene, and managing special health needs—is crucial to the developing child. Determination of specialized techniques for accurate educational assessment may also be important. To help develop an appropriate individualized program, assessment should focus on certain major areas.

Performance of Self-Help Skills What self-help skills a student has, what skills should be acquired, and what assistance is needed when certain self-help skills cannot be performed independently are vital pieces of information needed for planning a course of instruction. What a student can do currently and can be expected to do eventually in taking responsibility for special health needs is also important. Most often overlooked is assessment of how well each disabled individual can indicate to others how, when, and where to help.

Liz is able to indicate to her classmates how to help her set up her work station.

Extent of Mobility   Those involved in educating the physically disabled need to know how limited a student's mobility is, how the student moves from place to place, and what assistance the student needs in moving.

Accommodations Required for Physical Differences   A teacher must also know what adaptations or assistance will permit a student's participation in educational and leisure activities; what positions, postures, and other physical behavior should be encouraged or discouraged; and what special procedures (medical or emergency) may be necessary.

Level, Clarity, and Speed of Communication   Communication skills may range from just a few words to body movements or signals, to the use of communication boards or electronic communication devices or typing or handwriting, to highly intelligible speech. For those students with unintelligible speech or illegible handwriting, assessment helps describe discrepancies between levels of understanding and expressive ability. Five questions need to be answered:

1. In what ways and how clearly can the student communicate with (a) intelligible speech, (b) gesture language, (c) consistent body movement or signals for yes and no, (d) pointing at symbols on a communication board, (e) handwriting, (f) typing and an electronic communication device?

2. Does the student need extended time to respond?

3. What is the discrepancy between communication skills required by the student's environment and the student's actual skills?

4. How can the student's understanding and skill levels be assessed?

5. How can the student mark answers and record ideas?

Strategies and Special Devices to Facilitate Learning   It is essential to determine (1) what arrangements would enable the student to manage classroom equipment, such as pencils, papers, and books; (2) what behavior management techniques are appropriate; (3) how the student learns most quickly, through hearing or seeing for instance; (4) how the student can conserve energy at school; (5) what special procedures or materials would aid learning; and (6) what the top priority objectives are for learning outcomes.

Academic Achievement   Academic assessment should provide information about a student's strengths and weaknesses in each assessment area as well as a measure of how well the student can function in the school situation. Assessment information provides facts related to the instructional program and insight into varied considerations:

How does the student compare to others her age on grade-level proficiency tests?

What can the student do (and not do) in each basic academic area?

What is the student's potential in each academic and extracurricular subject studied at her grade level?

Assessment techniques used with nondisabled students can be used with some physically disabled students, although they may need to use adapted equipment, such as special pencil holders. Some disabled students can be given the same content but in a different test mode, perhaps on a tape instead of in print. Some students with disabilities use alternative methods to respond to test items: they may type or tell their answers to a scribe, *look* at one of four choices or kick when they hear their choice.

Assessment of physical and communicative self-sufficiency is also necessary. Functional skills must be measured to identify what the student will need to learn to do for herself. Skill objectives can be listed and records kept as to progress. If disabilities render a student unable to complete functional skills independently, the assessment process should evaluate the student's ability to communicate her need for assistance.

Special Help Required Assessment should also indicate what specialists are needed to work with a student or consult with the teacher and how their efforts can best be coordinated to benefit the student. Assessment of the student's environments, both present and potential, is imperative. The teacher's primary responsibility becomes to "note what environment it is and what discrepancies are present between skills required by the environment and skills acquired" (Mills & Higgins, 1984, p. 37).

Analyzing and defining components of those discrepancies reflect a major application of an assessment technique called *task analysis*. Task analysis may well be one of the most frequently employed methods of assessment with students with physical disabilities (Bigge, 1982). It can be used to analyze performance in every area of the curriculum, as well as to prepare students to interact in different kinds of daily life situations. After initial assessment task analysis continues to be of value as an instructional strategy.

Age-Level Distinctions

Early Childhood Observations of physically disabled children in voluntary activity can be one of the most effective assessment procedures. Observers can gain information about how the children communicate their desires and to what kinds of behaviors they respond. Do they ignore someone until he moves directly in front of them? Do they respond to simple verbal requests and warnings? Do they find some way to move themselves? What prompts them to move and to participate in an activity? Interviews with parents can provide additional helpful information.

School Age Academic achievement is a major assessment focus for school-age students following a regular or modified education curriculum. Assessment is a search to determine the relative effectiveness of alternative methods of doing schoolwork and taking tests, perhaps using standard keyboards on typewriters and computers, perhaps finding other alternatives for students who cannot use keyboards. Students with severe problems of physical dexterity can try different styles of switches that allow them to stop an electrically controlled scanner on desired letters, pictures, or words on a grid.

Secondary/Transition   Teachers often become the hub of assessment activities for secondary students. Special education teachers help regular teachers with traditional types of assessment activities involving students with disabilities. Perhaps anticipating the end of formal schooling and feeling concerned about their child's future, parents frequently become more intensely interested in assessment at this level. Also added to the assessment team at this stage are vocational rehabilitation personnel from state departments of rehabilitation. Potential employers and supervisors of work/study programs may provide work samples and opportunities for students to try jobs. Many students themselves take more responsibility for assessing their own skills, demonstrating an increased motivation to learn.

Intervention

Physical and educational programming are the two areas in which intervention usually begins for children with confirmed or suspected physical disabilities or health impairments.

Physical Management and Intervention

From the moment that physical problems are suspected or detected, intervention is crucial. There are numerous areas of concern.

Positioning and Seating   Sitting may be difficult for a child with physical disabilities. Positions should be found that will "enable him to use his hands to the best advantage, that will be easiest for eye-hand coordination and will present the least difficulties for balance" (Finnie, 1975, p. 229). Several sitting positions—including cross-legged sitting, side sitting, and regular chair sitting—may be secure and comfortable. Straps and other props are sometimes added to improve posture. Medical personnel and therapists should be asked to recommend positions for each child that aid development of desired posture and movements or discourage undesirable ones.

Positioning a child properly at a table or desk is another important consideration. Some students use trays attached to their wheelchairs and do not need any other work surface. When students do need some kind of table on which to work, the height of the tabletop should permit the student to rest her elbows on it comfortably and view materials on it easily. Tabletop height may also be used as a form of management: the height of the tabletop can be adjusted to encourage more functional body positions.

A raised desk top enables this student a more comfortable work surface.

Whether students use a wheelchair tray or some other surface, they should be able to obtain and put away their books and materials. Thus, placement of these objects needs to accommodate the student's range of arm motion, strength, and manipulative skills. If the student does not have a desk with usable drawers and compartments, organizers such as those used in offices may serve the purpose.

Mobility Individuals with disabilities should have the privilege of moving from place to place as independently as possible. Medical personnel and therapists can recommend appropriate procedures for achieving independent mobility without negatively affecting a child's physical functions. Young children who cannot walk alone are often taught to roll, crawl, or use crutches, walkers, or toy vehicles.

Architectural Accessibility Whether children with physical disabilities are educated in special settings or in regular schools, they frequently face physical barriers to their independent functioning and movement. These obstructions should be identified and removed. Ramps enable children in wheelchairs or on crutches to enter buildings easily. Toilet facilities, play areas, and drinking fountains must be located where individuals with physical limitations can have access to them. Grab bars or support railings should be installed beside drinking fountains, in toilet stalls, and near chalkboard sections.

In the classroom, furniture may need to be removed to make room for wheelchairs. Footrests and adjustable, swivel seats may be required. Special height-adjustable tables and cut-out or stand-up tables can provide additional help for students with special problems with sitting or standing. Special support devices can facilitate participation in activities that require sitting on the floor.

Special Equipment and Adaptations   As we have already noted, adaptive devices can often improve an individual's ability to function. These range from artificial limbs, wheelchairs, and crutches to typewriters and feeding, dressing, and toileting aids. The sooner needed devices are provided, the greater the individual's chance to develop some measure of independence and self-respect. Training with these aids is usually necessary. Teachers, therapists, and parents should all know how to help the disabled individual with the devices and should consult with each other regularly on the student's progress and changing needs.

Students should be taught early to manage common classroom materials, such as pencils and papers. They may, however, need to use adapted materials—special tabletops, clipboards, cups with handles, or special pencil holders—to prevent common inconveniences, such as dropping of pencils and other tools, slipping or torn and wrinkled papers, and illegible writing (see Figures 10-1, 10-2, and 10-3). Solutions can often be simple and inexpensive; the challenge is to find them.

Provision for Those with Multiple Disabilities   Individuals with physical disabilities often have one or more associated disabilities. A person with cerebral palsy, for example, may have problems related to learning, vision, hearing, speech, emotional adjustment, perceptual-motor involvement, or mental development (Cruickshank, 1976; Hall, 1984). Any combination of disabilities can place complex or unusual demands on intervention. Specialists should collaborate in deciding how best to help each student.

Some youngsters who have the type of cerebral palsy that causes excessive involuntary movements and who also have a severe visual disability may not obtain the maximum benefit from wearing glasses because they are unable to hold their heads still to focus carefully. Ordinarily, children who cannot read print because of visual impairment learn to depend on braille. However, children with cerebral palsy may not be able to read braille because they cannot control the gross movement of their hands or they do not have fine sensory discrimination in their fingertips. (This can quickly be assessed with a combination assessment-instruction curriculum such as that developed by Mangold, 1980.) In addition, hearing aids may be difficult to wear and use because the uncoordinated movements of these children cause excess, irritating noise that is amplified by hearing aids.

Teachers and other specialists must help students with multiple disabilities find ways to surmount or cope with any problems that affect learning. Ideally, every problem should be reduced or corrected. Realistically, priority objectives for each individual must be set. Most important, within whatever setting disabled students

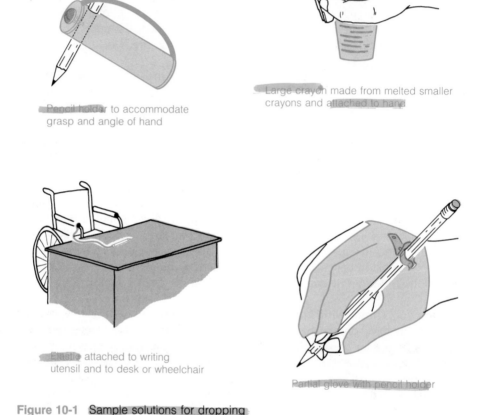

Pencil holder to accommodate grasp and angle of hand

Large crayon made from melted smaller crayons and attached to hand

Elastic attached to writing utensil and to desk or wheelchair

Partial glove with pencil holder

Figure 10-1 Sample solutions for dropping

receive their education, every effort should be made to help them become and remain *a part* of the group and prevent them from becoming and remaining *apart*.

Health and Disability Management In addition to managing the students' physical environment, teachers must be prepared to oversee the health needs of their disabled students. Teachers must understand not only the characteristics of various diseases and disabilities but also the precise care that should accompany them. For example, teachers should be aware that students with muscular dystrophy and cardiac conditions tire easily. Thus, they should encourage those students to take wheelchairs when they visit potential job sites or go to school events, even though they can walk around the classroom. With some impairments frequent absences from school may necessitate hospital or home instruction. Some handicapping conditions may change, either worsen or improve, and teachers must help

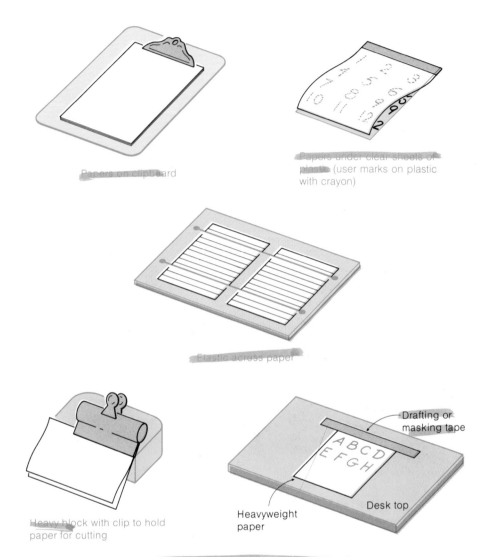

Papers on clipboard

Papers under clear sheets of plastic (user marks on plastic with crayon)

Elastic across paper

Heavy block with clip to hold paper for cutting

Drafting or masking tape

Heavyweight paper

Desk top

A B C D E F G H

Figure 10-2 Sample solutions for slipping, tearing, and wrinkling

students and families maintain close contact with medical personnel. For example, information on behavior changes that seem related to changes in medication is important in helping doctors find and maintain proper levels of medication to control the seizures of students with epilepsy. Students with spina bifida need instruction on personal hygiene and must be helped to develop awareness of increased odor, which can indicate infection related to bladder control problems.

The reaction and response of others to students with physical disabilities can be of critical importance, from both a physical and a psychological standpoint. The teacher must see that everyone involved understands that a student with recent brain trauma from a motorcycle accident can be knocked over easily, sometimes

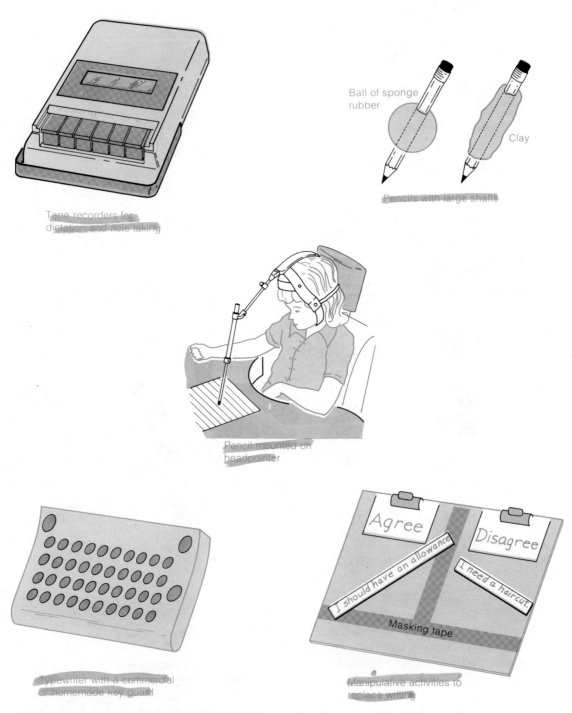

Tape recorders for dictation and note taking

Ball of sponge rubber

Clay

Pencils with large shafts

Pencil mounted on headpointer

Typewriter with a commercial or homemade key guard

Agree

Disagree

I should have an allowance

I need a haircut.

Masking tape

Manipulative activities to replace writing

Figure 10-3 Sample solutions for illegible writing

just by brushing against him; or that a jovial punch can cause life-threatening internal bleeding to a person with hemophilia. With certain physical handicaps (epilepsy or diabetes, for example) a student's condition can deteriorate rapidly and unexpectedly, and the teacher must be able to notice. As early as possible, the teacher should help students take over partial or full responsibility for their own health and disability management.

Instructional Intervention

Instructional intervention can have greater impact as a result of physical management and special equipment and adaptations. Nonetheless, much depends on what students write and say in class. When students cannot write or talk because of movement problems, teachers can gain optimal participation by following certain guidelines:

1. Assume that students with unintelligible speech understand at a higher level than their expression indicates; treat and teach them accordingly.

2. Invite students who cannot talk to show you how they communicate *yes*, *no*, I *don't know*, and *maybe* or *perhaps*.

3. Invite students to demonstrate for you all the ways they can let other people know what they want to say.

4. Respond constructively to students who cannot be understood.
    a. "Please repeat that again."
    b. "Please say that another way."
    c. "Show me by gesture."
    d. "Write, type, or point to the letters or words."

5. Repeat what you think students have tried to communicate, in order to clarify.

6. Find ways for students who cannot write or speak intelligibly to demonstrate increasingly difficult thinking skills.

7. Include all students in group learning experiences; phrase some questions so that disabled students can give yes/no answers, provide access to pictures and vocabulary boards, and assist students physically when necessary.

8. Give students time to respond.

Use of Task Analysis Task analysis, important in assessing physical abilities, is equally important as a strategy for instructing students with physical disabilities. It is based on the assumption that an individual's failure to perform is due to a lack of one or more of the skills involved. The performance of a student with a physical disability may follow one of several patterns: it may be adequate, incomplete, too slow, uncoordinated, or accomplished only through adaptive techniques or devices. Task analysis suggests the instructional orientation in each case.

After *adequate task completion* assessment and instruction can proceed to a more advanced task, a similar task of equivalent difficulty, or an entirely different task. In many instances disabled students may be able to perform tasks adequately because the tasks require only those body parts that are unaffected by disability. Teachers should emphasize such tasks. Some individuals with physical disabilities can proceed through a curriculum with no adaptations in materials or processes.

In the case of *incomplete task completion* we assume that the student is unable to accomplish one or more parts of the task. Figure 10–4 demonstrates one model for studying and assessing tasks tried but not accomplished. Analysis may suggest one of three instructional approaches:

1. Teach the unperformed skills so that the individual can finish the entire task in a usual manner.

2. Devise an alternative method of performing the uncompleted parts of the task.

3. Select a different task or goal to be accomplished.

Sometimes it is possible to teach parts of a task without revising the method or using special equipment or materials. It might be possible, for instance, to teach the child whose performance is described in Figure 10–4 to use her unreleased

---

Given the task of opening the classroom door and walking through it while using crutches, the student *performed* these parts of the task:
1. Walked to door
2. Stood in position to open door
3. Released hand from crutch to reach for knob
4. Reached knob
5. Grasped knob
6. Turned knob
7. Pulled door open
8. Released knob
9.

But *did not perform* these parts of the task:
1. Grasped the released crutch before door closed
2. Walked through doorway
3.
4.

Figure 10-4   Model for assessing tasks tried but not accomplished

SOURCE: From "Systems of Precise Observation for Teachers: Observation Guide to Accompany Film" by J. L. Bigge, 1970, Washington, DC: Department of Health, Education and Welfare, U.S. Department of Education, Bureau of Education for the Handicapped.

crutch as a door stop so that she can grasp her released crutch before the door closes and then move through the doorway.

For students who cannot perform some parts of a task in the usual manner, the teacher must find an alternate method or adaptive equipment. For example, a child who has control of only one hand cannot both grasp and turn the lid of a thermos. Perhaps he can be taught to hold the thermos between his legs while he unscrews the lid with his one usable hand. If completion of certain tasks is not a realistic goal, the teacher must set new goals. Some people with severe physical handicaps may never be able to feed themselves. An appropriate objective in such cases might be for them to indicate food preferences, to open their mouths voluntarily at the appropriate time, or to signal on a communication board that they need help. When a person is unable to perform a task, a different functional task should be found.

With *slow task completion* the pace must quicken. Children who require an hour or more to feed themselves an entire meal may be able to eat faster; others may need adaptive equipment—a plate with sides to keep food from falling off the edge or a spoon bent in a certain way to prevent spilling. In some tasks speed can be increased by eliminating unnecessary movements. The sixth-grade student who can complete math problems on a first-grade level but takes several minutes to do just one problem is another example of how slowness impedes functioning. Instruction may stress increasing speed, but it should also help the student learn to use a calculator for tasks of daily life, such as shopping and banking.

Uncoordinated task completion occurs when students with physical disabilities complete a task but with such uncoordinated movements that the results are not functional. Involuntary athetoid movements can cause a child to spill most of his milk as he picks up his glass or moves it jerkily to his mouth. When task analysis identifies this problem, instruction should focus on decreasing the effects of uncoordinated movements, with or without adaptations. The child might be taught to use a holder to stabilize the glass on the table and then drink with a straw. His handwriting might be improved if he sits on the unused hand to keep it from flailing; he can then focus attention on controlling the movement of the writing hand. Another child who might have trouble typing because she keeps hitting two keys at once could be given practice in localizing her stroke.

Adapted task completion may be the goal for individuals who are weak, lack coordination, or have missing or dysfunctional limbs. The goal of instruction then is to devise whatever alternative methods and support are needed. In the case of a young child who is paralyzed and can barely move his arms, removable, ball-bearing armrests attached to his wheelchair may help him feed himself. A spoon might be sewn into a mitt that fits over his hand. For individuals with cerebral palsy who cannot use their hands and arms, painting pictures becomes possible with head-pointer brushes attached to headbands. The challenge is always to devise additional adaptations that will permit the performance of even more complex tasks.

Psychosocial Development   Many individuals with physical handicaps also have problems of social and emotional adjustment. Crippling physical conditions frequently give rise to anxiety, frustration, and resentment. A supportive environment at home and in school can help relieve these feelings (see Carpignano, Sirvis, & Bigge, 1982). Psychological support services are often indicated. However, the response to the student's emotional stress must be balanced; the tendency to overprotect the individual is a natural reaction but may foster unhealthy, dependent relationships (Corbet, 1980).

The emphasis when instructing these students must always be on creating independence. Through independence many psychosocial problems related to self-esteem, self-confidence, and social interaction can be resolved or at least reduced. Even children whose conditions make them fragile and susceptible to injury can be taught to take responsibility for self-protection. Physical activities must often be modified, but the individual can succeed socially and academically in an otherwise normal educational program. Educational programming should include preparation for sedentary but mentally active vocational training and leisure.

The psychological problems manifested in youngsters with terminal illnesses are more difficult to cope with. The affected students, their peers, families, and teachers all need the perspectives that can be gained from death education programs. The teacher's task is to help the terminally ill student develop a concept of quality in a limited life span; educational programming can be a source of stability in a student's life. Thus, curricula for students with muscular dystrophy, cystic fibrosis, and terminal cancer should stress development and achievement of attainable short-term goals. Overindulgence should be avoided at all costs.

Age-Level Distinctions

Early Childhood   Staff intervention activities focus on increasing students' ability to help themselves and teaching them to attend to different situations. Increasing self-help involves finding ways for students without communication systems to tell others when they need toileting. It also involves training in the actual processes of eating, using a toilet, undressing, and dressing. A self-help curriculum begins here even though many children can do nothing for themselves at first and may even lack cognitive understanding. Some children in the same program may be able to help themselves, but most need training in when and how to do so.

In addition, students must learn to look at other people and attend to what those people are saying and doing; these are the rudimentary skills of attention education. To attend to other people, students with severe physical disabilities must learn to tolerate upright sitting positions, which may seem uncomfortable to them. After they learn to attend, we hope they will respond to cues from other people. As students learn to give their attention to situations, they can be taught to imitate what they see. They can begin to explore, perhaps with physical assistance from someone. In short, they increase their own awareness of their environment.

School Age   School-age intervention continues the efforts of early childhood but adds the basic subjects. Because of the time demands of different specialists and the students' slow work pace, the curriculum of physically disabled students is

All children have the right to the challenge and rewards of academics.

usually confined to the basic subjects. However, they should also be exposed to such subjects as career education, social studies, science, fine arts, and physical education. Computer technology can help to expedite the learning processes. It can expand and diversify the approaches to reading, spelling, vocabulary, and other language arts skills. Word processing capabilities can save time and effort in written work.

Microcomputers offer many advantages to students with poor hand coordination or low energy. Pressing keys is easier and quicker than writing by hand, and special adaptations are available for students with problems in physically accessing the keyboards. Key guards reduce the accidental pressing of unintended keys; expanded keyboards use a special connection that makes the computer think the user is pressing the computer keys; and special interfaces allow profoundly disabled students to use a switch to duplicate selection of characters on the keyboard.

Secondary/Transition   Ideally, interventions with older students focus on successful interventions from earlier years. Like younger students, secondary students may want help in finding alternatives to the usual ways of doing schoolwork. Handheld computers for notetaking may replace handwriting, which can cause much physical strain. Tape recordings of speeches produced on home computers with speech synthesizers may give nonspeaking students an opportunity to make oral reports. Students at this level devise many of these alternatives with help from special education teachers and their peers.

When students with disabilities have difficulty with secondary curriculum, other strategies may have to be employed. Sometimes handicapped students continue in regular classes and try to gain as much as they can. Others take less challenging classes. Still others take part of their coursework with a special education teacher, who can cover the content in a way that meets their learning needs and styles.

Extended work evaluations (vocational opportunities) give students and significant other persons a chance to devise creative approaches to work samples so that students may sometime join the work force. Effective adaptations include the use of a speaker phone so that dialing is not needed, special design of file drawers for wheelchair access, and a special lever to hold down a power switch on an electrical tool for an extended length of time. Senior citizen volunteers and retired engineers or other experts may be able to help design, build, or modify adaptive equipment or devices. Here again, task analysis is useful in determining helpful interventions.

Interdisciplinary Efforts

Professionals who provide services for students with physical and multiple handicaps have traditionally worked in semi-isolation. In the last two decades significant changes have occurred, involving increased interdisciplinary cooperation. With the advent of P.L. 94–142 and P.L. 98–199 professionals have had an opportunity to break down even further the rigid professional boundaries. The transdisciplinary approach facilitates collaboration among team members by encouraging a process of teaching and learning among them. As a result, staff should be able to function with increased unity of goals and intervention strategies (Sirvis, 1978; Williamson, 1978).

Programs for young children with physical and multiple handicaps tend to employ personnel from medical and allied health, educational, and social service disciplines. A transdisciplinary approach promotes the carry-over of intervention techniques. In this approach the entire team participates in the training of parents for implementation of home programs that supplement organized school programs. Most often, all team personnel are involved in direct service provision on an ongoing basis. Therapy and related interventions are provided within the context of the group to assure maximum use of time within a usually shortened day. In-class provision of therapy also increases the likelihood of skill generalization (Connor, Williamson, & Siepp, 1978; Hanson, 1984).

During the school-age program transdisciplinary interaction between health care and educational personnel is critical to programmatic success and skill generalization. Therapy goals for physical positioning and management can be incorporated into classroom programs. Educational goals for academic skill development can often be incorporated into therapy—for example, reinforcing knowledge of colors by color coding stairs used in development of mobility skills.

The emphasis on a secondary level may require that different personnel be included on the transdisciplinary team. As the need for therapy decreases, personnel who focus on postschool opportunities should become more involved in the program—rehabilitation counselors, vocational instructors, and therapeutic recreation personnel. Whenever possible, all personnel should provide interaction opportunities within the classroom (Brolin, 1982; Sirvis, 1980).

Curriculum Implications

Planning curricula for students with physical disabilities and health impairments is a complex undertaking that should involve a number of people: board of education members, administrators, regular teachers, classroom aides, special educators, therapists, vocational counselors, pupil service personnel, community agencies, medical personnel, parents, and the students themselves when appropriate. Suitable educational levels for students of similar ages may range from the most basic components of self-care tasks to academic content leading to advanced degrees.

Communications

Communications, as described by Bigge (in press), is a curriculum area that should be included in the course of study of physically disabled students. Objectives for most of these students are to learn to communicate what they want to say in a way that others can understand, whether in casual conversation or classroom discussion and testing, and to learn their schoolwork through means other than reading and writing, if they cannot read and write well. For the first time in history it is possible for persons with unintelligible speech to say all that they want to say and to have others understand them. Intensive and ongoing instruction is necessary to teach language usage as well as actual use of speech synthesizing devices.

Also difficult for some children is writing, because of poor motor control or weak arms. Through a communications curriculum they can be taught efficient alternative ways to record answers and express ideas. Tape recorders can be used by many students. In addition, problems can be written on large sheets of paper and placed on an easel so that a child can record her answers with a large crayon attached to an extension from a helmet.

A communications curriculum should also include instruction in keyboarding; typewriters and microcomputers can be used functionally even when a disability limits the typing to one hand. Electric typewriters are the easiest for most disabled students to handle. Metal guards placed over the keyboard prevent students from hitting more than one key at a time. The keys can be struck traditionally or in alternative ways—for example, with the eraser end of a pencil held in a student's hand, with a dowel stick attached to headgear, or with a mouth stick. With selected kinds of microcomputers, a special interface card and a single pedal switch can avoid the need to press keys altogether. Microcomputers can even permit disabled individuals to draw and paint.

Life Experience

Developing physical self-help skills is a priority in curriculum planning for disabled individuals of all ages. Program goals should focus on basic functional needs: eating and drinking, toileting, dressing and undressing, bathing, and managing nasal and oral hygiene. Poor coordination, muscular weakness, paralysis, loss of sensation, low vitality, and limb deficiency often prevent children and youth from completing tasks without aids. Special educators, therapists, rehabilitation specialists, and parents need to work together in assessing the physical problems in managing self-care tasks and in devising needed equipment to simplify those tasks—wheelchairs for one-handed operation, hand splints with spoons attached, remote controls for electronic appliances and learning aids.

To help disabled individuals become more independent, some school curricula now include life experience skills (Life Experience Program, 1976); The Source Book (Hale, 1983) is an excellent source of curriculum materials. The skills included—self-help, work, recreation and leisure—are all necessary to function independently in home and community environments. Often they are introduced to elementary-age students in career education programs. Stress is placed on an individual's ability to function in the community—for example, using public or private transportation, moving around the community in a wheelchair, asking strangers for directions, and locating and using community resources. Program goals are determined through task analysis of age-appropriate skills for each individual (Brown et al., 1979).

Career/Vocational Education

Throughout any curriculum there should be opportunities for developing task completion skills and other good work habits. These are important even for those who may never be employed. Some of the most profoundly handicapped may be taught to complete a task in sequence or to follow the directions given in a single work command or gesture; knowing how to perform even the simplest task reduces dependence. The more established work skills and behaviors become during the school years, the more prepared students will be for their futures—whether they involve volunteer jobs, home employment, sheltered or competitive work, or professional training.

More curricula should include lightly structured preparation for upcoming transition from school to community, from student to self-sufficient community participant, worker, even leader. For any task students must learn to compare their skills with those needed. If they find their skills inadequate, they should be taught to seek help to improve them. If improvement is not a realistic goal, even with specialized equipment and procedures, they must learn to explore alternative goals.

Many career education programs are following models that integrate the instruction of skills in several areas, emphasizing the interrelationships of skills needed for independence and responsible behavior as a worker at school, in the family, in a community, and on a job. This approach is believed to develop most fully each individual's potential for economic, social, and personal fulfillment (Brolin, 1982) and to prepare students to function in a variety of least restrictive current and subsequent school and nonschool environments (Brown et al., 1979).

Taking advantage of an AMI-GO's swivel seat, a young man enjoys leisure time.

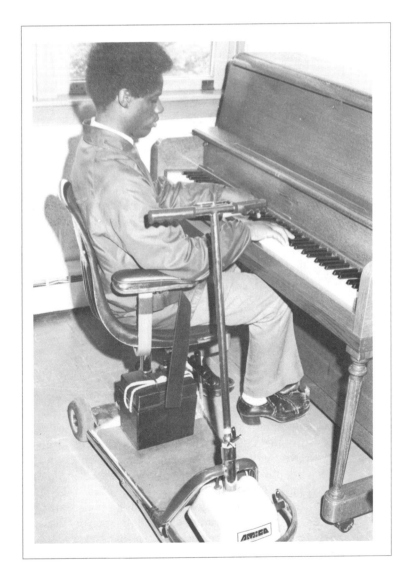

Recreation and Leisure Education

Like nondisabled persons in every community, individuals with physical disabilities and health impairments have a right to develop individual leisure life styles using community resources. Leisure education is critical to the development of attitudes and skills that will influence overall satisfaction during school years and in later life (Peterson & Gunn, 1984). Leisure concepts, values, and resource utilization can be incorporated into existing curricula in social studies, reading, math, and career education; it is important that the concepts be introduced early and continued throughout the curricula. Students should also be exposed to a variety of recreational activities in which they can engage, with or without adaptation for their physical disability (Sirvis & Cieloha, 1981).

Students should be taught the importance and the relevance of leisure to a satisfying life, should be led to recognize the importance of enjoyment in leisure experiences, and should be introduced to the concepts of choice and decision making in activities that provide pleasure. In the later elementary years children should be given ample opportunities to explore their environment and to identify leisure-related activities and resources. Focus should be on the integration of leisure into a satisfying, well-rounded existence.

School Subjects

Physically handicapped individuals should progress as far in the range and difficulty of regular school subjects as they are able. Those who can benefit from a curriculum for gifted students should be provided the opportunity to do so. When mental retardation or learning problems accompany a physical handicap, the curriculum may need to focus on functional academics. Sometimes the physically handicapped are not taught to their potential simply because they have limited hand use or unintelligible speech; adaptive devices should be used in such cases. We must not let the presence of a physical handicap cause us to underestimate a student's ability to participate in school subjects.

Age-Level Distinctions

Early Childhood   Motor and communication education permeate any early childhood curriculum for these students. Some who have severe motor problems must be taught to relax certain muscles so they can be toileted and fed. Promoting optimal postures and movement patterns for functional activities is an early objective. Another challenge is the location or development of adaptive devices and adaptive methodology to counteract or accommodate the results of physical disability. Other challenges lie in physical independence education: finding ways to teach young children with disabilities to start to manage their own physical needs.

Motor education does more than increase the quality of posture and movement and self-help skills. It also provides an opportunity for students to acquire the experiential learning upon which much other learning is based. It helps children do a variety of activities—move to a toy they want, put a piece in a puzzle, go down a slide. Thus, it provides the foundations for more difficult skills, and it provides some experiences upon which language and cognitive concepts can develop. Most important, it reduces dependence on others for what the child wants to do.

Many children with physical disabilities also have communication difficulties due to language delay and oral-motor incoordination. To prepare these students to function socially and academically in a variety of situations, teachers must collaborate with speech pathologists and parents to teach communication skills as aggressively as they teach academic readiness skills. Extensive discussion of curriculum guidelines and related assessment can be found in Connor, Williamson, and Siepp (1978) and Hanson (1984).

School Age   Striking differences exist in the curricula for disabled school-age students and their nondisabled peers: different kinds of curriculum components and different emphasis on social skill education.

The total course of study for a physically disabled student may include some of the regular curriculum components. However, it may also include components taught by a special education teacher or therapist. It will certainly focus on specific special education objectives based on each student's IEP. In most cases special education teachers provide direct instruction as well as consultation and coordination of the many facets of a student's curriculum.

Many disabled students have had limited interaction with groups of nondisabled persons. Thus, social skills education becomes important. In addition to the more obvious skills needed to make and keep friends, social skills education focuses upon developing self-advocacy. Self-advocacy teaches students to assert themselves comfortably and appropriately—to seek permission to tape lessons instead of writing them, for example, or to inquire about staying after school for Boy Scouts one afternoon a week instead of going home every day on the special education bus.

Secondary/Transition   Meeting all or part of graduation requirements is the goal of many secondary students with physical handicaps. These students need to pursue subjects and activities that are particularly motivating to them or that move them toward a specific role after graduation. Of course, many curriculum goals and objectives continue from the elementary years.

Because of the implications of their disabilities, many of these students require intense training in such areas as life experience and career/vocational education. Disabled students must be prepared with appropriate strategies for transition from public school: using public transportation, finding and maintaining a home for themselves, finding and using personal attendants, maintaining or improving their own physical condition, finding ways to obtain rehabilitation aids and social services, and directing any needed adaptations for their daily life, leisure, and employment.

Model Program

Henry H. North School is a neighborhood elementary school in Lansing, Michigan, which also houses preschool and elementary programs for students from a tri-county area who are hearing impaired or physically or otherwise health impaired (POHI). North School was built to facilitate mainstreaming of children with physical handicaps to whatever degree possible. This mainstreaming is partially achieved by the open-space pod design of the building; each pod contains three classrooms on one grade level. The inclusion of a multidisciplinary team of professionals serves to enhance the positive potential of mainstreaming efforts.

The school program actually begins prior to preschool with a program that provides services for infants and toddlers up to age 2 who reside in the Lansing School District. A multidisciplinary team integrates education and therapy services into group play periods. The major premise of this program is that parents are primary participants in the early intervention program, which provides only 2 hours each week in direct intervention at North School.

The preschool program provides social and play experiences and an academic base for future learning. Classroom personnel consider students as children first and work through each child's disability to achieve as normal a preschool experience as possible.

The first real mainstreaming experiences begin in the kindergarten classroom. Students are mainstreamed in accordance with their IEPs. Some attend the entire kindergarten session whereas others attend only a few hours each week. Because academic and social readiness are of great importance at this stage, full-day programs are provided for kindergarten students with physical handicaps. This scheduling allows for uninterrupted participation in the kindergarten program and opportunities to benefit from therapy services.

Mainstreaming continues through the elementary grades. Students continue to learn with their peers, thus providing an opportunity for all students to develop positive attitudes toward individual differences and necessary adaptations. Nondisabled students learn to provide assistance to their peers with physical disabilities. Older children who are mainstreamed are expected to increase their accountability and personal responsibility for academic success. A teacher consultant provides a variety of services to students and teachers and serves as a facilitator of therapeutic goals within the classroom experience.

Not all children in the POHI program are ready for the mainstream experience on a full-time basis. As academic discrepancies increase for older students with physical and multiple handicaps, there is often a demonstrated need for more specialized instruction. For these students part- or full-time placement in self-contained classrooms provides individualized instruction designed to meet their unique learning needs.

Physical, occupational, and speech and language therapies are provided as an integral and important component of the program. As often as possible, therapy is integrated into classroom experiences so that educational and therapy programs achieve maximum time and emphasis. Thus, an occupational therapist may provide feeding instruction during the regular classroom lunch period rather than removing the child for isolated instruction.

North School provides numerous other services, programs, and resources for students with physical handicaps. A pool program provided twice weekly focuses on gross motor, relaxation, and aquatic skills. Adaptive equipment, computers, and other electronic developments are provided when appropriate to help students achieve new levels of independence in education, recreation, mobility, and daily living skills. Staff development programs encourage all members of the multidisciplinary team to acquire expertise in new technology and intervention programs. Regular teachers are active members of the professional team.

When students complete their elementary schooling at North School, they proceed to a mainstreamed program at Dwight-Rich Middle School. A program at Everett High School is similar and includes a career education component for high school students with physical handicaps. For severely handicapped students aged 18 to 25, a life experience and survival skills program is also provided. Thus, the Lansing School District provides a full range of educational and related service alternatives for students with physical disabilities and health impairments. (Program description from the videotape "Going North: Mainstreaming the Physically Impaired in the Elementary School"; Malcolm R. Delbridge, program administrator, Lansing Public Schools)

Mainstreaming

The successful transition of a student from a special education setting into a regular classroom or school depends on many factors, including (1) the amount and kind of support services needed and available, (2) the responsibility for orientation taken by educational personnel, (3) the willingness of professionals to collaborate on programming, (4) the availability of transportation and aides or volunteers, and (5) architectural accessibility inside and outside the new school.

Age-Level Distinctions

Early Childhood With the advent of federal legislation, an increasing number of public programs, including Head Start, have become available for preschoolers with physical handicaps. Interdisciplinary efforts focus on physical skills and independence as well as socialization, self-help, and language development. Research supports the need for intervention prior to age 3 for children with physical and multiple disabilities. In response, federal legislation has opened the door for an increased number of public programs to provide services as soon as a problem is identified. In addition, private, usually nonprofit, organizations such as the United Cerebral Palsy Association, the National Easter Seal Society, and local agencies provide services for infants and very young children with specific handicaps. Typically, these early intervention programs offer centralized instruction to children and their parents as well as home instruction and visitation. Physical, occupational, and speech therapy is emphasized and coordinated with educational programming. The thrust at this age level is to *prepare* for mainstreaming.

School Age As mentioned earlier, some youngsters with physical handicaps are able to function in regular classes with no supportive help—for example, the child who has mastered the use of an artificial limb. Others may be able to succeed in the regular classroom if they receive special services, such as supplementary instruction; physical, occupational, or speech therapy; or counseling. Students with more severe or multiple handicaps may not be able to function in a regular classroom at all or may be able to participate in only limited activities. They may be enrolled in full- or part-time special classes designed to accommodate their needs, in regular or special schools, or even in residential facilities. Each student's individual needs must determine placement, to assure the most appropriate education in the least restrictive and most natural setting.

Secondary/Transition Secondary instruction focuses on academic and career education, as well as preparation for postsecondary training, school, employment, or other life situations. Of concern to educators is students' ability to participate fully in an appropriate secondary school experience. Teachers and students can explore numerous programmatic options, ranging from full participation in a regular high school program to limited participation and regular attendance at a workshop/training program. Lack of transportation, limited mobility, and physical incoordination are issues to be resolved in many cases. Above all, it must be remembered that each case is unique. It is conceivable, for instance, to place in a

Seriously handicapped children can participate in scientific field work.

regular class on a full-time basis a student who is physically dependent on others, does not possess many daily living skills, and is unable to speak or write to communicate. That same student may be able to communicate with yes/no head movements and meaningful facial expressions, to demonstrate on a typewriter a grade-level proficiency in reading and spelling, and to reveal in other ways interests and academic skills similar to those of nonhandicapped peers. Regular physical therapy treatments can be scheduled after school, and training in basic living needs can be received during summer school. Every disabled student deserves an individual-ized program.

Innovation and Development

As we recognize the unique needs of individuals with physical disabilities and health impairments, medical, technological, and societal advances should foster continued progress in treatment, intervention, and educational programming. Major advances and research efforts are focusing on developments in medicine, genetics, rehabilitation engineering, computer technology, and psychosocial development and growth. Current medical research efforts include the examination of neurophysiological aspects, surgical therapy, and adaptation resulting from exercise, drug intervention, and assistive devices. Research focused on the neuromuscular aspects of disability is looking at the use of biofeedback, for example, as well as the physical problems caused by traumatic brain injury (Fenton, 1981). Additional research has examined such unique procedures as spinal cord regeneration and the use of a computer to stimulate walking in individuals with paraplegia due to spinal cord injury.

Research also continues to focus on the origin of disabilities labeled *idiopathic* (cause unknown), such as epilepsy. Although the genetic origin of disabilities such as muscular dystrophy has been identified, we cannot yet alter the course of such diseases; genetic research has identified over 1500 diseases with genetic origin. However, the ability to identify carriers of such disabilities as muscular dystrophy, sickle cell anemia, and hemophilia will continue to have a significant impact on the nature of genetic counseling.

Rehabilitation engineering has emerged as a leading technological field. It encompasses the development of adaptive equipment and systems for seating, mobility, communication, and environmental control. The Lainey System is just one example. It is a technical system integrating components of communication, mobility, and computer access. The system incorporates a commercially available powered wheelchair, a microprocessor-based communication aid mounted on the back of the chair, and a computer system. The interconnecting units can be operated with a single control interface—the optical headpointer directed toward a clear selection panel mounted in front of the user. The communication aid controls the computer by wireless telemetry. The Lainey System can also provide remote control of appliances in the home or hospital—lamps, televisions, radios, page turners, and more. Another current focus of rehabilitation engineering, robotics (computer control of an external device, such as a mechanical arm), has been used

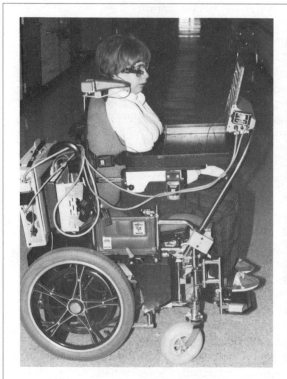 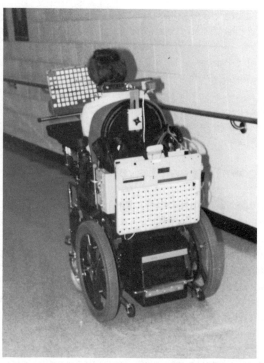

In the Lainey System, the student uses a head pointer to become independent. She can communicate, go where she wants, use a computer, and control lights and appliances.

experimentally with young children with severe physical handicaps. They were taught to control a robot to pour milk and do other chores they could not do for themselves (Behrmann & Lahm, 1984).

Research and development efforts continue in new and expanding areas. Medical and technological advances create new options for independence and participation for individuals with physical and multiple disabilities. Nonetheless, the need exists for continued quality in educational intervention so that technological and medical advances will support the growth and development of each individual.

Summary

The federal government has identified two categories of physical disabilities: orthopedic impairments and other health impairments. The causes of these disabilities are varied. Prenatal, perinatal, and postnatal factors must all be considered. Characteristics of these disabilities are diverse but include coordination problems, muscular weakness, paralysis, bone and joint problems affecting movement, and health impairments.

Transdisciplinary cooperation is vital to developing comprehensive programs that facilitate maximum development of each student. The process usually begins with interdisciplinary assessment of (1) performance of self-help skills, (2) mobility, (3) accommodation required for physical differences, (4) communication strategies and systems, (5) strategies and special devices that can make learning easier, (6) modes and styles of learning, and (7) special help required. Task analysis and behavioral observation are the assessment techniques most used.

Intervention focuses on numerous areas, including (1) physical management and intervention, (2) health and disability management, and (3) psychosocial development, again using task analysis as an instruction tool.

Curricular areas for students with physical disabilities and health impairments vary according to their age and disability characteristics. Of general concern are self-help and physical independence, communication, basic academic areas, computer applications, career education, and recreation and leisure education.

Students with physical handicaps and health impairments in regular classrooms may pose unique management problems. Teachers need to be thoroughly familiar with their students' disabilities in order to adapt the room, equipment, activities, or assignments. Service delivery systems at the elementary and secondary levels range from full integration in regular classes, to integration with support services, to special classes or special schools. Postsecondary arrangements include colleges, regional occupational centers, continuing education programs, and sheltered or competitive employment, depending on the severity of the disability and an individual's academic ability.

Research in medicine, rehabilitation engineering, and computer technology has contributed to the potential for increased independent functioning and a higher quality of life for individuals with physical disabilities.

Study Questions

1. What are some health impairments experienced by school children? List and describe several.

2. What are prenatal, perinatal, and postnatal causes of physical and health impairments? Give some of the conditions common to each.

3. Which disabilities result in hand-use limitations? Describe the nature of the limitations.

4. What are some possible psychological and social effects of nonvisible disabilities.

5. Which disabilities are not apparent at birth? Describe indications that alert persons to the presence of the disability.

6. What are some physical intervention strategies used with the physically disabled child or adolescent?

7. What are some modifications to the usual ways of doing school work? Briefly describe several situations in which modifications are needed; then describe the modifications.

8. Compare the emphases in curriculum content for disabled and nondisabled students in early childhood, school-age, and secondary/transition educational programs?

9. What are the special considerations in assessment of students with physical and health impairments?

10. What technological advances have impacted the self-reliance of persons with physical disabilities? Describe and explain.

11. What are some varied uses of task analysis with students with physical and health problems? Give some examples of each.

12. What are the roles of the different personnel involved in the educational and physical rehabilitation of students with physical disabilities and health impairments?

TIPS FOR HELPING

1. Assume until proven otherwise that students with unintelligible speech understand on a higher level than their expression indicates; treat and teach them accordingly.

2. If students are able to assist in the process, ask them what adaptations, special equipment, or teaching procedures work best for them.

3. Ask parents, therapists, or education specialists what special devices or procedures are needed to assist students.

4. Ask parents, therapists, and/or students what safety precautions are necessary.

5. Unless otherwise advised, give disabled students the opportunity to do what their peers do, even though their physical disability may cause them to seem uncoordinated.

6. Have volunteers assist with physical management so that students with disabilities can go on field trips and participate in special events and projects.

7. Openly discuss any uncertainties about when or how to aid a student with a disability.

8. Help nondisabled students and adults understand that characteristics such as drooling, unusual ways of talking, and physical awkwardness cannot be helped and should not be ridiculed.

9. Prepare yourself and your class for helping students with special needs.

10. Treat students with disabilities as normally as possible. Do not overprotect them; make them assume responsibility for themselves.

11

Hearing Impairments

Sheila Lowenbraun
University of Washington

Marie D. Thompson
University of Washington

Holiday shopping is a lively experience with Judy around. The animated almost-5-year-old moves swiftly through the crowded store checking frequently to see whether her mother and aunt are still in sight. She stops abruptly in front of a truck display. "I want that," she signs and says simultaneously, pointing at an overpriced model bulldozer. Mother says, "OK, honey, I know you want a truck; what else do you want Santa to bring you?" Judy thinks for a moment, smiles broadly, and signs, "I want two!" The dialogue continues as Judy falls in love with a gumball machine, a huge cardboard dollhouse, and various other display items. Mother and Aunt look at each other, grinning at the greed, and secretly thinking how marvelous it is that Judy wants something and can express her desires in no uncertain terms. Mother adds, "This year is the first year I could tell her about the holiday. I actually sat down and read her a story, and she understood it!"

Judy was diagnosed as severely hearing impaired at 28 months of age. At that time she had no speech and a receptive vocabulary of under 20 words. She relied on a primitive gesture system and some inappropriate behaviors such as biting and tantrums to express her needs. Judy now wears two behind-the-ear hearing aids. She attends a special school, where for 4 hours a day she gets specialized, individualized instruction in language, speech, auditory training, preacademics, music, and art; in addition, she has an opportunity to socialize with other preschool and school-age hearing impaired childen and nonhandicapped peers from a nearby Montessori school.

Since her diagnosis Judy has rapidly been making up for lost time. An excellent innate intelligence and a supportive extended family have helped. Also important is the fact that Judy has quite a bit of residual hearing, makes excellent use of her hearing aids, and has a good school program. It is now expected that she will be able to get at least part of her education in regular classes and will be able to attend college if she chooses.

At the checkout counter the salesperson looks pityingly at Judy, whose hearing aids are dangling from her ears, the result of a thwarted attempt to do a cartwheel in the aisle. "That's mine," Judy signs and says emphatically, her eyes wandering to a wind-up-robot display. The salesperson smiles gently and comments, 'She's a very normal little girl, isn't she? They always want everything!" Judy looks up at her mother and signs, "What she talking about?" A difficult question to answer.

Our perception of the world is based entirely on the information we derive through our five senses: touch, smell, taste, vision, and hearing. If any one of them is faulty, our understanding of the environment is changed. Of the five senses hearing and vision best allow us to perceive events occurring a distance away. Hearing is particularly valuable as a warning sense. We can hear in the dark, around corners, through closed doors, and above and below ourselves. Through hearing we receive the first indications of trouble in the environment.

Hearing has an additional vital function. It is the sense that normally developing children use to learn the language and speech skills requisite to social interaction and acquisition of academic skills. Through language children gain access to the accumulated knowledge, customs, and mores of their family, culture, and world. Even babies actively take in, process, and organize the language they hear. Like miniature linguists they recreate for themselves the language of their culture.

Hearing impaired children with intact central nervous systems have the same potential to learn language as any other children. However, they are deprived of linguistic input, which is the raw material for language acquisition. The challenge is to find other ways of getting linguistic messages to their central nervous systems as precisely and as quickly as possible so that hearing impaired children can acquire the communication skills necessary to function independently in social and academic contexts.

History

Hearing impairment has been identified as a human problem almost since the beginning of recorded history. We know of no efforts to educate the profoundly hearing impaired prior to the 15th century, but both Hebrew and Roman law included primitive classification systems for deafness. Hebrew law regulated three categories of hearing and communication disorders: (1) deaf people who could speak were allowed to transact business but not to own property; (2) people who could hear but were mute had no legal restrictions placed on them; and (3) those who were deaf and mute could not own property, engage in business, or act as witnesses. Roman law had similar regulations: (1) those who were deaf and dumb from birth were without legal rights or obligations; (2) those who became deaf and mute after learning to read and write were able to transact business; and (3) those who were deaf but could speak were not restricted in any way.

The first recorded effort to teach a deaf person occurred in Spain in the 16th century when a monk, Pablo Ponce de Leon, taught the firstborn son of a nobleman to speak in order that he might be legally able to inherit his father's property under the law of primogeniture. Slowly, education of the hearing impaired extended to common people. By the 18th century two opposing philosophies had arisen in Europe. The Abee de l'Epee in France used sign language to instruct and believed this to be the natural language of the deaf. However, in Germany Samuel Heinecke and in Great Britain Thomas Braidwood used speech to educate the deaf. The controversy over the better method began to be felt in the United States in the 19th century. Sent to Europe by concerned citizens of Hartford, Connecticut, to learn how to teach the deaf, Thomas Gallaudet was rejected in England by the clannish Braidwood family and ended up studying the manual method in France. In 1817 he established the first school for the deaf in America—the American Asylum for the Deaf and Dumb in Hartford. This school, now known as the American School for the Deaf, is still in existence. The first schools for the deaf to be founded on the principle of aural-oral communication were not established until 1867—Clark School in Northhampton, Massachusetts, and Lexington School in New York City.

At the International Convention held in Milan, Italy, in 1880, amidst enormous controversy, educators of the hearing impaired resolved to prefer the oral method of educating hearing impaired students, and subsequently many schools in the United States stopped using any form of sign language or fingerspelling for classroom instruction. In some residential schools, however, sign language continued to be used in extracurricular activities and in the dormitories; in deaf adult society American sign language continued to evolve. It was not until the 1960s, though, that people again began questioning the efficacy of the exclusively oral approach. By the 1970s, faced with some research evidence that the use of fingerspelling or sign language did not negatively affect speech or lipreading ability and had a positive effect on academic achievement, the majority of programs for the hearing impaired were using total communication for classroom instruction—a sign system, fingerspelling, residual hearing with amplification, speech and lipreading, and written language.

Education for the hearing impaired became universal in the United States through a system of state-supported residential schools, locally run day schools, and private schools. With the passage of P.L. 94–142 the population of these schools declined. Smaller, decentralized programs on public school campuses are now available in most communities, and hearing impaired children are being integrated into regular classroom activities.

The first college program for the deaf began in 1864, when Abraham Lincoln signed a bill creating Gallaudet College in Washington, DC, as a liberal arts college for the deaf. Gallaudet remained the only college program exclusively for the deaf until the 1960s, when the National Technical Institute for the Deaf (N.T.I.D.) and a demonstration network of regional community college programs were created. Gallaudet College remains, however, the only liberal arts college specifically for the deaf in the world (Moores, 1982).

Definition

Sound waves are produced by the to and fro movement of molecules. One complete movement back and forth constitutes a cycle. The number of cycles that occur per second determines the frequency of a sound. The term used to designate cycles per second is *hertz* (Hz); 1,000 Hz means that the frequency of the sound is 1,000 cycles per second. The human ear hears these frequencies as pitch. As frequencies decrease, pitch is lowered. As frequencies increase, pitch becomes higher. Although the human ear is sensitive to frequencies between 20 and 20,000 Hz, the most important frequencies are those between 500 and 3,000 Hz—the speech range. An increase or decrease of energy at any given frequency will cause a change in the intensity of the sound. Sound intensity is measured in *decibels* (dB) and is perceived as loudness. Normal hearing sensitivity begins at 0 dB for each frequency; that level represents the softest sound that an average person is able to hear and is called the hearing threshold. Higher numbers indicate louder sounds. For example, a quiet conversation would occur at about 20 dB.

Historically, definitions of hearing loss were based on the decibel levels at which humans responded to pure tone signals at different frequencies. A deaf person was defined as one who had a hearing loss of at least 90 dBHL (hearing level) at frequencies of 500, 1000, and 2000 Hz; such a person could hear nothing below the 90 dB level. Anyone with a lesser hearing loss was identified as hard-of-hearing; hard-of-hearing persons could have a hearing loss ranging from 20 to 90 dBHL. However, because the ability to understand and process speech is of far greater significance than simply responding to pure tones, new definitions were adopted by the Conference of Executives of American Schools for the Deaf (CEAD) in June 1975. These definitions are more functional because they emphasize the impact of the hearing loss on the development of language.

Hearing impairment. This generic term indicates a hearing disability that can range in severity from mild to profound. It includes the subsets of deaf and hard-of-hearing.

Deaf. A deaf person is one whose hearing disability precludes successful processing of linguistic information through audition, with or without a hearing aid.

Hard-of-hearing. A hard-of-hearing person has residual hearing sufficient for successful processing of linguistic information through audition, generally with the use of a hearing aid.

Prevalence

The 1984 report of the Office of Special Education and Rehabilitation Services stated that 48,659 hearing impaired children and youth (up to the age of 21) were served under P.L. 94–142 and P.L. 89–313 during the 1983–84 school year.

Causes

In the normally functioning ear sound waves enter through the auditory canal and move through the middle ear into the inner ear, which contains the cochlea (the organ of hearing) and the semicircular canals (the center of balance). In the process sound is changed into neural impulses, which travel along neural pathways to the brain. The brain then adds meaning to the impulses. Interference with any part of the transmission system can result in impaired hearing. It may involve a restriction in the range of frequencies received, distortion along the frequency spectrum, or an increase in the intensity needed to perceive a sound.

Conductive Hearing Loss

Impairment in the mechanical transmission of sound waves (sound conduction) through the outer and middle ear gives rise to conductive hearing losses. The outer ear, as illustrated in Figure 11-1, consists of the external ear (pinna) and a passage about 1 inch long and ¼ inch in diameter (the auditory canal), which terminates

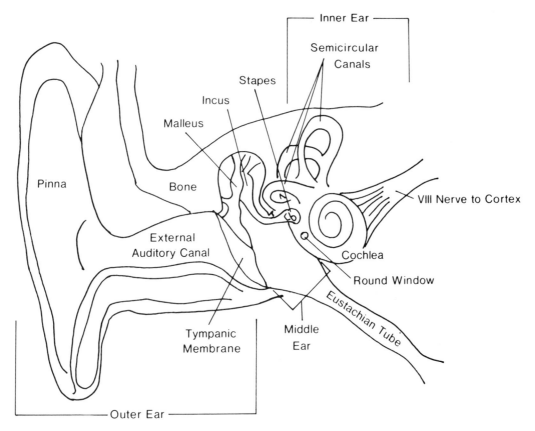

Figure 11–1 The peripheral portion of the auditory system

at the eardrum (tympanic membrane). Frequently, young children have an excess accumulation of wax in the external ear or fluid in the middle ear; these conditions interfere with sound conduction and produce a conductive hearing loss. Such problems are usually corrected through medication or surgery without special education placement.

The middle ear is a cavity 1 to 2 cubic centimeters in volume connected to the naso-pharynx by the Eustachian tube. It contains three tiny bones—the malleus, incus, and stapes—called the ossicular chain. The ossicular chain forms a bridge between the tympanic membrane and the entrance to the inner ear (round window). Sound waves are carried by the ossicular chain to the inner ear. The footplate of the last bone in the chain, the stapes, is embedded in the oval window. The most common cause of conductive hearing loss is inflammation or infection of the middle ear, called otitis media. It can usually be alleviated medically (Davis & Silverman, 1978).

Sensorineural Hearing Loss

Impairment within the inner ear interferes with the conversion of sound waves to neural impulses and is referred to as sensorineural hearing loss. Such losses not only reduce the intensity of the signal but also distort the sound perceived. Most children and youth enrolled in special education programs for the hearing impaired have this type of hearing loss. Unlike conductive losses, sensorineural losses cannot presently be reversed surgically or medically, and amplification is successful only in mild cases. A sensorineural hearing loss may be genetic in origin or may be caused by disease or injury. The loss can occur before, during, or after birth.

Genetic Hearing Loss

A hearing loss may be inherited as a single genetic trait or as part of a syndrome, such as Waardenberg Syndrome, which combines deafness with abnormal pigmentation and other problems; Ushers Syndrome, in which hearing loss is accompanied by progressive loss of vision; or Treacher Collins Syndrome, in which a conductive hearing loss is accompanied by facial anomalies. Deafness can be inherited as a dominant trait (14%), a recessive trait (84%), or a sex-linked disorder (2%).

At the present time more than 50 genetic syndromes have been identified in which hearing loss may occur, and genetic causes are thought to account for about 50% of all cases of deafness in children (Nance, 1976). In schools for the deaf it is common to find students who are the second or third generation of their families to attend. The high incidence of marriage between hearing impaired people is a factor in the high incidence of genetic hearing loss; however, most children who are genetically deaf have hearing parents who carried undetectable recessive genes for the condition. Children whose deafness is caused by a single dominant gene are usually born into families that already have experience with deafness. There is rarely additional injury to the central nervous system before birth, and the incidence of secondary handicaps in this population is no greater than in the population at large.

Nongenetic Hearing Loss

A sensorineural hearing loss may also be caused by disease or injury. Rubella, commonly called German measles, is a mild viral infection when it occurs in children or adults; however, when it is contracted by a woman during pregnancy, especially during the first 3 months, the developing fetus may be infected. Such an infection, which attacks the rapidly growing central nervous system, may cause the baby to be born with a hearing loss, defective vision, and/or irregularities of the heart and nervous system such as those associated with mental retardation and cerebral palsy. In 1968 a rubella vaccine was approved and is now routinely given to all preschool children. It has prevented rubella from reaching the epidemic proportions that had previously existed.

A more recently identified problem, for which there is presently no vaccine, is congenital cytomegalovirus infection (CMV). CMV is the most frequent viral infection in newborns (Williams et al., 1982) and is estimated to cause a hearing loss in one-third of these infants (Pass, Stagno, & Myers, 1980; Hanshaw & Dudgeon, 1978). Evidence suggests that CMV causes progressive hearing loss, which may prevent immediate identification. CMV can also cause mental retardation.

Hearing impairment can also occur at or near the time of birth as a result of complications in the birth process, such as prolonged labor, premature or abrupt birth (usually due to an accident), or difficulties that necessitate the use of obstetric instruments. Failure to breathe readily during or immediately after birth (apnea) is another commonly reported cause of hearing loss. When children's hearing loss is caused by apnea or by difficult birth, they are at high risk for other problem conditions, including mental retardation and cerebral palsy. Hearing impairment can be caused after birth by viral infections, such as mumps, measles, and meningitis. Otitis media, the inflammation of the middle ear mentioned earlier, can produce a permanent loss if it is a chronic condition. Trauma, accidents, high fevers, and drugs are factors in a small percentage of cases.

There is increasing concern over the incidence of hearing loss caused by excessive exposure to loud noises, specifically amplified sounds generated by rock bands and extensive use of portable headphone sets at high volume. Although the losses thus induced generally will not require special education, they may be sufficient to reduce the quality of life for adolescents and adults.

Characteristics

Degree of Impairment

Hearing losses can range from mild to profound. We describe the severity of loss in terms of decibels; the larger the number, the more severe the loss because the individual can hear nothing below the identified level. The impact on speech and language depends also on the frequencies involved; the greater the loss in the speech frequencies (500, 1000, 2000 Hz), the more severe the impairment. A hearing loss may be present in one ear (unilateral) or both ears (bilateral). Persons with unilateral hearing losses usually function normally and have problems only with locating the direction of sounds. Those with mild to moderate bilateral hearing losses (20 to 60 dB) can usually benefit from amplification. Those with severe loss (60 to 90 dB) can often be trained to use their residual hearing with amplification. The profoundly hearing impaired—those with bilateral losses of more than 90 dB—can sometimes derive benefit from amplification but often rely more on manual language and speech reading for communication.

It is important to remember that individuals are affected by a hearing loss in different ways. Nonetheless, we can identify some characteristics common to most severely and profoundly hearing impaired children. The degree to which they differ from normally hearing children and youth varies with age and other factors. Unless other handicaps are present, developmental differences in hearing impaired toddlers are minimal. As hearing impaired children grow older, however, they often fall behind in language comprehension and use, unable to keep up with the increased complexity and abstraction of the language system. Consequently, their academic, social, and emotional development may also be delayed.

Variables Affecting Education

Even a minimal hearing loss will affect language learning and influence educational progress. However, the extent of the handicapping effect will also depend on (1) the type of loss (conductive or sensorineural), (2) the degree of loss, (3) the age of onset, (4) the time of detection, (5) the time of intervention, (6) the home environment, and (7) the presence of other handicaps. Several variables of primary importance will be discussed here; type and degree of hearing loss are discussed elsewhere.

Age of Onset Some hearing losses occur at birth or prior to language learning (prelingual), whereas others occur after a child has learned the rudiments of a language system (postlingual). The age at which a hearing loss occurs is critical since the usual channel for normal language learning is the auditory system. From birth, parents constantly provide verbal input, and infants soon begin to analyze and store this information for future use.

Research has demonstrated that an unborn fetus responds to sound and that infants only a few days or weeks old use their hearing in order to discriminate between sounds (Moffit, 1971; Eimas, Siqueland, Jusczyk, & Vigout, 1971; Eilers & Minifie, 1975). Longitudinal studies of 9- to 18-month-old babies have demonstrated how older infants use the auditory system (Friedlander & Cyrulik, 1970). A toy that presented various auditory stimuli, such as music and the voices of different people reading and speaking, was placed in the crib. The babies selected the preferred presentation by pushing a button. A 12-month-old baby consistently chose to listen to a bright, cheery voice rather than his mother's monotonous one. A 14-month-old followed this pattern but after a few days listened to his mother's voice very carefully and never returned to the other voice.

At least 80% of language development has occurred by 3 years of age (McFarland & Simmons, 1980). A hearing loss that occurs after a child has learned spoken language (a postlingual loss) is less likely to cause severe educational problems than a prelingual loss. Children who experience a postlingual loss have had an opportunity to use the auditory system and practice their listening, speech, and language skills. Children who experience a prelingual hearing loss do not have the same opportunity to develop normally and require explicit teaching rather than simple exposure to ordinary language input. Although some help may be derived from observing lip movement, only 60% of English is visible on the lips, and that often looks confusingly similar. Thus, language learning becomes a very difficult and sometimes an almost impossible task. These children require a combination of teaching modes such as lip reading, the written word, and manual signing to supplement the imperfect auditory input.

Time of Identification and Intervention   It is essential to identify a hearing impairment as soon as possible so that both child and parents can participate in an intervention program. The further children move past the critical stage for language learning, the more difficult it becomes to learn language, especially the finer nuances of auditory discrimination and the complexities of the total linguistic system. The earlier children are identified and taught to use their residual hearing, the greater their chance to acquire the building blocks essential for more complex skills and to learn language in the same sequence as hearing children.

Another important part of early intervention is helping parents adjust to their child's hearing loss. Parental attitudes have a significant impact on the educational process. Parents who are themselves hearing impaired seem to be more accepting and more readily able to provide the communication and love essential for the mental health and educational achievement of their hearing impaired children. Parents with normal hearing, on the other hand, must often progress through the same five stages of grief identified with death—shock, denial, sadness, anger, and adaptation—before accepting and encouraging their hearing impaired child. Parents unable to move through these stages cannot provide the needed linkage with schools and service agencies and thus may interfere substantially with the full educational growth of their child. For this reason parent counseling is an important part of any intervention program.

Social Development

Normally, young children learn appropriate social interaction skills—such as turn taking, sharing, and the use of *please* and *thank you*—through language. Hearing impaired children are generally less socially mature than hearing children. This lack of social maturity is manifested in impulsivity and a related lack of responsibility and independence. Frequently, children with a hearing loss seem to disregard the feelings and misunderstand the actions of others. They typically exhibit a higher than usual degree of egocentricity and a low frustration level, which causes them to be demanding and act out if their demands are not met (Harris, 1978; Meadow, 1980).

Intelligence

The traditional method of evaluating intelligence is to use standardized intelligence tests that result in an IQ score. A 1968 review (Vernon) of 50 independent studies indicated that essentially the same distribution of intelligence exists

Hearing impaired students work at developing full and complete sentence patterns, which their teacher charts.

among hearing impaired and nonhandicapped populations when tested with performance tests rather than verbal intelligence scales. Hearing loss does not appear to affect intelligence as measured by performance intelligence tests.

Academic Achievement

The academic achievement of hearing impaired children contrasts poorly with their documented potential. Reading, which is based on language knowledge, is a major deficit area. One major longitudinal study showed national results of less than .3 of a grade improvement per year for a 3-year period (Trybus & Karchmer, 1977). When data were analyzed for subgroups, some information was obtained with implications for educating the hearing impaired: those making the greatest gains in reading were those students with more hearing, those with no additional handicaps, those who entered school early, and those who had two deaf parents.

Language

Severely and profoundly hearing impaired children usually have a smaller, more concrete vocabulary than do individuals with normal hearing. Their sentences are shorter and less complex. Hearing impaired students struggle with grammatical structure, often omitting plurals, tenses, possessives, prepositions, and other little words such as *a* and *the* that tend to be less concrete and adding words that do not belong, as in "I want for to go." Even as they begin to use longer sentences, these students still tend to use a very simple subject-verb-object order. Thus, their language is not so rich or subtle as that of individuals who hear normally. It must be remembered that the research in this area predates the widespread use of total communication in teaching the hearing impaired. New studies may indicate that language growth has improved with this method.

Speech

A common assumption is that the speech of severely and profoundly hearing impaired children is unclear because they do not articulate sounds correctly, but articulation is only part of the problem. Other factors, such as poor timing and rhythm, are involved. There is a tendency to prolong both stressed and unstressed syllables and to insert more and longer pauses than necessary, resulting in relatively slow speech. Variation of pitch is typically abnormal, and it tends to lack linguistic content. Thus, hearing impaired individuals often do not use the rising pitch we expect to hear at the end of a question or the falling pitch that indicates the conclusion of a declarative sentence. Nasality is frequently a problem also. Sounds such as *m*, *n*, and *ng*, which should be nasalized, may not be; others, such as vowels that should not be nasalized, are. Substituting one sound for another and prolonging the voicing of a single sound are other behaviors that contribute to unintelligibility in the speech of the hearing impaired.

Assessment

Audiological Assessment

The professional responsible for audiological assessment is an *audiologist*. This person usually holds a master's degree or doctorate from a department of speech and hearing sciences and is certified by the American Speech, Language, and Hearing Association. The instrument used to measure hearing is called an *audiometer*; it presents a series of carefully calibrated tones that vary in frequency (pitch) and intensity (loudness). Testing is done in a specially designed, soundproof booth or room, and the results are charted on a graph called an *audiogram*.

Speech audiometry refers to the various methods used to determine at what level children hear speech and how well the speech is understood. Testing of speech comprehension requires that the child have language; therefore, it is not possible to use the usual clinical test procedures with infants or young hearing impaired

The specialist using an audiometer measures a child's responses to varied frequencies and intensities.

children who have not developed language. Speech audiometry can use speakers or headphones; the materials can be either prerecorded or presented live.

The speech reception threshold (SRT) is the decibel level at which an individual can identify a speech stimulus 50% of the time. SRT is measured by presenting words at different intensity levels until a level is found at which the child can identify 50% of the words correctly. Children respond by looking toward the source of the speech (the loudspeaker), pointing to pictures, or actually repeating the words they hear. Once an SRT has been determined, the next task is to assess the ability of the student to understand speech under optimal listening conditions. Usually, lists of one-syllable words are presented through earphones or loudspeakers in the testing room. Test results are expressed in terms of the percentage of words that the child identifies correctly. Children with severe to profound hearing losses often have difficulty discriminating one word from another, and discrimination testing is often a difficult task for them.

Objective audiometry provides additional information about an individual's auditory system without requiring behavioral responses. One method is called impedance audiometry. It identifies a conductive hearing loss by the extent of stiffness or resistance to energy generated by the different sound pressure levels of an auditory stimulus. Another objective test, administered when children cannot be tested behaviorally because of retardation or developmental delay, employs electrodes placed on the scalp to pick up responses to auditory stimuli. The results obtained in these auditory brainstem response (ABR) or brainstem evoked response (BER) tests are averaged and recorded on a chart to show how the peripheral auditory system perceives high-frequency sound. ABR can presently measure reliably only the mid- to high-frequency range, although results of recent research give new hope for obtaining information about low frequencies as well.

Early Childhood   Although difficult, behavioral testing for hearing impairment is possible with infants as young as 0 to 5 months of age. Sounds are introduced through loudspeakers into a soundproof room. Although this method does not permit individual ear assessment, it does provide important information regarding hearing status at an early age and thus offers the opportunity for early intervention. Responses range from subtle ones (eye movements, increased activity, decreased activity) to a whole-body startle (Moro reflex). Extensive training and practice are necessary to be able to make accurate judgments about infant responses.

In testing the hearing of infants 5 to 24 months of age, sounds are often introduced through loudspeakers as for younger infants; however, some young children will accept headphones, which permit each ear to be evaluated individually. Responses are evaluated according to the normal head turns that infants make in response to sound at this age. In order to encourage the infant to continue responding to a sound, visual reinforcers such as animated toy animals are paired with the various sounds. Speech testing with this age group is limited to speech awareness for very young infants and object identification for those reaching the 24-month level. Object identification may not be possible with severely/profoundly hearing impaired children since most have not learned to use their residual hearing fully and exhibit a severe delay in language.

More precise measurement is possible after age 2. Earphones or a bone conduction oscillator (an instrument placed either on the bony structure behind the ear or on the forehead) can be used to evaluate hearing in each ear. Some 2-year-olds and most 3-year-olds are taught simple play procedures, such as placing a ring on a stick or dropping a block in a box, to use as responses to the auditory signal. At this age audiologists may begin to evaluate speech discrimination by having the child repeat words and point to pictures. However, these tasks may again be impossible for young severely/profoundly hearing impaired children. Impedence testing is often used with infants and very young children. ABR is usually used when children cannot respond behaviorally.

School Age Students in kindergarten and elementary school are asked to raise a hand each time they hear a signal. The stimuli are usually pure tones of known intensity and frequency presented to each ear individually through earphones or a bone oscillator. Thus, a threshold, the level of intensity at which each frequency is heard 50% of the time, is obtained for each ear. The results of testing are plotted on an audiogram. The 0 decibel (dB) level is the norm against which the individual's threshold is measured: it is the median threshold for a group of adults with normal hearing. Deviations from the 0 dB line indicate the additional intensity needed for an individual to hear a sound at a given frequency.

Testing results can show a sensorineural hearing loss (located in the inner ear) as seen in Figure 11-2 or a conductive hearing loss (located in the outer or

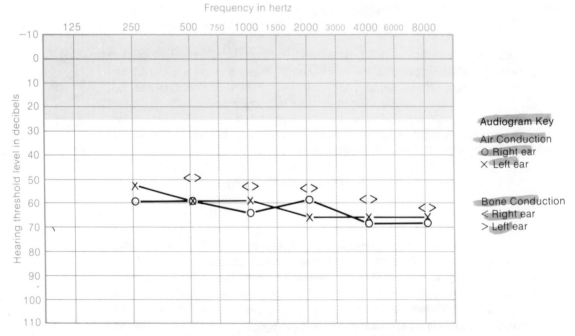

Figure 11–2   An audiogram depicting a bilateral sensorineural hearing loss
NOTE: Shading indicates acceptable range.

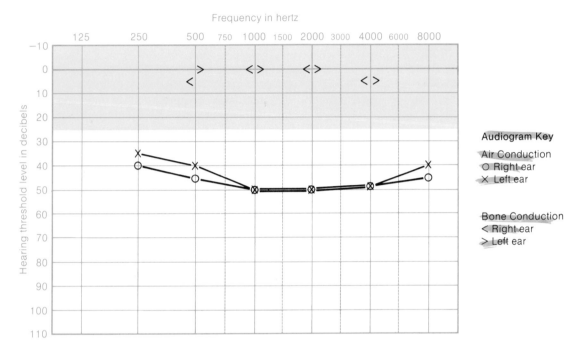

Figure 11–3   An audiogram depicting a bilateral conductive loss
NOTE: Shading indicates acceptable range.

middle ear) as seen in Figure 11-3. One can see that the degree of sensorineural loss might be called moderately severe and will certainly interfere with normal conversation whereas the conductive loss might be termed moderate and will not provide so much difficulty.

Secondary/Transition   Testing of older hearing impaired students follows the same format used with school-age students. Impedence testing would be a regular procedure for both school-age and secondary students, in addition to regular monitoring of the effectiveness of hearing aids.

Cognitive Assessment

The assessment of intelligence in hearing impaired children is complicated by the fact that standard IQ tests are largely verbal and rely heavily on the individual's linguistic competence. Such tests tend to confuse linguistic deprivation with intellectual impairment and thus erroneously indicate that a hearing impaired individual is retarded. It is critical that tests be selected that minimize the need for verbal language and be presented in a communication mode familiar to the student. At least two tests should be used (Vernon & Brown, 1964), and they should be administered individually (Hiskey, 1966). It is also important to have professionals who are familiar with hearing impaired children administer the tests, create a pleasant environment while testing, and assure that supportive data are available through additional measures.

Early Childhood   The Bayley Scales of Infant Development are well-standardized, developmental scales for children 2 to 30 months old with normal hearing (Bayley, 1969). Although some items on this instrument require auditory and/or language skills and thus necessitate a scoring adjustment, there are a sufficient number of other items that are of value. The Uzgiris-Hunt Ordinal Scales of Psychological Development (1978) are based on Piagetian theory and tasks. They are extremely helpful in evaluating certain cognitive skills of hearing impaired children up to 2 years of age, including nonverbal responses to cause-effect and means-end relationships, visual pursuit, association, and object performance.

The Smith-Johnson Nonverbal Performance Scale for 2- to 4-year-olds (Smith & Johnson, 1977) was designed for both hearing and hearing impaired children. Subtest directions are presented in pantomime, and the performance levels (below average, average, and above average) are age- and sex-referenced. Most of the items have been adapted from such well-known tests as the Gesell (1940) and Cattell (revised, 1960). There are 14 task categories, including pencil drawing, knot tying, paper folding, scissors use, completion items, and form discrimination.

School Age   One of the most widely used tests for the school-age population is the performance scale of the Wechsler Intelligence Scale for Children—Revised (WISC-R) (Wechsler, 1974). The performance scale was standardized using a hearing impaired sample (Anderson & Sisco, 1977) and, according to Sullivan and McCay (1979), was designed to evaluate the cognitive abilities of the hearing impaired population aged 6 through 17. Instructions may be given orally or modified by pantomime, visual aids, or total communication as necessary. IQ scores are derived from performance on six nonverbal subtests: block design, picture arrangement, picture design, object assembly, mazes, and coding. The Hiskey-Nebraska Test of Learning Aptitude (Hiskey, 1966) contains 12 nonverbal subtests, such as bead pattern memory, memory for color, spatial reasoning, and picture identification. Norms are provided for the hearing and hearing impaired, as are standardized pantomime instructions.

Another instrument, Raven's Progressive Matrices (Raven, 1948), can be used for individuals 9 years old and older. Some psychologists, however, think that it should be used with at least one other intelligence test. The Leiter International Performance Scale (Leiter, 1948) has been an extremely popular test for use with hearing impaired children because it is administered by pantomime and requires only nonverbal responses. Recently, though, questions have been raised about its standardization, reliability, and validity (Ratcliffe & Ratcliffe, 1979). Another appropriate test is the Nonverbal Test of Cognitive Skills (Johnson & Boyd, 1981). Nonverbal tests such as the Kaufman Assessment Battery for Children (Kaufman & Kaufman, 1982), designed for normally hearing children, can be adapted for the hearing impaired by modifying the communication mode. This change does destroy the statistical validity, but the results can still provide useful information for education. Only licensed psychologists, experienced and knowledgeable in the assessment of hearing impaired individuals, should conduct intelligence assessments; and conclusions about individual students should not be based on the results of just one test.

Secondary/Transition   As hearing impaired students become older, the availability of better tests and materials decreases. The Hiskey-Nebraska Test of Learning Aptitude can be used until 17 years of age; the WISC-R, until 16; the Leiter, until 18; and Raven's Progressive Matrices, into adulthood. An obvious problem is that after age 18 limitations of test materials preclude the development of a test battery.

Communication Assessment

Communication involves the use of language, speech, and the auditory system. The development of a communication system in a hearing impaired person is essential not only to transmit needs and desires but also to establish important social-emotional bonds. The assessment of communication in the hearing impaired, especially in the very young, is difficult because so much communication occurs in the verbal-auditory mode and most assessment tools have been developed accordingly. Still, there is evidence that hearing impaired children's language develops much like that of the nonhandicapped if given early input (Schlesinger & Meadow, 1972), and it may therefore be practical to evaluate the language of the hearing impaired according to normal developmental patterns.

Early Childhood   There are a few formal tests developed specifically for hearing impaired infants and preschoolers. The SKI-HI Language Development Scale was adapted from 19 different language development scales and is designed for use with hearing impaired children 0 to 5 years old. It reviews progress in both receptive and expressive areas and may be used by parents. The SKI-HI Receptive Language Test, designed for hearing impaired children 2 to 4 years old and at an equivalent developmental level, requires picture-pointing responses and measures comprehension of one to five elements of language: agent, action, object, attribute, and relation (Longhurst, Briery, & Emery, 1975). Another test that may prove helpful even though not specifically designed for the hearing impaired is the Communicative Intervention Inventory (Coggins & Carpenter, 1981). The CII is an observational system designed to clarify the function of language in developmentally young children. It focuses on what children intend when they gesture, vocalize, or verbalize. Parts of the Sequenced Inventory of Communicative Development evaluate a child's awareness and discrimination of auditory input as well as certain skills in receiving and expressing information (Hedrick, Prather, & Tobin, 1984).

Although none of these tests provides standardized scores, they do offer information on normal development and a means of gauging the functioning level of a hearing impaired child. They also provide a basis for choosing appropriate objectives for intervention. All can be presented either orally, gesturally, or through total communication. In addition, developmental profiles such as the Rockford Infant Development Scales (RIDES) can be extremely helpful because they evaluate the major areas of a child's development—personal-social/self-help, gross motor, fine motor, adaptive, and receptive and expressive language. Educationally, such an overview of a young hearing impaired child's skills is important because it helps identify what areas have been affected.

School Age Although some aspects of language of the school-age hearing impaired can be measured with the language portions of standardized achievement tests, such as the Stanford Achievement Test (SAT) (Madden et al., 1972), such tests neither evaluate all aspects of the linguistic system adequately nor provide information from which language goals and objectives can be derived. As is true for the preschool population, relatively few language tests are specifically designed and standardized for the school-age hearing impaired. However, since language is developmental and hearing impaired children seem to follow the developmental sequencing of their hearing peers, good language tests developed for school-age hearing children can provide valuable information regarding intervention. The results of such tests will provide the teacher with specific information about the functional language level of a child and, by applying known information about language development, will also provide a specific place for the teacher to begin instruction. Information pertaining to some language tests developed specifically for the hearing impaired can be found in Table 11-1.

Two additional tests reportedly used successfully with hearing impaired populations (Davis, 1974, 1977) are the Test for Auditory Comprehension of Language (TACL) (Carrow, 1973) and the Boehm Test of Basic Concepts (Boehm, 1971). The TACL is designed for children aged 3 through 7 and measures comprehension of different nouns, adjectives, verbs, adverbs, grammatical constructions, and syntax, using a picture-pointing response. The results can be converted to age scores and percentiles. The Boehm test evaluates mastery of concepts considered necessary to achieve in kindergarten through second grade and pinpoints areas where special instruction is needed. The results can be compared to norms for normally hearing and, to a limited extent, hearing impaired individuals of the same age.

Secondary/Transition Tests designed to evaluate specific areas of language deficits are not available for hearing impaired students older than 19. Those that can be used were identified previously—the Total Communication Receptive Vocabulary Test (to 17 years of age) and the Test of Syntactic Abilities (to 19 years of age). At this age level language ability can be approached indirectly through a reading test such as that found in the Peabody Individual Achievement Test (Dunn & Markwardt, 1970) for students in kindergarten through 12th grade. Samples of expressive language can be obtained and evaluated for appropriate use of grammar and syntax at any age.

Nonstandardized Testing The most accurate information about the language of hearing impaired children is usually obtained by skillfully using portions of many standardized and informal tests. Obtaining a sample of a hearing impaired student's expressive language can provide information about all aspects of language, including how the student uses language, an element not provided in most stan-

Table 11-1 Characteristics of language tests for the hearing impaired

Test Name	Age Range (in years)	Mode		Area Tested				Norm Group
		Receptive	Expressive	Vocabulary	Morphology	Syntax	Semantic Relationships	
SKI-HI Receptive Language Test (SKI-HI RLT)	3–6½	X		X			X	None
Test of Expressive Language Ability (TEXLA)	7–12		X		X	X		65 HI children, 17 hearing children
Test of Receptive Language Ability (TERLA)	7–12	X			X	X		92 HI children, 27 hearing children
Test of Syntactic Ability (TSA)	10–19	X				X		450 HI children
Total Communication Receptive Vocabulary Test (TCRVT)	3–12	X		X				77 hearing, 95 hard-of-hearing, 251 deaf children
Grammatical Analysis of Elicited Language (GAEL)	5–9		X		X	X		200 HI children, 200 hearing children
Maryland Syntax Evaluation Instrument (MSEI)	6–12		X			X		220 HI children

dardized tests. One of the most helpful informal instruments for evaluating expressive language competency is the Suggested Sequential Acquisition of Syntactic Structures for Hearing Impaired, which provides a framework for language learning that follows the Piagetian stages of cognitive development and can assist sequential, systematic educational planning (Streng, Kretschmer, & Kretschmer, 1978).

Speech is assessed using a variety of formal and informal tests, including articulation tests developed for normally hearing children. One of the better speech assessment tools, designed especially for use with hearing impaired students, is that of Ling (1976), which tests speech at both the phonological and phonetic levels and can be used with children of all ages (preschool through high school). Results are directly transferable to teaching goals.

Intervention

As soon as a hearing loss has been diagnosed and treated medically or surgically to whatever extent possible, the provision of a hearing aid is the first priority in intervention. Learning to use amplification and the remaining capacity for hearing is essential to the education of all hearing impaired children and youth. One or two hearing aids may be worn on the body, over the ear, or in the ear. Wherever they are worn, they perform the same function, and they have the same basic component parts. A microphone picks up sound waves and changes them to electric energy; an amplifier intensifies the energy; and a receiver changes the electrical energy back into a louder sound. The energy source for the hearing aid is a battery. Hearing aids may be selected or modified so that certain frequencies are amplified more than others.

Group hearing aids are often used in classrooms to enable the teacher to eliminate background noise and speak directly to the students. In this case a microphone is worn around the teacher's neck, and the room is encircled by a loop of wire that functions as a receiver or else radio frequency inserts are used, which fit directly into each child's hearing aid. The auditory information received, either through the loop or the insert, is transmitted to each student by the hearing aid. The newer FM systems can be connected directly to the student's personal hearing aid.

Modes of Communication

Educators agree that hearing impaired students require exacting instruction in all three aspects of language—content, syntax, and function. Yet almost from the time when efforts were first made to educate the hearing impaired, two approaches have been proposed and disputed. One group of authorities maintains that hearing impaired individuals should be educated to become as normal as possible. The goal of education in this view is to enable the hearing impaired to live in normal society and participate in the communication around them. To attain this goal, hearing impaired persons must learn to speak and read lips and use their residual hearing to whatever extent they can. These skills are extremely difficult to master, and

Using a FM amplification system, Lisa is learning to count. She says and signs the number as her teacher points.

proponents of aural-oral communication believe that if children are allowed access to a manual form of communication, they will select the easier method and never develop auditory or oral skills to their maximum potential.

Proponents of manual communication (through sign language or fingerspelling) in combination with oral training oppose this point of view. They believe that hearing impaired individuals should not be expected to achieve the impossible goal of normal but should be given the communication skills they need in any form possible—oral, manual, and written. With these skills, they assert, the hearing impaired can be integrated into the hearing world for work, can lead independent lives, and can choose to socialize with other hearing impaired persons as well as with normally hearing individuals.

The Aural-Oral Approach The aural-oral approach reflects the philosophy that hearing impaired individuals should be taught to hear and speak as normally as possible and that alternative modes of communication, such as fingerspelling or sign language, are crutches that hinder normalization (Simmons-Martin, 1972). It stresses making use of whatever hearing remains through amplification. Reception of sound is aided by speechreading, amplification, and the development of a kinesthetic feedback system for self-monitoring. Students are taught to speak, and reading and writing are introduced as additional methods for acquiring and using language.

In almost all cases of hearing impairment, some amount of hearing at one or more frequencies remains: few hearing losses are total. This residual hearing, if appropriately amplified, can be used as an aid in receiving and producing speech. An individualized program of auditory training is considered basic to success in learning how to receive (hear) speech.

However, since severely and profoundly hearing impaired children cannot receive all necessary information through the auditory channel, lipreading (speechreading) is used to supplement auditory input. Speechreading, defined as "the cor-

Learning about sound.

rect identification of . . . thoughts transmitted via the visual components of oral discourse" (O'Neill & Oyer, 1961), is complicated because some sounds that are different look alike on the lips (Jeffers & Barley, 1971). Another difficulty is that many speech sounds are hard to see or invisible in connected discourse.

Some information that is not accessible through speechreading may be obtained by feeling the movements of a speaker (taction). Touching the cheek and nose of the speaker can yield information as to whether a sound is voiced, voiceless, or nasal. This can be an aid in initially learning to form a sound (Calvert & Silverman, 1975). Individuals whose hearing is not impaired use their auditory system to monitor the speech they produce for correct articulation, volume, and pitch; some energy from speech sounds is returned to the auditory system of the speaker (called an auditory feedback loop). Sometimes the only feedback mechanism hearing impaired persons have is kinesthetic awareness—the internal feeling of their speech movements.

Speech does not develop naturally in severely and profoundly hearing impaired children. Even those who are fortunate enough to be diagnosed and receive amplification and instruction early need considerable help in developing speech that can be readily understood by unsophisticated listeners. They must be taught not only the sounds of the language as they occur in connected speech but also proper phrasing and pitch patterns. This training requires either a teacher of the hearing impaired or a communication disorders specialist with training in working with the deaf. Constant monitoring by hearing impaired individuals themselves, their teachers, their families, and other significant individuals in their environment is necessary to achieve habitual use of correct speech. If speech is not used and corrected consistently, it may deteriorate rapidly because of the lack of normal auditory feedback.

Manual Communication Modes   In manual communication, messages are sent by manipulating the fingers, arms, and upper torso and are received visually. Thus, the defective auditory-vocal channel is bypassed in favor of the intact visual-motor system. Those who advocate instruction in manual communication believe that general communication competence should be the goal for hearing impaired individuals.

Fingerspelling in America is based on a code of one-handed, manually formed symbols for each letter of the English alphabet, the ordinal numbers, and some punctuation (see Figure 11-4). Finger positions are discrete and easily learned; and after the code is mastered, any message that can be written can be sent and received. An expert in fingerspelling can send and receive spelled messages at about the speed of normal oral communication. The Rochester Method, developed at the Rochester School for the Deaf in New York, uses fingerspelling simultaneously with speech in the education of the hearing handicapped (1972). Fingerspelling eliminates the ambiguities that plague speechreading but is hard for young children to master.

American Sign Language (ASL) is a manual communication system in which the fingers, hands, arms, and upper torso are used in rapid communication of ideas. It has several thousand signs and a unique syntax that does not include

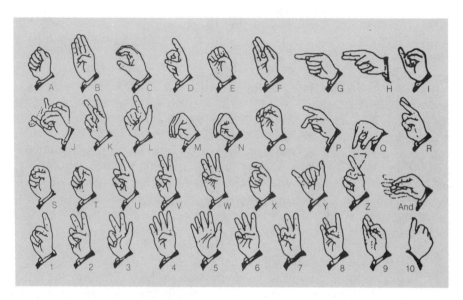

Figure 11—4 The fingerspelling code

such features as definite and indefinite articles, prepositions, forms of the verb *to be*, participles, and cases (Bergman, 1972). Verb tenses are communicated differently from English, and the vocabulary does not always permit full expression of the nuances of English—for example, *hot dog, frankfurter, wiener,* and *knockwurst*, which all have slightly different meanings in English, share one common sign in ASL. Although ASL is the communication system most often used in the adult deaf community and is, in its own right, a rich and beautiful language (see, for example, Klima & Bellugi, 1979), it does not convey the English language. For this reason many educators, fearing that its syntactic and semantic differences from English will interfere with learning reading and writing, consider it unsuitable for use with young hearing impaired students who are just learning English language skills. However, its use is often encouraged among older children so that they can better interact with the adult deaf community. There are a growing number of teachers and other professionals today who feel that deaf children should be taught bilingually, acquiring ASL and English skills simultaneously (Stewart, 1983).

Within the past 10 years, as interest has increased in sign language systems, a number of new, modified sign systems have been created to convey the English language in a manual mode. Manual English uses many ASL signs but adds signs for inflectional endings, pronouns, articles, and other structural elements. Like ASL, however, it communicates by ideas rather than morphemes. Other forms of sign language, such as Signing Exact English (SEE II), sign by morphemes rather than ideas (Gustason, Pfetzing, & Zawolkow, 1972). In selecting a SEE II sign, the word's spelling, sound, and meaning are considered. If any two of these are the same, the words are signed the same. Thus, the word *right* in "turn right," "right-of-way," and "right answer" would be signed the same, but *write* and *rite* would be signed differently. In ASL and Manual English different signs are used for different ideas. In all sign language systems signs are modified, usually by the fingerspelling position of the hand(s), to allow for expression of synonyms. For example, the word *beer* is signed with the fingers in the *b* position. The word *wine* uses the same sign with the fingers in the *w* position. Some concern has arisen over the ability of teachers and others to use Manual English or SEE II to accurately represent the English language (Marmor & Petitto, 1979; Kluwin, 1981).

Total Communication   Within the last 15 years education of the hearing impaired in the United States has been revolutionized by a new, combined aural-oral and manual communication approach. Known as *total communication*, this trend originated in the late 1960s with Roy Holcomb, a deaf teacher of the hearing impaired who is himself a parent of two hearing impaired children (Garretson, 1976). Advocates of this approach believe that any and all means of communicating with a hearing impaired person should be used as early as possible. The goal is not to establish a specific language system but to establish basic communication pathways as quickly and efficiently as possible. In practice, total communication uses primarily auditory training, speechreading, fingerspelling, variations of the sign system, reading, and writing in its approach to communication. If taught and used correctly, total communication uses all the components of an oral program plus

Oral and sign language are used together in a total communication approach.

sign language. Supporters of total communication share the philosophy that it is the "moral right of the hearing-impaired, as with normally hearing bilinguals, to receive maximal input in order to attain optimal comprehension and total understanding in the communication situation" (Garretson, 1976, p. 89).

In the past several years sign language has gained increasing exposure and aesthetic recognition by the hearing world, especially through the mass media. It is routine in some areas of the country to have an interpreter sign the local newscast on television. Some children's shows ("Sesame Street," for example) employ hearing impaired actors who sign and fingerspell, and even some commercials are interpreted. The National Theatre of the Deaf has gained worldwide recognition through exposure on television as well as live performances. The play *Children of a Lesser God* starred a congenitally deaf woman who signed throughout the play and won the 1980 Tony Award for best actress. Thus, a positive image is replacing the stigma of using sign language to communicate in the community at large.

Methods of Teaching Language

The primary goal of language instruction for hearing impaired individuals is to help them achieve the language fluency that they require to participate in and contribute to the accumulated knowledge of their society. Fluency of this sort involves the ability to correctly send and receive interpersonal communications and to use language as a tool for thinking. Those who believe that the hearing impaired community is a viable and valuable force set a secondary goal—fluency in manual communication. This enables hearing impaired children and youth to socialize with other hearing impaired individuals and allows them to tap the knowledge and resources of the deaf community as well as to interact with those in the hearing community who learn to communicate in sign.

We have known for a long time that language learning is slow and difficult for many prelingually severely and profoundly hearing impaired children. In the past, educators of the hearing impaired have attempted to remedy language defects through intensive programs of formal language instruction. Two primary methods have been employed: the grammatical method, which presents specific grammatical rules to guide the construction of sentences, and the natural method, which maintains that deaf children should learn language as hearing children do— through formulating linguistic hypotheses and testing them. In programs based on the natural method, language constructions and new vocabulary are introduced through extensive use in natural, meaningful situations. The situation may actually be carefully structured, but the grammatical principles to be acquired are in the mind of the teacher—the student is not consciously made aware of them (Hart, 1964). Called the mother's method, these programs have been advocated by such educators as Groht (1958) and Van Uden (1970).

A combination of these two methods and available knowledge about normal language development can provide hearing impaired children with the opportunity to learn language through structured teaching appropriate for the individual child's developmental level. A combined approach encourages the use of daily experiences to develop language use and, at the same time, identifies vocabulary and grammatical rules specific to the activity and the functional level of the child.

Laurie and her mother work on sentence structure.

Age-Level Distinctions

Early Childhood The importance of early intervention with young hearing impaired children (0 to 3 years old) and their families cannot be overemphasized. It is critical to reach the deaf child during the period when hearing children would normally be developing language and to assist parents in learning to communicate with and enjoy their child. During the past decade many states have established home intervention programs to assure that hearing impaired children receive training as soon as they are identified. Such programs are of particular importance to those for whom the cost of transportation is prohibitive and to families in rural areas without access to center programs. The program goal is to help the entire family adjust to the problems associated with the hearing impairment and learn to communicate with their child. These programs provide auditory training with hearing aids and initial instruction in speech and language, using an oral or a total communication approach. Training is accomplished primarily through visits to the home by a specially trained teacher. Visits are scheduled, insofar as possible, at times convenient for other family members and optimal for the child's learning. Such visits allow the hearing impaired child to receive training in his own environment, using meaningful, familiar objects. Group parent meetings, monthly newsletters, and counseling services are other elements of home intervention programs. Usually children can remain in these programs until they are of school age.

Early education for the hearing impaired is also offered through center-based programs. Programming varies from center to center. In some, several parents and children attend together, whereas in others only one child and parent are scheduled at a time. Group parent meetings may be a regular feature, and counseling services are often provided. The center-based program requirement that someone from the home accompany the child can present a problem. Family schedules may be disrupted, and some families may not be able to afford the cost of transportation. Thus, attendance may not be very good. A combination of a home- and a center-based program is often the best solution.

School Age   School-age hearing impaired children (3 to 21 years old) may be served in residential schools, which are private or state-maintained boarding facilities; day schools, which are public or private schools for the hearing impaired only; or day classes, which are self-contained classes within a normal public school setting. The term *day class* may signify one classroom of hearing impaired children in a single school district or a well-defined multiclass program serving several school districts on a contractual basis. An increasingly popular option for hearing impaired students who are able to use their hearing well and who have sufficient language and reading skills is the regular classroom with help from an itinerant teacher or special tutoring in a resource room.

Secondary/Transition   At the secondary level hearing impaired students fall into three groups: those who will go on to a 4-year liberal arts college, those who will pursue a community college/vocational program, and those for whom the high school program represents a terminal degree or certificate of attendance. For students who expect to go on to a 4-year college, the high school experience parallels that of nonhandicapped youth. They take a full range of academic subjects to earn an academic diploma. For students who are in integrated programs, much of the academic work may be taken in mainstreamed settings, very often with the support of interpreters. The interpreters translate the oral lecture or discussion into sign language; if the student's speech is not readily intelligible, they reverse the process, translating the student's signed comments into oral language so she can more fully participate in class discussions. Where students elect not to use sign language but still need help with comprehension in lecture settings, interpreters can orally interpret the lecture or discussion so that it is easier to speechread. Support of classroom notetakers is essential since it is virtually impossible to watch an interpreter or to speechread while taking notes. Students in residential schools who are going on to college also take regular academic classes but are usually not mainstreamed. At the conclusion of the high school program some students elect to go to regular 4-year colleges, using the support services of interpreters and/or notetakers. Others go to Gallaudet, the 4-year liberal arts college specifically for the deaf.

For those students going on to vocational, 2-year postsecondary schools, high school is largely devoted to improving reading and written language skills, acquiring independent living skills, and pursuing prevocational skills training and career exploration. Again, the students may be mainstreamed into high school prevocational classes with the aid of an interpreter.

Students for whom high school represents a terminal degree usually have low oral and written language skills and are not literate; that is, they read below fifth-grade level. Many are multiply handicapped. Secondary education for these students focuses on life skills training for independent living and preparation for competitive or sheltered employment. It is especially important for these students to practice the skills necessary for survival in the hearing world—things like notifying authorities in case of emergencies, filling out application forms, and banking money.

For all secondary hearing impaired students social development is an essential aspect of education. Many, perhaps most, severely or profoundly impaired individuals cannot fully integrate socially into the hearing world. At the high school level and beyond, when fluent verbal communication is necessary for socialization, hearing impaired individuals tend to be at a strong disadvantage. In most large cities, therefore, severely and profoundly hearing impaired people form a subsection of society with their own social clubs, leisure time activities, church services, athletic leagues, and communication styles. The language used by these people is usually American Sign Language (Hall, 1983). High school students become part of this system by socializing with other hearing impaired individuals through school, church activities, junior clubs, and athletic events. For the normally hearing parents of a hearing impaired adolescent, this is often a traumatic period. They begin to realize that their son or daughter is building a social life in a culture that is not theirs and using a language in which the parents are usually not fluent. They also realize that their son or daughter has a high probability of marrying another hearing impaired person and building a family within the deaf community.

Postsecondary education for hearing impaired students takes several forms. At Gallaudet College all classes are taught using sign language along with speech. A range of majors approximating that of many small liberal arts colleges is available. Gallaudet College also offers master's and doctoral degrees in fields related to deafness. These graduate-level programs are open to both hearing impaired and non–hearing impaired students. The National Technical Institute for the Deaf, located close to the Rochester (NY) Institute of Technology, offers a wide variety of vocational and technical degree programs. Some classes are segregated, but for technical classes hearing impaired students are integrated with nonhandicapped students and are supported by notetakers, interpreters, and tutors. There is also a national network of regional community college programs that offer support services to hearing impaired students. Students are mainstreamed into a wide variety of vocational and technical classes, again with the support of interpreters, notetakers, and tutors. Recently, Gallaudet College has been sponsoring continuing education classes in the Washington, DC, area and in other areas of the country where there are large concentrations of hearing impaired adults.

Curriculum Implications

Research during the past 20 years has provided substantial information regarding normal linguistic development that has important implications for instructing the hearing impaired. We have learned that the development of language begins at birth and proceeds very systematically. Children use their hearing to discriminate sounds and make sense out of what they hear. They hold that auditory language information long enough to sort out language rules, a process aided by a natural predisposition to language and cognition (Lenneberg, 1975). First they comprehend the suprasegmentals (the tonal or rhythmic patterns) of language; then they acquire the symbolic substance of the language, gradually learning the proper ordering of the code.

Initially, children's language is highly dependent on contextual cues. Children learn language in an open, natural environment where there are numerous nonlinguistic cues; and they communicate with gestures and combinations of gestures, vocalizations, and intonation patterns before they are capable of producing single-word utterances (Bates, Camaioni, & Volterra, 1975). At the single-word stage the relationship between language and cognitive development is apparent. For example, as children develop the notion of object constancy, their vocabulary enlarges to include functional terms such as *all gone*, *more*, and *no more*. From two-word sentences they progress to expanding vocabulary and gradually perfecting adult-type sentences. Hearing impaired children provided with linguistic input from birth go through these same developmental stages at approximately the same ages as do their hearing peers (Schlesinger & Meadow, 1972).

Age-Level Distinctions

Early Childhood   Ideally, an early intervention program should include certain components:

1. An enriched linguistic environment should be provided—full of contextual cues, gestures, sign language, and auditory-verbal input.

2. Hearing aids should be introduced, and training to use residual hearing should begin immediately to ensure that at least the auditory patterns of language (pitch change, intonational patterns, timing) are received.

3. Pragmatics (the functions of communication) should be introduced through the use of gestures, such as pointing, head nodding, and requesting. These gestures can be accompanied by vocalizations and/or signs.

4. Object concepts and labeling should be taught simultaneously.

5. Vocalization should be encouraged, and the speech sounds found in babbling should be used in play situations with parents to encourage the eventual use of speech.

Item 4 requires some explanation. Hearing impaired toddlers must be taught to notice the features that are relevant to object discrimination. As they perfect their knowledge of features, they expand their cognitive field, develop finer categories, and acquire new vocabulary. To learn two-word utterances that express a functional relationship, children must understand the significant differences between "this cookie" (a state of existence), "no cookie" (nonexistence), and "more cookie" (recurrence). This type of teaching at an early age is appropriately accomplished in the home, where it can occur on a continual basis and become a part of daily routines such as diapering, bathing, dressing, and playing games.

School Age   A number of curricula have been developed specifically for hearing impaired students. Some, such as the one developed by the Statewide Project for the Deaf in Texas (1978), are language centered and cover eight content areas as well as eight developmental areas. Others, such as the curriculum developed by the Kendall Demonstration Elementary School at Gallaudet College (1982), address five content areas. Some states, such as Oregon and Michigan, are developing their own curricula. Many curricula include areas of need specific to hearing impaired students, such as auditory training and speech. Although formats may differ, these curricula are generally based on normal developmental processes and provide a good framework within which to develop or find appropriate materials.

Since only a few materials for the hearing impaired are available commercially, standard materials for students with normal hearing are frequently used. However, subject matter in these materials—social studies, science, reading—is usually presented through linguistic structures too complex for most hearing impaired students. Thus, teachers must rewrite materials or work with students on specific language skills prior to introducing what is supposed to be the content of a course. Frequently, even materials created specifically for the hearing impaired must be modified to meet individual student needs.

Secondary/Transition   At the secondary and postsecondary levels the main problem facing hearing impaired students is the required rapid assimilation of large quantities of written material. Most hearing impaired students read at a level considerably below that of normally hearing peers. Unfortunately, hearing impaired students are also more dependent than their nonhandicapped peers on the written word as their source of information since they have less access to auditory media, such as audiotapes, telephones, television, and radio. Secondary curriculum must give considerable attention to improving reading and writing ability; at the same time teachers must simplify text material and supplement it with study guides, computer-assisted instruction, and other visual media such as captioned films and film strips.

Because of their relative lack of access to informal sources of information and because of the language barrier that often exists between hearing impaired students and their families, secondary students also need specific information on sexuality and sexual conduct, family life, legal rights and responsibilities, dealing with bureaucracies such as social security, and effective use of leisure time. For those hearing impaired students functioning at lower levels, the curriculum might parallel that offered to mildly mentally retarded students (see chapter 8) with a focus on prevocational and independent living skills.

Model Program

Each year the Early Childhood Home Instruction Program (ECHI) at the University of Washington serves approximately 30 young hearing impaired children (0 to 3 years old) and their families; typically, at least half of these children are multiply handicapped. Children and families are referred to the program by audiologists, pediatricians, and public health nurses as soon as a hearing impairment is identified. Service is provided through weekly home visits and a weekly classroom experience for families who wish to attend. In the latter situation the target children spend the morning in a classroom with a trained teacher of the hearing impaired, playing and learning with other children. Their siblings attend another class, also supervised by a trained teacher. The families of these children have an educational program that includes discussion of issues of concern to them and interaction with pediatricians, deaf adults, audiologists, counselors, psychologists, teachers, school administrators, and representatives of advocacy groups.

The major emphasis of the project, however, is home visitors working with families and children to promote all the precursor skills involved in language as well as language itself. The project utilizes total communication and is based on the belief that parents' natural teaching skills can be honed and augmented so that parents can further the development of their hearing impaired children. In addition to communicative and language skills, this training involves helping the children adjust to their hearing aids. The project believes that there are important advantages in educating young children in their natural environment, where siblings, other family members, and friends can be involved and where the resources of the home and natural family events can be utilized. Educational activities are integrated into regular routines as much as possible.

The project staff also works closely with the administrative and teaching personnel at the community schools in which project children will be placed when they reach the age of 3— to ensure the smoothest possible transition into public school programs. And the program provides a specially trained counselor to work with parents on both a group and an individual basis. Major emphasis in research within the ECHI program is directed toward (1) improving the communicative interaction between parents and children, (2) collecting data on first words of young, severely hearing impaired children using total communication for comparison with data from children with normal hearing, and (3) improving the training process for home visitors.

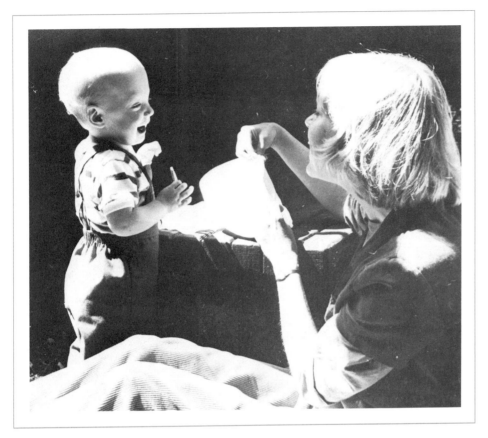

With special help a mother learns how to play with her 12-month-old hearing impaired son so that she stimulates language and intellectual growth.

Mainstreaming

The Least Restrictive Environment

Perhaps for no other group of handicapped people is there so much controversy over what truly constitutes the least restrictive educational environment mandated by P.L. 94–142. The environment that offers maximum opportunity for interaction with normal peers may also provide drastically inferior opportunities for communication with other hearing impaired students and adults as well as less than adequate support services. Indeed, some hearing impaired adults insist that the least restrictive environment for the hearing impaired is a segregated residential school, for only within such an environment can they communicate freely.

Many professionals, however, believe that placing hearing impaired students in carefully chosen regular education classes is academically and socially benefi-

Hearing impaired student can benefit from being in the regular class.

cial. Their position is probably valid if certain conditions hold. Hearing impaired students should be approximately the same chronological age, mental age, social age, and grade level as the students in the class they are entering. There should be an individualized education program as prescribed by P.L. 94–142. There should be appropriate support services, such as notetakers, interpreters, and tutors. And the receiving teacher should welcome the opportunity of having a hearing impaired student in the classroom. In addition, the hearing impaired students themselves, their parents, special education personnel, and other professionals involved in assessment must be consulted before placement, and provision for constant monitoring should be made. Those with a mild hearing loss and excellent language skills may spend a major part of every day in regular classes, perhaps receiving additional help through speech therapy or academic tutoring. More profoundly affected individuals, whose primary enrollment is in a special class or resource room, may be integrated for some specific academic subject areas or for social contact during nonacademic periods.

Age-Level Distinctions

Early Childhood   It is important for hearing impaired infants and young children to learn to interact with both adults and children. This interaction can be accomplished at first through visits with family friends with children. As some hearing impaired children reach the age of 2½ to 3 years, they may be able to enjoy a morning or two each week playing with other children in a regular preschool where the teacher is receptive. However, these ideal situations are complicated by many factors, including problems with the parents' acceptance of the hearing loss, the failure of relatives and friends to learn how to communicate with a hearing impaired child and a language delay so severe that normally hearing children do not want to be bothered with a hearing impaired peer. Often the hearing loss is not identified until 15 to 24 months, and the family life is so complicated by the newness of it all that formal mainstreaming is not possible.

School Age   As a hearing impaired child reaches the age of 3 years and moves into an academic setting, it may still be difficult to provide mainstreaming since normally hearing children do not begin public school until they are of kindergarten age or older. Many public schools do provide some interaction for 4- and 5-year-old hearing impaired children with normally hearing kindergarten children. For other children mainstreaming in private preschools or day-care facilities may be a practical approach.

As hearing impaired children become older, more opportunities for mainstreaming are available. Hearing impaired students who use total communication can be accompanied to regular classes by interpreters or classroom aides who sign proficiently. The well-organized teacher of the hearing impaired will plan ahead with the regular classroom teacher and provide tutoring in the particular content area. Coordinating efforts of this type increase the student's probability of success.

For those students who rely on the auditory system to receive information, it is important that the regular classroom provide good acoustics. Regular education teachers are often willing to wear a lavalier microphone around the neck in order to speak directly to the student and bypass the extraneous noise. It can also be helpful to employ the buddy system and have a student with normal hearing assist the hearing impaired student by making sure he is on the right page and by taking notes to help fill in what the hearing impaired student has missed.

Secondary/Transition   Academic mainstreaming for most severely or profoundly hearing impaired students at the secondary or postsecondary level is dependent on someone's ability to translate (from English to American Sign Language) or transliterate (from oral English to another mode, such as fingerspelling or Manual English). Information at the secondary and postsecondary levels is usually presented in oral lecture or discussion formats. Even the best speechreader has considerable trouble understanding oral communication in a large group, and the task becomes impossible when the lecturer walks around the room, turns around to write on the board, or digresses to a different topic without warning.

Interpreters, who are professionals certified by the National Registry of Interpreters for the Deaf (R.I.D.), mediate between the student and the oral information presented. Unless specifically hired for that purpose, interpreters are not tutors or student advocates; they are professional translators such as one might find at the United Nations. Mainstream teachers need to become accustomed to dealing with a student through an interpreter. For example, the teacher should look at the student rather than the interpreter when asking a question or receiving a response. The interpreter should not be addressed directly (e.g., "Do you think Dan understood that?") because the interpreter will simply convey those exact words to the student. Interpreters have the responsibility of knowing the communication level of their clients and modifying syntax and vocabulary accordingly. In technical fields interpreters need to be familiar with specialized vocabulary in order to fingerspell accurately and/or invent appropriate signs for frequently used technical terms.

Innovation and Development

Computer-Assisted Instruction

Microcomputer utilization offers one of the most promising areas for upgrading the education of hearing impaired children and youth. The special characteristics of computer instruction lend themselves to educating hearing impaired children. Computers are a basically visual medium, thus using a communication modality in which deaf students need not be handicapped. In addition, they are interactive, requiring frequent active participation in the learning process; the software may be self-paced; reinforcement and error correction are immediate; and branching in response to error analysis is possible.

Educators of the hearing impaired are just beginning to explore the dimensions of this new medium. At a March 1982 conference on microcomputers in the education of the hearing impaired, papers were presented on computer-assisted instruction as an aid to mainstreaming (Garvey, 1982) and as an adjunct to training in lipreading (Hight, 1982), fingerspelling (Johnston, 1982), reading (Prinz, Nelson, & Stedt, 1982), and math (Bardenstein, 1982).

By interfacing computers with telecommunication devices for the deaf (TDDs), deaf people can access the fast-growing world of electronic mail, bulletin boards, consumer services, and other benefits available to the hearing population, as well as communicate readily with other members of the deaf community. Computers are also being investigated as aids in diagnosis, record keeping, and individualized instruction.

A major challenge to educators in the future will be to enable hearing impaired students to take full advantage of this new and increasingly powerful tool. Computers are a visual medium, but their educational uses depend heavily on the ability to use language, and consequently upon the ability to read and write. Thus, we return again to the major job confronting all who deal with hearing impaired individuals—the development of adequate communication skills.

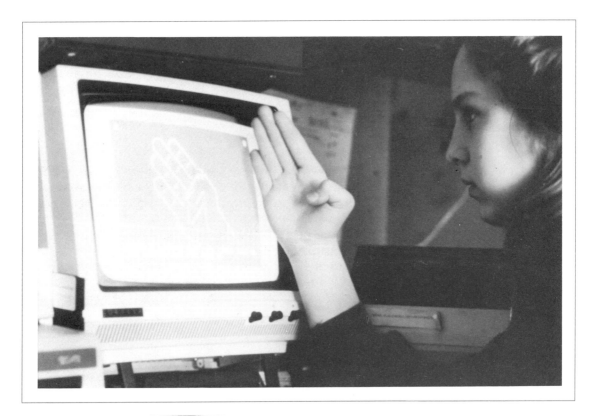

Computer instruction includes training in finger spelling.

Cochlear Implants

A cochlear implant is a device that is surgically placed in the ear. One part, a magnetic coil, is placed under the skin behind the ear. Another coil, an external one, is held in place by the implanted magnet. A wire extends from the implanted coil and ends in an electrode that is placed in the fluid within the cochlea (inner ear). The external coil is connected to an electrical pack that looks much like a body-type hearing aid. This pack can be worn in a variety of ways—in a pocket, on a belt, or in a pouch. A tiny microphone that can be hooked over the ear, clipped to a shirt collar, or worn on a barrette is also attached to the pack that houses the battery power for the system. The microphone picks up sounds that are carried to this pack or signal processor. The processor converts the sounds to electrical signals, which are transmitted through the implanted coils to the electrode in the cochlea, thereby stimulating electrical impulses in the auditory nerve. These impulses are then carried up through the auditory pathways to the brain.

The cochlear implant, unlike a hearing aid, does not change electrical impulses back to acoustical sounds. Rather, electrical impulses are carried directly through the system to the brain. Implant users have stated that sounds heard through an implant are different from sounds heard through a hearing aid. Evaluation for implant surgery involves many tests plus a general physical examination. The surgery to place the implant is usually performed under general anesthesia and involves opening the mastoid (the bony structure within the skull that leads to the middle ear) and the middle ear.

Summary

Sound waves move through the outer, middle, and inner ear and are changed into neural impulses, which are given meaning in the brain. Any interference with the transmission process can result in impaired hearing. A conductive hearing loss results from impairment in the transmission of the sound waves through the outer and middle ear and can usually be corrected. A sensorineural hearing loss results from impairment in the inner ear in the conversion of sound waves into neural impulses; it cannot be corrected. Hearing losses can be genetic or nongenetic—caused by disease or injury. Even a mild hearing loss affects learning; the impact of the loss is determined by a variety of variables. Social development is also affected.

Audiological assessment uses a variety of methods to measure the extent of a hearing loss. Cognitive assessment of hearing impaired children must avoid a linguistic emphasis. Intervention begins with a hearing aid, as early as possible. Thereafter, home-based or center-based programs or a combination of both may be the most effective during early childhood. More and more school-age students with hearing impairments are choosing regular education settings. Interpreters may facilitate mainstreamed placement for older students. Debate continues over the best method of instruction for hearing impaired students: the aural-oral approach or the manual approach. Total communication features both.

Hearing impaired children who receive linguistic input from birth develop language much like their hearing peers. Thus, early input is critical. Later, attention must be directed toward improved reading and writing skills and the provision of practical information. Mainstreamed educational placement must be carefully considered. Computer-assisted instruction offers great promise for the hearing impaired.

Study Questions

1. What is the distinction between a conductive hearing loss and a sensorineural hearing loss?
2. How is hearing measured (a) in adults and older children, (b) in preschool children, and (c) in infants and individuals with severe developmental delays?
3. What are some of the prenatal, perinatal, and postnatal causes of sensorineural hearing loss?
4. Discuss the general characteristics of the severely to profoundly hearing impaired pop-

ulation in terms of (1) intelligence, (2) language development, (3) speech development, and (4) social development.

5. What types of tests are appropriate for assessing (1) the cognitive abilities, (2) the academic achievement, and (3) the language development of hearing impaired children?

6. Describe the philosophy behind the aural-oral approach to educating hearing impaired children.

7. What are the components of total communication? What is the rationale for using this approach to communication?

8. Describe the differences between Manual English, fingerspelling, and American Sign Language.

9. What types of preschool programs are available to hearing impaired infants and their parents? Describe the advantages and disadvantages of each.

10. Discuss the range of placement options available to school-age hearing impaired children.

11. What postsecondary and continuing education options are available to hearing impaired adults?

12. How might regular curricula be modified for developmentally delayed hearing impaired students?

TIPS FOR HELPING

1. Seat the students where they can see your lip movements easily.

2. Do not speak too loudly, especially if the students are wearing hearing aids.

3. Avoid visual distractions, such as excessive makeup and jewelry, that draw attention away from your lips.

4. Avoid standing with your back to a window or bright light source; it throws your face in a shadow and makes speechreading difficult.

5. Avoid moving around the room or writing on the board while speaking. If possible, use an overhead projector, which allows you to speak and write while maintaining eye contact with the class.

7. During class discussions encourage the students to face the speaker even if this requires moving about the room.

7. When a manual interpreter is present, allow the interpreter and the student(s) to select the most favorable seating arrangements.

8. Write assignments and directions on the chalkboard, distribute mimeographed directions, or have a nonhandicapped student take notes on oral directions for hearing handicapped students.

9. Ask the handicapped students to repeat or explain class material to make sure they have understood it.

10. If a student has a hearing aid, familiarize yourself with its operation, but expect the student to assume responsibility for its care.

12

Visual Impairments

Rita Livingston
Illinois State University

The students in the kindergarten classroom are working on a mural. They are spread across the room, each busily coloring a section. Several children in the room have obvious disabilities. One child is visually impaired; however, what readily distinguishes her from her kindergarten peers is not her visual impairment but the fact that she is a head taller.

Angela is a rather quiet, shy student. Because of family circumstances, she is attending her third school this year. This school has a resource room available for children with visual disabilities. Angela is spending all morning with her kindergarten peers in a regular classroom; she will spend the rest of her school day with the resource teacher, who is trained to work with visually impaired children.

When she was about 2 years old, Angela's visual disability was identified. Her parents had noticed that she had difficulty focusing her eyes but were unsure whether there really was a problem. An ophthalmologist confirmed that Angela did have visual problems. However, Angela's parents were not told that educational assistance was available, despite the fact that they were living in a university community that prepares teachers of visually impaired learners. Consequently, Angela received no educational assistance until she entered her present school setting.

As Angela grew, her mother expected her to participate in most of the same activities that her brother enjoyed. For example, Angela was encouraged to play ball games even though she could not always see the ball coming toward her. Thus, she was not overly protected and learned to use her vision quite well. When Angela required plastic surgery after an accident, the surgeon expressed concern that she might have difficulty in school because of her limited vision and insisted that Angela be evaluated by a psychologist and/or educator.

Educational and psychological assessments show Angela to be on grade level in cognitive skills, fine and gross motor development, and auditory skills. Because she is having some difficulty with visual perception and visual motor skills, the teacher of visually impaired learners works with Angela on tasks to promote visual efficiency. According to her teachers, Angela is a fast worker and accomplishes many tasks in one day. By the end of the school day, however, Angela's eyes show signs of fatigue. The teachers alternate near and distance tasks to minimize her eye strain. Even though her eyes are tired, it is not harmful for Angela to use her vision. It would actually be more harmful if she did not. All indications are that Angela can learn visually, but because of her visual fatigue she will be taught listening skills to supplement the vision. In the first grade Angela will be provided with low vision aids— for example, magnifiers to enlarge regular print and a telescope to make overheads, films, and chalkboard work discernible from her seat. Some adaptations will probably be necessary in physical education, particularly for ball sports in which the ball moves at a high rate of speed toward the player (e.g., baseball and tennis).

Angela's teachers will monitor her progress in cognitive, motor, psychosocial, visual, and language skills to be sure that she develops in these areas along with her age peers. As Angela becomes better acquainted with her peers and as her home life begins to stabilize, teachers will be better able to assess her social interactions. As long as she continues to keep pace with her peers, she will probably be spending most of her school day in the regular classroom, while continuing to receive some services from a teacher of visually impaired learners.

Angela is classified is having low vision, a result of underdeveloped retinas. She also has field defects, strabismus (unbalanced eye muscles), and nystagmus (rapidly moving eyes). The images she sees are not clear, nor does she see in all parts of the normal 180° field.

In order to read, Angela will need enlarged print or special magnification devices. She probably will not require a special curriculum, just modification and adaptation of regular materials.

Normal vision is the result of a complex process of coordinated activities, photochemical reactions, and electrical impulses. Light rays, reflected from external images, must be bent, inverted, and focused, then converted into electrical impulses, relayed to the brain, and interpreted. A problem anywhere in the process will affect vision. Children with a visual problem so severe that they need materials other than print are classified as blind. They must learn about the world in different ways from those of their partially or fully sighted peers.

History

Formal education was not an option for individuals with visual impairments until 1784, when Valentin Haüy began the first school for the blind—the National Institute for the Young Blind in Paris. Prior to that time blind individuals either received no education or were educated at home. It was Haüy's ambition to teach blind individuals to read. One of his students, Louis Braille, developed the system of raised dots (braille) used by blind learners today.

In 1829 the first school for blind individuals in the United States was founded in Boston—the New England Asylum for the Blind. It is known today as the Perkins School for the Blind. Samuel Gridley Howe, who became its director in 1831, went to Europe to learn how blind individuals were being educated there. His subsequent report to the board of trustees was insightful and contrary to the prevailing philosophy; he argued that blind children deserved a well-rounded education.

By 1833 two more residential schools opened: the New York Institution for the Blind in New York City and the Pennsylvania Institution for the Instruction of the Blind in Philadelphia. At this point in history all individuals with a significant visual loss were considered blind and were educated through a tactual approach, which included reading braille.

In 1879 Congress passed legislation and appropriated funds establishing the American Printing House for the Blind (APH) in Louisville, Kentucky. APH provided books in both large print and braille, as well as educational materials for visually impaired school-age children. Legislation passed in 1931 allowed the Library of Congress to provide books for blind adults. A few years later recordings of books, "talking books," became available.

Education for visually impaired individuals occurred at home or in private or state residential schools until 1900, when the first public school classroom for blind children was opened in Chicago. In 1905 Cincinnati also established a classroom for blind students. Classes were begun in 1913 for the partially seeing. These classes were known as "sight saving classes" because the prevalent belief at that time was that sight needed to be conserved, that it would be damaged through use.

In 1938 Oakland, California, began the first itinerant program for students with low vision. The growth of such programs was influenced by two factors. First, legislation was passed allowing the students enrolled in local school programs to receive aids and appliances from the American Printing House for the Blind. Secondly, at this same time there was a sharp rise in the population of children who were visually impaired because of retrolental fibroplasia (RLF), and the parents of these children put pressure on local school systems to provide free public education. Nonetheless, residential schools continued to provide education for the majority of visually impaired students until the mid-1970s, when P.L. 94–142 allowed many students from residential schools throughout the country to attend their own local schools.

Definition

Formerly, all individuals with uncorrectable visual impairments were labeled blind, but terminology has changed over time. In this discussion the following definitions will be used:

> *Visual impairment.* Any reduction in central vision, peripheral vision, binocular vision, color vision, or visual accommodation because of malformation, dis-

Prescription lenses aid many visual impairments.

ease, or injury is a visual impairment. Many visual impairments can be corrected through prescription lenses or surgery. When vision is still limited after such interventions, a student may need special services to benefit from the educational process. Such individuals constitute the visually impaired population.

Visual functioning. How people use whatever vision they have is called visual functioning. The level of functioning is related to the amount of vision, motivation, expectations, needs, attitudes, training, and experiences of the individual (Barraga, 1983).

Visual efficiency. For educational purposes visual efficiency refers to "the degree to which the student can perform specific visual tasks with ease, comfort, and minimum time" (Barraga, 1983, p. 25).

Visually limited. Individuals who have difficulty seeing well under average circumstances are visually limited. They are considered to be sighted for educational purposes and in all other circumstances (Barraga, 1983). These individuals may require adaptations such as special lighting, prescriptive lenses, optical aids, or modified materials.

Low vision. Partially seeing is an outdated term that has been replaced by *low vision*. Low vision describes the condition of those students that are "still severely visually impaired after correction, but who may increase visual functioning through the use of optical aids, non-optical aids, environmental modifications and/or techniques (Corn, 1980, p. 3). For such students, near vision may be useful for reading printed materials and performing many school learning activities. Other low vision students may need to use tactual materials and supplement visual reading with braille. The distance vision of these students may be useful for only a few feet or perhaps much farther, depending on the size of the object to be viewed and the environmental conditions. These students need to be made aware of what they are seeing and encouraged to use their vision whenever possible.

Legal blindness. To qualify for services from federal agencies serving persons with visual impairments, an individual must meet the legal definition of blindness, which considers two visual aspects—central visual acuity and peripheral vision. Normal visual acuity is recorded as 20/20. The numerator of this fraction indicates the distance at which the individual can read the letter or symbol, usually on the Snellen Scale (see Figure 12–1). The denominator indicates the distance at which a person with normal vision could read the letter or symbol. Thus, a visual acuity of 20/80 means the person must be 20 feet from the letter or symbol to read what a person with normal vision could read 80 feet away. Legal blindness requires a "visual acuity for distance vision of 20/200 or less in the better eye with the best possible correction or field vision

Figure 12-1   Snellen Scale symbol chart

SOURCE: National Society for the Prevention of Blindness, 79 Madison Avenue, New York, NY 10016. Reprinted by permission.

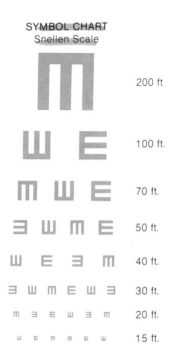

SYMBOL CHART
Snellen Scale

200 ft

100 ft.

70 ft.

50 ft.

40 ft.

30 ft.

20 ft.

15 ft.

no greater than 20 degrees" (National Society to Prevent Blindness, 1966, p. 10). This definition is also a part of P.L. 94–142. Individuals who are visually limited or have low vision may be legally blind.

Legal blindness. To qualify for services from federal agencies serving persons with visual impairments, an individual must meet the legal definition of blindness, which considers two visual aspects—central visual acuity and peripheral vision. Normal visual acuity is recorded as 20/20. The numerator of this fraction indicates the distance at which the individual can read the letter or symbol, usually on the Snellen Scale (see Figure 12–1). The denominator indicates the distance at which a person with normal vision could read the letter or symbol. Thus, a visual acuity of 20/80 means the person must be 20 feet from the letter or symbol to read what a person with normal vision could read 80 feet away. Legal blindness requires a "visual acuity for distance vision of 20/200 or less in the better eye with the best possible correction or field vision no greater than 20 degrees" (National Society to Prevent Blindness, 1966, p. 10). This definition is also a part of P.L. 94–142. Individuals who are visually limited or have low vision may be legally blind.

Educational blindness. In the educational setting *blind* is defined as totally without sight or with light perception only. Light perception is the ability to distinguish the absence or presence of light (Faye, 1970). Educationally blind individuals would be primarily tactile learners and would read with braille or auditory media. The perception of light would be useful in moving through the environment.

Prevalence

Visual impairment affects one of the smallest groups within special education; only approximately .1% of school-age children are visually impaired. Each January the American Printing House for the Blind (APH) surveys school-age children who qualify for service under the legal definition of blindness. Although 41,145 children were registered with APH in 1983, this figure does not reflect all visually impaired children being served in school programs (APH, 1984). It does not reflect numbers in postsecondary programs, and it also may not include children in the 0-to-3 age range. In addition, it is not known how many qualified individuals are not receiving services. In 1983, of the students receiving services in the schools, approximately 80% read printed materials. The remaining students read braille or listened to tapes, records, or human readers. This group included multihandicapped visually impaired students (APH, 1984).

Causes

The most common causes of visual problems relate to malformations or malfunctions of the eye. The cross section of the eye in Figure 12–2 depicts the parts of the eye referred to in the following discussion.

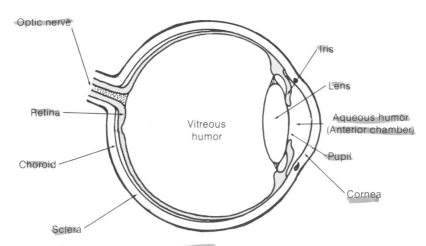

Figure 12-2   Cross section of the human eye

Structure and Function of the Eye

The eyeball is protected by the bony structure of the face and is controlled by six muscles that allow horizontal, vertical, and circular movements. The eyeball is composed of three main layers: the outer protective layer, the middle layer that nourishes the inner layer, and the photosensitive retina.

Light rays enter the eye through the transparent cornea, just behind which is the anterior chamber, filled with a clear fluid—the aqueous humor. The pupil is the opening created by the iris. The iris gives the eye its color and regulates the amount of light that passes through the pupil. Behind the iris is the lens. Slight changes in the shape of the lens alter the refraction of light from objects at different distances to maintain a clear image. The gelatinous vitreous humor helps the eyeball keep its form. Finally, the light rays reach the retina, where they come to a point of focus in the normal eye. The retina contains photoreceptor cells called rods and cones. Rods are more sensitive to movement and low levels of illumination. Cones enable us to see color and fine detail and function in daylight. Impulses travel along the optic nerve to the vision center in the brain. The brain then translates these impulses into a visual image, interprets the image, and gives it meaning.

Refractive Errors   Refraction is the bending of light. A malformation of the eye, lens, or cornea may result in a refractive error. Myopia (nearsightedness) results when the light is focused on a point in front of the retina rather than on the retina itself. The result is blurred vision, particularly for objects at a distance. Hyperopia (farsightedness) occurs when the light is focused on a point behind the retina. Near objects are usually blurred, although distant objects are more clear. When the cornea or lens has an imperfect curvature (waves), the image focused on the retina results in blurred vision; this condition is astigmatism. Many refractive errors can be corrected with eyeglasses or contact lenses.

Accommodation Problems   The lens and muscles of the eye change to assist the refractive process. When this does not occur, blurred vision results. Presbyopia affects many individuals about 40 years old or older, when the eyes no longer accommodate and make reading difficult. Eyeglasses for near visual tasks are usually prescribed.

Muscle Imbalance   An imbalance among the six eye muscles can result in double vision. When the two eyes are unable to focus on the same image, the condition is known as strabismus. In young children the brain may repress the image received from one eye, eventually destroying that eye's ability to function. This condition is known as amblyopia or anopsia ("lazy eye"). When the eyes jump—making rapid, jerky movements in an effort to obtain a single image—the condition is nystagmus.

Color Vision Impairment   An abnormality in color vision diminishes the ability to perceive differences in color. Most commonly this occurs with the red, blue, and/or green hues; and males are more likely to be affected than females. A total absence of color vision is very rare.

Prenatal Conditions   Most prenatal influences are hereditary and include conditions such as congenital cataracts, albinism, congenital glaucoma, myopia, and retinitis pigmentosa. Because the majority of these influences are hereditary, it is important that genetic counseling be available to all family members. Couples need to make informed decisions in their family planning.

When the lens of the eye becomes opaque, preventing the clear passage of light rays, a cataract has formed. Cataracts can be surgically removed and a new plastic lens implanted in place of the defective one. Contact lenses or eyeglasses can be used rather than or in conjunction with the lens implant. Albinism is a disorder that affects the pigmentation of the hair, skin, and/or eyes. Affected individuals often have poor acuity and are severely photophobic (sensitive to light). Glaucoma is the building up of aqueous fluid in the eye. The increased pressure causes damage to the eye tissue, resulting in a loss of vision. Symptoms develop slowly and are difficult to detect at first. One type of glaucoma is also painful. Retinitis pigmentosa, caused by changes in the retina, usually becomes evident about the time of puberty or slightly later. The inability to see well at night often is a preliminary sign, followed by a progressive loss of peripheral vision and central acuity that leads to severe low vision by age 40 to 60. Ushers syndrome is a combination of congenital deafness and retinitis pigmentosa.

Injuries   Retinopathy of prematurity (ROP) accounts for most of the cases in this category. This condition has also been known as retrolental fibroplasia (RLF), but a committee of international medical authorities has recommended that RLF be officially changed to ROP, a more accurate and inclusive term that is currently used by ophthalmologists. ROP is caused by the administration of oxygen at a certain level of concentration over an extended period of time to premature infants of low birth weight. Even though the cause has been known for many years, often the risk of eye damage must be weighed against the risk of death.

Accidents also account for loss of vision, although reports can be misleading. Often only one eye is involved, and the other retains normal vision. The National Society to Prevent Blindness estimates that 90% of all eye injuries could be prevented. It is especially important to enforce safety precautions on playgrounds and to use protective eyewear in such sports as racquetball and handball or in laboratory and shop work.

Neoplasms Eye tumors may be inherited, as in the case of retinoblastoma, a malignant tumor in the retinal layer that affects young children. Other tumors may occur in the brain or pituitary gland and cause damage to the optic nerve or occipital lobe of the brain.

Infectious Diseases Rubella (German measles) has been the leading cause in this category since the epidemic of 1964–65. All women of childbearing age need to determine their level of immunity to this disease prior to pregnancy. During the first trimester of pregnancy, when the eye structures of the fetus are developing, intrusion of the rubella virus can cause numerous abnormalities—hearing impairments, cardiac malformations, and mental retardation in addition to visual defects.

Characteristics

There are many myths concerning the extraordinary abilities of individuals with visual impairments. They are supposedly born with greater musical talent, more acute hearing or sense of touch, or better memory than the general population. Others claim the blind have an innate sixth sense or a naturally pleasant disposition (Lowenfeld, 1973). These myths are perpetuated by the stereotypic attitudes of society. Abilities or traits that happen to be superior in individuals with visual impairments are usually the result of constant use and/or practice. In contrast to the myths, several developmental areas are negatively affected by blindness—cognitive, language, motor, and social. Children with low vision may also exhibit deficits in these areas though not necessarily to the same extent as those individuals without vision from birth (Lowenfeld, 1971).

Cognitive Development

Infants normally learn about their world through imitation and integration of sensorimotor experiences. Children with severe visual limitations are denied the full range of experiences available to their sighted peers, and their early concept development is thus delayed. They cannot learn through imitation, nor can they move about and explore their environment as efficiently and effectively as other infants (Lowenfeld, 1973). In addition, the low vision child who receives blurred images forms faulty and imprecise concepts. Children with a small visual field have other problems. Like blind children they have a difficult time learning about objects and object relationships because the visual information they receive is too limited and fragmented to clarify the nature, function, and relationship of objects. This delay in forming the initial object concept affects the acquisition of other concepts—object permanence, causality, and spatial relationships—which, in turn, affects the acquisition of higher order skills, such as classification and conservation. Nonetheless, despite the delayed acquisition of all of these concepts during the preschool years, by school age (assuming early intervention) most are functioning at or only slightly below the levels of their sighted peers (Stephens & Grube, 1982).

Language Development

One consequence of the early concept delays is delayed language development. Although early vocalizations and verbal imitation may emerge at the expected ages, spontaneous word production may be delayed by 4 or more months (Fraiberg, 1977). In addition, some blind children develop verbalisms, which are words used without appropriate underlying concepts (Harley, 1963). For example, a child might know that mother uses a mixer when she bakes a cake, might understand what the mixer does, and might describe the sound, but when a mixer is placed in his hands, he might call it an iron. Like cognitive development the language development of severely visually impaired children progresses at a slower rate, but delays lessen significantly or disappear altogether by school age.

Motor Development

Loss of vision in and of itself does not retard motor development, but it does influence it (Fraiberg, 1977). As the realization develops that the hands are connected to the arms and that control of those limbs comes from within, the concept of body image begins to emerge. Movement and a fascination with objects develop early in the normal infant, as do hand coordination and imitation of body movements (Fraiberg, 1968). Although visually impaired children eventually develop spatial concepts, this area requires continuing educational intervention. The better the child's vision, the easier she is to teach (Fraiberg, 1968). Good body image forms the basis for learning to structure external space (Cratty & Sams, 1968). Acquisition of concepts of distance, directionality, laterality, body position in space, object position in space, and safe movement through space in familiar and unfamiliar environments usually requires direct intervention. Blind children may exhibit abnormal motor expressive skills, such as gait and posture, if early intervention does not occur (Cratty & Sams, 1968; Gibbs & Rice, 1974). Continued emphasis on movement and the development of gross motor skills is important throughout the elementary school years to enhance general physical health and to build the upper body strength necessary for reading braille or using optical aids.

Social Development

Blind individuals are handicapped more by the attitudes of others than by their visual impairment (Koestler, 1976; Scott, 1969). Four common attitudes toward individuals who are blind or "less fortunate" have been identified: "pity, because the individuals are seen as helpless, unhappy, or tragic figures; fear, because it could

Practice in fine motor skills.

happen to me or it might be catching; guilt, because I have not done enough for the blind; and discomfort, because many people do not know how to interact with a blind person" (Lowenfeld, 1975, pp. 245–246). One of Helen Keller's statements speaks to this issue: "Not blindness, but the attitude of the seeing to the blind is the hardest burden to bear" (Lowenfeld, 1975, p. 242). These attitudes interfere with the ability of blind persons to learn and practice the social skills that lead to interpersonal effectiveness.

One of the most influential factors in the child's social development is parental attitudes, which are, in turn, affected by the manner in which they are told about their child's visual impairment and the impressions they receive from the professional who first identifies the problem. Other factors affecting parental attitudes are the severity of the impairment and the etiology. Parents who believe their child has no vision adopt a pessimistic stance. If the eye condition is hereditary, there may be feelings of guilt and depression.

Young visually impaired children are often unable to participate in the nonverbal interactions so essential in establishing emotional bonds and learning appropriate social behavior (Warren, 1984). Totally blind children are often quiet and passive as infants, and they may not smile back at their parents or may smile at inappropriate times. They need to be cuddled and played with, but their responses to such affectionate overtures may not be the expected and may be misinterpreted. Parent-child play must be fostered through parental intervention because even play skills develop at a different rate in children with visual impairments. They display less creative and more functional uses for their toys than do their sighted peers (Parsons, 1982).

As these children mature, unhealthy parental attitudes contribute to the development of a negative self-concept. Attitudes of peers, teachers, and social agencies also affect the self-esteem of visually impaired individuals and thus their ability to function as productive members of society. One contributing factor is performance expectations, which may be either too high or too low.

Assessment

Many children with visual impairments are identified through routine examinations in day-care centers and preschool programs. Others are not identified until third or fourth grade, when the print size typically decreases and textbook formats become more complex. Alert teachers and parents can spot possible eye problems in their students and children by careful observation. Table 12–1 lists the possible trouble signs suggested by the National Society to Prevent Blindness (1977).

Vision screening in schools is an important practice and one supported by the National Society to Prevent Blindness. Some states require vision tests for all incoming students as well as students in selected grades. The most important screening instrument is one that measures visual acuity, such as the Snellen Scale

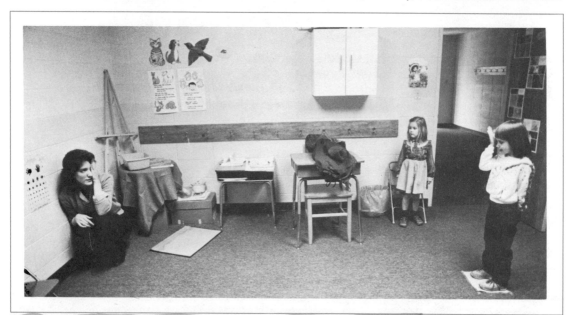

Early identification of visual impairments allows prompt and effective intervention.

Table 12-1 Signs of possible eye problems

Behavior

Rubs eyes excessively
Shuts or covers one eye, tilts head or thrusts it forward
Has difficulty reading or doing other work requiring close use of the eyes
Blinks more than usual or is irritable when doing close work
Is unable to see distant things clearly
Squints eyelids together or frowns

Appearance

Crossed eyes
Red-rimmed, encrusted, or swollen eyelids
Inflamed or watery eyes
Recurring sties

Complaints

Itching, burning, or scratchy feeling in eyes
Inability to see well
Dizziness, headaches, or nausea following close eye work
Blurred or double vision

shown in Figure 12–1. Screening usually involves tests for central visual acuity in both eyes, a test for astigmatism, and a test for strabismus. A test for hyperopia and a measure of near-point visual acuity may also be included to assess useful vision for reading. Several different materials or devices may be used—from wall charts or hand-held cards to more complicated tools or projectors.

If vision screening does reveal a problem, the next step is an eye examination, usually by an ophthalmologist, a medical doctor who specializes in the diagnosis and treatment of all defects and diseases of the eye. The ophthalmologist may prescribe lenses and/or medication, perform surgery, or carry out other medical treatment. Other vision specialists may also be involved. An optometrist is a licensed nonmedical practitioner who measures refractive errors, prescribes lenses, and fits contact lenses. An optician grinds the lenses prescribed by the ophthalmologist or the optometrist and may fit the lenses into frames and adjust the frames to the wearer.

Children with low vision may be referred to a low vision clinic to determine whether their visual efficiency can be increased through the use of special lenses, magnifiers, telescopic lenses, or electronic aids. If a special device is indicated, its proper use is taught at the clinic. Follow-up visits are scheduled to address any problems and to reassess the usefulness of any aids as eye conditions and individual needs change.

Functional Vision Assessment

Children in programs for the visually impaired have a wide range of visual abilities, which are affected by a number of factors: age of onset, level of visual acuity, nature of the condition (stable, fluctuating, or deteriorating), chronological age, other handicapping conditions (especially hearing loss), and motivation. Age of onset is a particularly important factor. Vision early in life facilitates a normal rate of concept development, motor development, and socialization; the child who had vision as an infant has some visual imagery, even if vision later deteriorates or is lost. The level of visual acuity and the nature of the condition also affect functioning. Stable conditions, slow deterioration, or sudden loss all have psychosocial implications. In addition, chronological age, the interaction of other handicapping conditions, personal motivation, and the expectations of others will all affect the individual's use of vision.

A functional vision assessment attempts to determine how well a student uses her available vision. It usually employs an informal checklist completed by a professional or group of professionals prepared to work with visually impaired learners. Members of the assessment team—which may include a teacher of visually impaired learners, an orientation and mobility specialist, a low vision specialist, and/or a low vision optometrist—observe the child in as many settings as possible.

A comprehensive functional vision assessment was developed by the Northern California Ad Hoc Committee on Assessment (Roessing, 1982). This criterion-referenced checklist includes skills necessary for academic tasks, mobility, and activities of daily living related to cooking and cafeteria use. The Program to Develop Efficiency in Visual Functioning (Barraga, 1983) has a low vision observation checklist and a diagnostic assessment procedure (DAP), which assesses a broad spectrum of visual abilities in a developmental sequence. Lesson plans are also available to teach needed skills.

Children with multiple handicaps present a special challenge for visual assessment. The Functional Vision Inventory for the Multiply and Severely Handicapped (Langley, 1980) is one example of an instrument for this population. The examiner uses a variety of stimuli and multiple trials to collect information about structural defects and behavioral abnormalities, reflexive reactions, eye movements, near vision, distant vision, visual field preference, and visual perception. To assess the motor, sensory, concept, and mobility skills of blind or low vision multihandicapped students, the Peabody Mobility Scale is useful (Harley, Wood, & Merbler, 1981).

General Assessment Considerations

There are several general assessment considerations when a child with a visual impairment is being evaluated. Factors related to the examiner, the environment, and interpretation of results may need closer attention than they would with a nonvisually impaired student.

Examiner Visually impaired students may be very distracted by odors. Strong scents of perfume or after-shave can present a problem. For low vision students bright colors or vivid patterns should be avoided; high contrast stripes tend to create the illusion of waves. In addition, the examiner must know the child well enough to make appropriate decisions regarding prescribed time limits, the orientation of the material (to maximize visual efficiency), use of visual aids and a defined space, as well as signs of visual fatigue.

Environment   Distractions should be kept to a minimum. Visual "noise" should be considered, too—clutter of irrelevant objects or pictures in the room, patterned working surface. Lighting conditions are also critical. Individual preferences and habits should be maintained. Glare should be avoided from light sources and from paper, such as glossy laminated cards. These considerations should be carried over to the classroom also.

Interpretation of Results   The evaluator's attitudes, beliefs, and values relative to visually impaired learners can influence the assessment procedures in subtle but profound ways. Mannerisms need not be considered unless they actually interfere with the completion of a task. However, the assessment instrument should be carefully previewed for visual orientation. ("How might a cardinal and an apple be alike?" Expected response: "They are both red.") The impact of the child's impairment must always be a primary consideration. Because of the heterogeneity of the visually impaired population, norms are difficult to establish for the instruments that have been developed for use with these individuals. Thus, the trend has been to use assessment results in planning appropriate intervention strategies rather than in comparing students. Swallow, Mangold, and Mangold (1978) have developed informal checklists on a broad range of developmental skills uniquely important for visually impaired learners. Included are such areas as visual functioning, unique academic needs, orientation and mobility, vocational skills, self-help, language, cognition, and psychomotor abilities.

Age-Level Distinctions

Early Childhood   In addition to vision, major assessment areas for young children include motor, social, conceptual, play, and speech/language development. Motor assessments should consider gross and fine motor skills and body image (the knowledge of body parts and the relationship of one's body to objects in space). The level of play skills as well as the functional and creative use of toys is usually assessed through observation. Visual efficiency is a critical factor to be monitored through all assessment procedures. Also, during the reading readiness phase the Roughness Discrimination Test (Nolan & Morris, 1965) may be given to potential braille readers. This assessment determines a student's ability to discriminate differences in textures in preparation for reading the braille characters. For potential visual readers size of print, spacing of letters, and level of visual fatigue become factors to be assessed. The Maxfield-Buchholz Social Maturity Scale for Blind Preschool Children (1957) is a standardized measure of social competency from birth to age 6. For visually impaired children with additional disabilities, the Revised Peabody Mobility Scale (Harley, Wood, & Merbler, 1981) can be used to assess motor, sensory, concept, and mobility skills.

School Age During the school years assessment often focuses on academic skills. General intelligence is often assessed through the verbal portion of the Wechsler Intelligence Scale for Children, Revised (WISC-R). For those students with enough vision the entire battery can be given. The Stanford Achievement Test (SAT) and Wide Range Achievement Test (WRAT) are two academic skill assessments available in braille and large print. With all assessment instruments the quality of braille transcription or print should be carefully evaluated prior to administration.

Secondary/Transition Most secondary students follow one of two educational options: college preparation or career/vocational training. Because visually impaired adults as a group are employed at a lesser rate than the general population (Kirchner & Peterson, 1979), secondary school or rehabilitation programs should emphasize skills needed to compete in the work force, as well as academics. Adequate or better-than-average job skills are not enough when self-confidence and interpersonal skills are inadequate. Likewise, those students interested in college must achieve more than academic success: they, too, must acquire the positive personal characteristics necessary for later entry into the work force. Therefore, assessment should focus on level of independence, mobility skills, self-esteem,

An enthusiastic workshop employee devises systems to keep track of things.

communication skills, grooming and personal hygiene, and personal mannerisms. Roessing (1982) has developed checklists to screen many of these skills at the secondary level. Many vocational assessments designed for sighted students can be used with visually impaired learners with few modifications (Scholl & Schnur, 1976).

Intervention

Special Equipment/Aids/Devices

Intervention with visually impaired learners often requires the use of special equipment, aids, and devices to make learning accessible and meaningful.

Optical aids for low vision learners include magnifiers, telescopes for viewing at a distance, and closed-circuit televisions (CCTV). Magnifiers can be mounted on the student's desk, held by hand, or attached to the head. Telescopes can be either monocular or binocular and can be mounted on glasses or held by hand. CCTVs use a camera to enlarge print that is displayed on a television screen. Letters can be magnified so greatly that one letter fills the entire screen. That much magnification is not very functional for reading but could be helpful in noting a specific

Closed-circuit television helps students with limited or low vision.

detail in a picture or drawing. Proper use and care of these aids must be taught. Nonoptical aids can be beneficial also. For example, a black felt-tip pen rather than a pencil makes greater contrast between the paper and the print; yellow acetate over a purple ditto increases legibility.

A typewriter is also an important aid for visually handicapped students. At the upper elementary, middle school, and secondary levels, the majority of these stu-

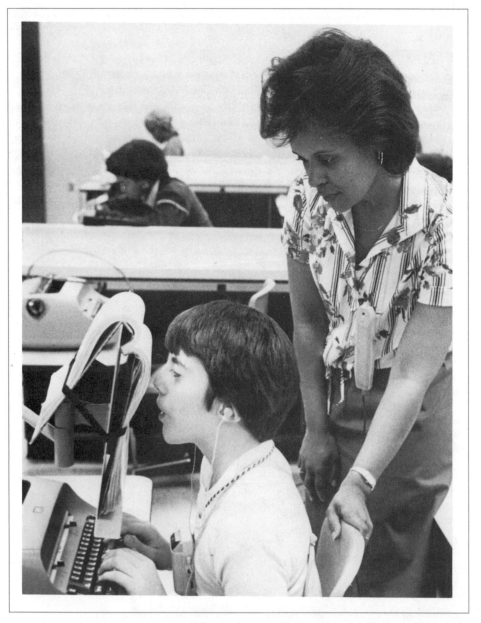

A sight and hearing impaired student uses special equipment in a regular typing class.

dents complete all assignments on a conventional typewriter. Instruction usually begins in about third or fourth grade and is often presented in conjunction with spelling instruction since there is considerable repetition in these areas.

Cassette recorders are used to take notes and to listen to taped books and lectures. Because visual or tactual reading is much slower for a visually impaired learner, auditory aids can increase speed without loss of comprehension. Modified recorders are available through APH to all registered visually impaired students. Talking book machines are modified record players used to play books recorded on discs, "talking books." Cassette tapes are beginning to replace the more cumbersome talking books.

Braille is a tactual language system. The basic braille unit, or cell, has potentially six dots in two columns and three rows. Each cell has a tactually distinguishable raised-dot pattern that represents a graphic symbol (see Figure 12–3). Two grades of braille are commonly used in the United States. Braille Grade 1 uses full spelling and consists of the letters of the alphabet, numbers, punctuation signs, and other signs unique to braille. Braille Grade 2 is a contracted system much like shorthand. It consists of Grade 1 braille plus 185 contractions and short-form words (e.g., the letter *c* stands for the word *can*, and *braille* is written *brl*), and it is used for most printed material. One configuration of dots within a cell can have several meanings, depending upon its position within the word. In the following sentence this configuration (⠲) has five separate meanings.

(Do)   (dis) a p p e (ar)   (be)(fore)   d a (dd) y   f (in) d s   (you)   (here)

Braille is written with a brailler (also called a braillewriter) or a slate and stylus. A brailler is a six-key machine that is manually operated. It types braille and is used for setting up math problems in addition to composition and notetaking. The slate and stylus is not so easy to use but is much quieter. The slate is a metal frame, like a template, with openings the size of braille dots; the stylus is a pointed

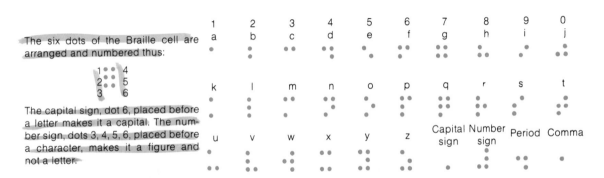

The six dots of the Braille cell are arranged and numbered thus:

1 ● ● 4
2 ● ● 5
3 ● ● 6

The capital sign, dot 6, placed before a letter makes it a capital. The number sign, dots 3, 4, 5, 6, placed before a character, makes it a figure and not a letter.

Figure 12-3   Braille alphabet and numbers

SOURCE: From the Division for the Blind and Physically Handicapped, Library of Congress, Washington, DC 20542.

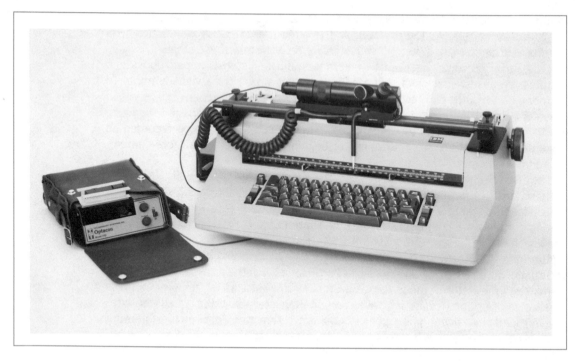

The Optacon adapts for use with other aids.

object used to emboss the dots. The slate and stylus are used most often for classroom notetaking. The braillewriter is a little cumbersome to carry around; the slate and stylus can be carried in a pocket or a large pencil case. The Cranmer Modified Perkins Brailler is a microcomputer added to the Perkins brailler. It can be interfaced with another microcomputer to become a braille printer or used as a separate unit. Because of the modifications it is capable of printing graphics.

There are two devices for electronic reading. The Kurzweil Reading Machine is a computerized system that converts printed materials into synthetic speech. The user places a book or other printed material face down above a scanner. The device automatically locates the first line of the text, and within a few minutes an electronic voice begins reading the material. Reading rate can be adjusted and words can be spelled out letter by letter if the user so desires. The Optacon, an optical-to-tactile-converter, is more widely used than the Kurzweil because it is portable, not much larger than a cassette tape recorder. The user moves a tiny camera across a line of print with one hand and reads the machine-produced letters with the other. The Optacon does not convert print to braille, as some mistakenly assume; it produces raised letters. As would be expected, reading speed is limited, but most feel that this disadvantage is far outweighed by the ability to gain independent access to a wide range of reading material (such as personal letters) that would otherwise be unavailable. Accessories are available to adapt the Optacon for use with a computer, an electronic calculator, a typewriter, and extremely small print.

The Cranmer abacus is an American adaptation of the Japanese abacus. A pocket-sized device that allows the user to perform advanced arithmetic calculations, the abacus is an invaluable aid for visually handicapped students. It permits much faster calculations than are possible with a brailler or a slate and stylus. A simple version of the abacus is the numberaid, which is used in the primary and early intermediate grades. Another device used in mathematics instruction is the cubarithm. It has a square frame surrounding a matrix of cells (16 × 16), into which small cubes fit. Each cube has braille digits on five of its faces and can be positioned into any cell for mathematical computation. Recent technological advances have also produced talking calculators that say the number or operational key that has been depressed as well as whatever answer has been calculated.

Technological devices to assist the visually impaired in independent travel include the Sonicguide, the Laser Cane, and the Mowat Sensor, which were introduced in chapter 2. The Sonicguide is an electronic mobility aid that transmits information about the locations and qualities of objects in the environment by means of high-frequency sound waves radiated from eyeglass frames. The user interprets the reflected sound waves through small ear tubes. Unfortunately, the Sonicguide does not detect drop-offs, so it must be used in conjunction with a cane or a guide dog. The Laser Cane has three thin beams of laser light that emit auditory and tactile signals to alert the traveler to drop-offs, obstacles directly ahead, and objects between chest and head height. The Mowat Sensor is a small, handheld instrument that conveys information about the travel path by means of vibratory signals.

There are numerous special materials and aids that are less exotic than the electronic devices described here but no less valuable to visually impaired students. These include audible sports equipment (balls and goal locators) for physi-

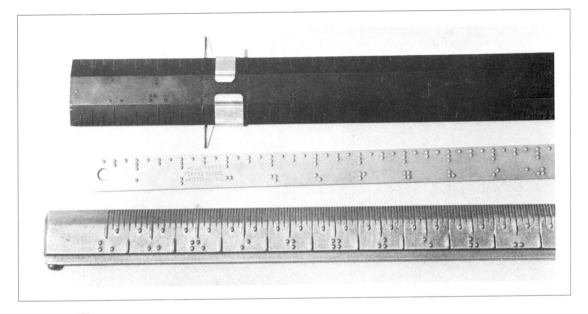

Braille rulers.

cal education as well as relief maps, globes, and braille atlases for the study of geography. Special science materials include science measurement kits with thermometers, spring balances, gram weights, and gravity specimens and simple machine kits with working models of pulleys and levers. There are also braille clocks and wristwatches, braille rulers, and even modified games such as Scrabble, bingo, checkers, and Parcheesi.

Age-Level Distinctions

Early Childhood Educational programs serving ages 0 to 3 focus on the parent as the teacher. In a home-based program an educational specialist visits the home and provides information about the developmental effects of impaired vision, available services, and support networks. Additionally, the specialist suggests activities that can minimize the effects of the impairment, provides instructional materials, demonstrates teaching strategies, observes and records the child's progress, and counsels the parents. Recommendations and activities are guided by each child's assessment results and IEP objectives.

Programs for toddlers and preschoolers are usually center based; the children (sometimes with their parents) are served in one location. The staff usually includes a counselor, an orientation and mobility specialist, a physical and/or occupational therapist, and a teacher. Often there are support group meetings for parents, and information about other resources such as community and state agencies is available. Many school districts have either home- or center-based programs; some use a combination of these approaches.

Many states provide public school services for visually impaired children as soon as they are 3 years old. These programs are most often preschool classes on public school campuses. The focus is to develop the skills necessary for school success. Efficient use of vision, gross and fine motor skills, socialization, positive self-esteem, mobility, and preacademic concepts are emphasized.

School Age There are numerous service delivery options for school-age visually impaired students. In regular classrooms they may be served by consulting teachers or itinerant teachers. Consulting teachers work closely with regular classroom teachers to individualize instruction for each impaired child. They recommend instructional methods and provide adapted materials and optical aids as needed. A disadvantage of this model is travel time. Since consulting teachers serve children in different schools and/or school districts, they usually spend considerable time traveling between schools. Unlike consulting teachers, who do not work directly with the students, *itinerant teachers* provide direct services. They teach specialized skills such as braille reading, use of the abacus and optical aids, activities to promote more efficient use of vision, and orientation and mobility. Like consulting teachers itinerant teachers serve several schools, and they often provide in-service training for regular teachers and administrators.

Some visually impaired students divide their time between a regular classroom and a resource room. A *resource room* is a specially equipped classroom where

Learning dexterity.

students receive specialized instruction in braille reading, typing, the use of slate and stylus for braille writing, the use of adapted or special equipment and aids, listening and daily living skills, and orientation and mobility. Instruction in the resource room also emphasizes visual efficiency and prevocational and vocational skills. An advantage of the resource setting is that expensive or large pieces of equipment and materials and other resources are concentrated in one location for use with several students. Many resource room teachers also assume responsibility for student and parent counseling.

Self-contained classrooms for visually handicapped students are much less prevalent than they were 10 years ago. A primary disadvantage of such classes is the reduced opportunities for visually impaired students to interact with their sighted peers. The teacher in such a setting is responsible for the entire curriculum. Typically students educated in a self-contained classroom are multihandicapped.

Most *residential schools* are state-supported facilities providing education, housing, and limited medical care for visually impaired residents. Whenever possible, resident students participate in local public school programs, where they may be served in resource rooms or self-contained classrooms. Since many students attending residential schools are multihandicapped, the latter arrangement is more common. There is some evidence of a promising national trend related to residential schools. As more visually impaired students are being educated in their own communities, residential schools are being reorganized to function more as a statewide resource. Because these schools can concentrate all their resources on the education of visually impaired children, they are able to provide assessment and training opportunities that may be unavailable in local districts. Many residential schools are now providing special short-term placements so that visually impaired learners can receive intensive training in specific skills—for example, mobility, activities of daily living, and use of the abacus and technological equipment. Even though the cascade model of least restrictive placement considers the residential school as the most restrictive, it is a viable educational alternative for short-term placements.

Secondary/Transition   Visually impaired college-age students and adults are eligible for services through state agencies that receive federal support. Most of the adults served have recently experienced a loss of vision, usually through trauma or disease. State departments of rehabilitation often provide centers where clients live for a short time to receive training in specific skill areas. Assistance is given in locating and using community, state, and federal resources and in securing employment. Some rehabilitation agencies also provide college preparation courses. However, most clients tend to be middle-aged or older and are more in need of assistance in daily living skills and adjustment to their impairment.

Curriculum Implications

The educational system's responsibility to visually impaired learners is the same as it is to nonimpaired students—to assist development and learning in academic, social, and physical domains. Compensatory instruction in any of these areas, as well as the use of special equipment and aids and the development of special materials will usually be assumed by certified special education personnel. Other instructional needs are the same for visually impaired students and their sighted peers and can be met by regular classroom teachers.

Age-Level Distinctions

Early Childhood   The broad goal of early education for young visually impaired children is to strengthen the unimpaired sensory channels. Special attention is given to the auditory, kinesthetic, tactual, olfactory, and gustatory senses in all activities. Cognitive and language training activities, for instance, use actual objects rather than plastic replicas. The object labels are always identified while the children explore the objects themselves tactually; many examples of different object concepts are provided so that the children learn the varied physical properties of objects. If you were to walk into a preschool classroom when the topic was fruit, you would see many different types of fruit and many examples of each type. The children might be tactually exploring some of the whole fruit, smelling and tasting smaller pieces of the fruit, or drinking fruit juice while the teacher calls their attention to similarities and differences in textures, tastes, and smells. Later they might take a field trip to a fruit market or grocery store and a fruit orchard.

Many self-care skills must also be taught at this age. Teachers take special care to explain to visually impaired children what is happening and what is going to happen at every step in any process. You might hear a teacher say, "I am placing the peanut butter jar in your left hand and the knife in your right hand. I am going to put my hand over yours on the knife to help you scoop some peanut butter from the jar. Then I will give you a cracker and help you spread it with peanut butter." Children with visual impairments are taught to take care of their toileting needs independently, and they are trained in basic grooming skills. Personal care items such as toothbrushes, combs, and hair brushes are marked with tactile identification so that the children can find their own items. They also learn the sounds and functions of personal and home-care devices, such as an electric razor, a blender, a vacuum cleaner, and a dishwasher.

One objective of fine motor training is to facilitate appropriate searching and grasping behaviors. Because young visually impaired children tend to use their hands in broad, sweeping motions, they fail to acquire precise search and grasp skills. The consequence, weak hands and fingers, is remediated by manipulation of clay and playdough and use of such objects as squeeze toys, busy boxes, and formboards with holes to finger. Spatial orientation is developed through play with blocks, nesting cups, pegboards, puzzles, and Tinker Toys. Potential braille users are prepared for reading by instruction in the shape of the basic braille cell and development of tactile discrimination, finger dexterity, hand and finger movements, light finger touch, the concept of book and page positions, and page-turning skills.

Gross motor activities teach children to reach for objects, which they do not do naturally because they do not see interesting things around themselves. Initially, sound-producing objects are used for these activities. Also, it is often necessary to teach transfer of objects from one hand to the other and use of both hands for handling some objects. In addition, early intervention programs use a variety of strategies to help children develop and maintain a positive self-image and learn to get along with others. Sharing, helping, and being polite are as important for visually impaired preschoolers as they are for their sighted peers.

School Age Even though most visually impaired students do not require a special curriculum, all will need at least some curricular modifications and adaptations. Materials must be provided in different media or modified and adapted; if special devices are indicated, students must be trained in their use. In addition, certain specialized areas of instruction must be included as appropriate.

Children with any residual vision are encouraged to use it and must be provided with training in how to use it most efficiently. A significant educational problem for these students is visual fatigue: they must expend a great deal of effort to distinguish the details of print. They should be encouraged to take frequent, short breaks; and their visual activities should be mixed with auditory and motor activities when possible. Also, favorable reading conditions—for example, proper lighting and appropriate print spacing—are critical.

Auditory training is also important for visually impaired students. To make maximum use of auditory instructional materials, they need well-developed auditory attention and discrimination skills. Listening instruction should utilize a variety of listening situations—environmental settings, formal presentations, informal conversations, and audio-reading of talking books and tape-recorded materials.

A smaller number of children require special instruction in braille reading and writing, which is usually begun in the first grade. Grade 2 braille is often taught

Learning to get around and read signs.

from the beginning so that children do not have to learn two distinct systems. Braille readers may be able to use the same basal reading series as their sighted peers since most reading series used in regular classrooms have been transcribed into braille. Initially, writing instruction centers around the use of a brailler; slate and stylus writing is not introduced until about the fifth grade.

The ability to move about independently, safely, and purposefully (mobility) is important for all individuals. Orientation refers to knowing one's position in space and in relation to objects in space. An orientation and mobility (O & M) instructor is trained to develop such skills and can teach visually impaired students movement through the environment, use of environmental cues, travel techniques, use of the long cane (white cane), and problem-solving techniques. Travel encompasses different environments, such as neighborhoods and business sections. When students are ready, they learn to use public transportation in localities where it is available. Knowledge of street patterns, traffic flow, and house numbering systems must also be taught to blind students.

Students who are recently impaired not only have to learn new skills and ways of functioning in the educational and home environments, but also have to deal with the psychosocial aspects of their visual loss. Some eye conditions (e.g., retinitis pigmentosa) do not manifest themselves until about the time of puberty and thus compound an already difficult time of life. Such students need the support of educational personnel, family, peers, and perhaps counselors. Peer support and/or parent support groups can often be beneficial.

Young students also need to begin developing the habits and skills that are necessary to maintain a job. Interpersonal skills, grooming, independent mobility, and task completion are examples of prevocational skills. Career awareness and exploration and vocational preparation are subsequent components of career education.

Secondary/Transition   A number of adjustments may be necessary for independent living. The most difficult of these, psychological adjustment, may require the assistance of a counselor. The recently impaired must learn the skills necessary to continue their employment or to be retrained for another job. They must also regain their self-confidence and learn how to care for personal needs and move around safely, efficiently, and purposefully in their environment. Adolescents have a different set of problems. Like their sighted peers, visually impaired adolescents are concerned with peer acceptance, a lack of dates, and an inability to drive. The problems of some students are compounded by the fact that their vision is deteriorating, necessitating more reliance on tactile and auditory learning. This can be a traumatic time psychologically.

High school is also a time when students are thinking of vocational pursuits. Visually impaired students must be informed about potential job opportunities and accompanying skill requirements. They must learn to function and travel independently and have the necessary personal skills to maintain a job. This is also a time when there is more direct contact with social agencies and rehabilitation services serving the visually impaired. Scott (1969) has commented that such agencies often force an individual into the social role of the blind man, much to his own detriment. Societal attitudes still make it difficult for a blind person to find a job, even

Independence in mobility is a skill requiring safety and practice.

when fully qualified and protected by laws prohibiting discrimination on the basis of handicap. Secondary students must begin to be more responsible for meeting their own needs. They must learn about available resources and the methods for ordering their own materials.

As mobility demands increase, a blind individual may choose to use a dog guide. Good orientation and mobility skills are still necessary since the dog can only follow the commands given by the owner. Several weeks of training are required before an owner and dog can safely travel together. State and local legislation does allow dog guides to accompany their masters into places where animals are normally not permitted (restaurants, hospitals, airplanes, hotels). However, individuals under 16 years of age and those with multiple disabilities are usually not permitted to obtain a dog guide.

Mainstreaming

Visually impaired students have been mainstreamed since the early 1900s. However, this system of education has not been without its problems. Careful attention must be given to the overall development of the visually impaired individual, par-

Model Program

The Austin Independent School District (A.I.S.D) serves visually impaired children and youth from birth through age 21. The program has several components: infant/parent (combined home- and center-based program), early childhood/special education (center based), elementary (itinerant and resource/self-contained), junior high (itinerant and resource), and high school (itinerant). In addition, a separate school program is available for multihandicapped visually impaired students. The A.I.S.D. program is comprehensive and is supported by extensive equipment and materials.

Itinerant staff members provide consultation to the regular classroom teachers and direct services to the visually impaired student. The itinerant teachers are more than academic tutors, although they may provide some instruction in reading and math. These teachers are responsible for instruction in visual efficiency, use of optical aids, concept development, social/emotional development, typewriting, listening skills, and more. For blind students, instruction is provided in the use of technology (Optacon, VersaBraille, computers, Cranmer Modified Perkins Brailler). Itinerant teachers also make sure that each student has the necessary materials and tangible aids to participate fully in the ongoing classroom activities. The secondary itinerant teacher helps students work toward greater levels of independence while providing assistance as needed. Career/vocational options are explored with the students, and assessments for vocational placement or college entrance are monitored. As new technology becomes available, the teacher instructs students on proper use and care.

Resource teachers are housed in one school, where they make every effort to ensure a successful mainstream experience. Some students have additional handicapping conditions that necessitate their spending almost the entire school day with the resource teacher. However, most participate in the regular classroom for a major part of the day.

The orientation and mobility instructors work with low vision and blind students to help them move safely, efficiently, and purposefully through their various environments. Orientation to the school building is of primary importance. Then additional skills are added, such as cane travel within the school, residential neighborhoods, business districts, and malls. Use of public transportation and movement within unfamiliar environments are taught also. Each skill is introduced according to the individual student's level of mastery and need.

The counselor for the visually handicapped program serves all levels. The younger children meet in groups to explore feelings and values. Older students may need individual sessions regularly or periodically to work on psychosocial needs. The counselor also works with the parents and siblings of visually impaired students.

ticularly the ability to live independently and become a contributing member of society. It will take the concerted efforts of all school personnel, students, and parents to make mainstreaming a positive experience for everyone involved (Orlansky, 1979). For school personnel multimedia materials such as *Good Start!* (AFB) provide information to assist in this endeavor. Materials available for regular classroom teachers give helpful suggestions for teaching visually impaired learners. *When You Have a Visually Handicapped Child in Your Classroom: Suggestions for Teachers*

(Martin & Hobin, 1977) tells teachers about what special devices a visually impaired child can use, how the child will work with printed materials, what services a teacher of visually impaired learners will provide, and what additional resources are available.

Personal care, independent living, financial planning, communication and socialization, human sexuality, and vocational preparation are areas that can easily be neglected when energy is focused on academic skills. When all such decisions are made by teachers and parents, visually impaired students become dependent, compliant, and docile individuals (Hatlen, 1979). Visually impaired students need to be able to organize their own space and time. Because these areas of concern are not generally a part of regular school curricula, it becomes important for teachers of the visually impaired to ensure that they are incorporated into each student's programming.

Innovation and Development

The explosion in technology has had an impact on access to the printed word. Computer programs are now available that transcribe print into Grade 2 braille. With appropriate software, an Apple IIe, a voice synthesizer, VersaBraille, and the Cranmer Modified Perkins Brailler, a braille reader and a print reader can quickly and efficiently communicate with each other. Braille writers in regular classrooms no longer need to wait for someone to transcribe their papers so that the teacher can grade them. And the classroom teacher can type worksheets or other information into the computer and have it printed in braille in a matter of minutes, rather than waiting for a day or more for the braillist to transcribe it. At this time such units are expensive, but the cost becomes more reasonable if a number of students are using the system.

Technological advances have also altered the vocational opportunities for visually impaired individuals. Monitors that display large print for low vision persons have opened job areas heretofore inaccessible. The visually impaired can now compete in the job market for positions as reservation clerks, computer programmers, and word processors. The challenge lies in convincing the business community that visually impaired workers are as qualified as their nonimpaired counterparts.

Biomedical advances also continue to aid visually impaired individuals. New surgical techniques are being refined. Artificial sight may even be possible for some blind individuals in the future. This innovation—implanting electrodes in the brain and connecting them to a small camera in an artificial eye—is in the early experimental stage. Eventually, it may be possible to provide the blend with a visual "prosthesis." And optics are being refined to allow higher quality magnification with less distortion around the edges and thus a larger field of vision.

Early intervention from birth to age 3 is receiving increased emphasis. The focus on utilization of vision is increasing across all age groups but particularly with young children. In the past, education of visually impaired learners placed an emphasis on the blind, perhaps because their impairment was more obvious. Currently the unique needs of low vision students are receiving more emphasis in teacher preparation programs and in service workshops, an appropriate trend since about 70% of the visually impaired population have low vision.

Summary

One of the oldest fields of special education is that of educating visually impaired students. The first school for the blind was opened by Valentin Haüy in Paris in 1784. His student, Louis Braille, devised the tactual form of reading still in use today. In the 1830s schools for the blind opened in the United States. Later the American Printing House for the Blind was established. Still later, significant legislation was passed, providing materials for visually impaired children and adults. Mainstreaming was introduced in the early 1900s.

To qualify for educational services, a visually impaired individual must meet the legal definition of blindness: 20/200 acuity in the best eye with the best correction or a visual field no greater than 20 degrees. Visual impairment is a low incidence disability, comprising about .1% of the school-age population. Refractive errors, lack of accommodation, and muscle imbalance are common among the general population and are usually easily corrected. Prenatal influences are the major cause of visual disabilities. Injuries, neoplasms, and infectious diseases are additional factors.

Individuals with visual impairments are not significantly different from their sighted peers in ability range or personality. However, blindness can affect cognitive, motor, and social development, especially if there is no early intervention. Attitudes of sighted individuals affect the social roles that visually impaired persons are forced to accept.

Vision screening by the National Society to Prevent Blindness can identify children with mild visual impairments at an early age. Teachers should be alert to signs of possible eye trouble. Referrals should be made to eye care specialists, ophthalmologists, or optometrists. Opticians can help with prescription lenses. Functional vision assessments determine how well and for what purposes a visually impaired student is able to use her vision. All assessments are affected by the examiner, the environment, and interpretation of the results.

A wide variety of service delivery systems are used by educators of the visually impaired. Infants are served through either home- or center-based programs. Early childhood intervention is usually center based. School-age students are served by a consulting, itinerant, or resource teacher. They can also be assigned to a self-contained classroom or special school; residential schools provide 24-hour programming. College-age students and adults may receive services through rehabilitation programs.

A number of additions may be made to regular academic curricula so that visually impaired children can receive optimal benefit from their educational experience. Mainstreaming was occurring for visually impaired students years before P.L. 94-142. Student progress must be monitored so that appropriate nonacademic skills are learned to enable these students to interact with and be accepted by their peers. The technology explosion, biomedical advances, emphasis on use of vision, and early intervention programs are all having an impact on the field of education for visually impaired students.

Study Questions

1. Why is visual impairment considered a low incidence disability?

2. Define the following causes of visual impairment: myopia, hyperopia, cataracts, albinism, amblyopia, astigmatism, glaucoma, and retinopathy of prematurity.

3. What is the difference between *educationally blind* and *low vision*?

4. What are the two criteria for legal blindness, and how is the definition used?

5. Define the following terms: *refraction*, *accommodation*, *photophobia*, *nystagmus*, and *color vision*.

6. Describe the following educational aids and tell how they are used: braillewriter, VersaBraille, Cranmer abacus, Optacon, slate and stylus, Kurzweil Reading Machine.

7. What is visual functioning? Visual efficiency? How are they different?

8. What is orientation and mobility?

9. What are the various methods of independent travel used by visually impaired persons?

10. What are the major service delivery models for students with visual impairments?

11. Which developmental areas are affected by a visual impairment? Why?

12. List the general assessment considerations for evaluating a visually impaired individual.

TIPS FOR HELPING

1. Focus on helping the student become independent; make the student accountable for routines and assignments expected of other students insofar as possible.

2. Have the student become familiar with the school and classroom as well as with regular and emergency routes and procedures, preferably before school opens.

3. Teach classmates how to serve as guides by allowing the student to grasp their arms at the elbow and walk with them.

4. Emphasize listening skills and, when possible, eliminate unnecessary, distracting noises in learning situations.

5. Encourage the student to use the sense of touch—to become familiar with objects by handling and feeling them.

6. Help the student gain the maximum benefit from any residual vision; make sure seating and lighting are optimal.

7. Enhance the student's conceptual understanding of the environment by describing people, animals, objects, or events as they are encountered and relating them to the sounds they involve.

8. Expose the student to as many practical experiences as possible and encourage participation in activities; avoid overprotecting the student from minor bumps, bruises, and the insults characteristic among peers.

9. Teach the student how to structure his environment in order to use it effectively; provide specific places for materials and personal belongings.

10. Assume responsibility for teaching curriculum content and identify available resources; specialists will need all the time allotted them to work with the student on specific skills to compensate for the visual handicap.

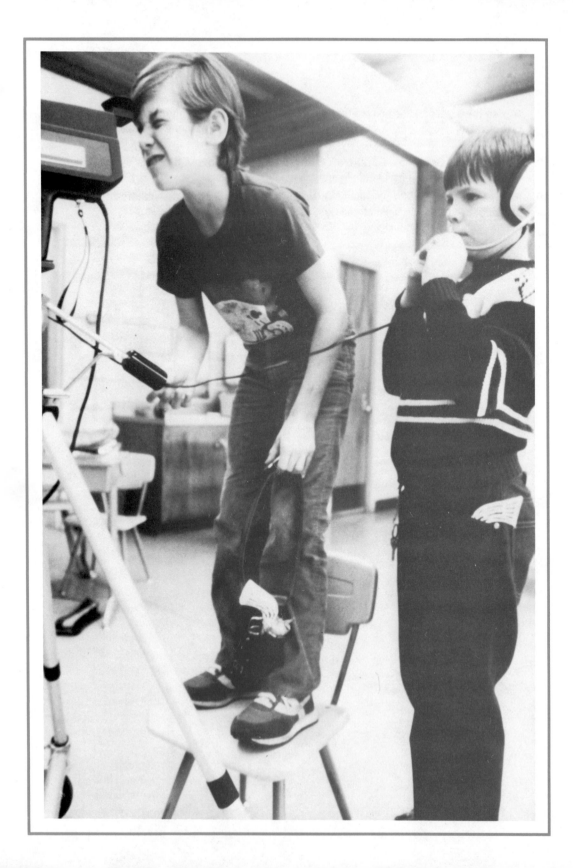

13

Gifted and Talented

Joan S. Wolf
University of Utah

Thomas M. Stephens
Ohio State University

Not only is Lisa classified as academically gifted, she is also talented in music. Her mother noticed that she was able to sing on key at approximately 14 months of age. She sang harmony as a preschooler and could sight-read alto notes in a musical by the time she was in first grade. At 6 Lisa started violin lessons. She progressed rapidly and added piano study at age 8. Lisa attended summer music camp, sang in the chorus in elementary school, played in the orchestra, and presently, as an eighth grader, is in the districtwide honors orchestra, a select group of young musicians in her school district.

Lisa is an unusual gifted child in that she is talented in many areas in addition to music. Her achievement test scores have consistently placed her well above grade level in reading and math skills. In sixth grade, for example, her scores on the Stanford Achievement Test ranged from 8.8 to 12.0

(grade level); she was at 12th-grade level in reading comprehension, listening comprehension, language, social science, and science. Her grades—almost all A's throughout her school career—also reflect her high level of achievement.

Lisa is an outgoing, friendly, sociable, independent girl who gets along well with her peers. She is well rounded with diverse interests. Although music is a great love, she is determined "to have music enrich my life, not dominate it." Some of Lisa's teachers recognized her outstanding ability and made attempts to individualize her instruction. Others were not able to deal effectively with her rapid progress and insisted she submit to drill, rote learning, and repetition. Because Lisa is basically patient and conforming, she coped with these situations by simply doing the work, even though it was often far below her ability level. Anxious to fit in with the other students, she never behaved in a way to call attention to her superior knowledge or abilities.

As a junior high school student, Lisa is enrolled in several advanced courses—notably science, algebra, and French. She continues her violin studies, and her career goals are focused on music. On the basis of Lisa's school career to date, it appears that she could be successful in a number of areas in addition to music. Opportunities for accelerated courses and interaction with other gifted students would be of benefit to her as she continues to explore career options and to develop her varied talents.

Gifted children and youth are so smart that they will make it on their own, say many. Certainly, some, like Lisa, do manage to get the best a system has to offer. But others may not. Many gifted students who are denied opportunities for challenging and stimulating learning experiences fail to realize their potential. Some become dropouts or deviants in a society that has ignored or even abused them. One observer attributes these failures primarily to the social and academic environments of the classroom (Whitmore, 1979, 1980).

Martin, a highly gifted college sophomore, made these comments on his educational experiences. "When I am a parent, I hope not to subject my children to the same sort of public education which I received. In looking back on my experiences, I feel that the values of individuality, creativity, tolerance, and sincerity which I would hope to pass on to my children were actively discouraged by my school environment. Conformity was the key to success both academically and socially,

and the standards to which one was expected to conform were often contrary to both my values and my personality.

"At the time I attended junior and senior high school, I was still attempting to establish a distinct identity, and I felt very threatened by the pressure to conform. I had a strong desire to make progress academically, but the opportunities seemed very limited. I did not have a great deal of respect for many of my teachers, who seemed more interested in passing the time than in teaching anything of significance. The combination of academic frustration and my desire not to conform created a very negative pattern of interaction between me and the school. I did much of my assigned work very haphazardly, if at all. This was easy for me to rationalize because teachers often assigned work that was hard to take seriously: word searches, crossword puzzle games, coloring maps. Then I would become upset when my grade was lowered, feeling that I had learned all that was possible from such a poor class.

"I did not make many friends in school until my junior year. I always felt more comfortable with my parents and their friends than with kids my own age. Although I scorned the kind of personal style necessary for social success in the school environment, I nevertheless found my lack of such success distressing. This added to my dislike of school in general. The worst year was 10th grade. I stopped attending many of my classes altogether and spent most of my time getting stoned. In my junior year fears about getting into college modified my behavior somewhat, and when I was a senior I actually had several stimulating (advanced placement) classes and became a much better student."

Concern for the gifted has waxed and waned throughout our history. Jefferson and his followers believed that trained leadership from the best minds was essential to the survival of a free world. Andrew Jackson's era was noted for its anti-intellectualism, and the attitudes of Jacksonian democracy seemed to prevail in the United States in the 1960s, when gifted education was at a low ebb (Huntington, 1975). Interest in the gifted has come with changing political and economic priorities, reflected in funding support at both state and national levels (Trezise, 1973).

Gallagher (1975) has suggested that present-day athletic programs represent a prototype for one kind of gifted education. Enjoying wide support in urban and rural settings in both small and large districts, they have high acceptance in our schools and are rarely subjected to criticism for exclusionary policies or elitism. Yet they do provide special opportunities for the physically talented—far better opportunities than exist for students whose talents lie elsewhere. Certainly those who are talented physically should continue to be encouraged, but much more commitment to other talents is greatly needed.

History

In the United States there have been three major movements in the education of gifted children and youth. Terman's studies, begun in the 1920s, focused on the intellectually gifted. His definition of giftedness (1925) was limited, based solely on IQ scores from individual intelligence tests. Although the methodology he used has been questioned, his work served to dispel or at least to diminish many of the stereotypes of gifted children prevalent at the time. The image of the physically frail, socially timid, emotionally retarded but intellectually able youngster did not stand up under his scrutiny. The Terman studies were continued by his associates and have been the source of a great deal of information about the gifted.

Programs for the gifted enjoyed increased interest and attention in the Sputnik era of the late 1950s. Science and math programs for the gifted were upgraded; the space race was on and talented scientists and technologists were in great demand. Yet with the advent of the sixties, the focus in education turned to civil rights, the war on poverty, and education of the handicapped.

Interest in the gifted was reawakened in the early 1970s. In 1972 Sidney Marland, the U.S. Commissioner of Education, reported to Congress that many of the estimated 2.5 million gifted students in our elementary and secondary schools were not being served and that more than half of the school administrators surveyed reported that there were no gifted students in their schools. Few could disagree with Marland's description of the gifted as our "most neglected and potentially productive group" (1972, p. ix). As a result of his report, the U.S. Department of Education created the Office of Gifted and Talented, and attention again turned to programs for the gifted.

Legislation and Policy

In 1976 the Special Projects Act provided $2.56 million to fund state and local proposals for service to gifted and talented students, and that amount has continued to rise. State and federal funds now support a wide variety of programs, and an increasing number of teachers are receiving preservice and in-service training

(Sisk, 1978). P.L. 95–561, the Gifted and Talented Children's Act, was signed in 1978, authorizing a minimum appropriation of $50,000 to each state education agency "to assist them in planning, development, operation and improvement of programs designed to meet the educational needs of gifted and talented children" (*Congressional Record*, 1978). Various advocacy groups, including the Council for Exceptional Children (CEC) and the Gifted Advocacy Information Network (GAIN), have been working to obtain increases in the actual level of federal appropriations for services to the gifted so that they more nearly approach the $25 million maximum authorized by Congress. Many states have their own local parent and professional advocacy groups providing information about and support for gifted programs in their communities.

Two important issues shaped programs for the gifted in the 1970s: the use of intelligence tests and the segregation of exceptional children in special classes (Tannenbaum, 1979). The equal rights movement has had a major impact on attitudes toward intelligence tests, especially as their use affected minority students. In some states abuses of IQ tests and reaction to them have resulted in laws barring their use (Tannenbaum, 1979). Grouping practices have also been affected; programs that provided for gifted students by clustering them together have become suspect, and the trend has been toward mainstreaming special students.

For gifted programs to continue to develop, state and local education agencies must recognize their significance. As of 1984, 48 states defined children who are exceptional by virtue of giftedness either in statute or in state education department regulations as a basis for providing programs (Nina Harrison, personal communication, December 26, 1984). Several states require the development of the same formal IEP for the gifted that is mandated for the handicapped in P.L. 94-142. Factors that seem to influence growth and maintenance of state funding for gifted programs are the existence of a full-time consultant in state government, the availability of state funds for local program development, and the existence of teacher-training programs (Sisk, 1978).

In 1981, when the federal government merged 30 separate educational programs into a $471 million block grant, programs for the gifted were among them. The U.S. Department of Education abolished the Office of Gifted and Talented and federal funding for the gifted and talented was reduced as a result, leaving many states struggling to maintain their programs. Professional and parent advocacy groups mobilized to promote more attention for the gifted. These advocacy groups paralleled the many commissions on the status of education in the nation, which called attention to the neglect of gifted and talented students as a major educational issue. These advocacy groups included the Coalition for the Advancement of Gifted Education and the Alliance of State Associations. In recent years the Council for Exceptional Children (CEC), the professional special education association, has increased its advocacy for gifted education.

In 1984 a measure entitled Education for the Gifted and Talented Children and Youth Improvement Act of 1984 was proposed. This bill would provide for federal grants or cooperative agreements with state education agencies to develop exemplary programs within the state and to promote the development and advancement of programs for gifted and talented children and youth through research. It would also provide grants to institutions of higher education and private nonprofit organizations for preservice and in-service teacher training.

Definition

In the past, *gifted* was a term applied primarily to those individuals who, according to intelligence tests, were far above average. The meaning it conveys today has changed somewhat, yet no universally accepted definition has been formulated. Several central issues regarding the nature of giftedness remain unresolved:

- What is intelligence and what role does it play in giftedness?
- What is creativity and what role does it play in giftedness?
- Should giftedness be defined in terms of performance or potential?
- What is talent and how does it pertain to giftedness?

Intelligence

The first problem is the nature of intelligence. Assuming we decide to define giftedness as intelligence far above average, we must then find valid instruments for assessing intelligence across all ages and populations. For years educators have relied on traditional, standardized intelligence tests to evaluate intellectual ability. One of these educators with an enormous impact on programs for the gifted, Lewis Terman, thinks that intelligence is manifested essentially in the ability to acquire and manipulate concepts (1954). Terman defines the gifted as those individuals who score at the upper end of the normal distribution of intelligence—the top 1%. Although the majority of subjects in the Terman study had IQ scores of 140 or above, a Binet score of 132 (2 standard deviations above the mean) was actually the cutoff. Terman's definition of giftedness is rooted in the assumption that intelligence can be measured, an assumption of great significance since it establishes a basis for valid prediction but an assumption that is open to question. Terman carefully distinguishes giftedness from talent and creativity. He views talent as a promise of unusual achievement but only when combined with high IQ scores. Creativity, he believes, is a personality factor different from both giftedness and talent.

Guilford later developed a different approach to the concept of intelligence (1967). He analyzed intelligence in terms of the specific abilities involved and arrived at a model that divides intellectual performance into three dimensions:

1. *Operation*. The categories included are cognition—discovering or recognizing data; memory—retaining newly gained information; divergent production—generating logical alternatives from given information; convergent produc-

tion—generating logical conclusions with emphasis on best response; and evaluation—comparing data to make judgments.

2. *Content.* The content forms in the Guilford model are figural—concrete forms; symbolic—symbols such as letters, numbers, or musical notes; semantic—concepts or ideas; and behavioral— information involving human interaction.

3. *Product.* The possibilities in the model are units—individual units of information; classes—sets of items grouped by common properties; relations—connections between items of information; systems—organized aggregates of information; transformations—changes or modifications in existing information; and implications—expected or predicted connections between items of information.

This model, shown in Figure 13.1, is known as the Structure of Intellect.

Guilford draws distinctions between those dimensions of intellectual performance that are not measured by standardized intelligence tests and those that are. Intelligence tests tend to measure convergent thinking rather than divergent thinking; most classroom activities tap convergent thinking as well. Teachers often have difficulty recognizing those who are divergent and highly creative. Guilford was one of the first to try to isolate characteristics of creative thought processes and to expand the definition of intelligence. Since the development of this model, other researchers have begun to investigate this area.

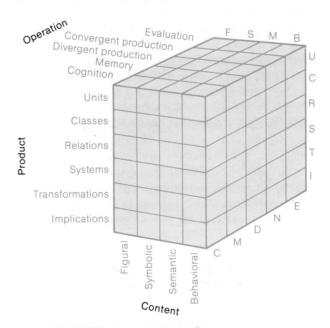

Figure 13-1   Guilford's Structure of Intellect Model

SOURCE: From The Nature of Human Intelligence (p. 63) by J. P. Guilford, 1967, New York: McGraw-Hill. Copyright 1967 by McGraw-Hill. Reprinted by permission.

Spirited discussion among psychologists has revolved around new definitions of intelligence. Sternberg (1984) suggests that intelligence tests are limited in their ability to predict school and job performance. He maintains that there is a need to find measures that go beyond the scope of intelligence tests and are more closely linked to behavior in the real world. He views intelligence as consisting of three major types of behaviors: problem-solving ability, verbal ability, and social competence. Conventional tests, he believes, do not measure these behaviors adequately.

Gardner (1984) claims that there is no general smartness; instead, people possess "several intellectual competencies or 'intelligences'" (p. 699). He proposes seven basic intelligences: linguistic, logical-mathematical, musical, spatial, body-kinesthetic, interpersonal, and intrapersonal. People will vary both in potential and in achievement in these domains.

Creativity

Definitions of giftedness have expanded to encompass creativity in addition to superior intellectual potential or performance. Creativity is generally defined as the process of bringing a new, different, and unexpected response to a situation. However, there is a lack of agreement concerning this definition. Defining the term limits the very notion of creativity, and people can be creative in many different ways. One useful definition of creativity emerges from Guilford's concept of divergent thinking, which he sees as the ability to produce many alternative ideas in problem-solving situations (Guilford, 1977). Those abilities that Guilford sees as most relevant to creative thinking are in his categories of divergent production and transformation. Khatena's notion of creativity as "the power of the imagination to break away from perceptual set so as to restructure ideas, thoughts, and feelings into novel and meaningful associate bonds" is also useful (1976, p. 316). Both Guilford and Khatena focus on the person who brings new, different, and unexpected responses to a situation and is a productive thinker and problem solver.

Torrance (1969) stresses creative thinking ability as a criterion for giftedness and identifies some of the appropriate characteristics:

- Fluency of ideas (the number of responses produced by a stimulus)
- Flexibility (shifts in thinking from one category to another)
- Originality (unusual or clever responses)
- Elaboration (adding details to basic ideas or thoughts)

According to Torrance, measurement of these qualities is an effective means of identifying gifted children and youth in culturally different or disadvantaged populations. He points out that IQ scores fail to identify large numbers of students in the top 20% of creative thinking ability.

There has been much discussion about the relationship of giftedness and creativity. Research suggests that most creative people are gifted, but not all gifted people are creative (Getzels & Jackson, 1962). Recent interest requires a distinction between academic giftedness and creativity. Studies of creativity and intelligence have revealed low correlations between creativity and the intelligence measured by an intelligence test. In one study correlations between the rated creativity of 60 eminent architects and their scores on an adult intelligence test were reported to be low (MacKinnon, 1962). In another, correlations between intelligence test scores and creativity as measured by divergent thinking tests were low (Getzels & Jackson, 1962). Still another investigation that attempted to correlate intelligence test and creativity scores supported these results (Torrance, 1962). A review of the literature reveals that most studies report positive but low correlations between the two factors for the general population with little or no correlation at the higher ability levels (Taylor & Holland, 1962).

Performance Versus Potential

Opinions differ as to whether above-average performance or the apparent ability to perform exceptionally well should be the criterion in determining giftedness. The 1958 yearbook of the National Society for the Study of Education defined a talented or gifted individual as "one who shows consistently remarkable performance in any worthwhile line of endeavor" (1958, p. 19). This widely accepted definition relies heavily on performance rather than potential. Some authorities, however, insist that potential should be a significant factor in identifying gifted individuals. Fliegler and Bish (1959), for instance, propose potential as an identifying characteristic of the gifted and maintain, too, that students whose ability is in the top 15% to 20% of the school population are gifted.

There are, of course, advantages and disadvantages to excluding potential from the definition. It is far simpler to evaluate performance—in intelligence as well as other areas. From an administrative viewpoint, therefore, it is more efficient to limit the definition to performance. On the other hand, by excluding those who perform poorly but seem to have high ability, we may deny educational services to those very young people who need them most—those whose exceptionality causes them difficulty in adjusting to regular educational and other environments. Thus, including potential in the definition encourages attention to gifted underachievers and bright youngsters from culturally different populations.

Talent

The concept of talent as part of the definition of giftedness was added in the 1970s and resulted in a broader definition (U.S. Senate Report, 1972). Some educators use the term *giftedness* to denote outstanding intellectual ability and the term *talent* to denote superlative skills in a specific area, particularly the arts. However, the terms are frequently used interchangeably.

Concern for the many aspects of giftedness is reflected in the definition adopted by the U.S. Department of Education in 1978:

> Gifted and talented children means children, and whenever applicable, youth, who are identified at the preschool, elementary, or secondary level as possessing demon-

A component of giftedness is talent.

strated or potential abilities that give evidence of high performance capability in areas such as intellectual, creative, specific academic, or leadership ability, or in the performing and visual arts, and who by reason thereof require services or activities not ordinarily provided by the school. (*Congressional Record*, 1978, H–12179)

The federal government's definition is important because it is applied in policy and funding decisions. However, individual states and school districts have developed their own definitions of giftedness within the relatively broad federal guidelines, and the resultant diversity contributes further to the uncertainty surrounding the current definition. Definitions of giftedness reflect the attitude of the times, and no one definition will ever be correct for all time. Indeed, Renzulli (1978) identifies some problems with the 1978 definition. Several of the areas, such as intellectual or creative ability, merely describe processes that can be brought to bear on a specific performance area and are not observable in themselves. Also, the definition fails to include motivational factors, such as devotion to hard work, quality output, interest in learning—all of which may have a strong impact on performance. Renzulli bases his definition of giftedness on three basic traits:

1. above-average ability in any area (intellectual ability or specific talent)

2. task commitment as reflected in a willingness to work hard and to produce at a high level

3. creativity as measured by generation of ideas or products

Clearly, the trend is toward broader and more general concepts. Since Terman's work, definitions have not been based on data or theory. Instead, they have evolved out of political and social movements, revealing the relationship between giftedness and society's values at various times in its history.

Prevalence

Prevailing attitudes determine not only who is designated gifted and talented but also what proportion of the population this group represents at any one time. When IQ scores were used as the sole criterion for identifying the gifted, a smaller proportion of the population was identified. Thus, as definitions of giftedness vary, so do prevalence figures. There may be only one child in a million, for example, who is highly gifted—who has an IQ of 180 or higher (Hollingworth, 1942). But the broader definitions of today produce higher prevalence figures. In a 1972 study prevalence was estimated at 3% to 5% (Marland), and that estimate was the one accepted by the Office of Gifted and Talented. However, when an IQ cutoff of 115 is used, 15% to 20% of the school population may be found to be gifted.

Causes

As a general rule, more gifted students are identified in programs that draw from higher socioeconomic groups and from preschool populations. Students from the dominant culture perform better on the pencil-and-paper tests often used to identify gifted individuals. In addition, the behavior and performance of young children can often be seen as different from that of their young peers, thus facilitating identification.

Gifted and talented youngsters can be found at every economic level and in every stratum of society, in all cultural, ethnic, and racial groups. Although we have found no way to predict or perfectly explain the occurrence of giftedness and talent, three factors do seem to contribute: heredity, prenatal and perinatal care, and early childhood environment. Various authorities have expressed the view that heredity—a purely biological factor—does play a role although no perfect correlation exists between the intelligence of parents and the intelligence of their children (Jensen, 1969). Prenatal and perinatal care often reflects the home environment of the family, with poor care more frequently reported at low socioeconomic levels. Hunt (1961) and White (1977) have both noted and discussed the importance of early environmental stimulation. According to Hunt, environmental stimulation is particularly important during the first 2 years of life if optimum development is to occur, a fact underscored by the negative effects of deprivation of environmental stimuli during early childhood. The interaction of heredity and environment seems to be a key in the development and nurturing of giftedness.

Characteristics

As the definitions of giftedness and talent have become broader, the number and variety of characteristics associated with this category of exceptionality have increased greatly. For the sake of simplicity, we will examine characteristics commonly found in individuals with high IQ scores as well as traits often seen in highly creative persons.

Characteristics of Individuals with High IQs

In 1925 Terman began a study of approximately 1,000 children with IQs of 130 or higher, a study that is still in process. Not only did he endeavor to discover what traits these children had in common, but he also followed their development into adulthood. Terman and his associates (Terman, 1925; Terman & Oden, 1959; Oden, 1968) observed some specific characteristics in these individuals:

fast learning ability

interest in reading biographies

scientific inclination

reading prior to entering school

enjoyment of learning

good abstract reasoning

good command of language

poor handwriting

only child

eldest child

born of older parents

good adjustment

good physical health

high scores on achievement tests

imagination

high energy level

Subsequent reports have confirmed most of Terman's findings (Gallagher, 1975). We should, however, be cautious in accepting some of his results, particularly those of his physiological measures indicating the above-average size, strength, and health of gifted children. In a 1964 study that compared 81 bright youngsters to their significantly less bright siblings, no significant differences were found in the physiques in each pair (Laycock & Caylor, 1964). It may well be that Terman's sample was skewed in favor of youngsters from higher socioeconomic levels whose superior physical development was a function of nutritional advantages. Of particular significance, however, were Terman's findings that gifted children tended to be superior intellectually, socially, emotionally, and morally, dispelling the traditional stereotype of the one-sided, socially withdrawn, and emotionally insecure "brain."

More recently, other intellectual traits have been identified as characteristic of academically gifted children:

Capacity for learning: Accurate perception of social and natural situations; independent, rapid, efficient learning of fact and principle; fast, meaningful reading, with superior retention and recall

Power and sensitivity of thought: Ready grasp of principles underlying things as they are; sensitivity to interference in fact, consequence of proposition,

The academically gifted are often curious.

application of idea; spontaneous elevation of immediate observations to higher planes of abstraction; imagination; original interpretations and conclusions; discriminatory power, quick detection of similarities and differences among things and ideas; able in analysis, synthesis, and organization of elements; critical of situations, self, and other people

Curiosity and drive: Mental endurance; tenacity of purpose; stubbornness, sometimes contrarily expressed as reluctance to do as directed; capacity for follow-through with extensive, but meaningful plans; curiosity about things and ideas; intrinsic interest in the challenging and difficult; versatile and vital interests; varied, numerous and penetrating inquiries; boredom with routine and sameness (Ward, 1975, pp. 63, 64)

Another approach defines three major categories of characteristics that distinguish the gifted: cognitive, emotional, and physical (Clark, 1979). On the basis of the characteristics identified, related needs and possible problems can then be deduced as a first step in assessment and program planning. For example, an unusual discrepancy between physical and intellectual development in the gifted may mean that gifted students need to be guided toward physical activities that they can find satisfying and that permit individualized progress. Thus, it may be desirable to encourage physical activity in those gifted students who stress mental activity to the detriment of physical development (Clark, 1979).

Characteristics of Highly Creative Individuals

The Getzels and Jackson study (1962) revealed some very important differences between highly intelligent and highly creative youngsters. Highly creative children tend to be nonconforming: they question, challenge, and even psychologically threaten some teachers who do not tolerate high levels of nonconformity. The following characteristics of creative youngsters have been compiled from various checklists (Lucito, 1974; Renzulli & Hartman, 1971):

generate a large number of ideas or solutions to problems and questions

are uninhibited in expression of opinion, sometimes radical and spirited in disagreement, tenacious

display a good deal of intellectual playfulness, fantasize, imagine not conforming, accept disorder, are not interested in details, do not fear being different

rely more on own evaluations that on those of others

build a reputation for having wild or silly ideas

display humor, playfulness, and relaxation in their creative products

Thus, some characteristics commonly ascribed to gifted children may be seen by teachers as negative rather than positive attributes. Seagoe's (1974) classification of characteristics with positive and negative valence is helpful. For example, children who have unusual abilities to see relationships may also have difficulty in accepting the illogical. Those students who have long attention spans and display persistent goal-directed behavior may be seen as stubborn and resistant to interruption or change. Clearly, the settings in which children learn and the adults involved in making judgments are influential.

Heterogeneity in the Gifted and Talented Population

The characteristics described here are frequently found in gifted and talented individuals. However, not all gifted and talented children will exhibit all of these characteristics. Indeed, the gifted and talented are a heterogeneous group. In addition to a wide range of interindividual differences, they exhibit a high degree of variability within themselves (intraindividual differences). An understanding of the characteristics of gifted children is further complicated because it is difficult to identify certain types of gifted youngsters. Some gifted children whose ability and performance are widely disparate are difficult to identify. Whitmore (1979) discusses these underachieving youngsters and points out that conventional characteristics will often exclude them from receiving any service. They are frequently seen as excessively aggressive or withdrawn and as having negative self-concepts.

Other special populations that contribute to the complexity of characteristics are the gifted/handicapped and the culturally different gifted youngsters. Because teachers tend to focus on deficits rather than strengths, handicapped students who are gifted in a specific area are rarely identified. In addition, the handicapping conditions of gifted children can interfere with their demonstration of superior ability (Maker, 1977). This same situation exists for culturally different gifted children who may have been raised in an environment that rewards certain types of behavior not consonant with conventional notions of giftedness. For example, in some Hispanic families there may be less reinforcement of children who are highly verbal. These children may seem somewhat reticent when they enter school and might be easily overlooked in screening for a gifted program. Although much has been written urging educators to be sensitive to the special characteristics of these populations, most programs still persist in using traditional methods of identification that rely on popular notions of gifted characteristics (Yarborough & Johnson, 1983).

Assessment

Many techniques have been used in identifying gifted and talented students. These include intelligence and achievement tests, tests of creativity, teacher nomination, and parent, peer, and self-nominations. Although none of these identification methods is adequate alone, each has a place in the identification process. When used in some logical combination, these approaches can strengthen our ability to identify gifted and talented students.

Assessing Aptitude (Intelligence)

Identification measures have traditionally included aptitude and achievement tests. Aptitude, or intelligence, tests usually provide IQ or other standard scores. The two individually administered intelligence tests most frequently used are the Stanford-Binet (Terman & Merrill, 1973) and the Wechsler intelligence scales (Wechsler, 1967, 1974, 1981). A recent addition to intelligence scales is the Kaufman Assessment Battery for Children (K-ABC) (1983). Another instrument with particular relevance for identifying culturally different gifted children is the System of Multicultural Pluralistic Assessment (SOMPA) developed by Jane Mercer (1978). The SOMPA is based on three assessment models—a medical model, a social system model, and a pluralistic model—each providing unique information about the individual. Performance in academic and nonacademic settings is assessed through standardized tests (e.g., the Weschler Intelligence Scale for Children—Revised and tests of physical and visual/motor functioning) and with the Adaptive Behavior Inventory for Children (ABIC), health history inventories, and sociocultural scales. One strength of the SOMPA is that a child's performance is evaluated not only against standard norms but also in comparison to children the same age from a similar sociocultural background. These comparisons yield estimates of learning potential that account for cultural differences.

Early Childhood   Formal intelligence tests are available for assessing giftedness in young children. These include the Stanford-Binet, the Wechsler Preschool and Primary Scale of Intelligence (WPPSI), and the recently introduced Kaufman-ABC. The Peabody Picture Vocabulary Test can also be used (Dunn, 1980).

However, because IQ scores of young children are not highly stable over time (Khatena, 1982), other means of identifying this population are important. These include behavioral checklists, parent interviews, and direct observation (Bauer & Harris, 1979; Kitano, 1982). These informal methods are particularly important with the culturally different and handicapped gifted. Some model programs for identifying and serving gifted and handicapped young children have developed such approaches. The RAPYHT (Retrieval and Acceleration of Promising Young Handicapped and Talented) project at the University of Illinois has outlined procedures for identifying gifted and talented preschoolers (ages 2½ to 5). These procedures, which are being replicated in many states across the country (Karnes, 1979), involve initial screening using a Preschool Talent Checklist, followed by a Preschool Talent Assessment Guide. Follow-up studies of the population involved in the RAPYHT program indicate excellent progress for these children in their subsequent school settings (Karnes, Schwedel, & Lewis, 1983), suggesting valid prediction of academic ability.

School Age   Intelligence tests measure a variety of abilities, including social, problem-solving, and abstract and concrete reasoning abilities. In addition, they give opportunities for both verbal and nonverbal responses. Not only do these tests provide valuable standardized information about a youngster's abilities and

TABLE 13-1 The Wechsler intelligence scales: A useful instrument for obtaining a profile of an individual's cognitive abilities

Test Category	Item Type	Example	Ability/Knowledge Tested
Verbal	Vocabulary	Define the word	Understanding of verbal concepts, quality and quantity of verbal expression
	Information	Who was the first U.S. president?	General information gained from environment
	Similarities	In what way are an accordion and a guitar alike?	Logical and abstract thinking, ability to recognize relationships between objects or ideas
	Comprehension	Why do bicycles have wheels?	Practical knowledge, social judgment
Attention and concentration	Digit span	Student repeats numbers forward and backward.	Rote memory and ability to attend
	Arithmetic	If I have *(x)* newspapers and sell *(y)*	Ability to manipulate number concepts
Visual organization	Picture arrangement	Student arranges a group of pictures in logical sequence.	Perception, visual comprehension, understanding of social situations
	Picture completion	Student identifies missing elements of pictures.	Ability to determine essential details, attention and concentration
Visual-motor	Object assembly	Student assembles picture puzzles.	Ability to organize parts into meaningful whole, perception of relationships, visual-motor coordination
	Block design	Student reproduces two-dimensional design with colored blocks.	Ability to apply logic and reasoning to space relationships and to analyze and reproduce a geometric pattern
	Coding	Student matches and copies symbols using simple shapes and numerals.	Visual-motor dexterity, ability to absorb new material

learning style, they also can provide significant nonstandardized information. For example, the Wechsler scales can yield a profile of a student's cognitive abilities, as shown in Table 13-1.

A new test of intellectual ability and achievement was introduced in 1983. The Kaufman-ABC (K-ABC) is an individually administered measure for use with youngsters from 2½ to 12 years old; it included gifted children in the sample used to develop norms. The developers describe the K-ABC as a measure built on a theory of intelligence that is based on two major types of skills. The first is termed *sequential* and includes sequential, analytic, and temporal processing skills; the second is termed *simultaneous* and involves spatial abilities and a holistic response to tasks. The K-ABC is designed to measure intelligence apart from achievement, with language or verbal skills playing a minimal role. The test gives the child opportunities to learn how to solve tasks and assesses ability on the basis of the processing style used. Because language or verbal skills play a minimal role in the assessment, the K-ABC has been proposed as a viable alternative for culturally diverse children (Haddad & Naglieri, 1984); it tends to identify more of this population than are found by traditional means.

Assessing Achievement

Sometimes special placement requires evaluation of achievement as well as aptitude. Tests that measure academic achievement are often group administered; performance is usually interpreted in terms of grade placement and/or percentiles. When placement is an issue, achievement measures should be directly related to the program's requirements. The structure of most achievement tests makes it possible to evaluate only specific areas in question. When standardized tests are used, specimen copies should be reviewed prior to purchase; reviews describing the instruments and their development and citing related research can be found in the Mental Measurement Yearbook (Buros, 1978). In addition to formal, standardized instruments, comprehensive test data from teachers can be valuable in assessing school achievement.

Assessing Performance in Nonacademic Areas

Talent in performance areas other than academic can sometimes be evaluated with standardized tests, but direct observation is a more valuable assessment technique. Methods of direct and daily observation of classroom performance have been systematized (Cooper, 1981). Often permanent products, a student's work, and other readily identifiable outcomes of performance are the best indicators of talent. These outcomes—for instance, drawings, creative writing, music performance, or a gymnastic feat—usually can be evaluated with relative objectivity by a committee of experts.

Assessing Creativity

If we view divergent response as a major aspect of creativity, we are faced with the difficult task of finding an objective measure. Measurement of divergence is, in several respects, contradictory to the notion of standardized testing, which is based on convergence—supplying the right answer. Nonetheless, several tests do exist that are purported to assess creativity. Perhaps best known are the Torrance Tests of Creative Thinking (TTCT) (1966), which were designed to measure four characteristics associated with creativity: fluency, flexibility, originality, and elaboration.

Interesting observations can be made of the students' individual development as they explore the dramatic arts.

Other Procedures for Identifying the Gifted and Talented

One widely used procedure for locating potentially gifted and talented students is teacher nomination, even though the ability of teachers to pick out the gifted in their classes has been open to question for some time. Early research in teacher nomination revealed that junior high school teachers did not locate gifted children well enough to place much reliance on their screening (Pegnato & Birch, 1959). These studies of teacher identification, however, required teachers to make global assessments of students' abilities. Such assessments were general and related more to good behavior, high grades, and the value systems of the teachers than to the students' abilities. More recent studies have shown that when teachers are given specific criteria, they are more accurate in identifying gifted children. Borland (1978) found positive correlations between teacher ratings and IQ but also found that teachers were more accurate in identifying gifted girls than gifted boys and gifted underachievers than gifted achievers. Borland's results confirm those of Jacobs (1971), who demonstrated that training teachers to identify gifted children increased their accuracy. In addition, instruments that focus on observable characteristics are now available for teachers to use in selecting gifted students and seem to be more reliable than teacher judgment alone.

One such behavioral checklist dealing with observable characteristics is the Scale for Rating the Behavioral Characteristics of Superior Students (Renzulli & Hartman, 1971), designed to obtain teacher estimates of students' characteristics in the areas of learning, motivation, creativity, leadership, communication, and the arts. Separate, weighted scores are obtained for each dimension, permitting emphasis on different areas. Some sample items from the Renzulli scale are included here:

is a keen observer; usually "sees more" or "gets more" out of a story, film, etc.

has unusually advanced vocabulary for age or grade level; uses terms in a meaningful way

has a large storehouse of information about a variety of topics

is easily bored with routine tasks

is interested in many "adult" problems, such as religion, politics, sex, race—more than usual for age level

displays a great deal of curiosity about many things; is constantly asking questions about anything and everything

is a high risk taker; is adventurous and speculative

displays a keen sense of humor and sees humor in situations that may not appear to be humorous to others

Lucito (1974) compiled a summary of traits generally associated with creative students, many of which are observable and, thus, can also be useful in identifying the gifted.

Other methods for identifying gifted children include parent, peer, and self-nomination. Parents are an excellent source of information about the strengths and weaknesses of their children. In a 1974 study parents who responded to a questionnaire asking whether their kindergarten children were gifted, according to stated criteria, correctly nominated 39 of a total of 58 children, for a 76% accuracy rate as compared to 22% for teachers (Ciha, Harris, Hoffman, & Potter, 1974). Classmates, too, can often provide significant information to aid in identifying the gifted and talented; even gifted and talented individuals themselves may be willing and able to identify their own special abilities and achievements.

Special Problems in Identifying the Gifted

Conventional methods of identifying gifted children often miss some special populations. Among these are the culturally different gifted, gifted females, the gifted handicapped, and gifted underachievers.

The Culturally Different Gifted   Even though gifted children may be found in every socioeconomic and cultural group, the schools have been more successful in identifying those in the majority or dominant culture. Indeed, the educational needs of many gifted children have not been well met because these children are more difficult to teach as well as to recognize. Now, at last, there is an increasing emphasis on identifying and serving culturally different gifted children (Frasier, 1980). Some of the difficulties in finding the culturally different gifted arose when concepts of giftedness were more limited and emphasized intellectual ability to the exclusion of broader concepts (Bernal, 1975). With current broader definitions of giftedness and the new willingness of school personnel to use a variety of screening and evaluation techniques and instruments, more children from minority cultural groups are now being identified. Some early studies of the Kaufman-ABC (McCallum, Karnes, & Edwards, 1984) indicate that the culturally different gifted are likely to score higher on this instrument than on the Stanford-Binet or Wechsler scales, which depend more on verbal skills.

Dissatisfaction with conventional procedures for identifying gifted students has led to the development of alternative methods. Renzulli, for instance, designed the Subcultural Indices of Academic Potential (1973), a test that requires students to assess their reactions to everyday situations and thereby produces a profile of their preferences, learning styles, and ways of approaching tasks. Another researcher attempted to identify and test for specific types of giftedness using Guilford's Structure of Intellect Model (Meeker, 1969)—an important step because it relates traditional intelligence measures to the nontraditional structure of intellect. Specific items on the Stanford-Binet Intelligence Test, for example, can be looked at in terms of the Structure of Intellect Model, and student strengths and weaknesses can be analyzed. Does the child do well on items requiring understanding of abstract words? Such a skill involves cognition, semantic content, and units. Does the child have trouble explaining why certain statements are foolish? Such a task involves evaluation, semantic content, and systems. In this way a child's performance can be analyzed for specific patterns of ability and disability, and teaching activities can be planned accordingly.

Another instrument for identifying the gifted is the Kranz Talent Identification Instrument (1982). This instrument is designed to raise awareness of the multiple criteria of giftedness in order to assist teachers in screening for talented children in their classes. Kranz uses a three-stage procedure in which teachers and administrators are prepared for the tasks of rating, screening, and selecting gifted and talented students. Input from parents is also a part of the process. The instrument trains professionals to focus on frequency, intensity, and quality of specific behaviors and intends to identify children from all ethnic and sociological backgrounds. Additional efforts have been made by Bernal (1972) to develop a means for identifying giftedness among Hispanic students in Texas and by Bruch (1972) to use an abbreviated form of the Stanford-Binet to identifying disadvantaged black youngsters.

Recent research indicates that one key factor in successful identification of culturally different gifted youngsters is teacher attitude (High & Udall, 1983). This study reported that culturally different students were not referred to gifted programs in the same proportion as Anglo students and that this lack of referrals may be related to negative teacher attitudes. In addition, the social and cultural milieu of a school seem to influence the way teachers evaluate students. In the same High and Udall study (1983) negative teacher attitudes seemed to be intensified in schools with large numbers of minority students. Teacher training is a key factor in the successful identification of minority students. Another variable influencing the low referral rate is the close relationship between learning characteristics on the checklists used, such as the Scale for Rating the Behavioral Characteristics of Superior Students (Renzulli & Hartman, 1971), and the majority culture's idea of positive school behavior. Attempts to develop alternative methods for identifying gifted students are relatively recent and will undoubtedly continue to receive increased attention.

Traditional assessment instruments can bypass gifted minority and female students.

Gifted Females Social expectations for women during the early decades of this century restricted them to the traditional roles of homemaking and teaching. In fact, Terman's study following a gifted sample into adulthood gathered data on the careers of the men only, because few women were expected to become professionals (Terman & Oden, 1959). Even today, women comprise approximately one-half of our nation's gifted and talented population but are conspicuously underrepresented in leadership roles (Fox & Tobin, 1978). Influenced by the civil rights movement of the sixties, attitudes have changed, and more options have opened up for women who want to assume nontraditional roles. Nonetheless, there remains a tendency among teachers to select different learning experiences for boys and girls (Welsh, 1977). It appears that in our culture, even today, women are not expected to succeed. For gifted women this is a serious problem. Their motivation to achieve conflicts with their fear that they will be rejected or considered unfeminine if they do. This conflict can result in ambivalence or even anxiety, which, in turn, impedes success (Horner, 1972).

There is little information available on assessing gifted females. However, some specific problems in identifying gifted females have been identified. These are related to differential treatment of males and females as well as different expectations on the part of adults and the gifted females themselves (Welsh, 1977). The key to better assessment of gifted females may lie in counseling and career development programs. Rodenstein, Pfleger, & Colangelo (1977) recommend some specific strategies.:

> a change in the opportunity structure of schools. . . . affirmative efforts to identify gifted and talented girls at an early age as well as a commitment to continuation of the identification process throughout the school years

> a reduction in overt barriers to pursuing opportunities for advanced work, thus allowing gifted females access to laboratories and other learning facilities where they may flourish

> broadening the scope of counseling and guidance services to include such programs as achievement motivation training and assertiveness training (p. 345)

A concerted effort to identify female role models in the school and community is also recommended, thereby encouraging gifted and talented women to explore and refine their abilities. Formation of support groups may also help to provide settings in which gifted females feel free to show their particular abilities and talents.

Gifted Handicapped Identification of the gifted handicapped depends on a willingness to focus on strengths rather than weaknesses. Wolf and Gygi (1981) reviewed some methods of identifying gifted learning disabled students, such as the use of individual intelligence tests (Hokansen & Jospe, 1976). Subtest scores can then be examined so that areas of high ability can be identified. Such an approach is useful, but it is not realistic to assume that it can be available to all those who need it.

Another method of assessing gifted handicapped students is direct observation. Such observation in natural settings may indicate variability in performance. Parent reports and self-evaluation may also be utilized. The learning disability would probably have to be fairly severe or the giftedness fairly extreme for teachers to become aware of performance discrepancies in the classroom.

Maker (1977) suggests three techniques to use in identifying gifted handicapped students. The first is a focus on potential rather than on demonstrated ability alone. The second is a comparison of the student with other handicapped students rather than with the general population. The third is observation of the student's skills in compensating for the disability. Observations of superior ability in reasoning and recognizing relationships (Given, 1977), intellectual curiosity, wide-ranging interests, and effective independent work can also be helpful in the assessment process. Such data can be good sources of information both for assessment purposes and for help in programming.

Gifted Underachievers   Another group of gifted students often missed in the assessment process is the gifted underachievers. Early studies attributed the problem to personality characteristics and/or family problems. There is some recent support for the premise that classroom conditions often contribute to the development of gifted underachievers. The maladjustment seen in this population is thought to be related to the interaction between the child, his personality and behavior, and the social environment of home and school (Whitmore, 1979, p. 47). It is clear that there are difficulties in identifying this population in a setting that may be contributing to the problem. Common procedures for finding these youngsters involve a comparison of performance on individual and/or group tests with academic achievement. Although this method will successfully identify many gifted underachievers, some will still be missed because of depressed test scores—especially gifted youngsters with emotional problems. Identification of these students must combine standardized test performance and a profile of achievement with teacher evaluation of social, emotional, and physical status. The use of behavior checklists is also crucial (Whitmore, 1980), and parent and student interviews can be extremely helpful.

Intervention

All schools have some gifted and talented students; many, however, make no special provisions for them. In those schools that do, services may be provided on an individual basis or through various administrative arrangements. Whatever the model of service delivery selected, gifted children will profit greatly from early intervention because they require more and qualitatively different experiences than other children of the same ages. It has been demonstrated that gifted children benefit specifically from early instruction in academic areas (Cassidy & Vukelich,

1978). According to Clark (1979), stimulation during the early years is a necessary requisite for the gifted child's optimal intellectual growth. Early nurturing of abilities can also bring forth latent talents, such as musical and mathematical aptitudes, which must be discovered and cultivated early. The majority of great talents are manifested before age 30, even though some great achievements, particularly in politics and historical research, do occur after age 45 (Lehman, 1953).

We should remember that for the gifted and talented, as for other exceptional students, it is important to individualize educational programs (Wolf, 1979). Individualization does not require having each of 25 gifted and talented students studying a different subject area. It does require dynamic and fluid grouping, a recognition that individuals learn at different rates, and an expectation that students will assume some responsibility for their own learning (Wolf, 1979; Wolf & Stephens, 1979).

Direct Services   Direct services are those the student receives through personal contact with service providers. They may be offered in the regular classroom, in the student's home school, or elsewhere. In the regular classroom the teacher may provide special attention, more challenging assignments, and enriched experiences. Outside the regular classroom gifted and talented students may be given part of their instruction by a resource teacher or by individuals in the community with specific expertise, in accelerated classes or in college or university courses.

Special counseling, tutoring, and interest development are other direct services that gifted and talented students may receive outside the regular classroom. Bright students typically need career counseling to be aware of the variety of career options open to them (Alexander & Muia, 1982). This type of guidance should begin early and extend throughout the school experience. It is essential that it be objective: the counselor's role should be to inform students about qualifications for specific careers, not to encourage or discourage early career commitments. Special tutoring can extend the subject matter range or depth normally available to students. Regular teachers or outside personnel can serve as tutors. Gifted students are frequently curious and do, with encouragement, develop a wide range of interests, which can be stimulated and developed through after-school clubs or groups that meet during school hours. Sometimes community resources can be tapped.

Indirect Services   Assistance in meeting the needs of gifted students may come from individuals who have no direct contact with the students themselves; these services are thus referred to as indirect. Consultants who provide teachers with suggestions, conduct or coordinate in-service training, and locate resources outside the schools are a common resource. Concerned and supportive principals and central district administrators can underscore the importance of programs for the gifted and talented and can help consultants gain access to teachers and parents. It is the job of administrators, too, to provide incentives for school personnel to identify and provide special programming for bright students—additional funds for enrichment materials or special field trips, for example. Special bulletins and journals on the education of the gifted and talented are another form of indirect service.

Independent Study Contracting

Independent study may involve the use of contracts established and agreed upon by the teacher, the student, and the parents when appropriate. Some contracts will not involve outside resources, whereas others may draw from the entire school system or even the community. Outlined here is an example of an independent contract arranged for Scott Martin in an attempt to meet some specialized needs in reading.

As a first step Scotty's teacher, Mrs. Webb, wanted to determine that he had indeed mastered with 95% accuracy all the basic skills that were part of the sixth-grade reading program. With a mastery test Mrs. Webb could be assured that there were no gaps in Scotty's reading skills background or could assist Scotty in filling any gaps that were disclosed.

Next, after assessing Scotty's reading interests, a decision was made to focus on modern science fiction writers. The various elements of the independent study contract were then worked out in the format shown in Figure 13-2. For this particular contract Scotty needed to examine the university course reading requirements before compiling his reading list. He then made a commitment to the contract as it was written. In fact, he was a major drafter of the contract, negotiating with his teacher the deadlines, methods of presenting the material, and evaluation criteria. The plan required the local university's permission for Scotty to enroll in a course in the English department and agreement from Scotty's parents to provide the necessary transportation.

Not all independent study contracts are so complex. Many can be carried out within the confines of the classroom and may simply involve a student's in-depth study of a topic studied less fully by the class. A student might contract to use different media and materials as part of his in-depth study, to develop a useful product, or in some special way to accomplish other specific objectives.

Bibliotherapy

Bibliotherapy, a counseling approach particularly suited to gifted children, is a technique of providing reading material on ways of dealing with problems (Wolf & Penrod, 1980). Because many gifted children are avid readers, teachers or counselors can often help them resolve personal crises by directing them to appropriate books or articles. This method is also useful with young gifted children. For example, a child may be having difficulty getting along with peers. Her teacher can use a source such as *The Bookfinder* (Dreyer, 1977) to identify fiction at an appropriate level that deals with peer relations. The child can then identify with the book's character in dealing with her problem. Full resolution can be facilitated by discussion of the book and opportunities to express feelings.

Independent Study Contract

Student: *Scott Martin*   Title of Study: *Modern Science*
Estimated Completion Date: *March 15, 1986*   *Fiction Writers*
MAIN QUESTIONS I PLAN TO EXPLORE:

A consideration of modern science fiction writers with focus on Heinlein, Asimov, Clarke, Herbert, Leguin

Comparison and contrast of these authors

MAIN SOURCES OF INFORMATION I PLAN TO USE:

University course on Modern Science Fiction Writers
Fall quarter M-W 8:00–9:30 a.m. Dr. Jones

Primary Sources:

Clarke: *Tales from the White Heart, 2001: A Space Odyssey*
Heinlein: *Paths Through Tomorrow*
Asimov: *The Foundation Trilogy*
Herbert: *Stand on Zanzibar, The Sheep Look Up*
Leguin: *The Left Hand of Darkness, The Earth Sea Trilogy*

Place and Format for Presenting My Study:

1. Written paper: Critique of Modern Science Fiction
2. One-week seminar on modern science fiction for fifth-sixth graders at Snowbird School
      I would like to have my study evaluated by this set of criteria

Written	Oral
Paper on critique of modern science fiction as seen in writings of Asimov, Heinlein, Clarke, Herbert, Leguin	*Presentation of one-week seminar on modern science fiction for fifth-sixth graders at Snowbird*
Course outline for one-week seminar	Teacher evaluation
	Student evaluation

Student's Signature _____

Date _____   Teacher's Signature _____

Parent's Signature _____

Figure 13-2 Example of an independent study contract

SOURCE: From "Individualized Educational Planning for the Gifted" by J. S. Wolf and T.M. Stephens, 1979, Roeper Review, 2(2), p. 12. Copyright 1979 by Roeper Review. Reprinted by permission.

Mentor Programs

In some programs arrangements are made for gifted and talented students to pursue a particular area of interest with an expert in the community. The goals and objectives as well as the particular learning activities are carefully delineated, and a time is set aside during the school day for the student to be with the mentor. Accountability is built in so that accomplishment of specific goals can be documented. An independent study contract or some other agreed-upon means can be used.

Colson, Borman, and Nash (1978) have described one program in which students have opportunities to examine career fields and then to work directly with a mentor in a chosen area. Activity logs are kept, and seminars are held in which students share experiences. Participating students have reported gaining insight into the life styles of those in their chosen fields as well as into their own needs and interests. Other populations have been identified from which mentors can be drawn. These include college students, particularly teacher trainees (Harris, 1984), as well as college professors (McCleary & Hines, 1983), parents and other adults in the community (Bridges, 1980), and older students with a particular area of expertise (Mattson, 1983).

Group Interaction with Peers

Even though independent study is a valuable educational tool for teaching the gifted and talented, opportunities for interaction with peers are equally important. The excitement of sharing knowledge and interests is both stimulating and motivating. The group setting allows opportunities for gifted students to learn from one another in an environment where unusual ideas are accepted and exciting discussions are plentiful. The group may include students of several ages or grades and may thus provide role models for younger gifted students. Emphasis should be on the topics or subjects studied and on the group process. Personal and social adjustment are enhanced by positive group experiences with gifted peers.

Early Admission and Concurrent Enrollment

Interaction with gifted peers may be enhanced through alternative programs that go beyond the walls of the classroom. For secondary students who are significantly advanced academically and who have social/emotional stability, settings beyond the high school environment may be particularly suitable. Early admission programs allow high school students, most commonly seniors, to enter college early without earning a high school diploma. Decisions are made on an individual basis. An early prototype of the early admission program was the Ford Foundation effort in the 1960s, in which selected youngsters throughout the country entered college at young ages. Results revealed that these students were as successful as older students in their university work and participated in extracurricular activities as well.

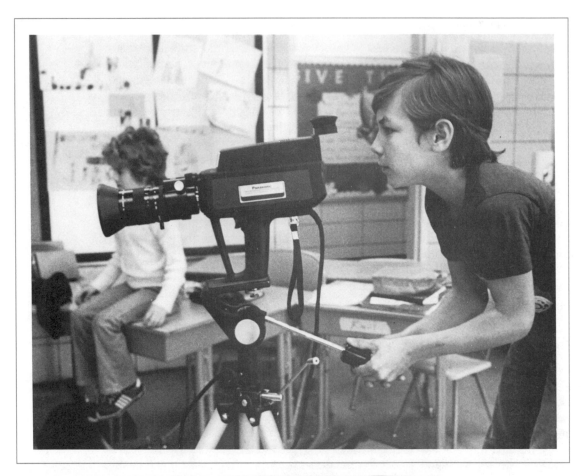

Students need hands-on experiences that can foster lifetime hobbies and careers.

A decision to admit some highly gifted youngsters to college may be made while they are still at an elementary age. Periodically we read about such young-sters. Mike Grost is one example (Grost, 1970). He entered college at 12, received his B.S. degree at 15, and developed an original mathematical theorem as a college senior. A recent article in the *New York Times* reported a decision for a 7-year-old girl to enter high school because of her exceptional abilities (1984). Reports of Coleman Miller's graduating from college at 15 and entering the California Institute of Technology as a graduate student in physics reveal another example of early admission policies. Although these youngsters represent extreme abilities, various modes of acceleration can be beneficial for the gifted.

One option of early admission programs is concurrent enrollment, in which high school students enroll in college classes for regular credit. These programs have been popular since the 1960s and are quite common today. Many institutions have reported that this select group of high school students have successfully completed college level courses taught by regular college faculty and containing regular college students (Voorheis, 1979) and have earned good to excellent grade point averages. Such a program allows gifted students intellectual stimulation and challenge and provides opportunities for them to interact with intellectual peers who may not be age-mates.

Teachers of the Gifted

An important key to effective intervention for the gifted rests in the teacher. Practically all teachers prefer students who learn quickly and are interested in their studies. However, even though gifted and talented students are eager learners, they also present teachers with frequent challenges that require tolerance and maturity. Teachers of the gifted must be personally secure; they must be able to accept the fact that their students may be more knowledgeable in certain areas and encourage them to seek even higher levels of learning.

There is little agreement on the specific qualities teachers of the gifted should have. We know generally that teachers who are excited about what they teach foster interest among bright students. At upper grade levels teachers must be knowledgeable in subject matter, willing to learn with their students, and capable of providing guidance and direction as students explore their intellectual interests. There is some evidence that successful teachers of gifted high school students are mature, experienced, emotionally well adjusted, and highly intelligent (Newland, 1962; Ward, 1961). In addition, they typically are knowledgeable about giftedness and express support for special attention to the gifted (Bishop, 1968).

Certain qualities seem to be characteristic of creative teachers at all levels: sensitivity and flexibility in their relationships with students, openness in thinking and activities, and respect and support for the individuality of each student (Kranyik & Wagner, 1965). Wyatt (1982) further addresses the important behaviors of supportive classroom teachers of the gifted: (1) providing an enriched classroom environment and differentiated curriculum; (2) involving students in independent investigations; (3) teaching process skills, the scientific method, and research skills; (4) providing options to accommodate learning styles; and (5) demonstrating knowledge about the gifted child. A recent study presented a profile of a gifted teacher (Mulhern & Ward, 1983) and included personal and professional characteristics (Fig. 13-3).

Does it make any difference if special provisions are made for the gifted? There are a few studies that indicate that gifted students do indeed benefit from special programs. Tremaine (1979) compared the achievements and attitudes of gifted high school graduates who had participated in special programs with those of gifted graduates who had not. He found that those enrolled in gifted programs had significantly more scholarships and awards, tended to elect difficult courses in high school, enrolled in college in higher numbers, and were involved in more school activities. No evidence was found of negative attitudes either toward those in special programs or from those in special programs.

Personal characteristics: The teacher is to present evidence of successful achievement(s) in each area prior to acceptance into the practicum.

Intellectual achievement: Is knowledgeable about a wide range of subjects and topics

Interpersonal skills: Is able to successfully establish a comfortable working relationship with both adults and students

Personal success: Has achieved success as a teacher or as a professional in some other field

Secure personality: Is at ease in most settings including those which are new and/or unknown

Intellectual curiosity: Is constantly seeking new solutions through continued learning

Organization: Has organized his personal life and maintains control over it

Leadership ability: Has demonstrated skills in leading people, especially young people, to successful accomplishment of a major undertaking

Professional characteristics: The teacher is to demonstrate successful attainment in each area.

Subject matter knowledge: In-depth command of one subject area and familiarity with several others

Information-handling skills: Ability to organize information into units for teaching gifted students

Classroom teaching skills: The ability to relate to gifted students within a classroom and to create an environment within which learning takes place

Diagnostic skills: The ability to use diagnostic tests and other tools to determine student educational needs.

Prescriptive teaching skills: The ability to design specific learning packages for students and to carry them out successfully

Program development skills: The ability to conceptualize a program for gifted students and to identify and organize the key elements related to its success.

Program leadership skills: The ability to convince a wide variety of persons about the appropriateness of a program for the gifted

Figure 13-3   Characteristics of a teacher for the gifted

SOURCE: From "A collaborative program for developing teachers of gifted and talented students" by J. D. Mulhern and M. Ward, 1983, Gifted Child Quarterly, 27 (4), p. 155. Copyright 1983 by Gifted Child Quarterly. Reprinted by permission.

Curriculum Implications

Sound instructional practices are necessary, regardless of any special provisions made for gifted and talented students. Terman believes that bright students should receive systematically differentiated instruction throughout their school experience because they learn differently (Seagoe, 1974). There is, in fact, general agreement that both the nature of the material and the rate of presentation may need modifying for gifted students. Although the objectives of instruction for the gifted are similar to those for other students, the approaches may differ. Emphasis should be on creativity, intellectual initiative, critical thinking, social adjustment, responsibility, and leadership. A common characteristic of academically gifted youngsters is their ability to grasp complex concepts and to master them easily. Their need for drill and practice is significantly less than that of average students. They should be taught concepts and principles rather than concrete facts, which are typically a natural part of their learning. The gifted learn inductively, too, responding to logic and reason (Tannenbaum, 1983). In short, bright students thrive on many new ideas and profit from moving through subject matter quickly in order to pursue interests in related areas, learning in depth and breadth.

Age-Level Distinctions

Many of the techniques that are appropriate for school-age gifted students can be applied in early childhood programs. Activities that promote inquiry and problem solving and encourage higher cognitive processes are particularly suitable. Opportunities for creative exploration are also important. Quattrocki (1974) describes an

In using scientific method, the gifted move beyond mere acquisition of information.

atmosphere in which young children can be creative as one that allows a child to be free from inhibition, to make novel combinations of ideas, and to express curiosity and imagination. Because gifted preschool children have a strong need to explore, a wide variety of materials should be available as well as time to explore them. Some support the Montessori method for the young gifted child (Tittle, 1984) since it encourages unlimited exploration with new materials.

The young gifted child may present some unique challenges to parents prior to school entry. The early talker, the precocious reader, the child who seems to absorb new ideas and concepts at a rapid rate can create problems in a household not prepared to provide needed stimulation. A variety of books and toys, opportunities for learning in informal situations, and interaction with other children in order to build social skills are important factors, along with parental willingness to respond to the child's interests and questions. One helpful approach brings gifted children together in a preschool program that responds to their needs and works with the parents in understanding the nature and needs of a young gifted child (Bauer & Harris, 1979).

For elementary and secondary gifted students subject matter is often modified in the same ways that instructional methods are. For instance, principles and concepts are emphasized, and students are encouraged to use deductive and inductive logic as well as other scientific tools, such as observation. Because most bright students are steeped in information, they are often taught the scientific method early, as a means of evaluating rather than merely assimilating knowledge.

Instructional Models

In this section we will examine three models useful in teaching segments of the gifted student population. The first, Bloom's taxonomy (1956), is designed to encourage thinking on higher levels. The second, Renzulli's Enrichment Triad Model (1977), is applicable for teaching the gifted within regular groups with a wide range of abilities. The third, a sequence for academic skills and concepts, is a generic model that we propose for teaching potentially gifted preschoolers (Stephens & Wolf, 1981).

Bloom's Taxonomy   Bloom's taxonomy (1956) is valuable both for the teacher in designing appropriate learning activities and for the students in their own direct learning. It is divided into cognitive and affective domains. The cognitive domain, which is applicable to the instruction of intellectually gifted students, consists of a hierarchy of skill areas, proceeding from the simple to the complex: knowledge, comprehension, application, analysis, synthesis, and evaluation. Table 13-2 clarifies the nature of each of these skill areas.

Most of the learning activities in a regular classroom focus on knowledge and comprehension. For gifted students, however, it is important to promote use of the higher level skills—application, analysis, synthesis, and evaluation. Figure 13-4 presents the taxonomy ladder of Bloom's cognitive domain and illustrates by the size of each piece in the triangles the appropriate emphasis on the specific skill areas for gifted and nongifted students. Often students are taught the Bloom model itself

Table 13-2 Behaviors and sample items from the skill areas in Bloom's cognitive domain

Skill Area	Behavior	Sample Items
Knowledge	Recall facts, definitions, observations	Define the word *cosmos*. Who spoke first? Where was the building located? What did the boys want? When did Columbus discover America?
Comprehension	State main ideas, describe, match items, compare and contrast	What happened during the experiment? What is the major theme of the play? How are the climates alike? How are they different?
Application	Apply rules and techniques to solve problems	What is the area of the social hall? Classify the short stories as comedy, tragedy, etc.
Analysis	Make inferences, find evidence to support generalizations, identify causes or motives	What can you conclude about the effect of communism on the economic life of the people? How would you characterize the platform of the Republican party on women's rights?
Synthesis	Make predictions, produce original material, solve problems	Give a title to this paragraph. What might happen if gold replaced the dollar as the economic standard?
Evaluation	Give opinions, judge quality of products, validity of ideas, and merit of solutions	Do you agree or disagree with this conclusion? What is your opinion? How would you improve . . . ? Do you think capital punishment is just?

so that they can understand the higher cognitive processes involved in learning and make decisions about how they want to acquire information.

Renzulli's Enrichment Triad Model   This model is particularly suited for teaching in a regular classroom the gifted with a wide ability range (Renzulli, 1977), but it can also be adapted for use in pullout programs for the gifted. It prescribes three types of enrichment: general exploratory activities, group training activities, and individual and small-group investigation of real problems.

   General exploratory activities are designed to expose all the students in the class to new subjects, topics, and/or experiences. They should serve as strong motivators, permitting discovery and exploration on various levels and extending beyond the regular content areas of the curriculum. Examples of these activities are going on

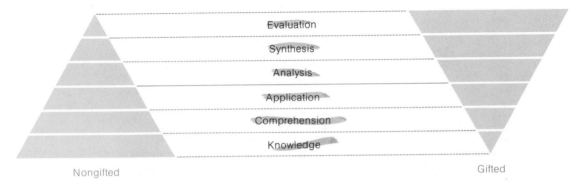

Nongifted   Gifted

Figure 13-4 Bloom's taxonomy ladder for the cognitive domain
SOURCE: From Growing Up Gifted *(p. 199) by B. Clark, 1979, Columbus, OH: Charles E. Merrill. Copyright 1979 by Bell and Howell Company. Reprinted by permission.*

a field trip, listening to a guest speaker, and watching a film or TV program on a new topic.

Group training activities are especially appropriate for students who show a high degree of interest and involvement during general exploratory activities. Students can usually work in groups, cooperating and learning from each other and building on the information gathered in exploratory activities as they learn research techniques and develop advanced mental processes. Thought processes that might be emphasized are brainstorming, classifying, and evaluating. Students might be asked first to think of all the possible ways their school could be used (brainstorm), then to categorize their ideas according to function or some other criterion (classify), and finally to suggest ways of improving the traffic pattern around the school building (evaluate). Two particularly important aspects of group training activities are a focus on higher level cognitive and affective processes and a wide range of response options. Communication and interaction skills, cooperation, and appreciation of other students' contributions are emphasized.

Individual and small-group investigation of real problems is the culmination of earlier activities: student learning takes shape as a final product. The emphasis is on investigative or creative work that is of the real world, not a contrived classroom activity; it is particularly suited for gifted children, requiring not only the skills of exploration and communication already developed but also the skills of organization and analysis needed to process the raw data meaningfully. A possible follow-up to earlier activities might question how traffic patterns around the school could be improved. The student would gather data in a real-life situation and then organize a compaign to modify traffic patterns. In the course of the campaign the student would need to communicate with significant community leaders, perhaps by submitting a letter to the editor in the local newspaper or appearing before the city council.

A Sequence for Academic Skills and Concepts Children with high academic potential typically show an interest in language acquisition, books, advanced ideas, and mathematics at an early age. These children can profit from systematic exposure to formal learning before they enter school. A sequence for academic skills

Encourage good students to communicate and cooperate as they investigate.

and concepts is a model for use by parents, teachers, and other child-care person-nel in helping potentially gifted preschoolers acquire concepts and skills in an efficient and correct manner (Stephens & Wolf, 1981). It permits teachers and parents to determine the level of mastery a young child has achieved on a specific skill or concept and provides a natural sequence for guiding the child toward total mastery.

Developmental learning theory suggests a natural sequence for the acquisition of early academic skills and concepts. The sequence, as shown in Table 13-3, specifies six phases in learning these beginning skills and concepts (Stephens & Wolf, 1981). This model provides a widely applicable teaching format that can be em-

Table 13-3 A sequence for academic skills and concepts

Phase	Behaviors	Examples
1. Discriminating and differentiating	Attend to details, match stimuli, see and hear similarities and differences	Identify common root words with suffixes
2. Labeling	Use names and other language symbols to identify stimuli, forms, and concepts	Name root words and suffixes
3. Copying and imitating	Copy, trace, or imitate responses in the presence of stimuli or immediately following exposure	Tell meaning of root words and words after suffixes are added
4. Reproducing to mastery	Respond from memory or in presence of visual, auditory, or other sensory cues; receive feedback in form of correction and/or encouragement	Tell meaning of root words before and after addition of suffixes
5. Practicing	Practice newly acquired skill and/or concept	Practice identifying root words before and after suffixes are added
6. Applying	Use mastered skill under direction of instructional agent	Demonstrate knowledge of root words, apply suffixes appropriately in oral and/or written speech

SOURCE: From "Instructional Models" by T. M. Stephens and J. M. Wolf, 1981, *Directive Teacher*, 3(3). Copyright 1981 by *Directive Teacher*. Reprinted by permission.

ployed in natural environments as well as in school programs for the very young gifted.

Instruction should begin at whatever phase has not been mastered and progress to the most advanced phase. For example, the manipulation of printed symbols through reading and writing often will not require passing through Phases 1 and 2 and aspects of Phase 3 because proper names and basic meanings for symbols will already have been acquired naturally. But when these symbols take on more complex meanings—for instance, when they must be understood in the context of printed passages—instruction may be necessary to achieve mastery. In this case instruction would begin within Phase 3.

These six phases do not always occur in the given sequence; learners can in some cases perform more advanced tasks prior to mastering easier ones. For example, children can sometimes copy or imitate responses (Phase 3) without having acquired correct labels (Phase 2). The extent to which the sequence is followed varies with the content, learner, and prior experiences.

Model Program

The Johns Hopkins University Center for the Advancement of Academically Talented Youth is a program that has its roots in the early 1970s study of mathematically precocious youth (SMPY). In 1971, 250 youngsters born between 1955 and 1961 were identified by their math performance on the Scholastic Achievement Test. They were selected for their strong mathematical reasoning ability (upper 1.5% of their age group in mathematical aptitude) and were encouraged to accelerate their educational programs, particularly in math and physical science. The Johns Hopkins program was initially limited to mathematically gifted students in Maryland but has been expanded over the years to serve youngsters gifted in verbal ability and those located in other geographic areas. The Johns Hopkins program and some prototypes are described here.

The Johns Hopkins University Center for the Advancement of Academically Talented Youth operates in Baltimore, Washington, DC, Philadelphia, Los Angeles, and four cities in New Jersey. Programs are offered throughout the year, with residential summer programs also available at Dickinson, Franklin, and Marshall Colleges in Pennsylvania. Twelve-year-olds are screened for this program in seventh grade; those who score in the top 3% on standard achievement tests, such as the Iowa Test of Basic Skills or the California Achievement Test, then take the Scholastic Achievement Test (SAT). To qualify for the Johns Hopkins program, they must score above the mean of college bound seniors (430 out of 800 for the verbal section and/or 500 out of 800 in math). Since 1972, 3,400 gifted adolescents have participated in the program.

The Talent Identification Program (TIP) is a summer program initiated in 1980 and located at Duke University in Durham, North Carolina. It includes 12- to 16-year-olds who score at least 550 in math and 500 in the verbal on the SAT. TIP makes special efforts to identify ethnic and racial minorities and offers financial aid to economically disadvantaged students. Participants also become eligible for special programs developed by TIP such as courses by mail on subjects ranging from literature, history, and Latin to chemistry, physics, and calculus. In addition, TIP produces the *Educational Opportunity Guide,* which lists 100 summer programs throughout 16 states in which these students may enroll.

The Rocky Mountain Talent Search operates at the University of Denver in Denver, Colorado. It includes seventh and eighth graders, 12 to 14 years of age, who have scored at the 95th percentile on total math or total verbal portions of standardized aptitude or achievement tests with national norms or who have received math scores of at least 450 or verbal scores of at least 430 on the SAT. A variety of courses are offered, ranging from math and computer science to philosophy and global issues. Cultural, recreational, and social events are scheduled for residential students. Some financial aid is available.

Much of the research on acceleration has come from the SMPY program and its satellites. Founder of the program, Julian Stanley, is a strong proponent of educational acceleration (1978). The intent of the SMPY program and others based on it has been to foster as much educational acceleration as is deemed appropriate with major input from the students themselves. Not only is such an approach cost effective for public education (Bereiter, 1976), but it is also beneficial to capable students who are eager to move quickly through the educational system to earlier creative accomplishment. Examination of the effects of acceleration on social and emotional adjustment indicates that students who participated in the SMPY program had enhanced feelings of self-worth and accomplishment, retained a more positive attitude toward education, displayed less egotism and arrogance, and had more time to explore hobbies and career options (Stanley, 1976).

Mainstreaming

Because gifted children have a wide variety of educational, social, emotional, and physical needs, it is important to have varied service options. The guide in selecting a service delivery pattern for any youngster should be "goodness of fit" (Vail, 1979). For gifted students, as for other exceptional children, the advantages and disadvantages of any arrangement should be considered in light of the particular needs of the student and her parents. Within the regular school system various administrative arrangements can be designed to accommodate the educational needs of exceptionally able students. Special grouping, early school admission and grade acceleration, and advanced placement are three such arrangements.

Special Grouping

In relatively large schools grouping may simply mean assigning all the gifted students of a particular age or grade level to one class. In smaller schools it is often necessary to include several age groups in special classes. A resource room, in which the gifted can spend part of their school day working with special teachers, represents another type of grouping.

At the junior and senior high school levels special grouping is often achieved through tracking, which clusters students in classes on the basis of expected performance. Past achievement or potential ability may be used to determine placement. A gifted or talented student may be in different tracks for different classes. In programs of this type self-selection often operates—students opt for those classes and tracks in which they are interested and for which they have prerequisite skills. Additional placement flexibility allows gifted individuals to receive advanced placement through proficiency exams and move through a given sequence of courses more rapidly. This is a particularly important option for gifted students. Special grouping arrangements are also useful for students with particular talents. Orchestra and band programs and advanced art classes, within the school and in the community, serve some of the needs of these students.

Early School Admission and Grade Acceleration

Some schools permit gifted students to enroll at earlier-than-usual ages, depending on psychological testing and trial placements. In some programs bright students can skip kindergarten or begin kindergarten early. In the primary grades students are seldom permitted to skip more than one grade because of the possible effect on social adjustment. Grade skipping can also be done in later years, although careful study of the individual student and parental approval are prerequisites. When a grade is skipped, the student should be provided with any supplemental instruction and personal assistance necessary to make the transition a smooth one. Research indicates that acceleration—a controversial issue for many years—is, in fact, an extremely viable option for many gifted students. It enables them not only to move through school at a faster pace but also to have increased opportunities for needed interaction with older classmates (Braga, 1971).

Advanced Placement

Advanced placement generally refers to college credit obtained by high school students. Some high schools offer advanced placement courses, for which students can receive credit at certain colleges. Other high schools allow gifted students to take courses at nearby colleges in addition to their high school work. Still other systems permit exceptionally bright students to skip one or more years of high school entirely and enter college early (Pressey, 1967).

Innovation and Development

Asked in a recent interview to identify some significant events in gifted education in the last decade, Gallagher cited Guilford's Structure of Intellect Model and innovations in curriculum development spawned by the National Science Foundation—both contributions of the 1960s. "The field of gifted," he noted, "has been running on the intellectual capital that was produced 20 years ago or more and what we're looking for now is some set of new discoveries or ideas or concepts that will be fit for the 1980s" (Wolf, 1981, p. 26). Unfortunately, we still lack definitive answers for many questions.

What Are the Most Effective Delivery Patterns for Serving the Gifted?

There is a need to examine the wide variety of program modes for the gifted and identify those patterns that are most successful for various types of gifted students. Should efforts be made to develop more self-contained programs? Is acceleration an option that should be more widely used? What are the variables to consider when planning programs? Can we relate the level of achievement of gifted students to the special services they received? What are the attitudes and perceptions of students in special programs? There are few studies examining these important questions.

What Is Appropriate Education for the Highly Gifted?

Early studies indicated more adjustment problems for the highly gifted, a finding confirmed in recent studies that point to some social/emotional problems among highly gifted youngsters (Webb, Meckstroth, & Tolan, 1983). Longitudinal studies are needed that will examine the educational needs of this population so that alternatives can be provided within the public and private sectors.

What Are the Critical Components of Effective Teacher Training for Those Working with Gifted Students?

More information is needed about teacher characteristics and appropriate training experiences for those who work with the gifted. Seeley (1979) has made an attempt to identify important characteristics and to develop a list of appropriate training experiences. Another study examined preparation needs of teachers of the gifted in in-service and university training programs (Rubenzer & Twaite, 1979). Much more remains to be done.

Future Directions

There are many significant developments that will influence the direction of this field. Prominent among them are the need for counseling of the gifted and the role of parents.

Counseling the Gifted   Counseling services in the schools are typically devoted to problem children or those who need support services in order to succeed. Yet gifted children have a great need for guidance also. They may face difficult career and occupational decisions, a lack of adult models, and uneven personal development and social mobility (Sanborn, 1979). School counselors should involve them in both individual and group counseling activities in order to attend to their concerns (Zaffrann & Colangelo, 1977). School counselors can also serve as an information source for teachers, administrators, and parents; and they can contribute to the field of gifted education through research and program evaluation. In addition, teachers of the gifted should be competent in basic counseling skills. They are in a central position to provide supportive counseling, career information, and referrals to professionals for more extensive help. With increasing efforts to provide appropriate education to the gifted and talented, counseling that is more specifically oriented to the unique needs of this population should become more widely available.

Parents of the Gifted   In recent years parents of the gifted have become more active and involved in their children's education. Their involvement has been on two levels—organizing parent groups to be advocates for all gifted children and participating in the education of their own children.

There are growing numbers of parent advocacy groups around the country (Nathan, 1979). Many have become advocates for gifted education as well as for their own gifted children. Parent activism has been a major factor in increasing funding, promoting local programs, and encouraging state consultants for the gifted to assume more active roles. Increasingly, parents are recognizing their role as agents of change in the school and community and are becoming concerned about improving their advocacy skills. Assistance has been provided in some regions through parent leadership groups, which cooperate with state consultants to offer education in advocacy techniques (Ginsberg & Harrison, 1977). Workshops in which parents role-play to become sensitized to the complexities of decision making have been particularly successful (Smith & Nevins, 1979).

In addition, an examination of current journals of gifted education reveals many examples of parent involvement in the educational process (Fine, 1977; Wolf & Stephens, 1984). Parents seem to be interested in working as team members with educators in order to meet their children's unique needs. Teachers are sometimes reluctant to view parents as resources; a common cry is "All parents think their children are gifted." However, recent studies have indicated that parents are an excellent and fairly accurate source of information, and parent identification of gifted children has proved to be more accurate than that of teachers (Ciha et al., 1974).

Nonetheless, many parents of gifted children are bewildered and frustrated about issues at home and school and want to develop basic parenting skills as well as specific strategies for encouraging learning at home and making good use of community resources. They often feel inadequate in their management of their children and uncertain about what is appropriate programming or how to stimulate and challenge their children in and out of school. Just as schools have become more involved in educating parents of handicapped children, there is a need for them to establish educational programs for parents of the gifted. There are, in fact, increasing numbers of such programs (Wolf & Stephens, 1984) under the sponsorship of parent groups, school districts, and universities. Some help is available, too, in written form; an examination of the literature yields several current works for parents (Vail, 1979). To meet the expanding role of the educator in parent education, there is also a need for increased training of professionals to deal with parents' concerns.

Summary

Support of programs for the gifted has waxed and waned in accord with social, political, and economic conditions. Although all gifted children are not yet identified and appropriately served, there is currently a high level of interest in meeting the needs of this population, and a wide variety of programs can be found nationwide. Professionals acknowledge some critical problems in identifying the gifted, especially those from culturally different environments, the gifted handicapped, and gifted underachievers.

No precise definition of giftedness is widely accepted. A major problem is deciding what intelligence is. Terman defined intelligence as the ability to acquire and manipulate concepts. Guilford analyzed it in terms of three dimensions of performance: operation, content, and product. He included intelligence as measured by tests and divergent thinking. Torrance, on the other hand, stressed creative thinking ability as a criterion for giftedness and attributed to it fluency of ideas, flexibility, originality, and elaboration. The federal government's current definition says the gifted and talented possess "demonstrated or potential abilities that give evidence of high performance capability in areas such as intellectual, creative, specific academic, leadership ability, or in the performing and visual arts." Renzulli has identified some problems with this definition; he defines giftedness as a combination of three factors—above-average ability, task commitment, and creativity.

There are many factors contributing to giftedness; these include heredity, prenatal and perinatal care, and early childhood environment. The gifted and talented exhibit individual as well as group differences; the highly creative may be very different from the highly intelligent, for example.

Major assessment techniques used to identify the gifted and talented include intelligence and achievement tests; creativity tests; and teacher, parent, peer, and self-evaluation. Talent in an academic area can be evaluated with standardized tests and/or direct observation. Two instruments used to assess creativity and gift-edness are the Torrance Tests of Creative Thinking and the Renzulli-Hartman Scales. Special efforts are being made to identify the culturally different gifted. Similar efforts need to be made to identify gifted females, the gifted handicapped, and gifted underachievers.

The range of services to broaden the learning opportunities for the gifted should include stimulation through community resources and extracurricular activities. Some of the services need to be provided outside the scope of the regular school program. Within the school system various arrangements exist for serving the gifted: special grouping and tracking, early school admission and grade acceleration programs, advanced placement classes, and concurrent enrollment programs.

There is no firm agreement on the characteristics that make teachers successful with the gifted. However, there are some personal characteristics that seem to be critical: a high level of intellectual achievement, good interpersonal skills, a secure personality, intellectual curiosity, and leadership ability. Additional professional characteristics needed are a strong command of subject matter, good information-handling skills, diagnostic and prescriptive teaching skills, and program development and leadership skills.

The curriculum for gifted students should stress conceptual, creative, and critical thinking as well as social adjustment, responsibility, and leadership. Bloom's taxonomy and Renzulli's Enrichment Triad Model provide frameworks for teaching the gifted. Other options include independent study contracting, the use of bibliotherapy, mentor programs, and group work with peers. Work needs to be done on counseling the gifted, encouraging career decisions, and involving parents in gifted programs.

Study Questions

1. Describe briefly the three major historical movements in the education of gifted children and youth, and relate each to the social, economic, and political forces existing at the time.

2. "Giftedness is relative to a given society's values at certain times in its history." Explain this statement and describe its effect on the accepted definition of giftedness.

3. Contrast commonly accepted views of intelligence and creativity. Consider the positions of Terman, Guilford, Gardner, Khatena, and Torrance.

4. What three factors seem to interact in contributing to giftedness?

5. Based on your reading here, generate a comprehensive list of characteristics of the gifted. Consider the opening profiles of Lisa and Martin as you generate your list.

6. Based on the literature, what are some characteristics of highly creative individuals?

7. Discuss the interindividual and intraindividual differences of gifted children.

8. What are some problems in the assessment of giftedness in very young children? What alternatives to traditional intelligence tests might be used?

9. What are some problems in the assessment of culturally different gifted youngsters? Of handicapped gifted youngsters? Of gifted females? Of gifted underachievers?

10. Contrast direct and indirect service provisions for the gifted.

11. Identify and discuss briefly the following intervention methods for the gifted; independent study contracting, bibliotherapy, mentor programs, group interaction techniques, early admission and concurrent enrollment.

12. Based on your reading about the personal and professional characteristics of successful teachers of the gifted, develop and defend your own list of important characteristics for teachers of the gifted.

13. Why is a differential curriculum important for gifted students? Base your answer on the learning characteristics of the gifted.

14. Clark argues that instruction for the gifted should emphasize the higher levels of Bloom's taxonomy (analysis, synthesis, evaluation). Explain and defend or refute this position.

15. Identify the various administrative arrangements commonly used in serving the gifted, and cite some advantages and disadvantages of each.

TIPS FOR HELPING

1. Make special arrangements for high-achieving students to take selected subjects in higher grades.

2. Introduce elementary-age students to research methods.

3. Teach debating skills and encourage students to sponsor and participate in debates on topics of their choice.

4. Provide access to computers and allow students to do their own programming.

5. Let students express themselves in art forms such as drawings, creative writing, and acting.

6. Make public services available and try to guide students to the resources they need; develop a catalog of resources, such as agencies providing free and inexpensive materials, local community services and programs, and people in the community with specific expertise.

7. Form interest clubs with students as officers.

8. Use a questioning technique to help students arrive at information or concepts—for example, hypothetical "what if" questions.

9. Provide learning experiences that go beyond the basic curriculum, drawing upon mentors in the community.

10. Emphasize concepts, theories, ideas, relationships, and generalizations.

14

Contemporary Changes in Special Education

Norris G. Haring
University of Washington

Linda McCormick
University of Hawaii

In the decade following the passage of P.L. 94–142, much has been accomplished. The exclusionary attitudes of the past have been replaced by a sense of responsibility to provide an education to all children, regardless of handicapping condition. Since the last edition of this book, in 1982, the total number of children receiving services each year under P.L. 94–142 has increased by 600,000; New Mexico, for many years the only state not applying for funds under this law, has now joined the other states in doing so. As noted in a recent report by SRI International (1982), handicapped children are being identified earlier, and those previously unserved or underserved are now beginning to receive appropriate attention.

During these years there have been great strides in legal commitments, teaching technologies, and professional preparation. With the help of new laws and the efforts of parents, advocates, and the handicapped

themselves, the processes of deinstitutionalization and normalization continue to advance, and exceptional individuals are becoming increasingly integrated into our communities. In addition, instructional techniques and curricula are more appropriate to the age of the individual and the nature of the handicap; our educational practices are more effective as the handicapped continue to make gains in essential learning skills. Finally, professional programs have expanded, to respond to the need for more trained professionals and new professional roles.

Yet there is still a great deal to be done. Certain groups within the handicapped population have not benefited so much from recent changes as others have. There are needs in the areas of research and professional training. And there are legal issues to be resolved. Preparing exceptional individuals for the realization of their potential and maximum integration into the community remains an ongoing priority.

As in the past, the future directions in special education will be determined by the interrelationship of a number of factors, such as governmental policy, public attitudes, research and development in education, and advances in medicine and technology. This chapter discusses some of the significant changes now going on in the field and offers some thoughts about what to expect in the years ahead.

Law, Litigation, and Educational Policy

Judicial and legislative activity during the past 2 decades has affirmed the basic right of handicapped persons to have their life circumstances determined by citizenship rather than disability. Both Congress and the courts have been involved in extending and guaranteeing educational opportunities. However, although federal laws provide important protections and guarantees, the process of implementing them has not been smooth or consistent. There is great variation among states and school districts and even among individual schools within a given district. In part these variations are due to differences of opinion about exactly what the laws mean. Many aspects are still being interpreted by the courts, by departments of education, and by district administrators. In particular, there is considerable debate, much of it in the courts, about precisely what is meant by the terms *appropriate*, *least restrictive environment*, and *related services* as used in P.L. 94–142. The lack of clear definitions in the law has slowed the pace of progress toward full implementation.

Appropriate Education

The provision of *appropriate education*, as the term is used in P.L. 94–142, has been a key issue in a number of court cases. The Rowley case is particularly significant because it was decided by the Supreme Court. Justice Rehnquist, who wrote the opinion for the Court, made this comment concerning what is meant by *appropriate*: "Noticeably absent from the language of the statute is any substantive standard prescribing the level of education to be accorded to handicapped children." The Court then proceeded to define *appropriate education* as "education sufficient to confer educational benefit upon the handicapped child" (*Rowley v. Board of Education of Hendrick Hudson Central School District*, 1982).

The Rowley case involved a deaf student who was denied the services of a sign language interpreter because she was making average progress without special assistance. The Supreme Court ruled that since the child was receiving substantial specialized instruction and related services, she was receiving an appropriate education under P.L. 94–142 and was not entitled to an interpreter. Most special educators consider the Rowley decision to be a narrow, or minimal, interpretation of the law and one that could threaten recent gains on behalf of handicapped students (McCarthy, 1983). There has even been a suggestion that services were denied because of the accompanying cost (Heaney, 1984). The consequence of this decision is that Amy Rowley, and others like her, will not be provided with services unless authorities formally confirm that they are necessary.

An example of a broader interpretation is the decision of the Pennsylvania courts in the case of *Fialkowski. v. Shapp* (1975). The Fialkowskis, the plaintiffs in this case, claimed that their two sons' education was inappropriate for several reasons, including the grouping together of students of widely different ages and handicapping conditions and the lack of age-appropriate curricula. In this case the court ruled that to be appropriate, a child's education must incorporate the most current, state-of-the-art techniques; in-service education for the teachers and extensive consultation were mandated to ensure the provision of quality services.

Other cases brought to the courts have dealt with the issue of an appropriate education in regard to school year length. *Armstrong v. Kline* (1979) was the original case that challenged the sanctity of the 180-day school year for children with severe handicaps. According to the federal court of appeals that heard this case, "severely and profoundly impaired" and "severely emotionally disturbed" children may be affected by prolonged interruptions in their educational programming, such as the summer vacations created by the 180-day school year. These children may lose many of the skills they have learned during the rest of the year unless instruction is continued through the summer months. More important, the degree of skill regression and the time required to recoup lost skills are usually much greater for these children than for others. Thus, the court found that the 180-day rule, because of the regression and recoupment problems it may impose, would prevent severely handicapped students from receiving the services enabling them to reach the educational goals and objectives specified in their IEPs.

Furthermore, the court found that the rigidity of the 180-day rule was incompatible with the emphasis of P.L. 94–142 on the needs of the individual student. Given the variety of handicapping conditions and the fact that no two IEPs are identical, a school district's blanket refusal to provide more than 180 days of schooling runs counter to the legal mandate that special education be tailored to the individual. Thus, if there is clear evidence that a handicapped student will regress significantly during a summer vacation, then that student is entitled to an extended school year.

This ruling has since been upheld by other courts. In all cases the court decisions have emphasized flexibility rather than rigidity and close attention to the individual case. Thus, for example, in *Bales v. Clarke* (1981) the court interpreted the *Armstrong v. Kline* ruling to mean that school districts are not legally compelled to offer summer programs to all students. Not all severely handicapped children regress during a summer vacation to the point of needing summer programs. All children regress academically to some extent during the summer months, yet no law requires them to attend summer school. In *Bales v. Clarke* there was no evidence that the child's regression was "extraordinary or irretrievable," and the school system was not obligated to provide year-round schooling.

Special educators stress the fact that *appropriate* cannot be defined on an a priori basis; the definition of what educational opportunities are appropriate for a particular student can be determined only by reference to outcomes. White (1982) notes that a "programmatic decision is appropriate to the extent that it results in an improvement in the pupil's life" (p. 35). Peck and Semmel (1982) contend that the definition of concepts such as *appropriate* requires two kinds of child-specific knowledge. The first kind of knowledge results from placing the student in a specific educational environment and then evaluating the specific outcomes of that placement according to developmental progress criteria, social validation criteria, and the effects of the arrangement on the student's peers. (Social validation criteria are concerned with the significance of the behavior change to parents and other important adults in the student's natural environment.) The second type of knowledge is based on an examination of the interaction of student characteristics and interventions in the classroom placement. It requires an evaluation of how variables such as peer characteristics, classroom activities, social climate, and teaching styles affect the student and whether they maximize the probability of successful instructional and social outcomes.

Least Restrictive Environment

According to P.L. 94–142 the term *least restrictive environment* (LRE) means that "to the maximum extent appropriate, handicapped children . . . are educated with children who are not handicapped." Special class placement, separate schooling, or other removal of handicapped children from the regular educational environment is prohibited unless "the nature or severity of the handicap is such that education in regular classes with the use of supplementary aids and services cannot be achieved satisfactorily" (Section 612 [5]). Section 504 of the Vocational Rehabilitation Act includes a similar mandate. Here again we are talking about decisions based on outcome data. The wording of the law suggests that students must demonstrate greater gains in a more restrictive placement before that placement can be justified.

Underlying the LRE is the philosophy of normalization (Wolfensberger, 1972). Normalization implies that the residential, educational, employment, and social and recreational conditions of persons with disabilities should be as close to those of their nondisabled peers as possible. Any restriction that limits the participation of disabled persons in the normal settings, patterns, and activities of community life is a violation of their legal and human rights and cannot be justified as a response to their disabling conditions.

In order to achieve independence and normal life styles, persons with disabilities need to learn a variety of skills. The most crucial variables affecting the acquisition of those skills are the contexts, goals, and procedures of major service delivery systems—particularly the educational system. Training provided in segregated settings does not prepare students to participate in integrated environments; it is all but impossible to achieve normal socialization in abnormal settings. Failure to maximize training opportunities in integrated settings is failure to prepare handicapped students for community living.

The LRE concept does not mean that every handicapped student must be in a regular classroom for the entire school day. However, it requires maximum integration for severely and mildly/moderately handicapped alike. According to Wilcox and Sailor (1982), operationalization of LRE for severely handicapped students requires that they be served in settings that meet these criteria: (1) there must be nonhandicapped, same-age peers present; (2) there must be opportunities for interaction with nonhandicapped, same-age peers; (3) the ratio of handicapped to nonhandicapped students should not exceed that of the population as a whole; (4) there must be equal access to educational and nonacademic facilities (e.g., the locker room after physical education class); (5) the same schedule for and organization of activities must be in effect; and (6) quality educational services must be provided. In addition, student characteristics and outcomes must be considered.

Related Services

Related services are defined by P.L. 94–142 as

> transportation and such developmental, corrective, and other supportive services as are required to assist a handicapped child to benefit from special education, and . . . speech pathology and audiology, psychological services, physical and occupational therapy, recreation, early identification and assessment of disabilities in children, counseling services, and medical services for diagnostic or evaluation purposes. The term also includes school health services, social work services in schools, and parent counseling and training. (34 C. F. R. 300–13)

Since 1975 there have been a number of court cases concerned with the precise parameters of related services. In most of these the controversy has centered on whether schools are required to provide psychotherapy, certain health services, physical plant accessibility, parent training and counseling, and/or extracurricular activities (Osborne, 1984).

The leading case addressing the provision of health-related services was *Tatro v. State of Texas* (1979). The district court ruled that catheterization was not a required related service. However, the appeals court reversed the decision, noting that without catheterization the child could not be present in the classroom and thus could not benefit from the educational services she was entitled to receive. This decision, which was later affirmed by the U.S. Supreme Court, helped to clarify the distinction between required related services and exempted medical services. The appeals court excluded from the related services category those health services that must be performed by a licensed physician.

It should be clear from these examples that special education law is not static but is in a process of continual refinement and evolution. The basic groundwork has been laid, but the details continue to be worked out, not only in the courts but also in Congress (which may pass new laws or amend old ones) and in policy decisions at the local, state, and federal levels. Differences in such factors as assessment procedures, staffing patterns, budgetary restrictions, and the skill, philosophy, and interests of staff continue to contribute to variations in the types of children served and the services provided.

Educational Programming and Practices

The focus of recent litigation and legislation has affected programming for handicapped individuals, in terms of both the policy decisions about the goals of education and the educational practices that serve those goals. More specifically, special educators have been working to upgrade educational programming in order to provide students with an appropriate transition and ultimate integration into community life, extend services to previously neglected populations, develop "best practices" in teaching, and explore the uses of new technology.

A Commitment to Full Integration

The emphasis on the least restrictive educational environment is part of the preparation of handicapped individuals for full integration into community life, it has become a major goal of programming for handicapped youth. Achieving this goal—especially for the severely handicapped—will require important changes in public and professional attitudes, a restructuring of programs and curricula, and coordination of individuals and agencies both inside and outside the educational system.

Although schools have made great progress in recognizing the value of at least partially integrated placement for the mildly and even moderately handicapped, there remains an assumption on the part of most educators that mixed education is neither appropriate nor beneficial for more severely handicapped students. The severely handicapped have traditionally been channeled into lifelong physical and social isolation, moving from separate classes to adult residential placements, sheltered workshops, and other institutions. Integration has been generally thought to be unproductive, if not actually harmful. Results of the latest research, however, are showing that

> physical proximity can influence the attitudes and behaviors of those involved positively. Furthermore, no detrimental findings associated with educational integration have been reported for either severely handicapped or nonhandicapped students. (Schutz, Williams, Iverson, & Duncan, 1984, p. 28)

The positive results of such interaction include, for the severely handicapped, appropriate social models and increased academic achievements; for the nonhandicapped, more accepting attitudes. In addition, the goal of integration is consistent with the legal principles underlying P.L. 94–142: the right of all citizens to benefit from education and other public services, the belief that society as a whole is influenced by the treatment of all its members, and those rights guaranteed to all citizens by the Constitution.

Productive interactions between severely handicapped students and their lesser handicapped or nonhandicapped peers do not occur spontaneously, however, any more than the severely handicapped can be placed in the competitive job market without special training and support. Both outcomes are possible but only with careful planning. In schools the first step is to achieve physical proximity. This involves a change from traditional practices of grouping all severely handicapped students in separate school settings, or even in separate wings of the regular school building. Side-by-side classrooms for same-age regular (mainstreamed) and special education classes are an appropriate and practical beginning. Placing students on the same time schedule; integrating them for lunch, assemblies, and other nonacademic activities; and giving them the same access to school facilities come next. The following step is to consciously structure activities that promote beneficial interactions—cooperative projects for small, heterogeneous groups; peer buddy and tutor systems; training of peers to act as models and give reinforcement; presentation of factual information on handicaps to the school population (Schutz et al., 1984); and pairing of regular students with a special friend for recreational activities (Voeltz, 1980, 1982). Research has shown that although regular education students prefer interactions with nonhandicapped or mildly handicapped peers, they do not automatically reject the severely handicapped; and with more contact their attitudes improve. Social skills training is an important component of integration-oriented curricula, along with functional training in such areas as self-care, daily living skills, and prevocational and vocational training.

Appropriate training of all students is one aspect of integration; another is commitment and support from the community. As Gaylord-Ross and Peck (1985) have noted, a critical policy shift is called for. Rather than asking, "Is this student too handicapped?" educators and policymakers must learn to ask, "Is this environment sufficiently supportive?" Throughout history we have come to see that societies are more likely than not to reject their handicapped members. Often, the rejection is unfair and inappropriate, at least in terms of the individuals' ability to contribute. Integrating the handicapped into society must be planned and purposeful; without the goal of full integration we tend to regress.

Transition The achievement of full integration implies appropriate educational programming for successful transition from schools to community. As Williams and his colleagues emphasize (Williams, Vogelsburg, & Schutz, 1985), the last few years of a handicapped student's schooling must be future oriented. There must be emphasis on the development of functional skills and the ability to apply these skills in environments outside the school—at home, in public and commercial locations, in vocational settings, and even in leisure activities. The educational program should take postschool opportunities and services into account.

For transition to succeed, there must be appropriate support systems within the community, including adequate public transportation, employment opportunities, availability of group homes or other local residential placements, and vocational and social services. There must also be cooperation among the key agencies concerned with the handicapped—vocational rehabilitation, developmental disabilities, and higher education facilities such as community colleges and vocational training institutions. Transition is a new field and one of great current interest to federal agencies. Federal funds have been available for leadership training and demonstration projects; the experiences and results will be analyzed and disseminated and should encourage the replication of successful strategies.

Teachers offer support for the transition from school to community.

Serving the Underserved

Another important area of ongoing change is the extension and improvement of services to particular groups within the handicapped population that have often been inadequately served. These groups include the youngest and oldest covered by P.L. 94–142 and those with mild or severe handicaps. Over the past several years the particular needs of each of these groups have won recognition, and progress has been made. However, in each case more attention is needed, and it is with these groups that we should see the greatest growth in the near future.

Early Intervention   Federal support for preschool handicapped education actually predates the passage of P.L. 94–142. The Head Start program, created in 1965, was beneficial to handicapped as well as disadvantaged children. It was, in fact, amended to reserve 10% of all placements for handicapped preschoolers. In 1968 Congress passed the Handicapped Children's Early Education Act, which provided funds for research and model demonstration projects devoted to developing and testing methods for educating the preschool handicapped population. P.L. 94–142 requires services for all handicapped young people between the ages of 5 and 17. It also gives states the option of serving those under age 5 and from 18 to 21.

This discretion is one reason that the preschool handicapped population has not been fully served. Other reasons include the lack of adequate funding, facilities, and experience.

Nonetheless, research has shown that preschool programs for the handicapped are both highly beneficial and cost effective. We have seen that there is potential for increasing the responsiveness of the brain through interventions in very early childhood. The earlier an infant with a handicap is identified and provided with educational services, the greater the potential for improving his educational prognosis. Today, almost all profoundly handicapped and the majority of severely handicapped children can be identified at birth or shortly thereafter; the majority of moderately handicapped, before they reach 18 months of age. Thus, in most cases it is possible to establish infant intervention and parent education programs early and avoid some of the problems that affect so many exceptional individuals later in life.

Nearly 20 years after Head Start's inception, a long-term study of 123 families showed striking differences between the children who had attended preschool programs and those who had not (High/Scope Educational Research Foundation, 1984). Two-thirds of the preschool group, compared to one-half of the control group, graduated from high school; and nearly twice as many continued their education past secondary school. The researchers estimated the cost benefits of preschool education at seven times the tuition cost. This finding is sustained by the U.S. Department of Education (1984):

> Early intervention with handicapped children results in a significant decrease in services required later; in some cases it eliminates or reduces services which would otherwise be needed when the child enters school, thereby resulting in notable cost savings. (p. xvi)

By 1984, 38 states had mandated preschool services for at least some portion of the birth to 5 population. These children were, in fact, the fastest growing group receiving special education services; they represented one-fourth of the total increase in children of all ages being served. The majority of the programs reported were for children over 3 years of age, but the number of infant and toddler services was growing.

In order to fully serve the preschool handicapped population we need refinements in infant identification and programming, total intensive care for premature and low birth weight infants, adequate numbers of trained staff, and a nationwide program of early screening, diagnosis, and intervention involving the cooperation of educators, pediatricians, developmental psychologists, pediatric nurses, and other trained professionals. Developments in curricula, teaching technologies, and professional training are leading the rapid maturation of this relatively new field. The next few years should bring important advances in the screening of all infants, the cooperation and coordination of those involved in serving this group, the development and dissemination of validated programs, and increased official commitment.

Secondary-School Handicapped These students, whether mildly or severely handicapped, have seldom received the intensive efforts that elementary-school handicapped children have received. As recently as 1972, 75% of all special education programs were at the elementary level (Martin, 1972). Heller (1981) indicates four principal reasons for the problem:

1. The traditional special education model of self-contained classes did not fit the traditional model of secondary teaching, which was and is organized around subject matter specialties. Rather than adjust the schools to better fit the students' needs, secondary students were more often expected to adjust to the structure of the school.

2. Most training programs for special educators were, until very recently, heavily oriented toward elementary teaching.

3. The heavy emphasis placed on vocational education for secondary handicapped learners resulted in less attention to other, equally important components of a comprehensive curriculum.

4. For too many years educators, including many special educators, assumed that secondary students who did not receive vocational education needed no particular special programming or accommodations in regular high school classes.

Recently, attention has been shifted to the education of handicapped teenagers and young adults, with particular emphasis on vocational training. In 1984 the U.S. Department of Education reported that 24 states had mandated—and many others had permitted—services for handicapped youth through age 21 (if they had not yet completed high school) and that this group was one of the fastest growing of those served under the federal law. Among other secondary/postsecondary trends noted by the department were the expansion of vocational assessment, an earlier start in prevocational skill training, and an increase in vocational staff to include both vocational specialists and local business people.

Programming for older handicapped students generally has two purposes: to build upon and expand the elementary level programs and to prepare students for transition from school to community. As Wilcox and Bellamy (1982) stress, the goals of secondary education for the handicapped should be essentially the same as those for their nonhandicapped peers—"participation in the mainstream of community life through vocational contributions, leisure pursuits, and independent living" (p. 233). Helping a handicapped person succeed in the mainstream depends heavily on helping the individual achieve some economic independence. Thus, career education and vocational training are essential. The development of vocational education programs for mildly and moderately handicapped students has been a concern of special educators for many years. Kolstoe's work (Kolstoe & Frey, 1965, Kolstoe, 1975) resulted in a three-phase program of work training for retarded adolescents, including initial work experience, on-the-job training, and permanent job placement. More recently, Brolin (1979, 1982) and his associates developed a com-

Vocational training is offered to handicapped students at the secondary level.

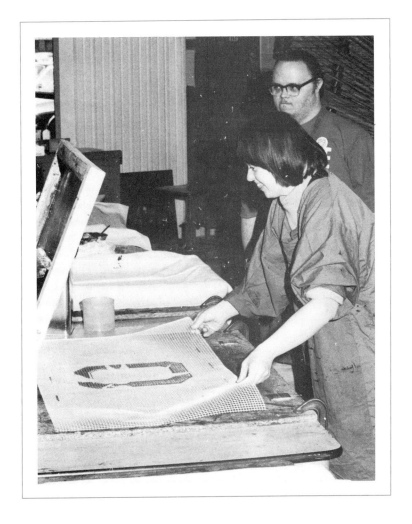

petency-based career education curriculum for mildly and moderately retarded students, with emphasis on daily living skills, personal-social skills, and occupational guidance and preparation.

Several special educators have also responded to the need for prevocational and vocational education for the more severly handicapped. Gold's early work (1972) recognized the potential of severely handicapped adults to develop vocational skills. His training sequences for assembling bicycle brakes, printed electronic circuits, and gas cap locks for automobiles are effective demonstrations in training severely handicapped adults. Bellamy (1976) followed with training sequences to develop a variety of marketable skills. Gaylord-Ross and colleagues (Gaylord-Ross, Forte, Storey, Gaylord-Ross, & Jameson, 1984) recommend that students' vocational training include short-term placements in several different employment settings. As an example, they trained severely handicapped interns to perform fairly complex tasks at sophisticated, high-technology job sites. Others, including Mithaug, have developed prevocational programs concentrating on establishing criteria for success in a sheltered workshop, particularly with severely handicapped adolescents (Mithaug & Haring, 1977). More than ever we are beginning to recognize the contributions that the handicapped can make to society and to offer them fuller opportunity for employment. Laws now guarantee that physical barriers may not prevent the handicapped from gaining access to their work sites. In addition, advances in instructional technology and behavioral science are promoting more effective intervention strategies, helping the handicapped to become more competent and independent members of our communities. In the future we will see increasing numbers of handicapped people competently performing jobs of all kinds, more fully integrated into more varied settings.

Mildly Handicapped   In discussions of service to the mildly handicapped, two problems are frequently cited. One is definitional. Since the passage of P.L. 94–142 the term *slow learner* has essentially been dropped from the educator's vocabulary. In its place are the terms used by state and federal laws to qualify students for special services—*learning disabled, mildly mentally retarded,* or *behaviorally disabled/emotionally disturbed.* In principle each of these conditions has quite different characteristics, but in practice the labels are often used interchangeably. For example, where services are available for a large number of students diagnosed as learning disabled, a large number tend to be identified. If the services are reduced, however, many of the same students may be relabeled and served in a different category. The result is a large, transient mildly handicapped population. Many

Regular classroom teachers want to know how they can best instruct the mainstreamed mildly handicapped.

studies are now underway to assess the extent of this problem and to propose ways of addressing it in future policy decisions.

A second, more urgent problem in serving the mildly handicapped is that of providing adequate support to teachers. It is obvious by now that these students can and should be fully integrated into regular classrooms, but this does not mean that they can be treated exactly like other students. They are, by definition, individuals with special needs; and their teachers need special training and extra effort to meet those needs. Finding time for this without neglecting many other responsibilities may seem to teachers like an overwhelming problem. Frequently, they opt to ignore those needs that they feel unable to meet. The focus in the future must be on providing appropriate training and staff support, to ensure that the benefits of integrated placement are fully realized.

The best gauge of our efforts with mildly handicapped students is whether they are completing secondary school. Unfortunately, the dropout rate has been quite high. Many states are now establishing statewide studies to analyze the problem and to identify and implement potential solutions.

Severely Handicapped   As our responsibility for educating all handicapped individuals has increased, professionals in special education have become more responsive to the moderately, severely, and profoundly handicapped. Since the 1970s there has been a national commitment to offer full educational services to those individuals historically denied them. Perhaps for the first time in history we have begun to realize that severely handicapped persons are capable of learning. And we are also beginning to understand that many unproductive behaviors of severely handicapped individuals—self-stimulation, blank stares, and the like—are in fact learned. Behaviors such as these result from a lack of systematically applied stimuli to promote the learning of other behaviors; they seem to be responses to the environment (Berkson, 1967; DeLissavoy, 1964), and their eventual effect is to compound already existing impairments.

The last few years have yielded more research than ever before in teaching the severely handicapped. Refinements in systematic instruction and curriculum sequences, advances in health technology and adaptive equipment, expanded early screening and identification, and more appropriate community services have all combined to offer the severely handicapped fuller, more normal lives. More and more we are coming to realize the crucial need for close and continued teamwork among professionals in medicine, nursing, occupational and physical therapy, communication disorders, psychology, social work, and community services. The problems of teaching the severely handicapped must be shared by all of these intervention and management disciplines.

In addition, we have recently made good headway in programming for severely handicapped students such as the deaf-blind, autistic, and severely mentally retarded. The deaf-blind, for example, have become a focus for special federal support, in an attempt to remedy many years of inappropriate services. It is expected that new teaching technologies for the severely handicapped will prove beneficial with deaf-blind students, and model demonstration projects are being established to assess this assumption. Programming for autistic children has also improved, partly because of the efforts of the National Society for Autistic Children (NSAC). Recently, the organization received federal funding to provide training for teachers and professionals working with autistic children around the country; the National Training Project is directed by Ann Donnellan and has been in operation since 1983.

Best Practices

Successful programming for all of these groups of handicapped students requires the use of teaching technologies that will adequately prepare each student for full participation in society. Such technologies are the current best practices in special education. They are the procedures, materials, activities, principles, and other environmental manipulations that have documented effectiveness. They are empirically validated concepts and strategies that demonstrate a strong and predictable relationship to positive student gains. Because they have broad application with special needs students (as well as more typical learners), these practices are among the most basic in the successful teacher's repertoire. Our discussion of the first three domains of best practices—classroom management, instructional organization, and lesson presentation—will be influenced strongly by a recent article by Englert (1984) in *Focus on Exceptional Children*.

Classroom Management   Successful teachers maintain a classroom environment conducive to attention and learning by establishing clear behavioral expectations, planning and teaching a signal system to elicit these behaviors, and providing immediate and appropriate consequences for compliance and noncompliance. Workable rules and routines are essential for teaching appropriate social behaviors and maximizing academic learning time. Brophy (1983) found that effective teachers actually provide instruction in classroom rules and routines for their students, much like that for academic behaviors.

Rules are first explained, posted, discussed, and justified. Then they are taught through modeling, rehearsal and practice, and feedback (Anderson, Evertson, & Emmer, 1980). The feedback may take one of two forms. Acceptable performance is praised with a specific reference to the rule that was followed. Inappropriate behavior occasions specific corrective feedback and rehearsal of an appropriate response alternative. Daily routines such as movement about the room, equipment use, and small-group procedures are described and explained as the need arises. Also, careful attention is given to arranging the physical environment to minimize disruptions resulting from children bumping into one another or classroom equipment.

Besides explicit instruction in classroom rules and routines, effective classroom managers demonstrate "withitness" and "overlappingness" (Brophy, 1979; Emmer, Evertson, & Anderson, 1980; Kounin, 1970). "Withitness" is the ability to monitor an entire class while providing direct instruction for a subset of students. Teachers who are with it know how to position themselves in order to maintain effective surveillance and make eye contact with any student. "Overlappingness" goes a step beyond withitness: the teacher is able to direct and respond to students who are outside the subgroup receiving direct instruction. In other words, effective classroom managers are able to do two things at the same time—without interrupting the flow of instruction.

Instructional Organization   Teachers who are effective organizers know how to schedule in order to maximize learning time, sustain high response rates, and maintain attention to academic tasks (Rosenshine, 1977). Two concepts are involved: academic learning time (ALT) and opportunity to respond. The first refers to the time students are engaged in academic-oriented behaviors; the second refers to the rate at which students emit specific academic responses.

In a comprehensive review of studies concerned with academic time analysis (conducted over a time span of more than 100 years) Borg (1980) found striking differences. Whereas academic instruction took up approximately 74% of the school day of second graders in the 1860s, only 47% of the school day of second graders in 1977–78 was taken up with academic subjects. Children between 1862 and 1926 received almost twice as many hours of reading instruction each day as the children observed in 1977–78. Two later studies confirmed this conclusion. Rosenshine (1980) and Good (1983) found that up to 50% of the school day in regular classrooms is allocated to noninstructional activities. Similar percentages have been reported in special education classrooms (Thurlow, Ysseldyke, Graden, & Algozzine, 1983).

As would be expected, the less time allocated for instruction, the fewer opportunities there are for children to respond. Thurlow et al. (1983) reported that some learning disabled students in their study averaged only 9 minutes per day in active reading practice, and only one-fourth of the 1.5 hours allocated for reading instruction for the entire class involved active responding (reading, writing, or speaking). Fox (1974) found that some inner city students averaged only 20 seconds per day in active reading practice.

As an instructional model, ALT was first developed in regular education. Fisher et al. (1980) define ALT as an observable measure of ongoing learning in the classroom. Any time spent by a student engaged in a task that the student can perform with success and that is directly related to an academic outcome is a measure of student learning. Among the principles of instruction derived from the ALT model are the following, drawn from a list of 14 by Fisher:

1. The amount of time that teachers allocate to instruction in a particular curriculum content area is positively associated with student learning in that content area.

2. The proportion of time that reading or mathematics tasks are performed with low success is negatively associated with student learning.

3. Increases in Academic Learning Time are not associated with more negative attitudes toward mathematics, reading, or school.

4. The teacher's accuracy in diagnosing student skill levels is related to student achievement and Academic Learning Time.

5. The teacher's prescription of appropriate tasks is related to student achievement and student success rate.

6. Specific feedback on academic performance is positively associated with student learning.

7. Structuring the lesson and giving directions on task procedures are positively associated with high student success.

8. A learning environment characterized by student responsibility for academic work and by cooperation on academic tasks is associated with higher achievement. (pp. 15–22)

If we were to condense these principles into a single statement, we would say that teachers must ensure that tasks are not too difficult for students, be consistent and specific in regard to expectations and accountability, increase the amount of instructional interaction, and increase the amount of ALT in desired areas.

Englert (1984) suggests three organizational techniques that can help teachers achieve maximum learning time and increased opportunities for academic responding: careful attention to scheduling and management, small-group instruction, and tutoring systems. Since even the amount of time allocated to instruction is positively associated with student learning (Berliner, 1981), it is reasonable to recommend revision of daily schedules. One way to increase time available for instruction is rigid adherence to lesson plans. Lessons should be consistently scheduled, intrusions should be minimized, and transitions between activities should be accomplished smoothly and quickly. To speed up transitions, Englemann (1982) suggests attention to teaching and rehearsal of transitions, use of a signal to mark the onset and termination of the transition, corrective feedback to children who are slow or disruptive, and reinforcement for quick and quiet transitions.

Small-group instruction is another means of increasing learning time; grouping permits a teacher to work directly with a larger number of students. In addition, group training may be a more effective instructional format for special needs students than individual training. Oliver and Scott (1982) found greater generalization when concept models were taught in a group format. Oliver (1983) also found equivalent or faster acquisition of nonvocal communication symbols in group training of severely handicapped adults (*if* the same symbol was being taught to each group member).

Tutoring systems are a third way to increase instructional time and provide students with greater opportunities for active responding. Successful tutoring programs are characterized by attention to tutor training and frequent measurement. They are probably most appropriate for developing sight vocabulary, reading fluency, spelling skills, and basic math facts.

In addition to maximizing academic instructional time, effective teachers find ways to ensure that students attend to and are actively engaged in their lessons. There are basically two types of learning situations in a classroom: teacher-directed lessons and independent seatwork. The latter is the more difficult for maintaining high task engagement. Englert (1984) suggests three management techniques to increase time-on-task for seatwork; monitoring, assuring a high correct response rate, and structure and accountability.

In order to manage seatwork effectively, teachers must circulate frequently during transitions to assist and to monitor progress. Both assistance and feedback

Tutoring increases instructional time.

should be immediate and continual (Englert & Thomas, 1982). A high correct response rate is particularly important with low-achieving students. Seatwork should be used for drill and practice, not for new skills instruction. Effective teachers also hold students accountable for their assignments. They keep track of completed work and student progress and require student assignments to be neat, accurate, and on time (Evertson & Emmer, 1982). Assignments that do not meet acceptable standards are redone.

Lesson Presentation   Effective teachers are aware of the need to use different procedures for different lesson phases. The teacher's role in the first phase of a lesson is to review what was learned the previous day, establish lesson rules and expectations, and prepare students for subsequent lesson activities. Teacher behaviors in the second phase of the lesson include modeling of the concept rule or procedures, providing many examples to illustrate the concept, and eliciting student responses (Becker & Carnine, 1980; Stevens & Rosenshine, 1980). Teachers should model and demonstrate how to use the target skill or concept and maintain high levels of accurate response through prompts and cues. In the third and final lesson phase teachers should provide additional opportunities for practice and systematic error correction when needed. Troublesome concept or skill elements should be repeated until there is a high rate of correct response.

In addition, effective teachers use three general instructional practices in all lessons—pacing, practicing for accuracy, and mastery learning. First, they maintain a brisk pace and a high rate of progress through the curriculum. Second, they provide opportunities for successful practice during teacher-directed lessons, reaching levels of 80% student accuracy or above. Third, they administer progress tests for regular evaluation of student mastery of target concepts and skills.

Generalization   The importance of independent living skills becomes more crucial the more severe a child's handicaps. Instructional time is at a premium; content and methods of instruction must be carefully chosen, and priorities must be clear. The teacher must focus on teaching not only specific skills but also the ability to use those skills whenever they are needed, at different times and under different conditions. This transfer of behavior, called generalization, is a key element in all instruction and especially in preparing the handicapped for transition from school to adult life.

In spite of the critical importance of generalization, it is rarely addressed in students' IEPs. In their study of severely handicapped students in two schools, for example, Billingsley and associates found that generalization was addressed in only 3% to 4% of the students' IEPs (Billingsley, Thompson, Matlock, & Work, 1984). The emphasis on functional skills was much better—they comprised about two-thirds of the total number of objectives in the IEPs. However, for the severely handicapped to make a successful transition from school to community life, both functional skills and generalization must be key elements of the educational program.

Stokes and Baer (1977) reviewed the existing literature on generalization to identify possible training strategies. They found the most common strategy to be "train and hope"; teachers anticipate that generalization will somehow be the fortuitous outcome of training. However, those authors also identified some systematic techniques for training generalization.

Training sufficient exemplars. Training occurs under a variety of conditions—in more than one setting, with more than one person, and with more than one instance or example. Effective teachers present sufficient examples to demonstrate the scope of the targeted concept or skill (i.e., "putting on a sweater" using a variety of sweaters). The precise number of examples depends on the student, the stimulus conditions, and the targeted response.

Programming common stimuli. This strategy derives from the assumption that the more similarity there is between the training setting and the setting where target behaviors are to occur, the greater likelihood there is of generalization. Thus, the training setting is made as similar as possible to the targeted setting where the skills will be used.

Sequential modification. This technique promotes generalization by providing training in all of the settings where the target behavior should occur.

Introduction of natural contingencies. Very often it is necessary to provide reinforcement on a continuous schedule during the acquisition phase of training. However, to increase the likelihood that new skills will be generalized, this method gradually discourages the student from expecting a reward every time a new behavior is performed. The frequency of reinforcement is diminished until it is similar to that in the natural environment.

Training loosely. Rather than applying rigid and tightly structured training procedures, this strategy emphasizes less controlled training with more varied conditions (e.g., instead of being told "Put on your shoes," the student may simply be handed a pair of shoes). This technique is based on the assumption that minimum control over training conditions promotes generalization to a broad class of stimuli.

Using indiscriminable contingencies. Consequences and schedules in the training setting are gradually replaced with those existing in natural settings. In this way naturally available consequences acquire reinforcing power by being paired with programmed consequences before the latter are discontinued. When a new behavior is not reinforced on a regular schedule, students have no way of knowing when a contingency is apt to occur. Consequently, they continue to perform the new behavior in hopes of receiving the reward whenever it is provided.

Mediating generalization. With this technique students are taught to monitor and manage their own behavior. They learn to be less dependent on others for behavior change and maintenance. They are able to acquire new skills and to behave appropriately without adult supervision.

In spite of their promise, none of these methods has been demonstrated to be completely effective. Not enough research has been conducted in controlled settings—in classrooms and homes with parents and teachers implementing the procedures. However, recent research efforts have provided some information with respect to facilitating generalization for severely handicapped students. The following factors seem to be necessary for teaching generalization effectively: (1) writing generalization objectives into each student's IEP; (2) reviewing all learning objectives for their functional value (i.e., Will the student really be using these skills?); (3) specifying examples of relevant and irrelevant stimuli in the training setting; (4) communicating with parents about each student's performance in both training and generalization settings; (5) structuring interactions with nonhandicapped or lesser handicapped peers; (6) varying the program setting and staff so that each student has a chance to practice skills in different places and under different managers (Billingsley, Haring, Liberty, Weisenstein, & White, 1984).

In addition, certain performance characteristics of students who are acquiring or perfecting a new skill may be critical to effective instruction. By examining such characteristics as the student's rate of performance, variability of performance, degree of accuracy, and weekly rate of progress, we can predict whether certain teaching strategies will lead to an overall improvement in the student's behavior. The next step would be to study the relationship between the student's patterns of learning and generalization of new skills. These patterns may provide a basis for predicting which strategies will facilitate generalization.

One related and rather controversial issue is the extent to which instruction should take place in natural settings. Frequently vocational training in secondary schools has included only career awareness classes and prevocational, or work support, skills. Preparation for a particular job was often reserved for postsecondary training programs. Some of the new approaches to vocational education, however, are placing students on job sites first and providing instruction on related skills in the context of the job experience (Bellamy, Rose, Wilson, & Clarke, 1982). By structuring the program around a natural setting, there may be increases not only in generalization but also in student responsiveness and in the usefulness and validity of the skills taught.

On the other hand, not everything can be taught effectively in natural settings; often they do not provide enough predictable opportunities for practice.

> The challenge . . . is to determine whether or not skills can be developed to an acceptable rate within an instructional environment and then transferred to the natural environment." (Billingsley, Haring, Liberty, Weisenstein, & White, 1984, p. vi)

Ecological Assessment   Handicapped students must be taught a variety of functional skills if they are to participate successfully in postschool domestic, vocational, leisure, and community environments. The procedures used by effective teachers to identify these skills, the natural environment cues for their performance, and naturally occurring reinforcers are called ecological assessment. It assures that present training addresses future skill needs.

One method of ecological assessment is an ecological inventory (Brown, Nietupski, & Hamre-Nietupski, 1976; Brown et al., 1980). It includes a variety of steps:

1. List the current and future environments where the student is apt to function (i.e., vocational, recreational-leisure, domestic, community).

2. Analyze the subenvironments of each current and future environment (one example of a community subenvironment might be a fast-food restaurant).

3. List and describe the activities that are necessary for functioning within the subenvironments (ordering food would be one activity in a fast-food restaurant).

4. Determine the skills or skill clusters the handicapped student needs to engage in each activity (ordering in a fast-food restaurant requires selection of items the student can afford, communicating the order to a person working behind the counter, and so on).

5. Develop a skill checklist with critical behaviors operationally defined and sequenced in the order in which they are performed.

6. Determine the student's status relative to each required skill.

7. Formulate instructional objectives to overcome identified skill deficits.

The final outcome of the ecological inventory is a set of instructional objectives directed toward the goal of independent functioning in important present and future environments.

New Technology

In the field of special education two applications of computer technology have especially great potential for the near future: highly individualized learning programs and communication devices. Among the latter some of the most promising include computerized improvements on tactile communications for the blind and a variety of devices that use the computer's potential to translate print into spoken sounds and vice versa. Examples include a voice synthesizer developed at the Artificial Language Laboratory at Michigan State University. It can be attached to a wheelchair and allows individuals with cerebral palsy to speak, by converting words typed into a keyboard into sound. Another device, which displays spoken words in written form rather like captioned TV news, is being tested in classes with deaf students at Rochester Institute of Technology. If the system works and is popular with students, it could replace interpreters in many secondary and postsecondary classrooms.

Until now, the promise of computers to provide self-directed, individualized instruction for handicapped students has been largely unrealized because of the scarcity of high quality educational software (Noble, 1984). As good software becomes available, it seems likely that computers will play a significant role in special education classes.

Personnel

The need for well-prepared special educators has long been recognized as a priority by policy makers and the administrators of special education programs. In fact, one of the first pieces of federal legislation that specifically addressed handicapped children, P.L. 85–926, was passed in 1958 and provided funds for the training of teachers to work with the mentally retarded. This act, expanded and incorporated into other legislation, has provided millions of dollars over the years to support the training of personnel to work with handicapped children and youth. P.L. 94–142 also addressed the need for professional preparation by requiring that states develop comprehensive plans for in-service training of both regular and special educators.

Shortages

Because P.L. 94–142 required major improvements in the way most school districts were addressing the needs of their exceptional students, it created an immediate and extensive need for more trained staff. The shortage of qualified special educators, as well as the need to provide special training for regular education teachers, has been a persistent problem in implementing the law.

Over 55,000 teachers were added to the ranks in the first 6 years after P.L. 94–142 took effect (U.S. Department of Education, 1984), yet almost every state continued to report a lack of teachers in rural and urban/inner city areas, as well as a shortage of teachers for secondary or older handicapped students and for the seriously emotionally disturbed (Smith-Davis, Burke, & Noel, 1984). An overall shortage is projected to continue well into the 1980s (Abramson & Hagarty, 1983), a result of teacher attrition and a general decrease in students choosing education as a career.

Attrition rates for special education teachers have always been higher than those for regular education teachers and are generally attributed to burnout, although there is little reliable research in this area. Abramson and Hagarty (1983) compared several different projections and concluded that a conservative estimate of attrition is around 6% a year. Based on the most current figures, this estimate means that about 15,000 special educators will leave the field each year.

The effects of such shortages on programs for the handicapped can be severe. School districts have responded with such undesirable solutions as increasing student/teacher ratios, busing students long distances to central classrooms, and relaxing the certification requirements for special education staff (Smith-Davis, Burke, & Noel, 1984). A longitudinal study of implementation of P.L. 94–142 (SRI, 1982) showed that local school districts were unable to develop programs they still needed because they lacked trained teachers.

Professional Standards and Certification

Despite these problems it remains essential that the quality of teacher preparation be high. One of the ways to control this quality is through certification, or licensing. Several related trends are emerging in special education today.

Since 1976 there have been three milestones in the movement toward professional standards in special education (Heller & Ridenhour, 1983). First, the National Council for Accreditation of Teacher Education (NCATE) approved and implemented a new standard pertaining to special education, which is now a part of NCATE's *Standards for the Accreditation of Teacher Education*: "The institution provides its graduates with the knowledge and skills necessary to provide an appropriate education for exceptional learners" (1979, p. 15). This standard does not require every college and university seeking NCATE accreditation to have a special education program, but it does require all colleges of education to provide their students with the knowledge and skills necessary for accommodation of exceptional learners in regular instructional settings. The second milestone was a resolution put before the 1981 delegate assembly of the Council for Exceptional Children (CEC), the largest special education professional organization. This resolution adopted by the assembly directed the Professional Standards Committee of CEC to expand its functions to include the development of a code of ethics and standards to govern preparation of teachers and professional practice. The third milestone was the approval of the 1982 CEC Board of Governors of the Professional Standards Committee's action plan for 1982–83.

The certification of teachers has long been a responsibility of state departments of education. In the early years of special education, few states required any special qualifications for teachers who worked with handicapped students (Martens et al., 1949). Gradually this situation has changed, and today special training is a certification prerequisite.

There are two basic types of special education certification: categorical and noncategorical. The first type requires training for a specific handicapped population, whereas the second type requires a basic core of course work and qualifies the teacher to work with a wide range of handicaps. Over the years the trend has been toward noncategorical certification. Currently, 26 of our states and territories offer this type, though many of them require additional course work or training for teachers of the severely handicapped, hearing impaired, and visually handicapped (Smith-Davis, Burke, & Noel, 1984).

Another trend in teacher certification, a response to the need to improve the quality of teachers, is minimum competency testing. Several states now require prospective teachers to pass competency tests before they can be certified. Thus, even those who have taken the required courses are not able to be licensed to teach unless they can demonstrate specific skills and knowledge. This movement is most apparent in regular education but is being expanded to include special educators as well.

Competencies

Exceptional students are those who require special arrangements and special instructional procedures or materials in order to learn successfully. To perform not only proficiently but almost automatically, in the way that a skilled surgeon does, the special education teacher needs a variety of carefully refined and well-established skills. Among those needed are the abilities to observe, analyze, and record behaviors critical to instruction. The ability to predict trends in student performance—to anticipate difficulties as well as sustained growth—is also crucial. Without the accompanying skill in formative measurement that can lead to new teaching interventions, a teacher may condemn a student to an inappropriate and consequently ineffective instructional plan.

In addition to these basic skills, the competent special education teacher must be fully familiar with the laws of behavior, understanding both the events in the environment that cue behaviors and the principles by which we can bring about behavioral change. The teacher must be able to identify the level at which a student is learning (acquisition, fluency, maintenance, generalization, or application) and specify an appropriate instructional procedure (shaping, molding, demonstration, modeling, cueing, drill, practice).

Horner, Holvolt, and Rinne (1976) have identified the following areas of competence for teachers of severely/multiply handicapped. For the most part, however, the listed skills are equally important for any special educator.

1. techniques for managing severe behavior problems

2. procedures for developing teacher-made instructional materials

3. skills in arranging the physical environment of a classroom to facilitate learning

4. basic principles of the acquisition of operant behavior

5. basic principles and techniques of measurement

6. basic principles of imitation training, generalization, discrimination, and maintenance

7. basic principles of task analysis

8. development and implementation of instructional programs

9. procedures used to develop curriculum sequences

In addition, the increasing use of computers in special education means that teachers must receive training in both the basic use of the equipment and the integration of computers into the total instructional program. Semmel, Cosden, Semmel, and Kelemen (1984) propose a two-tiered approach. In their model more teachers would be trained to a level of basic competency, able to use commercially available, off-the-shelf computer programs with their students. A few teachers with much more extensive training would have the skills to create educational programs and could serve as resource teachers, helping to design and prepare individualized instructional programs to fit each student's needs.

Beyond these specific skills, special educators must understand the roles of all the other professionals involved with exceptional youngsters and, perhaps most important, learn to support, cooperate with, and ask for help from the parents of the exceptional children with whom they work. Not only do legislation and the forces of parent advocacy demand this interaction, but so does the awareness that a handicapped student's educational needs do not end at the classroom door.

Staying Current

Special educators must stay informed about issues and trends in society as a whole and must remain responsive to the potential or actual implications of these trends. In addition, they must keep up on one kind of information that is often too dynamic to be learned from books or courses. That information varies somewhat from locale to locale and from year to year. It includes, for example, specific local procedures for observing legal due process in referring or placing an individual in special education, as well as procedures for maintaining confidentiality and for releasing legitimate information about a student. Every special education teacher has an obligation to become informed about such issues and responsibilities. The procedures for due process and confidentiality are now legal issues, and at least certain minimum requirements are in force in every state. But they were ethical issues long before the laws were passed, and informed teachers were paying careful attention to the rights involved even then. Like any other profession, special education demands current knowledge of the issues of the day.

Typically, one of the basic motives for entering special education is the desire to serve. In practice, the humanitarian motivation is necessary but hardly enough. Being effective, helping students learn and grow despite their handicaps, requires the kinds of competence just outlined and the determination to carry on even when success is far from dramatic. In addition, it requires a continuing effort to become even more effective. Like any scientist, special education teachers must change—to deal with new information and new procedures—and they must continually evaluate and refine their best efforts. In other words, special educators at all levels must assess themselves. They must collect information not only about their students' progress but also about the effectiveness of their own intervention. They must learn from their own teaching if they are to become truly responsive to their students.

Professional responsiveness must include the willingness to act as a handicapped person's advocate, in the face of pressures to undermine needed services. Recent cuts and shortages in funds have resulted in administrators in many school districts declaring unofficial moratoriums on identifying or placing additional students in costly special education programs. What should a teacher in such a district do? To whom does the professional owe primary allegiance?

> Individual educators should periodically review their personal reasons for entering the teaching profession. . . . More important than why they entered the field may be the question of current priorities. Do they wish to support children, even when their employment may be at stake? Do they intend to support the principal, superintendent, and/or school board, even when they may believe the responsible authorities are wrong? Do they want to get involved at all, regardless of which side of the controversy they are on? (Firth, 1981, pp. 491–492)

The commitment to continually assess our own competence and our own personal/social priorities is an essential part of becoming and remaining responsible professionals who serve exceptional learners.

Professional Roles

In addition to issues of teacher preparation, there are important topics and trends in the area of professional roles. Among the many changes that P.L. 94–142 brought about was the requirement that an IEP be formulated by a team of educators and the child's parents. During the formulation of the final regulations for implementing the law, there was some debate over the number of professionals who should attend the IEP meeting. Too little participation could result in communication problems or a fragmented program. On the other hand, too large a group could be inefficient and could easily overwhelm parents and stifle their participation. It is now generally recognized that a group of people, each representing a different area in the growth and learning of the handicapped student, must work together to make the best decisions about placement and services. Depending on the nature and extent of the learner's disability, different interactions will need to occur. Multidisciplinary or interdisciplinary cooperation are terms often used interchangeably in the field; however, some educators apply them to different levels of interaction among team members. A third level of interaction is transdisciplinary (Hart, 1977).

The *multidisciplinary team* is the oldest version of professional cooperation in serving the handicapped. Since most intervention programs for the more severely handicapped were attached to medical centers when this approach was developed, it is based on the medical model of intervention. The youngster is seen separately by various professionals, and their recommendations are sent to the teacher to implement. There is little consultation among group members; and when opinions are in conflict, the teacher has difficulty resolving the differences (Hart, 1977).

Members of an *interdisciplinary team*, in an approach that evolved out of the multidisciplinary model, meet to discuss the results of their findings and then offer recommendations to the teacher. Unfortunately, their recommendations are not always realistic or practical because they may fail to take into account the existing educational environment. An equally serious problem has been the lack of follow-up or feedback after evaluations and recommendations are made.

In a *transdisciplinary model*, as described by Haring and Billingsley (1984), professionals of different disciplines trade skills with and learn from each other; they exchange information in staff meetings and cross-skill training. The professional makeup of the team varies with each individual child and may include few or many members. One team member, usually the special education teacher, takes the lead in soliciting, synthesizing, and coordinating the input of the team. This person, together with the child's family, has the most frequent contact with the child and is most responsible for implementing the team's recommendations.

To accommodate the new demands of team planning, Bricker (1976) describes a new role for the teacher—that of educational synthesizer, a professional who can combine the observations and recommendations of other team members and incorporate them into daily intervention procedures for the student. This role is not limited to teachers; any member of the team can perform it as long as she (1) seeks appropriate information or techniques; (2) applies that information or those techniques to develop effective intervention strategies; and (3) implements those strategies to remediate problems or help the learner acquire new skills. As Iacino and Bricker (1978) note, "There are some activities that will remain in the province of a highly trained clinician, but it is becoming apparent that many forms of therapy may be effectively carried out by the classroom staff and/or parents" (p. 69).

In fact, the educational synthesizer is only one of four critical functions Iacino and Bricker (1978) envision for a new kind of teacher of the severely handicapped—the generative teacher. Such a teacher would serve also as a conceptualizer, someone with a broad knowledge of theory, curriculum, and behavioral technology who can develop new systematic programs rather than apply the all-too-common "cookbook" treatments. In addition, that teacher would instruct parents or other primary care providers and students in training to work with the severely handicapped. And finally, the generative teacher would develop and carry out evaluation of intervention efforts and share that information with all members of the educational team.

Issues Facing Professionals

Unfortunately, traditional roles and differences between disciplines can sometimes be obstacles to closer cooperation. There are some major issues that teams must resolve.

Territoriality   One of the pressing issues that threatens team cooperation is the question of who is best prepared to work with the handicapped learner. Nowhere is this problem more evident than in working with mildly handicapped children and youth, particularly those labeled learning disabled. Lieberman (1980) has painted a vivid picture of this lack of professional definition:

> This chapter in the territorial struggle and job market is currently being written. There are school systems where learning disabilities have been administratively placed under reading. There are school systems where it is taboo for a learning disabilities teacher to use a reading book lest she be caught by the reading teacher. If a child receives Title I reading help, he cannot go to the resource room. It is either one or the other. . . .
>
> Not only is everyone involved due to the multidisciplinary nature of the disorder; everyone claims that they are able to perform the same teaching functions that everyone else can. Reading specialists say that the vast amount of learning disabilities cases are reading failures and could be the province of remedial reading. Also they will say that their area of expertise is reading and that they know more about it than learning disabilities teachers. Similarly speech and language personnel are finding new strength in their psycholinguistic expertise as more and more learning disabilities professionals have bailed out of the ITPA. Process approaches have been overrun by occupational therapists. Are learning disabilities teachers in jeopardy? No. Most have seen the handwriting on the wall and have become "resource room teachers." Now they specialize in everything, which means that nothing can be attacked. Any one thing can be characterized as being such a small percentage of what the teacher does that it becomes a meaningless exercise to try to strip it away. (pp. 17, 18)

These problems are not just simple professional jealousies at work. As Lieberman implies, they are part of larger influences—like current patterns of teacher training and certification, economic pressures in a tight job market, funding tied to categorical labels, and confusion that results from overlapping categories. As Reynolds (1980) suggests:

> The current categorical approaches are not standing up. In fact, the funding systems and teacher-education programs that are based on categories have themselves become a part of the problem rather than a part of the solution. The old rule of the professional—"First, do no harm—is being violated. (p. 6)

Integration of Regular Education Teachers   Several specific strategies seem to offer some hope of lessening the resistance of regular classroom teachers to the mainstreaming of handicapped students. First, attitudes of regular teachers toward the handicapped must change. Since the confidence of regular teachers in their ability to teach exceptional learners appears to be related to their willingness to integrate them into their classes and since that willingness seems to increase with the number of special education courses they take (Stephens & Braun, 1980), such course work should become a part of every teacher training program. A second strategy is to give regular teachers in-service training in working with exceptional students. Another approach is to train special educators to become more effective consultants for regular educators; they must extend their contact with the regular classroom beyond the IEP encounter to a schedule of regular, sustained support. In addition, we need to offer regular educators more paraprofessional help in their classes, both to relieve the clerical burden of IEPs and to assist in direct instruction of students. As one government report indicates:

> Although paraprofessionals are successful in working with the handicapped and in helping to make busy classroom teachers more effective, relatively few paraprofessionals are available to the regular teacher. We estimate that only 48,000 paraprofessionals are used in the public schools, as compared with 1.9 million regular classroom teachers. (Comptroller General, 1976, p. 13)

Still another strategy is to help regular teachers increase their use of parent volunteers, peer tutors, and cross-age tutors to assist in the classroom.

Many, though not all, of these strategies require both the commitment of state and local education agencies and financial support for training and personnel. Yet as one observer has noted, "Attitude change can be neither legislated nor forced. . . . It takes time. It can best be accomplished via 'relearning by doing'" (Pappanikou, 1979, p. 52). Given time, the IEP and LRE requirements of P.L. 94–142 should bring about this change. All of the advances in providing services for exceptional individuals have taken time, but we cannot afford to be too patient. At the very least special educators must abandon territorial disputes in serving handicapped children and youth and involve as many professionals in the IEP process as can provide optimum service. The concept of the transdisciplinary team, with its commitment to shared responsibility and cooperation, is important in this effort.

Parent Involvement   Professionals must also pay more attention to parents, who should be key participants in any educational plan. Now, more than ever, we recognize that parent involvement is a critical element in the success of early intervention programs—and in the success of long-term programs for the severely and multiply handicapped as well. The value of keeping a handicapped child at home, in a normal family environment, must always be weighed against the high costs to the family, both financial and interpersonal. Parents who place their severely handicapped child in a publicly supported institution often pay nothing for that care. On the other hand, those who choose to keep their child at home must bear all of the normal costs of child care, as well as many of the extraordinary financial burdens associated with a handicapped child. In addition, those parents and other family members must share the daily demands and frustrations that are part of teaching and helping any severely handicapped person (the same kinds of demands and frustrations that special educators spend years preparing to manage). Without financial assistance and effective parent training programs, families may see no alternative but to place their children in institutions. During the last several years, more and more parents have joined with professionals in programs that establish consistent intervention goals and procedures across home and school settings. In the coming years we must expand these programs and work to remove the financial obstacles of keeping a handicapped child at home.

Conclusion

If we could somehow reduce the many complex elements in the history of special education and represent the developments graphically, the result would not be a straight line in any direction. Although we can generally identify progress in increased services accompanied by understanding and acceptance of exceptional citizens, the progress has not been smooth, consistent, or complete. There have been periods of rapid and of much slower growth. There have been setbacks. And certainly the progress in some areas has been more satisfactory than in others.

In the last two decades the field has taken a tremendous, unprecedented leap forward on many fronts. We are now in a time of continued but less dramatic growth with occasional reversals, such as the Rowley case. In many respects this is a time of consolidation, a time of weeding out approaches that have not proven successful and developing consensus around those that have. It is a time of closing gaps between those handicapped populations that have benefited most and least from recent efforts, between research and practice, between students' needs and available services. We can expect a continuation of trends toward balance and maturation of the field.

Other needed changes must come from society, in more accepting attitudes and a commitment to the principles that all individuals deserve the benefits of education and freedom and that all people should have opportunities to interact with and contribute to their community. This goal is already being sought by advocacy groups around the country. In the next decade we can expect expanded organization and continued pressure to extend such opportunities and to enforce the commitments already made.

Study Questions

1. Explain the ruling in the Rowley case and its implications for handicapped students.
2. If the term *appropriate* cannot be defined on an a priori basis, as some claim, then how should it be defined?
3. What is the normalization principle and what implications does it have for persons with disabilities?
4. What are some steps that schools can take to achieve positive interactions between severely handicapped students and their peers with less severe or no handicaps?
5. Describe recent trends in services for underserved populations.
6. Summarize the best practices in the following areas: classroom management, instructional organization, and lesson presentation.
7. Recent research efforts have provided some information about the issue of facilitating generalization for severely handicapped students. What are the factors that seem to be necessary for teaching generalization?
8. What is ecological assessment and how is it implemented?
9. What effects has P.L. 94–142 had on the discipline of special education?
10. Differentiate the multidisciplinary, interdisciplinary, and transdisciplinary team models.

Glossary

acuity   keenness of the senses; reception of external stimuli

adaptive behavior   behavior that meets standards of personal-occupational independence consistent with one's age and culture

advanced placement   option available to high school students whereby they may complete college level courses and receive college credit through examination

advocacy   providing support

amblyopia ex anopsia ("lazy eye")   inability to focus both eyes on same object (strabismus), sometimes resulting in brain's repression of image received from one eye; can eventually destroy that eye's ability to function

aphasia   severe language disorder affecting use of symbols; results from damage to central nervous system

apnea   failure to breathe readily during or immediately after birth

Applied Behavior Analysis   application and experimental evaluation of procedures for modifying significant human behaviors in practical situations

appropriate education   as used in P.L. 94–142, "education sufficient to confer benefit upon the handicapped child"

apraxia   impaired ability to organize motor commands to speech musculature which results in improper sequencing of sounds in word production

at-risk (infants)   infants who, for socioeconomic, health, physiological, or genetic reasons, face likely developmental delay

audiologist   someone certified in identification, measurement, and study of hearing and hearing impairments who recommends rehabilitative procedures

audiometry   various methods to assess hearing acuity

autism   see *infantile autism.*

behavior   overt response to a stimulus emitted voluntarily or elicited involuntarily

behavioral model   assumes that many forms of abnormal behavior are learned responses. Operant conditioning, respondent conditioning, and modeling are some of the mechanisms through which behaviors are acquired and regulated. Treatment involves environmental modifications of antecedent or consequent events

behavior disorders   behavior characteristics that (1) deviate from educators' standards of normality and (2) impair the functioning of that student and/or others. Manifested as environmental conflicts and/or personal disturbances and typically accompanied by learning disorders

behavior modification   systematic arrangement of environmental events (antecedent and consequent events) to produce specific changes in observable behavior. May include positive reinforcement, negative reinforcement, time-out, response cost, modeling, etc.

bibliotherapy   use of reading materials to help solve emotional problems and to promote mental health

Bilingual Education Act   law providing that non-English-speaking students are entitled to educational opportunities in their native language

blind   totally without vision or having light perception only

bonding   the process by which infants and parents become attached to each other through a series of reciprocal and rhythmical interactions

braille   system of reading and writing for the blind that uses embossed dots, named after its developer, Louis Braille

Brown v. Board of Education   case in which U.S. Supreme Court ruled that states may not provide "separate but equal" educational facilities; beginning of racial integration in U.S. schools and foundation for integration of handicapped students into regular classrooms

CAI   Computer-Assisted Instruction; includes drill-and-practice, tutorials, games, simulations, problem solving, and word processing

central visual acuity   sharpness or clarity of vision at the center or focal point of the visual field

cerebral palsy   disorder that is the result of damage to or maldevelopment of the brain

childhood schizophrenia   severe disorder of childhood, probably distinguishable from autism. Characterized by bizarre behavior patterns, distortions of thinking, and abnormal perceptions

cluttering   rapid, garbled speech with extra or mispronounced sounds and sometimes mixed-up sentence structure

CMI   Computer-Managed Instruction; system using computers for planning and to document student needs and progress and for data processing functions

cognitive disability   disorder in the formation or use of symbols and concepts during thinking, reasoning, planning, and problem solving

cognitive strategies   techniques that involve one in the self-control of one's own behaviors; strategies may include elements of self-instruction, self-monitoring, and self-reinforcement

communication   the whole spectrum of visual and auditory stimuli—facial expression, gestures, sounds, words, phrases—used to convey interpersonal messages

compulsory education   education required by state and/or federal law

conductive hearing loss   impairment in the mechanical transmission of sound waves through the outer and middle ear

congenital   present or arising from birth

content   of language, the meaning or semantic aspect

contingency contracting   contracting, usually written, that stipulates conditions for certain desired behaviors; conditions typically include precise behaviors desired, stated in clear and objective terms, the time period within which they are to be performed, and the consequences contingent upon successful performance

contributory conditions   situations that increase the risk of occurrence of a disability or disorder

creativity   the process of bringing a new, different, and unexpected response to a situation

cultural assimilation   relates to the "melting pot" concept whereby the entire American population is considered to be assimilated into a single race of people with similar life styles, values, language, and cultural patterns

cultural bias   inaccurate and/or distorted judgment based on cultural differences

cultural pluralism   appreciates and promotes cultural differences and recognizes unique contributions of various cultural groups to strengthen and enrich society

deafness   hearing disability that prevents processing of linguistic information through audition with or without a hearing aid

decibels (dB)   units of sound intensity perceived as loudness or softness

deinstitutionalization   effort to bring individuals in institutions into closest possible contact to the mainstream of normal society, either by removing them from institutions and placing them in alternative settings in the community or by changing the institution to permit more interaction with the outside community

developmental disability   severe, chronic disability attributable to a mental or physical impairment or combination of the two, which manifests itself before the age of 22 and results in substantial functional limitations

direct instruction   criterion-referenced, systematic instruction based on a subject's scope and sequence skills list; begins with lowest skill not mastered

disabled   having reduced functioning as a result of a physical deficit or a significant problem in learning or social adjustment; sometimes used more narrowly to refer to physical deficits or crippling conditions

disordered   having reduced functioning, particularly in academic achievement (e.g., learning disorders), social adjustment (e.g., behavior disorders), or oral language use (e.g., speech or language disorders)

Down's syndrome   a chromosomal disorder in which there is an extra chromosome in each somatic cell; a syndrome associated with characteristic flat facial features, mental retardation, and other congenital defects. Also called *mongolism*

drug therapy   major treatment for behavior and learning disorders, based on constellation of stimulant drugs such as amphetamines

due process   a right of a citizen to protest before any government acts to deprive him or her of the rights to life, liberty, or property

dyslexia   disorder characterized by failure to attain adequate reading skills

ecological model   assumes that behavior disorders are disturbances in interchanges between the individual and the social environment. Treatment is directed toward modifying the total ecological system

educable mentally retarded (EMR)   description for people who are mildly mentally retarded, achieve academically about 2 years slower than normal children during school age, and have a high probability of vocational independence

eligibility   determination as to whether a child qualifies for special educational and related services

emotional disturbance   See *behavior disorders*

endogenous   describing conditions of which the origins are inherent in the organism

epilepsy   seizure disorder caused by abnormal, excessive electrical brain discharges

etiology   origins or causes of a disease or condition, whether organic or environmental

exceptional   describing deviation from the norm, either by higher than average or lower than average performance or ability

exclusion component   one part of the P.L. 94–142 definition of *specific learning disability*, which excludes children whose learning problems are a result of physical or sensory handicap, mental retardation, emotional disturbance, or environmental, cultural, or economic disadvantages

exogenous describing conditions that originate outside an organism

extinction a procedure to weaken or eliminate problem behaviors by contingently withholding attention after a problem behavior occurs

fine motor skills small muscle actions such as those involved in eye-hand coordination, reaching, grasping, and object manipulation

fluency disorders interruptions of natural, smooth flow of speech by inappropriate hesitations, pauses, and/or repetitions

functional skills those tasks and activities most often required in routinely visited settings

gene specific segment of a DNA molecule that mediates transmission of inherited characteristics that influence an individual's development

gifted describing individuals who exhibit high levels of intellectual ability or who show potential for such development as demonstrated by their ability to think abstractly, solve complex problems, see relationships, and make generalizations

grammatical method method of teaching language to hearing impaired children by presenting them with specific grammatical rules for putting sentences together and then having them construct sentences using those rules

grant-in-aid a law that provides federal money to state and local governments to be spent for specific purposes in accordance with federal regulations

gross motor skills large muscle actions such as sitting, crawling, standing, and walking

habilitation provision of education and training opportunities that enable an individual to attain a level of independence commensurate with his or her potential

handicapped describing reduced functioning as a result of difficulty in responding to or adjusting to the environment because of intellectual, physical, or emotional problems

hard-of-hearing having sufficient residual hearing to process linguistic information through audition, usually with a hearing aid

hearing impairment hearing disability ranging from mildly to profoundly severe; includes *deafness* and *hard of hearing*

hydrocephalus abnormal blockage of cerebrospinal fluid in the cranial cavity; if not corrected, spinal fluid accumulates in the cranial cavity, enlarging the head and damaging the brain, usually causing mental retardation

hyperactivity behavior disorder characterized by excessive, nonpurposeful movement; restlessness, inattentiveness, impulsivity

hyperopia farsightedness; results in blurred vision for near objects

hypoactivity unnatural inactivity; passivity

idiopathic of unknown origin

imitation act of matching a modeled behavior, or behaving similarly to what is observed

impaired describing reduced functioning, often as a result of a sensory deficit (for example, loss of hearing or sight)

incidence actual occurrence of a condition, usually expressed as a percent of the total population; incidence estimates are usually higher than prevalence estimates, which include only the occurrences of the condition that are reported

incoordination lack of muscular control

independent study arrangement whereby a student works independently on a project or unit of study using methods, materials, and evaluation criteria agreed upon by the student and teacher

individualized education program (IEP)   educational program mandated by federal legislation in P.L. 94–142; designed and signed by parents, teacher(s), and any additional professionals needed to implement the program. The IEP reflects short- and long-term goals for the child for a year. Ensures confidentiality, placement in the least restrictive environment, and appropriate, individualized education

infantile autism   severe disorder of childhood, usually appearing by age 2 1/2. Characterized by lack of social participation, noncommunication, stereotypic behavior, and lowered cognitive and language abilities

institutionalization   placement in a collective, residential facility usually administered by the state and housing individuals labeled as mentally retarded or emotionally disturbed

integration   mixing of handicapped and nonhandicapped students in education and community environments

interindividual differences   differences between two or more individuals in a particular area; comparison of one person to another

intervention   design for changing an individual's behavioral, medical, or health status, or a change program itself

intraindividual differences   differences within one individual on several measures—considers strengths and weaknesses

IQ (Intelligence Quotient)   quantity derived in some systems by dividing chronological age into mental age and multiplying by 100 $[(MA/CA) \times 100]$

kinesthetic   describing neuromuscular sensing of the body parts' position in space

labeling   categorizing individuals by some group of like characteristics

language   arbitrary system of vocal symbols providing people with a way to interact and communicate. Nonverbal language involves signing, use of physical symbols, and body language

learning disability   a generic term referring to a heterogeneous group of disorders that are most evident in problems with acquisition and use of listening, speaking, reading, writing, reasoning, or mathematical abilities; presumed to be due to central nervous system dysfunction

least restrictive environment   the educational setting which is closest to full participation in the regular classroom but which still meets the exceptional student's special needs

legally blind   describing central visual acuity of 20/200 or less in the better eye after correction or peripheral vision reduced to an angle of 20 degrees or less in the better eye

limb deficiency   absence of one or more limbs, either as the result of postnatal disease or injury, or of a congenital problem

low vision   vision limited to seeing objects and materials within a few inches or feet away

mainstreaming   system for integrating handicapped students into regular classes, providing for their special needs through individualized instruction, tutoring, or their spending a portion of their day with a resource or special teacher

maladaptive behavior   inappropriate behavior or that judged as significantly below expectation for a specific age and cultural group

mental retardation   subaverage general functioning with impairment of adaptive behavior, manifested during developmental period—classified by etiology and severity; classifications by intellectual functioning are mild, moderate, severe, and profound

metacognition   refers to knowledge about and regulation of thinking processes

minimum competency testing   trend among some states to ensure that student promotions and graduations are based on mastery of certain basic skills

misarticulation   abnormal production of phonemes

mobility   the ability to move safely through the environment

mobility training   instruction to help visually impaired persons learn to travel independently in their home and community environments

modeling   behavior that is learned or modified by observing and imitating the actions of others

motor disorders   a broad term for disabilities related to muscle control and maintaining a straight and normal skeletal and muscular state

multicultural education   education that supports and encourages cultural pluralism

multihandicapped   demonstrating two or more disabling conditions

myopia   nearsightedness; results in blurred vision for objects at a distance

natural method   system of teaching language to hearing impaired children in carefully structured situations so they can learn through the process of hypothesis formulation and testing in sequences that closely follow language development of normal children

nature vs. nurture   issue of whether behavior can be attributed to hereditary or environmental causes

negative reinforcement   refers to strengthening a response by removal of an aversive event contingent upon the response being produced

neurological   pertaining to functioning of the central nervous system

normalization   a principle stating that care, education, and services for handicapped persons be available to permit them to function in a manner that approximates or equals what is normal in society

observational learning   learning that occurs from watching the behavior of others (models)

occupational therapist   a person registered and/or licensed to apply knowledge of the effects of occupation upon human beings to facilitate integration of biological, social, and psychological systems to attain or maintain maximum functioning in daily life tasks

operant conditioning   control of environmental stimuli so as to modify behavior

ophthalmologist   a physician who specializes in the care and treatment of the eyes

Optacon   device for translating print into tactile letters

orientation   ability to locate oneself in relationship to the environment or objects in the environment

partially sighted   describing central visual acuity between 20/70 and 20/200 in the better eye after correction

perceptual disorder   disorder resulting from inability to use one or more of the senses to recognize, discriminate, and interpret stimuli

perinatal   beginning with birth and extending through the first 3 or 4 weeks of life. Perinatal factors influencing child health include disorders of delivery, infections, prematurity, hypoglycemia, asphyxia, cardiac irregularities, respiratory difficulties, and factors that originated during the prenatal period

peripherals   any devices attached to a computer which are not part of the Central Processing Unit

peripheral vision   ability to perceive objects outside the direct line of vision

physical therapist   a person registered or licensed to apply knowledge or neurodevelopmental techniques to problems of feeding, positioning, ambulation, and development of other gross motor and fine motor skills

pinpoint   specify an observable behavior

play therapy   treatment approach in which play activities are used to establish rapport and communication between the child and therapist

positive reinforcement   refers to the increased probability of a response resulting from the application of a positive event

postnatal   pertaining to or occurring after birth

precision teaching   instructional procedure involving (1) pinpointing behaviors to be changed, (2) measuring frequency of behaviors, (3) designing instructional plan or intervention procedure, (4) measuring performance continuously and directly, and (5) graphing data to analyze trends and ensure that aims are met

prenatal   pertaining to the period before or occurring before birth

prevalence   reported occurrence of a condition, usually expressed as a percent of the total population. See *incidence*

prosthesis   an artificial device replacing a body part that was absent at birth or later removed

psychodynamic psychology   theories and therapies about behavior disorders, originally conceived by Sigmund Freud and revised by his many followers; emphasizes the importance of mental conflicts as causes of behavior disorders

psychoeducational model   adaptation of psychodynamic concepts for use with behaviorally disordered pupils in educational settings. Emphasis is on educational factors—abilities, interpersonal relations, skill level—in understanding and treating behavior disorders

psycholinguistic approach   emphasizes development of reception, association, and memory skills in the visual and auditory channels to alleviate learning problems

psycholinguistics   the psychological study of language and its effect on how the individual receives, processes, and expresses information

psychoses   profound behavior disorders of childhood; includes infantile autism and childhood schizophrenia

Public Law (P.L.) 94–142   Education for All Handicapped Children Act, requiring for all handicapped children "a free appropriate public education which emphasizes special education and related services designed to meet their unique needs"

public policy   law made or carried out by federal, state, and local governments

punishment   any event which immediately follows a behavior and results in the reduction or elimination of that behavior

Pygmalion effect   phenomenon whereby students' performances reflect preassigned classifications and preconceived expectations regardless of their abilities

reinforcement   any event or procedure which results in strengthening an existing behavior or teaching a new one

residential school   a school, usually self-contained, where students live, going home only for major holidays or summer vacation; many provide programs for preschool or elementary grades through secondary level

residual vision   vision that remains despite an impairment

resource room   a place where a teacher is available to work with individuals or small groups of students who have specific learning difficulties

response   a behavior following and resulting from a presented stimulus

right to due process   parents' and children's right to disagree with plan of goals and services of an individualized education program

robotics   general term for computer-operated devices which can simulate human functions

rubella   mild viral infection (German measles); if mother contracts during pregnancy, especially in the first trimester, infant may be born with hearing loss and/or defective vision, heart and nervous system anomalies

screening   process of identifying *provisionally* those children that require more complete assessment

self-contained day class   class composed entirely of exceptional children, usually all categorized under the same label (e.g., *educable mentally retarded, learning disabled*), who therefore do not participate in regular academic programs with their normal peers

sensorineural hearing loss   impairment of the inner ear or the eighth cranial nerve; reduces intensity of signal and may also distort the sounds received

sensory modality   systematic way of sensing the environment by use of hearing, vision, touch, etc. Each is a sensory modality

sheltered workshops   segregated vocational settings for the severely handicapped

social maladjustment   behavior that violates laws or community standards but conforms to standards of some social subgroup

spasticity   excessive tension of muscles and resistance to extension or flexion, as in cerebral palsy

speech   vocal transmission of language

speech pathology   an applied discipline made up of professionals with expertise in the remediation of verbal behavior disorders/delays

speech reception threshold (SRT)   decibel level at which one can identify a speech stimulus 50% of the time

spina bifida   a disorder in which a portion of the spinal cord is not enclosed by vertebral arches; usually a distortion of the spinal cord and roots results in a neurological disorder and related deformities

spinal cord injury   traumatic injury to the spinal cord that may result in paraplegia or quadriplegia

standard error of measurement   an estimate of the standard deviation of the population on which a test was normed

standardized tests   assessment instruments that meet certain reliability and validity criteria; include precise instructions for administration and scoring

stimulus   anything that serves to evoke a response, such as sound, light, shape, or sight

stuttering   speech disorder characterized by severe nonfluency

systematic instruction   process of instruction characterized by (1) systematic arrangement of conditions for learning, (2) initial assessment, (3) specification of objectives, (4) continuous measurement of performance, (5) instructional decisions based on performance measured, and (6) evaluation of overall effects of instructional conditions

tactile   receiving meaning from stimuli by using touch

talented   describing individuals who display superlative skills in a specific area as evinced by outstanding performance or products

task analysis   act of breaking down a skill into its behavioral components

teaching-family model   community-based group-home program developed by behavioral psychologists to help predelinquent youths learn socially adaptive skills

total communication   approach to teaching language to hearing impaired children that combines the aural-oral approach with manual communication

tracking systems   special grouping arrangements in which students of like ability and/or interest in a particular area are grouped together

trainable mentally retarded (TMR)   description (no longer widely used) for people who generally have an IQ of 25 to 50; indicates low rate of development; semidependence throughout life; potential for learning self-care and adjusting socially to family and neighborhood; not capable of profiting from a program for educable mentally retarded; may have physical and/or motor impairments and sensory deficits

trial placement   placing a student in a particular grade or grouping arrangement subject to evaluating its effectiveness. Often used for children given early admission to school or for acceleration (grade skipping)

use   of language, the pragmatic, functional, or social interaction aspect; the "why," "when," and "where" of language

visually limited   describing vision that is limited under average circumstances; with aids, materials, or assistance the person functions visually

voice disorders (voicing)   inappropriate intensity, pitch, and/or quality of vocal tone produced at the larynx and resonated in the pharynx, oral cavity, and sometimes the nasal cavity

References

CHAPTER 1

Abramson, M., & Hagerty, G. (1983). *A description of special education teacher training needs*. Unpublished manuscript, U.S. Department of Education, Special Education Programs.

Beez, W. V. (1968). Influence of biased psychological reports on teachers' behavior and pupil performance. *Proceedings of the 76th Annual Convention of the American Psychological Association*.

Blackard, K., Hazel, L., Livingston, S., Ryan, T., Soltman, S., & Stade, C. (1977). The interdisciplinary educational team. In N. G. Haring (Ed.), *The exceptional education training program: Vol. 3. Support services*. Seattle: University of Washington.

Comptroller General of the United States. (1976, September 28). *Training educators for the handicapped: A need to redirect federal programs*. Report to Congress.

Deno, E. (1970). Special education as developmental capital. *Exceptional Children*, 37, 229–237.

Elashoff, J. D., & Snow, R. E. (1971). *Pygmalion reconsidered*. Worthington, OH: Charles A. Jones.

Erickson, M. (1976). *Assessment and management of developmental changes in children*. St. Louis: Mosby.

Fine, M. J. (1970). Consideration in educating children with cerebral dysfunction. *Journal of Learning Disabilities*, 3, 132–142.

GAO cites overcounting problems with P.L. 94–142. (1980, September 15). *Department of Education Weekly*, 2–3.

Gaylord-Ross, R., & Pitts-Conway, V. (1984). Social behavior development in integrated secondary autistic programs. In N. Certo, N. Haring, & R. York (Eds.), *Public school integration of severely handicapped students*. Baltimore: Paul H. Brookes.

Gettinger, M. (1984). Measuring time needed for learning to predict learning outcomes. *Exceptional Children*, 51(2), 244–248.

Goldstein, K. (1927). Die lokalisation in der grosshirnrinde [The localization of brain damage]. *Handb. Norm. Pathol. Physiologie*, 10, 600.

Guess, D., & Siegel-Causey, E. (1985). Behavioral control and education of severely handicapped students: Who's doing what to whom? & why? In D. Bricker & J. Triler (Eds.), *Severe mental retardation from theory to practice*. Lancaster, PA: Lancaster Press, Council for Exceptional Children, Division of Mental Retardation.

Hall, R. V. (1979). *Opportunities to respond*. Poster session presentation at meeting of the Midwest Association of Behavior Analysis, Chicago.

Heward, W., & Orlansky, M. (1980). *Exceptional children: An introductory survey of special education*. Columbus, OH: Charles E. Merrill.

Hobbs, N. (Ed.). (1975). *Issues in the classification of children: A sourcebook on categories, labels, and their consequences* (Vol. 2). San Francisco: Jossey-Bass.

Johnson, J. L. (1969). Special education and the inner city: A challenge for the future or another means for cooling the mark out? *Journal of Special Education, 3,* 241–251.

Jones, R. L., & Wilderson, F. (1976). Mainstreaming and the minority child: An overview of the issues and a perspective. In R. L. Jones (Ed.), *Mainstreaming and the minority child.* Reston, VA: Council for Exceptional Children.

Kauffman, J. (1982). Social policy issues in special education and related services for emotionally disturbed children and youth. In M. Noel & N. Haring (Eds.), *Progress or change: Issues in educating the emotionally disturbed.* Seattle: University of Washington.

Martens, E., Elis, V., Graham, R., Lipton, E., Myer, L., Stanton, M., Stoddard, J., & Wagner, P. (1949). State legislation for the education of exceptional children. U.S. *Office of Education Bulletin,* No. 2, 23–57.

Martin, E. W. (1972). Individualism and behaviorism as future trends in educating handicapped children. *Exceptional Children, 38,* 517–525.

Minner, S., & Knutson, B. (1980). Improving vocational educators' attitudes toward mainstreaming. *Career Development for Exceptional Individuals, 3,* 93–100.

Minner, S., Knutson, R., & Aloia, G. (1979). *Concerns of vocational and special education teachers.* Unpublished manuscript, Amphitheater School District, Project EMPLOY, Tucson.

Nelson, R. (1980). The role of guidance in career education for handicapped students. In G. M. Clark & W. J. White (Eds.), *Career education for the handicapped: Current perspectives for teachers.* Boothwyn, PA: Educational Resources Center.

Neufeld, G. R. (1977). Deinstitutionalization procedures. *American Association for the Education of the Severely/Profoundly Handicapped Review,* 2(1), 15–23.

Pasanella, J. (1980). A team approach to educational decision making. *Exceptional Teacher, 1,* 1–2, 8–9.

Regan, M., & Deshler, D. (1980). Inservice training for vocational educators. *Career Development for Exceptional Individuals,* 44–52.

Reynolds, M. C., & Birch, J. W. (1977). *Teaching exceptional children in all America's schools.* Reston, VA: Council for Exceptional Children.

Rosenthal, R., & Jacobson, L. F. (1968). *Pygmalion in the classroom.* New York: Holt, Rinehart & Winston.

Rubin, R., & Balow, B. (1971). Learning and behavior disorders: A longitudinal study. *Exceptional Children, 38,* 293–299.

Sailor, W., & Haring, N. G. (1977). Some current directions in education of the severely/multiply handicapped. *American Association for the Education of the Severely/Profoundly Handicapped Review,* 2(2), 67–87.

Sartain, H. W. (1976). Instruction of disabled learners: A reading perspective. *Journal of Learning disabilities, 9,* 489–497.

Scheerenberger, R. C. (1983). *A history of mental retardation.* Baltimore: Paul H. Brookes.

Scranton, T. R., Hajicek, J. O., & Wolcott, G. J. (1978). Assessing the effects of medication: The physician and teacher team. *Journal of Learning Disabilities,* 205–209.

Silberman, C. E. (1970). *Crisis in the classroom: The reawakening of American education.* New York: Random House.

Smith-Davis, J., Burke, P. J., & Noel, M. M. (1984). *Personnel to educate the handicapped in America: Supply and demand from a programmatic viewpoint.* College Park, MD: University of Maryland, Institute for the Study of Exceptional Children and Youth.

Sontag, E., Burke, P. J., & York, R. (1973). Considerations for serving the severely handicapped in the public schools. *Education and Training of the Mentally Retarded,* 1973, 8, 20–26.

SRI International. (1982). *Local implementation of Public Law 94–142: Final report of a longitudinal study.* Menlo Park, CA: SRI International.

Stainback, W., & Stainback, S. (1984). A rationale for the merger of special and regular education. *Exceptional Children,* 51(2), 102–111.

Stick, S. (1976). The speech pathologist and handicapped learners. *Journal of Learning Disabilities,* 9, 509–519.

Tawney, J., & Gast, D. (1984). *Single subject research in special education.* Baltimore: Paul H. Brookes.

Tucker, D., & Horner, R. (1977). Competency-based training of paraprofessional teaching associates for education of the severely and profoundly handicapped. In E. Sontag, J. Smith, & N. Certo (Eds.), *Educational programming for the severely and profoundly handicapped.* Reston, VA: Council for Exceptional Children, Division on Mental Retardation.

U.S. Dept. of Education, (1984). The sixth Annual Report to Congress on the implementation of PL 94–142: The Education for All Handicapped Children Act.

Voeltz, L. (1984). Program and curriculum innovations to prepare children for integration. In N. Certo, N. Haring, & R. York (Eds.), *Public school integration of severely handicapped students.* Baltimore: Paul H. Brookes.

Wallace, G., & McLoughlin, J. (1979). *Learning disabilities: Concepts and characteristics* (2nd ed.). Columbus, OH: Charles E. Merrill.

Weintraub, F. J., & Ballard, J. (1982). Introduction: Bridging the decades. In J. Ballard, B. A. Ramirez, & F. J. Weintraub (Eds.), *Special education in America: Its legal and governmental foundations* (pp. 1–10). Reston, VA: Council for Exceptional Children.

White, O. R., & Haring, N. G. (1980). *Exceptional teaching* (2nd ed.). Columbus, OH: Charles E. Merrill.

Wilcox, B., & Bellamy, G. T. (1982). *Design of high school programs to severely handicapped students.* Baltimore: Paul H. Brookes.

Zettel, J. J., & Ballard, J. (1982). The Education for All Handicapped Children Act of 1975 (P.L. 94–142): Its history, origins, and concepts. In J. Ballard, B. A. Ramirez, & F. J. Weintraub (Eds.), *Special education in America: Its legal and governmental foundations* (pp. 11–22). Reston, VA: Council for Exceptional Children.

CHAPTER 2

Becker, H. J. (1983). *School uses of microcomputers.* New York: Center for Special Organization of Schools, Johns Hopkins University.

Behrmann, M. (1984). A brighter future for early learning through high tech. *Pointer,* 28(2), 23–26.

Behrmann, M. M., & Lahm, L. (1984). Foreword. In M. M. Behrmann & L. Lahm (Eds.), *Pro-*

ceedings of the national conference on the use of microcomputers in special education (pp. v–vi). Reston, VA: CEC.

Boraiko, A. A. (1982). The chip. *National Geographic, 162*(4), 421–456.

Budoff, M., & Hutten, L. R. (1982). Microcomputers in special education: Promises and pitfalls. *Exceptional Children, 49*(2), 123–128.

Cain, E. J. (1984). The challenge of technology: Educating the exceptional child for the world of tomorrow. *Teaching Exceptional Children, 16*(4), 238–241.

Center for Human Growth (1984). Weather Makers developed by Norma Jean Hemphill.

Chiang, A. (1978). Demonstration of the use of computer-assisted instruction with handicapped children. (Report No. 446-AM-60076A). Arlington, VA: RMC Research Corp. (Eric Document Reproduction Service No. ED 166913).

Clark, R. E. (1983). Reconsidering research on learning from media. *Review of Educational Research, 53*(4), 13, 445–459.

Dennis, J. R., & Kansky, R. J. (1984). *Instructional computing.* Glenview, IL: Scott, Foresman and Co.

Edwards, L. (1984). Teaching higher-level thinking skills through computer courseware. In M. M. Behrmann & L. Lahm (Eds.), *Proceedings of the national conference on the use of· microcomputers in special education,* 112–115. Reston, VA: CEC.

Evans, C. (1982). An invitation to the (near) future. *Today's Education, 71*(2), 14–17.

Feldman, D. (1979). The mysterious case of extreme giftedness. In A. Passow (Ed.), *The education of the gifted and talented: Seventy-eighth yearbook of the National Society for the Study of Education,* 20–59. Chicago: University of Chicago Press.

Hagen, H. (1984). *Microcomputer resource book for special education.* Reston: VA: Reston Publishing.

Hannaford, A. E. (1983). Microcomputers in special education: Some new opportunities, some old problems. *The Computing Teacher, 10*(6), 11–17.

Hannaford, A. E., & Taber, F. M. (1982). Microcomputer software for the handicapped: Development and evaluation. *Exceptional Children, 49,* 137–142.

Haring, N., Liberty, K., & White, O. (1980). *Data-based decision rules for instructional programs.* Unpublished monograph. Seattle: Child Development and Mental Retardation Center, University of Washington.

Hasselbring, T. S., & Hamlett, C. L. (1984). Planning and managing instruction. *Teaching Exceptional Children, 16*(4), 248–252.

Hill, E. W., & Bradfield, A. L. (1984). Electronic travel aids for blind persons. *Exceptional Education Quarterly. 4*(4), 74–89.

Hofmeister, A. M. (1983). *Microcomputer applications in the classroom.* New York: Holt, Rinehart, & Winston.

Kleiman, G., Humphrey, M., & Lindsay, P. H. (1981). Microcomputers and hyperactive children. In D. O. Harper & J. H. Steward (Eds.), *Run: Computer education* (pp. 12, 227–228). Monterey, CA: Brooks/Cole.

Lally, M. (1981). Computer assisted teaching of sight-word recognition for mentally retarded school children. *American Journal of Mental Deficiency, 85*(4), 13, 383–388.

LaVoy, R. W. (1957). Rick's communicator. *Exceptional Children* 23, 338–340.

Lloyd, J. W. (1984). How shall we individualize instruction—or should we? *Remedial and Special Education*, 5(1), 7–15.

McDermott, P. A., & Watkins, M. W. (1983). Computerized vs. conventional remedial instruction for learning-disabled pupils. *The Journal of Special Education*, 17(1), 13, 81–88.

Meyers, L. F. (1984). Unique contributions of microcomputers to language interventions with handicapped children. *Seminars in Speech and Language*, 5(1).

Palmer, J. T. (1984). Technology, career development, and special needs students. *Career Development for Exceptional Individuals*, 7(1), 3–11.

Papert, S. (1980). *Mindstorms: Children, computers, and powerful ideas*. New York: Basic Books.

Piaget, J. (1976). *The grasp of consciousness: Action and concepts in the young child*. Cambridge, MA: Harvard University Press.

Ruconick, S. K., Ashcroft, S. C., & Young, M. F. (1984). Making microcomputers accessible to blind persons. *Exceptional Education Quarterly*, 4(4), 9–22.

Schiffman, G., Tobin, D., & Buchanan, B. (1982). Microcomputer instruction with the learning disabled. *Journal of Learning Disabilities*, 15(9), 557–560.

Schneider, W., Schmeisser, G., & Seamone, W. (1981). A computer-aided robotic arm/work-table system for high level quadriplegics. *Computer*, 14(1), 41–47.

Smith, B., & Graystone, P. (1981). The handicapped typewriter. In *Proceedings of the fourth annual conference on rehabilitation engineering* (pp. 9–14). Washington, D.C.: Rehabilitation Engineering Society of North America.

Taber, F. M. (1983). *Microcomputers in special education*. Reston, VA: CEC.

Taymans, J., & Malouf, D. (1984). A hard look at software in computer assisted instruction in special education. *Pointer*, 28(2), 12–15.

Thorkildsen, R., Bickel, W. K., & Williams, J. G. (1979). Microcomputer/videodisc CAI package to teach the retarded. *Education and Industrial Television*, 11(5), 40–42.

Trifiletti, J. J. (1982). *Microcomputer-based instructional technology for children with learning disabilities*. Final Report. Hope Haven Association, Jacksonville, Florida. 13. pp.

Turkle, S. (1984). *The second shelf: Computers and the human spirit*. New York: Simon & Schuster, 23. pp.

Vanderheiden, G. C. (1977). *Nonvocal communication resource book*. Baltimore: University Park Press.

Walkington, P., & Babcock, E. (1984). Educational computing and the gifted child: A how-to approach. *Teaching Exceptional Children*, 16(4), 23, 266–272.

Watkins, M. W., & Webb, C. (1981). Computer assisted instruction with learning disabled students. *Educational Computer Magazine*, 1(3), 24–27.

Weir, S., Russell, S. J., & Valente, J. A. (1982). An approach to educating disabled children. *Byte*, 7(9), 342–360.

CHAPTER 3

Ainsworth, M. D. S. (1973). The development of infant-mother attachment. In B. M. Caldwell & H. Ricciutti (Eds.), *Review of child development research* (pp. 1–94). Chicago: University of Chicago Press.

Anderson, W., Chitwood, S., & Hayden, D. (1982). *Negotiating the special education maze.* Englewood Cliffs, NJ: Prentice-Hall.

Bailey, D. B., & Simeonsson, R. J. (1984). Critical issues underlying research and intervention with families. *Journal of the Division for Early Childhood, 9,* 38–48.

Becker, W. C. (1971). *Parents are teachers.* Champaign, IL; Research Press.

Benson, H., & Turnbull, A. (in press). Approaching families from an individualized perspective. In R. Horner, L. Voeltz, & H. Fredericks (Eds.), *Education of learners with severe handicaps: Exemplary service strategies.* Baltimore: Paul H. Brookes.

Berger, M., & Fowlkes, M. (1980). Family Intervention Project: A family network model for serving young handicapped children. *Young Children, 35* (4), 22–32.

Bernal, M. E., & North, J. A. (1978). A survey of parent training manuals. *Journal of Applied Behavior Analysis, 11,* 533–544.

Blacher, J. (1984). Sequential stages of parental adjustment to the birth of a child with handicaps: Fact or artifact? *Mental Retardation, 22,* 55–68.

Blacher, J., & Meyers, C. E. (1983). A review of attachment formation and disorder of handicapped children. *American Journal of Mental Deficiency, 87,* 359–371.

Bloom, B. S. (1982). The role of gifts and markers in the development of talent. *Exceptional Children, 48,* 510–522.

Bowlby, J. (1969). *Attachment.* New York: Basic Books.

Bristol, M. M. (in press). Issues in the assessment of single-parent families. *Journal of the Division for Early Childhood.*

DesJardins, C. (1980). *How to organize an effective parent/advocacy group and move bureaucracies.* Chicago: Coordinating Council for Handicapped Children.

Dewing, K. (1978). Family influences on creativity: A review and discussion. *Journal of Special Education, 4,* 399–404.

Dougans, T., Isbell, L., & Vyas, P. (1983). *We have been there: A guidebook for parents of people with mental retardation.* Nashville: Abingdon Press.

Drotar, D., Baskiewicz, A., Irwin, N., Kennell, J., & Klaus, M. (1975). The adaptation of parents to the birth of an infant with a congenital malformation: A hypothetical model. *Pediatrics, 56,* 710–717.

Featherstone, H. (1981). *A difference in the family: Living with a disabled child.* New York: Penguin.

Foster, M., & Berger, M. (1979). Structural family therapy: Application in programs for preschool handicapped children. *Journal of the Division for Early Childhood, 1,* 52–58.

Gabel, H., & Kotsch, L. (1981). Extended families and young handicapped children. *Topics in Early Childhood Special Education, 1* (3), 29–36.

Gallagher, J. J. (1979). Issues in education for the gifted. In A. H. Passow (Ed.), *The gifted and talented: Their education and development* (pp. 28–44). Chicago: University of Chicago Press.

Gallagher, J. J., Beckman, P., & Cross, A. H. (1983). Families of handicapped children: Sources of stress and its amelioration. *Exceptional Children*, 50, 10–19.

Gilliam, J. E., & Coleman, M. C. (1981). Who influences IEP committee decisions? *Exceptional Children*, 47, 642–644.

Goldstein, S., & Turnbull, A. P. (1982). Strategies to increase parent participation in IEP conferences. *Exceptional Children*, 48, 360–361.

Harris, S. L. (1983). *Families of the developmentally disabled: A guide to behavioral intervention*. New York: Pergamon Press.

Hill, R. (1949). *Families under stress: Adjustment to the crises of war separation and reunion*. New York: Harper.

Kozloff, M. (1973). *Reaching the autistic child: A parent training program*. Champaign, IL: Research Press.

McCubbin, H., & Patterson, J. (1983). The family stress process: The double ABCX model of family adjustment and adaptation. In H. McCubbin, M. Sassman, & J. Patterson (Eds.), *Advances and developments in family stress theory and research*. New York: Haworth Press.

Meier, J., & Sloan, M. (1984). The severely handicapped and child abuse. In J. Blacher (Ed.), *Severely handicapped young children and their families: Research in review* (247–272). New York: Academic Press.

Minuchin, S. (1974). *Families and family therapy*. Cambridge: Harvard University Press.

Moroney, R. (1981). Public social policy: Impact on families with handicapped children. In J. L. Paul (Ed.), *Understanding and working with parents of children with special needs*. New York: Holt, Rinehart & Winston.

National Committee for Citizens in Education. (1979). Unpublished manuscript serving as a basis for congressional testimony.

Olson, D., McCubbin, H., Barnes, H., Larsen, A., Muxen, M., & Wilson, M. (1983). *Families: What makes them work*. Beverly Hills, CA: Sage.

Olson, D., Russell, C., & Sprenkle, D. (1983). Circumplex model of marital and family systems: Vol. 1. Theoretical update. *Family Process*, 22, 69–83.

Patterson, G. R. (1977). *Families: Applications of social learning to family life*. Champaign, IL: Research Press.

Patterson, G. R., & Gullion, M. E. (1976). *Living with children: New methods for parents and teachers*. Champaign, IL: Research Press.

Roit, M. L., & Pfohl, W. (1984). The readability of P.L. 94–142 parent materials: Are parents truly informed? *Exceptional Children*, 50, 496–505.

Schilling, R. F., Gilchrist, L. D., & Schinke, S. P. (1984). Coping and social support in families of developmentally disabled children. *Family Relations*, 33, 47–54.

Simeonsson, R., & Bailey, D. (in press). Siblings of handicapped children. In J. J. Gallagher & P. Vietze (Eds.), *Research on families with retarded persons*. Baltimore: Paul H. Brookes.

Simeonsson, R., & McHale, S. (1981). Review: Research on handicapped children: Sibling relationships. *Child: Care, Health & Development*, 7, 153–171.

Stoneman, Z., & Brody, G. (1984). Research with families of severely handicapped children:

Theoretical and methodological considerations. In J. Blacher (Ed.), *Severely handicapped children and their families: Research in review*. Orlando, FL: Academic Press.

Strickland, B. (1983). Legal issues that affect parents. In M. Seligman (Ed.), *The family with a handicapped child: Understanding and treatment*. New York: Grune & Stratton.

Tseng, W. S., & McDermott, J. F. (1979). Triaxial family classification. *Journal of the American Academy of Child Psychiatry*, 18, 22–43.

Turnbull, A. P., & Strickland, B. (1981). Parents and the educational system. In J. L. Paul (Ed.), *Understanding and working with parents of children with special needs*. New York: Holt, Rinehart, & Winston.

Turnbull, A. P., Summers, J. A., & Brotherson, M. J. (1983). *The impact of young handicapped children in families: Future research directions*. Paper presented at the National Institute for Handicapped Research State-of-the-Art Conference on Parents' Roles in the rehabilitation of Their Handicapped Children up to Five Years of Age, Washington, DC.

Turnbull, A. P., & Turnbull, H. R. (1985). *Parents speak out* (2nd ed.). Columbus, OH: Charles E. Merrill.

Wikler, L., Wasow, M., & Hatfield, E. (1981). Chronic sorrow revisited: Parent vs. professional depiction of the adjustment of parents of mentally retarded children. *American Journal of Orthopsychiatry*, 51, 63–70.

Winton, P. (1981). *Descriptive study of parents' perspectives of preschool services: Mainstreamed and specialized*. Unpublished doctoral dissertation, University of North Carolina, Chapel Hill.

Winton, P. J., & Turnbull, A. P. (1981). Parent involvement as viewed by parents of preschool handicapped children. *Topics in Early Childhood Special Education*, 1(3), 11–19.

Winton, P., Turnbull, A., & Blacher, J. (1984). *Selecting a preschool: A guide for parents of handicapped children*. Austin, TX: Pro-Ed.

Witt, J. C., Mitler, C. D., McIntyre, R. M., & Smith, D. S. (1984). Effects of variables on parental perceptions of staffings. *Exceptional Children*, 51, 27–32.

Yoshida, R. K., Fenton, K. S., Maxwell, J. D., & Kaufman, M. J. (1978). Group decision making in the planning team: Myth or reality. *Journal of School Psychology*, 16, 237–244.

Ysseldyke, J. E., Algozzine, B., & Mitchell, J. (1982). Special education team decision making: An analysis of current practice. *Personnel and Guidance Journal*, 60, 308–313.

CHAPTER 4

American Association of Colleges for Teacher Education, Commission on Multicultural Education. (1973). No one model America. *Journal of Teacher Education*, 4, 264.

Baca, L. M., & Cervantes, H. T. (1984). *The bilingual special education interface*. St. Louis: Times Mirror/Mosby.

Baptiste, H. P., Baptiste, M. L., & Gollnick, D. M. (1980). *Multicultural teacher education: Preparing educators to provide educational equity*. Washington, DC: American Association of Colleges for Teacher Education.

Benavides, A. (1980). Cultural awareness training for the exceptional teacher. *Teaching Exceptional Children*, 12, 8–11.

Brown v. Topeka Board of Education. (1954). 347 U.S. 483, 493

Bureau of Census. (1981).

Cazden, C. B., & Leggett, E. (1981). Culturally responsive education: Recommendations for achieving Lau remedies II. In H. T. Trueba, G. Pung, & K. Au (Eds.), *Culture and the bilingual classrooms*. Rowley, MA: Newbury House.

Cole, M., & Bruner, J. S. (1971). Cultural differences and influences on psychological processes. *American Psychologist, 26*, 867–876.

Cole, N. (1981). Bias in testing. *American Psychologist, 36*, 1067–1077.

Dearman, N. B., & Plisko, V. W. (1981). *The condition of education*. Washington, DC: National Center for Education Statistics.

Diana v. State Board of Education, C. A. No. C–70–37 R.F.P. (N.D. Cal., 1970).

Dyricia S. v. New York City Board of Education. (1979). 79 Civ. 270.

Fuchigami, R. Y. (1980). Teacher education for culturally diverse children. *Exceptional Children, 46*, 634–641.

Fuhrmann, B. S. (1980). *Models and methods of assessing learning styles*. Paper presented to the Virginia Educational Research Association, Richmond.

Gearheart, B. R., & Weishahn, M. W. (1984). *The exceptional student in the regular classroom*. St. Louis: Times Mirror/Mosby.

Gottlieb, J., Cohen, L., & Goldstein, L. (1974). Social contact and personal adjustments as variables related to attitudes toward educable mentally retarded children. *Training School Bulletin, 71*, 136–148.

Greenleaf, W. (1980). *Work with* SOMPA. Paper presented at the Bureau of Education for the Handicapped-National Institute of Education conference Towards Equity in the Evaluation of Children Suspected of Educational Handicaps, Washington, DC.

Hoover, W. A. (1981). Analysis procedures and summary statistics of the language data. In A *longitudinal study of the oral language development of Texas bilingual children: Findings from the second year*. Paper presented at the International Reading Association Convention, San Antonio, TX.

Johnson, D. W., & Johnson, R. T. (1980). Integrating handicapped students into the mainstream. *Exceptional Children, 47*, 90–98.

Johnson, G. R. (1976). *Analyzing college teaching*. Manchaca, TX: Sterling Swift.

Jordan, C. (1981). The selection of culturally-compatible classroom practices. *Education Perspectives: Journal of the College of Education* (University of Hawaii), 20(1), 14–18.

Kagan, S. (1977). Social motives and behaviors of Mexican-American and Anglo-American children. In J. L. Martinez, Jr. (Ed.), *Chicano psychology*. New York: Academic Press.

Kaufman, A. S., & Kaufman, N. L. (1983). *Kaufman Assessment Battery for Children* (K-ABC). Circle Pines, MN: American Guidance Series.

Kagan, S., & Buriel, R. (1977). Field dependence-independence and Mexican-American culture. In J. L. Martinez, Jr. (Ed.), *Chicano psychology*. New York: Academic Press.

Kelley, T., Bullock, L., & Dykes, M. (1977). Behavioral disorders: Teachers' perceptions. *Exceptional Children, 43*, 316–318.

Killalea Associates. (1980). State, regional and national summaries of data from the 1978 civil rights survey of elementary and secondary schools. Prepared for the U.S. Office of Civil Rights, Alexandria, VA.

Langdon, H. W. (1982). Assessment and intervention strategies for the bilingual language-disordered student. *Exceptional Children, 50*(1). 37–46.

Larry P. v. Riles. (1974). 502 F 2nd. 963.

Lau v. Nichols. (1974). 414 U.S. 563.

Linder, T. W. (1983). *Early childhood special education.* Baltimore: Paul H. Brookes.

Lora v. New York City Board of Education. (1978). 456 F. Supp. 1211.

Madsen, M., & Shapira, A. (1970). Cooperative and competitive behavior of urban Afro-American, Anglo-American, Mexican-American and Mexican village children. *Developmental Psychology, 3,* 16–20.

Matluck, B. J., & Matluck, J. H. (1982). Formal English as a second language. *Topics in Language Disorders, 2*(4), 65–79.

Mercer, J. R. (1973). *Labeling the mentally retarded.* Berkeley: University of California Press.

———(1979). SOMPA: *System of Multicultural Pluralistic Assessment—Concepts and technical manual.* New York: Psychological Corporation.

National Foundation for the Improvement of Education. (1982, July 10). *Bilingual education fact sheet.* Washington, DC: NFIE.

Office of Civil Rights. (1982). 1980 *Elementary and Secondary Civil Rights Survey.* Washington, DC: OCR.

Parker, L. (1978). *Bilingual education: Current perspectives and synthesis.* Arlington, VA: Center for Applied Linguistics.

Pepper, F. C. (1976). Teaching the American Indian child in mainstream settings. In R. L. Jones (Ed.), *Mainstreaming and the minority child.* Reston, VA: Council for Exceptional Children.

Perrone, P. A., & Aleman, N. (1983). Educating the talented child in a pluralistic society. In D. R. Omark & J. G. Ericson (Eds.), *The bilingual exceptional child* (pp. 269–284). San Diego: College-Hill Press.

Reynolds, C. (1981). *Test bias: In God we trust: All others must have data.* Paper presented at the annual meeting of the American Psychological Association, Los Angeles.

Rodriguez, F. (1982). Mainstreaming a multicultural concept into special education: Guidelines for teacher trainers. *Exceptional Children, 49*(3), 220–227.

Rubin, R. A., & Balow, B. (1978). Prevalence of teacher identified behavior problems: A longitudinal study. *Exceptional Children, 45*(3), 102–113.

Spring, C., Blunden, D., Greenberg, L., & Yellin, A. (1977). Validity and norms of a hyperactivity rating scale. *Journal of Special Education, 11,* 313–321.

Tobias, S., Cole, C., Zibrin, M., & Bodlakova, V. (1981). *Bias in the referral of children to special services.* Paper presented at the annual convention of the American Psychological Association, Los Angeles.

Toronto, A. (1972). *A developmental Spanish language analysis procedure for Spanish-speaking children.* Unpublished doctoral dissertation, Northwestern University.

Wechsler, H., Suarez, A., & McFadden, M. (1975). Teachers' attitudes toward the education of physically handicapped children: Implications for implementation of Massachusetts Chapter 766. *Journal of Education*, 157, 134–141.

Witkin, H. A., Moore, C. A., Oltman, P. K., Goodenough, D. R., Friedman, F., Owen, D. R., & Raskin, E. (1977). Role of field-dependent and field-independent cognitive styles in academic evaluation: A longitudinal study. *Journal of Educational Psychology*, 69(3), 197–211.

Wong-Fillmore, L. (1981). Cultural perspectives on second language learning. *Teaching English as a Second Language Reporter*, 14(2), 23–31.

Ysseldyke, J. E. (1979). Issues in psychoeducational assessment. In D. Reschly & G. Phye (Eds.), *School psychology: Methods and roles* (pp. 247–260). New York: Academic Press.

Ysseldyke, J. E., & Algozzine, B. (1984). *Introduction to special education*. Boston: Houghton Mifflin.

Ysseldyke, J. E., Algozzine, B., & Allen, D. (1981). Participation of regular teachers in special education team decision making: A naturalistic investigation. *Elementary School Journal*, 82(4), 160–165.

Ysseldyke, J. E., Algozzine, B., Regan, R., Potter, M., Richey, L., & Thurlow, M. (1980). *Psychoeducational assessment and decision making: A computer simulated investigation*. Minneapolis: University of Minnesota, Institute for Research in Learning Disabilities.

Ysseldyke, J. E., Algozzine, B., Richey, L., & Graden, J. (1982). Declaring students eligible for learning disability services: Why bother with the data? *Learning Disability Quarterly*, 5(2), 37–44.

Ysseldyke, J. E., & Mirkin, P. K. (1981). The use of assessment information to plan instructional interventions: A review of the research. In C. Reynolds & T. Gutkin (Eds.), *A handbook for school psychology* (pp. 84–121). New York: John Wiley & Sons.

CHAPTER 5

Bachara, G. H., & Zaba, J. N. (1978). Learning disabilities and juvenile delinquency. *Journal of Learning Disabilities*, 11, 242–246.

Badian, N. A. (1976, April). *Early prediction of academic underachievement*. Paper presented at the meeting of the 54th Annual International Convention of the Council for Exceptional Children, Chicago. (ERIC Document Reproduction Service No. ED 122 500)

Baker, L. (1982). An evaluation of the role of metacognitive deficits in learning disabilities. *Topics in Learning and Learning Disabilities*, 2, 27–35.

Barsch, R. H. (1967). *Achieving perceptual-motor efficiency* (Vol. 1). Seattle: Special Child Publications.

Bateman, B. D. (1966). Learning disorders. *Review of Educational Research*, 36, 93–119.

Bender, L. (1968). Neuropsychiatric disturbances. In A. H. Keeney & V. T. Keeney (Eds.), *Dyslexia*. St. Louis: C. V. Mosby.

Bijou, S. (1973). Behavior modification in teaching the retarded child. In C. Thoresen (Ed.), *Behavior modification in education* (The Seventy-Second Yearbook of the National Society for the Study of Education). Chicago: University of Chicago Press.

Birch, J. (1974). *Mainstreaming: Educable mentally retarded children in regular classes*. Minneapolis: University of Minnesota, Leadership Training Institute/Special Education.

Boshes, B., & Myklebust, H. R. (1964). A neurological and behavior study of children with learning disorders. *Neurology*, 14, 7–12.

Brown, L., & Bryant, B. R. (1984). A consumer's guide to tests in print: The rating system. *Remedial and Special Education*, 5(1), 55–61.

Bryan, T. (1977). Learning disabled children's comprehension of nonverbal communication. *Journal of Learning Disabilities*, 10, 501–506.

Bryan, T. H., & Bryan, J. H. (1978). *Understanding learning disabilities* (2nd ed.). Port Washington, NY: Alfred.

Bryant, N. D. (1972). Subject variables: Definition, incidence characteristics, and correlates. In N. D. Bryant & C. Kass (Eds.), *Final report: LTI in learning disabilities* (Vol. 1) (USOE Grant No. OEG–0–71–4425–604, Project No. 127145). Tucson: University of Arizona.

Bryant, N. D., & Kass, C. E. (1972). *Leadership training institute in learning disabilities* (Vol. 1). Washington, DC: Office of Education, Bureau of Education for the Handicapped.

Busch, R. F. (1980). Predicting first-grade reading achievement. *Learning Disability Quarterly*, 3(1), 38–48.

Bush, W. J., & Giles, M. T. (1982). *Aids to psycholinguistic teaching* (3rd ed.). Columbus, OH: Charles E. Merrill.

Clements, S. D. (1966). *Minimal brain dysfunction in children* (NINDS Monograph No. 3, U.S. Public Health Service Publication No. 1415). Washington, DC: U.S. Government Printing Office.

Cone, T. E., & Wilson, L. R. (1981). Quantifying a severe discrepancy: A critical analysis. *Learning Disability Quarterly*, 4(4), 359–371.

Cook, J. M., & Welch, M. W. (1980). Reading as a function of visual and auditory process training. *Learning Disability Quarterly*, 3(3), 76–87.

Cordoni, B. (1982). A directory of college LD services. *Journal of Learning Disabilities*, 15, 529–534.

Cott, A. (1972). Megavitamins: The orthomolecular approach to behavior disorders and learning disabilities. *Academic Therapy*, 7, 245–259.

Coughran, L., & Liles, B. (1974). *Developmental Syntax Program*. Austin, TX: Learning Concepts.

Council for Learning Disabilities, Research Committee. (1984). Minimum standards for the description of subjects in learning disabilities research reports. *Learning Disability Quarterly*, 7(3), 221–225.

Cratty, B. (1971). *Active learning: Games to enhance academic abilities*. Englewood Cliffs, NJ: Prentice-Hall.

Cravioto, J. (1973). Nutritional deprivation and psychological development in children. In S. Sapir & A. Nitzburg (Eds.), *Children with learning problems*. New York: Brunner/Mazel.

Cravioto, J., DeLicardie, E. R., & Birch, H. G. (1966). Nutrition, growth and neurointegrative development: An experimental and ecologic study. *Pediatrics*, 38, 319.

Crawford, D. (1984). ACLD—R & D Project summary: A study investigating the link between learning disabilities and juvenile delinquency. In W. Cruickshank & J. Kliebhan (Eds.), *Early adolescence to early adulthood: Vol. 5. The best of ACLD*. Syracuse, NY: Syracuse University Press.

Critchley, M. (1970). *The dyslexic child* (2nd ed.). London: Heinemann Medical Books.

Cruickshank, W. M. (1976). William M. Cruickshank. In J. M. Kauffman & D. P. Hallahan (Eds.), *Teaching children with learning disabilities: Personal perspectives*. Columbus, OH: Charles E. Merrill.

————. (1983). "Straight is the bamboo tree." *Journal of Learning Disabilities, 16*, 191–197.

Deshler, D. D., Schumaker, J. B., Lenz, B. K., & Ellis, E. (1984). Academic and cognitive interventions for LD adolescents: Part II. *Journal of Learning Disabilities, 17*, 170–179.

Dunn, L. M., Smith, J. O., Dunn, L. M., Horton, K. B., & Smith, D. D. (1981). *Peabody language development kits* (rev. ed.). Circle Pines, MN: American Guidance Service.

Engelmann, S. E. (1977). Sequencing cognitive and academic tasks. In R. D. Kneedler & S. G. Tarver (Eds.), *Changing perspectives in special education*. Columbus, OH: Charles E. Merrill.

Feingold, B. F. (1975). Hyperkineses and learning disabilities linked to artificial food flavors and colors. *American Journal of Nursing, 75*, 797–803.

————. (1976). Hyperkineses and learning disabilities linked to the ingestion of artificial food colors and flavors. *Journal of Learning Disabilities, 9*, 551–559.

Fernald, G. (1943). *Remedial techniques in basic school subjects*. New York: McGraw–Hill.

Forness, S. R., Sinclair, E., & Guthrie, D. (1983). Learning disability discrepancy formulas: Their use in actual practice. *Learning Disability Quarterly, 6*(2), 107–114.

Gillingham, A., & Stillman, B. (1966). *Remedial training for children with specific disability in reading, spelling, and penmanship* (7th ed.). Cambridge, MA: Educators Publishing Service.

Grisé, P. J. (1980). Florida's minimum competency testing program for handicapped students. *Exceptional Children, 47*, 186–191.

Hallahan, D. P. (Ed.). (1980). Teaching exceptional children to use cognitive strategies. *Exceptional Education Quarterly, 1*, 1–102.

Hallahan, D. P., & Cruickshank, W. M. (1973). *Psychoeducational foundations of learning disabilities*. Englewood Cliffs, NJ: Prentice-Hall.

Hallahan, D. P., & Kauffman, J. M. (1982). *Exceptional children: Introduction to special education* (2nd ed.). Englewood Cliffs, NJ: Prentice-Hall.

Hallgren, B. (1950). Specific dyslexia: A clinical and genetic study. *Acta Psychiatrica Neurologica, 65*, 1–287.

Hammill, D. D., Goodman, L., & Wiederholt, J. L. (1974). Visual-motor processes: Can we train them? *Reading Teacher, 27*, 469–478.

Hammill, D. D., Leigh, J. E., McNutt, G., & Larsen, S. C. (1981). A new definition of learning disabilities. *Learning Disability Quarterly, 4*(4), 336–342.

Hammill, D. D., & McNutt, G. (1981). *Correlates of reading: The consensus of thirty years of correlational research* (Pro-Ed Monograph No. 1). Austin, TX: Pro-Ed.

Haring, N. G., & Schiefelbusch, R. L. (Eds.). (1976). *Teaching special children*. New York: McGraw-Hill.

Hermann, K. (1959). *Reading disability: A medical study of word-blindness and related handicaps*. Springfield, IL: Charles C. Thomas.

Horn, W. F., O'Donnell, J. P., & Vitulano, L. A. (1983). Long-term follow-up studies of learning disabled persons. *Journal of Learning Disabilities, 16,* 542–555.

Hresko, W. P., & Reid, D. K. (1981). Five faces of cognition: Theoretical influences on approaches to learning disabilities. *Learning Disability Quarterly, 4*(3), 238–243.

Kass, C. E. (1969). Introduction to learning disabilities. *Seminars in Psychiatry, 1,* 240–244.

Kaufman, A. (1976). A new approach to interpretation of test scatter on WISC-R. *Journal of Learning Disabilities, 9,* 160–168.

Kaufman, M. J., Gottlieb, J., Agard, J. A., & Kukic, M. B. (1975). Mainstreaming: Toward an explication of the construct. *Focus on Exceptional Children, 7*(3), 6–17.

Kavale, K. A., & Forness, S. T. (1983). Hyperactivity and diet treatment: A meta-analysis of the Feingold hypothesis. *Journal of Learning Disabilities, 16,* 324–333.

Kavale, K. A., & Mattson, P. D. (1983). "One jumped off the balance beam": Meta-analysis of perceptual-motor training. *Journal of Learning Disabilities, 16,* 165–173.

Keilitz, I., Zaremba, B., & Broder, P. (1979). The link between learning disabilities and juvenile delinquency: Some issues and answers. *Learning Disability Quarterly, 2*(2), 2–11.

Keogh, B. K., & Glover, A. T. (1980). The generality and durability of cognitive training. *Exceptional Education Quarterly, 1,* 75–82.

Kephart, N. C. (1971). *The slow learner in the classroom.* Columbus, OH: Charles E. Merrill.

Kershner, J., Hawks, W., & Grekin, R. (1977). *Megavitamins and learning disorders: A controlled double-blind experiment.* Unpublished manuscript, Ontario Institute for Studies in Education.

Kirk, S. A., & Gallagher, J. J. (1983). *Educating exceptional children* (4th ed.). Boston: Houghton Mifflin.

Kittler, F. J. (1970). The effect of allergy on children with minimal brain damage. In F. Speer (Ed.), *Allergy of the nervous system.* Springfield, Ill: Charles C. Thomas.

Knowles, B. S., & Knowles, P. S. (1983). A model for identifying learning disabilities in college-bound students. *Journal of Learning Disabilities, 16,* 39–42.

Lane, B. A. (1980). The relationship of learning disabilities to juvenile delinquency: Current status. *Journal of Learning Disabilities, 13,* 425–434.

Lee, L., Koenigsknecht, R. A., & Mulhern, S. T. (1975). *Interactive language development teaching.* Evanston, IL: Northwestern University Press.

Lerner, J. W. (1985). *Learning disabilities: Theories, diagnosis, and teaching strategies* (4th ed.). Boston: Houghton Mifflin.

Lindsley, O. R. (1964). Direct measurement and prosthesis of retarded behavior. *Journal of Education, 147,* 62–81.

Lloyd, J. (1980). Academic instruction and cognitive techniques: The need for attack strategy training. *Exceptional Education Quarterly, 1,* 53–63.

Lloyd, J., Cullinan, D., Heins, E. D., & Epstein, M. H. (1979). *Direct instruction: Effects on oral and written language comprehension* (Project EXCEL Working Paper No. 8). DeKalb: Northern Illinois University.

Loftus, G. R., & Loftus, E. F. (1976). Human memory: The processing of information. Hillsdale, NJ: Lawrence Erlbaum.

Loper, A. B. (1980). Metacognitive development: Implications for cognitive training of exceptional children. *Exceptional Education Quarterly*, 1, 1–8.

Lovitt, T. C. (1975). Applied behavior analysis and learning disabilities—Part II: Specific research recommendations and suggestions for practitioners. *Journal of Learning Disabilities*, 8, 504–518.

————. (1977). *In spite of my resistance: I've learned from children*. Columbus, OH: Charles E. Merrill.

————. (1978). Learning disabilities. In N. G. Haring (Ed.), *Behavior of exceptional children: An introduction to special education* (2nd ed.). Columbus, OH: Charles E. Merrill.

Maker, C. J. (1981). Problem solving: General approach to remediation. In D. D. Smith, *Teaching the learning disabled*. Englewood Cliffs, NJ: Prentice-Hall.

Mardell, C., & Goldenberg, D. (1975). For prekindergarten screening information: DIAL. *Journal of Learning Disabilities*, 8, 140–147.

Marge, M. (1972). The general problem of language disabilities in children. In J. V. Irwin & M. Marge (Eds.), *Principles of childhood language disabilities*. Englewood Cliffs, NJ: Prentice-Hall.

Mattes, J. A. (1983). The Feingold diet: A current reappraisal. *Journal of Learning Disabilities*, 16, 319–323.

McKinney, J. D. (1984). The search for subtypes of specific learning disability. *Journal of Learning Disabilities*, 17, 43–50.

McNutt, G., & Heller, G. (1978). Services for the learning disabled adolescent: A survey. *Learning Disability Quarterly*, 1(4), 101–103.

Meichenbaum, D. H. (1975, June). *Cognitive factors as determinants of learning disabilities: A cognitive-functional approach*. Paper presented at the NATO Conference on the Neuropsychology of Learning Disorders: Theoretical Approaches, Korsor, Denmark.

Mercer, C. D. (1983). *Students with learning disabilities* (2nd ed.). Columbus, OH: Charles E. Merrill.

Mercer, C. D., Forgnone, C., & Wolking, W. D. (1976). Definitions of learning disabilities used in the United States. *Journal of Learning Disabilities*, 9, 376–386.

Mercer, C. D., Hughes, C., & Mercer, A. R. (1985). Learning disabilities definitions used by state education departments. *Learning Disability Quarterly*, 8(1), 45–55.

Mercer, C. D., & Mercer, A. R. (1985). *Teaching students with learning problems* (2nd ed.). Columbus, OH: Charles E. Merrill.

Minskoff, E., Wiseman, D. E., & Minskoff, J. (1972). *The MWM program for developing language abilities*. Ridgefield, NJ: Educational Performance Associates.

Morsink, C. V. (1984). *Teaching special needs students in regular classrooms*. Boston: Little, Brown.

Murphy, M. L. (1976). *Idaho study of learning disabilities: Definition, eligibility criteria, and evaluation procedures*. Unpublished manuscript, State of Idaho Department of Education.

Myers, P. I., & Hammill, D. D. (1982). *Learning disabilities: Basic concepts, assessment practices, and instructional strategies*. Austin, TX: Pro-Ed.

Nelson, C. M., & Polsgrove, L. (1984). Behavior analysis in special education: White rabbit or white elephant? *Remedial and Special Education*, 5(4), 6–17.

Orton, S. T. (1937). *Reading, writing and speech problems in children*. New York: W. W. Norton.

Osgood, C. E. (1957). Motivational dynamics of language behavior. In M. R. Jones (Ed.), *Nebraska symposium of motivation*. Lincoln: University of Nebraska Press.

Otto, W., & Smith, R. J. (1980). *Corrective and remedial teaching* (3rd ed.). Boston: Houghton Mifflin.

Prillaman, D. (1981). Acceptance of learning disabled students in the mainstream environment: A failure to replicate. *Journal of Learning Disabilities, 14*, 344–346.

Quay, H. D. (1973). Special education: Assumptions, techniques, and evaluation criteria. *Exceptional Children, 40*, 165–170.

Rappaport, S. (1975). Ego development in learning disabled children. In W. M. Cruickshank & D. P. Hallahan (Eds.), *Perceptual and learning disabilities in children: Vol. 1. Psychoeducational practices*. Syracuse, NY: Syracuse University Press.

Raschke, D., & Young, A. (1976). The dialectic teaching system: A comprehensive model derived from two educational approaches. *Education and Training of the Mentally Retarded, 11*, 232–246.

Riegel, R. H., & Mathey, J. P. (Eds.). 1980. *Mainstreaming at the secondary level: Seven models that work*. Plymouth, MI: Wayne County Intermediate School District.

Rimland, B. (1983). The Feingold diet: An assessment of the reviews by Mattes, by Kavale and Forness and others. *Journal of Learning Disabilities, 16*, 331–333.

Roberts, G. H. (1968). The failure strategies of third grade arithmetic pupils. *The Arithmetic Teacher, 15*, 442–446.

Roddy, E. A. (1984). When are resource rooms going to share in the declining enrollment trend? Another look at mainstreaming. *Journal of Learning Disabilities, 17*, 279–281.

Rourke, B. P. (1978). Reading, spelling, arithmetic disabilities: A neuropsychologic perspective. In H. R. Myklebust (Ed.), *Progress in learning disabilities* (Vol. 4). New York: Grune & Stratton.

Schmid, R., Algozzine, B., Wells, D., & Stoller, L. (1980). *Final report: The national secondary school survey*. Unpublished manuscript, University of Florida.

Schumaker, J. B., & Deshler, D. D. (1984). Setting demand variables: A major factor in program planning for the LD adolescent. *Topics in Language Disorders, 4*(2), 22–40.

Schumaker, J. B., Deshler, D. D., Alley, G. R., & Warner, M. M. (1983). Toward the development of an intervention model for learning disabled adolescents: The University of Kansas Institute. *Exceptional Education Quarterly, 4*, 45–74.

Silver, L. B. (1975). Acceptable and controversial approaches to treating the child with learning disabilities. *Pediatrics, 55*, 406–415.

Slingerland, B. H. (1971). *A multisensory approach to language arts for specific language disability children: A guide for primary teachers*. Cambridge, MA: Educators Publishing Service.

Smead, V. S. (1977). Ability training and task analysis in diagnostic/prescriptive teaching. *The Journal of Special Education, 11*(1), 113–125.

Smith, R. M., Neisworth, J. T., & Greer, J. G. (1978). *Evaluating educational environments*. Columbus, OH: Charles E. Merrill.

Smith, R. M., Neisworth, J. T., & Hunt, F. M. (1983). *The exceptional child: A functional approach* (2nd ed.). New York: McGraw-Hill.

Speece, D. L., & Mandell, C. J. (1980). Resource room support services for regular teachers. *Learning Disability Quarterly,* 3(1), 49–53.

Spring, C., & Sandoval, J. (1976). Food additives and hyperkinesis: A critical evaluation of the evidence. *Journal of Learning Disabilities,* 9, 560–569.

Stephens, T. M. (1977). *Teaching skills to children with learning and behavior disorders.* Columbus, OH: Charles E. Merrill.

Strauss, A. A., & Lehtinen, L. E. (1947). *Psychopathology and education of the brain-injured child* (Vol. 1). New York: Grune & Stratton.

Tjossem, T. D. (1976). Early intervention: Issues and approaches. In T. D. Tjossem (Ed.), *Intervention strategies for high risk infants and young children.* Baltimore: University Park Press.

Treiber, F. A., & Lahey, B. B. (1983). Toward a behavioral model of academic remediation with learning disabled children. *Journal of Learning Disabilities,* 16, 111–116.

Unger, K. (1978). Learning disabilities and juvenile delinquency. *Journal of Juvenile and Family Courts,* 29(1), 25–30.

U.S. Department of Education. (1968). *First annual report of National Committee on Handicapped Children.* Washington, DC: U.S. Department of Health, Education, & Welfare.

————. (1977). Assistance to states for education of handicapped children: Procedures for evaluating specific learning disabilities. *Federal Register,* 42(250), 65082–65085.

————. (1984). *Sixth annual report to Congress on the implementation of P.L. 94-142: The Education for All Handicapped Children Act:* Washington, DC.

Vogel, S. A. (1982). On developing LD college programs. *Journal of Learning Disabilities,* 15, 518–528.

Wallace, G., & McLoughlin, J. A. (1979). *Learning disabilities: Concepts and characteristics* (2nd ed.). Columbus, OH: Charles E. Merrill.

Weller, C. (1980). Discrepancy and severity in the learning disabled: A consolidated perspective. *Learning Disability Quarterly,* 3(1), 84–90.

Wepman, J. M., Cruickshank, W. M., Deutsch, C. P., Morency, A., & Strother, C. R. (1975). Learning disabilities. In N. Hobbs (Ed.), *Issues in the classification of children* (Vol. 1). San Francisco: Jossey-Bass.

White, O. R., & Haring, N. G. (1980). *Exceptional teaching: A multimedia training package* (2nd ed.). Columbus, OH: Charles E. Merrill.

Wiederholt, J. L. (1974). Historical perspectives on the education of the learning disabled. In L. Mann & D. Sabatino (Eds.), *The second review of special education.* Philadelphia: Journal of Special Education Press.

Wiig, E. H., & Semel, E. M. (1976). *Language disabilities in children and adolescents.* Columbus, OH: Charles E. Merrill.

————. (1984). *Language assessment and intervention for the learning disabled* (2nd ed.). Columbus, OH: Charles E. Merrill.

Wong, B. (1979). The role of theory in learning disabilities research: Part I. Analysis of problems. *Journal of Learning Disabilities,* 12, 585–595.

Wong, B. Y. L. (1982). Understanding learning disabled students' reading problems: Contributions from cognitive psychology. *Topics in Learning and Learning Disabilities*, 1, 43–50.

Ysseldyke, J. E., & Salvia, J. (1974). Diagnostic-prescriptive teaching: Two models. *Exceptional Children*, 41, 181–185.

Ysseldyke, J. E., Thurlow, M., Graden, J., Wesson, C., Algozzine, B., & Deno, S. (1983). Generalizations from five years of research on assessment and decision making: The University of Minnesota Institute. *Exceptional Education Quarterly*, 4, 75–93.

CHAPTER 6

Achenbach, T. M. (1974). *Developmental psychopathology*. New York: Ronald Press.

Achenbach, T. M., & Edelbrock, C. S. (1978). The classification of child psychopathology: A review and analysis of empirical efforts. *Psychological Bulletin*, 85, 1275–1301.

Apter, S. J. (1982). *Troubled children/troubled systems*. New York: Pergamon Press.

Axline, V. M. (1969). *Play therapy* (2nd ed.). New York: Ballantine Books.

Azrin, N. H., & Besalel, V. A. (1980). *How to use overcorrection*. Austin, TX: Pro-Ed.

Bandura, A. (1973). *Aggression: A social learning analysis*. Englewood Cliffs, NJ: Prentice-Hall.

———. (1978). The self system in reciprocal determinism. *American Psychologist*, 33, 344–358.

Barkley, R. A. (1983). Hyperactivity. In R. J. Morris & T. R. Kratochwill (Eds.), *The practice of child therapy*. New York: Pergamon Press.

Bash, M. A., & Camp, B. W. (1980). Teacher training in the Think Aloud classroom program. In G. Cartledge & J. F. Milburn (Eds.), *Teaching social skills to children*. New York: Pergamon Press.

Becker, W. C., Madson, D. H., Arnold, C. R., & Thomas, D. R. (1967). The contingent use of teacher attention and praise in reducing classroom behavior problems. *Journal of Special Education*, 1, 287–307.

Berne, E. (1964). *Games people play*. New York: Macmillan.

Bettelheim, B. (1950). *Love is not enough*. New York: Macmillan.

Bosco, J. J., & Robin, S. S. (1980). Hyperkinesis: Prevalence and treatment. In C. K. Whalen & B. Henker (Eds.), *Hyperactive children: The social ecology of identification and treatment*. New York: Academic Press.

Bower, E. M. (1969). *The early identification of emotionally handicapped children in school* (2nd ed.). Springfield, IL: Charles C. Thomas.

Brolin, D. E., & Kokaska, C. J. (1979). *Career education for handicapped children and youth*. Columbus, OH: Charles E. Merrill.

Bullock, L. M., & Brown, R. K. (1972). Behavioral dimensions of emotionally disturbed children. *Exceptional Children*, 38, 740–742.

Camp, B. W., & Bash, M. A. (1981). *Think aloud: Increasing social and cognitive skills—A problem-solving program for children* (primary level). Champaign, IL: Research Press.

Camp, B. W., & Ray, R. S. (1984). Aggression. In A. W. Meyers & W. E. Craighead (Eds.), *Cognitive behavior therapy with children*. New York: Plenum.

Cantor, S. (1982). *The schizophrenic child.* Montreal: Eden.

Cartledge, G., & Milburn, J. F. (1980). *Teaching social skills to children.* New York: Pergamon Press.

Catania, A. C. (1975). The myth of self-reinforcement. *Behaviorism, 3,* 192–199.

Chan, K. S., & Rueda, R. (1979). Poverty and culture in education: Separate but equal. *Exceptional Children, 45,* 422–431.

Cohen, S. I., Keyworth, J. M., Kleiner, R. I., & Brown, W. L. (1974). Effective behavior change at the Anne Arundel Center through three different minimum contact interventions. In R. Ulrich, T. Stacknik, & J. Mabry (Eds.), *Control of human behavior* (Vol. 3). New York: Scott, Foresman.

Conners, C. K. (1980). *Food additives and hyperactive children.* New York: Plenum.

Conners, C. K., & Werry, J. S. (1979). Pharmacotherapy. In H. C. Quay & J. S. Werry (Eds.), *Psychopathological disorders of childhood* (2nd ed.). New York: John Wiley & Sons.

Cullinan, D., & Epstein, M. H. (1979a). Administrative definitions of behavior disorders: Status and directions. In F. H. Wood & K. C. Lakin (Eds.), *Disturbing, disordered, or disturbed?* Minneapolis: Advanced Institute for Trainers of Teachers for Seriously Emotionally Disturbed Children and Youth.

————. (Eds.). (1979b). *Special education for adolescents: Issues and perspectives.* Columbus, OH: Charles E. Merrill.

————. (1984). Patterns of maladjustment of behaviorally disordered male students. *Behavioral Disorders, 9,* 175–181.

Cullinan, D., Epstein, M. H., & Kauffman, J. M. (1982). The behavioral model and children's behavior disorders: Foundations and evaluations. In R. McDowell, F. Wood, & G. Adamson (Eds.), *Teaching emotionally disturbed children.* Boston: Little, Brown.

————. (1984). Teacher ratings of students' behaviors: What constitutes behavior disorders in school. *Behavioral Disorders, 10,* 9–19.

Cullinan, D., Epstein, M. H., & Lloyd, J. (1983). *Behavior disorders of children and adolescents.* Englewood Cliffs, NJ: Prentice-Hall.

Denton, D. L., & McIntyre, C. W. (1978). Span of apprehension in hyperactive boys. *Journal of Abnormal Child Psychology, 6,* 19–24.

Edelbrock, C., & Achenbach, T. M. (1980). A typology of child behavior patterns: Distribution and correlates for disturbed children aged 6–16. *Journal of Abnormal Child Psychology, 8,* 441–470.

Epstein, M. H., & Cullinan, D. (1979). Special education for adolescents: An overview. In D. Cullinan & M. H. Epstein (Eds.), *Special education for adolescents: Issues and perspectives.* Columbus, OH: Charles E. Merrill.

————. (1984). Research issues in behavior disorders: A national survey. *Behavioral Disorders, 10,* 56–59.

Epstein, M. H., Cullinan, D., & Rose, T. L. (1980). Applied behavior analysis and behaviorally disordered pupils: Selected issues. In L. Mann & D. A. Sabatino (Eds.), *The fourth review of special education.* New York: Grune & Stratton.

Epstein, M. H., Cullinan, D., & Sabatino, D. A. (1977). State definitions of behavior disorders. *Journal of Special Education, 11,* 417–425.

Fagen, S. A., Long, D. J., & Stevens, D. J. (1975). *Teaching children self-control.* Columbus, OH: Charles E. Merrill.

Feindler, E. L., Marriott, S. A., & Iwata, M. (1984). Group anger control training for junior high school delinquents. *Cognitive Therapy and Research, 8,* 299–311.

Feingold, B. F. (1975). *Why your child is hyperactive.* New York: Random House.

Ferster, C. B., & Culbertson, S. A. (1982). *Behavior principles* (3rd ed.). Englewood Cliffs, NJ: Prentice-Hall.

Firestone, P., & Martin, J. E. (1979). An analysis of the hyperactive syndrome: A comparison of hyperactive, behavior problem, asthmatic, and normal children. *Journal of Abnormal Child Psychology, 7,* 261–274.

Gersten, J. C., Langner, T. S., Eisenberg, J. B., Simcha-Fagen, O., & McCarthy, E. D. (1976). Stability and change in types of behavioral disturbance of children and adolescents. *Journal of Abnormal Child Psychology, 4,* 111–127.

Gilbert, G. M. (1957). A survey of "referral problems" in metropolitan child guidance centers. *Journal of Clinical Psychology, 13,* 37–42.

Glasser, W. (1969). *Schools without failure.* New York: Harper & Row.

Glidewell, J., & Swallow, C. (1968). *The prevalence of maladjustment in elementary school.* Chicago: University of Chicago Press.

Glueck, S., & Glueck, E. (1968). *Delinquents and non-delinquents in perspective.* Cambridge: Harvard University Press.

Goldstein, A. P., Sprafkin, R. P., Gershaw, N. S., & Klein, P. (1980). *Skillstreaming the adolescent.* Champaign, IL: Research Press.

————. (1983). Structured learning: A psychoeducational approach for teaching social competencies. *Behavioral Disorders, 8,* 161–170.

Graham, P. J. (1979). Epidemiological studies. In H. C. Quay & J. S. Werry (Eds.), *Psychopathological disorders of childhood* (2nd ed.). New York: John Wiley & Sons.

Greenwood, C. R., Walker, H. M., & Hops, H. (1977). Issues in social interaction/withdrawal assessment. *Exceptional Children, 43,* 490–501.

Grinspoon, L., & Singer, S. (1973). Amphetamines in the treatment of hyperkinetic children. *Harvard Educational Review, 43,* 515–555.

Handleman, J. S. (1981). A model for self-contained classes for autistic type youngsters. *Education and Treatment of Children, 4,* 61–70.

Haring, N. G., & Phillips, E. L. (1962). *Educating emotionally disturbed children.* New York: McGraw-Hill.

Harris, T. (1976). *I'm ok, you're ok.* New York: Avon.

Heaton, R. C., Safer, D. J., & Allen, R. P. (1982). A contingency management program for disruptive junior high school students: A detailed description. In D. J. Safer (Ed.), *School programs for disruptive adolescents.* Baltimore: University Park Press.

Heaton, R. C., Safer, D. J., Allen, R. P., Spinnato, N. C., & Prumo, F. M. (1976). A motivational environment for behaviorally deviant junior high school students. *Journal of Abnormal Child Psychology, 4,* 263–275.

Hetherington, E. M., & Martin, B. (1979). Family interaction. In H. C. Quay & J. S. Werry (Eds.), *Psychopathological disorders of childhood* (2nd ed.). New York: John Wiley & Sons.

Hewett, F. M. (1968). *The emotionally disturbed child in the classroom.* Boston: Allyn & Bacon.

Hresko, W. L., & Brown, L. (1984). *Test of Early Socioemotional Development.* Austin, TX: Pro-Ed.

Huntze, S. L., & Grosenick, J. K. (1980). *National needs analysis in behavior disorders: Human resources in behavior disorders.* Columbia: University of Missouri.

Jessness, C. F. (1975). The Youth Center Project: Transactional analysis and behavior modification programs for delinquents. *Behavioral Disorders, 1*(1), 27–36.

Kauffman, J. M. (1980). Where special education for disturbed children is going: A personal view. *Exceptional Children, 46,* 522–529.

————. (1981). *Characteristics of children's behavior disorders* (2nd ed.). Columbus, OH: Charles E. Merrill.

Kauffman, J. M., & Kneedler, R. D. (1981). Behavior disorders. In J. M. Kauffman & D. P. Hallahan (Eds.), *Handbook of special education.* Englewood Cliffs, NJ: Prentice-Hall.

Kazdin, A. E. (1977). Assessing the clinical or applied significance of behavior change through social validation. *Behavior Modification, 1,* 427–452.

————. (1978). *History of behavior modification: Experimental foundations of contemporary research.* Baltimore: University Park Press.

————. (1980). *Behavior modification in applied settings* (2nd ed.). Homewood, IL: Dorsey Press.

Kazdin, A. E., & Wilson, G. T. (1978). *Evaluation of behavior therapy: Issues, evidence, and research strategies.* Cambridge, MA: Ballinger.

Koegel, R. L. (1981). *How to integrate autistic and other severely handicapped children into a classroom.* Austin, TX: Pro-Ed.

Koegel, R. L., Russo, D. C., & Rincover, A. (1977). Assessing and training teachers in the generalized use of behavior modification with autistic children. *Journal of Applied Behavior Analysis, 10,* 197–205.

Koegel, R., & Schreibman, L. (1981). *How to teach autistic and other severely handicapped children.* Austin, TX: Pro-Ed.

Kohlberg, L., LaCrosse, J., & Ricks, D. (1972). The predictability of adult mental health from childhood behavior. In B. B. Wolman (Ed.), *Manual of child psychopathology.* New York: John Wiley & Sons.

Lahey, B. B., & Ciminero, A. R. (1980). *Maladaptive behavior: An introduction to abnormal psychology.* Glenview, IL: Scott, Foresman.

Lakin, K. C. (1983). Research-based knowledge and professional practices in special education for emotionally disturbed students. *Behavioral Disorders, 8,* 128–137.

Lansing, M. D., & Schopler, E. (1978). Individualized education: A public school model. In M. Rutter & E. Schopler (Eds.), *Autism: A reappraisal of concepts and treatment.* New York: Plenum Press.

Liebert, R. M., Neale, J. M., & Davidson, E. S. (1973). *The early window: Effects of television on children and youth.* New York: Pergamon Press.

Liebert, R. M., & Wicks-Nelson, R. (1981). *Developmental psychology* (3rd ed.). Englewood Cliffs, NJ: Prentice-Hall.

Lippman, H. S. (1962). *Treatment of the child in emotional conflict* (2nd ed.). New York: McGraw-Hill.

Litow, L., & Pumroy, D. K. (1975). A brief review of classroom group-oriented contingencies. *Journal of Applied Behavior Analysis, 8,* 341–347.

Long, K. A. (1983). Emotionally disturbed children as an underdetected and underserved public school population: Reasons and recommendation. *Behavioral Disorders, 9,* 46–54.

Long, N. J. (1974). Nicholas J. Long. In J. M. Kauffman & C. D. Lewis (Eds.), *Teaching children with behavior disorders: Personal perspective.* Columbus, OH: Charles E. Merrill.

Long, N. J., & Newman, R. G. (1976). Managing surface behavior of children in school. In N. J. Long, W. C. Morse, & R. G. Newman (Eds.), *Conflict in the classroom* (3rd ed.). Belmont, CA: Wadsworth.

Lovaas, O. I. (1977). *The autistic child.* New York: Irvington.

Lovaas, O. I., & Newsom, C. D. (1976). Behavior modification with psychotic children. In H. Leitenberg (Eds.), *Handbook of behavior modification and behavior therapy.* Englewood Cliffs, NJ: Prentice-Hall.

Maslach, C. (1978). Job burnout: How people cope. *Public Welfare, 36,* 56–68.

Meichenbaum, D. H. (1977). *Cognitive-behavior modification.* New York: Plenum.

Menninger, K. (1963). *The vital balance.* New York: Viking Press.

Mesibov, G. B. (1983). Current perspectives and issues in autism and adolescence. In E. Schopler & G. B. Mesibov (Eds.), *Autism in adolescents and adults.* New York: Plenum.

Metz, A. S. (1973). *Number of pupils with handicaps in local public schools, Spring, 1970.* Washington, DC: U.S. Government Printing Office.

Meyen, E. L. (1982). An introductory perspective. In E. L. Meyen (Ed.), *Exceptional children and youth: An introduction* (2nd ed.). Denver: Love.

Mischel, W. (1971). *Introduction to personality.* New York: Holt, Rinehart & Winston.

Monat, A., & Lazarus, R. S. (1977). *Stress and coping: An anthology.* New York: Columbia University Press.

Morris, R. J., & Kratochwill, T. R. (1983). *Treating children's fears and phobias.* New York: Pergamon Press.

Morse, W. C. (1965). The crisis teacher. In N. J. Long, W. C. Morse, & R. G. Newman (Eds.), *Conflict in the classroom.* Belmont, CA: Wadsworth.

————. (1971). The crisis or helping teacher. In N. J. Long, W. C. Morse, & R. G. Newman (Eds.), *Conflict in the classroom* (2nd ed.). Belmont, CA: Wadsworth.

————. (1976). The helping teacher/crisis teacher concept. *Focus on Exceptional Children, 8*(4), 1–11.

Morse, W. C., Cutler, R. L., & Fink, A. H. (1964). *Public school classes for the emotionally handicapped: A research analysis.* Washington, DC: Council for Exceptional Children.

Nathan, P. E., & Harris, S. L. (1980). *Psychopathology and society* (2nd ed.). New York: McGraw-Hill.

Nye, R., Short, J., & Olson, V. (1958). Socio-economic status and delinquent behavior. *American Journal of Sociology, 63,* 381–389.

Oliver, L. I. (1974). *Behavior patterns in school of youths 12–17 years* (National Health Survey, Series 11, No. 139, U.S. Department of Health, Education, & Welfare). Washington, DC: U.S. Government Printing Office.

Paternite, C. E., & Loney, J. (1980). Childhood hyperkinesis: Relationship between symptomatology and home environment. In C. K. Wahlen & B. Henker (Eds.), *Hyperactive children: The social ecology of identification and treatment.* New York: Academic Press.

Pattavina, P. (1984). Generic affective competencies: A model for teaching socially and emotionally disturbed adolescents. In S. Braaten, R. B. Rutherford, & C. A. Kardash (Eds.), *Programming for adolescents with behavioral disorders.* Reston, VA: Council for Children with Behavioral Disorders.

Pauling, L. (1968). Orthomolecular psychiatry. *Science, 160,* 265–271.

Phillips, E. L., Phillips, E. A., Fixsen, D. L., & Wolf, M. M. (1972). *The teaching-family handbook.* Lawrence: University of Kansas Printing Service.

Polsgrove, L. (1979). Self-control: Methods for child training. *Behavioral Disorders, 4,* 116–130.

Polsgrove, L., & Reith, H. J. (1980). A new look of competencies required by teachers of emotionally disturbed and behaviorally disordered children and youth. In F. Wood (Ed.), *Teachers for secondary school students with serious emotional disturbance.* Minneapolis: University of Minnesota.

Prugh, D. G., Engel, M., & Morse, W. C. (1975). Emotional disturbance in children. In N. Hobbs (Ed.), *Issues in the classification of children* (Vol. 1). San Francisco: Jossey-Bass.

Quay, H. C. (1979). Classification. In H. C. Quay & J. S. Werry (Eds.), *Psychopathological disorders of childhood* (2nd ed.). New York: John Wiley & Sons.

Quay, H. C., Glavin, J. P., Annesley, F. R., & Werry, J. S. (1972). The modification of problem behavior and academic achievement in a resource room. *Journal of School Psychology, 10,* 187–198.

Redl, F. (1959). The concept of the life space interview. *American Journal of Orthopsychiatry, 29,* 1–18.

Redl, F., & Wineman, D. (1951). *Children who hate.* New York: Free Press.

Rhodes, W. C. (1970). A community participation analysis of emotional disturbance. *Exceptional Children, 37,* 309–314.

Rimland, B. (1969). Psychogenesis versus biogenesis: The issues and the evidence. In S. C. Plog & R. B. Edgerton (Eds.), *Changing perspectives in mental illness.* New York: Holt, Rinehart & Winston.

Roberts, J., & Baird, J. T. (1972). *Behavior patterns of children in school* (DHEW Publication No. [HSM] 72–1042). Washington, DC: U.S. Government Printing Office.

Robins, L. N. (1966). *Deviant children grown up.* Baltimore: Williams & Wilkins.

————. (1979). Follow-up studies. In H. C. Quay & J. S. Werry (Eds.), *Psychopathological disorders of childhood* (2nd ed.). New York: John Wiley & Sons.

Rose, T. L., Epstein, M. H., Cullinan, D., & Lloyd, J. (1981). Academic programming for behaviorally disordered adolescents: An approach to remediation. In G. Brown, R. L. McDowell, & J. Smith (Eds.), *Educating adolescents with behavior disorders.* Columbus, OH: Charles E. Merrill.

Rosen, B. M., Bahn, A. K., & Kramer, M. (1964). Demographic and diagnostic characteristics of psychiatric clinic out-patients in the U.S.A., 1961. *American Journal of Orthopsychiatry, 34,* 455–468.

Ross, A. O. (1980). *Psychological disorders of children* (2nd ed.). New York: McGraw-Hill.

Routh, D. K. (1980). Developmental and social aspects of hyperactivity. In C. K. Whalen & B. Henker (Eds.), *Hyperactive children: The social ecology of identification and treatment.* New York: Academic Press.

Russo, D. C., & Newsom, C. D. (1982). Psychotic disorders of childhood. In J. R. Lachenmeyer & M. S. Gibbs (Eds.), *Psychopathology in childhood.* New York: Gardner.

Rutter, M., & Schopler, E. (Eds.). (1978). *Autism: A reappraisal of concepts and treatment.* New York: Plenum.

Rutter, M., Tizard, J., Yule, W., Graham, P., & Whitmore, K. (1976). Isle of Wight studies, 1964–1974. *Psychological Medicine, 6,* 313–332.

Safer, D. J., & Allen, R. P. (1976). *Hyperactive children: Diagnosis and management.* Baltimore: University Park Press.

Safer, D. J., Heaton, R. C., & Parker, F. C. (1982). A contingency management program for disruptive junior high school students: Results and follow-up. In D. J. Safer (Ed.), *School programs for disruptive adolescents.* Baltimore: University Park Press.

Sarason, S. B., & Doris, J. (1979). *Educational handicap, public policy, and social history: A broadened perspective on mental retardation.* New York: Free Press.

Schopler, E., & Mesibov, G. (Eds.). (1983). *Autism in adolescents and young adults.* New York: Plenum.

Schopler, E., Reichler, R. J., & Lansing, M. (1980). *Individualized assessment and treatment for autistic and developmentally disabled children* (Vol. 2). Baltimore: University Park Press.

Schreibman, L., & Mills, J. I. (1983). Infantile autism. In T. H. Ollendick & M. Hersen (Eds.), *Handbook of child psychology.* New York: Plenum.

Schultz, E. W., Hirshoren, A., Manton, A. B., & Henderson, R. A. (1971). Special education for the emotionally disturbed. *Exceptional Children, 38,* 313–319.

Schwartz, B. (1984). *Psychology of learning and behavior* (2nd ed.). New York: W. W. Norton.

Seymour, F. W., & Stokes, T. F. (1976). Self-recording in training girls to increase work and evoke staff praise in institutions for offenders. *Journal of Applied Behavior Analysis, 9,* 41–54.

Skinner, B. F. (1957). *Verbal behavior.* New York: Appleton-Century-Crofts.

————. (1968). *The technology of teaching.* New York: Knopf.

Szasz, T. S. (1960). The myth of mental illness. *American Psychologist, 15,* 113–118.

Tawney, J. W., & Gast, D. L. (1984). *Single subject research in special education.* Columbus, OH: Charles E. Merrill.

Thomas, A., & Chess, S. (1977). *Temperament and development.* New York: Brunner/Mazel.

Walker, H. M., & Buckley, N. K. (1973). Teacher attention to appropriate and inappropriate classroom behavior: An individual case study. *Focus on Exceptional Children, 5,* 5–11.

Walker, H. M., Hops, H., & Greenwood, C. R. (1984). The CORBEH research and development model: Programmatic issues and strategies. In S. C. Paine, T. C. Bellamy, & B. Wilcox (Eds.), *Human services that work*. Baltimore: Paul H. Brookes.

Walker, H. M., McConnell, S., Holmes, D., Todis, B., Walker, J., & Golden, N. (1983). *The Walker social skills curriculum: The* ACCEPTS *program*. Austin, TX: Pro-Ed.

Werry, J. S. (1979a). The childhood psychoses. In H. C. Quay & J. S. Werry (Eds.), *Psychopathological disorders of childhood* (2nd ed.). New York: John Wiley & Sons.

————. (1979b). Organic factors. In H. C. Quay & J. S. Werry (Eds.), *Psychopathological disorders of childhood* (2nd ed.). New York: John Wiley & Sons.

Willis, D. J., Swanson, B. M., & Walker, C. E. (1983). Etiological factors. In T. H. Ollendick & M. Hersen (Eds.), *Handbook of child psychopathology*. New York: Plenum.

Wilson, R. (1984). A review of self-control treatments for aggressive behavior. *Behavioral Disorders, 9*, 131–140.

Zabel, R. H., Boomer, L. W., & King, T. R. (1984). A model of stress and burnout among teachers of behaviorally disordered students. *Behavioral Disorders, 9*, 215–221.

Zilboorg, G., & Henry, G. W. (1941). A *history of medical psychology*. New York: Norton.

CHAPTER 7

Aram, D. M., & Nation, J. E. (1980). Preschool language disorders and subsequent language and academic difficulties. *Journal of Communication Disorders, 13*, 159–170.

Aronson, A. E. (1981). Dysarthria. In T. J. Hixon, L. D. Shriberg, & J. H. Saxman (Eds.), *Introduction to communication disorders* (pp. 407–447). Englewood Cliffs, NJ: Prentice-Hall.

Bailey, D. B., & Wolery, M. (1984). *Teaching infants and preschoolers with handicaps*. Columbus, OH: Charles E. Merrill.

Baker, H., & Leland, B. (1967). *Detroit Tests of Learning Aptitudes*. Indianapolis: Bobbs-Merrill.

Bankson, N. W. (1977). *Bankson Language Screening Test*. Baltimore: University Park Press.

Bates, E. (1976). *Language and context: The acquisition of pragmatics*. New York: Academic Press.

Bernthal, J. E., & Bankson, N. W. (1981). *Articulation disorders*. Englewood Cliffs, NJ: Prentice-Hall.

Bloom, L. (1970). *Language development: Form and function in emerging grammars*. Cambridge: MIT Press.

Bloom, L., & Lahey, M. (1978). *Language development and language disorders*. New York: John Wiley & Sons.

Boone, D. R. (1980). Voice disorders. In T. J. Hixon, L. D. Shriberg, & J. H. Saxman (Eds.), *Introduction to communication disorders* (pp. 311–352). Englewood Cliffs, NJ: Prentice-Hall.

Bowerman, M. (1976). Semantic factors in the acquisition of rules for word use and sentence construction. In D. Morehead & A. Morehead (Eds.), *Normal and deficient child language* (pp. 99–179). Baltimore: University Park Press.

Brown, R. (1973). A *first language, the early stages*. Cambridge: Harvard University Press.

Bruner, J. (1975). The ontogenesis of speech acts. *Journal of Child Language, 2*, 1–19.

Bzoch, K., & League, R. (1971). *The Receptive-Expressive Emergent Language Scale.* Gainesville, FL: Computer Management.

Chomsky, N. (1957). *Syntactic structures.* The Hague: Mouton.

Cromer, R. (1974). The development of language and cognition: The cognitive hypothesis. In B. Foss (Ed.), *New perspectives in child development* (pp. 184–252). New York: Penguin Education.

Deshler, D. D., Alley, G. R., Warner, M. M., & Schumaker, J. B. (1981). Instructional practices for promoting skills acquisition and generalization in severely learning disabled adolescents. *Learning Disability Quarterly, 4,* 415–421.

Deshler, D. D., Schumaker, J. B., Alley, G. R., Warner, M. M., & Clark, F. L. (1981). Social interaction deficits in learning disabled adolescents—Another myth? In W. M. Cruickshank & A. A. Silver (Eds.), *Bridges to tomorrow; Vol. 2. The best of* ACLD. Syracuse, NY: Syracuse University Press.

Donahue, M., Pearl, R., & Bryan, T. (1982). Learning disabled children's syntactic proficiency during a communicative task. *Journal of Speech and Hearing Disorders, 47,* 397–403.

———. (1983). Communicative competence in learning disabled children. In H. Bialer & K. Gadow (Eds.), *Advances in learning and behavioral disabilities* (Vol. 2). Greenwich, CT: JAI Press.

Dore, J. (1979). What's so conceptual about the acquisiton of linguistic structures? *Journal of Child Language, 6,* 129–138.

Duchan, J. F., & Palermo, J. (1982). How autistic children view the world. *Topics in Language Disorders, 3*(1), 10–15.

Fluharty, N. B. (1978). *The Fluharty Preschool Speech and Language Screening Test.* Boston: Teaching Resources.

Frankenburg, W. K., & Dobbs, J. B. (1970). *Denver Developmental Screening Test.* Denver: Ladocao Project & Publishing Foundation.

Fredericks, H. D. B., Baldwin, V., Grove, D., Moore, W., Riggs, C., & Lyons, B. (1978). Integrating the moderately and severely handicapped preschooler into a normal day care setting. In M. J. Guralnick (Ed.), *Early intervention and the integration of handicapped and nonhandicapped children* (pp. 191–206). Baltimore: University Park Press.

Hammill, D. D., Brown, V. L., Larsen, S. C., & Wiederholt, J. L. (1980). *Test of Adolescent Language: A multidimensional approach to assessment.* Austin, TX: Services for Professional Educators.

Hammill, D. D., & Larson, S. (1974). The relationship of selected auditory perceptual skills and reading ability. *Journal of Learning Disabilities, 7,* 429–435.

Hammill, D., & Wiederholt, J. L. (1973). Review of the Frostig Visual Perception Test and the related training program. In L. Mann & D. Sabatino (Eds.), *The first review of special education* (Vol. 1, pp. 33–48). Philadelphia: Grune & Stratton.

Hart, B., & Risley, T. (1975). Incidental teaching of language in the preschool. *Journal of Applied Behavior Analysis, 7,* 243–256.

Hart, B., & Rogers-Warren, A. (1978). Milieu approach to teaching language. In R. L. Schiefelbusch (Ed.), *Language intervention strategies* (pp. 193–235). Baltimore: University Park Press.

Hedrick, E. P., Prather, E. M., & Tobin, A. (1984). *Sequenced inventory of communications development* (rev. ed.). Seattle: University of Washington Press.

Hymes, D. (1971). Competence and performance in linguistic theory. In R. Huxley & E. Ingram (Eds.), *Language acquisition: Models and methods* (pp. 3–28). New York: Academic Press.

Keenan, E. (1977). Making it last: Repetition in children's discourse. In S. Ervin-Tripp & C. Mitchell-Kernan (Eds.), *Child discourse*. New York: Academic Press.

Kirchner, D. M., & Skarakis-Doyle, E. (1983). Developmental language disorders: A theoretical perspective. In T. M. Gallagher & C. A. Prutting (Eds.), *Pragmatic assessment and intervention issues in language* (pp. 215–246). San Diego: College-Hill Press.

Kirk, S., McCarthy, J., & Kirk, W. (1968). *The Illinois Test of Psycholinguistic Abilities* (rev. ed.). Urbana, IL: University of Illinois Press.

Lee, L. (1971). *Northwestern Syntax Screening Test (NSST)*. Evanston, IL: Northwestern University Press.

McCormick, L. (1984). Review of normal language acquisition. In L. McCormick & R. Schiefelbusch (Eds.), *Early language intervention* (pp. 35–38). Columbus, OH: Charles E. Merrill.

Menyuk, P. (1983). Language development and reading. In T. M. Gallagher & C. A. Prutting (Eds.), *Pragmatic assessment and intervention issues in language* (pp. 151–170). San Diego: College-Hill Press.

Menzel, E. W. (1969). Naturalistic and experimental approaches to primate behavior. In E. Williams & H. Rausch (Eds.), *Naturalistic viewpoints in psychological research*. New York: Holt, Rinehart & Winston.

Miller, J. F. (1983). Identifying children with language disorders and describing their language performance. In J. Miller, D. E. Yoder, & R. Schiefelbusch (Eds.), *Contemporary issues in language intervention* (pp. 61–74). Rockville, MD: American Speech-Language and Hearing Association.

Miller, J. R., Campbell, T. F., Chapman, R. S., & Weismer, S. E. (1984). Language behavior in acquired childhood aphasia. In A. Holland (Ed.), *Language disorders in children* (pp. 57–100). San Diego: College-Hill Press.

Nelson, K. (1977). The conceptual basis for naming. In J. MacNamara (Ed.), *Language learning and thought* (pp. 117–136). New York: Academic Press.

Newcomer, P., & Hammill, D. (1982). The Test of Language Development—Primary. Austin, TX: Pro-Ed.

Panagos, J. M., & Griffith, P. L. (1981). Okay, what do educators know about language intervention? *Topics in Learning and Learning Disabilities*, 1(2), 69–82.

Perkins, W. H. (1980). Disorders of speech flow. In T. J. Hixon, L. D. Shriberg, & J. H. Saxman (Eds.), *Introduction to communication disorders* (pp. 449–490). Englewood Cliffs, NJ: Prentice-Hall.

Piaget, J. (1952). *The origins of intelligence in children* (M. Cock, Trans.). New York: International Universities Press.

———. (1954). *The construction of reality in the child*. New York: Basic Books.

———. (1962). *Play, dreams and imitation in childhood*. New York: W. W. Norton.

Pickering, M. (1981). Consulting with the classroom teacher to promote language acquisition and usage. *Topics in Learning and Learning Disabilities*, 1(2), 59–68.

Rees, N. S. (1981). Saying more than we know: Is auditory processing disorder a meaningful concept? In R. W. Keith (Ed.), *Central auditory and language disorders in children* (pp. 40–87). Houston: College-Hill Press.

———. (1983). Language intervention with children. In J. Miller, D. E. Yoder, & R. Schiefelbusch (Eds.), *Contemporary issues in language intervention* (pp. 309–316). Rockville, MD: American Speech-Language and Hearing Association.

Ruder, K. F., Bunce, B. H., & Ruder, C. (1984). Language intervention in a preschool/classroom setting. In L. McCormick & R. Schiefelbusch (Eds.), *Early language intervention* (pp. 268–297). Columbus, OH: Charles E. Merrill.

Schery, T., & Glover, A. (1982). *The Initial Communication Processes Scale.* Monterey, CA: Publishers Test Service.

Schlesinger, I. (1971). Production of utterances and language acquisition. In D. Slobin (Ed.), *The ontogenesis of grammar* (pp. 63–101). New York: Academic Press.

Schumaker, J. B., & Deshler, D. D. (1984). Setting demand variables: A major factor in program planning for the LD adolescent. *Topics in Language Disorders*, 4(2), 22–40.

Shriberg, L. D. (1980). Developmental phonological disorders. In T. J. Hixon, L. D. Shriberg, & J. H. Saxman (Eds.), *Introduction to communication disorders.* Englewood Cliffs, NJ: Prentice-Hall.

Silva, P. (1980). The prevalence, stability and significance of developmental language delay in preschool children. *Developmental Medicine and Child Neurology*, 22, 768–777.

Skinner, B. F. (1957). *Verbal behavior.* New York: Appleton-Century-Crofts.

Slobin, D. I. (1970). Universals in grammatical development in children. In G. B. Flores d'Arcais & W. J. M. Levelt (Eds.), *Advances in psycho-linguistics.* New York: American Elsevier.

Stark, J., & Wallach, G. P. (1980). The path to a concept of language learning disabilities. *Topics in Language Disorders*, 1(1), 1–14.

Stevenson, J., & Richman, N. (1976). The prevalence of language delay in a population of 3-year-old children and its association with general retardation. *Developmental Medicine & Child Neurology*, 18, 431–441.

Striffler, N., & Willig, S. (1981). *Communication Screen: A preschool speech-language tool.* Tucson: Communication Skill Builders.

U.S. Department of Education. (1984). *Sixth annual report to Congress on the implementation of P.L. 94–142: The Education for All Handicapped Children Act.* Washington, DC.

U.S. General Accounting Office. (1981). *Disparities still exist in who gets special education.* Washington, DC: U.S. General Accounting Office.

Van Riper, C. (1978). *Speech correction: Principles and methods* (6th ed.). Englewood Cliffs, NJ: Prentice-Hall.

Wiig, E. H. (1982). Communication disorders. In N. G. Haring (Ed.), *Exceptional children and youth* (3rd ed., pp. 81–109). Columbus, OH: Charles E. Merrill.

———. (1984). Language disabilities in adolescents: A question of cognitive strategies. *Topics in Language Disorders*, 4(2), 41–58.

Wiig, E. H., & Semel, E. M. (1980). *Language assessment and intervention for the learning disabled.* Columbus, OH: Charles E. Merrill.

CHAPTER 8

Alabiso, F. (1977). Inhibitory functions of attention in reducing hyperactive behavior. *American Journal of Mental Deficiency, 77,* 259–282.

American Psychiatric Association. (1980). *Diagnostic and statistical manual of mental disorders* (3rd ed.). Washington, DC: Author.

Baumeister, A. A., & Brooks, P. H. (1981). Cognitive deficits in mental retardation. In J. M. Kauffman & D. P. Hallahan (Eds.), *Handbook of special education* (pp. 87–107). Englewood Cliffs, NJ: Prentice-Hall.

Becker, C. W., & Carnine, D. W. (1980). Direct instruction: An effective approach to educational intervention with the disadvantaged and low performers. In B. B. Lahey & A. E. Kazdin (Eds.), *Advances in clinical child psychology* (Vol. 3, pp. 429–473). New York: Plenum.

Begab, M. J. (1981). Issues in the prevention of psychosocial retardation. In M. J. Begab, H. C. Haywood, & H. L. Garber (Eds.), *Psychosocial influences in retarded performance: Vol. 1. Issues and theories in development* (pp. 3–19). Baltimore: University Park Press.

Belmont, J. M. (1966). Long-term memory in mental retardation. In N. R. Ellis (Ed.), *International review of research in mental retardation* (Vol. 1). New York: Academic Press.

Bijou, S. W. (1966). A functional analysis of retarded development. In N. R. Ellis (Ed.), *International review of research in mental retardation* (Vol. 1, pp. 1–19). New York: Academic Press.

Biklen, D., & Bogdan, R. (1977). Media portrayals of disabled people: A study in stereotypes. *Bulletin (Interracial Books for Children), 8*(6&7), 4–9.

Bray, N. W. (1979). Strategy production in the retarded. In N. R. Ellis (Ed.), *Handbook of mental deficiency: Psychological theory and research* (2nd ed., pp. 699–737). Hillsdale, NJ: Lawrence Erlbaum.

Brolin, D. (1982). *Vocational preparation of retarded citizens* (2nd ed.). Columbus, OH: Charles E. Merrill.

Brolin, D., & Kokaska, C. (1985). *Career education for handicapped children and youth* (2nd ed.). Columbus, OH: Charles E. Merrill.

Brown, S. M., & Robbins, M. J. (1979). Serving the special education needs of students in correctional facilities. *Exceptional Children, 45,* 574–579.

Bruininks, R. H. (1977). *Manual for the Bruininks Oseretsky Test of Motor Proficiency.* Circle Pines, MN: American Guidance Service.

Bruininks, R. H., Warfield, G., & Stealey, D. S. (1978). The mentally retarded. In E. L. Meyen (Ed.), *Exceptional children and youth: An introduction* (pp. 196–261). Denver: Love.

Campbell, L. W. (1968). *Study of curriculum planning.* Sacramento: California State Department of Education.

Cegelka, P. T., & Prehm, H. J. (1982). *Mental retardation: From categories to people.* Columbus, OH: Charles E. Merrill.

Clark, G. M. (1975). Mainstreaming for the secondary educable mentally retarded: Is it defensible? *Focus on Exceptional Children, 7*(2), 1–5.

Cohen, R. L. (1982). Individual differences in short-term memory. In N. R. Ellis (Ed.), *International review of research in mental retardation* (Vol. 11, pp. 43–77). New York: Academic Press.

Coulter, W. A., & Morrow, H. W. (1978). The future of adaptive behavior: Issues surrounding the refinement of the concepts and its measurement. In W. A. Coulter & H. W. Morrow (Eds.), *Adaptive behavior: Concepts & measurement* (pp. 215–225). New York: Grune & Stratton.

Crain, E. J. (1980). Socioeconomic status of educable mentally retarded graduates of special education. *Education and Training of the Mentally Retarded,* 15(2), 90–94.

Deshler, D. D., Lowrey, N., & Alley, G. R. (1979). Programming alternatives for learning disabled adolescents: A national survey. *Academic Therapy,* 14, 389–397.

Dettre, J. H. (1983). Bridges to academic success for young at risk children. *Topics in Early Childhood Special Education,* 3(3), 57–64.

Dunn, L. M. (1968). Special education for the mildly retarded—Is much of it justifiable? *Exceptional Children,* 35, 5–22.

————.(1973). Children with mild general learning disabilities. In L. M. Dunn (Ed.), *Exceptional children in the schools: Special education in transition.* New York: Holt, Rinehart & Winston.

Edgerton, R. B. (1967). *The clock of competence: Stigma in the lives of the mentally retarded.* Berkeley: University of California Press.

Facts on mental retardation. (1973). Arlington, TX: National Association for Retarded Citizens.

Gottlieb, J. (1981). Mainstreaming: Fulfilling the promise? *American Journal of Mental Deficiency,* 86, 115–126.

————.(1982). Mainstreaming. *Education and Training of the Mentally Retarded,* 17, 79–82.

Gottlieb, J., & Budoff, M. (1973). Social acceptability of retarded children in nongraded schools differing in architecture. *American Journal of Mental Deficiency,* 78, 15–19.

Gottlieb, J., Gottlieb, B. W., Schmelkin, L. P., & Curci, R. (1983). Low- and high-IQ learning disabled children in the mainstream. *Analysis and Intervention in Developmental Disabilities,* 3, 59–69.

Gottlieb, J., & Leyser, Y. (1981). Facilitating the social mainstreaming of retarded children. *Exceptional Education Quarterly,* 1(4), 57–69.

Gottlieb, J., Semmel, M. I., & Veldman, D. J. (1978). Correlates of social status among mainstreamed mentally retarded children. *Journal of Educational Psychology,* 70, 396–405.

Gresham, F. M. (1982). Misguided mainstreaming: The case for social skills training with handicapped children. *Exceptional Children,* 48, 422–433.

Grossman, H. J. (Ed.). (1973). *Manual on terminology and classification in mental retardation.* Washington, DC: American Association on Mental Deficiency.

————.(1977). *Manual on terminology and classification in mental retardation.* Washington, DC: American Association on Mental Deficiency.

————.(1983). *Classification in mental retardation.* Washington, DC: American Association on Mental Deficiency.

Hallahan, D. P., & Kauffman, J. M. (1976). *Introduction to learning disabilities: A psycho-behavioral approach.* Englewood Cliffs, NJ: Prentice-Hall.

————.(1982). *Exceptional children: Introduction to special education* (2nd ed.). Englewood Cliffs, NJ: Prentice-Hall.

Hardman, M. L., & Drew, C. J. (1975). Incidental learning in the mentally retarded: A review. *Education and Training of the Mentally Retarded,* 10, 3–9.

Hawaii Transition Project. (1984). Honolulu: University of Hawaii, Department of Special Education.

Haywood, H. C. (1979). What happened to mild and moderate mental retardation? *American Journal of Mental Deficiency, 83,* 429–431.

Hewett, F. M., & Forness, S. R. (1977). *Education of exceptional learners.* Boston: Allyn & Bacon.

Johnson, N. M., & Chamberlin, H. R. (1983). Early intervention: The state of the art. In *Developmental handicaps: Prevention and treatment* (pp. 1–23a). Washington, DC: American Association of University Affiliated Programs for Persons with Developmental Disabilities.

Kaufman, A. S., & Kaufman, N. L. (1982). *Kaufman Assessment Battery for Children.* Circle Pines, MN: American Guidance Service.

Kehle, T. J., & Barclay, J. R. (1979). Social and behavioral characteristics of mentally handicapped students. *Journal of Research and Development in Education, 12*(4), 46–56.

Keilitz, I., & Miller, S. L. (1980). Handicapped adolescents and young adults in the justice system. *Exceptional Education Quarterly, 1*(2), 117–126.

Keogh, B. K., & Daley, S. E. (1983). Early identification: One component of comprehensive services for at-risk children. *Topics in Early Childhood Special Education, 3*(3), 7–16.

Keogh, B. K., & Kopp, C. B. (1978). From assessment to intervention: An elusive bridge. In F. Minifie & L. Lloyd (Eds.), *Communication and cognitive abilities—Early behavioral assessment* (pp. 523–547). Baltimore: University Park Press.

Kirk, S. A. (1964). Research in education. In H. A. Stevens & R. Heber (Eds.), *Mental retardation: A review of research* (pp. 57–99). Chicago: University of Chicago Press.

Knowles, M. (1978). *The adult learner: A neglected species* (2nd ed.). Houston: Gulf.

Kolstoe, O. P. (1976). *Teaching educable mentally retarded children* (2nd ed.). New York: Holt, Rinehart & Winston.

Lambert, N., & Windmiller, M. (1981). AAMD *Adaptive Behavior Scale—School Edition.* Monterey, CA: Publishers Test Service.

Lawrence, E. A., & Winschel, J. F. (1975). Locus of control: Implications for special education. *Exceptional Children, 41,* 483–490.

Lazar, I., & Darlington, R. (1982). Lasting effects of early education: A report from the consortium for longitudinal studies. *Monographs of the Society for Research in Child Development, 47.*

MacMillan, D. L. (1982). *Mental retardation in school and society* (2nd ed.). Boston: Little, Brown.

MacMillan, D. L., & Borthwick, S. (1980). The new educable mentally retarded population: Can they be mainstreamed? *Mental Retardation, 18,* 155–158.

MacMillan, D. L., Meyers, C. E., & Yoshida, R. K. (1978). Regular class teachers' perceptions of transition programs for EMR students and their impact on the students. *Psychology in the Schools, 15,* 99–103.

Marsh, R. L., Friel, C. M., & Eissler, V. (1975). The adult MR in the criminal justice system. *Mental Retardation, 13*(2), 21–25.

Mascari, B. G., & Forgnone, C. (1982). A follow-up study of EMR students four years after dismissal from the program. *Education and Training of the Mentally Retarded, 17,* 288–292.

McCormick, L., & Kawate, J. (1982). Kindergarten survival skills: New directions for preschool special education. *Education and Training of the Mentally Retarded, 17,* 247–251.

Mercer, C. D., & Mercer, A. R. (1981). *Teaching students with learning problems.* Columbus, OH: Charles E. Merrill.

Mercer, J. R. (1973). *Labelling the mentally retarded.* Berkeley: University of California Press.

———. (1975). Sociocultural factors in educational labeling. In M. J. Begab & S. A. Richardson (Eds.), *The mentally retarded and society: A social science perspective* (pp. 141–157). Baltimore: University Park Press.

Mercer, J. R., & Lewis, J. P. (1977). *System of Multicultural Pluralistic Assessment: Parent Interview Manual.* New York: Psychological Corporation.

Mesinger, J. F. (1976). Juvenile delinquents: A relatively untapped population for special education professionals. *Behavior Disorders, 2,* 22–28.

Meyen, E. L. (1984). Mental retardation: Issues in perspective. In E. L. Meyen (Ed.), *Mental retardation: Topics of today—Issues of tomorrow* (pp. 1–4). Washington, DC: Division on Mental Retardation of the Council for Exceptional Children.

Meyen, E. L., & Moran, M. R. (1979). A perspective on the unserved mildly handicapped. *Exceptional Children, 45,* 526–530.

Morgan, D. I. (1979). Prevalence and types of handicapping conditions found in juvenile correctional institutions: A national survey. *The Journal of Special Education, 13,* 283–295.

Office of Civil Rights Report. (1980). Washington, DC: U.S. Department of Health, Education, and Welfare, Office of Education.

Palmer, F. H., & Andersen L. W. (1981). Early intervention treatments that have been tried, documented, and assessed. In M. J. Begab, H. C. Haywood, & H. L. Garber (Eds.), *Psychosocial influences in retarded performances:* Vol. 2. *Strategies for improving competence* (pp. 45–68). Baltimore: University Park Press.

Patrick, J. L. & Reschly, D. J., (1982). Relationship of state educational criteria and demographic variables to school-system prevalence of mental retardation. *American Journal of Mental Deficiency, 86,* 351–360.

Patton, J. R. (1984). *Changes in the mild mental retardation population: A continuing phenomenon.* Unpublished manuscript.

Payne, J. S., & Patton, J. R. (1981). *Mental retardation.* Columbus, OH: Charles E. Merrill.

Payne, J. S., Patton, J. R., & Beirne-Smith, M. (1985). *Mental retardation* (2nd ed.). Columbus, OH: Charles E. Merrill.

Payne, J. S., Patton, J. R., Kauffman, J. M., Brown, G. B., & Payne, R. A. (1983). *Exceptional children in focus* (3rd ed.). Columbus, OH: Charles E. Merrill.

Polloway, E. A. (1984). The integration of mildly retarded students in the schools: A historical review. *Remedial and Special Education, 5*(4), 18–28.

Polloway, E. A., Payne, J. S., Patton, J. R., & Payne, R. A. (1985). *Strategies for teaching retarded and special needs learners.* Columbus, OH: Charles E. Merrill.

Polloway, E. A., & Smith, J. E. (1982). *Teaching language skills to exceptional learners.* Denver: Love.

President's Committee on Mental Retardation. (1976). *Mental retardation: Century of decision.* Washington, DC: U.S. Government Printing Office.

———. (1978). *Hello world.* Washington, DC: U.S. Government Printing Office.

Ramey, C. T., & Finkelstein, N. W. (1981). Psychosocial mental retardations: A biological and social coalescence. In M. J. Begab, H. C. Haywood, & H. L. Garber (Eds.), *Psychosocial influences in retarded performance*: Vol. 1. *Issues and theories in development* (pp. 65–92). Baltimore: University Park Press.

Robinson, N. M., & Robinson, H. B. (1976). *The mentally retarded child* (2nd ed.). New York: McGraw-Hill.

Rogers-Warren, A. K., & Poulson, C. L. (1984). Perspectives on early childhood education. In E. L. Meyen (Ed.), *Mental retardation: Topics of today—Issues of tomorrow* (pp. 67–87). Washington, DC: Division of Mental Retardation of the Council for Exceptional Children.

Seligman, M. E. (1975). *Helplessness: On depression, development, and death*. San Francisco: W. H. Freeman.

Simner, M. L. (1983). The warning signs of school failure: An updated profile of the at-risk kindergarten child. *Topics in Early Childhood Special Education*, 3(3), 17–27.

Smith, J. D., & Polloway, E. A. (1983). Changes in mild mental retardation: Population, programs and perspectives. *Exceptional Children*, 50, 149–159.

Smith, J. E., & Payne, J. S. (1980). *Teaching exceptional adolescents*. Columbus, OH: Charles E. Merrill.

Soeffing, M. (1975). Abused children are exceptional children. *Exceptional Children*, 42, 126–133.

Sparrow, S. S., Balla, D. A., Cicchetti, D. V. (1983). *Vineland Adaptive Behavior Scales*. Circle Pines, MN: American Guidance Service.

Spitz, H. H. (1966). The role of input organization in the learning and memory of mental retardates. In N. R. Ellis (Ed.), *International review of research in mental retardation* (Vol. 2, pp. 29–56). New York: Academic Press.

Spradlin, J. E., (1963). Language and communication of mental defectives. In N. R. Ellis (Ed.), *Handbook of mental deficiency* (pp. 512–555). New York: McGraw-Hill.

———. (1968). Environmental factors and the language development of retarded children. In S. Rosenberg & J. H. Koplin (Eds.), *Developments in applied psycholinguistic research*. New York: Macmillan.

Staats, A. W. (1975). *Social behaviorism*. Homewood, IL: Dorsey Press.

Staats, A. W., & Burns, G. L. (1981). Intelligence and child development: What intelligence is and how it is learned and functions. *Genetic Psychology Monographs*, 104, 237–301.

Stebbins, L. B., St. Pierre, R. G., Proper, E. C., Anderson, R. B., & Cerva, T. R. (1977). *Education as experimentation: A planned variation model*: Vol. 4. *An evaluation of follow through*. Cambridge, MA: Abt.

Stephens, W. E. (1972). Equivalence formation by retarded and nonretarded children at different mental ages. *American Journal of Mental Deficiency*, 77, 311–313.

Strichart, S. S., & Gottlieb, J. (1983). Characteristics of mild mental retardation. In T. L. Miller & E. E. Davis (Eds.), *The mildly handicapped student* (pp. 37–65). New York: Grune & Stratton.

Tarjan, G., Wright, S. W., Eyman, R. K., & Kerran, D. V. (1973). Natural history of mental retardation: Some aspects to epidemiology. *American Journal of Mental Deficiency*, 77, 369–379.

Terman, L. M., & Merrill, M. A. (1973). *The Stanford-Binet Intelligence Scale* (3rd rev.). Boston: Houghton Mifflin.

Tjossem, T. J. (1976). *Intervention strategies for high risk infants and young children.* Baltimore: University Park Press.

Torgesen, J. K. (1982). The learning disabled child as an inactive learner: Educational implications. *Topics in Learning & Learning Disabilities, 2*(1), 45–52.

Tucker, J. (1980). Ethnic proportions in classes for the learning disabled: Issues in nonbiased assessment. *Journal of Special Education, 14,* 93–105.

Turnbull, H. R., & Barber, P. (1984). Perspectives on public policy. In E. L. Meyen (Ed.), *Mental retardation: Topics of today—Issues of tomorrow* (pp. 5–24). Washington, DC: Division on Mental Retardation of the Council for Exceptional Children.

Walker, H. M., McConnell, S., Walker, J., Clarke, J. Y., Todis, B., Cohen, G. & Rankin, R. (1983). Initial analysis of the ACCEPTS curriculum: Efficacy of instructional and behavior management procedures for improving the social adjustment of handicapped children. *Analysis and Intervention in Developmental Disabilities, 3,* 105–127.

Wechsler, D. (1974). *Wechsler Intelligence Scale for Children—Revised.* New York: Psychological Corporation.

Winschel, J. F., & Ensher, G. L. (1978). Educability revisited: Curricular implications for the mentally retarded. *Education and Training of the Mentally Retarded, 13,* 131–138.

Woodcock, R. W., & Johnson, M. B. (1977). *Woodcock-Johnson Psycho-Educational Battery.* Hingham, MA: Teaching Resources.

World Health Organization. (1978). *International Classification of Diseases* (9th rev.). Washington, DC: Author.

Zeaman, D., & House, B. J. (1963). The role of attention in retardate discrimination learning. In N. R. Ellis (Ed.), *Handbook of mental deficiency.* New York: McGraw-Hill.

Zigler, E. (1966). Research on personality structure in the retardate. In N. R. Ellis (Ed.), *International review of research in mental retardation* (Vol. 1). New York: Academic Press.

———. (1973). The retarded child as a whole person. In D. K. Routh (Ed.), *The experimental psychology of mental retardation.* Chicago: Aldine.

CHAPTER 9

Abramowicz, H. K., & Richardson, S. A. (1975). Epidemiology of severe mental retardation in children: Community studies. *American Journal of Mental Deficiency, 80,* 18–39.

Armstrong v. Kline, Civ. Action No. 78–172 (E.D. Pa. June 21, 1979).

Azrin, N. H. & Foxx, R. M. (1971). A rapid method of toilet training the institutionalized retarded. *Journal of Applied Behavior Analysis, 4,* 89–99.

Azrin, N. H., Schaeffer, R. M., & Wesolowski, M. D. (1976). A rapid method of teaching profoundly retarded persons to dress by a reinforcement-guidance method. *Mental Retardation, 14*(6), 29–33.

Azrin, N. H., Sneed, T. J., & Foxx, R. M. (1973). Dry bed: A rapid method of eliminating bedwetting (enuresis) of the retarded. *Behavior Research and Therapy, 11,* 427–434.

Baker, B. L., Seltzer, G. B., & Seltzer, M. M. (1977). *As close as possible. Community residences for retarded adults.* Boston: Little, Brown.

Barton, E. S., Guess, D., Garcia, E., & Baer, D. M. (1970). Improvements of retardates' mealtime behaviors by time-out procedures using multiple baseline techniques. *Journal of Applied Behavior Analysis, 3,* 77–84.

Bates, P., & Renzaglia, A. (1982). Language game instruction: Use of a table game. *Education and Treatment of Children, 5*(1), 13–22.

Baumeister, A. A. (1978). Origins and control of stereotyped movements. In C. E. Meyers (Ed.), *Quality of life in severely and profoundly mentally retarded people: Research foundations for improvement* (pp. 353–384). Washington, DC: American Association on Mental Deficiency.

Bayley, N. (1969). *Bayley Scales of Infant Development.* New York: Psychological Corporation.

Berkson, G., & Landesman-Dwyer, S. (1977). Behavioral research on severe and profound mental retardation (1955–1974). *American Journal of Mental Deficiency, 81,* 428–454.

Blatt, B., Ozolins, A., & McNally, J. (1979). *The family papers: A return to purgatory.* New York: Longman.

Braddock, D. (1977). *Opening closed doors: The deinstitutionalization of disabled individuals.* Reston, VA: Council of Exceptional Children.

Browder, D., Snell, M., & Ambiogio, B. (1984). *Using time delay to transfer stimulus control within the behavioral chain of vending machine use with a comparison of training sites.* Unpublished manuscript.

Brown, L., Branston, M., Hamre-Nietupski, S., Johnson, F., Wilcox, B., & Gruenwald, L. (1979). A rationale for comprehensive longitudinal interactions between severely handicapped students and nonhandicapped students and other citizens. *AAESPH Review, 4,* 3–14.

Brown, L., Branston, M. B., Hamre-Nietupski, S., Pumpian, I., Certo, N., & Gruenwald, L. (1979). A strategy for developing chronological age appropriate and functional curricular content for severely handicapped adolescents and young adults. *Journal of Special Education, 13,* 81–90.

Brown, L., Branston-McClean, M. B., Baumgart, D., Vincent, L., Falvey, M., Schroeder, J. (1979). Using the characteristics of current and subsequent least restrictive environments in the development of curricular content for severely handicapped students. *AAESPH Review, 4,* 407–424.

Brown, L., Nietupski, J., & Hamre-Nietupski, S. (1976). The criterion of ultimate functioning and public school services for severely handicapped students. In M. A. Thomas (Ed.), *Hey don't forget about me!* (pp. 2-15) Reston VA: Council for Exceptional Children.

Bruininks, R. H., Woodcock, R. W., Weatherman, R. F., & Hill, B. K. (1984). *The Scales of Independent Behavior.* Allen, TX: DLM Teaching Resources.

Caro, P., & Renzaglia, A. (1984). *Parent implemented instruction of contingency awareness and head control in young severely handicapped children.* Unpublished manuscript, University of Virginia.

Cronin, K. A., & Cuvo, A. J. (1979). Teaching mending skills to retarded adolescents. *Journal of Applied Behavior Analysis, 12,* 401–406.

Crosson, J. (1969). A technique of programming sheltered workshop environments for training severely retarded workers. *American Journal of Mental Deficiency, 73,* 814–818.

Dennis, C. M. (1980). *Top-down curriculum for Richard.* Unpublished manuscript, University of Virginia.

Doleys, D. M., Stacy, D., & Knowles, S. (1981). Modification of grooming behavior in adult retarded: Token reinforcement in a community-based program. *Behavior Modification, 5,* 119–128.

Dubose, R., & Langley, M. (1977). *The Developmental Activities Screening Inventory.* Boston: Teaching Resources.

Eyman, R. K., & Call, T. (1977). Maladaptive behavior and community placement of mentally retarded persons. *American Journal of Mental Deficiency, 82,* 137–144.

Eyman, R. K., Moore, B. C., Capes, L., & Zachofsky, T. (1970). Maladaptive behavior of institutionalized retardates with seizures. *American Journal of Mental Deficiency, 75,* 651–659.

Eyman, R. K., O'Connor, G., Tarjan, G., & Justice, R. S. (1972). Factors determining residential placement of mentally retarded children. *American Journal of Mental Deficiency, 76,* 692–698.

Favell, J. E., McGinsey, J. F., Jones, M. L. (1980). Rapid eating in the retarded: Reduction by nonaversive procedures. *Behavior Modification, 4,* 481–492.

Fialkowski v. Shapp, 405 F. Supp. 946 (E.D. Pa. 1975).

Foster, R. (1974). *Camelot Behavioral Checklist.* Lawrence, KS: Behavioral Systems.

Goetz, L., Schuler, A., & Sailor, W. (1979). Teaching functional speech to the severely handicapped: Current issues. *Journal of Autism and Developmental Disorders, 9,* 325–343.

Gold, M. (1972). Stimulus factors in skill training of retarded adolescents on a complex assembly task: Acquisition, transfer, and retention. *American Journal of Mental Deficiency, 76,* 517–526.

Gollay, E., Freedman, R., Wyngaarden, M., & Kurtz, N. R. (1978). *Coming back: The community experiences of deinstitutionalized mentally retarded people.* Cambridge, MA: Abt Books.

Grossman, H. J. (Ed.). (1983). *Classification in mental retardation.* Washington, DC: American Association on Mental Deficiency.

Gruber, B., Reeser, R., & Reid, D. H. (1979). Providing a less restrictive environment of profoundly retarded persons by teaching independent walking skills. *Journal of Applied Behavior Analysis, 12,* 285–297.

Guess, D., Sailor, W., & Baer, D. (1976). *Functional speech and language training for the severely handicapped.* Lawrence, KS: H & H Enterprises.

Halle, J. W., Marshall, A. M., & Spardlin, J. E. (1979). Time delay: A technique to increase language use and facilitate generalization in retarded children. *Journal of Applied Behavior Analysis, 12,* 431–439.

Hamilton, J., Allen, P., Stephens, L., & Duvall, E. (1969). Training mentally retarded females to use sanitary napkins. *Mental Retardation, 7*(1), 40–43.

Haring, N. G., White, O. R., Edgar, E. B., Affleck, J. Q., & Hayden, A. H. (1981). *The Uniform Performance Assessment System.* Columbus, OH: Charles E. Merrill.

Haskett, J., & Hollar, W. (1978). Sensory reinforcement and contingency awareness of profoundly retarded children. *American Journal of Mental Deficiency, 83,* 60–68.

Hill, J., Wehman, P., & Horst, G. (1982). Toward generalization of appropriate leisure and social behavior in severely handicapped youth: Pinball machine use. *Journal for the Association of the Severely Handicapped, 6,* 38–44.

Horner, R. D., & Keilitz, I. (1975). Training mentally retarded adolescents to brush their teeth. *Journal of Applied Behavior Analysis, 8,* 301–319.

Horner, R., Lehren, B., Schwartz, T., O'Neill, C., & Hunter, J. (1979). Dealing with the low production rates of severely retarded workers. *AAESPH Review, 4,* 202–212.

Hunter, J., & Bellamy, G. T. (1976). Cable harness construction for severely retarded adults: A demonstration of training technique. *AAESPH Review, 1,* 2–13.

Intagliata, J. C., Wilder, B. S., & Cooley, F. B. (1979). Cost comparison of institutional and community based alternatives for mentally retarded persons. *Mental Retardation, 17(3),* 154–155.

Janssen, C., & Guess, D. (1978). Use of function as a consequence in training receptive labeling to severely and profoundly retarded individuals. *AAESPH Review, 3,* 246–258.

Katz, S., & Yekutiel, E. (1974). Leisure time problems of mentally retarded graduates of training programs. *Mental Retardation, 12(3),* 54–57.

Kennedy, J. F. (1962). Statement regarding the need for a national plan in mental retardation (Oct. 11, 1961). In *National action to combat mental retardation.* Washington, DC: U.S. Government Printing Office.

Knapczyk, D. R. (1983). Use of teacher-paced instruction in developing and maintaining independent self-feeding. *Journal for the Association of the Severely Handicapped, 8,* 10–16.

Lambert, N., Windmiller, M., Cole, L., & Figueroa, R. (1975). AAMD *Adaptive Behavior Scale: Public School Version* (1974 revision). Washington DC: American Association on Mental Deficiency.

Lancioni, G. E., & Ceccarani, P. S. (1981). Teaching independent toileting within the normal daily program: Two studies with profoundly retarded children. *Behavior Research of Severe Developmental Disabilities, 2,* 79–96.

Landesman-Dwyer, S., & Sackett, G. P. (1978). Behavioral changes in nonambulatory profoundly mentally retarded invididuals. In C. E. Meyers (Ed.), *Quality of life in severely and profoundly mentally retarded people* (pp. 55–144). Washington, DC: American Association of Mental Deficiency.

Leonard, J. (1981). 180 day barrier: Issues and concerns. *Exceptional Children, 47,* 246–253.

Marchant, J., & Wehman, P. (1979). Teaching table games to severely handicapped students. *Mental Retardation, 17,* 150–52.

Marchetti, A. G., McCartney, J. R., Drain, S., Hooper, M., & Dix, J. (1983). Pedestrian skills training for mentally retarded adults: Comparison of training in two settings. *Mental Retardation, 21,* 107–110.

Matson, J., & Andrasik, F. (1982). Training leisure-time and social-interaction skills to mentally retarded adults. *American Journal of Mental Deficiency, 86,* 533–542.

Matson, J. L., DiLorenzo, T. M., & Esveldt-Dawson, K. (1981). Independence training as a method of enhancing self-help skills acquisition of the mentally retarded. *Behavior Research and Therapy, 19,* 399–405.

Milunsky, A. (1983). Genetic aspects of mental retardation: From prevention to cure. In F. J.

Menolascino, R. Neman, & J. A. Stark (Eds.), *Curative aspects of mental retardation: Biomedical and behavioral advances* (pp. 15–25). Baltimore: Paul H. Brookes.

Moon, M. S. (1982). *The effects of nonhandicapped peer participation and different reinforcement procedures on the maintenance of performance of fitness activities in severely handicapped adolescents.* Unpublished doctoral dissertation, University of Virginia.

Nelson, G. L., Cone, J. E., & Hanson, C. R. (1975). Training correct utensil use in retarded children: Modeling vs. physical guidance. *American Journal of Mental Deficiency, 80,* 114–122.

Nutter, D., & Reid, D. H. (1978). Teaching retarded women a clothing selection skill using community norms. *Journal of Applied Behavior Analysis, 11,* 475–487.

O'Brien, F., & Azrin, N. H. (1972). Developing proper mealtime behaviors of the institutionalized retarded. *Journal of Applied Behavior Analysis, 5,* 389–399.

O'Brien, F., Bugle, C., & Azrin, N. H. (1972). Training and maintaining a retarded child's proper eating. *Journal of Applied Behavior Analysis, 5,* 67–73.

O'Connor, G. (1976). *Home is a good place: A rational perspective of community residential facilities for developmentally disabled persons.* Washington, DC: American Association on Mental Deficiency.

Pennsylvania Association for Retarded Children v. Commonwealth of Pennsylvania, 343 F. Supp. 279 (E.D. Pa. 1972).

Renzaglia, A., Bates, P., & Cless, T. (1978). Manual sign training for a nonverbal profoundly retarded individual utilizing an instructional table game. In O. Karan (Ed.), *Habilitation practices with the severely developmentally disabled* (Vol. 2). Madison, WI: Research and Training Center in Mental Retardation.

Richmond, G. (1983). Shaping bladder and bowel continence in developmentally retarded preschool children. *Journal of Autism and Developmental Disorders, 13,* 197–203.

Robinson, N. M., & Robinson, H. B. (1976). *The mentally retarded child: A psychologieal approach* (2nd ed.). New York: McGraw-Hill.

Roos, P. (1979). Custodial care for the "subtrainable"—revisiting an old myth. *Law and Psychology Review, 5*(Fall), 1–14.

Rusch, F. R. (1983). Competitive vocational training. In M. Snell (Ed.), *Systematic instruction of the moderately and severely handicapped* (2nd ed., pp. 501–523). Columbus, OH: Charles E. Merrill.

Rusch, F. R., & Mithaug, D. (1980). *Vocational training for mentally retarded adults: A behavior analytic approach.* Champaign, IL: Research Press.

Rynders, J. E., Johnson, R. T., Johnson, D. W., & Schmidt, B. (1980). Producing positive interaction among Down syndrome and nonhandicapped teenagers through cooperative goal structuring. *American Journal of Mental Deficiency, 85,* 268–273.

Sailor, W., Guess, D., Goetz, L., Schuler, A., Utley, B., & Baldwin, M. (1980). Language and severely handicapped persons. In W. Sailor, B. Wilcox, & L. Brown (Eds.), *Methods of instruction for severely handicapped students* (pp. 71–105). Baltimore: Paul H. Brookes.

Sailor, W., & Mix, B. (1975). *The TARC Assessment Systems.* Lawrence, KS: H & H Enterprises.

Saunders, R., & Sailor, W. (1979). A comparison of three strategies of reinforcement on two-choice learning problems with severely retarded children. *AAESPH Review, 4,* 323–333.

Scheerenberger, R. C. (1982). Treatment from ancient times to the present. In P. T. Cegelka & H. J. Prehm (Eds.), *Mental retardation: From categories to people* (pp. 44–75). Columbus, OH: Charles E. Merrill.

Schleien, S. J., Ash, T., Kiernan, J., & Wehman, P. (1981). Developing independent cooking skills in a profoundly retarded woman. *Journal for the Association of the Severely Handicapped,* 6, 23–29.

Schleien, S., Wehman, P., & Kiernan, J. (1981). Teaching leisure skills to severely handicapped adults. An age-appropriate dart game. *Journal of Applied Behavior Analysis,* 14, 513–519.

Snell, M. E. (1982a). Analysis of time delay procedures in teaching daily living skills to retarded adults. *Analysis and Intervention in Developmental Disabilities,* 2, 139–156.

———. (1982b). Characteristics of the profoundly mentally retarded. In P. Cegelka & H. Prehm (Eds.), *Mental retardation: From categories to people.* Columbus, OH: Charles E. Merrill.

Sobsey, R., & Orelove, F. P. (1984). Neurophysiological facilitation of eating skills in children with severe handicaps. *Journal for the Association of the Severely Handicapped,* 9, 98–110.

Sontag, E., Burke, P. J., & York, R. (1973). Considerations for serving the severely handicapped in the public schools. *Education and Training of the Mentally Retarded,* 8, 20–26.

Sontag, E., Certo, N., & Button, J. E. (1979). On a distinction between the education of the severely and profoundly handicapped as a doctrine of limitations. *Exceptional Children,* 45, 604–616.

Sosne, J. B., Handleman, J. S., & Harris, S. L. (1979). Teaching spontaneous functional speech to autistic-type children. *Mental Retardation,* 17(5), 241–244.

Sowers, J., Rusch, F. R., & Hudson, C. (1979). Training a severely retarded young adult to ride the city bus to and from work. *AAESPH Review,* 4, 15–23.

Sprague, J. R., & Horner, R. H. (1984). The effects of single instance, multiple instance, and general case training on generalized vending machine use by moderately and severely handicapped students. *Journal of Applied Behavior Analysis,* 17, 273–278.

Stark, J. A. (1983). The search for cures of mental retardation. In F. J., Menolascino, R. Neman, & J. A. Stark (Eds.), *Curative aspects of mental retardation: Biomedical and behavioral advances* (pp. 1–11). Baltimore: Paul H. Brookes.

Sternat, S., Messina, R., Nietupski, J., Lyon, S., & Brown, L. (1977). Occupational and physical therapy services for severely handicapped students: Toward a naturalized public school service delivery mode. In E. Sontag, N. Certo, & J. Smith (Eds.), *Educational programming for the severely handicapped* (pp. 263–278). Reston, VA: Council for Exceptional Children.

Strain, P., McConnell, S., & Cordisco, L. (1983). Special educators as single-subject researchers. *Exceptional Education Quarterly,* 4(3), 40–51.

Taylor, S. (1982). From segregation to integration: Strategies for integrating severely handicapped students in normal school and community settings. *Journal for the Association of the Severely Handicapped,* 8, 42–49.

Thompson, G. A., Jr., Iwata, B. A., & Poynter, H. (1979). Operant control of pathological tongue thrusts in spastic cerebral palsy. *Journal of Applied Behavior Analysis,* 12, 325–333.

van den Pol, R. A., Iwata, B. A., Ivanic, M. T., Page, T. J., Neff, N. A., & Whitley, F. P. (1981). Teaching the handicapped to eat in public places: Acquisition, generalization and maintenance of restaurant skills. *Journal of Applied Behavior Analysis,* 14, 61–69.

Voeltz, L. M. (1980). Children's attitudes toward handicapped peers. *American Journal of Mental Deficiency, 84,* 455–464.

————. (1982). Effects of structured interactions with severely handicapped peers on children's attitudes. *American Journal of Mental Deficiency, 86,* 180–190.

Vogelsburg, R. T., & Rusch, F. R. (1979). Training severely handicapped students to cross partially controlled intersections. AAESPH *Review, 4,* 264–273.

Wehman, P. (1981). *Competitive employment.* Baltimore: Paul H. Brookes.

Wehman, P., & Marchant, J. (1977). Developing gross motor recreational skills in children with severe behavior handicaps. *Therapeutic Recreation, 11,* 48–54.

Wehman, P., Renzaglia, A., Berry, G., Schutz, R., & Karan, O. (1978). Developing a leisure skill repertoire in severely and profoundly handicapped persons. AAESPH *Review, 3,* 162–172.

Weiskopf, P. E. (1980). Burnout among teachers of exceptional children. *Exceptional Children, 47,* 18–23.

Westling, D. L., Koorland, M. A., & Rose, T. L. (1981). Characteristics of superior and average special teachers. *Exceptional Children, 47,* 357–363.

Westling, D. L., & Murden, L. (1978). Self-help training: A review of operant studies. *Journal of Special Education, 12,* 253–283.

Zigler, E., & Balla, D. A. (1977). Impact of institutional experience on the behavior and development of retarded persons. *American Journal of Mental Deficiency, 82,* 1–11.

CHAPTER 10

Anderson, E. M., & Spain, B. (1977). *The child with spina bifida.* London: Methuen. (Distributed in the U.S. by Love Publishers, Denver)

Anderson, H. (1981). *The disabled homemaker.* Springfield, IL: Charles C. Thomas.

Batshaw, M. L., & Perret, Y. M. (1981). *Children with handicaps: A medical primer.* Baltimore: Paul H. Brookes.

Behrmann, M. M., & Lahm, L. (1984). Babies and robots: Technology to assist learning of young multiply disabled children. *Rehabilitation Literature, 45,* 194–201.

Bigge, J. L. (1982). *Teaching individuals with physical and multiple disabilities* (2nd ed.). Columbus, OH: Charles E. Merrill.

Bigge, J. L. (in press). *Curriculum strategies for students in special education.* Palo Alto, CA: Mayfield.

Bleck, E. E. (1982). Cerebral palsy. In E. E. Bleck & D. A. Nagel (Eds.), *Physically handicapped children: A medical atlas for teachers* (2nd ed., pp. 59–132). New York: Grune & Stratton.

Bleck, E. E., & Nagel, D. A. (Eds.). (1982). *Physically handicapped children: A medical atlas for teachers* (2nd ed.). New York: Grune & Stratton.

Bobath, K. (1980). *A neurophysiological basis for the treatment of cerebral palsy* (Clinics in Developmental Medicine No. 75). Philadelphia: Lippincott.

Bobath, K., & Bobath, B. (1975). Cerebral palsy. In P. Pearson & C. E. Williams (Eds.), *Physical therapy services in the developmental disabilities* (pp. 31–113). Springfield, IL: Charles C. Thomas.

Brolin, D. E. (1982). *Vocational preparation of persons with handicaps* (2nd ed.). Columbus, OH: Charles E. Merrill.

Brown, L., Branston-McClean, M., Baumgart, D., Vincent, L., Falvey, M., & Schroeder, J. (1979). Using the characteristics of current and subsequent least restrictive environments in the development of curricular content for severely handicapped students. *American Association for Education of the Severely and Profoundly Handicapped Review*, 4, 407–424.

Carpignano, J. L., Sirvis, B., & Bigge, J. L. (1982). Psychosocial aspects of physical disability. In J. L. Bigge (Ed.), *Teaching individuals with physical and multiple disabilities* (2nd ed., pp. 110–137). Columbus, OH: Charles E. Merrill.

Christiansen, R. O., & Hintz, R. L. (1982). In E. E. Bleck & D. A. Nagel (Eds.), *Physically handicapped children: A medical atlas for teachers* (2nd ed., pp. 269–277). New York: Grune & Stratton.

Chutorian, A. M., & Engel, M. (1982). Diseases of the muscle. In J. A. Downey & N. L. Low (Eds.), *The child with disabling illness: Principles of rehabilitation* (2nd ed., pp. 291–347). New York: Raven Press.

Connor, F. P., Williamson, G. G., & Siepp, J. M. (1978). *Program guide for infants & toddlers with neuromotor and other developmental disabilities*. New York: Teachers College Press.

Corbet, B. (1980). *Options: Spinal cord injury and the future*. Newton Upper Falls, MA: National Spinal Cord Injury Foundation.

Corrigan, J. J., & Damiano, M. L. (1983). Blood diseases. In J. Umbreit (Ed.), *Physical disabilities and health impairments: An introduction* (pp. 167–174). Columbus, OH: Charles E. Merrill.

Crain, L. S. (1984). Prenatal causes of atypical development. In M. J. Hanson (Ed.), *Atypical infant development* (pp. 27–55). Baltimore: University Park Press.

Cruickshank, W. M. (Ed.). (1976). *Cerebral palsy: A developmental disability* (3rd ed.). Syracuse, NY: Syracuse University Press.

Denhoff, E. (1976). Medical aspects. In W. M. Cruickshank (Ed.), *Cerebral palsy: A developmental disability* (3rd ed., pp. 29–71). Syracuse, NY: Syracuse University Press.

Denhoff, E., & Robinault, I. (1960a). *Cerebral palsy and related disorders*. New York: McGraw-Hill.

————. (1960b). *Definitions and a developing concept*. New York: McGraw-Hill.

Donovan, W. H. (1981). Spinal cord injury. In W. C. Stolov & M. R. Clowers (Eds.), *Handbook of severe disability* (Stock No. 017–090–00054–2, pp. 65–82). Washington, DC: U.S. Government Printing Office.

Downey, J. A., & Low, N. L. (Eds.). (1982). *The child with disabling illness: Principles of rehabilitation* (2nd ed.). New York: Raven Press.

Federal Register, August 23, 1977, 42 (163), 42474–42518.

Fenton, J. (Ed.). (1981). *Research directory of rehabilitation research and training centers, fiscal year 1980*. Washington, DC: U.S. Department of Education.

Finnie, N. R. (1975). *Handling the young cerebral palsied child at home* (2nd ed.). New York: E. P. Dutton.

Goldenberg, E. P. (1979). *Special technology for special children*. Baltimore: University Park Press.

Goldenson, R. M. (Ed.). (1978). *Disability and rehabilitation handbook*. New York: McGraw-Hill.

Hale, G. (Ed.). (1982). *The source book for the disabled.* New York: Holt, Rinehart & Winston.

Hall, D. M. B. (1984). *The child with a handicap.* Boston: Blackwell Scientific Publications.

Hanson, M. J. (Ed.). (1984). *Atypical infant development.* Baltimore: University Park Press.

Hanson, V. (1983). Juvenile rheumatoid arthritis. In J. Umbreit (Ed.), *Physical disabilities and health impairments: An introduction* (pp. 240–249). Columbus, OH: Charles E. Merrill.

Harvey, B. (1982). Cystic fibrosis. In E. E. Bleck & D. A. Nagel (Eds.), *Physically handicapped children: A medical atlas for teachers* (2nd ed., pp. 255–263). New York: Grune & Stratton.

Holm, V. (1982). The causes of cerebral palsy. *Journal of the American Medical Association, 247* (10), 1473–1477.

Howell, L. (1978). Spina bifida. In R. M. Goldenson (Ed.), *Disability and rehabilitation handbook* (pp. 560–564). New York: McGraw-Hill.

Huckstep, R. L. (1955). *Poliomyelitis.* New York: Churchill Livingstone.

Jacobs, I. B. (1983). Epilepsy. In G. H. Thompson, I. L. Rubin, & R. M. Bilenker (Eds.), *Comprehensive management of cerebral palsy* (pp. 131–137). New York: Grune & Stratton.

Koehler, J. (1982). Spinal muscular atrophy. In E. E. Bleck & D. A. Nagel (Eds.), *Physically handicapped children: A medical atlas for teachers* (2nd ed., pp. 477–481). New York: Grune & Stratton.

Life experience program: An alternative approach in special education. (1976). San Jose, CA: Office of the Santa Clara County Superintendent of Schools.

Link, M. P. (1982). Cancer in childhood. In E. E. Bleck & D. A. Nagel (Eds.), *Physically handicapped children: A medical atlas for teachers* (2nd ed., pp. 43–58). New York: Grune & Stratton.

Low, N. L. (1982). Seizure disorders in children. In J. A. Downey & N. L. Low (Eds.), *The child with disabling illness: Principles of rehabilitation* (2nd ed., pp. 121–144). New York: Raven Press.

Lyle, R. R., & Obringer, S. J. (1983). Muscular dystrophy. In J. Umbreit (Ed.), *Physical disabilities and health impairments: An introduction* (pp. 100–107). Columbus, OH: Charles E. Merrill.

Mackie, R. (1945). *Crippled children in American education.* New York: Teachers College, Columbia University.

————. (1969). *Special education in the United States: Statistics 1948–1966.* New York: Teachers College, Columbia University.

Mangold, S. (1980). *Developmental program of tactile perception and braille letter recognition.* Castro Valley, CA: Exceptional Teaching Aids.

Marquardt, E. G. (1983). A holistic approach to rehabilitation for the limb-deficient child. *Archives of Physical Medicine and Rehabilitation, 64*(6), 237–242.

Mills, J., & Higgins, J. (1983). *The assessment for non-speech communication.* San Diego: California Publications.

————. (1984). An environmental approach to delivery of microprocessor-based and other communication systems. *Seminars in Speech and Language, 5*(1), 35–45.

Molnar, G. E. (1983). Musculoskeletal disorders. In J. Umbreit (Ed.), *Physical disabilities and health impairments: An introduction* (pp. 108–116). Columbus, OH: Charles E. Merrill.

National summary of handicapped children receiving special education and related services under P.L. 94–

142 & P.L. 89–313, 1980–1981. Washington, DC: U.S. Department of Education, Office of Special Education and Rehabilitation Services.

Perterson, C. A., & Gunn, S. L. (1984). *Therapeutic recreation program design: Principles and procedures* (2nd ed.). Englewood Cliffs, NJ: Prentice-Hall.

Proceedings of the Second International Conference on Rehabilitation Engineering combined with the RESNA *Seventh Annual Conference.* (1984). Bethesda, MD: Rehabilitation Engineering Society of North America.

Rab, G. T. (1983). The hip. In M. E. Gershwin & D. L. Robbins (Eds.), *Musculoskeletal diseases of children* (pp. 539–559). New York: Grune & Stratton.

Shotick, A. L. (1976). Mental retardation. In W. M. Cruickshank (Ed.), *Cerebral palsy: A developmental disability* (3rd ed., pp. 421–458). Syracuse, NY: Syracuse University Press.

Sirvis, B. (1978). Developing IEPs for physically handicapped students: A transdisciplinary viewpoint. *Teaching Exceptional Children,* 10(3), 78–82.

———. (1980). Career education for the severely handicapped. In G. M. Clark & W. J. White (Eds.), *Career education for the handicapped: Current perspectives for teachers.* Boothwyn, PA: Educational Resources Center.

Sirvis, B., & Cieloha, D. (1981). Recreation and leisure skills. In J. Umbreit & P. Cardullias (Eds.), *Educating the physically handicapped: Curriculum adaptations* (Vol. 4, pp. 53–63). Reston, VA: Council for Exceptional Children.

Thompson, G. H., Rubin, I. L., & Bilenker, R. M. (Eds.). (1983). *Comprehensive management of cerebral palsy.* New York: Grune & Stratton.

Umbreit, J. (Ed.). (1983). *Physical disabilities and health impairments: An introduction.* Columbus, OH: Charles E. Merrill.

U.S. Department of Education. (1984). *Sixth Annual Report to Congress on the Implementation of* P.L. 94–142: The Education for All Handicapped Children Act. Washington, D.C.

Viscardi, H. (1972). *But not on our block.* New York: Eriksson.

Wald, J. R. (1971). Crippled and other health impaired and their education. In F. P. Connor, J. R. Wald, & M. J. Cohen (Eds.), *Professional preparation for educators of crippled children* (pp. 94–99). New York: Teachers College Press.

Williamson, G. G. (1978). The individualized education program: An interdisciplinary endeavor. In B. Sirvis, J. W. Baken, & G. G. Williamson (Eds.), *Unique aspects of the* IEP *for the physically handicapped, homebound, and hospitalized.* Reston, VA: Council for Exceptional Children.

Wright, B. A. (1960). *Physical disability—A psychological approach.* New York: Harper & Row.

———. (1983). *Physical disability—A psychosocial approach.* New York: Harper & Row.

CHAPTER 11

Anderson, R. J., & Sisco, F. H. (1977). *Standardization of the* WISC-R *performance scale for deaf children* (p. 1). Washington, DC: Gallaudet College, Office of Demographic Studies.

Bardenstein, L. (1982, September). MELBORP (math drill and practice). *American Annals of the Deaf,* 127 (5), 659–664.

Bates, E., Camaioni, L., & Volterra, V. (1975). The acquisition of performatives prior to speech. *Merrill-Palmer Quarterly*, 21, 205–226.

Bayley, N. (1969). *Bayley Scales of Infant Development*. New York: Psychological Corporation.

Bergman, E. (1972). Autonomous and unique features of American Sign Language. *American Annals of the Deaf*, 117(5), 20–24.

Boehm, A. E. (1971). *Boehm Test of Basic Concepts*. New York: Psychological Corporation.

Calvert, D., & Silverman, S. R. (1975). *Speech and deafness: A text for learning and teaching*. Washington, DC: A. G. Bell Association for the Deaf.

Caniglia, J., et al. (1972). *Appletree*. Beaverton, OR: Dormac.

Carrow, E. (1973). *Test for Auditory Comprehension of Language*. Austin, TX: Learning Concepts.

Cattell, R. (1960). *The measurement of intelligence of infants and young children* (rev. ed.). New York: Psychological Corporation.

Coggins, T., & Carpenter, R. (1981). The communicative inventory: A system for observing and coding children's early intentional communication. *Applied Psycholinguistics*, 2, 235–251.

Davis, H., & Silverman, S. R. (1978). *Hearing and deafness* (4th ed.). New York: Holt, Rinehart & Winston.

Davis, J. (1974). Performance of young hearing-impaired children on a test of basic concepts. *Journal Speech and Hearing Research*, 17, 342–351.

———. (1977). Reliability of hearing-impaired children's responses to oral and total presentation of the test of auditory comprehension of language. *Journal Speech and Hearing Research*, 42, 520–527.

Dunn, L. M., & Markwardt, F. C. (1970). *Peabody Individual Achievement Test*. Circle Pines, MN: American Guidance Service.

Eilers, R. E., & Minifie, F. D. (1975). Tricative discrimination in early infancy. *Journal of Speech and Hearing Research*, 18, 158–167.

Eimas, P. D., Siqueland, E., Jusczyk, P., & Vigout, J. (1971). Speech perception in infants. *Science*, (1970). 171, 303–306.

Friedlander, B., & Cyrulik, A. (1970). *Automated home measurement of infants' preferential discrimination and loudness levels*. A presentation to the American Speech and Hearing Association.

Garretson, M. D. (1976). Total communication. *Volta Review*, 78(4), 88–95.

Garvey, M. (1982, September). CAI as a supplement in a mainstreamed hearing impaired program. *American Annals of the Deaf*, 127(5), 613–616.

Gesell, A. (1940). *The first five years of life*. New York: Harper Brothers.

Groht, M. A. (1958). *Natural language for deaf children*. Washington, DC: Volta Bureau.

Gustason, G., Pfetzing, D., & Zawolkow, E. (1972). *Signing exact English*. Rosemoor, CA: Modern Sign Press.

Hall, S. (1983). Train-gone-sorry: The etiquette of social conversations in American Sign Language. *Sign Language Studies*, 41, 291–309.

Hanshaw, J. B., & Dudgeon, J. A. (1978). Congenital cytomegalovirus. *Major Problems in Clinical Pediatrics*, 17, 97–152.

Harris, R. I. (1978). Impulse control in deaf children. In L. Liben (Ed.), *Deaf children: Developmental perspectives.* New York: Academic Press.

Hart, B. O. (1964). A child-centered language program. *Proceedings of the International Congress on the Education of the Deaf.* Washington, DC: U.S. Government Printing Office.

Hedrick, D. L., Prather, E. M., & Tobin, A. R. (1984). *Sequenced inventory of communication development.* (rev. ed.) Seattle: University of Washington Press.

Hight, R. (1982, September). Lip-reader trainer: Teaching aid for the hearing impaired. *American Annals of the Deaf,* 127(5), 564–568.

Hiskey, M. S. (1966). *Nebraska test of Learning Aptitude.* Lincoln, NE: Union College Press.

Jastak, J. F., & Jastak, S. R. (1978). *The Wide Range Achievement Test (Revised).* Wilmington, DE: Jastak Associates.

Jeffers, T., & Barley, M. (1971). *Speechreading (lipreading).* Springfield, IL: Charles C. Thomas.

Johnson, J. O., & Boyd, H. F. (1981). *Nonverbal Test of Cognitive Skills.* Columbus, OH: Charles E. Merrill.

Johnston, D. (1982, September). DEAFSIGN: A series of computerized instructional programs for the teaching of sign language. *American Annals of the Deaf,* 127(5), 556i–558.

Karchmer, M. A., & Trybus, R. J. (1977). *Who are the deaf children in "mainstream" programs?* (Series R, No. 4). Washington, DC: Gallaudet College, Office of Demographic Studies.

Kaufman, A. S., & Kaufman, N. L. (1982). *Kaufman Assessment Battery for Children.* Circle Pines, MN: American Guidance Service.

Klima, E., & Bellugi, U. (1979). *The signs of language.* Cambridge: Harvard University Press.

Kluwin, T. N. (1981). The grammaticality of manual representations of English in classroom settings. *American Annals of the Deaf,* 126, 417–421.

Leiter, R. (1948). *The Leiter International Performance Scale.* Chicago: Stoelting.

Lenneberg, E. (1975). The concept of language differentiation. In N. O'Conner (Ed.), *Language, cognitive defects, and retardation* (pp. 89–142). London: Butterworth.

Ling, D. (1976). *Speech and the hearing impaired child: Theory and practice.* Washington, DC: A. G. Bell Association for the Deaf.

Longhurst, T., Briery, D., & Emery, M. (1975). SKI-HI *Receptive language test,* Project SKI-HI. Logan: Utah State University.

Madden, R. G., Gardner, E. F., Rudman, H. C., Karlsen, B., & Merwin, J. C. (1972). *Stanford Achievement Test special edition for hearing-impaired children.* Washington, DC: Gallaudet College.

Marmor, G. S., & Petitto, L. (1979). Simultaneous communication in the classroom: How well is English grammar represented? *Sign Language Studies,* 23, 99–136.

McFarland, W., & Simmons, B. (1980). The importance of early intervention with severe childhood deafness. *Pediatric Annals,* 9, 13–19.

Meadow, K. (1980). *Deafness and child development.* Berkeley: University of California Press.

Miller, J. F. (1964). Practices in language instruction. *Exceptional Children,* 30, 355–358.

Moffit, A. (1971). Consonant cue perception by 20–24 week old infants. *Child Development,* 42, 717–731.

Moores, D. (1982). *Educating the deaf: Psychology, principles and practices* (2nd ed.). Boston: Houghton Mifflin.

Nance, W. E. (1976). Studies of hereditary deafness: Present, past and future. *Volta Review,* 78(4), 6–11.

O'Neill, J. J., & Oyer, H. J. (1961). *Visual communication for the hard of hearing.* Englewood Cliffs, NJ: Prentice-Hall.

Pass, R. F., Stagno, S., & Myers, G. J. (1980). Outcome of symptomatic congenital cytomegalovirus infection: Results of long-term longitudinal follow-up. *Pediatrics,* 66, 758–762.

Prinz, P., Nelson, K., & Stedt, J. (1982, September). Early reading in young deaf children using microcomputer technology. *American Annals of the Deaf,* 127(5), 529–535.

Quigley, S., & Desmond, J. (1979). TSA *Syntax Program.* Beaverton, OR: Dormac.

Quigley, S. P., Steinkamp, M. W., Power, D. J., & Jones, B. W. (1978). *The Test of Syntactic Abilities.* Beaverton, OR: Dormac.

Ratcliffe, K. J., & Ratcliffe, M. W. (1979). The Leiter scales: A review of validity findings. *American Annals of the Deaf,* 124(1), 38–45.

Raven, J. (1948). *Progressive matrices.* New York: Psychological Corporation.

The Rochester Method as a vehicle for improving the education of deaf children., Rochester, NY: Rochester School for the Deaf. (1972).

Schlesinger, H., & Meadow, K. (1972). *Sound and sign: Childhood defense and mental health.* Berkeley: University of California Press.

Simmons-Martin, A. (1972, December). Oral-aural procedure: Theoretical basis and rationale. *Volta Review,* 74, 541–551.

Smith, A. J., & Johnson, R. E. (1977). *Smith-Johnson Nonverbal Performance Scale.* Los Angeles: Western Psychological Service.

Stewart, D. (1983, summer). Bilingual education: Teachers' opinions of signs. *Sign Language Studies,* 39, 4.

Streng, A. H., Kretschmer, R., & Kretschmer, L. (1978). *Language, learning, and deafness: Theory, application, and classroom management.* New York: Grune & Stratton.

Sullivan, P., & McCay, V. (1979). Psychological assessment of hearing-impaired children. *School Psychology Digest,* 8(3), 271–290.

Trott, L. A. (1984). Providing school psychological services to hearing-impaired students in New Jersey. *American Annals of the Deaf,* 129(3), 319–323.

Trybus, R., & Karchmer, M. (1977). School achievement scores of hearing impaired children: National data on achievement status and growth patterns. *American Annals of the Deaf Directory of Programs and Services,* 122, 62–69.

U.S. Department of Education. *Sixth Annual Report to Congress on the Implementation of the Education of the Handicapped, Act,* 1984.

Uzgiris, I. V., & Hunt, J. M. (1978). *Assessment in infancy: Ordinal Scales of Psychological Development.* Urbana: University of Illinois Press.

Van Uden, A. (1970). *A world of language for deaf children.* Rotterdam, The Netherlands: Rotterdam University Press.

Vernon, M. (1968). Fifty years of research on the intelligence of hard of hearing children: A review of the literature and discussion of implications. *Journal of Rehabilitation of the Deaf*, 1(4), 1–12.

Vernon, M., & Brown, D. W. (1964). A guide to psychological tests and testing procedures in the evaluation of deaf and hard-of-hearing children. *Journal of Speech and Hearing Development*, 29(4), 414–423.

Wechsler, D. (1974). *Wechsler Intelligence Scale for Children (Revised)*. New York: Psychological Corporation.

White, A. H. (1977). *Maryland Syntax Evaluation Instrument*. Sanger, TX: Support Systems for the Deaf.

Williams, W. D., Murdina, M. D., LaFeuers, N., Taber, L., Catlin, F. I., & Weaver, T. G. (1982). Symptomatic congenital cytomegalovirus. *American Journal of the Disabled Child*, 138, 902–905.

Zinkus, P. W., Gottlieb, M. L., & Shapiro, M. (1978). Developmental and psychoeducational sequelae of chronic otitis media. *American Journal of the Disordered Child*, 132, 1100–1104.

CHAPTER 12

American Printing House for the Blind. (1983). *Annual report*. Louisville, KY.
———. (1984). *Annual report*. Louisville, KY.
Barraga, N. C. (1983). *Visual handicaps and learning*. Austin, TX: Exceptional Resources.

Corn, A. (1980). *Development and assessment of an inservice training program for teachers of the visually handicapped: Optical aids in the classroom*. Unpublished doctoral dissertation, Teachers College, Columbia University.

Cratty, B. J., & Sams, T. A. (1968). *The body image of blind children*. New York: American Foundation for the Blind.

Davidson, I., & Nesker Simmons, J. (1984). Mediating the environment for young blind children: A conceptualization. *Journal of Visual Impairment and Blindness*, 78, 251–255.

Faye, D. D. (1970). *The low vision patient*. New York: Grune & Stratton.

Fletcher, J. F. (1980). Spatial representation in blind children: 1. Development compared to sighted children. *Journal of Visual Impairment and Blindness*, 74, 381–385.

Fraiberg, S. (1968). Parallel and divergent patterns in blind and sighted infants. *Psychoanalytic Study of the Child*, 23, 264–300.

———. (1977). *Insights from the blind*. New York: New American Library.

Fraiberg, S., Siegel, B., & Gibson, R. (1966). The role of sound in the search behavior of a blind infant. *Psychoanalytic Study of the Child*, 19, 113–169.

Gibbs, S. H., & Rice, J. A. (1974). The psycholinguistic characteristics of visually impaired children: An ITPA analysis. *Education of Visually Handicapped*, 6, 80–88.

Harley, R. K. (1963). *Verbalism amoung blind children*. New York: American Foundation for the Blind.

———. (1980). An orientation and mobility program for multiply impaired blind children. *Exceptional Children*, 46, 326–331.

Harley, R. K., Wood, T. A., & Merbler, J. B. (1981). Peabody Mobility Scale. Chicago: Stoelting.

Hatfield, E. M. (1975), Why are they blind? *Sight Saving Review, 45*(1), 3–22.

Hathaway, W. (1959). *Education and health of the partially seeing child.* New York: Columbia University Press.

Hatlen, P. H. (1979). *Important concerns in the education of visually impaired children* (MAVIS Sourcebook 5). Boulder, CO: Social Science Education Consortium.

Jankowski, L. W., & Evans, J. K. (1981). The exercise capacity of blind children. *Journal of Visual Impairment and Blindness, 75,* 248–251.

Juurmaa, J. (1967). *Ability structure and loss of vision.* New York: American Foundation for the Blind.

Kirchner, C., & Peterson, R. (1979). Employment: Selected characteristics. *Journal of Visual Impairment and Blindness, 73,* 239–242.

Koestler, F. A. (1976). *The unseen minority.* New York: David McKay.

Landau, B., Gleitman, H., & Spelke, E. (1981). Spatial knowledge and geometric representation in a child blind from birth. *Science, 213,* 1275–1277.

Langley, M. B. (1980). *Functional vision inventory for the multiple and severely handicapped.* Chicago: Stoelting.

Lowenfeld, B. (1950). Psychological foundation of special methods in teaching blind children. In P.A. Zahl (Ed.), *Blindness.* Princeton, NJ: Princeton University Press.

————. (1971). *Our blind children.* Springfield, IL: Charles C. Thomas.

————. (1973). *The visually handicapped child in school.* New York: American Foundation for the Blind.

————. (1975). *The changing status of the blind: From separation to integration.* Springfield, IL: Charles C. Thomas.

Martin, G. J., & Hobin, M. (1977). *Supporting visually impaired students in the mainstream.* Reston, VA: Council for Exceptional Children.

Maxfield, K. E., & Buchholz, F. (1957). *Social Maturity Scale for Blind Children: A guide to its use.* New York: American Foundation for the Blind.

National Society to Prevent Blindness. (1966). *Manual on use of the NSPB standard classification of causes of severe vision impairment and blindness: Index of diagnostic terms pertaining to severe vision impairment and blindness.* New York: Author.

————. (1976). *Annual report for 1975.* New York: Author.

————. (1977). *Signs of possible eye trouble in children* (Pub. G–112). New York: Author.

Nolan, C. Y., & Morris, J. E. (1965). *Roughness Discrimination Test.* Louisville, KY: American Printing House for the Blind.

Orlansky, M. D. (1979). *Encouraging successful mainstreaming of the visually impaired child* (MAVIS Sourcebook 2). Boulder, CO: Social Science Education Consortium.

Parsons, S. (1982). *An exploratory study on the patterns of emerging play behavior in young children with low vision.* Unpublished doctoral dissertation, University of Texas.

Roessing, L. J. (1982). Functional vision: Criterion-referenced checklists. In S. S. Mangold

(Ed.), A *teacher's guide to the special educational needs of blind and visually handicapped children*. New York: American Foundation for the Blind.

Santin, S., & Nesker Simmons, J. (1977). Problems in the construction of reality in congenitally blind children. *Journal of Visual Impairment and Blindness*, 71, 425–429.

Scholl, G., & Schnur, R. (1976). *Measures of psychological, vocational, & educational functioning in the blind and visually handicapped*. New York: American Foundation for the Blind.

Scott, R. A. (1969). *The making of blind men*. New York: Russell Sage Foundation.

Spenciner, L. J. (1972). Differences between blind and partially sighted children in rejection by sighted peers in integrated classrooms, grades 2–8. In B. S. Tuckman (Ed.), *Conducting educational research*. New York: Harcourt Brace Jovanovich.

Stephens, B., & Grube, C. (1982). Development of Piagetian reasoning in congenitally blind children. *Journal of Visual Impairment and Blindness*, 76. 133–143.

Stephens, B., Grube, C., & Fitzgerald, J. (1977). *Project PAVE (Final Report)*. Washington, DC: U.S. Department of Health, Education, and Welfare, Bureau of Education for the Handicapped.

Swallow, R., Mangold, S., & Mangold, P. (Eds.). (1978). *Informal assessment of developmental skills for visually handicapped students*. New York: American Foundation for the Blind.

Sykes, K. C. (1972). Print reading for visually handicapped children. *Education of Visually Handicapped*, 4, 71–75.

Warren, D. H. (1981). Visual impairments. In J. M. Kaufman & D. P. Hallahan (Eds.), *Handbook of special education*. Englewood Cliffs, NJ: Prentice-Hall.

———. (1984). *Blindness and early childhood development*. New York: American Foundation for the Blind.

CHAPTER 13

Alexander, P. A., & Muia, J. A. (1982). *Gifted education: A comprehensive roadmap*. Rockville, MD: Aspen Publication.

Bauer, H., and Harris, R. (1979). Potentially able learners (P.A.L.s): A program for gifted preschoolers and parents. *Journal for the Education of the Gifted*, 2, 214–219.

Bereiter, C. A. (1976). SMPY in social perspective. In S. Keating (Ed.), *Intellectual talent: Research and development*. Baltimore: Johns Hopkins University Press.

Bernal, E. A. (1975). A response to educational uses of tests with disadvantaged subjects. *American Psychologist*, 30, 93–95.

Bishop, W. (1968). Successful teachers of the gifted. *Exceptional Children*, 39, 317–325.

Bloom, B. S. (Ed.). (1956). *Taxonomy of educational objectives: Handbook 1. Cognitive domain*. New York: David McKay.

Borland, J. (1978). Teacher identification of the gifted: A new look. *Journal for the Education of the Gifted*, 2(1), 22–32.

Braga, J. (1971). Early admission: Opinion vs. evidence. *The Elementary School Journal*, 72(1), 35–46.

Bridges, R. D. (1980). Mentors open new careers and hobby vistas for youth. *Phi Delta Kappan*, 62, 199.

Bruch, C. (1972). *The ABDA: Making the Stanford-Binet culturally unbiased for disadvantaged black children*. Paper presented at the Southeastern Invitational Conference on Testing Problems, University of Georgia, Athens, GA.

Buros, O. K. (1978). *The mental measurement yearbook* (8th ed.). Highland Park, NJ: Gryphon Press.

Cassidy, J., & Vukelich, C. (1978). Providing for the young academically talented: A pilot program for teachers and children. *Journal for the Education of the Gifted*, 1(1), 70–76.

Ciha, I., Harris, R., Hoffman, C., & Potter, M. W. (1974). Parents as identifiers of giftedness, ignored but accurate. *Gifted Child Quarterly*, 18, 191–195.

Clark, B. (1979). *Growing up gifted*. Columbus, OH: Charles E. Merrill.

Colson, S., Borman, C., & Nash, W. R. (1978). A unique learning opportunity for talented high school seniors. *Phi Delta Kappan*, 59(8), 542–543.

Congressional Record. (1978, October 10), H–12179.

Cooper, J. O. (1981). *Measuring behavior* (2nd ed.). Columbus, OH: Charles G. Merrill.

Dreyer, S. S. (1977). *The bookfinder*. Circle Pines, MN: American Guidance Service.

Dunn, L. M. (1980). *Peabody Picture Vocabulary Test*. Circle Pines, MN: American Guidance Services.

Fine, M. J. (1977). Facilitating parent-child relationships for creativity. *Gifted/Creative/Talented*, 21(4), 487–499.

Fliegler, L., & Bish, C. (1959). Summary of research on the academically talented students. *Review of Educational Research*, 29, 408–450.

Fox, L., & Tobin, D. (1978). Broadening career horizons for gifted girls. *Gifted/Creative/Talented*, 4, 18–22.

Frasier, M. M. (1980). Screening and identification of gifted students. In J. B. Jordan & J. A. Grossi (Eds.), *An administrative handbook on developing programs for the gifted and talented*. Reston, VA: Council for Exceptional Children.

Gallagher, J. (1975). *Teaching the gifted child* (2nd ed.). Boston: Allyn & Bacon.

Gardner, H. (1984). Assessing intelligence: A comment on testing intelligence without IQ tests. *Phi Delta Kappan*, 65, 699–700.

Getzels, J., & Jackson, P. (1962). *Creativity and intelligence*. New York: John Wiley & Sons.

Ginsberg, G., & Harrison, C. H. (1977). *How to help your gifted child*. New York: Simon & Schuster.

Given, B. K. (1977). Reaching the learning disabled gifted. In J. H. Orloff (Ed.), *Creativity and the gifted/talented child*. Falls Church, VA: Northern Virginia Conference on Gifted Talented Education.

Goertzel, V., & Goertzel, M. (1962). *Cradles of eminence*. New York: Little, Brown.

Grost, A. (1970). *Genius in residence*. Englewood Cliffs, NJ: Prentice-Hall.

Guilford, J. P. (1967). *The nature of human intelligence*. New York: McGraw-Hill.

———. (1977). *Way beyond the IQ*. Buffalo, NY: Creative Education Foundation.

Haddad, F. A., and Naglieri, J. A. (1984). The Kaufman Assessment Battery for Children: An alternative to present approaches. *Directive Teacher*, 6, 12–13.

Harris, R. A. (1984). Mentorship for the gifted. *Gifted/Creative/Talented*, 33, 8–9.

High, M. H., and Udall, A. J. (1983). Teacher ratings of students in relation to ethnicity of students and school ethnic balance. *Journal for the Education of the Gifted*, 6, 154–166.

Hokansen, D. T., & Jospe, M. (1976). *The search for cognitive giftedness in exceptional children.* New Haven, CT: Project SEARCH.

Hollingworth, L. (1942). *Children with above 180 IQ.* Yonkers on Hudson, NY: World.

Horner, M. S. (1972). Toward an understanding of achievement-related conflicts in women. *Journal of Social Issues*, 28, 157–175.

Hunt, J. M. (1961). *Intelligence and experience.* New York: Ronald Press.

Huntington, S. (1975). The United States. In M. Croziers, S. Huntington, & J. Watanuki (Eds.), *The crisis of democracy: Report on the governability of democracies to the trilateral commission.* New York: New York University Press.

Jacobs, J. C. (1971). Effectiveness of teacher and parent identification of gifted children as a function of school level. *Psychology in the Schools*, 8, 140–142.

Jensen, A. R. (1969). How much can we boost IQ and scholastic achievement? *Harvard Education Review*, 39(1), 1–123.

Karnes, F. A., & Collins, E. C. (1979). State consultants in gifted education: A valuable resource. *Roeper Review*, 2, 7–10.

Karnes, M. B. (1979). Young handicapped children can be gifted and talented. *Journal for the Education of the Gifted*, 2, 157–172.

Karnes, M. B., Shwedel, A. M., & Lewis, G. F. (1983). Long term effects of early programming for the gifted/talented handicapped. *Journal for the Education of the Gifted*, 6, 266–278.

Kaufman, S. A., & Kaufman, N. L. (1983). *Kaufman Assessment Battery for Children.* Circle Pines, MN: American Guidance Service.

Kenmare, D. (1972). *The nature of genius.* Westport, CT: Greenwood Press.

Khatena, J. (1976). Major directions in creativity research. In J. Gowen, J. Khatena, & P. Torrance (Eds.), *Educating the ablest.* Itasca, IL: Peacock.

———. (1982). *Educational psychology of the gifted.* New York: John Wiley & Sons.

Kitano, M. (1982). Young gifted children: Strategies for preschool teachers. *Young Children*, 38(1), 14–24.

Kranyik, R. D., & Wagner, B. A. (1965). Creativity and the elementary school teacher. *Elementary School Journal*, 66, 2–9.

Kranz, B. (1982). *Kranz Talent Identification Instrument.* Moorehead, MN.

Laycock, F., & Caylor, J. S. (1964). Physiques of gifted children and their less gifted siblings. *Child Development*, 35, 63–74.

Lehman, H. (1953). *Age and achievement.* Princeton, NJ: Princeton University Press.

Lucito, L. (1974). The creative. In R. Martinson (Ed.), *Identification of the gifted and talented.* Ventura, CA: Office of the Ventura County Superintendent of Schools.

MacKinnon, D. (1962). The nature and nurture of creative talent. *American Psychologist, 17,* 484–495.

Maker, C. J. (1977). *Providing programs for the gifted handicapped.* Reston, VA: Council for Exceptional Children.

Marland, S. (1972). *Education of the gifted and talented* (Report to Congress by the U.S. Commissioner of Education). Washington, DC: U.S. Government Printing Office.

Mattson, B. D. (1983). Mentors for the gifted and talented: Whom to seek and where to look. *Gifted/Creative/Talented, 27,* 10–11.

McCallum, R. S., Karnes, F. A., & Edwards, R. P. (1984). The test of choice for assessment of gifted children: A comparison of the K-ABC, WISC-R and Stanford-Binet. *Journal of Psychoeducational Assessment, 2,* 57–63.

McCleary, I. D., & Hines, S. (1983). Expanding horizons: University professors serve as mentors for gifted middle-graders. *Phi Delta Kappan, 64,* 661–662.

Meeker, M. (1969). *The structure of intellect: Its interpretation and use.* Columbus, OH: Charles E. Merrill.

Mercer, J. (1978). SOMPA, *System of Multicultural Pluralistic Assessment.* New York: Psychological Corporation.

Mulhern, J. D., & Ward, M. (1983). A collaborative program for developing teachers of gifted and talented students. *Gifted Child Quarterly, 27,* 152–156.

Nathan, C. N. (1979). Parental involvement. In A H. Passow (Ed.), *The gifted and talented: Their education and development* (The 78th Yearbook of the National Society for the Study of Education, Part 1). Chicago: University of Chicago Press.

National Society for the Study of Education. (1958). *Education for the gifted* (57th Yearbook, Part 2). Chicago: University of Chicago Press.

Newland, T. (1962). Some observations on essential qualifications of teachers of the mentally superior. *Exceptional Children, 29,* 111–114.

New York Times, (1984, May 7). High school classes set for a 7 year old. p. A4.

Oden, M. (1968). The fulfillment of promise: 40-year follow-up of the Terman gifted group. *Genetic Psychology Monographs, 77,* 3–93.

Pegnato, C. W., & Birch, J. W. (1959). Locating gifted children in junior high schools: A comparison of methods. *Exceptional Children, 25,* 300–304.

Pressey, S. L. (1967). "Fordling" accelerates ten years after. *Journal of Counseling Psychology, 14,* 73–80.

Quattrocki, C. G. (1974). Recognizing creative potential in preschool children. *Gifted Child Quarterly, 18,* 74–80.

Renzulli, J. S. (1973). Talent potential in minority group students. *Exceptional Children, 39,* 437–444.

———. (1977). *The Enrichment Triad Model: A guide for developing defensible programs for the gifted and talented.* Mansfield Center, CT: Creative Learning Press.

———. (1978). What makes giftedness? Reexamining a definition. *Phi Delta Kappan, 60,* 180–184; 261.

Renzulli, J. S., & Hartman, R. K. (1971). Scale for rating behavioral characteristics of superior students. *Exceptional Children*, 38, 243–248.

Rodenstein, J., Pfleger, L. R., & Colangelo, N. (1977). Career development of gifted women. *Gifted Child Quarterly*, 21, 340–347.

Rubenzer, R. L., & Twaite, J. A. (1979). Attitudes of 1200 educators toward the education of the gifted and talented: Implications for teacher preparation. *Journal for the Education of the Gifted*, 2, 202–213.

Sanborn, M. P. (1979). Differential counseling needs of the gifted and talented. In N. Colangelo & R. Zaffrann (Eds.), *New voices in counseling the gifted*. Dubuque, IA: Kendall/Hunt.

Seagoe, M. V. (1974). Some learning characteristics of gifted children. In R. V. Martinson (Ed.), *Identification of the gifted and talented*. Ventura, CA: National/State Leadership Training Institute on the Gifted/Talented.

Seeley, K. R. (1979). Competencies for teachers of gifted and talented children. *Journal for the Education of the Gifted*, 3, 7–13.

Sisk, D. (1978). Education for the gifted and talented. A national perspective. *Journal for the Education of the Gifted*, 1(1), 5–24.

Smith, B., & Nevins, C. (1979). Sole support vs. soul support. *Gifted/Creative/Talented*, 10, 44–47.

Stanley, J. C. (1976). The study of mathematically precocious youth. *Gifted Child Quarterly*, 20, 246–283.

———. (1978). Educational non-acceleration: An international tragedy. *Gifted/Creative/Talented*, 3, 3–5, 53–57, 60–63.

Stephens, T. M., & Wolf, J. S. (1981). Instructional models. *Directive Teacher*, 3(3), 5–6.

Sternberg, R. J. (1984). Testing Intelligence without IQ tests. *Phi Delta Kappan*, 65, 694–698.

Tannenbaum, A. J. (1979). Pre-sputnik to post-Watergate concern about the gifted. In A. H. Passow (Ed.), *The gifted and the talented: Their education and development* (The 78th Yearbook of the National Society for the Study of Education, Part 1). Chicago: University of Chicago Press.

———. (1983). *Gifted children. Psychological and educational perspectives*. New York: Macmillan.

Taylor, C., & Holland, J. (1962). Development and application of tests of creativity. *Review of Educational Research*, 32, 91–102.

Terman, L. M. (Ed.). (1925–1959). *Genetic studies of genius* (Vols. 1–5). Stanford, CA: Stanford University Press.

———. (1954). The discovery and encouragement of exceptional talent. *American Psychologist*, 9, 221–230.

Terman, L. M., & Merrill, M. A. (1973). *Stanford-Binet Intelligence Scales*. Boston: Houghton Mifflin.

Terman, L. M., & Oden, M. (1959). The gifted group at mid-life: Thirty-five years' follow-up of the superior child. In L. M. Terman (Ed.), *Genetic studies of genius* (Vol. 5). Stanford, CA: Stanford University Press.

Tittle, B. M. (1984). Why Montessori for the gifted? *Gifted/Creative/Talented*, 33, 3–7.

Torrance, E. P. (1962). *Guiding creative talent*. Englewood Cliffs, NJ: Prentice-Hall.

————. (1966). *Torrance Tests of Creative Thinking*. Princeton, NJ: Personnel Press.

————. (1969). Creative positives of disadvantaged children and youth. *Gifted Child Quarterly*, 13, 71–81.

Tremaine, C. D. (1979). Do gifted programs make a difference? *Gifted Child Quarterly*, 23, 500–517.

Trezise, R. (1973). Are the gifted coming back? *Phi Delta Kappan*, 54, 687–688.

U.S. Senate Report of the Gifted and Talented Subcommittee on Labor and Public Welfare. (1972, March). Washington, DC:

Vail, P. (1979). *The world of the gifted child*. New York: Walker.

Voorheis, P. (1979). Concurrent high school-college enrollment. *Educational Record*, 60, 305–311.

Ward, V. (1961). *Educating the gifted*. Columbus, OH: Charles E. Merrill.

————. (1975). Basic concepts. In W. Barbe & J. Renzulli (Eds.), *Psychology and education of the gifted*. New York: Irvington.

Webb, J. T., Meckstroth, E. A., & Tolan, S. S. (1983). *Guiding the gifted child*. Columbus, OH: Ohio Psychology.

Wechsler, D. (1967). *Wechsler Preschool and Primary Scale of Intelligence*. New York: Psychological Corporation.

————. (1974). *Wechsler Intelligence Scale for Children—Revised (WISC-R)*. New York: Psychological Corporation.

————. (1981). *Wechsler Adult Intelligence Scale—Revised*. New York: Psychological Corporation.

Welsh, G. S. (1977). Personality correlates of intelligence and creativity in gifted adolescents. In J. C. Stanley, W. C. George, & C. H. Solano (Eds.), *The gifted and the creative: A fifty-year perspective*. Baltimore: Johns Hopkins University Press.

White, B. L. (1977). Early stimulation and behavioral development. In A. Oliverio (Ed.), *Genetics, environment, and intelligence*. New York: Elsevier/North Holland.

Whitmore, J. R. (1979). The etiology of underachievement in highly gifted young children. *Journal for the Education of the Gifted*, 3, 38–51.

————. (1980). *Giftedness, conflict and underachievement*. Boston: Allyn & Bacon.

Wolf, J. (1979). Education of the gifted: Some critical issues. *Insight: A Forum for Leaders and Policy Makers in Western Education*, 2, 15–20.

————. (1981). An interview with James Gallagher. *Directive Teacher*, 3, 25–27.

Wolf, J., & Gygi, J. (1981). Learning disabled and gifted: Success or failure. *Journal for the Education of the Gifted*, 4(3), 199–206.

Wolf, J., & Penrod, D. (1980). Bibliotherapy: A classroom approach to sensitive problems. *Gifted/Creative/Talented*, 15, 52–54.

Wolf, J., & Stephens, T. M. (1979). Individualized educational planning for the gifted. *Roeper Review*, 2, 11–12.

————. (1984). Training models for parents of the gifted. *Journal for the Education of the Gifted*, 7(2), 120–129.

Wyatt, F. (1982). Responsibility for gifted learners—A plea for the encouragement of classroom teacher support. *Gifted Child Quarterly, 26,* 140–143.

Yarborough, B. H., & Johnson, R. A. (1983). Identifying the gifted: A theory-practice gap. *Gifted Child Quarterly, 27,* 135–138.

Zaffrann, R. T., & Colangelo, N. (1977). Counseling with gifted and talented students. *Gifted Child Quarterly, 21,* 305–321.

CHAPTER 14

Abramson, M., & Hagarty, G. (1983). *A description of special education teacher training needs.* Unpublished paper, U.S. Department of Education, Special Education Programs.

Anderson, L. M., Evertson, C. M., & Emmer, E. T. (1980). Dimensions in classroom management derived from recent research. *Journal of Curriculum Studies, 12,* 343–346.

Armstrong v. Kline. 476 F.Supp. 583 (E.D. Pa., 1979), 3. Medical Disability Law Reporter, 317.

Bales v. Clark. F.Supp. 1366 (1981).

Becker, W. C., & Carnine, D. W. (1980). Direct instruction: An effective approach to education intervention with the disadvantaged and low performers. In B. B. Lahey & A. E. Kazdin (Eds.), *Advances in clinical child psychology* (pp. 429–473). New York: Plenum.

Bellamy, G. T. (Ed.). (1976). *Habilitation of severely and profoundly retarded adults: Reports from the Specialized Training Program* (Vol. 1). Eugene: University of Oregon.

Bellamy, G. T., Rose, H., Wilson, D. J., & Clarke, J. Y. (1982). Strategies for vocational preparation. In B. Wilcox & G. T. Bellamy (Eds.), *Design of high school programs for severely handicapped students.* Baltimore: Paul H. Brookes.

Berkson, G. (1967). Abnormal stereotyped motor acts. In J. Zubin & H. F. Hunt (Eds.), *Comparative psychopathology: Animal and human.* New York: Grune & Stratton.

Berliner, D. C. (1981). Academic learning time and reading achievement. In J. T. Guthrie (Ed.), *Comprehension and teaching: Research views* (pp. 203–226). Newark, DE: International Reading Association.

Billingsley, F., Haring, N., Liberty, K., Weisenstein, G., & White, O. (1984). *Investigating the problem of skill generalization* (2nd ed.). Seattle: University of Washington.

Billingsley, T., Thompson, M., Matlock. B., & Work, J. (1984). Generalization and the educational ecology of severely handicapped learners: A descriptive study—second project year. In *Institute for education of severely handicapped children: Washington Research Organization annual report FY 83–84* (U.S. Department of Education Contract No. 300–83–0634). Seattle: University of Washington, College of Education.

Borg, W. R. (1980). Time and school learning. In C. Denham & A. Liebman (Eds.), *Time to learn* (pp. 27–72). Washington, DC: National Institute of Education.

Bricker, D. D. (1976). Educational synthesizer. In M. A. Thomas (Ed.), *Hey, don't forget about me.* Reston, VA: Council for Exceptional Children.

Brolin, D. E. (1979). *Life-centered career education: A competency-based approach.* Reston, VA: Council for Exceptional Children.

————. (1982). *Vocational preparation of handicapped individuals* (2nd ed.). Columbus, OH: Charles E. Merrill.

Brophy, J. E. (1979). Teacher behavior and its effects. *Journal of Educational Psychology, 71,* 733–750.

————. (1983). Classroom organization and management. *Elementary School Journal, 83,* 254–285.

Brown, L., Flavey, M., Vincent, L., Kaye, N., Johnson, F., Farrara-Parish, P., & Gruenewald, L. (1980). Strategies for generating comprehensive, longitudinal and chronological age appropriate individual education programs for adolescent and young adult severely handicapped students. *Journal of Special Education, 14,* 199–215.

Brown, L., Nietupski, J., & Hamre-Nietupski, S. (1976). The criterion of ultimate functioning and public school services for the severely handicapped student. In M. A. Thomas (Ed.), *Hey, don't forget about me* (pp. 2–15). Reston, VA: Council for Exceptional Children.

Comptroller General of the United States. (1976, September 28). *Training educators for the handicapped: A need to redirect federal programs* (Report to Congress). Washington, DC: U.S. Government Printing Office.

DeLissavoy, V. (1964). Head-banging in childhood: A review of empirical studies. *Pediatrics Digest, 6,* 49–55.

Dokecki, P. R., & Newbrough, J. R. (1983). The legacy of Nicholas Hobbs: Editors' introduction. *Peabody Journal of Education, 60,* 1–2.

Emmer, E. T., Evertson, C. M., & Anderson, L. M. (1980). Effective management at the beginning of the school year. *Elementary School Journal, 80,* 219–231.

Englemann, S. (1982). Dear Ziggy. *Direct Instruction News, 1*(3), 5.

Englert, C. S. (1984). Measuring teacher effectiveness from the teacher's point of view. *Focus on Exceptional Children, 17*(1), 1–14.

Englert, C. S., & Thomas, C. C. (1982). Management of task involvement in special education classrooms. *Teacher Education and Special Education, 5,* 3–10.

Evertson, C. M., & Emmer, E. T. (1982). Effective management at the beginning of the school year in junior high classes. *Journal of Educational Psychology, 74,* 485–498.

Fialkowski v. Shapp. 405 F.Supp. 946 (E.D. Pa., 1975).

Firth, G. H. (1981). "Advocate" vs. "professional employee": A question of priorities for special educators. *Exceptional Children, 47,* 486–493.

Fisher, C. M., Berlinger, D. C., Filby, N. N., Marliave, R., Cahen, L. S., & Dishaw, M. M. (1980). Teaching behaviors, academic learning time, and student achievement: An overview. In C. Denham & A. Lieberman (Eds.), *Time to learn.* Washington, DC: National Institute of Education.

Fox, R. G., (1974). *The effects of peer tutoring on oral reading behavior of underachieving fourth grade pupils.* Unpublished doctoral dissertation, University of Kansas.

Gaylord-Ross, R., Forte, J., Storey, K., Gaylord-Ross, C., & Jameson, D. (1984). *Community-referenced instruction in technological work settings.* Unpublished manuscript, San Francisco State University, Department of Special Education.

Gaylord-Ross, R., & Peck, C. A. (1985). Integration efforts for students with severe mental handicaps. In D. Bricker & J. Filler (Eds.), *Serving the severely retarded: From research to practice.* Reston, VA: Council for Exceptional Children.

Gold, M. W. (1972). Stimulus factors in skill training of retarded adolescents on a complex assembly task: Acquisition, transfer, and retention. *American Journal of Mental Deficiency, 76,* 517–526.

Good, T. L. (1983). Classroom research: A decade of progress. *Educational Psychologist, 18,* 127–144.

Haring. N., & Billingsley, F. (1984). Systems change strategies to ensure the future of integration. In N. Haring & R. York (Eds.), *Public school integration of severely handicapped students: Rational issues and progressive alternatives.* Baltimore: Paul H. Brookes.

Hart, V. (1977). The use of many disciplines with the severely and profoundly handicapped. In E. Sontag, J. Smith, & N. Certo (Eds.), *Educational programming for the severely and profoundly handicapped.* Reston, VA: Council for Exceptional Children, Division of Mental Retardation.

Heaney, J. P. (1984). A free appropriate public education: Has the Supreme Court misinterpreted Congressional intent? *Exceptional Children, 50,* 456–462.

Heller, H. W. (1981). Secondary education for handicapped students: In search of a solution. *Exceptional Children, 47,* 582–583.

Heller, H., & Ridenhour, N. (1983). Professional standards: Foundation for the future. *Exceptional Children, 49*(4), 294–298.

High/Scope Educational Research Foundation. (1984). *Changed lives: The effects of the Perry preschool program on youths through age 19.* Ypsilanti, MI: High/Scope Press.

Horner, R. D., Holvolt, J., & Rinne, T. (1976). *Competency specifications for teachers of the severely and profoundly handicapped.* Unpublished manuscript, University of Kansas.

Iacino, R., & Bricker, D. (1978). The generative teacher: A model for preparing personnel to work with the severely/profoundly handicapped. In N. G. Haring & D. D. Bricker (Eds.), *Teaching the severely handicapped* (Vol. 3). Seattle: American Association for the Education of the Severely/Profoundly Handicapped.

Kolstoe, O. P. (1975). Secondary programs. In J. M. Kauffman & J. S. Payne (Eds.), *Mental retardation: Introduction and personal perspectives.* Columbus, OH: Charles E. Merrill.

Kolstoe, O. P., & Frey, R. (1965). *A high school work-study program for mentally subnormal students.* Carbondale: Southern Illinois Press.

Kounin, J. (1970). *Discipline and group management in classrooms.* New York: Holt, Rinehart & Winston.

Lakin, K. C., & Bruininks, B. H. (1985). Contemporary services for handicapped children and youth. In R. H. Bruininks & K. C. Lakin (Eds.), *Living and learning in the least restrictive environment* (pp. 3–22). Baltimore: Paul H. Brookes.

Lieberman, L. (1980). Territoriality—Who does what to whom? *Journal of Learning Disabilities, 13,* 15–19.

Martens, E., Elis, V., Graham, R., Lipton, E., Myer, L., Stanton, M., Stoddard, J., & Wagner, P. (1949). State legislation for the education of exceptional children. U.S. *Office of Education Bulletin, 2,* 23–57.

Martin, E. W. (1972). Individualization and behaviorism as future trends in educating handicapped children. *Exceptional Children*, 38, 517–525.

McCarthy, M. M. (1983). The Pennhurst and Rowley decisions: Issues and implications. *Exceptional Children*, 49, 517–522.

Mithaug, D. E., & Haring, N. G. (1977). Community vocational and workshop placement. In N. G. Haring & T. J. Brown (Eds.), *Teaching the severely handicapped* (Vol. 2). New York: Grune & Stratton.

National Council for Accreditation of Teacher Education. (1979). *Standards for the accreditation of teacher education*. Washington, DC: U.S. Government Printing Office.

Noble, D. D. (1984). Jumping off the computer bandwagon. *Education Week*, 4(5), 21, 24.

Oliver, P. R. (1983). Effects of teaching different tasks in group versus individual training formats with severely handicapped individuals. *Journal of the Association for Persons with Severe Handicaps*, 8(2), 79–91.

Oliver, P. R., & Scott, T. L. (1982, November). *Comparative effectiveness of group and individual training in programming generalized language skills with severely handicapped individuals*. Paper presented at the meeting of the Association for the Severely Handicapped, Denver.

Osborne, A. G. (1984). How the courts have interpreted the related services mandate. *Exceptional Children*, 51(3), 249–252.

Pappanikou, A. (1979). Mainstreaming. *Teacher Education and Special Education*, 2, 51–55.

Peck, C. A., & Semmel, M. I. (1982). Identifying the least restrictive environment (LRE) for children with severe handicaps: Toward empirical analysis. *Journal of the Association for the Severely Handicapped*, 7(1), 56–63.

Reynolds, M. C. (Ed.). (1979). *A common body of practice for teachers: The challenge of Public Law 94–142 to teacher education*. Minneapolis: National Support Systems Project.

———. (1980). Categorical vs. noncategorical teacher training. *Teacher Education and Special Education*, 2, 5–8.

Rosenshine, B. (1977). Review of teaching variables and student achievement. In G. D. Borich & K. S. Fenton (Eds.), *The appraisal of teaching: Concepts and process* (pp. 144–120). Menlo Park, CA: Addison-Wesley.

———. (1980). How time is spent in elementary classrooms. In C. Denham & A. Lieberman (Eds.), *Time to learn*. Washington, DC: National Institute of Education.

Rowley v. Board of Education of Hendrik Hudson Central School District. 102 S.ct. 3034 (1982).

Schutz, R. P., Williams, W., Iverson, G. S., & Duncan, D. (1984). Social integration of severely handicapped students. In N. Certo, N. Haring, & R. York (Eds.), *Public school integration of severely handicapped students: Rational issues and progressive alternatives*. Baltimore: Paul H. Brookes.

Semmel, M. I., Cosden, M. A., Semmel, D. S., & Kelemen, E. (1984). Training special education personnel for effective use of microcomputer technology: Critical needs and directions. *Special Services in the Schools*, 1(1), 63–82.

Smith-Davis, J., Burke, P. J., & Noel, M. M. (1984). *Personnel to educate the handicapped in America: Supply and demand from a programmatic viewpoint*. College Park, MD: University of Maryland, Institute for the Study of Exceptional Children and Youth.

SRI International. (1982). *Local implementation of Public Law 94–142: Final report of a longitudinal study*. Menlo Park, CA: SRI International.

Stevens, R., & Rosenshine, B. (1980). Advances in research on teaching. *Exceptional Education Quarterly, 2,* 1–9.

Stevens, T. M., & Braun, B. L. (1980). Measures of regular classroom teachers' attitudes toward handicapped children. *Exceptional Children, 46,* 292–294.

Stokes, T. F., & Baer, D. M. (1977). An implicit technology of generalization. *Journal of Applied Behavior Analysis, 10,* 349–367.

Tatro v. State of Texas. 481 F.Supp. 1224 (N.D. Tex., 1979).

Thurlow, M. L., Ysseldyke, J. E., Graden, J., & Algozzine, B. (1983). Instructional ecology for students in resource and regular classrooms. *Teacher Education and Special Education, 6,* 248–254.

U.S. Department of Education. (1984). *Sixth annual report to Congress on the implementation of Public Law 94–142: The Education for All Handicapped Children Act*. Washington, DC: U.S. Department of Education.

Voeltz, L. M. (1980). Children's attitudes toward handicapped peers. *American Journal of Mental Deficiency, 84,* 455–464.

———. (1982). Effects of structured interactions with severely handicapped peers on children's attitudes. *American Journal of Mental Deficiency, 86,* 380–390.

White, O. (1982). Child assessment. In B. Wilcox & R. York (Eds.), *Quality education for the severely handicapped* (pp. 29–79). Falls Church, VT: Quality Handcrafted Books.

Wilcox, B., & Bellamy, G. T. (1982). *Design of high school programs for severely handicapped students*. Baltimore: Paul H. Brookes.

Wilcox, B., & Sailor, W. (1982). Service delivery issues: Integrated educational systems. In B. Wilcox & R. York (Eds.), *Quality education for the severely handicapped* (pp. 277–302). Falls Church, VT: Quality Handcrafted Books.

Williams, W., Vogelsberg, R. T., & Schutz, R. P. (in press). Programs for secondary-age severely handicapped youth. In D. Bricker & J. Filler (Eds.), *Serving the severely retarded: From research to practice*. Reston, VA: Council on Exceptional Children.

Wolfensberger, W. (1972). The principle of normalization and its implications to psychiatric services. *American Journal of Psychiatry, 127,* 291–297.

Contributors

Norris G. Haring is currently professor of education/special education at the University of Washington and principal investigator of the Western Technical Assistance Region (WESTAR), a technical assistance project for early intervention funded by the Bureau of Education for the Handicapped and located at the University of Washington in Seattle.

Dr. Haring received his B.A. from Kearney State Teachers College in 1948; his M.A. from the University of Nebraska—with study at the Merrill-Palmer Institute and a Ford Foundation Fellowship in Child Development and Family Life—with a major in psychology in 1950; and his Ed.D. in special education from Syracuse University in 1956.

As an educator, Dr. Haring has served as instructor in education at Syracuse University from 1954 to 1956; director of special education for the Arlington Country Public Schools in Arlington, Virginia, from 1956 to 1957; associate professor and coordinator of special education at the University of Maryland from 1957 to 1960; professor of education, associate professor of pediatrics, and educational director of the Children's Rehabilitation Unit at the University of Kansas Medical Center from 1960 to 1965; and adjunct professor in the Department of Pediatrics at the University of Washington from 1966 to 1978.

Dr. Haring served as founding president of the Association for Severely Handicapped from 1975 to 1978. He has special interests in research in systematic instruction with both mildly and severely handicapped children.

Linda McCormick is an associate professor of special education at the University of Hawaii and coordinator of the Early Childhood Handicapped Graduate Teacher Preparation Program. She received her Ph.D. from George Peabody College of Vanderbilt University in 1973. In addition to primary professional commitments to early language acquisition and infant and preschool intervention, she has published numerous articles on, and consults to, application of the transdisciplinary service delivery model. Prior to joining the faculty of the University of Hawaii, Dr. McCormick was a member of the graduate faculty at the University of Alabama in Birmingham and was associated there with the Center for Developmental and Learning Disorders. She is a consultant to numerous public and private agencies in Hawaii, providing workshops and teaching courses for various universities in the South Pacific, an active member of several professional organizations, and a reviewer for numerous journals.

Donald B. Bailey, Jr., is the director of early childhood research at the Frank Porter Graham Child Development Center at the University of North Carolina at Chapel Hill. He also serves as clinical assistant professor at the university's division of special education. He taught mildly and moderately retarded preschoolers in Chapel Hill prior to earning his Ph.D. in early childhood special education at the University of Washington. Dr. Bailey has written extensively on assessing and teaching young children.

June L. Bigge is a professor of special education at San Francisco State University. She received the Ed.D. with honors from the University of Oregon. Before she began university teaching, she taught regular first grade, classes of children with physical and multiple disabilities in a specal education school, individuals with severe learning disabilities in regular classes, and physically disabled students who received most of their education in regular classes. Currently, she is reducing her university load and is teaching microcomputer use to students with physical disabilities in the public schools.

Dr. Bigge is a past president of the DOPH (Division of the Physically Handicapped) of the Council for Exceptional Children. Her publications include *Teaching Individuals with Physical and Multiple Disabilities*, 2nd ed. and she is currently completing another book, *Strategies for Curriculum Development for Students in Special Education*.

Philip C. Chinn is a professor and department head at East Texas State University. He was formerly the special assistant to the executive director for minority and handicapped concerns and development at the Council for Exceptional Children. Dr. Chinn has taught educable mentally retarded students in Louisville, Kentucky; was a work-study coordinator for high school students in Texas; taught emotionally disturbed and retarded students at the state reformatory in Hawaii; and has been a teacher educator in special education for 13 years.

He has co-authored textbooks on mental retardation, the communication process with parents of exceptional children, and multicultural education. In addition, he has authored numerous articles, monographs, and chapters in books.

Douglas Cullinan is a professor in the Department of Learning, Development, and Special Education at Northern Illinois University, where he teaches students in the bachelor's, master's, and doctoral programs in special education. He has taught emotionally disturbed and mentally retarded pupils in public schools and educationally handicapped occupants of a state detention facility. He has also worked with handicapped pupils as a consultant to school districts and on federally funded grants. Dr. Cullinan has researched and published articles on various topics related to special education for children and adolescents. He serves on the editorial boards of *Behavioral Disorders, Education and Treatment of Children, Learning Disability Quarterly,* and *Remedial and Special Education.* He co-authored with Mike Epstein *Information/Edge: Behavior and Emotional Disorders,* a quarterly newsletter of developments relating to students with behavior disorders.

Michael H. Epstein is an associate professor in the Department of Learning, Development, and Special Education at Northern Illinois University. His previous experiences include 5 years of teaching learning and behaviorally handicapped pupils in both public schools and residential settings.

   Dr. Epstein has authored numerous journal articles and books dealing with handicapped children and adolescents, particularly in the areas of behavior disorders and applied behavior analysis.

   Dr. Epstein received a B.S. in business (1969) and an M.S. Ed. in special education (1971) from American University and an Ed.D. in special education from the University of Virginia (1975). He holds memberships and editorships with several professional journals and organizations.

Rita Livingston teaches courses in special education and in the visually impaired sequence at Illinois State University. After receiving her M.Ed. and Ph.D. from the Universiy of Texas at Austin, she taught at the Texas School for the Blind and as an itinerant/resource teacher in the Austin Independent School District. Dr. Livingston is active in the Council for Exceptional Children, having served on the board of directors and as secretary for the Division of Visually Handicapped. She has presented numerous in-service sessions for teachers on how to work with visually impaired students.

Sheila Lowenbraun teaches education at the University of Washington. There she has directed a program for teachers on working with hearing impaired children for the past 15 years. Her research, writing, and consulting work focus on how to best implement the least restrictive environment for the hearing handicapped.

After earning a degree in zoology at Barnard, she changed her career goal to education of hearing impaired children. Her choice led her to a master's degree in teaching the hearing impaired from Teachers College, Columbia University. For the next several years she taught multiply handicapped/deaf adolescents, many from New York's inner city. She returned to Columbia for her Ph.D. Prior to her present position, she taught at Colorado State College.

Cecil D. Mercer is a professor of education at the University of Florida and codirector of the University of Florida Multidisciplinary Diagnostic and Training Program. In 1974, he received his Ed.D. in special education from the University of Virginia. Dr. Mercer has written extensively on educating exceptional children, including the two major works *Students with Learning Disabilities* and *Teaching Students with Learning Problems*.

Dr. Mercer remains involved in the educational programs of exceptional children through his participation in the learning disabilities program at Shands Teaching Hospital in Gainesville. In addition, he coaches Dixie Youth and Dixie Boys baseball.

James M. Patton teaches in the special education mild/moderate program at the University of Hawaii/Manoa. Having experience in secondary, elementary, and adult special education, Dr. Patton is particularly interested in lifelong learning for the mentally retarded, laws concerning the handicapped, and teaching math and science to exceptional students. Currently he is researching the unique needs of college students who have learning problems. Dr. Patton earned his M.Ed. and Ed.D. from the University of Virginia.

James S. Payne currently serves as dean of the College of Education of the University of Mississippi, having taught education at the University of Virginia for 14 years. He earned with honors an Ed.D. in special education/mental retardation from the University of Kansas. To his teaching he brings a wealth of information from his experiences in counseling, hiring, and training the retarded in restaurant and custodial services; planning a sheltered workshop; and directing a Head Start preschool program. Since 1975 he has chaired the Association for Retarded Citizens Education Committee. He has helped develop a training package for ARC, has authored many articles and books, and serves as a consultant and lecturer on special education and sales motivation.

Adelle M. Renzaglia is an assistant professor at the University of Illinois at Urbana-Champaign, where she teaches courses in the graduate program for teachers of the severely handicapped. She also directs a federally funded model program designed for severely and profoundly handicapped school-age students. The major thrust of the model is community-based instruction and integration of handicapped students with their nonhandicapped peers. Dr. Renzaglia earned her Ph.D. at the University of Wisconsin. Throughout her courses, workshop presentations, and journal articles, she stresses a functional curriculum and systematic instruction for the handicapped in work, home and leisure.

Barbara Sirvis is the assistant dean of the College of Applied Life Studies at the University of Illinois at Urbana-Champaign. She began her career working as a classroom teacher of children with physical and multiple disabilities. She has taught in self-contained preschool classes piloting a transdisciplinary approach and in secondary resource room programs. She has also worked in clinical and community-based therapeutic recreation programs. Prior to her current position, she was assistant professor in the Departments of Recreation and Leisure Studies and Special Education at San Francisco State University. She earned her Ed.D. at Teachers College, Columbia University.

An active member of the Council for Exceptional Children, she currently serves as governor-at-large, U.S. on the executive committee on the board of governors. She serves as a consultant, external evaluator, and workshop presenter for programs in both special education and therapeutic recreation. Her publications include several articles and book chapters on special education and therapeutic recreation.

Martha E. Snell teaches special education at the University of Virginia and is the associate editor of the *Journal of the Association of the Severely Handicapped*. After graduating from Michigan State University in social science, she worked as a ward supervisor in an institution for the mentally retarded. She then earned an M.Ed. in special education and taught mildly retarded children. While completing her doctorate, also at Michigan State University, she coordinated an in-service training project for teachers of the severely handicapped. For the past 14 years she has consulted and participated in workshops for many school districts, group homes, and training schools. She has authored numerous books and articles; her most recent writing and research focus on preparing educators to teach the severely and profoundly handicapped.

Thomas M. Stephens is a professor and chairman of the Department of Human Services Education at the Ohio State University. He previously has worked as a classroom teacher, a psychologist, a school administrator, and a teacher educator. Dr. Stephens was the first state director of gifted education in the Ohio Department of Education.

An author of six textbooks and the Criterion Referenced Curriculum system, Dr. Stephens has published numerous articles and monographs on various aspects of special education. In addition, he and Dr. Joan Wolf have coauthored two monographs about teacher-parent conferences.

Marie Thompson is an associate professor in the program for hearing-impaired, College of Education, University of Washington, and an adjunct associate professor in Speech and Hearing Sciences. Her extensive experience includes teaching the hearing and visually impaired, implementing and directing an early intervention program for hearing impaired children from birth through three years of age and their parents for 12 years, and supervising handicapped programs in the Seattle Public Schools. She coordinated programs for hearing-impaired and deaf-blind students in Washington for four years and has received numerous federal and state grants relating to these two populations. Her research and publications also reflect her interest in both hearing-impaired and deaf-blind children.

Pamela J. Winton is a research associate at the Carolina Institute for Research on Early Education of the Handicapped at the University of North Carolina at Chapel Hill. She has served as a consultant in the field of special education in Concord, New Hampshire, and in Livonia, Michigan. She has written extensively on parental involvement in the education of handicapped children and on the effects of mainstreaming on families.

Joan S. Wolf is an assistant professor, Department of Special Education, at the University of Utah. She began her career as an elementary school teacher. Having completed an M.A. in school psychology and a Ph.D. in special education, she is certified as a teacher, a school psychologist, and a supervisor in the area of learning disabilities. She has worked with learning disabled and gifted youth and has been active in gifted program development. She has written numerous publications and has conducted many workshops on the gifted. Dr. Wolf currently serves as director of Graduate Studies and Gifted Education at the University of Utah.

Name Index

Subject Index